The Neurofeedback Book

Also by Michael Thompson & Lynda Thompson

Setting up for Clinical Success with the Procomp^{+}/Biograph

Also by William Sears & Lynda Thompson

The A.D.D. Book:
New Understandings, New Approaches to Parenting Your Child

The Neurofeedback Book
An Introduction To Basic Concepts in Applied Psychophysiology

Michael Thompson & Lynda Thompson

Introduction by Joel Lubar

Published by:

The Association for Applied Psychophysiology and Biofeedback
Wheat Ridge, Colorado USA
2003

COPYRIGHT © 2003
by
Michael Thompson

All rights reserved.

First Edition

Drawings by Amanda Reeves

Disclaimer: This text is intended only as a guide for professionals who are learning about the field of neurofeedback. It is published for teaching purposes only and none of this constitutes medical or psychological advice. None of the suggestions are to be taken as treatment protocols.

Professionals will learn about treatments from their colleagues in appropriate professional learning situations. This book is only a broad overview and guideline that will hopefully assist readers with an introduction to the field.

Note to readers: **The Neurofeedback Book** is being published at this time as a "working document". It is expected that reader input will help to improve this working document to allow a better referenced, more accurate and complete, second edition. The authors want to take this opportunity to invite you, the readers, to give us feedback concerning this book. We wish to thank you for your anticipated help which will be used to improve this introductory text for practitioners in this important field.

Table of Contents – Broad Overview

Acknowledgments
A Word from the Authors
Introduction by Joel Lubar

Table of Contents

PART ONE
What Neurofeedback is & the Science Behind It

SECTION I - What Neurofeedback Is and the Science Behind It.

SECTION II - Origin of The Electroencephalogram (EEG)

SECTION III - The EEG: Frequencies & Normal & Abnormal Waveforms

PART TWO:
Assessment and Intervention

Section VI - The Basics Of Assessment & Intervention, 128

Section VII - Autonomic Nervous System (ANS) and Skeletal Muscle Tone Assessment (EMG)

PART THREE

Acknowledgements

Our mentors and teachers in this field are extraordinary scientists and wonderful individuals – intelligent, innovative, rigorous and, also, friendly. One of them should have written this book but they all are too busy doing cutting edge work, so it got left to us to interpret a field they created.

Our training in biochemistry, physiology, medicine and psychology gave a background to neurology, neuroanatomy, the EEG, biofeedback and learning, but our introduction to the use of the EEG for biofeedback training (neurofeedback) came from Joel Lubar. In 1992 Dr. Lubar was giving one of his classic introductory workshops in Fort Lauderdale on "A Non-medication Approach to Treating ADD" and somehow the Biofeedback Society of Florida pamphlet arrived on our doorstep - February in Florida instead of Toronto? That seemingly easy choice led to our discovery of the field. Then came more training with Tom Allen in Florida, Joel and Judy Lubar in Tennessee, Frank and Mary Diets in Arizona, and Susan and Siegfried Othmer in California. Within the year ADD Centres Ltd. was born out of our joint practices that dealt to a large extent with learning disabilities, attention deficit disorder and children who had Asperger's syndrome and autism. Then Barry Sterman's address at the Northwestern Biofeedback Society meeting in Banff in November of 1993 made it clear there was plenty more to master. We took further training in full cap assessment techniques taught by George Fitzsimmons, a psychologist in the Department of Education at the University of Alberta. He had also been taught by Joel Lubar and had started the first neurofeedback centre in Canada at the University of Alberta called the Neuronal Re-regulation Programme. Since then there has been regular attendance at meetings of the Association for Applied Psychophysiology and Biofeedback, the Society for Neuronal Regulation, Future Health's Winter Brain meetings, plus pleasant forays to the Biofeedback Foundation of Europe and the World Congress of Psychophysiology.

The warmth of people in this field and the generous way that everyone shares their knowledge is perhaps the most impressive feature of the neurofeedback community. In addition to Joel Lubar and Barry Sterman, pioneers like Joe Kamiya, Tom Budzynski and Peter Rosenfeld were welcoming and ready to share knowledge from the first time we met them in Key West at an early Rob Kall Winter Brain meeting. George Fuller von Bozay modeled combining biofeedback with neurofeedback, which has become a mainstay of our approach. Jay Gunkelman added an element of fun and constructive drive that, along with the lectures by Bob Thatcher, made us dig out Michael's neuroanatomy and electroencephalography textbooks, plus his neurology notes and diagrams from a year spent dissecting the brain. Vendors and manufacturers are, likewise, great sources of information. Frank Diets has been unfailingly patient in teaching about things electronic in response to Michael's calls. His wife Mary has always assisted us in understanding the fine points of biofeedback. Hal Myers, Larry Klein and their staff at Thought Technology have assisted at every turn. Hal and Larry are indefatigable proponents of our field and add Canadian content, as does the ever innovative Paul Swingle. Lexicor staff contribute significantly to education and trained our son James in 19-channel intricacies. There are also behind the scenes heroes like Francine Butler, Executive Director of AAPB, and Judy Crawford, Director of Certification (and heart and soul) of BCIA. As we got to the point that we could share what we had learned, we presented papers about our clinical work and started being invited to give workshops. We have been privileged to teach in Canada, the United States, Australia, Israel, Switzerland, Germany, Norway, and China and our thanks go to all those professionals whose questions and discussion have continually pushed us to revise our concepts and techniques.

For this text, Barry Sterman reviewed the section on QEEG and contributed brain map examples. Jay Gunkelman also shared EEG examples and his extensive experience in reading EEGs. Joel Lubar wrote the section on LORETA and kindly contributed the introduction to the book. Bonny Beuret of the Lerninstitut Basel in Switzerland deserves particular thanks for her reading of the manuscript and helpful editing. The talented Amanda Reeves produced the drawings and worked on typing several early drafts of the manuscript. Our children must have a special thanks for putting up with their parents being buried in manuscripts for the last four years. They have each made their own unique contributions. James has written the chapter on Statistics and Research design and has worked with us at international meetings presenting on the training of athletes and executives. Aaron, the newest Dr. Thompson in the family, helped with scientific references and Katie put us straight on what learning strategies are useful in high-school and university settings.

This book represents our inchoate strivings to understand a fascinating and fast moving field and to share that knowledge. The new discipline of neurofeedback spans diverse domains of knowledge: neuroscience, anatomy, physiology, electroencephalography, psychology, learning theory, biofeedback, electronics and electrical engineering, measuring devices, physics, computers, statistics and research design, therapeutic interventions, stress management, sports psychology, metacognition, sleep research, pharmacology, nutrition, and the list goes on. If you feel a bit overwhelmed, that is appropriate. After more than a decade in the field, we still do, too.

Yet you should not feel discouraged. It is possible to learn enough of the necessary bits from each of the complementary disciplines to make a start at applying your knowledge to help people learn to self regulate. Then you keep learning more from clients and from colleagues. We gratefully acknowledge what clients, in particular, have taught us this past decade. Our hope and purpose in writing this book is that your learning curve will be a little easier and more efficient than ours. We have tried to give you "the basics" in one place. In return, we expect that you will be contributing your experience to the field in the next decade.

A Word from the Authors

Welcome to the field of neurofeedback. Once you enter, you will never be bored and you will never stop learning. There is always more to master and it keeps one both curious and humble.

Sharing Our Bias With You:

Biofeedback and neurofeedback are tools that assist individuals to learn self-regulation skills that improve their functioning. These tools may be used in two general ways. The first is an educational or training use. The candidates for this are students, athletes and persons who wish to optimize their performance in school, jobs, sports or even interpersonal relationships. This educational intervention is done by the individual, most often with the help of a teacher, trainer or coach who has specialized training in biofeedback and/or neurofeedback. The second use is a therapeutic one. The feedback tools assist the therapist to help a client or patient to manage symptoms or overcome a disorder, disease, condition (e.g., substance abuse) or an emotional difficulty. In this case, a health care professional is helping a patient and the biofeedback and neurofeedback are one part of the treatment plan.

We chose the term 'tool' for feedback because the analogy is that neurofeedback equipment is a lot like exercise equipment. We are facilitating exercise for the brain. An exercise machine may be used by an individual at home, in a gym or at school with the assistance of a trainer or coach. You certainly need to know something about the equipment and how to use it, plus the individual doing training should have a training regimen designed by someone knowledgeable at the outset. That is like the first – educational - use of neurofeedback. Analogous to the second use would be exercise equipment in a hospital or clinic when a physiotherapist is doing rehabilitation. The use depends on the presenting situation: a person is doing exercise either for self-improvement or because they are a patient requiring treatment. Similarly, neurofeedback is used either for training clients or for treating patients.

Just as with an exercise machine, one must not attribute undue power to the use of biofeedback or neurofeedback equipment. The goals of the user may often be achieved using other techniques; meditation, relaxation, yoga, cognitive training, metacognitive strategies to name just a few. EEG biofeedback, however, is usually more efficient. Training can be done quite rapidly using modern technology as compared to these other techniques. Neurofeedback can also be combined with other interventions.

For the most part our focus is on an educational approach both at our ADD Centre and in this book. Thus we talk of trainers who have a coaching role, rather than therapists, when describing who is helping the student or client learn self-regulation. Topics such as alpha-theta training, which is appropriately used by therapists, will receive less discussion in this book than will approaches that improve attention and concentration. Tension, distractibility, lack of ability to quickly shift between broad and narrow focus, poor organization and inability to sustain concentration all interfere in work, school and sports. Helping people to have more flexible brains and to be able to produce a state that is calm, alert and focused is what we specialize in and do every day at our ADD Centre. We *add* to a person's self-regulatory skills using neurofeedback. How we do this and why we do this (i.e., the scientific underpinnings) is the subject of this book.

Overview of this Book:

This book is written to assist you in understanding the basis of neurofeedback and the fundamentals of how to do EEG biofeedback. Note from the outset that we do not yet know the precise mechanisms by which EEG biofeedback works. Ours is an empirical field based on observed outcomes. There is a lot of science behind it. As Dr. John Basmajian stressed in his address at the AAPB convention in 2000, we do not have to be apologetic in the least about our field because it is solidly research based. (Basmajian is, himself, a biofeedback pioneer who demonstrated in the 1960's that you could do single motor neuron training.) Understand that our knowledge is still growing and much of what is written today may be obsolete in a few years time.

Part One begins with questions. What is biofeedback? Why use an EEG? What kind of learning takes place? How is the EEG produced? What can be observed with the EEG? How does the EEG instrument detect and display this information? Neuroanatomy related to neurofeedback is covered and includes the following: the synapse, nerve conduction, the structure of the cortex, the fundamentals of pyramidal cells, inhibitory cells, the influence of subcortical structures on the EEG and some aspects of what is known about the functions of the ganglia and the lobes of the brain.

Part Two, attempts to answer the question of how and why one does biofeedback (BFB) combined with neurofeedback (NFB). It includes how to do a NFB assessment, artifact the data and carry out NFB training. It also includes a brief BFB stress assessment detailing what sensors are used, what they represent and how to carry out a combined NFB + BFB training session. Included is mention of other techniques that may accelerate the learning process, with particular emphasis on a detailed look at metacognition.

Part Three, contains information about research design and statistics. It is written by our eldest son James Thompson who is a graduate student in Human Physiology. He is closer to these topics than his parents. Understanding basic concepts in these areas is vital, not only for doing research but for evaluating intelligently the research done by others. We want everyone in the field of neurofeedback to continue in the scientific vein in which our field was first conceived.

Current and Future Status of Neurofeedback

Our understanding of where neurofeedback fits in the larger realm of neuroscience and how it works is still primitive. Compare it to Galileo's stunning deduction that the earth revolved around the sun, with our world just a minor part of a large solar system. His basic ideas were resisted, but were not disproven and they eventually were accepted and refined with further astronomical discoveries. Our field is still

in the new-idea-being-resisted stage, but it will eventually become mainstream for the simple reason that it works. We all look forward to neuroscience advancements leading to increased understanding of how neurofeedback works and the most efficient ways to use this valuable tool.

Self-regulation will become a major part of health maintenance in the 21st century. Two powerful reasons underlie this assertion. First, self-regulation aided by biofeedback and neurofeedback is effective in managing a wide range of conditions, many of which do not respond readily to traditional medical approaches. Secondly, the cost to society is much less since the focus is on maintaining health with self-regulation rather than being passive in receiving help when things go wrong. Self-regulation is a learning method that engenders a long term positive change. Pharmaceutical methods, for example, are only effective as long as the medication is continued and are costly in the long term. Self regulation is health, not illness, oriented.

Why isn't neurofeedback better accepted in some quarters? Why is neurofeedback largely ignored? One reason is that it is outside the scope of most health care professionals' training. It is an enormous conceptual shift for many with biochemical or neurological training and experience to move from a psychopharmacological model to an educational model using biofeedback. If you have no experience with something, you may not even perceive it. The natives reportedly did not see Cortez' ships in the bay because they had no prior experience of big, wooden floating things that could transport people across vast oceans. Accept that neurofeedback is not yet on the radar screen for most people, but be assured that awareness is growing. The internet is spreading the word faster than the scientific publications are.

We all have a responsibility to do things right so that the word that spreads is favorable. Aim for success with every client. Keep in mind the advice to promise less and deliver more.

Notes to the Reader

1. The terms *EEG biofeedback* and *neurofeedback* (NFB) are used interchangeably in this text. Other terms in common usage are *neurotherapy* and, simply, *brain wave biofeedback*. Whatever the term, the process involves monitoring brain electrical activity, displaying it as an *electroencephalogram* (EEG), and giving the client instant information, thus feedback, about what their brain is doing.

2. The term *BIOFEEDBACK* (BFB) is used when the information given back to the client involves autonomic nervous system modalities or muscle electrical activity. Muscle contractions are measured and shown with an electromyogram (EMG tracing). The other modalities commonly used are temperature, heart rate, respiration rate, and skin conductance, which is also called electrodermal response (EDR), or the inverse of EDR, galvanic skin response (GSR).

3. We suggest that you, yourself, use *metacognitive strategies* while reading this book. In other words, go beyond (*meta*) regular thinking and perceiving (*cognition*) and be aware of how you are thinking, how you best learn and remember new material. To start off right, apply active reading strategies. **Before opening the rest of this book,** first think about what you would like to know and how you would design such a text. Second, scan the major headings, then the sub-headings, and think about how your design matches or differs from the one we decided to use. Third, review the intent of the book, as described here in this *Word from the Authors*. Fourth, begin to read in whatever chapter seems most useful to you. Throughout your reading, please generate questions and try to find the answers, either here or in other texts. These steps encourage emotional involvement which helps you remember the material. Make sure you have a personal reason for bothering to read this text.

Important note concerning pronoun use and *gender neutrality.*

In keeping with the government's policy in our province, in the text we have, for the most part, adopted the use of *they, their, themselves* instead of *he/she, his/her, himself/herself* even when the sentence would normally require the singular. For example, you may find a phrase such as, the client changed *their* theta wave amplitude, which is traditionally grammatically incorrect but has now become the correct way to speak and write in our jurisdiction.

In addition, we have used American and British/Canadian/Australian spelling interchangeably.

4. Disclaimer:

This text is a short primer about a broad field. For this reason everything is simplified. Simplification may be overdone and errors do occur. Also, we put the criterion of "doneness" ahead of perfection. So, when you find errors, please let us know by writing to us at 50 Village Centre Place, Mississauga, ON L4Z 1V9 Canada. We will attempt to put corrections that we make from your suggestions onto our website: www.addcentre.com or on to the AAPB website: www.aapb.org. Your feedback will also contribute to an improved second edition of this text.

THE
NEUROFEEDBACK
BOOK

An Introduction to The Neurofeedback Book

Joel F. Lubar Ph.D,
BCIA-Senior Fellow, BCIA-EEG, Fellow ISNR
Professor, University of Tennessee
Co-Director,
Southeastern Biofeedback and Neurobehavioral Institute

I am very pleased to have this opportunity to write the forward for Drs. Michael and Lynda Thompson's new book "The Neurofeedback Book". Neurofeedback has been around a long time, since the 1960s when it was only called EEG biofeedback. We have waited more than 40 years for the advent of a true textbook of neurofeedback. The Neurofeedback Book fulfills this need beautifully and in great detail. This book is written for people at all levels of knowledge in the field from beginners to those who are very advanced. The writing style is clear and straightforward.

 The Thompson's book begins with basic science dealing with the definitions of biofeedback and neurofeedback and a rather detailed discussion regarding EEG in terms of its generation, and its normal and abnormal manifestations. The genesis of the EEG in terms of its emergence from activity both at the cellular level and intra-cortical dynamics and thalamocortical pacemakers is very complex. This text does a fine job of sorting these out and elaborating them in Part One. There is a very detailed coverage of the terminology that is germane to the EEG literature such as coherence, phase, asymmetry, synchrony, and basic terms such as frequency, magnitude different waveforms and many others. The majority of the material that one would need in preparation for certification in the area of EEG biofeedback is contained in this volume. The basic neurophysiology and basic science behind EEG is well outlined both in terms of its historical importance as well as the present state of knowledge. The book contains numerous excellent illustrations both in black and white as well as in color showing different types of EEG phenomena including topographic brain maps and comparisons of clinical cases with normative databases.

There is a wealth of clinical information contained in the volume dealing with most of the common disorders that are currently treated both medically and with behavioral medicine approaches including neurofeedback. There are illustrations of different types of feedback displays from a variety of different instruments. Considerable effort is expended in discussions of clinical procedures including assessment, psychophysiological profiling, combining conventional biofeedback with neurofeedback, and tracking patient progress. The Thompsons describe in detail their metacognitive approach for working with attentional and learning disorders.

One important part of the book is the detailed list of references and the whole section of multiple choice questions that are tied to the BCIA blueprint areas for EEG biofeedback Certification. This again emphasizes the value of The Neurofeedback Book as a primer for new certificants and as a review for those seeking recertification or additional certifications in the field. In summary, The Neurofeedback Book should be read and reread by all in the field and should be made available for University courses in psychophysiology and behavioral medicine. It provides a wealth of material for patients in treatment using neurofeedback approaches and for educating professionals in health care who might refer patients for treatment or who might be considering embarking on the neurofeedback-neurotherapy endeavor.

PART ONE

WHAT NEUROFEEDBACK IS AND THE SCIENCE BEHIND IT

This section contains a brief overview of definitions, learning theory, origin of the EEG, instrumentation and neuroanatomy. In each of these areas it is expected that the reader will have had undergraduate courses. This section is meant only to give a short review of the area as it pertains to the use of neurofeedback. The reader is encouraged to review their own basic textbook on neuroanatomy. The section on instrumentation and electronics goes into detail that is not necessary for most neurofeedback practitioners but is important in understanding the differential amplifier and the importance of impedance.

x

SECTION I
What Neurofeedback Is and the Science Behind It

What is biofeedback in general and EEG biofeedback in particular? *Definition, Description & Overview of Biofeedback, Learning Theory, and Neurofeedback Applications.*

A. What is Biofeedback

Biofeedback is the use of instrumentation to mirror psychophysiological processes of which the individual is not normally aware and which may be brought under voluntary control (George Fuller, 1984).

Think of *Bio* as referring to biology, the science of life, and all those dynamic processes which are going on all the time in our bodies. The brain with its 100 billion neurons runs this whole dynamic organization. The nerves carry its messages to every corner of the human body. Through the action of neurotransmitters, neuromodulators and neurohormones, every cell in the body can be influenced by the brain. When you give the brain information you influence the system. Biofeedback simply means "*feeding*" information "*back*" to the individual who generated the bio-signals in the first place.

One example of *feeding back bio*logical information is heart rate variability biofeedback. When the heart runs faster, something in the nervous system is related to this increase. In this case it is a portion of the *autonomic* nervous system called the *sympathetic* nervous system. In our body there is always a balance of stimulating and slowing, excitation and inhibition. In the example of heart rate, slowing of the heart corresponds to its being released from sympathetic stimulation, which speeded it up. The *parasympathetic system* (more specifically, the vagus nerve which has branches to many of our internal organs) takes over control of heart rate, inhibiting or slowing down the heart.

Biofeedback for this modality involves using an instrument which monitors heart rate variability and displays this virtually instantly in "real time" to the client whose cardiac activity is being measured. The display is the feedback and it usually has both a visual and auditory component.

Biofeedback implies more than just a *passive* measurement. It implies an *active* involvement of the client. *Biofeedback* is done so that the client will become actively involved in controlling their own physiology; hence the term *applied psychophysiology*

EEG biofeedback, (or neurofeedback) is based on two basic tenets: that brain electrical activity – the electroencephalogram or EEG - reflects mental states and that the activity can be trained. Electrical activity being produced in the brain can be displayed on a computer screen virtually instantly (within approximately 50 to 100 milliseconds with modern equipment). The display is in the form of a line with a mixture of waves. Most people are familiar with the electrocardiogram (EKG) that represents the electrical activity of the heart. The EEG is similar but less regular. It looks rather like waves on the surface of a lake. Like waves on a lake, what we observe is always a complex sum: small little waves with low amplitude and little force or power, like those produced by a gentle breeze run at a high frequency, whereas larger waves (high amplitude, more power), like the waves produced by a ferry boat, run at a slower frequency. The little ripples change amplitude and frequency with each gust of wind – and are thus desynchronous. The larger waves, however, roll by in a more regular synchronous fashion. We have already noted that there is a different *generator* for each of these types of waves, those from the ferry boat versus those from the wind. Indeed we could imagine a smaller motor boat going by and producing a regular, synchronous, wave of a little higher frequency but less power than those from the much larger ferry boat. The little ripples may ride on top of the larger waves and the surface activity is constantly changing. This analogy can be kept in mind when watching the EEG on the computer screen.

Similarly, in the case of the EEG, waves which come from different *generators* (cortex, thalamus) are different in frequency. The raw EEG contains all these different frequencies in a single wavy line, faster waves riding on top of slower waves.

EEG biofeedback involves recording this information using electrodes placed on the scalp and *displaying* it, that is *feeding it back,* on a computer display screen. As the client a*lters their own mental state* it changes the amplitudes of various brain wave frequencies. The client sees this change as it is reflected by various displays on the computer monitor and attempts to alter their brainwave pattern to achieve a predefined goal. In this manner the client learns to *self-regulate. It is a learned normalization of EEG patterns (Sterman).* To summarize, advanced electronics and mathematical computations have made it possible to convert EEG patterns into images on a computer monitor. Learning to change the computer image reflects self-regulation of the EEG. Self-regulation of the EEG requires that the client self regulate underlying mental states which were responsible for that EEG pattern. Since the EEG patterns reflect system changes in thalamus-basal ganglia-cortical interchanges, the person is actually learning self-regulation of this complex dynamic neural system.

It is well established in science that a positive reward for a behaviour is followed by an increase in the probability of that behaviour recurring. (Edward Thorndike's Law of Effect). The production of particular brainwave patterns is the behaviour we reward when doing EEG biofeedback. The reward is information about success using sounds and visual displays provided by a computer. Rewarding a behaviour (or a sequence of neurophysiological occurrences) therefore 'shapes' the contributing components of that sequence in a way that results in an increased frequency of that behaviour sequence recurring (Sterman 2000). Shaping is done through a process which is termed *operant conditioning.*

The term *operant conditioning* originally reflected the fact that the behaviours being trained resulted in a series of learned responses which constituted an operation(s) or observed action on the environment. Advances in techniques demonstrated that internal changes such as skin temperature or heart rate could also be influenced in this manner. External rewards could thus influence physiological changes in the body (Sterman 2000). The operations were no longer on the external environment and a new term for this type of work emerged. After much discussion in the 1960's, it came to be called *biofeedback.*

When we reward changes in neuronal behaviour, using a tool called the electroencephalogram (EEG) which reflects changes in neuronal activity, we use the term EEG biofeedback or neurofeedback. The evidence that EEG biofeedback can produce significant and sustained physiological changes was well documented as far back as the early 1970's. (For references see the review by M. Barry Sterman, entitled "EEG Markers for Attention Deficit Disorder: Pharmacological and Neurofeedback Applications". *Child Study Journal*, Vol. 30, No. 1, 2000)

Biofeedback is **not a new invention**. Biofeedback is a universal, natural, biological process. A simple example is learning to ride a bicycle. If a child is 7 or 8 years, old he can learn, usually in half an hour, put his bike down for the winter and then ride again without relearning in the spring. How is this possible? The answer is *natural neurofeedback.* Instead of a biofeedback instrument on the desk we have one inside our body, in the inner ear, called the vestibular apparatus. It consists of fluid inside tiny semicircular canals which detect movement in all directions. This information is instantly sent to the brain along the auditory pathways (just like neurofeedback displays are sent by the optic and auditory pathways). The brain assimilates the data and, far faster than one can consciously think about what is happening, adjusts the muscles. The result is that the child is balanced on the bicycle. The means for learning was a kind of internal *neurofeedback.* Other ways of gaining control over brain states that have been practiced for centuries include yoga, meditation, and martial arts.

Treatment versus Training

Treatment, for the most part, implies passivity. Taking a medication or undergoing a surgical procedure are examples of 'passive' involvement of the patient. Learning (training) is an active process that requires some motivation and repetition of exercises.

B. What can be Measured?

1. Concerning Biofeedback

In many forms of *biofeedback* we measure functioning of the autonomic (sympathetic and parasympathetic) nervous system. You may think of the word *autonomic* as meaning 'automatic'. Decades ago western scientists thought that this portion of our nervous system, which governed the actions of our internal organs (for example the heart, blood vessels, lungs, gastrointestinal system, bladder and so on), was not under conscious control. On the other hand, Eastern practitioners in places like India and China have practiced controlling aspects of these systems for thousands of years. As a Greek once said, "nothing new under the sun."

Western science made a leap forward in the 1900's when it, too, recognized that humans are capable of consciously learning how to *self-regulate* much of their own physiology. It became clear that we could regulate autonomic biological functions such as: peripheral skin temperature, electrodermal responses (sweating), heart rate, and the synchrony of heart rate with respiration which is called respiratory sinus arrhythmia (RSA). In addition, we now use the term *biofeedback* to refer to control of muscle tension (EMG). How to assess and self regulate each of these physiological functions is dealt with in a later section.

2. Concerning Neurofeedback

In *neurofeedback* we measure the frequency and amplitude of different brain waves. These are recorded by means of small electrodes (sensors) placed using a highly conductive electrode paste on the surface of the scalp. The electrode records evidence of electrical activity produced by the underlying neurons (nerve cells) in the brain. This recording is called an *electroencephalogram (EEG)*. *Electro* because you are measuring electricity (the potential difference between two electrodes), *encephalo* which refers to brain and *'gram'* which means writing. Older machines use pens which draw the brain waves on paper that is rolled past the pen. Current technology uses a computer display of the waves. The raw EEG shows the morphology (shape) of the waves, the amplitude (how high the waves are from peak to trough) and the frequency (how many waves there are in one second). Waves with different frequencies occur together, often with faster waves riding on slower waves. Different EEG patterns correspond to different mental states. For example, there are different patterns for sleep and wakening, for focused concentration and problem solving compared to drifting off and day dreaming, for impulsive, hyperactive states versus calm, reflective states and so on.

A *quantitative electroencephalogram* (QEEG) involves not just recording the EEG but doing measurements; that is, quantifying data concerning the amount of electrical activity occurring at particular frequencies (say, 4 Hz.), or across defined frequency bands (say, 4-8 Hz.). The electrical activity is usually expressed either as amplitude, measured in microvolts (μV) or millionths of a volt, or as power, measured in picawatts (pW). The raw EEG shows brainwaves, amplitude and wave forms seen as a function of time. The QEEG uses computer algorithms that transform this raw EEG into quantitative displays that assist the clinician to recognize deviations from normal. You can do a simple QEEG using 3 leads. The electrodes comprise a positive (+ ve) lead, a negative (- ve) lead and a ground. The ground is not truly a ground wire in modern instruments; it performs a type of electrical or instrument housekeeping which results in a good quality recording. The EEG instrument (the *electroencephalograph*) measures the potential difference between the +ve and the -ve leads. The positive lead is called the *active* lead and is usually placed over the area you wish to record and measure. The –ve lead, called a *reference* electrode, is usually placed over a relatively inactive area electrically such as the mastoid bone or an ear lobe. This is called a referential placement. It is also possible to measure the *potential difference* between two active electrode sites on the scalp. This kind of *sequential* recording gives much lower amplitudes as compared to a *referential* recording. The potential difference between the two active sites is also dependent on the ***phase*** of the waveforms being measured and compared. Imagine that you were measuring and comparing the amplitude of 2 waves running at 9 cycles (or waves) per second. Cycles-per-second (cps) is called Hertz (Hz) named after Heinrich R. Hertz, a German physicist who died in 1894. If one of these waves registered +6 μv and the other +4 μv the difference would be 2 μv. On the other hand, if the first measured +6 μv and the second – 4 μv the algebraic sum or difference between the two sites would be much higher, namely, 10 μv.

This same kind of comparison or measurement between pairs of electrodes can be done for many more leads placed at different locations on the scalp. Usually 19 leads at active sites are used and it is called a *full cap* assessment. This term arises from the fact that this type of assessment may utilize a soft, thin, cloth cap (a popular one was developed by Marvin Sams), which looks very like a swimmer's bathing cap. The cap has tiny electrodes sewn into it. The data from a full cap assessment can be quantified in various ways. The clinician can look at power, percent power (percent of a certain bandwidth compared to the total power of all bandwidths), coherence, comodulation and phase. (These terms will be discussed later.) It can also be compared to a normal database, with several from which to choose. This is discussed in the section on *assessment* in Part II. There are research centers, where they are trying to improve the spatial information from an EEG recording, that use even more electrodes, sometimes over 200.

Another, newer, experimental method of describing information concerning electrical activity is called LORETA (*low resolution electrical tomography assessment*) This is a mathematical process which looks at surface EEG information and infers what activity is occurring in areas a little deeper in the cortex It was first developed by Roberto Pasqual-Marquis in Zurich. At this time these data appear to be correlating very well with MRI (*magnetic resonance imagery*) findings. However, LORETA is very sensitive to many kinds of artifact. In future we may be using LORETA derived information to guide neurofeedback interventions.

Note that EEG, though it lacks the spatial resolution possible with imaging techniques such as MRI or PET, has the best temporal resolution. You can see what the brain is doing over time very accurately. EEG also has the advantage of being non-invasive whereas other mapping techniques often involve injections of radioactive material. With the PET (*positron emission tomography*) scan a radioactive form of oxygen is injected. Positrons are given off. These collide with electrons. The result is 2 gamma rays or photons that are detected by the scanner which calculates their source. Metabolically active regions of the brain have an increased demand for oxygen and thus regions of increased (or decreased) blood flow can be identified. These other techniques are well accepted by the scientific community and EEG data correspond well to the other measures. With Attention Deficit Disorder, for example, the slowing of the EEG in the central and frontal regions parallels decreased glucose metabolism shown on PET scans and decreased blood flow seen on SPECT scans in the frontal region.

3. Event Related Potentials (ERPs):

An ERP is a measure of brain electrical activity which occurs as a response to a specific stimulus. The EEG, on the other hand, is a measurement of spontaneous and on-going activity in the brain. ERPs are usually thought of as being *time-locked* to a specific stimulus. There are interesting exceptions to this. For example, ERPs have been found at the exact time when a stimulus was expected but when there was no actual external stimulus present (Sutton, Teuting, Zubin & John, 1967). The definition of an ERP as proposed by Vaughn in 1969 stated that the ***ERP is a brain response that shows a stable time relationship to actual or anticipated stimuli.***

In North America there is not a lot of overlap between people using ERPs and those doing neurofeedback, but research in these two ways of looking at brain electrical activity are complementary. The ERP research literature is much larger and, because conditions are carefully controlled, it has more scientific respect. Most often ERPs are measured at FZ,

CZ, and PZ (see the 10-20 electrode system diagram for these locations) and amplitude and scalp distribution are among the variables measured. Amplitudes of one common measurement called the P300 are usually highest parietally and lowest in the frontal region. Research has shown that ERPs can distinguish between different clinical conditions so they are used in diagnosis. The most common application is the use of ERPs by audiologists to test hearing since the presence of the response indicates the brain has responded to the sound even if the person cannot give a verbal response.

Most ERPs are only made visible by averaging many, many samples (at least twenty and sometimes several thousand samples). Specific ERPs, in a given individual, come a set time interval after the stimulus and are always the same waveform. When sufficient samples are averaged, the ERP deflections are consistent and will remain whereas other brain activity will be random and will therefore cancel out. Vaughn suggests four types of ERPs: sensory, motor, long-latency potentials and steady-potential-shifts. The sensory ERPs are those evoked by sight, sound, smell and touch. Auditory ERPs occur with a negative peak at about 80–90 msec, and a positive peak at about 170 msec, after the stimulus. These together are called the N1-P2 complex. It occurs in the auditory cortex in the temporal lobe (Vaughn & Arezzo, 1988). Motor ERPs precede and accompany motor movement and are proportional in amplitude to the strength and speed of muscle contraction. They are seen in the precentral area (motor cortex).

Long-latency potentials reflect subjective responses to expected or unexpected stimuli. They run between 250 and 750 msec after the stimulus. The most often mentioned ERP is a positive response called the P300. It comes approximately 300 msec after an *odd-ball* stimulus, although it can be later, depending on variables such as age and processing speed. Children with ADD tend to have a slower P300 than their non-ADD age peers. An *odd-ball* refers to a meaningful stimulus which is different than the other stimuli in a series. An example is a high tone in a series of low tones or hearing your name when a list of names is being read aloud. The P300 (sometimes shortened to just "P3") indicates that the brain has noticed something. The P300 was apparently discovered by Sutton, Barron and Zubin in 1965. The orienting response is also seen as an ERP. A switch in attention evokes what can be termed P3a. Engagement operations may evoke parietal P3b responses. Disengagement may evoke a frontal-central P3b response.

One important negative long-latency potential is the N400 (Kutas & Hillyard 1980). It occurs as a response to unexpected endings in sentences or other semantic deviations. The lyrics of the song, *Oh Suzanna,* "It rained all night the day I left, the weather it was dry. The sun so hot, I froze to death. Suzanna don't you cry." would presumably evoke a series of N400 responses.

An example of a *steady-potential shift* is one that occurs after a person is told that they must wait after a signal (warning) and then respond to an event. It is a kind of *anticipation* response. It is seen as a negative shift which occurs between the warning signal and the event. This type of steady-potential shift is called a *contingent negative variation (CNV)* (Walter, Cooper, Aldridge, McCallum & Winter, 1964.)

ERPs have been investigated as an aid to diagnosis. For example, using *go-nogo paradigms,* there are response differences between ADHD children and normals. In a 'go' condition the subject performs an action in response to a cue. A green light is an example of a cue that says you can cross the street. A 'go' stimulus produces alpha desynchronization. In a 'nogo' condition the subject withholds acting in response to a cue that indicates he is not to act. A red light at a street corner is an example of a cue that says you must withhold a response and not cross the street. In this case the subject must suppress a prepared action. There is motor inhibition. Following a 'nogo' stimulus there is an initial desynchronization followed by synchronization in the frontal and occipital areas. These ERP responses are impaired in ADHD. The ERP amplitudes are higher in normal subjects. It has been demonstrated that 20 sessions of beta training, in subjects diagnosed with ADHD, can result in a dramatic increase in the ERP response (Grin-Yatsenko, Kropotov, 2001). At the time of writing, Yuri Kropotov's group in St. Petersburg, Russia, were doing work using ERPs that should help elucidate the areas of the cortex that are involved in discrimination tasks. Peter Rosenfeld, at Northwestern University near Chicago, USA, has been working on the use of ERPs in lie detection. He has found a different scalp distribution regarding the amplitude of the P300 when someone lies. Interestingly, when the amplitudes of P300 are graphed at Fz-Cz and Pz there is a straight line when subjects are telling the truth and a crooked line when lies are told Rosenfeld, 1998).

ERPs can also be used to demonstrate the effects of injury. For example, Kropotov has shown that an auditory ERP will decrease if there is an injury in the left temporal-parietal area (auditory cortex) but will increase if the damage is in the frontal area. This increase indicates a loss of inhibition from the frontal to the temporal lobe.

4. Event-Related-Desynchronization (ERD)

Event-Related-Desynchronization (ERD) refers to the observation that increased cognitive or sensory workload results in a decrease in rhythmic slow wave activity and an increase in desynchronized beta activity. When the task is completed there is *post-reinforcement-synchronization* (PRS) of the EEG. M. Barry Sterman describes these patterns in his work concerning EEG measurements in top-gun pilots. He notes that this synchronization phase is self-rewarding. It seems almost as if the brain rewards itself with a little rest – a burst of synchronous alpha waves – after completing a task. Sterman also found that a pilot would shift from faster brain wave activity (beta) to alpha when he was on overload; for example, attempting an impossible landing in the simulator. Thus alpha can reflect different things under different conditions - in these instances, either a very brief rest or giving up. Nothing is ever simple regarding the complex human brain. It is best to learn early that you must live with a bit of ambiguity in the field of neurofeedback.

5. Slow Cortical Potentials (SCPs)

The major work in this area is carried out in Europe prinicipally by researchers such as Nils Birbaumer, at the University of Tuebingen, Germany and by John Gruzelier, of the Psychology department at the Imperial College of Medicine in London. The equipment most of us are using for assessment and for neurofeedback in North America will not measure these slow cortical potentials. SCPs are

very slow waves that indicate the shift between positive and negative. These shifts underlie the electrical activity we are usually measuring.

There is great interest in this meticulous work. Gruzelier examined slow cortical potentials in patients with schizophrenia. Birbaumer has been able to teach subjects with severe amyotrophic lateral sclerosis (ALS or Lou Gehrig's disease), who could not speak or move or otherwise communicate, to consciously make a positive or negative shift like an on-off switch and thus communicate. He has used this to assist them to mark letters of the alphabet and thus slowly write sentences. He has also demonstrated that a shift to electro-positivity can decrease voltages of the normal AC (alternating current) activity of the brain. It may even halt an epileptic discharge.

C. Early findings with the EEG:

(For further description of the history of the field of neurofeedback the reader should consult Jim Robbins' book *A Symphony in the Brain*.)

1. History

The earliest measurements of electrical patterns in the brain were done with animals. These findings, using a string galvanometer to measure the activity, were reported in 1875 by a British scientist named Richard Caton. In the 1920's Hans Berger, a German psychiatrist, made detailed recordings and observations using his own son as the subject. He observed a pattern of uniform electrical waves in humans that he labelled as the first order waves. This came to be known as *alpha rhythm*, with reference to the first letter of the Greek alphabet. He also observed periods when these waves were absent, the pattern of waves was smaller and desynchronous. This pattern was called *beta*. His studies indicated that when people had their eyes closed the alpha rhythm was prominent but when they opened them it was greatly reduced, thus linking the alpha rhythm to the brain resting. Berger's observations, published in 1929, are still valid today. He gave not only the Greek letter designations to the field, he also coined the word electroencephalogram and the abbreviation EEG. His findings were replicated by two British scientists, Adrian and Matthews in 1934, which brought the field of EEG into the English scientific literature.

In 1958 psychologist Joe Kamiya, using careful scientific methods, demonstrated that a person could correctly identify when they were producing alpha waves but subjects were not able to say precisely how they were making that discrimination. Kamiya had one subject say "A" or "B" to indicate if he was in the state. By the third day he scored 400 correct guesses in a row! Kamiya noted later that he was fortunate in finding a subject so attuned to his own mental state as it increased his motivation to do more studies. This early finding is important when considering neurofeedback, which requires individuals to change their mental state according to feedback based on the brain waves they are producing. Research investigating the EEG as it relates to consciousness and awareness has continued for almost half a century. Thomas Hardt, for example, has done EEG recordings with Zen Buddhist monks in Japan and continues to research questions of consciousness at his center in San Francisco.

M. Barry Sterman, working with cats in the late 1960's at the University of California Los Angeles, demonstrated that they could be trained using a method called *operant conditioning* to increase a specific spindle-like brain wave pattern which ran at a frequency between 12 to 19 cycles per second. He gave the spindle like activity between 12 and 15Hz. the name *sensorimotor rhythm (SMR)*.

We are grateful to Dr. Maurice Barry Sterman for allowing us to use the picture below which was taken in his Lab during his brilliant experiments that for the first time demonstrated that brain waves could be operantly conditioned.

Closely following on this discovery was his observation that cats that had increased their SMR activity were resistant to seizures caused by exposure to hydrazine, a toxic chemical used in rocket fuel. This hydrazine had been causing seizures in air force personnel exposed to it during rocket fuelling operations. He tried the same operant conditioning to increase SMR in human patients with epilepsy and found that it decreased the frequency, duration and severity of seizures, and sometimes totally controlled their seizures. This effect has been successfully reproduced in other laboratories, as reviewed in Sterman's article published in the January 2000 issue of *Clinical Electroencephalography* January 2000. (That whole issue of *Clinical EEG* is devoted to neurofeedback and it is definitely recommended reading.)

Another physiological psychologist who was already working with EEG, Joel Lubar, came from the University of Tennessee to UCLA on a National Science Foundation grant to work for an academic year with Sterman. The observation had been made that many seizure disorder patients had hyperactivity and became calmer with SMR training. The question arose as to whether SMR training might be beneficial for children with hyperactivity. Margaret Shouse, a graduate student with Lubar at the time, decided to direct her doctoral thesis effort to this question. Using many outcome measures, she found that a significant number of the children she provided with SMR training objectively benefited. Building on earlier work concerning the EEG and on these findings, they published a paper on the neurofeedback treatment of an ADHD child (Shouse and Lubar, 1976 and 1979). Lubar has continued his work on operant conditioning for ADHD at the University of Tennessee. Lubar discovered that measuring the theta / beta ratio was a key to differentiating between normal and ADHD clients. Joel Lubar and his wife Judith, a social worker, have now amassed over 25 years of experience using the EEG for assessment and treatment. The Lubars have taught hundreds of professionals and students, and are responsible for much of the research in this field particularly with respect to using neurofeedback for people with ADD.

2. Some Applications that Use the EEG

a. Clinical Electroencephalography

The primary (medical) use of the EEG is **not for most readers of this text.** *Clinical encephalography* is used to detect and analyze transient events in the EEG that are abnormal. These events have a known clinical significance. An example is spike and wave activity that may be observed in a seizure disorder. This is largely the domain of neurologists and electro-encephalographers.

The role of the neurofeedback provider is fundamentally different from that of a neurologist. Neurology is a medical specialty wherein the EEG is used for the detection of abnormalities such as seizure disorders, space occupying lesions (tumors and aneurisms) and arteriovenous malformations. The neuro-feedback practitioner's interest usually lies in an entirely different area, that is, normal EEG waves and variations on normal. What is the foreground for our work is just background for the neurologist. Our assumption is that the neurofeedback client has their own medical practitioner and will always have their medical problems handled through that professional or by referral to a medical specialist. Neurofeedback training can be a helpful adjunct to medical treatment. It does not replace it.

b. Assessment Using Quantitative Electroencephalography

The second use of the EEG is to distinguish patterns that indicate a person is an appropriate candidate for neurofeedback training. Patterns should correspond to the history given by the client. This work involves the use of *quantitative electroencephalography* **(QEEG)**. This describes the spectral characteristics of the EEG. It may reveal differences from normal databases that would not easily be perceived by visual inspection of the raw EEG. The differences usually involve comparing amplitudes of different frequency bands to expected values and / or examining the communication between different areas of the brain. This information is used for planning a neurofeedback (NFB) training regimen.

Another use of the brain maps generated by QEEG methods is to look at patterns found in different diagnostic groups. E. Roy John and Leslie Prichip at New York University in Manhattan have done this in collaboration with psychiatrists at Bellevue Psychiatric Hospital and have published extensively (John, 1989). They can predict medication response in those with depression, for example, thus increasing the chances of choosing the correct class of antidepressant (SSRI versus tricylic anti-depressants) at the outset of treatment.

NFB practitioners observe the EEG waveforms and distinguish electrical frequency patterns for the purpose of setting up a training program to meet their clients' objectives and assist them to gain a degree of *self-regulation*. Normal brain wave patterns have been found to correspond to various mental states. We have detailed this in the section on 'States of Consciousness and Band Widths'. In brief, it has been found that delta activity, 0.5 –3 Hz, is found in sleep and also in conjunction with learning disabilities and brain injury. Theta waves, 4-7 Hz, are seen in drowsy, states which are also states in which some quite creative thoughts may occur. Low alpha, 8-10 Hz, is found in dissociative states, some kinds of meditation, and tuning out from external stimuli (daydreaming). High alpha, 11-12 Hz, can be found associated with creative reflection as well as relaxed calm states of optimal performance. Sensorimotor rhythm frequencies, 13–15 Hz. imply being motorically calm with reflection before action. Low Beta waves, 16-20 Hz, are associated with singular focus, external orientation and problem solving, while higher beta frequencies may be found in association with anxiety (above 20 Hz) and rumination (around 30 Hz). Note that there is overlap in the frequency bands (theta may be defined as 3-7, 4-7, or 4-8 Hz, for example). There are also shifts with age, moving to the right along the frequency spectrum (frequency on a horizontal spectrum increases as you move from left to right thus 7 Hz in a child may be 8 Hz activity in an adult). Indeed, in young children, for example, alpha wave forms may have a frequency of 7 Hz.

Correlations of Band Widths to Mental States

Frequency Bands	Correlations
0.5-3 Hz Delta	Movement or eye blink artifact. Brain damage. Learning disabilities. The dominant frequency in infants.
3-5 Hz Low Theta	Tuned out. Sleepy.
6-7 Hz High Theta	Internal orientation, important in memory recall, can be very creative but may not recall ideas for very long after emerging from this mental state unless these ideas are consciously worked on and developed. Not focused on external learning stimuli such as reading or listening. The dominant frequency in young children.
7.5-8.5 Hz	Visualization
8-10 (or 11) Hz Low Alpha	Internally oriented and may be observed in some types of meditation. It is possible but rare to have a dissociative experience when totally in this state. Adults (eyes closed) have alpha as the dominant frequency.
12 Hz (11-13 Hz) High Alpha	Can correlate with a very alert broad awareness state. This can be a readiness state seen especially in high level athletes. Persons with high intelligence often demonstrate a higher peak alpha frequency.
13-15 Hz SMR	When this corresponds to sensory motor rhythm (only over the central cortex: C3, Cz, C4) it can correlate with decreased motor and sensory activity combined with a mental state that maintains alertness and focus. Appears to correlate with a calm state, decreased anxiety and impulsivity. It may also correlate with a decrease in involuntary motor activity.
16-20 Hz Beta	Correlates with active problem solving cognitive activity. It requires more beta when you are learning a task than when you have mastered it.
19-23 Hz	This may correlate with emotional intensity including anxiety
24-36 Hz	Can correlate with ruminating which is most often negative
~ 27 Hz (Elevated in the mid 20's)	May correlate with family history of addiction
38-42 Hz Sheer (Gamma)	Cognitive activity – related to attention and increasing it may help to improve learning disability. It is also referred to as a 'binding' rhythm. It may also be seen at the moment of correcting balance.
44 – 58 Hz	Reflects the effect of muscle activity on the EEG
60 Hz (50 in Europe & Australia)	Usually electrical interference

In the above table the frequency brackets used for each name are approximate. To emphasize this we have used different bandwidths throughout the text in this book. The practitioner should always state explicitly the frequency he is training.

The heavy black lines separate 4 regions that we talk about in the training section of this text. For example, below 10 Hz the waves are usually referred to as slow waves. (Fast waves are those above 10 Hz.). Above 19 Hz is often referred to as high-beta. In training both the slow waves and the high-beta are often discouraged.

c. Learning Self-Regulation

The third use of the EEG is for learning self-regulation of brain wave patterns through operant conditioning. Using the information contained in the EEG the person is given feedback and the reward is information about successfully producing the desired patterns in the EEG. For example, we may ask a client with symptoms of Attention Deficit Disorder to practice holding a mental state wherein they decrease theta (and/or low alpha) while at the same time raising SMR (and/or low beta). The mental state which corresponds to this is calm, alert, focused concentration. This will be discussed in detail in Section VIII.

D. Learning Theory and Neurofeedback

There are two basic learning paradigms, Operant Conditioning (Instrumental Learning) and Classical (Pavlovian) Conditioning. Both are relevant to neurofeedback.

1. Operant Conditioning or Instrumental Learning:

This type of learning is based on **The Law of Effect** which can be simply stated thus: W*hen you reward behaviour you increase the likelihood of its recurrence.* This law was first stated by Edward Thorndike in 1911. He mainly studied cats in puzzle boxes where the cats had to figure out how to get out of the box to get food that was visible just outside the box. He concluded that responses to a particular situation that were followed by satisfaction were more likely to occur when the animal was again in that situation. (That is, rewarded responses were more likely than were responses that were followed by discomfort. In this case, things that did not work resulted in the cat staying hungry). This is also known as Trial and Error Learning since Thorndike's cats tried a lot of things that did not work, like mewing and scratching, before they figured out how to get out of the box by pulling on a string or stepping on a treadle. On subsequent trials they did not bother with the other behavior but immediately did the thing which got them out of the box and to the food.

Skinner took Thorndike's Law of Effect and refined it by introducing the idea of operant classes. An *operant* is a response that operates on the environment. Skinner thus emphasizes the function of a behavior. Having a temper tantrum or smiling nicely are in the same class of operants if they both produce attention from the parent. Skinner's operants are voluntary behavior and this distinguishes these responses from classically conditioned reflexive responses. (See below.) In what came to be known as Skinner

Boxes a pigeon would be trained to peck at a disc or a rat would learn to press a lever (operant behaviors) with food as a reinforcer. Further experiments established the importance of schedules of reinforcement; for example, a variable reinforcement schedule is more resistant to extinction than a continuous reinforcement schedule. (Hence the problem with gambling where an occasional big payoff is highly reinforcing and results in behavior that is hard to eliminate.) Skinner and other behaviorists also introduced concepts of secondary reinforcement, shaping and chaining. They investigated how to apply the principles when training animals and also in human learning. When shaping behaviour you reward successive approximations to the behaviour, for example, you might reward your dog for lying down as a first step in training him to roll over. In general, operant conditioning can be used for the learning of responses that are under voluntary control. Motivation is a factor and the reward must be meaningful or desired.

Operant conditioning occurs frequently in everyday life. When a young child is asked to do 10 math questions which that child considers very boring, then an external reward each time they finish a question (with a double reward if it is correct) may help. If rewards are abruptly stopped, the math behavior may quickly extinguish. If the child is just occasionally rewarded (partial reinforcement) then the math homework completion will be more resistant to extinction. The child finds that they finish the homework more quickly and get out to play. Soon the child may finish the work quickly and correctly just with the knowledge that they will then have earned free time. The play time is a secondary reinforcer. This may turn into what parents call a good habit as they grow older. The essential factor in *operant conditioning* is that *when you reward behavior you increase the likelihood of its recurrence.*

2. Classical Conditioning or Autonomic Conditioning:

Classical conditioning is a term that refers to another type of learning. It was originally described by Pavlov in Russia as a conditioned, or learned, reflex. Pavlov had studied the reflex involved when a dog salivates at the presentation of food. He *paired* ringing a bell with the delivery of meat powder, and the dog "learned" to salivate at the sound of the bell. The food was an unconditioned stimulus that produced an unconditioned response (salivation). When the conditioned stimulus, the bell, was paired with the presentation of meat powder it came to elicit an almost identical conditioned response of salivation. Pavlov also did *second order conditioning* with a light coming on just before the bell, without any meat. The light, too, came to elicit salivation.

True classical conditioning can only be done when there is a reflex response to begin with, so it is really restricted to autonomic nervous system responses, and does not apply to new behaviour. Motivation is largely irrelevant. Emotional conditioning, which is a subset of classical conditioning, occurs when any gut reaction, from anxiety to relaxation, is paired with a neutral object. An example would be a person who liked to fly developing a fear of flying after a particularly rough flight that terrified them. In a similar vein, a young child (or the family dog for that matter) may get excited and run to the front door when he hears it open because that sound has been paired with father coming home to play with him. In this case father's arrival home is an unconditioned stimulus that elicits increased excitement/autonomic arousal in the child and the family dog.

John Watson conducted an (in)famous experiment that demonstrated acquisition and generalization of a fear response. He conditioned fear of a white rat in little Albert, an 11-month old child who loved to touch and explore things, by making a loud noise as Albert reached for the rat. The fear generalized to other white furry objects (rabbits, cotton, Santa mask, Watson's white hair). In **classical** conditioning the conditioned stimulus *automatically elicits* a conditioned response after it has been paired a sufficient number of times with an unconditioned stimulus that elicits an autonomic response. This is why motivation is irrelevant in this kind of learning. Watson also coined the term "behaviorism", which he used in a lecture in 1912, though it was Skinner and operant conditioning, rather than Watson with his work using classical conditioning, who became known as the great Behaviorist.

3. What kind of learning occurs with EEG-Biofeedback?

a. Operant Conditioning

In Sterman's seminal work with cats back in the 1960's the production of brain wave patterns, that came to be known as sensorimotor rhythm, was rewarded with milk and chicken broth. In our work with EEG biofeedback operant conditioning occurs when the client is rewarded for finding a mental state which results in his meeting the thresholds which have been set for designated slow and fast waves. This is rewarded with visual and auditory feedback, usually using a game-like display. There may be secondary rewards of praise or tokens, which may be exchanged for little rewards. It seems that the human brain will learn with information about success as the reward. Soon the person can get into the desired mental state quite rapidly. It is similar to training them to hit a tennis serve. At first it is awkward and difficult. If they practice exactly the same swing many times, it becomes automatic. With motor training coaches estimate that between 1500 and 5000 correct repetitions of a movement are needed for it to be automatic. With neurofeedback the general rule of thumb (at least for managing ADD symptoms) is a minimum of 40 training sessions.

In *operant conditioning* of brain waves the student operates on the display by changing their mental state until rewards are received. The student practices this many times. After enough practice moving to that state becomes almost automatic. At that juncture our job in neurofeedback is to facilitate the transfer of this skill to other situations, such as the classroom or when doing homework. For this a second step of pairing the desired mental state with doing an academic task can be helpful. This second step is hypothesized to involve *classical conditioning*.

The basic principle is that when you reward production of a particular brain wave pattern with auditory and visual feedback, then that information acts as a reward and you increase the likelihood of recurrence of that brainwave activity. The human brain will work for information.

b. Classical Conditioning

Classical conditioning occurs when the desired mental state of focused concentration is paired with carrying out an academic task during the neurofeedback training session. This is done by having the student find the desired mental state of focused concentration, which corresponds to decreased slow wave and increased fast wave activity in the EEG, using the operant conditioning paradigm described above and then *pairing* that mental state with doing an academic task. The fact that the desired mental state is being retained is evidenced by continued auditory feedback even if the visual focus is on text or a math question. If the auditory feedback should stop, the student is instructed to return their attention to the NFB display screen until they again have a steady feedback state. Then they resume the academic task.

We increase the likelihood of the student approaching academic tasks in this focused mental state during everyday life by pairing the mental state with learning metacognitive strategies during their neurofeedback training. Then, when they are at school or doing homework and consciously think of the strategy they should immediately go into the desired state of focused concentration, (For more on metacognition, see chapter XII) which is the physiological state they were in when they learned the strategy.

c. Other Relevant Learning Paradigms

i. Shaping

Shaping refers to conditioning by successive approximations. Animal trainers use shaping extensively and can get animals to do extraordinarily complex behaviors by rewarding little steps in the desired direction. Rewarding a behaviour or a sequence of neurophysiological occurrences *shapes* the contributing components of that sequence in a way that results in an increased frequency of that sequence occurring (Sterman, 2000). Shaping is done when you reward a small shift in the microvolt level of a particular frequency band and then, as the client is successful, you change the threshold to make it a little more difficult. This is part of *operant*

conditioning. When working with people with Attention Deficit Disorder, for example, you reward a shift toward more mature patterns, which means reducing the dominance of slow wave activity in the theta range.

ii. Incidental or 'Associative' Learning

Incidental or 'Associative' Learning occurs when things get unintentionally paired with reinforcers. The red light that indicates muscle activity on some neurofeedback instruments would be an example. Although it is necessary to reduce EMG induced artifact in the EEG, you do not want the less important information regarding EMG activity to be more prominent than the reward for the mental state you are training. If the client focuses mostly on the EMG light, your learning curve for EEG changes may take longer. You may want it prominent at first, however, so that the client learns to reduce EMG so that they get quality feedback with less artifact. This *associative learning* can be both a help and a hindrance. We want the associations to be with things such as strategies which they can take with them and transfer to situations outside of the office. In our training we change times of day, materials used, instruments, feedback screens, and trainers. We don't want a transference cure due to a desire to please a particular client, we want a change in EEG patterns. Our hope is to reduce to a minimum this type of pairing to stimuli which only occur in the office situation.

iii. Secondary Reinforcers

Secondary reinforcers, such as praise and tokens, can be used to further reinforce learning of brain wave states. The tokens can be exchanged for prizes to help motive a child. This is particularly useful for children with ADD who tend only to be able to focus if something is inherently interesting to them or becomes interesting because there is a tangible payoff for doing it. Skinner would call the tokens a "*generalized conditioned reinforcer*" since they can be used for a variety of self-selected rewards. Money has the same role for adults who work for that reward. Whatever you use as a reinforcer must be desired by the person learning or they will not be motivated to work for it. Remember that motivation is only important in operant conditioning. Classical conditioning relies on reflexive responses.

iv. Generalization:

In its simplest form, this term means that what the client learns in the office doing neurofeedback will also occur at other times, places and with other people and tasks. We know that the ability to *generalize* is severely impaired in some disorders such as autism.

We have already touched on the importance of taking generalization into account and used the example of having the student use metacognitive strategies during the training session and then use the same strategy when starting a task outside of the centre. There are many methods you can use. For example, a young child can turn on the state by looking at the top of their pencil and focusing steadily on it for few seconds then gradually broadening that focus to include the book or the black board. For persons who are tense we recommend breathing techniques which we have already paired with an advantageous mental state in the training sessions. An obvious method used by coaches is the warm up exercises for athletes. Getting the client to use self-cueing of some kind, like a word ('focus') or movement (sitting straight, breathing calmly) that has been paired with the production of the desired state can promote generalization.

The observation that the results of neurofeedback training generalize is something that sets it apart from other treatments for ADHD. The use of medication does not produce generalization of improved behavior or neater handwriting when the drug wears off. Behavior modification that works in one class does not usually generalize to another class or to the playground where the same contingencies and rewards are not in place.

v. Extinction:

In classical conditioning *extinction* occurs when the conditioned stimulus is no longer paired with the unconditioned stimulus over a number of trials. In operant conditioning it occurs when a behavior is no longer reinforced ('rewarded'). Since we want to have lasting effects, we want the response (production of the desired mental state) to be resistant to extinction. This is why secondary reinforcers are important. Pavlov found that even after several years a conditioned response could be restored to full strength with a few trials, so relearning is much more rapid than original learning. Sometimes having a client who has ADD back for a few refresher training

sessions is a good idea if things seem to slip in terms of concentration.

When you train a person to do a particular skill, their ability will decrease over time unless the skill is practiced. However, if there is *intermittent reinforcement* of the skill the tendency to lose the skill to the point of it being *extinguished* altogether is markedly decreased. In real life, the student should receive positive reinforcement, (praise, better grades) for their new ability to self-regulate attention which should further reinforce the "behavior" (mental state).

Note: Learning theory alone does not explain why neurofeedback results appear to last. Most people working in the field hypothesize that structural changes in the brain are also a factor. Changes in the production of neurotransmitters or the way they operate at the synapse may also occur. The mechanisms for immediate change and for lasting change have not yet been established.

D. Which Conditions are Appropriate for Neurofeedback Interventions

1. Diagnosed Conditions in which NFB may be Helpful

The list of conditions for which there is considerable research, including controlled studies, published in peer-reviewed journals is short at the time of writing. It is important to distinguish, as the AAPB/SNR joint guidelines discuss (La Vaque et al., 2002), between validated applications, those with some support, and those that are experimental. Seizure disorders and Attention Deficit Disorder are in the first group. Treatment of depressed mood, treatment of alcoholism and addictions, helping those with *closed head injuries* (CHI)/ *traumatic brain injury* (TBI) and work with children who have learning disabilities would be in the second group. Applications that look promising due to clinical reports of improvement but which are not yet verified include Tourette Syndrome and other movement disorders, (Parkinson's disease, dystonia), Asperger's Syndrome and high functioning autism, "brain brightening" in the elderly, obsessive compulsive disorder, and generalized anxiety disorder. When anxiety is part of the symptom picture, it makes sense to include biofeedback.

The work on seizure disorders is well reviewed by Sterman (2000). Joel Lubar has been the leader in research in Attention Deficit Disorder. A multi-site study has established norms for theta / beta ratios (Monastra, Lubar, et al. (1999). Vince Monastra recently published research showing that improvements in ADHD symptoms achieved with neurofeedback continued after training, whereas improvements with stimulant medication alone were not sustained when the drug was withdrawn (Monastra, 2002).

2. A Therapeutic Procedure to be used by an Experienced Psychotherapist

Neurofeedback can be used as an adjunctive procedure in psychotherapy. This use is based on the observation that slow wave activity, particularly in the theta range, can be associated with a *hypnagogic state* (the state we all experience between wakefulness and sleep) that allows for what Sigmund Freud termed primary process thinking. (Note: *Hypnopompic* refers to the partially conscious state preceding wakening.) In the hypnagogic state the client is not consciously evaluating the ideas that drift through their mind or float up from their "unconscious". This training comes under the heading of Alpha-Theta training. There has been considerable work done with alcohol dependency starting with Peniston's work (Peniston & Kulkosky, 1990). It will be briefly described in the interventions section of this book.

3. Optimizing Performance

This type of work is not usually within the purview of health-care professionals, though a professional such as a psychologist may do the initial evaluation. Training sessions can be carried out by coaches, trainers and teachers.

Training that combines neurofeedback with biofeedback allows the participant to have a flexible brain, for example being able to produce calm, relaxed yet alert, focused concentration with appropriate reflection before action. A diverse population may benefit from this type of work since difficulties with attention span, concentration or being a bit impulsive interferes with the student using their full intellectual potential or with executives and athletes reaching their top functioning.

Many children currently (incorrectly) diagnosed with ADHD fall into this group. This group would fall into Thom Hartmann's description of the 'Hunter' mind. They can hyperfocus when there is something of interest that they want to pursue, but have difficulty with time management and with concentration for things that are boring or slow-paced. They do not qualify for a formal diagnosis of ADHD as one could not say their functioning is impaired by their ADHD symptoms to a clinically significant degree, but they are underachieving. The underachievement is frustrating to them, their teachers and their parents. Without intervention, there may be "impairment" as they get into high school or university. Neurofeedback training can play a preventive role in such cases, giving the child self-regulation skills so that their behaviour and learning improves over time rather than worsening.

A second group for optimal performance training would be athletes. Sports require both intense concentration and an ability to shift mental states quickly. Golfers, for example, must analyze the shot they need to make, taking myriad things into consideration, (wind, lie of the ball, distance to the green or the hole, etc.). This mental work requires beta activity, but they must shift into alpha to release their shot effortlessly. This training can help an athlete find the zone where performance in their sport seems effortless and automatic. Jim Robins wrote a magazine piece called, "The Mental Edge" about athletes and neurofeedback.

A third group who make prime candidates for optimal training comprise executives. They often work under intense pressure and to tight time lines, so they need to be able to handle stress and work efficiently. This requires good management of their psychophysiology. For example, breathing techniques quickly produce a calm state. They must shift gears mentally to switch from careful observation and/or listening to processing and making decisions. It is a great asset to be able to choose your state: calm and reflective, or energetic and enthusiastic, depending on what kind of interaction you want to have with colleagues. Adults other than business people can also benefit. We have worked with a graduate student who improved her concentration and organization in order to complete the thesis requirement for her degree. On another occasion we assessed a university professor who had an impressive curriculum vitae with over 150 publications (articles) but he had felt unable to sustain his focus to complete a book.

Another application for optimal performance is with music performance. Rae Tattanbaum has reported her work at meetings and John Gruzelier has done some elegant controlled research with students at the Royal Conservatoire in London, England (AAPB proceedings, 2002). The results over two years were impressive enough that NFB became part of the curriculum at the Royal Conservatoire in the fall of 2002. It seems that whatever level you are at you might reach a higher level with some training. Remember that optimal performance is considered an experimental application of neurofeedback as it does not yet have a sufficient, published research base to be considered an established application.

4. Assessing Efficacy

A joint "Efficacy Task Force" of the Association for Applied Psychophysiology and Biofeedback (AAPB) and the Society for Neuronal Regulation (SNR) developed standards for efficacy research methodology and a template for rating the level of efficacy of each application. Two articles about this important endeavour were published in 2002, appearing in both *Applied Psychophysiology and Biofeedback* and in the *Journal of Neurotherapy*. They are entitled "Task Force Report on Methodology and Empirically Supported Treatments: Introduction" (Moss & Gunkelman, 2002) and "Template for Developing Guidelines for the Evaluation of the clinical Efficacy of Psychophysiological Interventions (La Vaque & Hammond, 2002). Readers are referred to these two important papers. They are meant to be used as the

foundation for a series of scientific reviews and practice guidelines to be published by both societies.

A literature review is beyond the scope of this text. There exists a *Byers' Neurotherapy Bibliography* published in 1992 and available through the AAPB bookstore. For a more current source, a helpful listing of articles, arranged according to conditions in which neurofeedback has been applied, has been compiled by Hammond and is available on the web at www.isnr.org. It primarily includes outcome studies and case reports. Look for "Comprehensive Neurofeedback Bibliography" under Neurofeedback Archive on the website of the International Society for Neuronal Regulation. (The "International" was added to the SNR name as of 2003 in recognition of the Australian and European chapters of that society.) As of mid-2003 the Hammond's list included:

- Epilepsy
- ADD/ADHD, Learning Disabilities & Academic- Cognitive Enhancement
- Anxiety Disorders, PTSD, & Sleep Disorders
- Depression, Hemispheric Asymmetry, & Anger
- Addictive Disorders
- Brain Injury, Stroke, Coma, & Spasticity
- Chronic Fatigue syndrome, Fibromyalgia, & Autoimmune Dysfunction
- Pain & Headache
- plus a dozen other conditions with single case studies

SECTION II
Origin of the
Electroencephalogram (EEG)

Please remember during all of the following that despite the knowledge contained in text books and articles, what is really known at this time about the brain could be likened to what Galileo knew of astronomy. Many break-throughs have been made in neuroscience, especially during the Decade of the Brain in the 1990's, but the field is still in its infancy. Nonetheless, what we are beginning to understand is fascinating and much of it is relevant to our work in neurofeedback. The discovery of greater *neuroplasticity* is one such relevant finding. It is not just that we start life with billions of neurons that get pruned, but our brains can make new neurons and grow new connections among existing neurons throughout our lives. For an interesting and readable account of brain function in the elderly see the book *Aging with Grace* in which David Snowdon provides a popular account of the research known as the Nun Study.

A. Definition:
1. What is an EEG?

The brain's *neurons* communicate by the conduction of electrical currents along *dendrites* and axons. Chemical conduction using *neurotransmitters* occurs at the *synaptic junctions* between nerves. It is somewhat like a huge complex city that is dependent on its electrical wiring. The analogy immediately fails, however, because the brain is far more complex. Each of the billions of neurons has thousands of connections, though it is postulated that there are only four synapses separating any two neurons in the brain. (That last fact comes from a German neuroscientist by the name of Poppel who was interviewed for a Lufthansa flight magazine article published in April, 2002. The source attests to how popular the world of neuroscience has become.) Perhaps the worldwide telephone network is a better analogy than a city's

electrical system since there are local, regional, and wide-spread connections. For fast, long distance communication the brain uses myelinated fibres (white matter) just like fiber optic cable in telephone systems is faster than regular cable for voice transmission. We have not yet discovered the equivalent of satellite transmission, though perhaps there is an as yet undiscovered brain equivalent that would explain telepathy – the phenomenon that first got Hans Berger interested in brain activity.

The *electroencephalograph* is an instrument that detects and amplifies the electrical activity in the brain. The EEG instrument measures the potential difference between pairs of small electrodes (sensors) placed on the surface of the scalp using a highly conductive medium. This is usually a conductive electrode paste such as 10-20 Conductive Paste or Elefix, although saline solutions are also used. The electrodes record electrical activity produced by certain neurons (nerve cells) called pyramidal cells in the brain. The resulting recording is called an *electroencephalogram (EEG)*, e*lectro* because you are measuring electricity (the potential difference between the activity at two electrodes) *encephalo* which refers to brain and '*gram*' which means writing. Many hospital instruments still use pens which actually draw the brain waves on paper which is rolled past them. The instruments used for neurofeedback purposes display the results on a computer monitor. In either case, one has a wave-like line that shows the amplitude of the electrical activity over time. Different frequencies can be seen in the tracing/display. The unit of measurement for the frequencies is cycles per second, or Hertz (Hz), named for Heinrich Hertz, a German physicist who died in 1894. For amplitude it is usually measured in microvolts, or millionths of a volt. Different frequency ranges correspond to different mental states; for example, alpha (8-12 Hz activity) is a resting state.

2. Why bother with the EEG?

In general, the EEG is helpful as a way of monitoring brain activity because it is non-invasive and has excellent temporal resolution. In these respects it is better than imaging techniques like PET and SPECT, though they have better spatial resolution. You know what the brain is up to from moment to moment when you look at the dynamic EEG; that is, which areas are resting and which are active.

There is interesting research on how brain map patterns can correspond to diagnostic categories. Studies done with American whites, American blacks, Scandinavians and Chinese have all yielded similar results. E. Roy John in his March, 2000 presentation at the annual meeting of the Association for Applied Psychophysiology and Biofeedback (AAPB), gave an overview of the neurometric approach that he has developed at his Brain Research Labs, Department of Psychiatry, New York University. Since 1973 he has used the EEG to produce brain maps and with his colleagues, notably his wife Leslie Prichep, he has done mathematical transformations of the data to find patterns that correspond to diagnostic categories. This is painstaking work and they have 2008 values in their matrix that plots electrode placements by frequencies. In the AAPB presentation they noted that the utility of their eighty-two diagnostic classifications, which can discriminate with 85-90% accuracy, lies in being able to predict treatment response. For example, in the elderly there is a 94% correct discrimination between depression and dementia. This information has important treatment ramifications, particularly in terms of which drugs the psychiatrist will prescribe. ADD can be distinguished from normals with 90% accuracy using their neurometric approach and they can build a discriminant function that distinguishes between responders and non-responders to stimulant drugs even when the symptom picture is the same. John has noted that, among the advantages of using the EEG, are the findings that it is stable over time and culture free.

Using a single channel placement at CZ, the multi-site study led by Vince Monastra and Joel Lubar established theta to beta power ratios that had even higher sensitivity for distinguishing between ADHD subjects and those in the control group (Monastra et al, 1998).

Whereas John's and Prichep's findings have mainly been used by psychiatrists to guide drug treatment, the finding that interests neurofeedback practitioners is that the patterns found by means of the EEG can be changed through neurofeedback. These changes can ameliorate symptoms or optimize performance. Here is a summary of *six good reasons for using the EEG,* both diagnostically, and for changing brain and behavior patterns through the learning process called operant conditioning, which came to be known as neurofeedback.

First, **mental states can be "defined" by the EEG.** Certain frequency *bandwidths* correspond to particular mental states. These were described for each commonly used bandwidth (such as theta, 4 to 8 Hz.) in Section I above. Examples are: theta – internally-oriented, drowsy, drifting off, memory retrieval and visualizing; alpha - internally-oriented, contemplative, perhaps day dreaming, and/or meditative states; SMR – calm states where individuals reflect before acting, beta - alert, problem solving, often externally-oriented states.

Second, certain **brain wave patterns** (and we are referring here to normal brain waves, not abnormal ones as are found in seizure disorders) **correspond to common disorders** or syndromes. A good example is the high theta and low beta pattern (high theta/beta ratio) found in persons diagnosed with attention deficit disorder (Monastra et. al, 1998).

Third, both animals and **humans can learn to alter their brain wave pattern** by means of operant conditioning/EEG biofeedback. The earliest work was done in the 1960's with Sterman demonstrating that cats could increase a particular rhythmic pattern in the 12-15 Hz range that he named sensorimotor rhythm or SMR for short. Increasing these frequencies was found to be associated with a reduction in sensory input being relayed to the cortex and a reduction in motor output.

Fourth, both animals and **humans show changes in behavior when they have learned to change their brain wave frequency patterns** by means of operant conditioning. Again, the earliest work was that of Sterman, now Professor Emeritus at UCLA, with cats. The means of operant conditioning of brain waves used with the cats was that they were rewarded with a milk and chicken broth mixture as they produced SMR. The cats became still, yet alert, as they increased SMR. When the contingencies were changed and they were rewarded for reducing SMR, they learned that, too, and they became twitchy cats, flicking their ears and tails. Further work demonstrated that this training to increase SMR resulted in the cats being resistant to seizures. Once work was begun with human subjects who had epilepsy it was noted that as they reduced the frequency and severity of seizures, their symptoms of hyperactivity were also reduced. This led to applying the techniques with hyperactive children. Work done principally by Dr. Joel Lubar at the University of Tennessee over the last 25 years has demonstrated that children can learn to decrease slow waves in the theta range and increase fast waves in the beta range resulting in a marked increase in attention, with decreased impulsivity and hyperactivity. Other variables that changed included statistically significant improvements in their performance on traditional intelligence tests (Weschler Intelligence Scale for Children), on continuous performance tests (Test of Variables of Attention, TOVA), and in school performance. Work with athletes has demonstrated that differences between experts and intermediate level individuals can be clearly distinguished with the EEG (Landers, 1991). Promising work is now being carried out in the area of improving athletic performance.

Fifth, brain maps using 19 active electrodes can **help distinguish psychiatric syndromes.** Much of this work has been done by E. Roy John at New York University, as noted above. The brain maps help predict response to medication. When excess alpha is found centrally, (above the cingulate gyrus), 80% of patients diagnosed with Obsessive Compulsive Disorder will respond to SSRIs. In OCD patients with central theta, only 20% responded. In a similar vein, Richard Davidson (1998) found that depressed individuals show less activation (higher alpha) in the left frontal lobe. Elsa Baehr and associates have demonstrated that depressed patients can respond positively to operant conditioning using the EEG (Baehr, Rosenfeld, Baehr & Earnst, 1999).

Sixth, brain maps using 19 active electrodes can **demonstrate communication patterns** between different areas of the brain. The terms used for this kind of work are *coherence* and *comodulation*. As mentioned earlier data from full cap (19-lead) assessments can be compared to *normative data bases.* Databases have been developed by E. Roy John, Frank Duffy, Robert Thatcher, William Hudspeth, and M. Barry Sterman. Statistical comparisons may demonstrate too little or too much communication between areas of the cortex. This information can then be used to do training that helps individuals overcome some of the symptoms of various disorders. Coherence training may prove to be particularly useful with mild closed head injuries. The approach is to do training that normalizes the EEG.

In conclusion, this section's main point is that mental states can be changed through neurofeedback. The change can be targeted toward normalization or towards optimal performance.

a. Target: Normal Patterns

Operant conditioning can move a client *towards normal patterns* when used to produce a mental state which is relaxed, calm, reflective, alert, focused, with appropriate degree of movement. These changes may overcome symptoms of ADHD or decrease symptoms of some seizure disorders. Indeed, neurofeedback is considered to be among the 'preferred treatments' for these two conditions, as noted in the section concerning biofeedback on the National Institutes of Health website for alternative and complementary medicine. NFB may also ameliorate symptoms in anxiety, depression, addiction, movement disorders, and closed head injury. It may improve difficulties in socializing, as found in Asperger's syndrome or in high functioning autism, though there is less published literature for these applications.

b. Target: Optimal Performance

Operant conditioning of brain wave patterns can move an athlete or a business person *towards optimal performance* for work situations, academic and athletic performance. Again, there needs to be more work published. There are intriguing results from studies such as John Gruzelier's regarding improved music performance particularly with respect to the interpretive, emotive aspects of performance.

3. How is it Possible that the very Small Voltages Produced by Nerve Cells can be Detected?

Electrical activity that we measure comes from the cortex. More precisely, each pyramidal cell acts rather like a little battery to produce a dipole. Dipoles are important because, to detect electricity, we must have a potential difference between two points. The cortical site, such as Cz, will have electrical activity beneath the sensor due to the dipole created when a pyramidal cell is activated. The site to which it is referred, such as the nose, mastoid bone, or an ear lobe, is usually much less electrically active.

This electrical activity depends on special characteristics of the pyramidal cell. Other cells in the cortex do not have this ability to create dipoles though they do influence the pyramidal cells. Roberto Pascual-Marquis from Switzerland (proceedings, Society for Neuronal Regulation annual meeting, 2000) who has done brain research in Zurich and who developed LORETA, has given an eloquent explanation which is summarized below.

B. The Physiological Basis of the EEG

The EEG is defined as the difference in voltage between two different recording locations plotted over time. (Fisch, 1999). The EEG is generated by the synchronous activity of postsynaptic inhibitory and excitatory potentials involving large groups of cortical pyramidal cells. These pyramidal cell's postsynaptic potentials form an *extracellular dipole layer*. "This dipole layer parallels the surface of the cortex projecting opposite electrical polarities towards the cortical surface compared to the innermost layers of the cortex." (Fisch, 1999). The postsynaptic potentials have a long time duration (15-200 milliseconds). These potential changes summate and the EEG records the potential (+ve or –ve) directed towards the electrode on the surface of the scalp.

The charge will differ depending on whether an excitatory post synaptic potential (EPSP) or inhibitory post synaptic potential (IPSP) has been generated in the area of the cortex beneath the electrode. The standard electrode used in neurofeedback is called a macro-electrode and it detects the activity of a very large number of neurons beneath it. (Microelectrodes are much smaller, less than 2 microns in diameter, and are used for measurements of electrical activity within the brain, as, for example, in animal research when the electrodes are implanted beneath the skull.) Each electrode can measure the electrical activity of an area of about six square centimeters, (6 cm^2). Action potentials which travel down the axons or dendrites of these cortical cells have a very short time duration (1 ms) and that electrical activity does not significantly contribute to the EEG.

If how all of the above happens is already clear to you, you can skip the rest of this section. If you wish a bit of review, the next sections will explain about action potentials, post-synaptic potentials and the current thinking about mechanisms that govern the production of the EEG.

1. Pyramidal Cells
a. Terms
Sink = where positively charged cations entered the cell leaving a negative charge in the extracellular space. The *sink* may be at the base, middle or apex of a pyramidal cell dendrite.
Source = where current leaves a cell
Dipole = electric field between source and sink.

Macrocolumn The neurons in the cortex are arranged in groups called macrocolumns. Each column consists of a group of cells several millimeters in diameter and 6 layers deep. These groups contain pyramidal cells, stellate cells (excitatory) & basket cells (inhibitory). They also contain glial cells. The *glial* cells outnumber the pyramidal cells. These cells are important for their role in supporting pyramidal cells; providing nutrition, removing waste products, and giving structural support.

b. Measurement of Post-synaptic Potentials
In the following diagrams the nerve axon that is connecting with the pyramidal cell is excitatory. If it were inhibitory, then the electrical charges marked on the diagrams in the extra-cellular space would be opposite to those shown. The positive (+ve) would be negative (-ve).

Example #1, an excitatory post synaptic potential (EPSP) at the *distal* end of a pyramidal cell dendrite.

Influx of sodium makes for what is known as an active *sink* at the level of the synaptic input from another cell's axon. An active *source*, which is positive, is created outside the pyramidal cell body at the other end of the dendrite. The negative charge (sink) is created outside the cell when sodium, which has a positive charge, rushes into the dendrite due to chemical changes that make the surface more permeable to sodium. This in-rush of positive ions into the distal end of the dendrite, as shown in the diagram opposite, leaves a negative charge outside the portion of that dendrite next to the surface of the scalp and just under our electrode. Inside the dendrite the positive charge is towards the surface of the cortex and the negative end of this intracellular dipole is toward the pyramidal cell body.

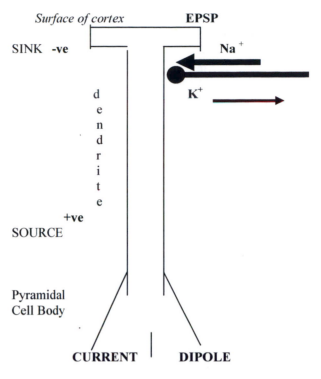

The voltage measured by an electrode on the surface of the scalp above this pyramidal cell's dendrite (and referenced to a point some distance away from it) would be *negative*. It would be measuring an **EPSP** (excitatory post-synaptic potential). An **IPSP** (inhibitory post-synaptic potential) is not shown in this diagram. Inhibitory neurotransmitters make the surface membrane less permeable to sodium, yet potassium (also with a positive charge) continues to be released so the charge outside the dendrite's membrane would be positive. The electrical charge detected by an electrode on the surface of the scalp above this site would then be positive. That is it would be opposite to the reading on the surface of the scalp produced by an EPSP at the distal end of the pyramidal cell dendrite.

Example #2, an excitatory post synaptic potential (EPSP) at the *proximal* end of a pyramidal cell dendrite.

If the synaptic connection took place near the base (cell body) of the pyramidal cell, then the active sink (-ve) is closer to the soma (body) of the pyramidal cell and the 'source'(+ve) would be at the distal end of the dendrite, closer to the cortex.

The voltage measured by an electrode on the surface of the scalp above this pyramidal cell's dendrite and referenced to a point some distance away from it would be *positive*. The current dipole is in the opposite direction to the first example.

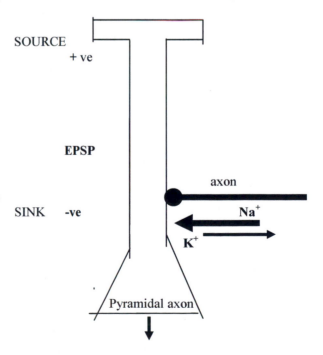

c. Conditions For Current Detection

Having looked at this diagrammatic representation of a pyramidal cell, we must ask ourselves how such small voltages could possibly be detected. The simplest way of understanding this has again been provided by Pascual-Marquis. He explains that four conditions must exist before there is sufficient electrical activity to allow for detection at the surface of the scalp.

i. Directionality

What would happen if the pyramidal neurons were arranged haphazardly?

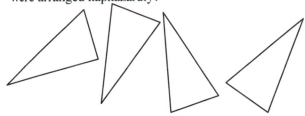

The contribution of these pyramidal cells would sum to zero and no EEG would be detected.

However, pyramidal cells in the cortex are lined up perpendicular to the surface, though not as perfectly as in this schematic diagram because of the convolutions of the cortex.

ii. Synchronicity

Cells must be firing together in a synchronized fashion to produce current flow. If all the cells were firing randomly rather than at the same time, then the sum of their potentials would be close to zero at any given point in time.

This simultaneous firing is possible. One clear mechanism that effects timing concerns subcortical structures controlling the rhythm of firing in the cortex. The clearest contributor is the thalamus. We have already noted how it controls theta, alpha and SMR patterns.

iii. Similarity of Position (Proximal or Distal)

The same thing must be happening at precisely the same time for the majority of cells within a cluster or macrocolumn of neurons. We must have the **simultaneous** occurrence of discharge at the synapses of the axons which connect to the dendrites of the pyramidal cells **at the same level on the dendrite**. The *post synaptic potentials* (**PSPs**) will then be of the same charge; for example, all will have a sink near the top of the dendrite leaving a negative charge near the surface of the cortex.

iv. Valence

The valence (+ve or –ve) must also be the same for virtually all of the pyramidal cells within a spatial cluster or they will cancel each other out. Thus it has to be the **SAME TYPE of input** (excitatory or inhibitory) for virtually all the pyramidal cells within a cluster.

These 4 conditions are well established. They are the basis of the production of an electrical charge (+ve or –ve) that can be measured on the scalp and recorded as the EEG.

Note: The pyramidal cell is the only neuron whose dendrite can produce an action potential (dendrites normally produce excitatory and inhibitory slow potentials which can summate at the axon hillock to produce an action potential.)

2. How Neurons Communicate.

The job of neurons is to communicate with other neurons. They do this through an exquisitely designed system that involves both electrical and chemical transmission of information.

a. The Nerve Cell Resting Potential

Think of the cell as a castle. The castle is at peace and sits in a *resting state*. The enemy outside the wall will enter the castle if they can breach the wall. To conduct an impulse a breach has to be made in the castle wall. The defenders, on the other hand, will repair the wall and force the enemy troops out again in order to return to a resting state. In the case of nerve cell walls a breach can be affected in two ways: chemical or electrical.

In the resting state neurons have what is called a *resting potential*. The resting potential is just the potential difference between the inside and the outside of the cell. It measures between −50 and −100 mV. The inside of the cell is negative compared to the outside. When at rest this potential is about minus seventy millivolts (-70 mV). Think again of the membrane as a castle wall. Inside the cell or 'castle' are high concentrations of negatively charged large protein and amino acid anions (A^-), a positive cation, potassium (K^+), and a low concentration of chloride (Cl^-) which is negative. Outside the cell wall is the opposite array: high concentrations of sodium (Na+) and chloride and a low concentration of potassium. There is also another important positive ion outside the cell wall, calcium Ca^{2+}. It will come into our discussion later when we discuss presynaptic neurotransmitter release. The main point to remember is that under special circumstances sodium, potassium and chloride can all cross the membrane (castle wall); but think of the very large negative protein anions as immobile in the sense that they cannot cross the wall.

The overall resting −ve charge inside the membrane or cell (with the sodium kept out of the castle and the potassium kept in) is maintained by an active process which requires energy. This process, referred to as a *sodium-potassium pump*, transports ions against diffusional and electrical gradients. By means of this process sodium (+ve) is transported out of the cell and potassium (+ve) in. Sodium (Na) is kept at a concentration about 10 times higher outside the cell than inside. Sodium must be transported out against both the +ve electrical state outside and against its own concentration gradient (higher outside). Potassium, on the other hand, is just transported in against a concentration gradient.

b. Why Doesn't This Electrical Difference Dissipate?

The membrane is about 50 times more permeable to potassium than sodium. Potassium will diffuse slowly out of the cell due to the concentration gradient. This will make the inside of the cell even more negative, which will compete with the concentration gradient for attracting the potassium. If this was the only process that was going, on, the membrane would reach an *equilibrium potential for potassium ions* of about −85 mV. However, there is a small steady influx of sodium due to both its concentration gradient and the negative internal electrical charge. This produces a *resting potential* of about −70 mV. This second process will, in turn, encourage more potassium to leave the cell in an attempt, so to speak, to move toward the *potassium resting potential* of −85 mV. This tends to encourage more sodium to enter the cell. If this *leakage* of both sodium and potassium continued, the potassium and sodium gradients would gradually be lost. As mentioned above, an active process called the *sodium-potassium pump*, which requires continual energy input (adenosine triphosphate (ATP) is the source), is necessary to prevent this. It pumps a little more sodium out than it allows potassium in and thus maintains the −70 mV *resting potential* (negative inside the cell) (Campbell, 1996).

c. The Postsynaptic Potential
How do nerve cells connect, resulting in an EPSP or an IPSP?

i. The Synapse
In the previous diagrams of the pyramidal cell the line with a bulbous end represents an axon from another cell. The bulbous end represents the *synaptic terminal*. The synaptic terminal releases neurotransmitters, which attach to specific receptor sites on the *post-synaptic membrane* of the pyramidal cell's *dendrite*. These axons may come from *excitatory* neurons such as *stellate* cells, *inhibitory* neurons such as the *basket* cells or from other kinds of neurons, including other pyramidal cells or neurons at deeper levels, such as those in the thalamus.

The axon ends at a synaptic terminal. It can be at the top or at the bottom of the large dendrite. The arrival of the axon's nerve impulse at this *synaptic terminal* results in an influx of Ca^{2+}. These calcium channels are activated when the membrane potential is held below about −65 mV for approximately 50-100 ms. The resulting rise in Ca^{2+} concentration inside the synaptic terminal results in the small vesicles filled with neurotransmitters to fuse together and, then, to fuse to the inside of the presynaptic membrane. Then the neurotransmitter is released through the presynaptic membrane into the synaptic cleft. The neurotransmitter crosses the synaptic space and attaches to a specific receptor site (protein) on the dendrite and causes the postsynaptic membrane to become temporarily permeable to specific ions. The post-synaptic potentials can be either excitatory (depolarize the membrane) or inhibitory (hyperpolarize the membrane).

ii. Excitatory Post-Synaptic Potential (EPSP)

If the neurotransmitter and the post synaptic receptor site are *excitatory* then the membrane (the sheath of the dendrite) becomes permeable to sodium. It enters the cell because of the negative charge inside the cell and because of the concentration gradient with more sodium being outside the cell membrane. This results in a drop in the potential difference from a starting point of about −70 mV inside compared to outside of the membrane. The membrane begins to *depolarize*. (Remember from the previous discussion that it is not the electrical activity of the action potential that is measured when recording an EEG but, rather, the charge left in the extracellular space as the sodium rushes into the cell.) If more than one EPSP overlaps in time (*temporal summation*) or two or more presynaptic endings release neurotransmitters at the same time (*spatial summation*), then the internal potential of the postsynaptic area may begin to depolarize and reach about −50 mV. At this point it will reach what is called the *threshold potential*. The membrane potential will suddenly change to a positive internal potential of about 10mV. The membrane is said to be *depolarized* and this will initiate another process called the *propagation* of a nerve impulse. This process is discussed below under 'action potentials'.

iii. Inhibitory Post-Synaptic Potential (IPSP)

If the neurotransmitter is *inhibitory,* then the opposite process occurs. The change in membrane permeability allows potassium ions to exit from the cell, and negatively charged chloride ions, which are in high concentration outside the cell, move into the cell due to the concentration gradient. (This movement happens despite the fact that the electrical gradient is not in favor of their movement in.) This makes the potential difference move in an even more negative direction, inside versus outside the cell. This is called *hyperpolarization*. This makes it less likely that sufficient depolarization will occur to cause an action potential. Two amino acids which are *inhibitory* transmitters are gamma amino butyric acid (GABA) and glycine.

iv. Summation

EPSPs and IPSPs *summate*. This is an important concept both for understanding what is measured in the EEG and for understanding a completely different process, the *action potential*. In the first case, the EEG, we are not able to detect the change when a single pyramidal cell receives input from an axon. As previously noted, we can only detect a positive or negative charge in the extracellular space, compared to a relatively neutral reference point, if the dendrites of a very large number of pyramidal cells receive axon input that is the same, (either EPSP's or IPSP's) at the same time. It is the summation of these inputs that may result in an electrode placed on the scalp detecting either a negative or a positive charge.

With respect to the generation of an action potential, perhaps it is just common sense that the same principle applies. A single input might not depolarize a membrane to the point where it will suddenly go through complete depolarization. Several similar inputs along the dendrite may bring it to this point. It is an algebraic sum, so that the inhibitory inputs subtract from the effect of excitatory inputs and can prevent the membrane from reaching its *threshold potential*. Once it reaches its threshold potential, however, it is an all or none phenomenon.

d. Neurotransmitters

In most instances it is the receptor site that governs whether a transmission will be *excitatory or inhibitory*. Receptor sites respond to neurotransmitters, specialized brain chemicals that are needed to conduct nerve signals from one neuron to another.

i. Acetylcholine

The most common neurotransmitter is acetylcholine. Acetylcholine is the excitatory neurotransmitter at neuromuscular junctions. In the central nervous system (CNS) it may be either excitatory or inhibitory. It is the neurotransmitter in the parasympathetic division of the autonomic nervous system. It is involved in recording memories in the basal forebrain and the hippocampus and is deficient in Alzheimer's disease. In the reticular activating system it has a role in attention and arousal. It is also involved in the control of the stages of sleep.

There are 3 other groups of neurotransmitters that you will commonly encounter in your reading, but keep in mind that this is a partial list: there are well over two hundred neurotransmitters.

ii. Biogenic Amines

The first group is the **biogenic amines** (catecholamines) including: norepinephrine, dopamine. Norepinephrine and dopamine are derived from the amino acid *tyrosine*. There are also a second group called the **indole** amines and they include serotonin. Serotonin is derived from the amino acid *tryptophan*. Dopamine is generally excitatory, serotonin is usually inhibitory and norepinephrine is both. The common neurotransmitter in the sympathetic portion of the *autonomic nervous system* is norepinephrine.

Dopamine has been researched with respect to many disorders. LSD and mescaline may produce their hallucinogenic effects by binding to dopamine receptors. Schizophrenia may involve an excess of dopamine and Parkinson's is related to a reduction in dopamine. It is hypothesized (Malone et al.) that ADHD is associated with reduced dopaminergic activity in the left hemisphere and increased noradrenergic activity in the right hemisphere. It is the principle neurotransmitter in the brain's reward or pleasure circuit. This circuit involves the structures along the medial-forebrain-bundle pathway described below in the section on neuroanatomy.

Too much dopamine has been reported in the following conditions: hallucinations; psychosis, including the *positive symptoms* of schizophrenia such as paranoia; Tourette's Syndrome; obsessive compulsive disorder (agitation & repetition); and in overly excited states including euphoria and mania.

Amphetamines and cocaine are catecholamine agonists. They block the reuptake of dopamine and noradrenaline from the synaptic cleft and thus increase the availability of these transmitters to the post-synaptic neuron. This effect in the nucleus accumbens may be important in understanding the excitatory effects of these drugs and their ability to create a chemical 'high'. Alcohol, nicotine and caffeine can also increase dopamine in the nucleus accumbens.

Too little dopamine has been reported in Parkinson's disease with its tremor and inability to start movement, with the *negative symptoms* of schizophrenia including lethargy, misery, catatonia & social withdrawal, in adult Attention Deficit Disorder and in addictions.

Norepinephrine arises principally from neurons located in the locus coeruleus. This nucleus is described in the section on neuroanatomy. It has connections through the medial-forebrain-bundle to the hypothalamus. Its primary excitatory function in the central nervous system (CNS) is related to arousal and attention. It is released during stress and may be a part of the fight or flight response, and it is involved in emotions such as fear, anxiety and possibly mania. It is also thought to have a role in learning and the formation of memories. Too little norepinephrine may be associated with depression and too much with mania. It may be in excess in some anxiety disorders. It may, however, be depleted in patients who have had chronic stress.

Serotonin (5-hydroxy-trypamine [5-HT]) is produced in the brain stem and released by the Raphe nuclei. It is primarily an inhibitory neurotransmitter. It is involved in the regulation of pain, mood, appetite, sex drive and in falling asleep. It may also be involved in memory. It is a precursor for melatonin which, in turn, is important in biological rhythms. Low levels of serotonin are thought to be related to a number of psychiatric disorders including depression, obsessive compulsive disorder (OCD) and aggression. Selective serotonin reuptake inhibitors (SSRIs) are used to treat these conditions.

iii. Amino Acids
The second group of neurotransmitters is the *Amino Acids*. This group includes the two inhibitory transmitters: gamma amino butyric acid (GABA) and glycine. It also includes glutamate and aspartate, which are excitatory transmitters. The anxiolytic medications (benzodiazepines), alcohol, and barbiturates may exert their effects by potentiating the responses of GABA receptors. GABA will open both potassium and chloride channels and thus hyperpolarize the neuron and make it more difficult for that neuron to be depolarized. The neuron is effectively inhibited.

GABA is possibly the most important inhibitory neurotransmitter in the CNS. The entire CNS is a system in which, when a neuron is stimulated, a feedback loop is activated to inhibit or stop that neuron from continuously firing. These feedback loops often use the neurotransmitter GABA. This is the braking and stabilizing mechanism of the CNS.

Glycine is found in the lower portions of the brain stem and in the spinal cord. In tetanus (lock-jaw) the bacteria releases a glycine blocker. The removal of glycine's inhibitory effects is responsible for the muscles contracting continuously.

Glutamate is essential in learning and memory and in an important process called *long term potentiation (LTP)*. Long term potentiation is the process whereby a post synaptic cell changes (is enhanced) in response to episodes of intense activity across the synapses. It is thought to be crucial to memory storage. Further research is needed to show whether long term potentiation is due to an increase in neurotransmitter receptors, increased synaptic connections or both. Whatever the mechanism, the post synaptic cell can depolarize more in response to a neurotransmitter. How this takes place may be as follows: glutamate activates what is called a non-"N-methyl-D-aspartate" receptor causing an influx of sodium into the post-synaptic terminal.

This depolarization has the effect of displacing magnesium (Mg^{2+}) which is blocking a second "N-methyl-D-aspartate" receptor site. This site is then activated by glutamate with a resultant influx of calcium ion (Ca^{2+}). This influx of Ca^{2+} results in the activation of other 'messenger' pathways and the release by the post-synaptic cell of a *paracrin'*. A paracrine is a chemical that is released by a cell and then acts to alter cells in its immediate vicinity. In this case it may act on the pre-synaptic ending and enhance the release of the neurotransmitter glutamate. The post-synaptic membrane also appears to be changed in this process to become more sensitive to glutamate. It is theorized that the post-synaptic cell may develop more glutamate receptors (Silverthorn, 1998). The importance of this for our work in neurofeedback is that it could be another important theoretical framework for understanding how only a few sessions of neurofeedback might result in sustained changes in the CNS.

iv. Neuropeptides
The third group of neurotransmitters is the *neuropeptides*. These are short chains of amino acids. They are responsible for mediating sensory and emotional responses. Among them is *Substance P* which mediates the perception of pain. Measurements of substance P in the cerebral spinal fluid (CSF) are assisting clinicians in the diagnostic work-up of persons suffering from fibromyalgia. The *endorphins* are also neuropeptides. They function at the same receptors that receive heroin and morphine and are thought of as naturally occurring analgesics and euphorics. They are found in the limbic system and the midbrain. The ventral tegmental area of the midbrain and the nucleus accumbens in the frontal lobe have opiate receptors (see neuroanatomy section). A third type of neuropeptide is **neuropeptide Y (NPY) / polypeptide YY (PPYY)**. This substance is found in the hypothalamus and may be related to food intake and eating disorders.

3. Action Potentials
There are two processes which can lead to membrane depolarization. The first is the response to a neurotransmitter. Traditionally, we thought this occurred just at *synaptic terminals* (electrochemical connections between neurons),

but it is now accepted that there are receptors at many sites along an axon and neurotransmitters in the extracellular fluid can float some distance from the site of their release and attach to these receptors. The second process is a *voltage sensitive* change. This refers to the fact that depolarization in one section of a neuron will activate depolarization in the adjacent portion of the neuron. This raises the question of why nerve impulses are not chaotic, running in both directions. We will discuss first the creation of an *action potential* and then demonstrate why the impulse runs only in one direction.

As mentioned at the beginning of this section, the postsynaptic potentials created in the extracellular space outside the pyramidal cells' dendrites are of a relatively long duration and summate in a manner that can be detected by an electrode on the surface of the scalp. Sustained postsynaptic potentials may cause current to flow along the surface of a cell body or dendrite. The area of the neuron at the base of that neuron's axon is called the *axon hillock*. This is the *integrating* center of the neuron. The depolarizing changes in the cell may summate to the point where the potential at the axon hillock is changed sufficiently (critical level is >10 mV and the critical change is a move from the *resting level* of about -70 mV to the *threshold for excitation* -55 mV) such that the membrane suddenly loses its charge and an *action potential* is produced and propagated along the axon to the next synapse. The electrical change is a temporary reversal in charge along the cell membrane. It is about 110 mV and lasts about 1ms. It is all or nothing. This sudden change has the effect of inducing a similar change in the adjacent membrane that is in a *resting state* and so a current is propagated down the axon. The permeability of the adjacent membrane to sodium suddenly increases about one thousandfold over that of the *resting state*. It is, however, unidirectional. It is not propagated in the reverse direction due the structure of the *gateways* for sodium. There are two gates for sodium. The first opens instantly when activated by an appropriate chemical or an electrical change. The second is a relatively slow *gate* which closes shortly after sodium enters the cell and will not open again until its resting state is again achieved. While the active sodium pump is removing sodium from the interior of the cell to reestablish the old negative resting potential, the slower gate stays closed. Therefore, a second depolarizing stimulus cannot open this gate. This insensitive time is called the *refractory* period. Thus the current can only be propagated in one direction down the axon. The potassium gates are slow to open in response to depolarization compared to the first sodium gate and, thus, potassium flowing out of the cell is present during, and assists in, the repolarization phase. Indeed, it is these potassium channels that cause a bit of an *undershoot* and hyperpolarization at the end of the repolarization phase. *Action potentials* are very brief local currents. They are not what is being measured in the EEG.

The changes in the cell membrane affecting the permeability of K+ and Na+ are known as the *Hodgkin Cycle*. The sodium-potassium pump uses energy to maintain a resting potential and that resting potential allows the neuron to respond quickly to a stimulus; just as a poised arrow is ready for flight, so the energy it requires is well justified.

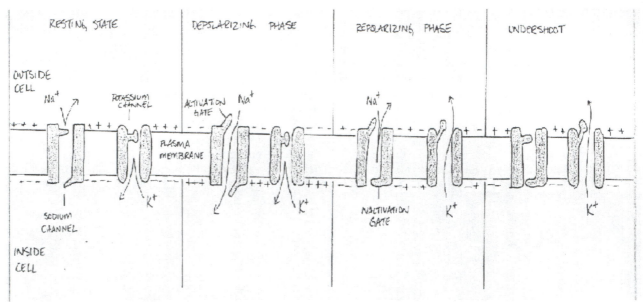

Schematic Diagram of a Receptor Site to Show the Progression of Electrical Changes in the Hodgkin Cycle (After Campbell, 1996)

A note on two types of synaptic receptor sites: The post-synaptic receptors discussed here are also called **ionotropic** because when a neurotransmitter binds to this type of receptor, an ion channel is opened. Their action is local and is very fast (a millisecond). (You may also hear the term "nicotinic" receptor. Nicotine will lock acetylcholine receptor channels in the open state. Nicotinic receptors are a type of ionotropic receptor for acetylcholine and are the type of receptors that open ion gates at neuromuscular junctions of striated muscles and at some neuronal synapses. Also, a slightly different type of nicotinic receptor is found in the autonomic nervous system (ANS).)

Metabotropic receptors are a different type of receptor. In contrast to the ionotropic receptors, the effect of their action is diffuse and slow (seconds to minutes). Their action involves the production of secondary chemical 'messengers' which can influence the metabolism of cells and produce long-lasting changes. You may also hear the term **muscarinic**. *These are a type of metabotropic receptor. Muscarinic acetylcholine receptors are found in the smooth muscles of the pupils, glands, blood vessels and so on.*

The reason for mentioning that there are different types of receptors is that, in future, we may discover that some of neurofeedback's lasting effects may come about, in part, due to .

effects on receptors that cause a change in the metabolic activity of neuronal pathways.

Since action potentials are *all or none* the strength of a nerve impulse is governed only by the *frequency* of action potentials. The action potential itself begins at a single site. The impulse is propagated by a series of depolarizations and resultant action potentials. The speed of transmission is increased by an increased first, by axon diameter and second, by a process called *salutatory* (from the Latin to leap) conduction. This second process is enabled by myelinization of the axon. There are gaps in the myelin sheath called *nodes of Ranvier* and the action potential *jumps* between these nodes skipping the myelinated region in between. Think of myelinated axons as being the superhighways with faster speeds. (Campbell, Neil A. et al.)

A note on Myelinization: Myelinization in the cortex differs from that in the peripheral nervous system. In the latter Schwann cells form the myelin sheath, whereas in the cortex the myelin is generated by oligodendroglia cells. Myelin contains fat and this produces the white colour. The deeper layers of the cortex are thus called white matter, whereas the upper layers are grey matter. In the spinal cord and peripheral nervous system the white matter is on the outside and grey matter on the inside – the reverse of the brain where the grey matter is on the outside. Grey and white matter have different densities, as well as different colouring since the fat holds more water. When there is a head injury, the grey and white matter will move at different speeds due to their different densities. The resultant sheer forces lead to diffuse axonal injury (DAI). This type of injury can be detected in the EEG though it may not show up using brain imaging techniques, such as magnetic resonance imaging (MRI). The EEG also has better temporal resolution than MRI. On the other hand, MRI does have better spatial resolution as it can look at deeper structures. The use of mathematical transformations known as LORETA may improve the spatial information that an EEG can yield.

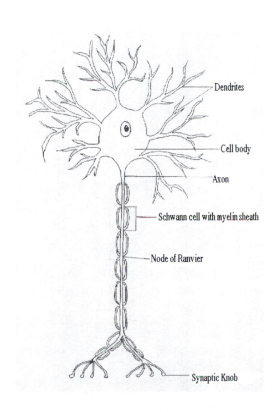

Schematic Diagram of an Axon Showing Schwann Cells.
The speed of transmission along a nerve fiber is increased by an increased axon diameter and by a process called *salutatory* (from the Latin to leap) conduction. This second process is enabled by *myelinization* (cells of Schwann in the peripheral nervous system) of the axon. There are gaps in the myelin sheath called *nodes of Ranvier* and the action potential *jumps* between these nodes skipping the myelinated region in between.

4. Other Cortical Cells

We have already mentioned *inhibitory cells*. The clearest example of these are the numerous *basket* cells which are found throughout the cortex. *Stellate cells* (so named because they look star shaped) are excitatory. Only the pyramidal cells create dipoles which can be measured on the scalp. They act like little batteries with positive and negative poles and produce current. Other cortical cells **do not contribute** directly to the electricity recorded by the EEG. They do contribute indirectly, however, in so far as they influence the pyramidal cells.

Glial cells are actually more numerous in the cortex than are pyramidal cells. They provide the infrastructure and support the pyramidal cells. Glial cells provide nourishment and remove waste so they are important for an efficient brain. It is reported that Einstein's brain had a higher than expected number of glial cells.

5. Subcortical Influences

Like the *basket* (inhibitory) and *stellate* (excitatory) cells in the cortex, cells in the sub cortical structures do not contribute directly to the electrical potential which we are measuring. These cells are not *dipoles*. They do, however, influence the pyramidal cells. In general terms, one can say that the thalamus is the major pacemaker that influences rhythmic activity – theta, alpha, and SMR.

a. Thalamic Pacemakers

There are over 100 billion neurons in the brain and 97% of neuronal connections are within the cortex. But this activity is modulated by thalamic pacemakers, so the influence of thalamocortical connections (representing only about 1% of the neural connections) far outweighs their number. Thalamic pacemakers produce different cortical rhythms depending upon which cortical loops they activate. The thalamic cells are *relay cells* that may be either in an *active* (relay or *working*) mode or in a stand-by (idling) mode. The stand-by or idling mode is one where these cells are not, for example, receiving cortical input. In this circumstance these thalamic cells hyperpolarize. They then fire in a bursting, oscillating, pattern Anderson and Anderson (1968) proposed that thalamo-cortical cells send fibers to the cortex. These fibers give off branches that go to interneurons which then inhibit the thalamic activity. Then the thalamic neurons recover and go again into excitation. They give off another synchronized volley which goes both to the cortex and to the thalamic inhibitory interneurons. If this inhibition lasted $1/10^{th}$ of a second, then the rebound oscillatory (cyclic) excitation would occur 10 times per second and would be recorded as an alpha wave. The nucleus reticularis (one of the many nuclei within the thalamus) has such intrinsic pacemaker properties and is responsible for the EEG sleep spindle. This type of activity is, in general, responsible for rhythmic wave patterns. Sterman's research with cats demonstrated that if thalamo-cortical connections are cut, the brain produces no theta, alpha or SMR, just delta.

Interruptions to this kind of rhythmical activity (*desynchronization*) can occur as a response to input from ascending neuronal systems that produce arousal in part through "activation of ascending cholinergic projections of the basal forebrain and brainstem and projections from the raphe nuclei and locus coreuleus" (Fisch, p14). Understanding how both synchronous and desynchronized EEG activity is produced is key to understanding EEG biofeedback's usefulness.

Lubar states, "Changes in the cortical loops, as a result of learning, emotion, motivation, or neurofeedback for that matter, can change the firing rate of thalamic pacemakers and hence change their intrinsic firing pattern". He also notes that changes in this intrinsic firing pattern mean changes in mental state. In work with clients who have ADD this usually means that slow waves have been decreased and SMR increased. *(Joel Lubar, 1997 after Nunez)*

The diagram below is given to emphasize cortico-thalamic communication.

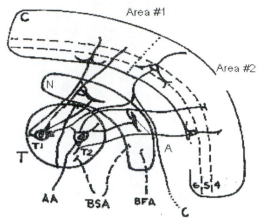

Figure with thanks to Maurice Barry Sterman after Sherman and Guilery.

T = Thalamus; AA = Ascending Afferents
C = Cortex; 6,5,4, are layers in the cortex;
BFA Basal Forebrain Afferents to the reticular nucleus of the thalamus. BSA = Brain Stem Afferents.

Just above 'A' is an axon from a pyramidal cell in layer 6 to T2 (Thalamic sensory relay nucleus). Note how the axon gives off a branch that goes to the reticular nucleus of the thalamus (N) which, in turn, sends an inhibitory axon to the thalamus to stop the firing of the nucleus on which that cortex axon terminated.

This diagram emphasizes cortico-thalamic interaction. There are two principles schematically represented here. First, 'Area #1' of the cortex is shown to send axons down to the sensory relay nucleus of the thalamus. This can influence the thalamus to pay attention to (*facilitate*) or turn off (*inhibit*) attention to specific sensory inputs. Second, Area #1, (imagine it to be, say, visual) communicates to T2 (a thalamic association nucleus) which in turn communicates with the cortical 'Area #2' which has a different function than cortical Area #1. This is why, if you were to cut cortical connections along the dotted line between Area #1 and Area #2, these areas would still be observed to be communicating with each other.

6. Cortical Electrical Communication

a. Macrocolumns

The pyramidal cells and their surrounding support cells (stellate and basket cells) are arranged in groups. Each vertical column contains hundreds of pyramidal cells. The columns are parallel to each other and at right angles to the surface of the cortex. Many adjacent groups may receive the same afferent axonal input and thus fire in unison allowing for a large enough potential that is measurable at the surface of the scalp. Each pyramidal cell may have more than 100,000 synapses. At least 6 cm^2 of cortex with synchronous activity is necessary to obtain a reliable scalp EEG recording. (Dyro, 1989). The amplitude of the recording will, of course, vary with the amount and type of tissue between the electrode and the cortex. Children, for example, have thinner skulls and higher amplitude EEG. It should be understood that you cannot tell from the EEG whether the potential under your electrode is generated by IPSPs or EPSPs. Research has shown, however, that in a seizure discharge the spike is produced by excitation and the slow wave by inhibition.

b. Resonant Cortical Loops

Cortical to cortical connections are far more abundant than thalamic to cortical connections as has been noted above. EEG rhythmicity occurs due to direct thalamic influence and may also occur due to these interconnections between groups of cortical cells (Traub et al, 1989).

Understanding the electrical activity of the cortex that is detected by the EEG must, in addition, include some comment on the frequencies produced which correlate with different distances between columns of cells within the cortex. Joel Lubar has given a lucid overview of this (Lubar, 1999). He explains that distance is one of the factors that dictates the frequency of the waves which are detected in the EEG. Subcortical rhythmic influences, such as those arising from thalamic nuclei, are the other major factor. A simplified way of looking at this is as follows.

The cortex works in terms of three major resonant loops. They are:

1. Local: This loop of electrical activity is between macrocolumns that are close neibours. It appears to be responsible for high frequency (> 30Hz) gamma activity.

2. Regional: This loop of electrical activity is between macrocolumns which are several centimeters apart. It appears that this activity is in the range of intermediate frequencies: alpha and beta.

3. Global: This loop of electrical activity is between widely separated areas, for example, frontal-parietal and frontal-occipital regions. Areas can be up to 7cm apart. The activity produced is in the slower frequency range of delta and theta activity.

All three of these resonant loops can operate spontaneously or be driven by thalamic pacemakers.

Clinical Tip:

When you work with clients it is often helpful for them to realize that their EEG does change with stimulation. They can close their eyes then you can have them open their eyes. The client will observe that occipital alpha, and often alpha in central locations, is suppressed by visual stimulation. If you observe the wicket shape of a mu rhythm at C3 or C4, then this can be suppressed by voluntary movement such as closing their fist on the opposite side of their body from the observed rhythm. It is of real interest to ADHD children and their parents that they can observe theta production, then suppression of theta with a concomitant increase in beta (16-18 Hz) activity either frontally or centrally, when they retrieve information to do a math problem and then do the calculation and produce an answer. The trainer can also run the EEG during a boring task when theta or low alpha predominates (specific frequency is unique to the individual) then pause the EEG and ask the client what was happening. Most clients respond that they had started the task then drifted off. Whereas it is true that theta is sometimes an important active state, crucial for memory retrieval, for example, the ADHD subject tends to go into this state inappropriately and remain there oblivious to what a teacher or parent is saying. It is the ability to appropriately self regulate the mental states that is assisted by neurofeedback. In the early stages of working with a client the forgoing exercises may be a helpful means for allowing the client to observe that they can self regulate their brain activity and that this regulation is reflected in the recorded EEG rhythms.

c. Communication Linkages

It has already been mentioned that most of the communication (more than 95%) going on in our brain appears to occur between cortical areas, much of it in the same hemisphere. Less than 5% is due to thalamo-cortical connections yet these connections have tremendous influence on what we observe in the EEG. Steriade, in Ottawa, Canada, demonstrated that when the cortex was cut communications remained between distant parts of the cortex (Steriade, 1990). This communication, therefore, is posited to be relayed subcortically through the thalamus. **Synchronous activity** is usually due to thalamic influence. It may also be associated with cortical lesions or seizure activity.

The transmission of a signal through a **volume conductor** is nearly at the speed of light. Examples of volume conductors are cerebral spinal fluid (CSF), brain tissue, skull and scalp. Thus similarly appearing waves occurring at the same moment in time at non-adjacent sites probably originate from the same generator. If there is a time delay then this must involve a synapse and therefore a different cellular origin. (Fisch, 1999, p16)

d. Corticocortical Coupling

Coupling is a term that has relatively recently begun to be used. Coupling means to join two objects, as in coupling between train cars. It is beginning to appear that for any particular mental state there is an optimal coupling between different areas of the brain.

i. Hypercoupling

To quote Lubar, "Neocortical **states** associated with **strong corticocortical coupling** are called **hypercoupled** and are associated with global or regional resonant modes." Hypercoupling thus means that large resonant loops are involved. Biochemically it appears that the dominant neurotransmitter in this type of coupling is serotonin. **Hypercoupling** is said to be appropriate for states such as **hypnosis & sleep**

and also for **visualization.** Hypercoupling is also correlated with decreased attention.

ii. Hypocoupling

Hypocoupling is associated with small regional and local resonant loops and thus higher frequencies. Biochemically it appears that the neurotransmitters involved in this type of coupling are acetylcholine, norepinephrine, and dopamine. Hypocoupling is said to be appropriate for **information acquisition, complex mental activity and increased attention.**

We generally **use NFB to train** people to produce activity associated with hypocoupling and **resonance in local and regional areas** in order to be capable of better attention and better learning. Although what we are measuring is cortical activity, regulation of this activity may be primarily controlled from subcortical structures, principally the links from the thalamus to macro-columns of cortical cells.

SECTION III
The EEG: Frequencies & Normal & Abnormal Waveforms

The electroencephalograph is an instrument that detects the alternating electrical currents which are produced by groups of neurons in the brain. The resulting recording is called an *electroencephalogram (EEG)*.

A. Definitions and Descriptions of Common Terms

1. Quantitative EEG
a. Definition
QEEG refers to Quantitative EEG. This term is used when the software that analyzes the EEG signal quantifies different aspects of the EEG. In this step something is gained and something is lost. This process does not reflect information about specific morphology (shape) of waves or about the relative abundance of certain types of waves but it makes it easier for you to visualize, in broad terms, what may be going on. The computer is able to display these numerical values in a table as a spectrum of amplitude plotted against frequency, or as a topographic map showing activity at different electrode sites.

b. Normative Data Bases
Comparisons can also be made to normative data bases. Suffice it to say that a number of different databases are available for purchase and services exist to interpret 19-lead assessments. Databases/interpretation software currently available include (in alphabetical order) those by Frank Duffy, William Hudspeth, E. Roy John,

Robert Thatcher, SKIL (Sterman Kaiser Imaging Labs).

c. Amplitude and Power
Typically the QEEG will provide information about amplitudes in microvolts (uV) and power in picawatts (pW) for specific frequencies at specific sites. Calculations concerning ratios, standard deviations, and other statistics are also done. Usually QEEG refers to a 19-lead assessment but values from one active location can also be quantified. A single active electrode at CZ, for example, was used to generate theta/beta power ratios comparing individuals with ADHD to controls in the multisite study done by Monastra, Lubar, Green, and Linden (1999). The term QEEG is therefore independent of the number of sites and channels used in gathering the information.

The interpretation of a 19 channel QEEG is not for the beginner in the field of neurofeedback and so it will just be touched upon in this text. Examples from 19-lead assessments will sometimes be shown.

d. The EEG Spectrum (The Frequency Domain) – Fast Fourier Transform (FFT)

i. Transformation from Time to Frequency Domain
The transformation from the *time related domain* of the raw EEG to the *frequency domain* for statistics is carried out by a mathematical calculation called a *Fast Fourier Transform*

(FFT). Jean Baptiste Fourier showed that any repetitive signal could be broken down into a series of sine waves. The breaking apart of a complex wave into its component sine waves may be called a Fourier analysis. Fisch notes that, "The FFT function is based on the fact that any signal can be described as a combination of sine and cosine waves of various phases, frequencies and amplitudes" (Fisch, p.125). Squaring these Fourier coefficients may be done to give a *power spectrum* which shows the power measured in picowatts (pW) between frequencies at a particular point in time. This type of display is used, for example, in summarizing information in the A620 assessment program designed by Joel Lubar for the electroencephalograph manufactured by Stoelting Autogenics. The spectrum used in other programs, such as the BioGraph, is in microvolts (an *amplitude spectrum*) which corresponds better to the raw EEG but does not show such dramatic differences between frequency band magnitudes since the units are smaller. (Squaring a microvolt ratio approximates a ratio in picowatts, however, variability in the measurements that make up the averages used in the ratio can alter this approximation.) It should be noted, however, that the EEG is not truly made up of only sine wave signals and the EEG frequencies will sometimes have harmonics. Nevertheless power spectra are reasonably accurate and a valuable tool used in assessment work with the EEG.

ii. Absolute Band Values & Ratios

Absolute band values are calculations based on the area under the spectral curve for that frequency band (for example, 4-8 Hz). Dividing two *absolute band values* to obtain a ratio (such as a power ratio for theta / beta calculated as the value of 4-8 Hz activity divided by the pW value of 13-21 activity theoretically approximately corrects for skull and tissue thickness differences between individuals. This is the rationale behind doing studies comparing these ratios in individuals who have difficulties with attention span (Monastra et al, 1998; Jansen, 1995; Mann, 1992).

iii. Cautions

Remember: once you have 'quantified' the EEG, you have values and pictures (spectra and topographic brain maps) which have no information about wave morphology or about how frequently a particular wave form appeared in the EEG. Spikes and waves are not evident in this information. The topographic maps also do not help with localization of an activity. Topographic maps are a technique for displaying the scalp distribution of EEG activity from a large number of electrode sites. They show clearly what electrode positions have maximal power of a particular frequency band in the EEG. However, one must be very cautious in drawing conclusions from these maps. Remember that a few very high amplitude waves may give the same value as extensive lower amplitude bursts of the same frequency. The analysis is also prone to artifact effects so the EEG data must be carefully examined and artifacts removed before the quantitative analysis is done. **It is imperative that you keep referring back to the raw EEG** before coming to any conclusions about the data. Topographic maps are impressive, but keep in mind that there are only 19 'real' values from a 19-site assessment. All the values indicated by the colours between these points are interpolated (estimated). The only way to improve spatial resolution is to increase the number of channels. However, for the purposes of neurofeedback applications this has very little increased value.

2. Wave Forms, Frequencies, Phase & Synchrony

a. Morphology

Morphology (or waveform) refers to the shape of a wave. The following terms are only briefly defined in this basic text because you are probably not going to use them but you may hear about them in lectures you attend.

i. Regular & Irregular Waves

Regular waves may be sinusoidal or may be arched (wickets) or saw-toothed (asymmetrical, triangular). *Irregular* waves are constantly changing their duration and shape.

ii. Monophasic / Biphasic / Triphasic, Transients, Complexes and Rhythmic Wave Forms

A wave is *monophasic* if it goes either up or down, *biphasic* if it goes up and down and *triphasic* if it has 3 such components. A *transient* wave is one that stands out as different against the background EEG. A *complex* is a sequence of 2 or more waves which is repeated and recurs with a reasonably consistent shape. (Fisch, p.145). Sinusoidal waves like alpha waves or spindle waves (such as sleep spindles or the similar waves called *sensorimoter rhythm*) are described as being *rhythmic*.

b. Activity: Generalized versus Lateralized Waves

The activity which is observed may be generalized, lateralized or focal. *Generalized* waves are widespread and diffuse occurring at the same time in most of the channels being recorded. The origin may be inferred by finding that the wave is maximal in one location as seen in a referential recording or by observing a phase reversal in a sequential (bipolar) recording. *Lateralized* waves are those more frequently observed on one side of the head. This distribution of waves often may represent an abnormality. *Focal* waves are localized to one site or area.

c. Phase

Waves may be *in phase*. This would mean that the troughs and peaks of the waves in one area were occurring at the same time in another area of the brain. If they do not coincide, then they are *out of phase*. However, the waves may go up and down in a similar manner consistently but not quite coincide. There would then be a *time delay* which is expressed as a *phase angle*. If the angle was 180°, then the peaks would point in opposite directions and it would be called a *phase reversal*.

Note from Fisch: "Phase: (1) Time or polarity relationships between a point on a wave displayed in a derivation and the identical point on the same wave recorded simultaneously in another derivation. (2) Time or angular relationships between a point on a wave and the onset of the cycle of the same wave. Usually expressed in degrees or radians." (Fisch, p 450)

Note: For the term "derivation" you can substitute the word 'channel'. Derivation refers to the process of recording from a pair of electrodes in an EEG channel (Fisch 443).

d. Synchrony

If the same kind of waves occurred simultaneously on both sides of the head, they would be in phase and *bisynchronous*. Waves that occur in different channels without a constant time relationship to each other are called '*asynchronous*' (Fisch, p.152)

3. Dominant Frequency and Age

Age is a factor in determining the dominant frequency in the EEG. The dominant frequency, measured with eyes closed in adults, is typically in the alpha range, around 9 to 10 Hz. It is generally reported that higher peak alpha frequencies are found in brighter people; that is, the adult whose eyes closed peak alpha is at 11 Hz probably has a higher IQ than an individual whose peak alpha is at 9.5 Hz. Higher is not necessarily better, however; Tom Budzynski noted that some of the brilliant Silicon Valley scientists he has worked with have very high alpha but are quite brittle. In the frontal and central regions below age 3 delta is dominant. From 3 to about age 5 theta is dominant. Low alpha becomes dominant around age 6 to 8 and then it gradually moves to a higher frequency alpha around 10 Hz as the individual reaches adolescence. It is important to keep the developmental aspects of the EEG in mind when working with different age groups. What would be considered excess theta in a 12 year old client with ADD would be quite normal in a 4 year old.

4. Rhythms and Asymmetries.

a. Alpha

Alpha amplitude is normally higher on the right but this difference should not exceed 1.5 times (Gibbs, & Knott, 1949). The alpha rhythm should exceed 8 Hz in adults. If it never exceeds 8 Hz, this is probably abnormal. A difference of 1 Hz in frequency of the dominant alpha rhythm between the two hemispheres indicates an abnormality in the hemisphere with the lower frequency (Fisch p185, 187). Alpha rhythm is found predominantly in the posterior region (occipital leads) and, apart from prefrontal alpha, (which according to Fisch should be considered eye movement artifact until proven otherwise) frontal and central predominance of alpha is abnormal.

Alpha rhythm is usually blocked, or at least attenuated, with eye opening. The absence of any reduction is abnormal as is unilateral blocking (Bancaud's phenomenon). Eyes closed alpha represents an alert awake state and alpha attenuates as the person becomes drowsy and theta increases.

Alpha is most strongly associated with the visual system and seems to correlate with a resting state with decreased visual input.

b. Beta

Beta activity is found >13 Hz in adults. It is desynchronized rather than being rhythmic. It is almost always a sign of normal cortical functioning. Asymmetry in beta between hemispheres should be no more than 35% of the amplitude of the side with the higher amplitude. If the difference is greater than this, then the side with the lower amplitude may be abnormal. (Fisch, p.181)

B. States of Consciousness, Wave Forms and Bandwidths

1. Historical Context

Different wave forms are seen in different frequency ranges. A very simple analogy can be made to waves on a lake. There are very large waves produced when a ferryboat goes by, smaller, regular waves when an outboard motor boat passes, and little irregular or desynchronized ripples when a gust of wind blows across the lake. Alternating current goes positive, then negative, then positive again. Alternating current will, therefore, produce 'waves' when graphed over time. This was first described by Richard Caton in England in 1875 when he used a string galvanometer to show electrical activity from the cortex of rabbits and displayed the waves by shining a light that made the waves visible as a shadow on the wall. Hans

Berger, in the 1920's, was the first to record and report on the human EEG. He used paper recordings with a series of pens linked to the different EEG channels. That continued to be the method until computers offered the possibility of a digitalized signal that could be displayed on a computer screen. Some hospital EEG recordings are still done on paper, but neurologists are also switching over to computer displays rather than paper recordings.

2. Frequency Band Widths
a. Frequency Ranges

Before describing *bandwidths* it is important to understand that the *frequency* of a wave is just the number of those waves produced in one second. If you imagine that a motorboat produced 4 waves that passed a dock in one second, each wave lasted for 250 ms. The frequency of this wave would be 4 cycles per second (cps). This is usually called 4 Hz. *Hz* is an abbreviation from the name of the physicist Henrich Hertz who first described waves this way in the late 1800's. 4 Hz is in the *theta* range as we will describe below. The EEG is merely a wavy line. This line consists of waves of many different morphologies (shapes) and frequencies measured in terms of the number of waves in one second. You may have faster waves riding on slower waves. All the frequencies are mixed together in the wavy lines we call an EEG.

Bandwidths refer to frequency ranges. For example, the easily identified, relatively high amplitude, synchronous alpha wave is seen when we close our eyes and it usually runs in a frequency range between 8 and 12 cycles per second (Hz). However, alpha waves may also run more slowly, especially in children, at just 6 or 7 Hz, or, they may be faster, 13 or 14 Hz. It is the morphology and not just frequency that determines whether it is alpha. Location and amplitude offer further clues. A *typical bandwidth* or frequency range is not static. The following section discusses some *typical bandwidths* and the age and/or mental state when a particular band width is most frequently observed.

b. The Spectral Array

To make it easier to see which bandwidths are at high amplitudes and which are at low amplitudes during different mental states and activities, a *spectral array* is used. This is a **histogram** showing the amplitudes for each frequency usually from 2 to 32 Hz or more. It is helpful to have a spectral array that goes a little above 60 Hz so that you can easily detect electrical interference. High 60 Hz activity can also indicate poor impedance readings reflecting a poor contact between the electrode and the skin. (In Europe, Asia and Australia it is 50 Hz.) To understand what a spectrum is, imagine that you have 61 containers or bins in a row. Then you ask the computer to pull out of that very complex EEG, which has waves at all the different frequencies, all the waves at 1 Hz and put them in the first bin. You ask it to do the same with all waves at 2 Hz and place them in the second bin, then all those at 3 Hz into the third bin and so on for each frequency up to 62 Hz. Then you tell the computer to display these bins as a histogram with the height of each bin or column representing the power of that frequency in picawatts (or the amplitude in microvolts, depending on which EEG instrument you are using). The extremely fast modern computers can do all the mathematics (called *Fast Fourier Transform*, FFT) to give you this graphic picture in milliseconds. The amplitudes usually decrease fairly uniformly as you move from 2 Hz to 62 Hz in part because the skull attenuates the faster frequencies more than slower frequencies. Thus, when you see a sharp rise (or dip) in any particular bandwidth, that pattern is different than you would usually expect. The exception to this general rule is that adults with eyes closed will have a dominant frequency in the alpha ranges. There will be a blip (a sudden increase in amplitude) representing the alpha activity.

c. Magnitude and Amplitude

We spoke above of the magnitude of the wave being the power expressed in picawatts. The amplitude is the height of the EEG wave measured in microvolts (μv), a millionth of a volt. In most equipment each bin or bar in the histogram represents the average **amplitude** of that frequency of the EEG over one second in time. The relationship between the two measures is that power (pW) is the square of the amplitude (μv) x 6.14. Thus power measurements will yield larger measures.

d. Sensitivity and Gain

EEG instruments have been calibrated in order to give you an accurate estimate of the amplitudes of the EEG waves. This amplitude measurement is based on a comparison of the EEG signal to the height of a wave of a calibrated signal. Your amplifier has its amplification rated in terms of *sensitivity* and *gain*. Thus amplifiers have known *sensitivities* which are recorded as a number of μv/mm. (A higher sensitivity means lower amplification of the recording.) Thus, if a calibration signal of 50 μv causes a deflection of the wave of 7 mm, then this amplifier has a *sensitivity* of 7 μv/mm. Therefore any signal that is 4 mm in height would be 28 μv (7 mm x 4 μv) in strength or *amplitude* (see Fisch, p45, p149). (This discussion assumes that the calibration signal was recorded at the same *filter* and *gain* settings.) You will adjust *sensitivity* when you read an EEG if you work with different age groups because children have much higher amplitude waves than adults. You will decrease sensitivity and thus lower the amplification of the recording for children.

Gain refers to a ratio of the voltage of a signal at the output of the amplifier to the voltage of the signal at the *input* of that amplifier. Thus a gain of 10V / 10μv = 1 million. You will see *gain* mentioned in the specifications for your amplifier. It will probably be recorded in *decibels*. A gain of 1 million (or 10^6) is 120 decibels. A simple way to calculate this is to multiply 20 times the power to which 10 is raised. (20 x 6 = 120 decibels)

3. Correspondence of Mental States to Typical Band Widths

There is nothing inherently good or bad about any frequency or any frequency range. All frequencies are appropriate at certain times or for certain tasks. The most flexible and efficient brains seem able to change quickly from one frequency range to another depending upon task demands. Think of frequency ranges being like gears in a car, you need them all and you want to be able to shift smoothly and quickly between them.

a. Delta

0.5-3 Hz (0.5-3 cycles or waves in one second) waves are called **Delta**. This is the dominant wave form in infants. These waves appear to originate in the cortex (layer V) and correlate with periods of reduced pyramidal cell neuronal activity. These waves are found during sleep at all ages. Stage four sleep will be more than 50% delta waves. They may also be seen in the waking state in infants, in some learning disabled children and in people with brain damage. Delta activity is the dominant activity in normal infants up to about 6 months of age. Caution: Eye blinks and eye movements can produce waves that look like delta.

b. Theta

3-7 Hz, 4-7 Hz or 4-8 Hz waves are called **Theta**. For the most part the origin of this rhythm appears to be in the thalamus and in the limbic system (septal area). Hippocampal theta had been recorded in rats and more recently in humans. It appears to be related to memory retrieval and to the ability to control responding or not responding to stimuli. These waves dominate the EEG from about 6 months to around 6-7 years of age. In older clients, predominance of these waves in the waking state appears to be associated with being drowsy and tuned out from what others may be discussing or from conscious observations of the environment. It is thought that this kind of theta arises from thalamic nuclei. You might still be walking and not trip over objects in your path or bump into things as these actions are rather automatic. You might even think of some very creative things when in this state since it corresponds to the hypnagogic state before sleep onset. Indeed, Thomas Edison reportedly took naps with a small metal ball in his hand and a metal pie plate on the floor beneath each hand. When he went into a creative mental state just before falling fully asleep his muscles would relax, his hands would open and the ball hitting the plate would wake him. He would immediately write down his ideas. Psychotherapists use this mental state to allow a patient to freely bring up memories, fantasies and associations. Waves at 7 Hz may also be seen when a person is visualizing. In peak performance states you will observe brief rises in about 6 to 8 Hz during cognitive processing of information. Perhaps this is indicating some visualization techniques are being utilized or perhaps the theta reflects functions to do with memory and cognition. The point where the power spectra for alpha amplitude intersects with that for theta is called the *transition frequency*. Excessive amounts of theta are typical in individuals with Attention Deficit Disorder.

c. Alpha

8-12 Hz waves are called **Alpha** if they have a regular sinusoidal form. The origin of this rhythm also appears to be in the thalamus. These symmetrical waves are seen in about 90% of people when they close their eyes. These waves are the dominant frequency of the EEG (measured with eyes closed) after 9 –11 years of age and through adulthood. We like to think of alpha as one kind of 'resting' state. When you finish solving a problem (for example, a pilot landing a plane or a child answering a multiplication question) the brain appears to 'rest' briefly in alpha. When teaching children about brain waves, we often joke that the brain is a very lazy organ. It will take a rest (in alpha) whenever it can. We often *'reflect'* on a problem in alpha and it may be quite a creative state. Clients who feel anxious and stressed may show decreased alpha. Alpha dominates the EEG measured at a central location when a person is daydreaming and also when a person is meditating (at least those meditation traditions that encourage an inner focus, as in yoga). You also see increased alpha when someone smokes marijuana and the increased alpha (eyes open) may persist for a couple of days.

i. Low Alpha

8-10 Hz is often referred to as **low alpha**. (Low here refers to the frequency range, not the amplitude of the waves. To be more accurate, what we refer to, as *'low alpha'* is alpha below that individual's peak, eyes closed, alpha frequency. This peak frequency may decrease with age or cognitive deterioration. As noted previously, brighter individuals usually demonstrate a higher *peak-alpha-frequency*. Meditation often is associated with an alpha state. It is a calm and relaxing state but it is also a state in which we are not attending to the world around us. We are in our own head so to speak. When students ask, "Isn't alpha really good?" we may answer that it is, but remind them that going into a meditative mental state in the classroom or boardroom won't be appreciated. You want the mental state to match the situation. Both low alpha and theta rhythms demonstrate diurnal variations. Higher amplitudes of these waves are observed around 11 A.M., 1 P.M. and 3 P.M. The degree of change in amplitude and the exact times vary between individuals and may also vary with fatigue. The peaks are independent of food intake. These diurnal variations are important to the professional who is doing pre and post EEG measurements. To compare data these measurements should be done at the same time of day.

ii. High Alpha

11-12 Hz (or 11 –13 Hz) may be referred to as **high alpha.** The bandwidth 11-12 Hz is associated with a mental state of open awareness. An open awareness implies being capable of responding to a wide range of changes in one's environment. In athletics this state is associated with fast reflexes and accurate responses. The awareness of a professional goalie in hockey or soccer or a black belt martial artist about to fight several opponents would likely be reflected in 12 Hz activity (though this has not been researched in real life situations). It is also associated with the mental and physical calm required in that readiness state before action: for example, the moment just prior to and during the release of an arrow by an archer (Landers, 1991). Open awareness is part of being in the zone, the ideal mental state achieved by top performers in most any field of endeavor. Encouraging the production of 11-13 Hz activity is probably the most common goal in neurofeedback optimal performance training.

d. Beta

Beta waves are above **12 Hz.** Except for sensorimotor rhythm, as described below, beta waves are produced in the brain stem and the cortex. In the cortex beta indicates local activity in a specific area beneath your active electrode. When producing beta we are usually awake, alert, externally-focused, logical, problem solving, attentive. It will be seen when we are listening to a speaker or solving a problem. However, we may also be tense and anxious. Beta rhythm is normal but an asymmetry of >35% may indicate an abnormality on the lower amplitude side (Fisch, 1999, p192). Excessive beta, on the other hand, may be due to medications such as benzodiazepines or barbiturates. This broad range of beta can be broken down into smaller frequency ranges which correspond to more precise kinds of cortical functioning as follows:

i. Sensorimotor Rhythm

13–15 Hz is called **sensorimotor rhythm (SMR)** when it is found across the sensor-motor strip. As noted in the history paragraph, this frequency range does not have a Greek letter name as Sterman named it more recently (1967). It is a very specific **spindle-like** waveform produced in the ventral-basal nucleus of the thalamus. It too is a kind of 'resting' wave state. It occurs when there is a decrease in the activity of the sensory and motor pathways which run through the thalamus, that is, it occurs when there is less attention paid to sensory input and when there is decreased motor output. It is necessary, but not sufficient, to be still for this rhythm to be produced. There is a change in muscle tone such that the person (or cat, or monkey in Sterman's early experiments) is mentally alert without muscles being tense. It is measured across the sensorimotor strip of the cortex and these frequencies found elsewhere would be called beta. The waveform in other areas of the cortex would also be different: desynchronized fast waves, not a spindle like rhythm. Note that the spindle shape of the waves is very apparent when microelectrodes are implanted in the brain as in Sterman's early experimental work, but it is not so easily seen in recordings from the scalp. SMR appears to be associated with a calm mental state with increased reflecting-before-acting. It is thus important to train up (increase) SMR in those who have problems with hyperactivity and / or impulsivity.

ii. Low Beta

16–20 Hz we often refer to as **low beta.** We refer to it as *problem-solving beta*. Of course this beta is found from 12 to 15 Hz and sometimes at frequencies higher than 20 Hz. It can be easily demonstrated for children and their parents by having them watch the EEG and a spectral array, (a histogram of the amplitudes of each frequency) while you ask the child to multiply, say 7 x 8. This can be quite dramatic. Momentarily, activity around 17 Hz suddenly increases in amplitude and at precisely the same time, theta waves and low alpha (8-10 Hz) waves decrease in amplitude if the child can do the math.

iii. High Beta

Beta spindling
This refers to bursts of beta waves in a rising and falling spindle-like pattern. Although it can be less than 20 Hz, most spindles involve fast beta, above 20 Hz. They can be associated with epileptic auras. It may be due to a disease process and cortical irritability. It can be seen in ADHD. In Part II of this book we discuss how training down beta in the area involved may

correspond to a decrease in the client's symptoms.

19–21 Hz or 20–23 Hz Beta is often observed to be raised (above the levels of the beta between 16–18 Hz) in anxious clients. It may correlate with emotional intensity. You must check with each client to establish if a rise in this area is correlated with productive cognitive work, productive but too intense work, or unproductive intense or anxious thinking.

Note: It is crucial that the neurofeedback practitioner always check what their client is experiencing. It is important that you check without suggesting what you think a particular frequency band should represent.

24–36 Hz Beta is often seen to be at very high amplitudes in clients who are worried and ruminating. These clients often feel 'stressed-out'. They may be hyper-vigilant. We may also note a peak around the mid-20's in individuals if they or others in the family have a problem with alcohol or substance abuse. It may be a marker for a tendency to deal with anxiety by using alcohol or drugs. Higher frequency ranges of beta (>30 Hz) is sometimes referred to as *gamma*.

iv. Sheer Rhythm

38–42 Hz Beta is sometimes referred to as **Sheer** rhythm after David Sheer who did some work in the 1970's concerning enhancing 40 Hz activity. This particular rhythm has been observed to be important in learning. It may correspond to a type of attention where the subject is bringing together different aspects of an object into a single percept. It is, therefore, referred to by some clinicians as a *binding* rhythm and is thought to be associated with peak performance. Research at Penn State University, State College Campus, has shown that athletes on a balance board, instructed to lean as far forward as they can, show 40 Hz activity at the moment they correct their balance to prevent falling. An athlete who has suffered a concussion shows poorer balance and does not show the 40 Hz increase. We are, therefore, careful not to include this range of beta in any *inhibit* range we use to eliminate interference (see under artifacts) from muscle electrical activity (EMG).

e. Ambient Electrical Activity

50 Hz in Europe, Israel, Australia or **60** Hz in North America often represents interference from electrical activity in the room. If it is raised, it is a good warning to check all possible sources of unwanted electrical artifact, including your electrode connections. Sometimes lowering the impedance readings between each of your connections will be sufficient to lower this frequency as *common mode rejection* means the pre-amp will not amplify that frequency. Note, too, that when impedances are different between sites currents can be induced in the leads leading to electrical artifact. Other possible sources of ambient current include lamps, extension cords and any electrical appliance, such as a pencil sharpener.

f. EMG

EMG: Fast sharp waves or 'H' forms are seen when there is EMG (electromyogram) interference. The frequency of most muscle activity is higher than 60 Hz but it is of high voltage. It will overwhelm the instrument's filters and interfere with the accurate reading of brain waves at lower frequencies. In our work with the EEG it is called an *artifact*, that is, electrical activity of non-cortical origin. EMG artifact will proportionately inflate the lower amplitude higher frequencies more than high amplitude slower frequencies.

4. Broad Descriptive Terms used in Neurofeedback:

a. Slow Waves:

This term usually refers to any waves running at a rate less than 12 Hz. These include delta, theta and alpha waves.

b. Fast Waves:

This term usually refers to any waves running at a rate greater than 12 Hz. (12 Hz may be slow or fast depending on whether the waveform you are referring to is alpha or SMR/beta respectively.)

C. Wave Forms Not Frequently Encountered in Neurofeedback Work:

1. Lambda Waves

Lambda waves are positive saw-tooth shaped waves usually found in the occipital region. They are 'evoked' by visual scanning or looking at detailed material. They last about 100-250 msec. They are infrequently observed in typical hospital EEGs because these recordings are done with eyes closed. You may see them quite frequently if you do full cap assessments because you might be recording while the subject is reading. Lambda is only considered abnormal if the waves are markedly asymmetrical. This can suggest an abnormality on the side with a lower amplitude (Fisch p193). We will just mention, not focus, on this wave form in the discussions in this basic text.

In the figure below, Gunkelman notes that the lambda waves are sharp downward deflections (positive) that may be seen repeatedly when the subject is reading.

Lambda during reading

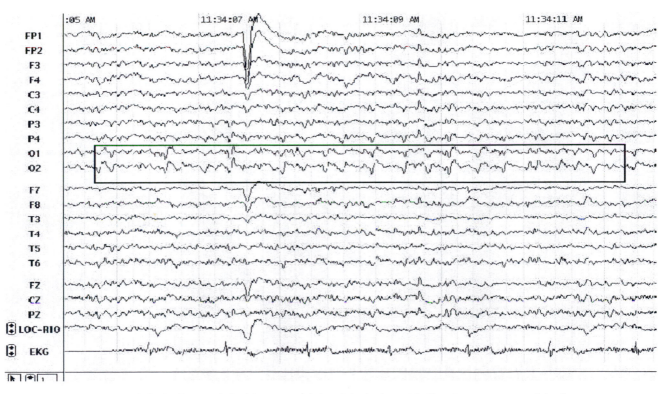

Lambda is the occipital downward (positive) sharp deflection seen repetitively

Thanks are extended to Jay Gunkelman for sharing this example.

2. Mu Waves

Mu waves may fool you. They look like alpha waves and are usually found in the 7-11 Hz frequency range. Mu is usually observed at C3 and C4. Because many of you will be working with clients who have difficulty with attention and concentration, it is important that you distinguish this activity from central alpha which may be a marker for certain types of ADD. Mu is blocked by making a fist. This blocking of Mu is, for the most part, on the *contra-lateral side* (the side of head opposite the side of the body where the client made the fist). You may also try having the client close their eyes and then open them. When they open their eyes, alpha is blocked but Mu will remain in the central region. The only real indication of an abnormality with Mu is if it is found only on one side of the head. Though most people do not produce Mu, it is considered a normal variant. It may be found in about 7% of the population. However, Mu is found in a much higher proportion of clients who have ADHD.

Morphology:

- **Mu** waves have a pointed top and bottom rounded (or, alternatively, a rounded top and a pointed bottom.) It is, therefore, often referred to as a *wicket* rhythm. This wave shape is monomorphic rather than sinusoidal.

- Contrast this with biphasic waves which have 2 points like those seen with EMG (muscle activity).
- Contrast it also with sinusoidal waves characteristic of alpha (usually not pointed).

It is reasonably safe to say that, for the most part, you will not normally see alpha centrally without it also being observed in the occipital and parietal regions.

Figure below shows an example of Mu waves seen at F4-C4 in a longitudinal sequential montage.

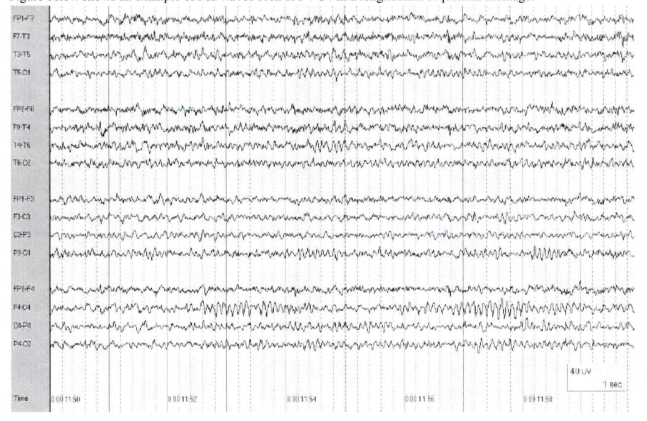

Laplacian Montage, note Mu at C4 – aC4.

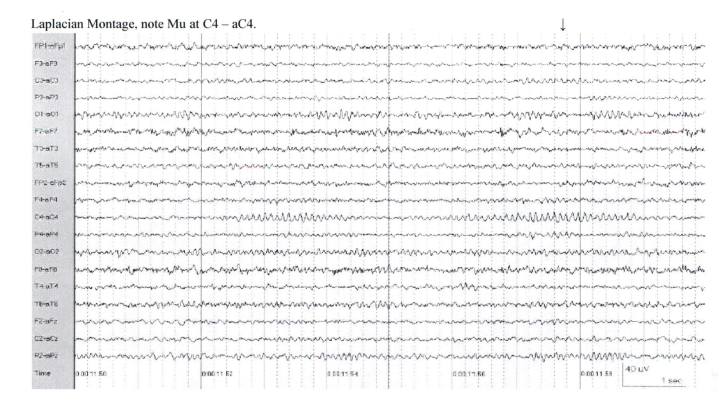

3. Waveforms Less Commonly Seen In NFB Work

As we stated at the beginning of this section on waves, waves may be described as: *regular* such as a burst of theta waves, or *irregular* such as a burst of theta with beta waves riding on top. Waves may be described as *sinusoidal*, such as a burst of alpha waves. They may be said to be *spindle-like* (e.g., SMR) beginning small and building up in amplitude then falling off in a spindle shape, a shape familiar to those who know the weaving trade. Less often waves may be described as *sharp* or *spiked* or as combinations of these, *spike-and-wave* or *poly spikes* or complexes.

a. Spikes

Spikes: These waves have a duration of 20-70 ms. This wave looks just like its name says. It is a spike and it would hurt if you sat on it. The spike is a distinct wave form in terms of its rate of climb & descent. A spike's amplitude is usually higher than other background activity, about 40-100 µv.

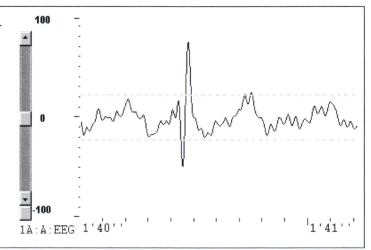

Although this sample of EEG is from a woman who has a seizure disorder and this sample is a spike, the morphology is that of **a myogenic spike biphasic**. In other words it is muscle generated and goes in two directions. There is **not** an "after-following" slow wave, the hallmark of cerebral spikes. A spike with an after-following slow wave is the wave form that is characteristic of seizures. This is an interictal sample from a client who has partial complex seizures. Note also the high amplitude slow wave activity. However, since the electrode was placed 1 cm above a point, 1/3 of the way along a line drawn from external ear canal to the lateral canthus of the eye (appropriate for picking up interictal activity) it is also a placement that is liable to detect a lateral rectus spike, which reflects electrical activity from the muscle involved in lateral eye movement The spike may appear without visible movement of the eye since these spikes are like a single motor unit (SMU), not a contraction. This spike is thus an artifact (electrical activity not of cerebral origin). (Thanks to Jay Gunkelman for interpretation.)

b. Spike & Wave:

Uniform 3 per second spike and wave 'pairs' are characteristic of an absence (petit mal) seizure. Note very high amplitude (>160 µv) of these waves.	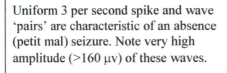 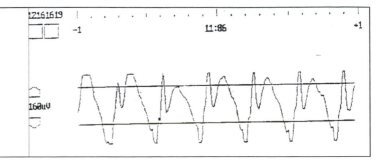

c. Sharp Waves:

These waves have a duration of 70-200 ms. They do not have as sharp a point as a 'spike' and are more like the tip of a pencil rather than the needle-like spike. They are described as having a high velocity segment. They are bi-directional. **(See figure under 'i' below)**

d. Sharp Transients:

These are groups of sharp waves. If they are in infrequent bursts, then they are usually just called *non-specific*. However, *complexes* containing spikes and sharp waves which are repeated may represent *interictal* (between seizures) epileptiform activity. This kind of activity may occur between seizures in a patient who has epilepsy. It is possible to have complexes which last for a few seconds but which do not correspond to any observable clinical manifestations of a seizure. In such cases the term *subclinical electrographic seizure pattern* may be used.

e. Paroxysmal discharge

A *Paroxysmal discharge* refers to one or more wave that stand out from the rest of the EEG activity. They usually begin and end abruptly. Although they may be seen in patients who clinically present with a seizure disorder, they may also be seen in people who have never had a seizure, particularly when a person is drowsy.

i. Epileptiform Paroxysmal Discharge

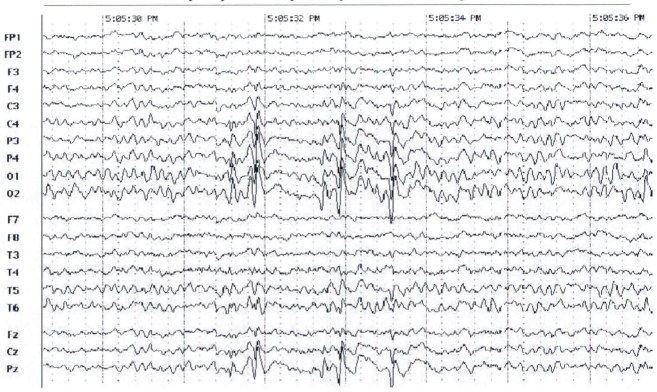

This epileptiform paroxysmal discharge sample has been provided by Jay Gunkelman.

ii. Paroxysmal hypnogogic hypersynchrony

This term refers to synchronous, slightly notched, sine waves that are higher in amplitude than surrounding waves and run at about 3-5 Hz. The burst may last for a couple of seconds. You may see this in normal children when they are sleepy.

f. Sleep spindles, V waves & K complexes,

Sleep spindles look like SMR spindles and are in the same frequency range: 12-15 Hz. Like SMR they are maximal over the central regions. Apparently they arise from a different generator and are only present during sleep and are seen in stage II. V waves occur during sleep and are negative with an amplitude of up to 250 µV and a duration of less than 200 ms. K complexes are seen in stage II sleep and are sharp, negative and of high amplitude followed by a longer duration positive wave. People doing neurofeedback are not concerned with the specialized field of reading sleep EEGs so these waves are mentioned but most practitioners will never encounter them in practice.

g. Square waves:

This term refers to a fundamental frequency plus harmonics. This terminology is familiar to musicians. On the EEG it may look like a slow wave theta or delta with faster, lower amplitude (beta) waves riding on top. A harmonic is a whole number multiple of the fundamental frequency. With a number of harmonics riding on the fundamental wave, the waveform becomes visually squared off. The first harmonic of a theta wave that is seen in the EEG is usually lower in amplitude than the fundamental frequency and three times its frequency. Examples are shown in the intervention section of this book.

h. Slow Waves
i. Localized slow waves:
These waves are under 8 Hz and may indicate a localized lesion (for example, a stroke) or abnormality (for example, migraine, transient ischemic attack, mild head injury, supratentorial brain tumors). The tentorium is a large in-folding of dura matter (connective tissue) separating the cerebellum below from the cerebrum above. Child tumors are more frequently inferior and adult tumors, superior, to the tentorium. (The other indentation of dura separates the two cerebral hemispheres, on the dorsal surface, and is called the falx cerebri.) Delta is usually surrounded by theta in these instances. The delta doesn't respond to manoeuvres such as eye opening or hyperventilation. Deep lesions (such as those in the internal capsule) do not show focal delta but may result in hemispheric or bilateral delta. (Fisch, p.349)

ii. Bilaterally synchronous slow waves:
These may be seen in children when they are drowsy. However, in an alert resting adult these delta waves may indicate deep midline structural damage. They may appear intermittently in bursts and be higher in amplitude than surrounding wave forms. This phenomenon may be due to diffuse gray matter damage. Frontal intermittent rhythmical delta activity has the acronym FIRDA. Interictally 3 Hz waves of this kind may be seen in some clients who have absence seizures.

iii. Generalized asynchronous slow waves:
These waves (<8 Hz) occur over both hemispheres but demonstrate no constant time relationship one side to the other. They are seen in normal individuals who are sleepy and in children who have a fever. However, a marked amount of these slow waves may indicate an abnormality (usually quite nonspecific and seen in such disorders as: migraine headaches, head injuries, high fever, encephalopathies, degenerative diseases, dementia, and in some clients with Parkinson's). Generalized asynchronous slow waves are the most common and least specific EEG abnormality. You should always have this checked out by a neurologist. (See Fisch, p.363-376 for a detailed discussion.)

iv. Continuous irregular delta:
Polymorphic delta results from lesions affecting white matter.

i. Abnormal Beta
Neurologists may view an isolated reduction in beta as a fairly reliable sign of local damage. When beta activity is asymmetrical, it is said to be abnormal on the side with less beta if the difference is > 35%. (Note: An asymmetry in alpha activity needs to be > 50% to be considered abnormal.) Decreased beta may also be seen during a migraine attack. A reduction in amplitude of all waves occurs for a few seconds after a seizure and a localized decrease in alpha and beta may be seen for a short time (from seconds to a few minutes) after a focal seizure.

j. Abnormal Amplitude:
There is, generally speaking, no upper limit. The lower limit is 20 microvolts in any channel in any montage during eyes closed wakefulness with exceptions that include alerting, mental effort, eyes opening, anxiety or drowsiness.

A **bilateral decrease in alpha** may be due to anxiety or a disorder, usually toxic or metabolic. A general **increase in beta** is usually due to tranquilizers or sedatives. (Fisch, p.407) **Slowing of alpha**, that is, a lower peak alpha frequency, may be a sign of head injury.

A **unilateral reduction of alpha** may indicate an abnormality. If this occurs while doing mental arithmetic in eyes closed condition, it may indicate abnormalities in the ipsilateral parietal or temporal lobe. (Westmoreland, 1998) Failure on one side to block alpha on eye opening may also indicate a lesion in these areas, and is known as Bancaud's phenomenon.

D. Sleep

1. Normal Stages of Sleep
Most readers of this text will not be recording during sleep. We will, therefore, give just a brief overview of the wave patterns seen during normal sleep.

Wakefulness with eyes closed: Alpha dominates and is highest in the occipital leads while beta may dominate the frontal leads.

Stage I: Alpha attenuates and irregular slow waves dominate the EEG in the frequency range of 1 to 7 Hz.

Stage II: This light sleep phase is characterized by the appearance of V waves, sleep spindles and posterior occipital sharp transients (POSTs).

Stage III: In this stage high amplitude delta waves begin to appear. POSTs are still present and sleep spindles may be present as well.

Stage IV: More than half the record will be delta waves at a frequency of 2Hz or less.

REM: This refers to a rapid eye movement phase in which the subject is usually dreaming and may recall the dreams on awakening. The EEG is characteristically of low voltage and despite prominent theta and the lower frequency alpha, it may look much like an awake recording. There is a distinct lack of muscle tone which is different from the awake state.

Sleep is cyclic through the night beginning with stage I and proceding to stage II, III, and IV and then going briefly back to stages III and II and into REM before beginning the cycle again with stage I sleep. Each cycle is between 80-120 minutes long. The percentage of time spent in stages III and IV decreases with age.

2. Sleep Disorders

Many trainers using NFB will see clients who have Attention Deficit Disorder and one must keep other pathological conditions in mind when making a differential diagnosis. The marker for A.D.D. (increased theta) is also found in individuals who have either narcolepsy or sleep apnea. In clients who have *narcolepsy* REM sleep will occur at sleep onset. However, people who do not have narcolepsy but take a day-time nap, may also show REM onset at the beginning of their nap. Multiple naps with a very short time before falling asleep (less than 5 minutes) all beginning with REM sleep may indicate narcolepsy. Sleep deprivation for any reason may result in excessive daytime drowsiness and REM onset naps.

Frequent long periods (> 10 seconds) without breathing may indicate sleep apnea. It is most common in people who snore and those who are obese. Essentially what happens in this disorder is that the airway becomes obstructed when the person is asleep. Their muscles relax allowing fat to fold in and close off the airway, or they may have enlarged tonsils or adenoids that produce the blockage. The result is poor quality sleep, periods of reduced oxygen flow to the brain and a daytime EEG that looks very drowsy with lots of slow waves. If you have any question about these disorders you should have the client checked out by the appropriate medical professional.

An excellent book that covers all aspects of sleep is *The Promise of Sleep* by William Dement.

E. Abnormal EEG Patterns

This is not the subject of this book. The only reason for describing and showing a few abnormalities is to **warn you to refer these persons immediately to the appropriate medical practitioner.** You may do NFB training for many years and never see any abnormal pattern unless, of course, you are using neurofeedback to treat people who have a seizure disorder or a head injury. When you do see abnormal wave patterns, it will hopefully be in people who have already been the subject of neurological evaluation and so you know what you are dealing with in their EEG.

It is nevertheless possible that you might see an unusual pattern. What might it look like? The following are just a few selected examples.

1. Seizures – General Description:

Seizures are usually brief periods of motor, sensory, mental or autonomic disturbances of sudden onset, often accompanied by a change in consciousness and paroxysms of unusual EEG activity. They may be followed by a brief period of paralysis of that function which was most involved in the seizure. Recurring seizures due to a cerebral abnormality are termed *epilepsy*. This is as opposed to a seizure caused by a reaction to a transient circumstance, such as alcohol withdrawal, hypoglycemia or fever. A single febrile seizure in an infant is thus not an indicator of epilepsy.

Seizures are described by different terms. The first set of terms you may encounter are: symptomatic, idiopathic and cryogenic. *Symptomatic epilepsy* is defined as seizures resulting from a cerebral disorder. *Idiopathic epilepsy* are seizures in a patient without any identifiable cause who has had a normal neurological examination. *Cryptogenic epilepsy* is the term used when the patient has seizures without an identifiable cause but who has a cognitive impairment and/or neurological deficits.

a. Generalized Seizures

There are over a hundred different kinds of seizures. Although certainly an unwanted abnormality, there are a number of famous people who had seizures including Charles Dickens, Vincent Van Gogh and Sir Isaac Newton.

Generalized seizures involve both hemispheres. Examples are a tonic-clonic seizure, myoclonic seizure or an absence seizure. A *tonic* seizure involves flexion of muscles. The contraction may last up to a minute and there is loss of consciousness. A *clonic* seizure is characterized by rhythmic myoclonic movements lasting for one or more minutes and associated with loss of consciousness. The combination termed a *tonic-clonic seizure (or Grand Mal Epilepsy in older texts)* you will not forget once you have seen it. The client loses consciousness followed by sustained *tonic* contractions. The client turns blue (cyanotic) and their heart rate and blood pressure rises. After about 15 seconds rhythmic *clonic* movements begin. This progresses to violent jerking and the client may bite their tongue. This phase lasts for about 30 seconds. Incontinence may occur.

Atonic seizures refer to a sudden loss in muscle tone.

The *myoclonic* seizure is characterized mainly by sudden, brief, flexor muscle contractions. It can cause the patient to fall and can, therefore, be dangerous.

b. Partial Seizures

Partial seizures involve a single area in just one hemisphere. If consciousness is not impaired it is termed a *simple partial seizure*. If change in consciousness is involved, it is termed a *complex partial seizure*. A partial seizure may be motor, sensory (burning, tingling or other sensations), autonomic (sweating, flushing, epigastric sensations) or psychological (distortions of cognition, including time; feelings, including fear and anger; hallucinatory and so on). An example of a simple motor partial seizure would be the sudden loss of expressive or receptive language (aphasic seizure).

Complex partial seizures (temporal lobe seizures) usually involve the inferior and medial part of the temporal lobe. It is generally accepted that Joan of Arc had a seizure disorder which was the source of her visions. Now that a localization for religiosity has been identified in the temporal lobe (see Rita Carter, p.13) it is interesting to speculate about the focus of St. Joan's seizure activity.

2. The EEG in Seizure Disorders

a. Spike-and-Wave Pattern

The EEG activity may be *ictal* (during the seizure) or *interictal* (between seizures). It may be *localized* or *generalized*. Thalamic projections appear to be involved since suppression of thalamic function abolishes spike-and-wave discharges. This early *centrencephalic* theory (Penfield & Jasper 1954) has been modified to include the primary role of the cortex in seizure propagation and of the reticular formation in modulating cortical excitability (corticoreticular theory, Fisch, p.300).

Focal epileptiform activity often consists of localized spikes and sharp waves seen in a few neighbouring electrodes. This activity may be surrounded by irregular slower waves or followed by an after-going slow wave. Focal spike and sharp waves may appear before and after a generalized discharge. (Fisch, p.271)

There are many disorders which may show epileptiform activity. These are the purview of neurologists not neurofeedback practitioners. One rare disorder, *Landau-Kleffner syndrome,* is characterized by a progressive disturbance of language comprehension and speech. The spike and wave complexes are in the temporal region.

Another pattern that involves speech shows central bisynchronous spikes associated with Rhett's syndrome. This disorder of females is associated with slow decrease in motor and language skills beginning often in the second year of life. Hand wringing is a prominent symptom. There are generalized complex partial or simple motor seizures which end by about age 10. After this time the EEG is dominated by delta activity.

Absence Seizures

Generalized 3 Hz high amplitude spike and slow wave activity is a pattern you may see, if you evaluate a lot of children for ADHD, Inattentive Type. This pattern is characteristic of *absence seizures* (petit mal epilepsy). Someone with this problem is often mistakenly thought to be daydreaming and inattentive when, in fact, an unrecognized absence seizure disorder is the primary reason for the child's lack of attention in the classroom. There is no loss of muscle tone. Inattentiveness is momentary. If you tell the client something during the attack there will be no memory of it afterwards. They just stare off into space and nothing registers for a few seconds. These children may or may not also have ADD but the seizure disorder must be the first problem to be addressed.

Sample of EEG from F1000 instrument showing an absence seizure activity in an 8 year old girl.

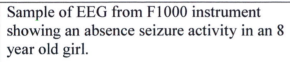

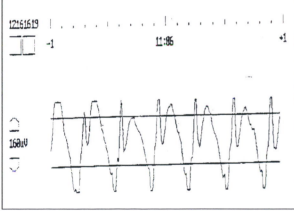

Figures on the left

Note the very high amplitude of these recordings.
The first figure on the left is the raw EEG, 11 minutes into the session. It demonstrates the typical 3 per second spike and wave pattern seen in absence seizures (petit mal). Note the very high amplitude, >160 μV.

This 8 year old girl was sent due to 'tuning–out' during classes.

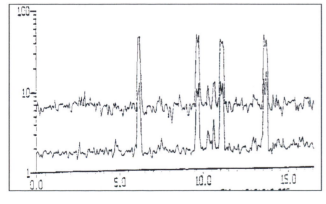

In the second figure on the left the top line represents slow wave (4-8 Hz) and the bottom, fast wave (16-20 Hz). This diagram is included to demonstrate both the frequency of these seizures (four in the course of 15 minutes) and the very high amplitude of the waves.

Focal slow wave activity may suggest a focal brain lesion.

Note: Spike-and-wave patterns may sometimes appear with no relationship to a seizure disorder. (Fisch, p.333)

c. Non Spike and Wave Pattern

Non spike and wave patterns are also found in some seizure disorders. For example, bursts of rhythmic slow waves may be seen in temporal or frontotemporal regions in complex partial seizures. Detailed descriptions of the EEG in seizure disorders may be found in any basic neurology textbook.

Illustrations of a Seizure Disorder:

In Figure 1, shown below, the subject is a 16 year old boy who has tonic-clonic (grand mal) seizure activity. Note the spikes with following slow wave.

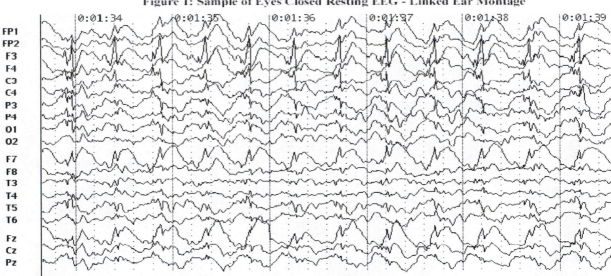

Figure 1: Sample of Eyes Closed Resting EEG - Linked Ear Montage

The figure opposite is a topometric display from the SKIL program. It compares the subject to the SKIL data base for theta, 4 – 8 Hz.. The light gray lines are 2 standard deviations (SD) above and below the heavy black line (joined squares) which shows the data base average. The joined circles (red line) are the subjects values in the 4-8 Hz theta range. Note the high values at F3 and P4. Time of day correction is on.

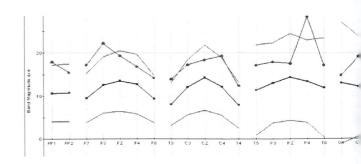

Below is a 'brain map' display of the same data.

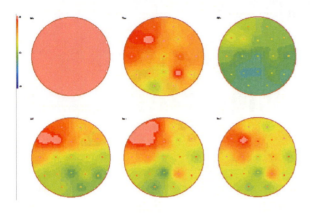

In this brain map the amplitude range is between 0 and 28.5 μV. Note high F3 and P4 theta.

In keeping with these EEG observations, this 16 year old boy, in addition to tonic-clonic seizure activity, also exhibited symptoms similar to Asperger's Syndrome. His affect appeared flat, he spoke slowly without emotional intonation. At times he would laugh inappropriately. He did not seem to appreciate social innuendo and lacked social responsiveness.

Below the same data are displayed in 1 Hz frequency bins and compared to the SKIL normative data base at 3 SD. Red is above the mean and dark blue is below the mean. The dull brick colour seen in the 1 Hz display is the farthest from the mean.

The figure below is a comparison with the SKIL data base at 3 SD. Note the very high theta and beta activity in the left frontal region.

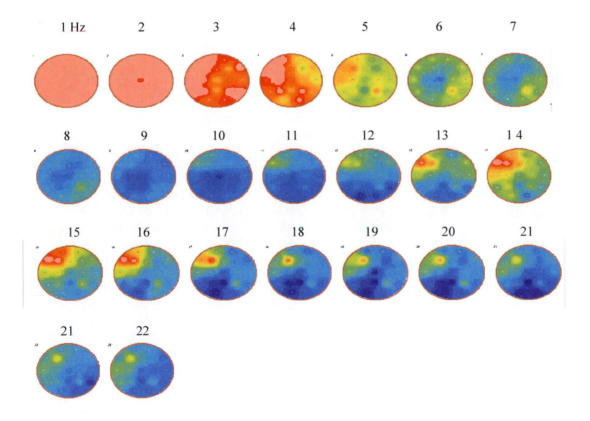

SECTION IV
Measuring the EEG:
Instruments & Electronics

What we are measuring when we monitor the EEG using an electroencephalograph is the potential difference between pairs of small electrodes. The voltages measured are in millionths of a volt. We can induce voltage differences of thousands of volts just by rubbing our feet on the carpet and approaching another person. The obvious dilemma and question is, how does the EEG instrument detect the tiny voltages produced by groups of neurons in our cortex and eliminate the influence of enormous voltages from extraneous sources? First let's consider what '*potential difference*, '*current*', and '*resistance*' mean.

You probably recall from high school physics that for a direct current (DC), such as you have in a flashlight run by batteries, there is a relationship between potential difference measured in volts, current measured in amperes, and resistance measured in ohms. The relationship was described by the German physicist Georg Ohm in 1826 as Potential Difference (V) = Current (I) x Resistance (R). A similar formula describes this relationship for alternating currents (AC). AC is what you get from a wall plug and also what is measured by an EEG. The formula is: Voltage (V or E) = Current (I) x Impedance (z). Impedance is a more complex construct than resistance because its calculation requires measurements of not only the resistance of the conductor but other factors such as capacitance, inductance and the frequency of the alternating current. These terms and impedance measurements will be described in more detail later in this text.

In these formulas *current* is the rate of electron flow through a conductor. It is measured in '*amperes*'. *Potential difference* may be thought of as the force or pressure that causes the electron current to flow in one direction. Thus the current flows due to the potential difference between source (-ve site) and destination (+ve site). The *resistance* (or impedance with AC

current) is the opposition to this flow inherent in the material through which the current is flowing. Thus R and z both refer to the opposition to the flow of electrons through the conducting circuit. Opposition to electron flow is high in substances such as rubber where most of the atoms contain outer electron layers that are full. This increases the resistance of the electron in the outer layer to being dislodged. These substances make good insulators and very poor conductors.

Current measures the rate of transfer of electric charge from one point to another. (Your utility company measures the number of electrons passing through the meter in each second. They measure it in *amperes* where an ampere = 6.28 x 10^{18} electrons [coulomb]). *Electrical charge* refers to the negative charge carried by electrons. Electrons orbit around their nucleus but at different orbiting distances that may be thought of as *energy levels*. Each energy level contains a precise number of electrons. Nearest to the nucleus are 2 electrons. In the next level there are 8, and in the third level there are 16 electrons. It is the electrons in the outermost layer that are responsible for electricity. This electron layer may be incompletely filled. When this is the case, the electrons in that layer are less tightly held in place and collisions may dislodge them. Imagine that a loose electron acts like a billiard ball. It collides with another electron, is captured by the atom it collided with but that atom's electron is sent off on a different course to strike the next atom and so on in a chain reaction. It is this sequence that is responsible for what we know as an electric current.

In our work with neurofeedback we use the potential difference between a +ve and a –ve electrode as a measure of the *amplitude* of the EEG signal. For brain waves this is expressed in microvolts (μV). A microvolt is a millionth of a volt.

An analogy that is often quoted is the flow of water from a water tower. The height of the tower dictates the pressure that will move the water through a pipe. Pressure is like potential difference (voltage) in an electrical circuit. The rate of flow of the water is the 'current'. The diameter of the pipe corresponds to resistance in the electrical circuit. A small diameter pipe will resist the flow of the current. The current can be increased either by increasing the pressure (a higher water tower) or decreasing the resistance (a wider pipe).

The brain produces an alternating current. This current may be thought of as a sine wave. To measure the amplitude of this wave we usually measure from the top of the positive wave to the top of the negative wave and we term this a *peak to peak* measurement.

A. The EEG Instrument
How Does My System *'Read'* the EEG Signal and Keep Out Unwanted Electrical Activity?

The scalp electrodes used for neurofeedback are macro-electrodes (>5mm) which are detecting microvolt differences between electrodes at two different sites. A microvolt is a millionth of a volt. Merely walking closer to the client can induce currents in the wires and in virtually any room that you will be using for NFB there will be many other electrical influences which can affect the recording. Perhaps the simplest and most dramatic example is static electricity: rub your feet on the rug and put your hand out towards your neighbour and a spark will jump between you. The potential difference between you and your client can climb to more than 1000 volts. Thus the first step in measuring the EEG involves an instrument called a *preamplifier*. It amplifies this tiny microvolt difference by more than 100,000 times and does not amplify the other electrical signals. The second step is to change the alternating analog current to the digital form that the computer can work with by a process called *sampling*. The third step is to take this digital signal and display it in a manner that makes it easier to read by *filtering*, which means showing the portion of the EEG which is of interest to us and filtering out the rest of the

signal. The next sections will describe these processes in more detail.

1. Amplification:
Why a *preamp:* The preamp amplifies the EEG current by a huge amount so that other influences in the environment will be small and inconsequential in comparison to the amplified EEG current. It only amplifies the differences in voltage between inputs. Your electrodes are picking up tiny amounts of electrical current. You are measuring millionths of a volt (microvolts). Just walking towards your client after rubbing your shoes on a carpet can create a voltage difference between you and your client of thousands of volts. This will induce an electrical current in the wires attaching your client to the amplifier. Long wires may pick up more induced electrical changes. Thus having short wires that run to a preamp that is placed on the clients shoulder, or even on the headband, should reduce the problem. (There is less wire that can act like an antenna.) Other instruments have the preamp in the same box as the encoder, which means longer wires and more distance along which other electrical activity can be picked up. Having a well shielded cable is one way to handle the problem of long wires. Cables for the Focused Technology's F1000 equipment, for example, have an extra wire wound inside to pick up extraneous current so that it does not have much influence on the wires carrying current from the electrodes. Some instruments such as Thought Technology's Procomp+ and the Infinity instruments have a preamp which can be clipped onto the client's collar. Thus the wires from the electrodes to the preamp can be short.

Whether the instrument has a preamp close to the electrodes, well shielded cables from electrodes to amplifier, or both, the goal is to reduce the amount of induced electrical current affecting the system.

The preamplifier is a small unit that, ideally, would be placed as close to the electrode site as possible because, once amplification has taken place, ambient electrical field effects will have much less influence on the recorded EEG. In Sterman's research with TopGun airforce pilots there was a preamp built into the cap worn by the pilot at each electrode site. This is an elegant but very expensive solution to the problem of wires between the electrode and the preamp picking up unwanted current.

Calibration of a full cap EEG instrument is done by applying a standard voltage to all input channels. This ensures that the voltage read is accurate and that all inputs are amplifying and filtering the signal in the same way. Most neurofeedback instruments do not require calibration measurements before each use. You would only calibrate if you suspected a problem. We recommend that practitioners have two EEG instruments. When a problem is suspected the trainer can rapidly plug the clients electrodes into the second instrument to check the readings.

How does the amplifier work: The amplifier detects and amplifies differences between 2 inputs. It amplifies changes in the signals to each input to the same degree but in opposite directions, referenced to an electrical reference built into the amplifier. It does this by reversing the polarity of the second input so that the two currents are effectively subtracted. The amplifier only amplifies this difference between the two inputs; hence it is correctly called a differential amplifier. In this way the amplifier is said to *reject* signals that are in common to both inputs. This is called 'common mode' rejection. The machine is wired so that greater negativity at input 1 than input 2 causes an upward deflection of the signal.

(Note: Your ground wire, on the client's scalp, does NOT go to the ground in the sense that we call the third wire on an electrical plug, a ground wire. Think of the term "ground" when referring to your third electrode as an 'electrical housekeeping' wire. True ground is no longer the reference point for measurements. (Frank Diets, electrical engineer who made the F1000 biofeedback / neurofeedback instrument, personal communication.)

The *common mode rejection ratio* is the ratio of the common mode input voltage divided by the output voltage (Fisch, p43). This ratio should be greater than 100,000. Failure of this system to eliminate external common mode artifact is likely due to either a difference in impedance between the two electrodes and/or a poor 'ground' connection.

A second amplification is carried out after signals are filtered. This is called *single ended amplification* because it just compares a single input with the 'ground' and amplifies that signal.

2. Filtering:

Your computer amplifier has two filters which help to minimize distortions that could make it quite difficult for you to read the EEG. These are the *high pass filter* and the *low pass filter*. In some instruments this filtering is done in the *preamp* that has input from three electrodes (positive, negative, and ground) and which is placed between those wires and the *encoder* which sits on the desk. In other instruments it is in the same box on the desk with the encoder. Filtering takes place after the differential amplification and before the second, single-ended, amplification. A third type of filter called a *notch* filter is present in some instances to filter out a narrow band of activity such as 60 Hz. These filters do not just cut off waves below or above them. It is a more complex process of attenuating the unwanted frequencies, that is, reducing their amplitude by a set percentage. You may read about this process in a basic EEG textbook such as Fisch, (page 46-54). An unavoidable, unwanted effect of the low pass filter is that the filter can distort artifact potentials (such as muscle artifact) by lowering the amplitude and slowing the observed frequency with the result that the waves may look as if they are cerebral in origin.

a. High-Pass Filter:

The *high pass filter* is meant to attenuate waves (reduce the amplitude) that come in at a frequency below its cut off. It lets *pass through* it waves higher than its cut off frequency. It is not an all-or-none type of filtering but a gradual elimination of frequencies. Most of our instruments have high pass filters at 1 or 2 Hz because we are usually only looking for wave forms above 3 Hz when doing EEG biofeedback. In hospital work, however, lower frequencies are considered for interpretation of the EEG. Instruments such as the Procomp+ or Infinity have their high-pass filter set at a lower frequency (0.5 Hz). Delta waves can be clearly seen with this instrument, though you must be careful to distinguish between delta and eye movement artifact.

In some EEG instruments, such as the Lexicor, this high pass filter may be turned on or off if they are reading the EEG. You will usually have it on during feedback. A low cut off gives an EEG that includes delta, which may be useful. However, it means that any interference which is sufficient to overload this high pass filter, such as the start up of an air-conditioner or a pump, may result in a spurious signal while the amplifier takes time to recover. The resulting EEG may have the appearance of a single square wave several seconds long (with spurious harmonics up through beta). There are pros and cons to every design and, as we discuss instrumentation, you will frequently find that the engineers had to make decisions based on trade-offs. Remember that a high-pass filter is set at a low number such as 0.5 Hz or 2 Hz. It is therefore sometimes called a low frequency filter.

b. Low-Pass Filter

The *low pass filter* is meant to only let through, for our observation, waves below its cut off point. Many biofeedback instruments have a low pass at approximately 32 Hz. Thus frequencies higher than this are not registered. The F1000 has a digitally tunable low pass filter. It is set to 61 Hz for an on-line FFT display that goes out to 63 Hz. During feedback, however, it is set to 45 Hz to reduce the influence of 50 / 60 Hz interference. The ProComp+ and Infinity low pass filter is also above 61 Hz. This higher cut off point allows us to observe the EEG at higher frequencies. This is important when we are attempting to distinguish cortical activity, for example, ruminative activity around 30 Hz, or cognitive 'binding activity' (Sheer rhythm) around 40 Hz, from activity in these frequency ranges that may be due to muscle (EMG) artifact. Electrical activity from lights, computers, extension cords, etc. is usually very regular and distinct on the EEG and can be seen at 60 Hz in North America or at 50 Hz in Europe, Asia and Australia.

Other sources of interference may be more of a problem to very sensitive instruments than they are to some other less sensitive or older instruments due to a very low *noise level allowance*. The 'boosters' which Trucker's 'boosters' for their 2-way radio communications, for example, may result in a rise in amplitude starting at high frequencies and moving down to lower ones like surf in Hawaii.

c. Band Pass Filters

A *band pass* is just the frequency range (for example, 4 to 8 Hz) that is chosen by the practitioner to use either for statistical comparisons or for neurofeedback. In neurofeedback the practitioner chooses frequency bands to inhibit or to enhance. How these are chosen is described in the intervention section of this book. Some software computer systems allow the practitioner to choose both the type of filter (IIR, FIR, FFT) and the width of the frequency band that is desired for statistics or for neurofeedback training. In other systems the type of filter is chosen by the engineer who designed the program and it cannot be changed.

3. Sampling Rate

The original EEG can be said to be in an 'analog' or continuous wave form. This wave must be broken up into tiny parcels or samples to be used by your computer. Breaking up the continuous wave into small pieces is called *sampling*. This sampling is performed by an analog to digital (A/D) converter. It may be located in the *encoder* of the Procomp+ and in the interface board of the instrument. Modern inputs to the encoder always use female plugs. Female plugs are used because they cannot accidentally be connected to a power source, an error that could be damaging to both equipment and the person connected to that equipment.

A fast sampling rate is crucial for obtaining accurate information. The maximum frequency that can be reconstructed in a filter is based on the *Nyquist* principle. It is half the sampling rate frequency. Technically then, 128 samples per second would allow you to view frequencies up to about 64 Hz although, in practice, instruments with this sampling rate usually just handle frequencies up to 32 Hz.. This is the basis of the F1000 on-line spectral display and also approximately the rate read by the Lexicor at the time of writing. Other instruments such as the ProComp+ biofeedback systems and the Neuronavigator have a sampling rate of 256 samples per second or greater. Thought Technology's Infinity can offer choices of sampling rates up to 2000 samples per second. Faster sampling rates allow the practitioner to more accurately observe higher frequency wave forms. For example, a sampling rate of 256 cps can accurately show frequencies of ¼ that rate or 64 cycles a second (Hz). Although a division by 2 is acceptable, as a rule-of-thumb most manufacturers divide the sampling rate by 4 to get an approximate maximum frequency for accurate EEG wave frequency analysis. Thus to get an EEG spectrum that goes accurately to about 64 Hz we want an instrument that will sample at rate of 256 samples per second and for 32Hz you can sample at 128 samples per second. High sampling rates are necessary for analytical analysis of single waveforms. It is referred to as *over-sampling* and 8x to 16x the frequency being analyzed is a common standard.

The sampling rate of 64 cycles per second used by some older instruments allowed a faster FFT calculation. This was an important consideration with older, slower computers. The trade-off with respect to sampling rate vs. breadth of frequency range is that higher sampling rates take longer for calculation and this can slow down the feedback. Today's fast computers make this less of a problem.

A sampling rate which is too slow will make the analog signal incorrectly appear to be running at a slower frequency than it actually is. This effect is called *aliasing*.

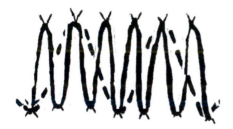

In the above diagram the actual wave is the solid line and the incorrectly interpreted wave is the dashed line. The true wave is theta at 6 Hz. This is seen if 13 samples ('x' points on the drawing) are taken. If only 5 samples are taken then the line drawn between the points makes it appear as if the EEG wave form is delta at 2 Hz.

If you draw for yourself a wave sampled at 42 samples per second and then draw a second wave just using every third sample or 14 of those samples, you will see that the first wave is 21 Hz while the second is only 7 Hz.

In addition to having an assigned *sampling* rate the *analog to digital converter* (ADC) also is assigned a *voltage range* and a *bit number*. The number of 'bits' refers to the number of amplitude levels that can be resolved. An 8 bit ADC will have 2^8 or 256 amplitude levels. This would be ± 128 discrete voltage levels in the voltage range allowed by that ADC. Too few *bits* means that small increases in voltage will be overemphasized. Too narrow a voltage range means that a large voltage change would be cut off.

4. Types of Filters:

Three types of digital filtering are: *finite impulse response (FIR)*, *infinite impulse response (IIR)* and *fast Fourier transform (FFT)*. The FFT filter can provide a much sharper cut off than the FIR filter. Both of these filters correct to give reasonably accurate phase relationships. The FIR filter computes a moving average of digital samples. The number of points which are averaged is termed the *order* of the filter. Some instruments such as the ProComp+/Biograph allow you to choose both the *order* and the type of filter. Each filter attenuates the same frequency ranges in a slightly different manner; for example, an IIR filter has a much sharper slope than an FIR filter.

The implications for the practice of neurofeedback lie in the realization that when you sample a certain frequency range, say 4-8 Hz, the frequencies outside that range are attenuated but not entirely eliminated. In particular, the frequencies at each end of the range will get through to a certain extent due to the shoulders (degree of slope) on either side of the filter.

The following two diagrams are illustrations taken from the Procomp+Biograph instrument. They compare an FIR Blackburn filter in the first diagram with an IIR Butterworth filter for the same bandwidth 13-15 Hz.

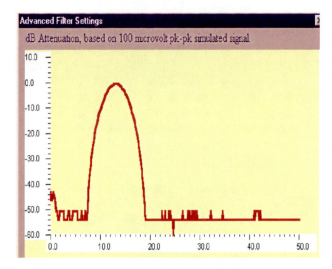

Advanced Filter Settings
dB Attenuation, based on 100 microvolt pk-pk simulated signal.

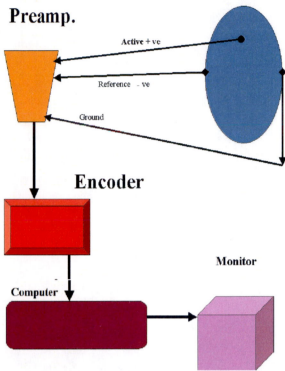

Preamp.

Active + ve

Reference - ve

Ground

Encoder

Monitor

Computer

Illustration of a NFB System

This diagram shows the basic functions usually carried out by software programs in the encoder and the computer.

Filtering may be digital (hexagon) or FFT (oval).

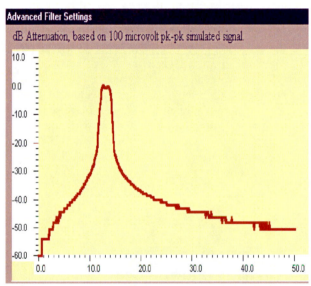

Advanced Filter Settings
dB Attenuation, based on 100 microvolt pk-pk simulated signal.

We use the IIR filter for doing statistics because we find that we get more consistent results. However, when a fine tuned analysis is done, it demonstrates that the IIR filter is so narrow and precise that 13-15 Hz may actually turn out to just be 14 Hz activity. The exact range depends on the "order" of the IIR filter. Without getting too complicated just remember a simple rule-of-thumb: whatever filter you use, you must use that same filter for all your statistics because different filters give quite different statistical values for each bandwidth.

This diagram shows a 3 lead referential placement. The active lead is placed at Fz and the reference is on the left ear. The ground has been placed on the right ear.

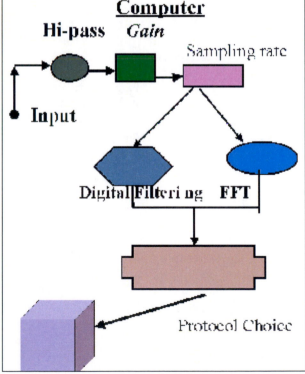

Computer

Hi-pass   Gain   Sampling rate

Input

Digital Filtering   FFT

Protocol Choice

A *Fast Fourier Transform (FFT) filter,* which is a program inside your computer, can take the EEG information and mathematically transform it to give an average voltage for a specific frequency over a specified time frame. This in turn produces a histogram where the x-axis is frequency in Hertz and the y-axis is amplitude in microvolts or power in picawatts. This type of graphic display can help you show students and parents different mental states in a way they can understand and picture. For example, recall the example we mentioned earlier about asking the student to do a multiplication question in his head. Stop the recording immediately after they answer. Now go back and replay this data to show how the brain activity changed. You may see a sequence such as the following: Theta went up in the left frontal area when they were trying to recall the answer from memory. Then when they actually were figuring it out beta increased. Then theta dropped and beta remained high as they calculated and gave you the answer.

Computations used to be quite slow for FFT filters but computers now run at >700 megahertz. This has speeded this process considerably so it is now possible to use FFT displays for feedback.

the electrodes immediately surrounding it which is called a *Laplacian* montage. For a full discussion of Laplacian mathematics which relate to EEG analysis see Hjorth's 1980 article. Each *montage* is just a mathematical reworking of the data which can easily be done by the computer software. Examples of the same data shown with sequential and Laplacian montages were used in the examples of measures in the last section (III, C, 2).

Each of these different ways of looking at the data will have both advantages and disadvantages. The *sequential* (bipolar) and *Laplacian* montages are good for viewing highly localized activity. This would be of more value to neurologists. The *common reference montage,* on the other hand, is excellent for detection of widely distributed currents and for analyzing asymmetry. It is also very good for the detection of artifacts. It is not so useful for viewing localized activity. A sequential (bipolar) recording may register a lower value for theta and, relatively, a higher value for beta than a referential recording. This is because theta is a more generalized activity than beta and will be canceled out by the differential amplifier in the sequential recording to the extent that it is found at both sites.

5. Montage Reformatting

Montage reformatting is a process whereby one can take different views of the same data referencing one electrode site to any other site or combination of sites. In NFB we usually use the ear lobe or the scalp over the mastoid bone as a reference site. This is because, compared to other sites on the scalp, these sites have very little electrical activity. We can then assume that changes which we are recording are due to the site on the scalp where we have positioned our *active* electrode. In a full-cap assessment linked ears are often used in what is termed a *common electrode reference montage.* When we do a *sequential* or *bipolar* recording we are referencing two electrodes to each other. In a full cap assessment *sequential (bipolar) montages* may be done using adjacent pairs of electrodes in the 10-20 placement system. In a nineteen lead recording the computer can do a number of different *montages.* It could, for example, reference an active electrode to an average of all the other electrodes (*average reference montage*). It could reference it to the average of

6. Electrical Terms

Electrical Outlets:

Electrical wires are color coded. Generally black carries the main current and would then be the dangerous wire. White usually is neutral and carries the current returning from the instrument. Green would then be the ground. However, **don't trust this generalization** – always read the color coding for any wired apparatus that you are using and always have a professional electrician handle the electrical wiring in your centre. Colors can be confusing. The EEG wires we use commonly use a different color coding than the one described above that electricians use.

Capacitors:

Capacitors are formed by two conductors separated by an insulator such as air. A capacitor will store a charge. Where this concept can be of importance to you is in giving you some understanding of why it is preferable not to use extension cords to your instrument. If there is a gap between the extension cord and the plug you have created a capacitor. Current can actually flow between the wires (from the black to the green).

Optical Isolation:

In our work steps are taken to protect the patient. Optical Isolation is one such step. This term refers usually to a process where we separate the encoder from the computer by a glass wire. The digital current from the encoder is changed to an optical form for transmission to the computer. The computer converts it back to a digital form for computer analysis. Apart from the very high speed of optical transfer, it has the added advantage of protecting ('isolating') the patient from the electrical connection of the computer to the wall circuit. Ordinary electrical current cannot be conducted through this glass wire, optical connection from the computer to the encoder. The encoder must, therefore, have its own electrical source. This is usually a battery source with very low current produced.

B. Electrical Artifacts

The manufacturer of your EEG instrument has attempted to minimize artifacts in the EEG recording. There are also precautions you can take when you put on the electrodes. Nevertheless, despite having a good instrument and taking appropriate precautions, you will observe electrical artifacts. You must be able to identify waves that are not due to neuronal activity. This section deals just with electrical artifacts. Other kinds of artifact, such as those due to eye blinks or EMG, are covered in another section.

1. What may Interfere

Electrical wires act as antennae. They will pick up 60 Hz activity (50 Hz in Europe and Asia). This activity is always present in our offices.

One of the biofeedback trainers didn't like fluorescent lighting in the office. He brought in an old standing lamp. It took several days for us to realize that this was the reason we weren't able to get the EEG equipment in that office space to work properly. Bad wiring in an old lamp can ruin your EEG record!

The electrode wires can also pick up some frequency outputs from a nearby radio station. Truckers with CB boosters can give your machine and you a small ulcer! They are illegal in many jurisdictions because of their effects on hospital equipment. However, this law does not seem to make any difference to the booster users. These boosters may overwhelm the amplifier's high pass filter and be observed as high amplitude surges at a variety of frequencies.

Even movement of people in the room may have an effect. Potential differences between objects in the environment and the wires to your electrode, which is on the client's scalp, can induce current in the wires. The simplest example of this is static electricity produced when you rub your leather-soled shoes on the rug and approach another person with hand outstretched. This can produce a spark. What we didn't know when we playfully did this as children was that there could be as much as 3,000 to10,000 volts difference between the two of us. Think of yourself as a container of negatively charged electrons compared to your client. You know that negative repels negative. As you approach your client you actually induce a current in the wires. But Ohm's law states that voltage = current x resistance ($V = IR$). You are changing the current I. Therefore, the voltage will change. It will change at frequencies controlled by the rate of your approach. Electric wiring in the room, lights and other instruments can all have the effect of inducing unwanted currents. They will induce current at frequencies associated with their source. Electrical wiring in North America, for example, has a frequency of 60 cycles per second. This can be clearly seen at a very high amplitude on the spectrum display unless you do a good job of making sure that impedances are the same at the electrode sites so that your differential amplifier will *reject* this voltage.

2. What Can You Do to Minimize these Problems

a. Troubleshooting Pointers for the Office

Many electrical artifacts will be from a source that affects all of your wires equally. Your instrument has a differential amplifier. It will only amplify waves that are different in phase and magnitude between each pair of sites. Effectively it is *rejecting* that which is in common. (Common mode rejection will be explained in more detail later in this chapter.) However, the 60 Hz source such as your electric lighting, can be common to both electrodes but appear different when the waves reach the amplifier. This could occur if the connection between the scalp electrode site and the amplifier was different for the two electrodes. The amplifier might then compare the electrical activity from these two electrode inputs and, because the waves appear to be different, amplify this difference in voltage between the two electrodes. The amplifier's common-mode-rejection would not come into play. Then this induced interfering signal would be amplified and ruin your EEG recording.

Thus you want to reduce differences between each site and your amplifier as much as possible. Several steps may help you to do this. First, your electrodes should all be made of the same material. This is usually gold or tin. You should not have two metals at the site as would occur if some of the gold plate had worn off one of your electrodes. Electrodes should be carefully cleaned after each use. In addition dead skin has a very high resistance. When you measure potential difference (voltage) it is proportional to current (I) and to the resistance to direct electrical (DC) current flow. You will recall this relationship is described by the equation V=IR (Ohm's law). Impedance (z) is just the term that replaces R when you are talking about the resistance to the flow of an alternating current (AC). Brain waves that we work with in neurofeedback are AC not DC. For us the relevant formula is v=iz. Therefore it follows that if you did an excellent site preparation at site 'A' and lowered the impedance at this site, but you did no preparation at a second site 'B', although the voltage induced at each site came from a common source, by the time it reached the amplifier it would not appear to be the same.

It might not then be rejected.

If you pay careful attention to site preparation as measured by your impedance readings and you clean your electrodes between each use then you should minimize most electrical interference.

Other hints to minimize the effects of induced changes are as follows. Don't let your electrode wires form loops or move during the recording. Have either specially shielded wires (as with the F1000) and/or the preamplifier as close as possible to the electrode site and have the wires between the electrode and the preamplifier as short as possible. Using a headband like those used by tennis players keeps the wires stabilized and reduces movement. Braiding loose wires will help equalize the effect on all wires but specially protected wires are best. In more sophisticated wiring, such as the special shielded wires in the F1000, induced current will flow harmlessly to the amplifier through the wire's special covering and to the ground. (With unprotected wires, when the resistance of the amplifier is high, it flows to your client.)

In addition, remove any equipment that seems to produce interfering signals.

We run a learning center. The teaching staff regularly use pencils. One enterprising trainer put an electric pencil sharpener in a training room. For days we examined the equipment, carefully redid site preparations, changed electrodes, turned off all electrical lighting but to no avail. The EEG signal could be read but the readings for fast waves were too high. By accident one of us unplugged the pencil sharpener. All electrical interference disappeared. This interference was present even when the sharpener was not in use.

Even extension cords can distort the EEG signal.

The authors were presenting at a professional meeting. A member of the audience was attached to the instrument. The EEG signal was virtually unreadable. The connection to the amplifier and the encoder were all changed but to no effect. The author then decided it must be something to do with the hotel's wiring. The first step to check this was to disconnect the extension cord and run on batteries. All interference disappeared. It turned out that the extension cord had been responsible for the artifact.

The building's electrical wiring may induce electrical artifact into the system.

The author was invited to work with the senior vice presidents of a large firm. The EEG feedback system that worked perfectly in his office showed completely overwhelming interference with extremely high amplitudes observed from 56 to 63 Hz. Amplitudes at other frequency bands varied from day to day. The only way to do the neurofeedback sessions was to run them using a laptop on battery power.

We **strongly recommend** that you try your EEG equipment in any new office you intend to rent. On one occasion an associate in a very old building (wall plugs were for 2 pronged plugs) had to run copper wires out the window to the ground to obtain good grounding and decrease interference. On another occasion a colleague couldn't run his equipment from his old office (because an engine somewhere in the building was interfering). Every time the engine started in the basement his EEG amplifier was overwhelmed and the EEG flattened for several seconds. He rented another office. In an office we were about to rent I demonstrated the electrical interference to the landlord before I signed the lease. The landlord agreed to run special wires to our offices that were not connected to any other outlets. This avoided our having interference when other offices and cleaners turned on equipment using wiring that was connected to our electrical wiring. When you check a new office site, do it at several different times of day.

b. Simple Equipment Troubleshooting

In the foregoing discussion we have recommended that you do your best to limit the number of sources of electrical activity that might interfere with your equipment. You have unplugged all unnecessary electrical equipment and turned off other equipment such as cell phones. You should also try increasing the distance between your EEG amplifier and your computer. If you have done all these steps and you still have high 60 Hz activity and/or unexplained EEG activity or inactivity, then begin to check your equipment in a logical stepwise manner.

i. Begin by checking impedances, offsets and electrodes.

The EEG amplitude dropped. The readings were lower in amplitude than last day. However, the proportions of one frequency to another seemed reasonably appropriate. The theta/beta ratio appeared close to that which was observed in the last two sessions. The EEG looked normal to a trainer who had only done a few hundred hours of work with EEGs. However, she intuitively felt it just wasn't right and called in a more experienced trainer. They checked impedances and changed wires to no avail. Then the EEG suddenly went flat. The client was changed to another EEG instrument to finish their session.

The next day the same machine appeared to be working perfectly. Then, after a couple of hours, it again suddenly dropped in amplitude and after a few minutes went flat. Humidity and overheating were both considered but these were not felt to explain the sudden occurrence of this problem. The EEG paste was changed for a tube used in another room where the instrument was working. Finally the author was called. The first question asked was, "What are the offsets?" These had been checked by the more senior trainer. He replied that they seemed high for the scalp electrode. He, therefore, replaced this electrode. He noted, however, that the high impedances remained for this site even when he put on three other brand new electrodes. He had even moved the child, with these same electrodes still attached, to a different amplifier (different EEG instrument) and the connections all worked perfectly.

The author tried a short wire electrode from a different batch of electrodes. The offset dropped from 85 to 5 and the EEG on the apparently faulty machine has run perfectly ever since.

A second phenomenon had been observed with this same machine when the above problem was investigated. The trainer found that, instead of a flat line when he removed one of the three electrodes at the end of the cable to the amplifier, waves suddenly appeared on the screen. It was as if he was getting an EEG with only two electrodes inserted into the connection to the amplifier. In our centers we always insist that the trainers have a way of looking for high frequency artifact. In this case the trainer was able to see a regular spiky high amplitude, high frequency artifact. He recognized that this did not represent an EEG but was a complex electrical artifact.

There are several points that come out of this example. First, unless you have EEG instruments from more than one manufacturer and can compare EEGs on different instruments, you might be fooled into thinking you were getting a normal EEG when what you were recording was either an incorrect (low amplitude) EEG or artifact. Second, it is possible to get a whole batch of faulty new electrodes. Third, it is helpful to be able to check offset as well as impedance. A high offset tells you that there is a problem with your wire. It may look fine on the outside but be broken on the inside. Fourth, to an inexperienced person, complex electrical artifact can mimic a poor EEG. Fifth, it is always helpful to have experienced back up when things don't look quite right. The following corollary to this is: Never underestimate the importance of the technical support department of your equipment manufacturer.

ii. Make Sure The Computer to Encoder (or Amplifier) Connections are Working Properly

When you do not appear to be detecting the EEG on the monitor there are a series of steps you can take to identify and correct the problem. First make sure that your encoder (encoder/amplifier) is detected by your computer. Put your hand over the end of the place where electrodes are inserted. For example, this could be a cable end in the A620 or a preamp in the Procomp$^+$ or Infintiy. Now move your hand and shake the cable. Waves may appear where an EEG should be on the display screen. This is a simple way to demonstrate that there is still a connection from the computer to this point. Some instruments will show a sign on the display screen that states whether or not the computer is detecting the encoder.

On multi-channel encoders, if the computer is not detecting the encoder/amplifier for the EEG, check to see if other channels on the encoder/amplifier work, such as a second EEG channel or an EMG, temperature or EDR channel. If nothing is detected, then check your connections (an optical cable in modern instruments) and check the batteries in the encoder itself. Try replacing the wire or optical cable from the encoder (or amplifier) to the computer. If changing the connection does not work, try putting the wire or the optical cable into the port on a different computer and seeing if the encoder is detected by that computer. If it is, then you may have to reload the program and/or repair the first computer. It could be a hardware fault in the first computer. However, before doing anything dramatic, do try plugging your computer into a different wall outlet. (*We have had both a faulty wall outlet and a faulty extension cord.*)

If all of these steps fail, try replacing the whole encoder with one that is working on another computer. In 99% of cases you will have identified the problem by this point. However, if you haven't, call the technical support for your system.

The EEG was a flat line. "Dr. R" did each of the steps above but no encoder was detected by the program in the computer. She phoned the manufacturer and a new replacement encoder arrived the next morning by courier. It worked.

It is important to have a good relationship with your supplier. Some companies do respond immediately. However it is important that you have carried out reasonable trouble shooting before you call. Again, it is very helpful to have more than one of each type of EEG equipment if you are doing a lot of neurofeedback / biofeedback work. Even cars, stoves, refrigerators, and washing machines break down and it can happen to computers and EEG equipment, too.

iii. If the encoder is detected but the EEG is not being recorded, check the connections from encoder to the scalp:

If the encoder is detected but the EEG is not being recorded, then we usually begin troubleshooting working from the head down. There is a saying in clinical medicine that applies here, "Common things are common". Look for simplest errors first. The fault usually lies in a wire. Often it is one of the electrode wires. Try replacing each electrode in turn. If the EEG is still flat or of poor quality then replace the wire that attaches the preamplifier (which may be clipped to the client's shoulder) to the encoder (on the desk). This is the second most common problem. Wires do break. If the problem persists, then try replacing the cable from the preamplifier to your short electrode wires. If these steps fail to solve the problem, then try replacing the preamplifier itself.

All of the difficulties that are mentioned above can be expected to occur over time. It is wise to have back-up electrodes and cables. Ideally one should also have a back-up EEG instrument and computer to avoid down-time when there are problems with an instrument. At our center we have EEG instruments from 8 different manufacturers. All of them will puzzle you with little glitches from time to time.

3. What The Manufacturer Has Done To Minimize Artifact – The Differential Amplifier

The amplifier *differentially* amplifies the electrical information it receives. This means that signals of the same frequency which are different *in magnitude and phase* at each site are magnified while signals which are the same are not magnified.

For example, signals which differ may be magnified at the preamp by a factor which is more than 100,000 times greater than the amplification of changes which are in common in <u>magnitude and phase</u> between the 2 electrodes. A number of current instruments have a common mode rejection ratio much higher than 100,000/1. Every 20 decibels (DB) multiplies the ratio by 10. Thus a voltage amplification of 10/1 is 20 decibels. 100/1 is 40 DB. Modern instruments may be rated as 120 DB which is 1,000,000 /1. This effectively acts to *reject* the unwanted <u>common</u> artifactual currents.

Examples of things that might be in common are jaw or neck muscle tension, heart electrical activity or spurious electrical changes in the environment. The latter might be caused by people moving in the room, electrical lighting, wall outlets, pencil sharpeners, an electric razor,

a tape recorder, a CD player, a hair drier, an extension cord and so on.

4. Electrical Artifact at Only One Site

Unfortunately not all 'electrical artifacts' (extraneous noise) are in common to all electrodes. An important example is **electrode movement**. Movement of an electrode creates a new waveform with its own frequency but only in that electrode's connection to the amplifier. It is a DC potential created by galvanic action between the electrode, skin and conductive paste. With movement there is a change in the geometry of this *galvanic cell*. It will alter what may be termed V_{offset}. Try having your client move their head or wiggle one of their ear lobes. You may observe a large slow wave artifact in addition to a high frequency artifact. Getting a very good connection that shows low impedances is one way to minimize this. Another helpful trick is to put the electrode wire under a head band so that small head movements will not result in wire movement near the electrode site.

If the jar of electrode paste is left open to the air for long periods of time, or if the paste is frozen in transport during the winter, changes may occur that interfere with the paste's adhesive and conductive qualities. This paste should be replaced.

C. Differential Amplifier

<u>Important Note</u>: **This section is purposefully both too brief and too oversimplified from the point of view of anyone experienced in electronics. Nevertheless, we hope it will be helpful to those who have a clinical or teaching background and less knowledge of electronics.**

1. What are we measuring?

Briefly, the amplifier receives input from the positive active electrode and the negative reference electrode and it measures the difference between these two inputs: Thus the EEG which we observe is: $V_{measured}$ (+ve) from site #1 - $V_{measured}$ (- ve) from site #2 at frequencies we specify. (V = voltage, +ve =

positive, -ve = negative) It is the potential difference ('V' in microvolts) between 2 electrodes. Why do we call one site positive and the other negative? Let's look at this in slightly more detail.

2. The Differential Amplifier

a. General Description

The original concept for the differential amplifier came from the work of Thomas Edison. The actual amplifier, however, was not developed until the 1930's. In simplest terms just think of the electrode at one site going to the preamp. There is a potential difference between the site on the scalp and a 'comparison' within the amplifier that involves your third electrode, which you call a *ground*. Many years ago the comparison actually was with 'ground'. As noted previously, in modern amplifiers there is not any direct connection of your client to the ground. The measurement and calculations are done within the amplifier. Now visualize the wire from the second site entering at another point in the amplifier. Think of the first site being positive and the second negative. Often a +ve sign is seen on the electrode that you use as your *active* electrode and a –ve sign is on the other or reference electrode. In reality the polarity for the second electrode connection is changed in the amplifier such that the second input is *inverted* and becomes –ve with respect to the first electrode which is +ve.

These two potential differences, the active site to the amplifier (+ve) and the reference site to the amplifier (-ve), are compared. Any voltage which is the same in both will therefore cancel out. Thus any induced electrical activity from another source such as a nearby lamp (60 Hz) should be the same frequency, amplitude and *in phase* on both wires. The *+ve wire*, so to speak, from the active electrode will, in this case, be the mirror image of the *-ve* wire from the reference site with respect to this 60 Hz current and the two will cancel out and therefore NOT be amplified. The EEG, on the other hand, will be different as recorded in each of these wires and, therefore, will not cancel out and will be

amplified. Thus the difference, between the two EEG voltages that have simultaneous input to the amplifier, is amplified. This is the unique function of a *differential* amplifier. This concept is represented in the diagrams below by conventional circuit diagrams. The active (+ve) electrode and the reference (-ve) electrodes enter the amplifier on the left and the output voltage is seen on the right. The ground is represented by parallel horizontal lines.

Conventional Circuit Diagram For an Amplifier (A)

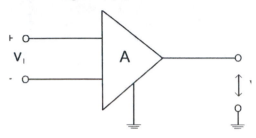

Schematic Representation of a Differential Amplifier

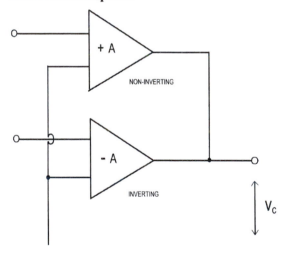

In the next diagram the 60 Hz electrical interference signal has come equally into both inputs of the differential amplifier. This *common mode* signal is, therefore, cancelled out and does not appear in the output. The alpha wave is high amplitude on the top, active (+ve) electrode and much lower amplitude on the bottom, referential (-ve) electrode. When these are subtracted and amplified, a very nice picture of alpha appears at the output.

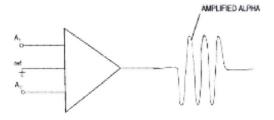

In summary: the amplifier detects and amplifies differences between 2 inputs. It amplifies changes in the signals referenced to the *ground* of the amplifier (an internal calculation not a direct ground). It does this by reversing the polarity of the second input so that the two electrical inputs are effectively subtracted. The amplifier only amplifies this difference between the two inputs; hence it is correctly called a *differential amplifier*. In this way the amplifier is said to *reject* signals that are in common to both inputs. This is called *common mode rejection*.

b. Common Mode Rejection Ratio

The *common mode rejection ratio* is the ratio of the common mode input voltage divided by the output voltage. This ratio should be > 100,000 in newer instruments. Failure of this system to eliminate external common mode artifact is likely due to either a difference in impedance between the two electrodes and/or a poor *ground* connection.

The importance of having almost the same impedance at all electrode sites can now be better appreciated. If the impedances were very different, then the induced voltage from a common electrical source would not appear the same when the *differential* amplifier compared the active and reference inputs. Therefore it would not cancel out and might, therefore, be amplified. This would result in a large artifact in the recording. This is, therefore, a good point at which to review impedance in a little more detail.

3. How Can You Get the Best Quality EEG

a. Impedance: Rationale

In the foregoing we have recommended having good impedance readings for all electrodes. The most frequent reason put forth for this is to ensure that artifacts in common to all electrodes are seen to be the same by the differential amplifier. A second reason is to ensure that the amplitude of the EEG recorded in different sessions is comparable. High impedance will decrease the amplitude of the EEG record. A third, less often cited reason, is that good connections may result in your recording less electrode movement artifact (discussed above). These are different considerations. Below we will discuss the first problem, ensuring that common artifact inputs are rejected.

Impedances should be virtually the same between all pairs of electrodes. As previously noted, if impedances differ, then even if the interference (for example a 60 cycle *noise* from lights, motors and so on) is the same at each site, it may "appear" to be different and so the *common mode rejection* by the amplifier will not eliminate it appropriately. Your first step on seeing a high 60 Hz bar on the spectrum output of your instrument is to immediately stop feedback and check your impedances. You almost invariably will find that one electrode has come loose! This has changed 'z' impedance at the electrode site. You must redo your prep and retest impedances. Let's learn a little more detail about this.

b. What is Impedance?

i. Definition

Electrode impedance may be defined as the *resistance to alternating electrical current flow*. You should distinguish this from the electrical term *resistance*. Resistance is the inability of a part of an electrical circuit to allow the passage of a *direct* (constant voltage) current (Fisch p44). Since the EEG is an alternating current, we must deal with impedance measures. You should always check impedance for each electrode site using a specially constructed impedance meter that passes a weak alternating current that mimics an EEG frequency produced by neuronal alternating potentials. The current flows from the selected electrode, through the scalp to all other electrodes connected to the meter. The current is at 10 Hz to approximate a common EEG frequency. Ohm's Law for a direct current is V=IR. However, for an alternating current this becomes v = iz where 'z' is the impedance of the circuit. This is what we are dealing with because electrical activity we measure in the brain is AC not DC. Both resistance 'R' and impedance (z) are measured in ohms. In a DC circuit, when a potential difference occurs between two points, then instantly a current flows and will flow as long as that potential difference remains. In an AC circuit the current will instantly flow but will not remain flowing.

Mathematically (when inductance is not a major factor):

Impedance (z) = √(square root of)[R^2 + (10^6 / $2\pi fC)^2$]

where π is 3.14, f is the frequency of the alternating current in Hz, and C is the capacitance.

ii. Capacitance

You are not expected to be an expert in electronics. However, there are a couple of points to be learned by looking at this formula. First, C(capacitance), which is measured in microfarads (μF), refers to the storage of electrons.

Note that *capacitance* refers to the storage of electrical energy on two parallel *plates* of conductive material separated by an insulating material. **Capacitors block the flow of direct current** while an **inductor (described below) impedes the flow of alternating current**. The electrons flow into the capacitor and then away from the capacitor as the current alternates. Capacitors are an important element in biofeedback circuits. Capacitance is, therefore,

an essential consideration in calculating impedance.

A capacitor consists of two conductors separated by a resistance. It introduces a time factor because current will rise instantly, then the capacitor stores electrons with the result that the current will gradually decrease over time. Thus DC current is stopped and only AC current can pass. Cell walls act as *capacitors*. So do your electric wires that run from the client to the preamp.

If C and f were held constant (as they would be in a DC circuit) then the 'z' would vary directly with R. However, this is not the case in an AC circuit. The formula shows that 'z' will go up as C goes down. 'z' also varies inversely with frequency. Thus, as frequency increases, the measured impedance will rapidly decrease. For this reason a standard measurement must be introduced so that we are all talking in the same language. The international standard is that we use a 10 Hz frequency (AC) when measuring impedances for our electrode sites.

iii. Inductance

Inductance (Note: This is mentioned for completeness but is not an important consideration for the work of neurofeedback practitioners.)

We have **not** considered this factor in our standard equation for impedance. However, if in an instrument an alternating current passed through a wire that lay within a second coil of wire, then the changing magnetic flux that is produced around the first wire will induce a voltage in the second wire. This induced voltage in the coiled wire has the opposite polarity to the original. It will oppose a change in current flow within the original wire. This counter voltage is called *inductance* and its unit of measurement is the *Henry (L)*. This is another type of resistance but in this case it is to alternating current flow and is called *inductive resistance* (X_L). It is calculated in the following manner:

$$X_L = 2\pi fL$$

In this equation f is frequency(Hz) and L is the inductance of the element under consideration and its unit of measurement is the 'Henry'. (Cohen, 1989, p.323 – 335).

If inductance was a factor in the circuit, then the formula for impedance would be changed (enlarged) to include both capacitance (as discussed previously) and inductance. The formula for impedance becomes:

$$Z = \sqrt{(square\ root\ of)}\left[\ R^2 + (2\pi fL - 10^6 / 2\pi fC)^2\right]$$

Note: For the majority of readers electrical formulas are not really important. We include them only when we think that they may be helpful in giving an overview to the reader. An expert in electronics can easily find what we have included to be far too simplistic. These experts should read appropriate textbooks on instrument design and use this textbook only for its clinical explanations.

c. Can the client feel anything when impedance is measured?

Yes, a few young children and the occasional adult have been able to detect a tingling feeling when impedances were checked. The manufacturer of your meter should have met electronic standards which guarantee that the amount of current is entirely within safe limits. Your instrument will be run by batteries which further assures you that no dangerous connection with a high voltage or current is being applied. Likening the sensation to a cat tickling their ear may be useful. Measuring devices may use either a sine wave or a square wave. Therefore, if one meter gives a sensation, you can try a different type of impedance meter. Some manufacturers build an impedance check into their instruments. You should ask about the criteria to see if they are adequate.

d. What Are Acceptable Impedance Readings

The impedance (resistance to the flow of alternating current) at the electrode site should be as low as possible. As a rule of thumb, < 5 kohms impedance in all combinations of leads with < 1 Kohm difference between leads is excellent and meets research standards. If you do this then differences due to resistance when measuring 'V' at different electrode sites become negligible compared to differences that are proportional to actual current at the source.

The resistance of the instrument's amplifier is a constant. It will be different in different instruments. In the voltage-divider-formula given below you will be able to see that when the amplifier resistance is very high, then the resistance (impedance for our purposes since EEG is an alternating current) at the electrode site will have less effect on measured voltage as compared to systems with an amplifier that has a low input resistance.

e. What May Occur If You Don't Measure Impedances:

Without good consistent connections (low impedances) you may not be giving quality feedback and your amplitude readings and, therefore, threshold settings will change from day to day. If impedance differs between electrode pairs, then any movement can cause spurious readings. The most common problem is either that the trainer has been pressed for time and has not tested impedance or something has occurred to alter the electrode connections during the session. Perhaps the impedance readings were good after the hook-up was first done but something has disturbed the connection (client rubbed their ear or scratched their head, pulled on a wire, etc.) When impedance is retested, it may be found that the impedance between electrodes is not only high but is quite different between pairs of electrodes. Correcting this will usually mean the raw EEG appears clean and smooth.

John was training a hyperactive child. The child liked to scratch his ears. Part way through the session there appeared to be excessive fast wave activity. The amplitude readings for the child's beta and SMR were above the usual readings for that client. The impedances were rechecked and found to be quite different between electrodes.

When the impedances were improved the high beta activity (24-32 Hz) reading dropped from 10 –15 μv to 4 μv. The 45-58 Hz activity dropped to < 2 μv. The SMR and beta amplitudes moved from falsely high amplitudes to readings which corresponded to that client's last session. John started a keep-your-hands-still game with this child. This involved the child balancing a token on the back of each hand while doing feedback. John rewarded him at the end of each two minute time span for having the tokens still there. The child felt very good about it and got rewards. The electrodes stayed in place and quality feedback was received.

If you are calculating a potential difference, you want to ensure that your measurement of electrical activity actually reflects the neuronal activity at the sites being used (or lack of it in the case of the reference electrode). The above example demonstrates a case where the client would not receive accurate feedback unless care was taken to monitor the EEG and assure that the quality of that EEG is maintained throughout the session.

f. Why Modern Amplifiers are More Forgiving – The Voltage Divider Model

You will hear it said that with high input impedance in the amplifier measuring electrode impedance is not important. Certainly it is far less critical than in older equipment. However, the above example is one from a session on a very high input impedance amplifier. Certainly, the old low impedance amplifiers required a lot of exacting attention to impedances at the electrode sites. Why this is so may be understood (albeit in a superficial way) by a brief introduction to what is termed the *voltage-divider-model* as briefly explained below.

Note: Most readers can skip the section below that is in italics as it is not crucial to understanding these fine points in order to do neurofeedback. It is provided for those who want the in-depth information.

Where does the term "voltage divider" come from?

This term is commonly used when discussing changing sensitivity on a recording instrument. You are all aware of how an adult EEG may be very low amplitude compared to the very high amplitudes observed in young children. To read the EEG on your display screen you must change the sensitivity and, therefore, the size of the EEG on your screen. To allow the operator to change the sensitivity of the instrument a chain of resistors, in series, are attached to the output of

a differential amplifier. A current passes through the resistors ($R_1 + R_2 + R_3$). Then, by Ohm's law, $V = (R_1 + R_2 + R_3)$ I. (alternatively: $I = V \div (R_1 + R_2 + R_3)$). If all 3 resistors were the same then, if the switch was placed after the first resistor, the out-put would be 1/3V and if placed after the 2nd resistor it would be 2/3 V. This chain of resistors wired to a switch is called a 'voltage divider'. The total voltage will divide itself across the three resistors in proportion to their values.

The same voltage divider concept applies to the measurements being made by the amplifier. Initially, imagine the 'differential' amplifier as being two amplifiers. (This was diagrammed above.) In this example, for each electrode, there are at least two resistances we must consider. Because we are discussing an 'alternating current', the term 'impedance' must be substituted for the word 'resistance'. You can think of the voltage being changed by the resistances to current flow. This means that the output voltage is proportionate to each impedance according to the formula:

$V_{output+} = V_+$ x $Z_{amplifier} \div (Z_{site+} + Z_{amplifier})$ for the +ve electrode site and

$V_{output-} = V_-$ x $Z_{amplifier} \div (Z_{site-} + Z_{amplifier})$ for the −ve electrode site.

Thus the first impedances (Z_{site+} and Z_{site-}) are at the level of the scalp and the active(+) and reference (-) electrodes. We want these impedances to be very low. The second impedance($Z_{amplifier}$) is at the input to the amplifier and we want it to be very high. If this is done then the voltage measured will be much more related to the input impedance of the amplifier and more forgiving of different impedances at the electrode sites because the voltage will have divided itself across these impedances in proportion to their magnitudes. As the amplifier impedance becomes very large, the voltage measured at the amplifier will very closely approximate the true EEG voltage.

Now let us imagine the whole circuit (not just each electrode going to the amplifier):

When you think of the connections between the scalp and the amplifier, imagine that when you make the final connection then a current can flow. It flows, in this hypothetical example, in a circle (circuit). The current is generated in the brain and flows out one site around through the amplifier and back through the other site and the brain. For schematic purposes just imagine three impedances to the flow of this current. These impedances are in series. The three are: the first electrode site(Z_{site+}), the amplifier, and the second electrode site (Z_{site-}). You will then measure the voltage (potential difference) across the large resistor (impedance to flow) in the amplifier ($Z_{amplifier}$).

By Ohm's law, $I = V/R$. Again, change R to Z (impedance) because we are dealing with alternating current.

Then for the active electrode you would have:

$$I = V_{+(input)} / (Z_{site+} + Z_{amplifier}) \text{ and}$$

$$\text{for the reference electrode:}$$
$$I = V_{-(input)} / (Z_{site-} + Z_{amplifier}).)$$

(Strictly speaking we should use lower case letters for V (or E) and for I and Z when we are discussing alternating rather than direct (AC not DC) currents. In order to make it a little easier to read, we have not followed this convention in this section.)

For the voltage output of the entire differential amplifier substitute for I in the Ohm's law equation ($V = ZxI$) for our hypothetical circuit and get:

$$V_{output+} = Z_{amplifier} \times [V_{(input\ to\ amplifier)} \div (Z_{site-} + Z_{site+} + Z_{amplifier})].$$

Thus if the impedances at the two sites are very small,l and the impedance at the amplifier very large, then the output voltage will be relatively independent of the impedances at the two electrode sites. It will vary with the EEG input voltage which is then amplified.

4. Brief Summary

In review, potential differences between objects in the environment and the wires to your electrode on the client's scalp can induce current in the wires. As we approach our client we actually induce a current in the wires. But $v = iz$ (voltage = current x impedance). You are changing 'i'. Therefore, the voltage will change. It will change at frequencies controlled by the rate of your approach. Electric wiring in the room, lights and other instruments can all have the effect of inducing unwanted currents. They will induce current at frequencies associated with their source. Electrical wiring in North America, for example, has a frequency of 60 cycles per second. This can be clearly seen at a very high amplitude on the spectrum display unless you do a good job of decreasing impedance at the electrode sites. If you do a good job, the common mode rejection function of the amplifier will eliminate this artifact. You hope that all interfering induced currents will be the same in all the wires and, given that you have impedances which are very close between each pair of electrodes, that they will be rejected by the amplifier.

In more sophisticated wiring, such as the special shielded wires in the F1000 (no longer being manufactured), induced current will flow harmlessly to the amplifier through the wire's special covering and to the ground. With unprotected wires the resistance of the amplifier is high so it flows to your client.

You can minimize the effects of these undesirable electrical interferences by using shielded cables or having shorter wires, which is possible if you have a preamp very close to the electrode site. You can reduce differences between electrodes by paying careful attention to site preparation (dead skin has very high resistance and hair spray acts as an insulator). Measure your impedance and clean your electrodes between each use. Also remove any electrical equipment that seems to produce interfering signals.

Now you know a little about how the manufacturer of your EEG instrument has attempted to minimize artifacts in the EEG recording. Nevertheless, all these mechanisms can be overwhelmed or by-passed. The neurofeedback practitioner must still be able to identify waves that are not due to neuronal activity.

SECTION V
Neuroanatomical Structures, Connections and Neurochemistry

A. General Orientation

The scope of this section is to give an overview of neuroanatomy and neurophysiology as it pertains to our understanding of the EEG, as well as to behaviours involving attention, impulsivity, memory, learning, executive functions, connation (emotion plus cognition), speech, reading, involuntary motor activity and emotions. A basic knowledge of neuroanatomy is essential in order to understand recent literature which quotes findings from studies that have used techniques such as MRI, PET scans, SPECT scans and LORETA.

It is important to review a few basic points concerning the cortex and sub-cortical structures and to recognize the importance of communication between structures. Keep in mind that neurophysiology is not precisely understood. Only some of the rudiments are beginning to be elucidated. Thus different ideas will be found in different texts.

It should be understood by the reader that there is quite a bit of redundancy in this section and that this is intentional: first, because learning neuroanatomy is difficult so a bit of repetition is helpful and, second, so that one can consult a sub-section and find it comprehensive without reading everything that came before.

Teaching even a short course on neuroanatomy and physiology is beyond the scope of this book.

This section is limited to:
1. A brief overview of Neuroanatomy and the general functions of different parts of the nervous system.
2. A discussion of aspects of the neocortex and of subcortical structures that contribute to functions which can be influenced by NFB training such as memory, attention span, speech and language, reading and involuntary movement.

Note: You may rightly feel that this section jumps from one theory to another. This is a reflection of the present state of knowledge. It is rather like having a few hundred pieces and attempting a thousand piece jigsaw puzzle. We are trying to understand where they fit. We don't pretend that it can be done accurately, however, the few pieces we can match do help us understand a little bit about observed behaviour and why our EEG biofeedback may have a positive influence.

1. Getting your Directions
a. Basic Terms
The front of the brain behind the forehead is called the *anterior* or *rostral* portion. The back of the head is *posterior*. The top of your head is termed *superior* or *dorsal*. The under surface is *inferior* or *ventral*. Each side of the brain would be said to be *lateral*. The portion of a lobe of the brain facing into the middle of your head would be termed *medial*. Your back is said to be a *dorsal* surface whereas your front is *ventral*. Note the overlap in terms: dorsal can mean either top or back; ventral can mean either below or front. As a memory trick, think of the dorsal fin on a fish. It is on the fish's back and on top as he swims.

b. Sections of the Brain
If you stand at the *lateral* side of a brain and slice that brain with your knife pointing away from you and across the brain from left to right (ear to ear) and you cut from the top dorsal surface down to the base or ventral surface, then you have made a **coronal** or *transverse* section.

If you stand in front of the brain and hold your knife in a horizontal plane from front to back on one side of the head and you slice across so that you could now lift off the top of the brain, then you have made a **horizontal** section.

If you stand in front of the brain with your knife reaching from the front to the back and slice it from its dorsal to its ventral surface, then you have made a *sagittal* section. You will often encounter textbook pictures of a midsagittal section because this neatly slices the brain in half so that you may see the *medial* surfaces of the left and right hemispheres.

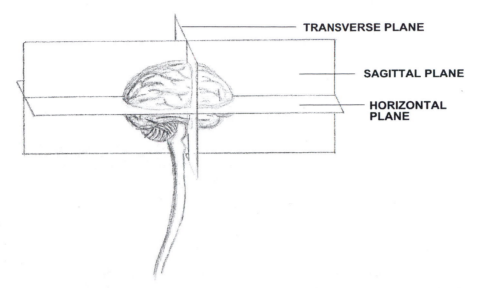

c. Gyrus, Sulcus and Fissure

A *gyrus* is a broad ridge of cortex and a *sulcus* is a dip or valley in the cortex. A *fissure* refers to a very deep dip or valley. (Don't get too confused. The terminology here can get quite formidable and it may be slightly different in different textbooks.) One good neuroanatomy text (Smith, 1961, p157 & p171) calls the separation or groove bordered above by the frontal and parietal lobes and inferiorly by the temporal lobe and medially by the insula, the 'lateral fissure' one time and the 'lateral sulcus' another. A basic biology text (Carlson,1984, p98) refers to the same groove as the 'lateral fissure'. People generally agree that the large groove between the two hemispheres is a 'fissure', the longitudinal (cerebral) fissure.

The two hemispheres are separated by the longitudinal cerebral fissure.

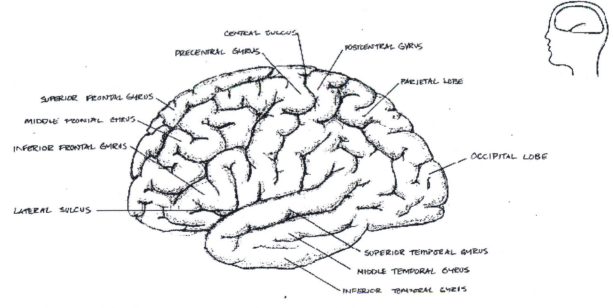

Lateral Aspect of the Cerebral Hemisphere (after Smith, 1962)

d. The Tentorium and The Falx Cerebri

The *tentorium* is a large in-folding of *dura matter* (connective tissue) separating the cerebellum below from the cerebrum above. Child tumors are more frequently inferior and adult tumors, superior to the tentorium. The other indentation of dura separates the two cerebral hemispheres, along the dorsal surface and is called the falx cerebri. When folded in the dura matter forms a hard ridge. When there is a blow to the head the neurons in the cortex can be damaged as they hit this tentorium if the force is from above or damaged by the falx cerebri (if the force is lateral). Thus, a person can sustain medial damage even though the blow is on the side of the head.

e. Gray and White Matter

Gray matter refers to the cell bodies of the neurons, their unmyelinated axons and dendrites and various types of support cells, especially glial cells (1/2 the cells in the brain, which support pyramidal cells) *Glial* cells include: *astrocytes* (providing nutrition and structural support, and act like phagocytes and form the *blood-brain barrier*), *microglia*, & *oligodendroglia* which, like the Schwann cells in the peripheral nervous system (PNS) produce myelin for the fibers in the CNS. There are about $3x10^{10}$ neurons in the human cortex. Gray matter is found in the cerebral cortex, the corpus striatum, and the septal region.

White matter refers to areas that contain mainly myelinated axons. The *myelin sheath* of the nerve fibers are responsible for the white colour. The "superhighways" of the brain that allow for high-speed transmission of signals are a part of the white matter. White matter is less dense due to its fat content. *Myelinization* is not complete until the 2nd decade of life. Thus a teenager's brain is very much a work-in-progress and executive functions, such as inhibition, are not well developed. Myelinization allows for faster transmission of nerve impulses. There is more white matter in right cerebral hemisphere (Tom Budzynski, *SNR 2001*) than the left cerebral hemisphere since there is more long distance communication there. Budzynski compares the right hemisphere to the functions of an Apple computer which uses more pictures and Gestalt organization and contrasts this to the left hemisphere that has sequential organization comparable to PC computers. He notes that the abilities tested on a standard IQ test are overwhelmingly left hemisphere functions.

f. Blood Supply – Overview

The brain weighs only about 1400 grams (2.5-3 pounds) yet it receives more than 20% of cardiac output, 25% of the oxygen and 25% of the glucose available to the body. The *internal carotid arteries* supply the rostral portion and the *vertebral arteries,* which join to form the basilar artery, supply the posterior or caudal portion of the brain. There are connections between these two great arterial supplies. The anterior cerebral artery runs anterior off the internal carotid artery. The medial cerebral artery runs laterally off the internal carotid artery. The posterior cerebral arteries arise from the basilar artery. (See the end of this section for more detail.)

g. Meninges and CSF

The entire brain is covered by a layer of connective tissue. The outer layer is called the *dura* matter. The middle layer is termed the *arachnoid* membrane. The inner layer, which caries the smaller blood vessels, is called the *pia* matter. There is a gap between the pia matter and the arachnoid membrane called the subarachnoid space. This space is filled with cerebrospinal fluid (CSF). Large blood vessels pass through this space. This arachnoid membrane and the CSF is only present in the central nervous system (CNS). The CNS comprises the brain and spinal cord. The peripheral nerves and the autonomic ganglia are covered by fused pia and dura matter. Large chambers filled with CSF are called the lateral *ventricles* (two of them, one on each side) and the third and fourth ventricle. These ventricles are connected to each other. The fourth ventricle is connected to the **central canal** of the spinal cord.

A bridge of neural tissue called the *massa intermedia* passes through the middle of the third ventricle. It connects the two lobes of the thalamus. It may be missing in some normal people. This communication link is of interest since it may help explain why training SMR on one side of the brain will have an equal effect on the opposite side. That finding suggests that there is good communication between the two lobes of the thalamus. This may be one way that we can understand how EEG patterns that depend on thalamo-cortical connections can spread across both hemispheres.

Approximately half the CSF is replaced in about 3 hours (half-life). There is about 125 ml of CSF in an adult brain. CSF is produced by the *choroid plexus.* It flows from the fourth ventricle to the subarachnoid space via the *foramen of Magendie* (a single opening) and the *foramina of Luschka* (two openings). ('Foramen' means a small opening. The plural is 'foramina'.) Blockage of the flow of CSF can result in a condition known as hydrocephalus.

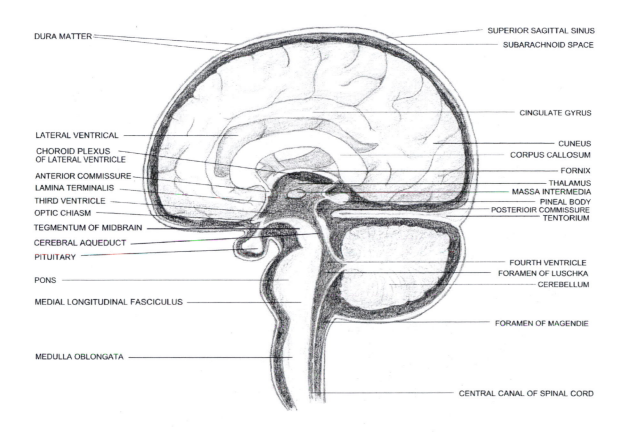

Lateral Aspect of the Brain (after Carlson, 1986)

B. Neuroanatomical Structures

1. Introduction and Overview

This section begins with a brief overview of the basic anatomical structures in the brain. This is followed by a description of the development of selected major internal features of the forebrain. Early development leads naturally into an overview of the communication linkages within the hemispheres, between the hemispheres, and between the hemispheres and the diencephalon, midbrain and spinal cord. This basic neuroanatomy overview will be followed by a section on the functions of the principle lobes and nuclei of the brain.

The brain may be thought of in three major parts: *forebrain, midbrain* and *hindbrain.* In broad general terms, the forebrain is responsible for higher reasoning, the midbrain for emotions an motivations, and the hind brain for survival, instincts and automatic responses. Note that other ways of describing these divisions are also possible; for example, looked at phylogenetically, we have a reptilian brain surrounded by the limbic system which, in turn, is wrapped in the neocortex. For an articulate discussion of how this triune (three-in-one) brain structure relates to human emotions, read *A General Theory of Love* by Thomas Lewis, Fari Amini and Richard Lannon, three psychiatrists from three different generations of psychiatric thought. It attempts to blend psychoanalytic concepts with psychobiology / drug effects and more recent neuroscience discoveries.

2. Forebrain (Telencephalon and Diencephalon)

a. Cerebral Hemispheres

Two symmetrical cerebral hemispheres are covered by the cerebral cortex and contain the basal ganglia and the limbic system. The cerebral cortex is grooved (*sulci* and *fissures*). The tissues between the sulci are called *gyri*. The EEG which we record comes from the cortex or *gray matter*. The cortex is subdivided into frontal, parietal, temporal and occipital lobes. A *central sulcus* separates the frontal and parietal lobes. The *lateral fissure* separates the frontal and parietal lobes from the temporal lobe. Most of the surface of the hemispheres is covered by what is termed the *neocortex*. The neocortex has 6 layers. (This is, perhaps, the best definition of a mammal, an animal with a six-layered cortex.) The pyramidal cells constitute the largest part of the third and fifth layers. The granular cells are present in higher numbers in the third and fourth layers while the fusiform cells are found in the sixth layer.

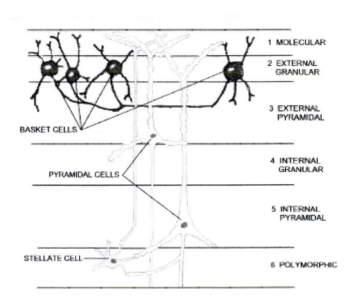

Schematic Representation of the Neocortex (after Smith, 1962)

On the medial surface the edges of the hemispheres have another type of cortex called the *limbic* (limbus means 'border') cortex. A portion of this is called the *cingulate* cortex. It lies between the cingulate sulcus and the corpus callosum. The septal region includes a portion of the cingulate gyrus, the superior frontal gyrus and cortex anterior to the lamina terminalis. The septal area is important for its role in consciousness.

The hemispheres are connected by large bands of white matter or *commissures*. The largest of these is called the *corpus callosum*. These fibres are myelinated and, therefore, white in colour. *Axon* connections unite homotropic (same site) areas in the right and left cerebral hemispheres.

The *central sulcus* divides the motor (rostral) and the sensory (caudal) cortex. This part of the cortex sends motor commands and receives sensory (touch, temperature, pain) information that has been relayed from the periphery by specific areas in the thalamus. The axons come from peripheral sensors (specific information) and ascend, for the most part, in the dorsal column of the spinal cord to cross over to the opposite side in the medial lemniscus to synapse in the ventral posterior nucleus of the thalamus before continuing to the somatosensory cortex of the postcentral gyrus of the parietal lobe.

The visual cortex is located in the occipital area and the auditory cortex in the temporal lobe within the lateral fissure.

The remainder of the cortex is called *association cortex.* In the frontal lobes the association cortex is involved in important cognitive functions including executive functions such as planning.

b. Limbic System

The limbic system consists of the *hippocampus, amygdala and septum* in the telencephalon, and in the diencephalon, the *anterior thalamic nuclei and the mammillary body*. The major axon connecting 3 parts of this system is referred to as the *fornix*. It connects the anterior thalamic nuclei with the hippocampus and the mammillary bodies. These connections will be discussed in the next section.

c. Amygdala

The *amygdala* is located in the rostral end of the temporal lobe. It has 2 groups of nuclei: corticomedial and basolateral. The older

corticomcedial nuclei project axons through the *stria terminalis* to the hypothalamus and forebrain. The newer basolateral nuclei project through the *ventral amygdalofugal pathway* to the hypothalamus, preoptic region, septal nuclei, midbrain tegmentum and periaqueductal gray matter. The amygdala receives input from thalamus, hypothalamus, midbrain, and the temporal lobe. (See diagram under 6c of this section.)

The *amygdala* is also connected to the tail of the caudate and to the *uncus*. In part the grey matter of the uncus is continuous with gray matter of the amygdala. It is at the rostral end of the hippocampal cortex. The *fornix* or 'arch' connects the hippocampus with the anterior thalamic nuclei and the mammillary body. As previously noted, the hippocampal cortex has connections with the frontal, parietal and temporal lobes and the cingulate via the cingulum. Thus the amygdala has connections to all the areas concerned with emotions, the autonomic nervous system and the endocrine system. Animal experiments involving electrical stimulation of the amygdala result in aggression while bilateral removal of the amygdala can result in a tame animal that appears indifferent to danger. It is involved in having affect (like or dislike) towards others. It is an integral part of the system that controls autonomic and endocrine responses to emotional states.

The amygdala is also important in memory. It appears to lay down unconscious memories which bring back an autonomic nervous system - body state information - which accompanied the emotions evoked by the event (Carter, 1995). This is particularly evident with respect to traumatic memories. (Contrast this with the hippocampus which is involved in laying down conscious memories.)

It is rather as if the thalamus is the 'hub' of the wheel with connections radiating like the spokes of a wheel to every corner of the nervous system. The amygdala and hippocampus are rather like the gearshift, governing, in many ways, aspects of thinking, feeling and behaviour.

d. Basal Ganglia

The structures that comprise the basal ganglia include the globus pallidus, caudate nucleus and the putamen. The basal ganglia – thalamic system is involved in the selection of actions

(Kropotov & Etlinger, 1999). For appropriate executive actions this system must flexibly select sensations, cognitions and motor actions and also inhibit inappropriate sensations, motor actions or irrelevant thoughts (Kropotov, 1997).

The basal ganglia are involved in the motor system and are also important in NFB work because of their importance in movement disorders, including Tourette's, Parkinson's and dystonia. They also play a role in learning.

e. Striatum

The striatum comprises the putamen and caudate and is thus a sub-division of the basal ganglia. (Recall that the term *'Basal Ganglia'* refers to the globus pallidus, caudate nucleus and the putamen.) The striatum interconnects with the substantia nigra. It is important for automatic movements. In Parkinson's disease dopamine producing cells are depleted in the substantia nigra. The striatum is also involved, however, in higher functions. It appears that it may play an important role in the selection of which

'program' will be acted upon. Its connections through the globus pallidus may, in turn, result in a release of inhibition of specific thalamic nuclei. This may facilitate focus both by the cortex and by the superior colliculus (which orients the person in the selected direction).

Normally, the striatum exerts a balanced inhibition of the globus pallidus (GP). The GP normally inhibits parts of the thalamus. Inhibiting the GP thus allows the thalamic neurons to be in a relay mode. These neurons can then facilitate the transfer of sensory and other signals to the cortex. In ADHD it is hypothesized that the striatum exerts too little inhibition on the GP which, in turn, will increase its inhibition of the thalamus. When this occurs, it is hypothesized that the thalamus goes into standby mode and the executive functions such, as engagement and disengagement operations, are impaired. (DeLong, 1990; Sterman, 2000; Kropotov, 1997) It allows the thalamus to facilitate the cortical elements of a selected program. (Kropotov, 1999)

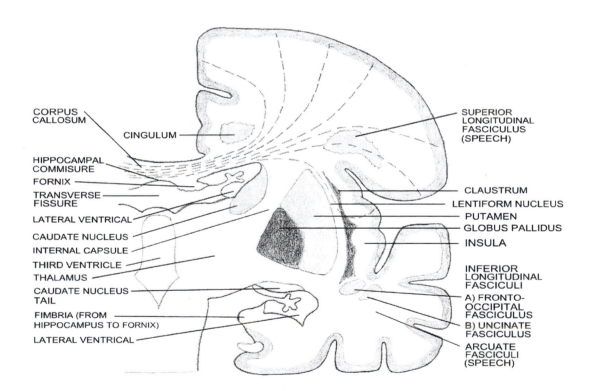

Schematic Diagram of a Transverse Section Through the Right Cerebral Hemisphere (After Smith 1962)

3. Diencephalon

The diencephalon lies between the telencephalon and the midbrain and contains the thalamus and the hypothalamus.

a. Thalamus

The name thalamus comes from the Greek word for inner chamber according to some and 'antechamber' according to others. Both are appropriate in meaning because it is an inner structure and, like an antechamber, things pass through the thalamus to go elsewhere. All sensory information except smell passes through the thalamus before going on to the cortex. It has two lobes connected by the *massa intermedia* which goes through the third ventricle. The nuclei within the thalamus project to specific areas of the cerebral cortex. Their connecting fibers are called *projection fibers* or *axons*. **The lateral *geniculate*** nucleus of the metathalamus projects to the visual cortex. The ***medial geniculate nucleus*** projects to the auditory cortex. The ***ventroposterior*** nucleus projects to the somatosensory cortex. The ***ventrolateral nucleus*** projects information from the cerebellum to the motor cortex. The ***anterior nuclei*** project information from the mammillary bodies (nuclei of the hypothalamus (Smith, p.68)) to the cingulate gyrus. The ***midline nuclei*** and the ***reticular nuclei*** partially encapsulate the thalamus and project to other areas of the thalamus and cortex in feedback loops which are important in our understanding of EEG rhythms. (after Smith, 1961, p.96, 185)

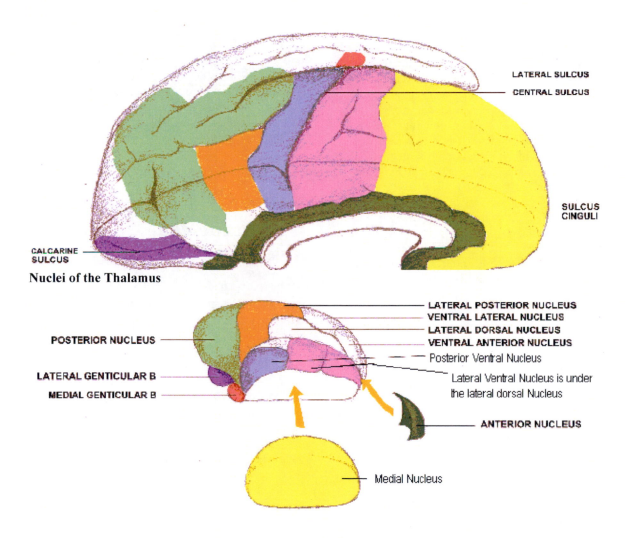

Nuclei of the Thalamus

*The above diagram is colour coded to demonstrate how specific areas (nuclei) in the thalamus link to specific areas in the cortex. (**Note:** The temporal lobe (at top of figure) has been "folded up" to show the auditory area (red).) (After Smith, 1962)*

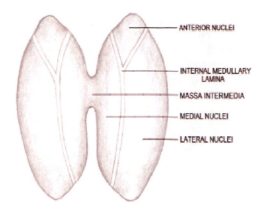

Schematic Diagrams of the Thalamus (after Smith, 1962).

b. Hypothalamus:

The hypothalamus sits under the thalamus and on either side of the third ventricle. The *optic chiasm* is just anterior to the pituitary stalk which comes out of the base of the hypothalamus. Just anterior to this is an area which will come up in lectures on NFB and brain function, it is the *preoptic area.* It is important in our work with BFB because it is involved in the control of the autonomic nervous system. It is also a keystone in the control of the endocrine system. The pituitary gland is attached to its base and thus, as Carlson humorously puts it, this system is responsible for "the survival of the species – the so called 4 F's: fighting, feeding, fleeing and mating". (Carlson, p. 104)

Even maternal behaviour appears to be hard wired to a certain degree. The medial preoptic area, which contains estrogen receptors, is important for nurturing the young. It is linked to the hypothalamus.

4. Midbrain (Mesencephalon)

The midbrain comprises the tectum and the tegmentum. The *tectum* or roof of the mesencephalon contains the superior and inferior colliculi. The superior colliculi are part of the visual system and are involved in visual reflexes and reacting to moving stimuli (Carlson, p. 107). The inferior colliculi are part of the auditory system. The auditory pathways synapse in the inferior colliculi and proceed on to the medial geniculate nucleus (part of the metathalamus of the diencephalon (Smith, p.90)) and then the auditory cortex. The *tegmentum* is an extension of the subthalamus and includes the anterior portion of the *reticular* formation, the *red nucleus,* the *substantia nigra, periaqueductal gray* matter and the *ventral tegmental area.* The substantia nigra projects fibers to the caudate nucleus. Its production of dopamine is reduced in Parkinson's disease. The red nucleus is crucial in our understanding of how increasing SMR may assist clients who are hyperactive and also those who suffer from movement disorders, such as dystonia and Parkinson's disease. The reticular formation contains over 90 nuclei and networks of neurons extending down into the brain stem. It receives all kinds of sensory information and communicates with the thalamus, cortex and spinal cord. It is crucial to our understanding of sleep, arousal and attention. The periaqueductal gray matter is involved in fighting and mating in animals. The ventral tegmental area secretes dopamine and projects to the basal forebrain (median forebrain bundle). It is involved in learning and has been implicated in schizophrenia.

5. Hindbrain (Metencephalon, Myelencephalon)

The *Metencephalon* comprises the Cerebellum and the Pons. The *Myelencephalon* contains the medulla oblongata. The *cerebellum* like the cerebrum is covered with cortex. It is involved in coordination and motor performance. Damage results in jerky, exaggerated movements on the same side of the body as the lesion. The *pons* lies on the ventral surface of the cerebellum and is involved in sleep and arousal. The myelencephalon consists of the *medulla oblongata.* It is involved in the functioning of the lungs and the heart. It is also implicated in the maintenance of skeletal muscle tone.

An important nucleus in the hindbrain which has connections to the forebrain, is the *Locus Coeruleus.* It is important in the production of the neurotransmitter norepinephrine. This is thought to be important in attention deficit disorder, as will be discussed later in this chapter.

C. Early Development of the Forebrain

1. Development

The easiest way to learn the anatomy and the interconnections between areas in the brain is to make a mental picture of how the brain developed.

During the early stages of development, in the embryo what eventually becomes the brain is just a tube of neural tissue, an extension of the spinal cord. The rostral end of this tube develops as an *association* mechanism to detect sensory inputs and coordinate and direct motor actions. Four bulges appear along this hollow tube. These become the *forebrain (telencephalon), the connecting portion of the forebrain to the midbrain (Diencephalon), the midbrain and the hindbrain*. At the rostral end, in the bulges that become the telencephalon, the outer aspect of the walls becomes the cellular gray matter while more medial aspects contain the myelinated white matter of the interconnecting axons of these nerve cells. (This is the reverse of the rest of the 'tube' that becomes the dienephalon, midbrain, hindbrain and spinal cord where the gray matter is more central and the white matter more peripheral.) The hollow part of this tube becomes enlarged into four spaces containing cerebral spinal fluid. These spaces are called ventricles.

****

Schematic Diagram of The Developing Brain (after Smith, 1962)

2. Ventricles

Gradually the 'bulges' in the rostral end of the neural tube take on more definition. Each side of the most rostral end of the tube, the telencephalon, bulges out laterally. These lateral bulges of neural tissue will become the left and right cerebral hemispheres. Imagine blowing out a rather thick-walled balloon on either side of the rostral end of the neural tube. The hollow centres of each of these bulges of neural tissue expands to become the left and right *lateral ventricles*. Instead of air, like a balloon, they are filled with fluid called *cerebral spinal fluid* (CSF). A small tube at the anterior end of these two lateral ventricles remains to connect them to the original hollow center of the tube. This little tube is called the *interventricular foramen* **(foramen of Monro).** The hollow portion of this part of the brain, called the diencephalon, enlarges and is called the *third ventricle*. It is located in the center of the diencephalon between two masses of neurons in the lateral walls of this tube. This grey matter thickening in the lateral walls of the diencephalon will become the left and right lobes of the thalamus. The sensory pathways ascending up the spinal cord (the caudal end of 'the tube') will synapse here before going on to the left and right cerebral hemispheres.

Each lateral ventricle lies in a C-shaped form anteroposteriorly from the frontal lobe (anterior horn) back past the interventricular foramen through the parietal lobe (body) and down and forward again into the temporal lobe (inferior horn). It has a 'tail' into the occipital lobe (posterior horn) from the middle point of this C-shaped formation. In the lateral wall of the anterior horn, the body, and the temporal horn can be seen the caudate nucleus. It ends as a bulge in the tip of the inferior horn. This bulge of gray matter is the amygdala. In the body of the ventricle, at its inferior medial corner where the caudate is juxtaposed to the diencephalon, is the choroid plexus. This plexus, which produces CSF, runs medially from its attachment to the diencephalon-caudate juncture to attach to the fornix (described later). The 'body' portion of the lateral ventricle has the corpus callosum above it and a medial wall, the septum pellucidum. The choroid plexus remains attached to the caudate and coextensive (Smith, p.205) with the fibers forming the fornix (and fimbria) all the way around the C-shaped curve to the tip of the inferior horn.

3. Development of the Corpus Striatum

A mass of neural tissue in the floor of each of these lateral ventricles expands. It becomes very large filling most of the ventricle. What had been an oval shaped ventricle space now becomes squeezed into a 'C' shape over (and medial), around the posterior aspect and under this mass of cells. This large cellular outgrowth into the left and right lateral ventricles is now adjacent to the lateral wall of the diencephalon. It is called the *corpus striatum.* (Note that this term is somewhat confusing since it is different than the term "*striatum*" which comprises only the putamen and caudate as described in B2e above. [Smith, 198-203].) The corpus striatum is made up of the *lentiform* nucleus, the *caudate*, the *amygdala* and the *claustrum.* The *lentiform nucleus* is so named because it is shaped rather like a lens between the diencephalon and a relatively thin section of the cortex lateral to it called the *insula.* This lentiform nucleus comprises the *putamen* laterally, the *globus pallidus* medially, and inferiorly at its base, the *innominate substance* containing the *anterior perforated area*.

As you are now surmising, all these nuclei, which you keep hearing about, came originally from the same mass of tissue which grew out of the original floor of the left and the right lateral ventricles. As it grew, so did its connections to the diencephalon and midbrain. Therefore, the amount of connecting tissue posterior to the interventricular foramen and the lateral aspect of the diencephalon necessarily had to thicken. A small portion of the medial wall of the lateral ventricle remained paper-thin with no nerve cells invading it. This portion is the choroid membrane that contains capillaries and partly encircles the attachment of the hemisphere to the diencephalon. All the rest of the neuronal tissue that was forming the walls of the lateral ventricles was also thickening. This outer skin of our imaginary balloon was becoming differentiated into 6 layers which would form the cerebral cortex. The true definition of a mammal, as mentioned before, is a creature with a 6-layered cortex.

4. Development of the Internal Capsule

Naturally the emerging neocortex was not just forming as a disconnected mass. The neurons in this emerging cortex were maintaining their original afferents, those connections going to the new cortex from the caudal end of the tube, the spinal cord, to the rostral end via the diencephalon's thalamic links to the cerebral hemispheres. These neurons also preserved *efferent* connections (from the new cortex) to the rest of the original neural tube. Some of these efferent and afferent fibers went through the bulge of neural tissue forming on the base of the lateral ventricle called the corpus striatum and they eventually formed a thick band called the *internal capsule.* Thus this internal capsule pierced the corpus striatum resulting in the caudate portion of the corpus striatum looping around the anterior part of the internal capsule then coursing above it in a posterior direction. Below (inferior to) the internal capsule lies the putamen and globus pallidus. Medial to it lies the thalamus in the diencephalon.(See diagrams under 2e above and under 6e below.)

The afferent sensory fibers within the internal capsule came from sensory organs via the thalamus on their way to the sensory cortex. All senses except smell go through the thalamus firrst. Smell goes directly to the brain (including parts of the cortex and amygdala) and secondarily to the thalamus along its own olfactory tract. The motor cortex sends its efferent axons down through the internal capsule to sweep over the left and right lateral aspects of the diencephalon as the *crus cerebri*. This becomes the *basis pedunculi* on the ventral surface of the midbrain. At the caudal end of the pons segment of the hind brain the basis pedunculi becomes the *pyramid.* The pyramid runs along the ventro-lateral surface of the medulla. Then the fibers enter the spinal cord and *cross over* to the opposite side to become the *lateral corticospinal tract* which innervates the skeletal muscle system.

5. Communication Links
Brief Overview of the Major Communication Pathways

a. Commissures
These are large bundles of fibers that link the two hemispheres. Think of these bundles as the highway links between countries.

i. Corpus Callosum
The word **commissure** means connection. The largest connection between the hemispheres is the *corpus callosum.* Developmentally, the first commissure to unite the hemispheres was a cellular or gray matter one. The cells were derived from the septal region. (See diagram under 6c below.) These cells invaded the anterior wall (*lamina terminalis*) of the foramen (interventricular foramen) between the left and right lateral ventricles. Large bands of fibers connecting, first, the anterior portions of the hemispheres, and then the posterior portions were added to this commissure creating the connecting links between these portions of the hemispheres. Fibers of the corpus callosum going laterally after reaching the lateral border of the ventricle dove downwards, medial to the insula, and gave a thin white matter cover to the lateral aspect of the lentiform nucleus. This white matter 'cover' is called the *external capsule.* The corpus callosum grew thicker and as it grew in a posterior direction it formed a canopy over the diencephalon. The space between this canopy and the diencephalons became known as the *horizontal fissure.* (See diagram under B2e above)

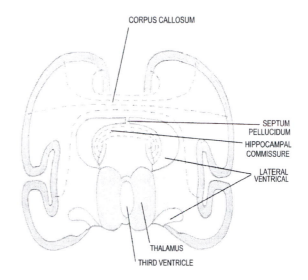

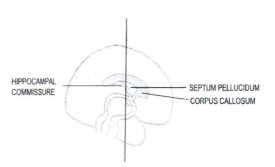

Schematic Diagram of a Transverse Section Through the Cerebral Hemispheres and the Diencephalon. (after Smith, 1962)

ii. Anterior Commissure
Two other small commissural bands exist. The first is at the anterior/inferior portion of the corpus callosum. This point was the developmental origin of the corpus callosum just in front of the interventricular foramen. This band of fibers is the *anterior commissure.* It connects the neocortical areas in the temporal lobes. The anterior commissure pierces the corpus striatum and passes below the internal capsule to fan out in the anterior portion of the temporal lobes.

iii. Hippocampal Commissure
The other commissural band of axonal fibers is the *hippocampal commissure.* It is a thin lamina in the inferior border of the septum pellucidum coursing posteriorly from the interventricular foramen across the top of the diencephalon to become part of the *fornix* which runs along and

connects to the hippocampus on each side. This will be described below. (See diagram below and also the diagram under B2e above.)

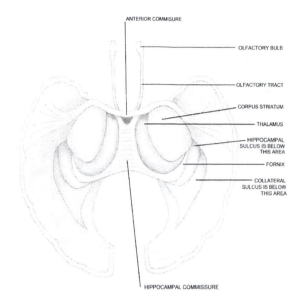

Schematic Diagram, Horizontal Plane, to show the Anterior and Hippocampal Commissures. (after Smith, 1962)

b. Association Fibers (within either the left or right cerebral hemisphere)

i. Short Association Fibers
These 'U' shaped fiber bands link adjacent gyri. Think of these as the major roads within a city.

ii. Long Association Fibers
These fiber bands link large areas of the cortex that are long distances from each other. Think of them as the super highways. There are four major such bands of association fibers: the cingulum, the superior longitudinal fasciculus band the inferior longitudinal fasciculus which contains 2 bundles of fibers.

(1.) The Cingulum
If you were to look at *a sagittal section* of the cerebral hemisphere just lateral to the midline, you would see the large association communication bundle of fibers for the limbic system. As noted previously, the limbic cortex is a C-shaped region on the medial surface of the cerebral hemisphere. It includes the cingulate gyrus, parahippocampal gyrus, hippocampus and

the parolfactory area. It has connections with the frontal, parietal and temporal lobes. It connects to these lobes through the *cingulum* in the cingulate and parahippocampal gyri. It is a bundle of long association fibers which is at the core of the limbic system. It is involved, therefore, in the conscious perception of emotions.

(2.) The Superior Longitudinal Fasciculus
Imagine another sagittal section but this time cut more laterally. Now, pretend you are now standing beside the brain looking the other way at it, that is, looking towards the center of the brain. In this view you would see a large bundle of *association* fibers which course above the insula and between the frontal lobe, the occipital lobe and, after turning around the end of the lateral sulcus, the temporal lobe. One possible important function of this communication system is speech.

(3.) The Inferior Longitudinal Fasciculus
In the same kind of view (sagittal section) you will also see two smaller bundles of fibers at the inferior border of the insula. The top bundle of fibers run from the frontal to the occipital poles. Below these are shorter association fibers joining the orbital cortex with the temporal pole called the *uncinate fasciculus*.

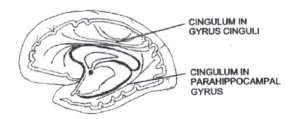

Sagittal Section to Show Cingulum (after Smith, 1962)

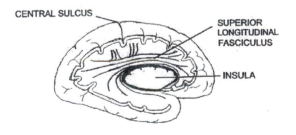

Sagittal Section ((looking from the lateral aspect of the hemisphere towards the midline)) to show the Superior Longitudinal Fasciculus. (after Smith, 1962)

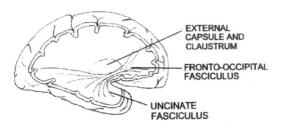

Sagittal Section (looking from the lateral aspect of the hemisphere towards the midline) to show the Inferior Longitudinal Fasciculus.
(after Smith, 1962)

6. Development of Important Connections Between the Hemispheres:

The Role of the Neural Tissue in the Vicinity of the Anterior Wall of the Third Ventricle.

a. Lamina Terminalis – One Keystone

In the foregoing description of the early development of the rostral end of the neural tube we described the growth of the corpus striatum. We noted that connections to and from the original neural tube had extended into each cerebral hemisphere behind the interventricular foramen within that thickened wall of the cerebral hemisphere immediately lateral to the diencephalon.

Now let us consider the wall of the third ventricle anterior to the foramen magnum. This anterior wall of the third ventricle is called the *lamina terminalis.* It remains very thin. At first, the connection here between the two hemispheres consisted of grey matter from the septal region of the medial-frontal part of the developing cerebral hemispheres. These cells from the septal region had invaded this anterior wall of the third ventricle that had been the rostral end of the embryonic neural tube. The

lamina terminalis lies between the optic chiasma below and the anterior commissure (temporal lobes – memory functions) above.

b. Septal Area & Anterior Perforated Area – More Keystones

The gray matter immediately anterior to the lamina terminalis on each side is the septal region which plays a role in consciousness. The septal region connects to the cingulate gyrus and the superior frontal gyrus. Thus the septum is a small section of the medial surface of the hemisphere adjacent (and connected) to the lamina terminalis. Developmentally, cells from the septum invade the lamina terminalis with the right hemisphere thus connecting at this point with the left. As this connection thickens, it forms the anterior commissure and the corpus callosum. The anterior commissure contains some fibers from the olfactory tract. Most of its fibers, however, connect the temporal lobes. The septum helps to form the *septum pellucidum,* a thin anterior vertical partition below the cerebral commissure (corpus callosum) and between the right and left lateral ventricles. It is immediately adjacent and connected to the subcallosal gyrus (part of the septal area). The subcallosal gyrus goes along the anterior border of the lamina terminalis to the *anterior perforated area.* The subcallosal gyrus is immediately posterior to the paraolfactory area which is next to the anterior end of the cingulate gyrus.

Anterior Perforated Area

The *anterior perforated area* (APA) is an area which is perforated by small blood vessels which supply the corpus striatum. This area forms the inferior medial part of the innominate substance of the lenticular nucleus. It borders posteriorly with the *amygdala.* The amygdala is continuous anteriorly with the innominate and with the putamen. It is also connected to the *uncus.* In part, the grey matter of the uncus is continuous with gray matter of the amygdala. Anterior to the anterior perforated area, the lentiform nucleus joins the caudate. The olfactory bulb is quite easy to see in most medial sagittal sections. It attaches by a visible stalk to the anterior border of the anterior perforated area. The APA is beside the anterior half of the ventral (inferior) surface of the diencephalon. At the lateral aspect of the APA is the insular neocortex. (See diagram under c. below.)

c. Hypothalamus, Septum & Anterior Perforated Area

A 'Hub' of Communication Pathways

Thus far we have seen that the olfactory bulb sent a stalk of fibers to the anterior perforated area. Fibers went on to the septum and the amygdala. Fibers connect the anterior perforated area, the septum, and the amygdala to the **hypothalamus.** The hypothalamus lies below the thalamus and is continuous with the septal area and with the anterior perforated substance. Thus, the amygdala connects either rather directly to the hypothalamus via the APA or, indirectly, by a long circuitous route via the stria terminalis. Complementing this back door route is a septal region 'back door' to the dentate and hippocampus via the *longitudinal stria.* The longitudinal stria consists of fibers that arose in the hypothalamus, go to the septal area, then the subcallosal gyrus, penetrate through the corpus callosum, run posterior to the splenium, then go around this curve to descend and run anterior to the dentate. (Smith, p.188) (Note figure on page 87.)

The hypothalamus is critical in the regulation of blood pressure, pulse rate, body temperature and perspiration. It is involved in all the body's homeostatic mechanisms. It is important in hunger, thirst, water balance, sexual behaviour and lactation. It is important for our biological clock and, thus, our circadian rhythms. It is, with the amygdala, an integral player in our fight or flight responses. The lateral aspects of the hypothalamus appear to be involved in both pleasure and anger. The medial portions seem to be more involved in aversion. The anterior hypothalamus is involved in parasympathetic activity and the posterior portion is part of the sympathetic system. Modulation of affective responses may also involve the hypothalamus. Thus the hypothalamus, with its influences on the endocrine system (the pituitary gland develops as an extension of the ventral hypothalamus) and the autonomic nervous system, is essential to homeostasis and to our emotional responses to our environment.

How these Structures Relate to the Fear Response

More than 100 years ago, a Swiss psychlogist, Édouard Claparède, reported that a woman patient who had severe amnesia could nevertheless acquire a fear response. She unconsciously and automatically associated his handshake with pain after he had pricked her hand with a pin when he was shaking hands with her. Although she could not recall who he was the next day (although she had been introduced to him on a daily basis for some time), she automatically withdrew her hand when he extended his.

Joseph LeDoux, Cornell University, studying conditioned fear in the 1980's, found that rats could not learn when a portion of their thalamus called the auditory thalamus was removed. He concluded that the auditory cortex, which is responsible for integration of sounds into conscious awareness, was not involved in the automatic fear response. He discovered that a second connection went from the auditory thalamus directly to the lateral nucleus of the amygdala and hence to the central nucleus. The central nucleus of the amygdala links to brain stem areas that control autonomic responses, such as changes in breathing, heart rate, skin temperature and skin conduction. These changes occur as a response to a fear-producing stimulus. The amygdala also controls the automatic 'freezing' of motion that occurs when a sudden, fear-producing stimulus, like the sound of the rattler of a rattlesnake, is detected. It is an extremely fast automatic response (often to an emotional memory) that occurs long before the conscious brain (cortex) can figure out what is going on (*declarative memory*) and initiate a voluntary response (*procedural memory*). Declarative memory is laid down by the hippocampus. Emotional memory seems to be 'marked' by amygdala connections in a way that gives it primary importance before conscious thinking can occur. To take control of this automatic response initiated by the central nucleus of the amygdala an animal has to learn to shunt the stimulus from the lateral nucleus to the basal nucleus of the amygdala. The basal nucleus links to brain areas that can initiate a new, helpful, action. Beta-blockers, used to help people who have had a traumatic experience, do not block the automatic emergence of the memory but do decrease the emotionally driven autonomic responses. These drugs may gradually make the uncomfortable responses to the memories decrease.

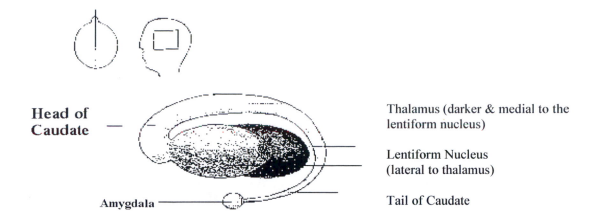

Head of
Caudate ——

Thalamus (darker & medial to the
lentiform nucleus)

Lentiform Nucleus
(lateral to thalamus)

Amygdala ————

Tail of Caudate

**Diagrammatic Sketch (Sagittal section) looking from left lateral aspect to medial, to show some
relationships of the basal ganglia to the thalamus.**

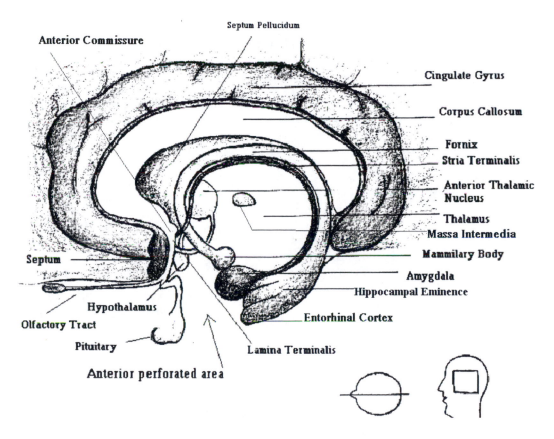

Septum Pellucidum

Anterior Commissure

Cingulate Gyrus

Corpus Callosum

Fornix
Stria Terminalis

Anterior Thalamic
Nucleus

Thalamus
Massa Intermedia

Mammilary Body

Amygdala
Hippocampal Eminence

Entorhinal Cortex

Septum

Hypothalamus

Olfactory Tract

Pituitary

Lamina Terminalis

Anterior perforated area

Midsagital Diagramtic Representation of the Diencephalon and Surrounding Forebrain (After Smith
1962)
Note 1:   The stria terminalis joins the fornix at the interventricular foramen and then terminates on the
hypothalamus.
Note 2:   The fornix joins the hippocampus to the hypothalamus and the mammillary body and these
connect to the subthalamus, tegmentum and the red nucleus (Smith 85, 187).
Note 3:   The stria terminalis joins the amygdala with the hypothalamus.

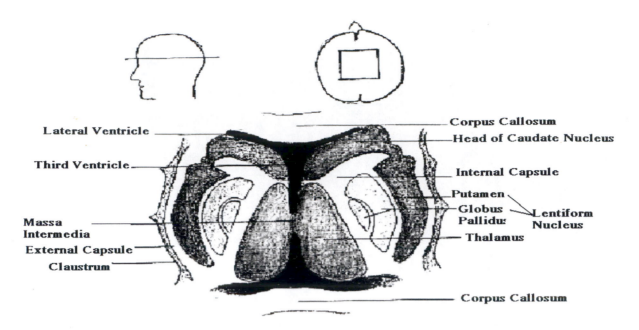

Horizontal Section of the Diencephalon and Surrounding Forebrain Structures (after Smith, 1962)

Labels on diagram:
Lateral Ventricle
Third Ventricle
Massa Intermedia
External Capsule
Claustrum
Corpus Callosum
Head of Caudate Nucleus
Internal Capsule
Putamen
Globus Pallidus
Lentiform Nucleus
Thalamus
Corpus Callosum

d. The Hippocampus – Another Keystone

If you now visualize the anterior, superior, lateral corner of the diencephalon (thalamus and hypothalamus), you will recall that the balloon-like bulge which grew out laterally still had to remain attached. Think of the skin of this 'balloon' at this point of attachment becoming the medial portion of the cortex of the cerebral hemisphere. The inferior portion of this cortex is a primitive cortex with fewer layers than the rest of the *neocortex* and it is called *archicortex*. It has only three layers as compared to the neocortex which has 6 layers. At its anterior end this archicortex connects with the amygdala and the anterior perforated area. At the posterior end it is continuous with what is termed *entorhinal cortex* in the wall of the hippocampal sulcus and this gives rise to the fibers of the fornix that eventually connect with the hypothalamus. The *fornix* or 'arch' also connects the hippocampus with the anterior thalamic nuclei and the mammillary body. In addition, the hippocampal cortex has connections with the frontal, parietal and temporal lobes. It is connected with the cingulate via the cingulum, a large band of association fibers. The subcallosal gyrus + the parolfactory area + the cingulate gyrus + the parahippocampal gyrus + the hippocampal formation, together, form the limbic system. The limbic system links directly to the amygdala, hypothalamus and thalamus. Papez suggested as early as 1937 that this system's interconnections with the frontal, parietal and temporal lobes was at the basis of sensing emotions. The hippocampus, thus, has connections to the areas concerned with emotions, the autonomic nervous system, the endocrine system and consciousness. It is perhaps not surprising that it plays a key role in understanding the laying down of memory and recall. It is the hippocampus that allows the animal to compare the present situation with past memories of similar situations. This is an important function for survival.

e. Development of Linkages

There are connections between the hemispheres and complex linkages between nuclei in the hemispheres and the brain stem. In addition, there are very important connections between the limbic system, the extrapyramidal motor system and decision making portions of the cerebral hemispheres.

i. The Anterior Commissure

We have already noted that a commissure is a connection and that, developmentally, the first commissure to unite the hemispheres was a cellular or gray matter one. The cells were derived from the septal region which invaded the anterior wall of the third ventricle (*lamina terminalis*) anterior to the foramen (interventricular foramen) between the left and right lateral ventricles. The fibers connecting, first, the anterior portions of the hemispheres and then the posterior portions were then added to this commissure forming the connecting links between the hemispheres. The commissure grew thicker and formed a canopy over the diencephalon. We also described above the two other, smaller commissural bands. The first, located at the anterior/inferior portion of the corpus callosum (the developmental origin of the corpus callosum just in front of the interventricular foramen) is the **anterior** commissure which connects the neocortical areas in the temporal lobes. It pierces the corpus striatum and passes below the internal capsule to fan out in the anterior portion of the temporal lobe.

of the fornix. The fornix contains **commissural fibers** that cross to the other cerebral hemisphere allowing for connections between the right and left hippocampal formations. It also contains **projection** fibers that course anteriorly to the *lamina terminalis*. There, by the *interventricular foramen,* these fibers descend into the diencephalon, enter the superior surface of the hypothalamus and continue on to make connections with the medial part of the mammillary body. (As previously noted and diagrammed above, fibers from the stria terminalis arise in the amygdala and join the fornix as it enters the hypothalamus anterior to the interventricular foramen.)

ii. Hippocampal Commissure and The Fornix

The other band is the **hippocampal** commissure which goes across the top of the diencephalon to become part of the **fornix.** The fornix connects to the hippocampus in each hemisphere. Along the hippocampal sulcus is the hippocampal formation containing the hippocampus and the dentate nucleus. This hippocampal cortex connects with the *entorhinal cortex* anterior to it and to the bulb of cortex there called the *uncus* which is continuous with the amygdala and the anterior perforated area as noted above. (See figure below.) This entorhinal cortex is the origin

iii. Mammilo-Thalamic Tract

In the mammillary body the fibers synapse with connections in the **mammilo-thalamic tract** which connects to the **anterior nucleus of the thalamus**. In addition this **tract connects to the cingulate** gyrus. It has **other fibers** descending through the **subthalamus** to the **tegmentum** of the midbrain and the **red nucleus.** The red nucleus connects to the muscle spindles in the skeletal muscles. These connections to the amygdala can be important in understanding the automatic fear response.

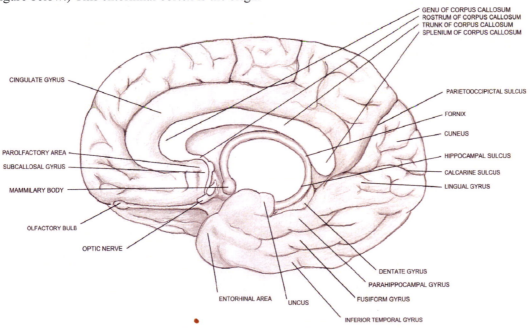

Midsagital Diagramtic Representation of the Diencephalon and Surrounding Forebrain (after Smith 1962)

f. Brief Summary

The foregoing has described a complex network of connections that links areas of the brain that are concerned with emotions, the autonomic nervous system and the extrapyramidal motor system. These connections imply an interrelationship between the limbic, autonomic and motor systems. These interconnections may influence skeletal muscle tone through the red nucleus and muscle spindles. This aspect may be of importance to us when we are theorizing about the effects of NFB combined with BFB in improving the quality of life of clients with movement disorders. Reducing hyperactivity and other kinds of unwanted motor activity, such as movements in dystonia or tics in Tourette's syndrome, is perhaps also facilitated by these interrelationships. As we increase SMR and practice diaphragmatic breathing, thalamo-cortical loops are affected and, perhaps, also there are other inter-connected networks which are affected.

In addition, recall that we mentioned above that fibers of the fornix (which comes from the hippocampus) connect with the hypothalamus and that the *fornix* also connects the hippocampus with the anterior thalamic nuclei and the mammillary body. In addition to this, the hypothalamus connects to the *medial nucleus of the thalamus* which connects, in turn, with the *prefrontal* and the *parietal* cortex. This provides a connection from the cingulate to the prefrontal cortex. This kind of connection is important in our discussion of such disorders as obsessive compulsive disorder (OCD).

7. Motor Pathways: Cortex to Spinal Cord

a. Voluntary Control – Pyramidal System

The *pyramidal* motor pathways from the cortex descend as the *corticobulbar* (voluntary movement via cranial nerves) and the *corticospinal* (voluntary movement via the spinal nerves) tracts. A third tract, the *corticopontine* tract, activates the cerebellum to coordinate muscles involved in these movements. These tracts descend through the internal capsule to the *crus cerebri* on the lateral aspect of the diencephalon to become the *basis pedunculi* of the midbrain running in this basal or ventral position through the pons segment to become the *pyramid* on the lateral surface of the medulla. From here they enter the spinal cord and *cross over* to the opposite side to become the *lateral corticospinal tract.* They cross over and, thus, the motor cortex of the left side of the brain controls motor movements on the right side of the body and visa versa. The *internal capsule* is called *internal* because it is medial to the lentiform nucleus and *capsule* because it has the appearance of forming a layer over this nucleus (medial and superior). The *internal capsule* is like a fan. The handle is the crus cerebri (basis pedunculi). This contains the motor pathways. The fan portion opens up between the caudate above and the lentiform nucleus below.

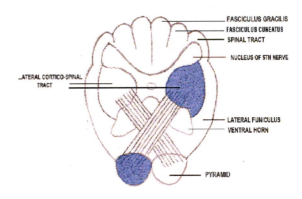

Section of Spinal Cord at the level of the Medulla Oblongata (after Smith, 1962)

The above schematic diagram is at the level of the medulla oblongata at the point where the motor fibers of the pyramid cross the midline and descend in the cortico-spinal tract. The uncrossed sensory fibers in the fasciculus gracilis and fasiculus cuneatus synapse and then cross the midline just above the section of the medulla shown above and become a ventral fiber tract, the medial lemnsicus. Here they join the sensory fibers, in the ventral spinal thalamic tract, that had crossed earlier in the spinal cord. This sensory tract called the medial lemniscus ascends to the diencephalon and the thalamus.

Note: There is also an external capsule. Fibers of the corpus striatum going laterally dive downwards medial to the insula and give a thin white matter cover to the lateral aspect of the lentiform nucleus and are called the external capsule. In so doing these fibers detach a chunk of grey matter from the corpus striatum which is called the claustrum. As previously noted, the anterior fibers of the corpus callosum course into the frontal lobe, and the posterior ones into the occipital lobe.

b. Extrapyramidal Motor Control

The cortex also has *extrapyramidal motor* areas (premotor). The pathways from these areas have many intervening synapses in different areas of the motor system. These areas include the nuclei within the *corpus striatum* - including the lenticular nucleus (putamen & globus pallidus) - which send fiber bundles to the *subthalamic* nucleus. The first bundle pierces the posterior limb of the internal capsule (lenticular fasciculus) and the second courses around the anterior border of the internal capsule (ansa (loop) lenticularis). At this juncture (subthalamus) fibers from the lenticular nuclei cross the midline. They connect, in the midbrain, with the *red nucleus*, the *substantia nigra,* and the *reticular formation* and from there descend to influence (extrapyramidal) the striated muscles. This influence differs from that of the pyramidal tract motor pathways in that these extrapyramidal paths are not discrete to individual muscles, but rather, involve movement of whole portions of the body such as a limb. Damage within this system results in awkwardness, not paralysis. The many ascending and descending connections with other nuclei in the midbrain, such as the red nucleus, may result in rigidity and/or tremor.

8. Sensory Pathways: Spinal Cord to Cortex

The sensory pathways in the spinal cord are labeled in the figure below. Note the different pathways for different aspects of sensation: light touch, proprioception (position sense), pain (dual pathways) and temperature. These pathways will ascend to synapse in the thalamus before ascending to the sensory cortex. These will not be discussed in further detail in this textbook.

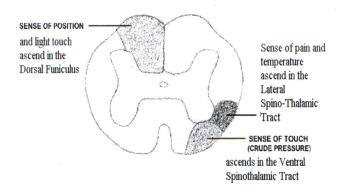

Section of Spinal Cord to Show Sensory Pathways (after Smith, 1962)

D. Functional Significance of the Lobes of the Brain

1. The Cerebral Hemispheres – a broad overview

a. Frontal Lobes

The frontal lobes have an anterior portion termed *prefrontal*. The prefrontal areas are involved in executive functions: the voluntary control of attention, the inhibition of inappropriate and/or unwanted behaviour, the planning of actions and executive decision making. They have a role in the maintenance of arousal and the temporal sequencing of complex entities such as the expression of compound sentences. They are not fully developed until the second decade of life, which helps explain why teenagers are more spontaneous and reactive than adults. The symptoms of ADHD are, in large measure, attributable to frontal lobe dysfunction or under-activation. The more posterior portion of the frontal lobes is involved, to a large extent, in motor functions and speech.

i. The Left Hemisphere

The left hemisphere is involved in speech, articulation and writing. It has a major role in auditory and verbal representation. Object naming and word recall reside in this hemisphere. It is also involved in the representation of visual images evoked by auditory input. The left hemisphere functions also encompass letter and word perception and recognition. Thus, there is representation of abstract verbal forms and perception of complex relationships.

The left frontal lobe regulates speech production and syntax. It can regulate attention, inhibit actions and switch responses. It is usually involved in analytic, sequential processing. It can utilize speech (inner dialogue) to regulate behaviour. It is responsible for operations that require sequencing, such as those one can test by asking the client to recite a series of numbers or count backwards by 7's. As previously noted, Tom Budzynski uses the analogy of the left hemisphere being a PC computer running on DOS, whereas the right hemisphere is like a Macintosh computer.

Left hemisphere dominance is usually thought of as being characterized by a lack of emotion, introversion, goal-directed thinking and action with an internal locus of control. Processing may tend to be slow and serial in keeping with the tendency to be careful and sequential. The aptitudes tested on IQ tests are largely left hemisphere functions. The dominant neurotransmitter is dopamine.

ii. The Right Hemisphere

The right cerebral hemisphere is also important in the regulation of attention and in the inhibition of old habits. It is more involved, however, in sensing the Gestalt (image of something) and in parallel processing. It attends to spatial relationships. It is more responsible for the representation of geometric forms. It is also responsible for orientation in space and holistic perceptions. Though one typically thinks of language being in the left hemisphere, the emotional aspects of language, such as the information conveyed by intonation, are a right hemisphere function.

Right hemisphere dominance is usually thought of as being characterized by distractibility, stimulus seeking behaviour, seeking novelty and change, being emotionally involved and expressive and extroverted. There may tend to be an external locus of control. There may be more of a tendency for hysterical, impulsive and even manic behaviours. Processing tends to be fast and simultaneous in keeping with the Gestalt or holistic tendencies. The dominant neurotransmitter is noradrenaline which is associated with speeding up activity and serotonin which may be thought of more as slowing down activity. (Tucker, 1984) The cortex under F8 may be related to social appropriateness and the emotional aspects of behaviour. Disturbances may result in impulsivity, aggressiveness and disinhibition.

For a readable book about the temperament and style of children who seem more ruled by this hemisphere, get *Right-Brained Children in a Left-Brained World.*

Right Brained or Left Brained

Sometimes people talk of boys being more right brained. Piaget used the terms, *assimilate* and *accommodate*. The right hemisphere is more responsible for assembling descriptive systems, (*accommodation*) that in making changes that broaden the existing cognitive structure. Dominance in these functions leads to seeking regularities in a new Gestalt through experimentation. This is an inductive reasoning process. It occurs in response to new information and leads to understanding abstract information and making generalizations. Persons who excel in this kind of thinking can adapt to new things. They can look at evidence and extend their thinking into something else; that is, generate a hypothesis. Children who have Asperger's syndrome share with autistic children deficiencies in these kinds of functions.

The left hemisphere is responsible for integrating and applying these well formed descriptive systems; that is, *assimilate* the new information (bring in and make part of) into an existing cognitive structure. This is a process of deductive construction of previously developed schemata. In deductive processes the individual can take evidence and come to a conclusion. Example: The cows are all lying down under the trees, there is distant thunder - I deduce it may rain.

Left hemisphere dominance should make it easier to follow set rules. The child with Asperger's does better in situations where there are well set rules. Unlike the Autistic child, the child with Asperger's syndrome may do very well verbally, a left hemisphere function. (see also Rourke, 2001).

iii. In Both Hemispheres
The central area of the cortex which is anterior to the central sulcus governs skilled movements. Posterior to the central sulcus it registers sensations.

b. Temporal Lobes
The temporal lobes are responsible for auditory processing and, on their medial aspect in the hippocampus, for short term and working memory. They receive frontal input (possibly inhibitory via the uncinate fasciculus), limbic input and parietal sensory inputs. They may play a large role in the integration and comprehension of new information and on the emotional valance of thoughts and behaviours.

c. Parietal and Occipital Lobes
The occipital and parietal lobes are involved in visual acuity. The visual recognition of simple shapes is registered posteriorly in the occipital lobes. As one moves forward (anterior) there is an ever increasing complexity of pattern recognition. The parietal lobes process raw sensory information into perceptions. Understanding these perceptions is then carried out by the frontal lobes. Which sensory inputs then make it to conscious awareness may be governed by the dorsolateral frontal cortex. On the left side this is approximately under the F7 electrode and disturbances in this area may correlate with distractibility.

Interestingly, parietal high alpha training (encourage higher amplitude above 10 Hz) may result in a decrease in low alpha (below 10 Hz) frontally (diffuse alpha projection system) and shift the mean frequency of alpha to a higher level (posterior specific projection system). When done in the left hemisphere this, can reduce dysphoria and increase alertness and attention.

d. Medial and Basal Zones of the Cerebral Hemispheres
As a broad general statement these areas are involved in affective processing. The orbital and medial prefrontal cortex is strongly connected to all of the limbic areas and, in particular, to the amygdala. It is primarily involved in affective processing. All aspects of emotional processing and attaching emotional significance to events (a function of the amygdala) involve these areas. The medial prefrontal cortex may also be involved in turning off the amygdala's fear systems. If there is damage here, fear would not be properly controlled. Therefore fear and anxiety might persist inappropriately and the autonomic center outputs of the hypothalamus presumably could then lead to observable symptoms of anxiety. The ventromedial prefrontal region is important in learning concerning social interactions. The lateral nucleus of the amygdala is critical in assigning emotional valance to events. The central nuclei of the amygdala are more involved in emotional expressions including flight or fight responses. Dysfunction in the interconnections between the orbital and medial wall of the prefrontal cortex and the amygdala and/or dysfunction in the lateral and central nuclei of the amygdala may therefore lie at the root of some of the difficulties encountered in the autistic spectrum disorders (Shultz, 2000).

As previously noted, the limbic cortex is a C-shaped region on the medial surface of the cerebral hemispheres. It includes the cingulate gyrus, parahippocampal gyrus, hippocampus and the parolfactory area. In addition to the forgoing, the Basal-Forebrain area is involved in sleep-wake regulation. Concept organization is also a function of this area (Robert Thatcher – personal communication).

E. Disorders Involving Cortical Functioning

1. Importance
Increasingly, NFB practitioners may be doing full cap assessments on a wide variety of clients. These assessments can reveal hyper and hypo communication links between different cortical

areas. Since NFB using coherence and/or comodulation training can perhaps help to normalize these communication links, it is important that we have a general understanding of the cortical areas involved. A basic dictum is that you base your NFB training on understanding how the client's difficulties correspond to the EEG assessment findings, coupled with your knowledge of brain function and correlations between EEG patterns and mental states. Two case examples may help to clarify this. (These cases will be expanded in Part II, Section VI under 'Interventions'.)

Troy, age 13, was completely oblivious to the meaning of emotions expressed by others. He appeared baffled rather than angry, worried or saddened by loudly expressed anger towards himself or other people. He appeared flat or, alternatively, overly excited with events that would be expected to evoke emotions. He did not express emotions appropriately either verbally or non verbally. His behaviour was impulsive and, as with many autistic children, it could be best understood if one assumed an underlying anxiety. He was in a general learning disability class for very low functioning children. He had no friends. Troy had been diagnosed as severely autistic at the children's hospital and, independently, by two other psychiatrists. He did have language skills but did not always respond to questions. Sometimes he would burst out laughing and flail his arms without any external stimulus being apparent.

The right hemisphere's involvement in the expression (anterior) and understanding (parietal-temporal) of emotional communications has been known for many years. The underlying major symptom of anxiety coupled often with inexplicably impulsive outbursts and/or actions are well known in individuals who have autistic spectrum disorders or Asperger's syndrome. The calming effect of right-sided (C2, C4) SMR training in anxious and impulsive individuals has also been demonstrated. Therefore, the use of 13-15 Hz augmentation and decrease in the 'tuning out' dominant slow wave (3-10 Hz range) made good sense both neurologically and from experience. His initial EEG profile showed excessive theta and low alpha (alpha below 10 Hz) that contrasted with a sharp drop in activity above 12 Hz.

The degree of success which Troy reached was not expected and we wish to be very cautious about making too much of the success with Troy and a small number of other children until large case series replicate this work. Over the course of a year he took 80 NFB sessions. He was placed in a normal classroom when he entered high school at age 14 and, by tenth grade, took several advanced courses. He was socializing and new friends in his class asked him to their birthday parties. Of course, he was still recognizably different but he had begun a 'new' life. A seven year follow-up was done by telephone and his father reported that Troy was in University and did not want anyone to ever know he used to have a problem.

Roger, a 32 year old man, could not read the signs at the race track where he took care of horses or even the menu at McDonald's. He was a thoughtful, sincere, hard working man who was engaged to a woman who had gone to university and was a voracious reader. He had been in special education at school and had tried literacy courses as an adult in order to learn how to read but to no avail. His fiancé learned of neurofeedback and encouraged him to try the training. The active electrode was placed just anterior to Wernicke's area and he was taught basic reading skills (phonetic awareness plus some sight words) at the same time as he achieved activation of this area (lowered his dominant slow wave and raised beta (16-18 Hz). After 60 sessions he had achieved his objectives and was able to read the cards at his next birthday party and simple novels. He had achieved functional literacy. (This example will be expanded in the next section.)

2. Damage Within The Cerebral Cortex

Most NFB practitioners are not trained in neurology so this section gives a few examples of higher cortical functioning which involve the connections between different areas of the cortex. An overview of a small selection of disorders that are related to dysfunction of different areas in the cortex is perhaps the easiest way to make sense of, and remember, the functions of cortical areas.

a. Right Cerebral Hemisphere Problems

Recognition and Expression of Emotions

Recognition of emotions appears to involve the **right brain, posterior to the central sulcus.** Damage to the right temporal-parietal region has been found to impair an individual's ability to detect differences in tone of voice which conveys emotional meaning (Tucker, 1977).

Anterior right hemisphere lesions impair the **expression of emotion** both non-verbally and verbally. Electrodermal responses (EDR) also demonstrate reduced reaction to emotionally-loaded stimuli in patients with right hemisphere damage (Morrow, 1981).

Recognition that damage to the **right frontal lobe** could result in euphoria and emotional indifference is long standing (Carlson, p.674 after Babinski, 1914). The term *anosognosia* is applied when the person seems to ignore, and even be completely oblivious to, paralysis of their left side. This is due to right hemisphere damage. Damage to the left hemisphere, on the other hand, may result in depression.

Although we recognize the meaning of language with the left hemisphere, the meaning of innuendo and tone is recognized in the right hemisphere. When we speak, our voice conveys emotional information through intonations, melody and rhythm. We put emphasis on different aspects of what we are saying. These aspects of speech are called *prosody*. This aspect of speech can be present even when the individual is making no sense at all, a condition called Wernicke's aphasia. However, the opposite is also true. The person may construct speech accurately and yet not put across the meaning appropriately due to a lack of correct intonation. Prosody is a function of the right hemisphere. Expression is frontal, comprehension is more posterior (Ross, 1981). A person could, for example, express their own emotions but not recognize the emotions expressed by others if the dysfunction is in the right temporal-parietal region

b. Left Cerebral Hemisphere Problems

i. Agnosia

Agnosia means a failure to know. (Agnosia in general may be thought of as a failure to **perceive**.) This is a higher level function and it, therefore, implicates a cortical dysfunction, not just a sensory problem. A person who had visual agnosia could see but would not be able to visually *identify* the items that they could see in their immediate environment. Oliver Sachs, a neurologist who writes reflective books about his interesting patients, describes a case of agnosia in
The Man Who Mistook His Wife for a Hat.

Apperceptive agnosia refers to an inability to recognize objects based on their shape. He would distinguish color, hue and size but not shape. He could walk along the sidewalk and not trip over objects placed in his path. This client would not be able to copy a drawing, a common test used by psychologists. A more specific type of visual agnosia is *prosopagnosia,* where the client is not able to recognize faces. These higher level functions appear to reside in the **medial** aspect of the **occipital and posterior temporal cortex bilaterally**. At an even higher level of functioning the person may be able to perceive an object correctly and even copy a picture correctly. However, they are not able to name the object just from sight (*perception defect*). (They can name it if they feel it so 'naming' is not the key problem.) This is called *associative visual agnosia.* In this case the visual associative cortex may be normal and speech is normal but the connections (white matter) between these areas and areas used in naming and verbalizing may be damaged.

ii. Anomia

A defect in the **associative cortex involved in speech and language is** both similar and yet different than a defect in the visual *associative cortex.* A person with a difficulty in speech and language might have what is called *anomia.* Like the person with a visual agnosia they can both see and recognize an object, such as a tricycle, but be unable to name it. They have a general difficulty with retrieving names. Even without the object in sight they might be trying to talk about a trycycle but be completely unable to come up with the right name for it. They might, however, describe its function and they will recognize the name if you remind them.

The **temporal lobe** contains the *auditory association cortex.* The parietal lobe association cortex contains areas responsible for **localization in space and perception of space.** Damage to these areas will result in corresponding deficiencies.

c. Parietal Lobe Damage

The parietal lobes are involved in the integration of sensory information and perception of the body. They are also involved in the perception of spatial relationships between objects around us. Lesions to the left and right parietal lobes can have quite profound effects on our functioning.

Lesions to the parietal lobes can result in a loss of awareness, and neglect, of body parts and surrounding space (parietal lobe lesions). *Gertsmann's syndrome* occurs when there is damage to the **left** parietal lobe. It comprises left-right confusion, *agraphia, acalculia, aphasia* and *agnosia.* **Right** parietal lobe damage may include difficulty drawing, *constructional apraxia* (difficulty making things) and *anosognosia* (denial of deficits). Damage to **both sides** causes *Balint's syndrome* which includes *ocular apraxia* (inability to control gaze) and *simultagnosia* (inability to integrate components of a visual scene) and *optic ataxia* (inability to accurately reach for an object with visual guidance).

Clearly all the association areas are constantly communicating with the frontal lobes in order for us to make meaningful decisions concerning movements and speech.

i. Apraxia
Damage to the frontal lobe, parietal lobe and corpus callosum can result in motor apraxia. *Apraxia* means 'without action'. It is the inability to execute a learned movement. As noted above *constructional apraxia* refers to an inability to construct or even to draw an object. Perception of geometrical relations is commonly tested in standard psychological testing before beginning NFB. It is due to lesions in the right parietal cortex.

ii. Limb Apraxia – An Example of Complex Interconnections Involving Limb Movement
A limb apraxia refers to unintended movements of a limb. If you ask a patient to pretend he is screwing in a screw, your command is analyzed in the left parietal lobe (*Wernicke's* area). The interpretations are communicated to posterior areas in the parietal lobe, the left prefrontal cortex and the left motor association cortex and other areas. These connections evoke memories of how to do this action and begin the process of coordinating the actions. The resulting decisions must be conveyed in the anterior portion of the corpus callosum to the right hemisphere and to the correct portions of the motor association cortex and then to the precentral motor cortex to control the movements of the left arm. Damage at the site of transfer (corpus callosum) to the right hemisphere will interfere with the left arm doing the desired movements. Damage to the *left motor precentral gyrus* will interfere with movements of both arms. The right arm is partially or completely paralysed and the left will not perform the task properly. Damage even earlier in the sequence described above might involve the posterior regions of the parietal lobe and would affect the appropriate movements of both limbs.

d. Complex Interactions Between Hemispheres

i. Functions: Speech, Language, Reading and Writing
Preschool children who show the symptoms of ADHD have an extraordinarily high incidence of speech and language disorders (Love & Thompson, 1988). It is also known that these children have a higher incidence of reading disorders once they are in school. It has been known for many years that certain areas of the left hemisphere are involved in speech and in reading. Using NFB to encourage the child (or adult) to increase fast wave and decrease slow wave activity over particular areas of the left hemisphere can produce improvements in language development, a decrease in articulation difficulties and improved ability to read.

During neurofeedback training of clients suffering from speech output problems, it makes sense to place the electrode over *Broca's area* and near C3 over the motor cortex when the symptoms are related to speech output. The electrode is usually placed over Wernicke's area and the insula for reading difficulties. Gradually, however, the training will become a little more sophisticated. It will be based on full cap assessments and on data which can demonstrate that certain areas of the brain are communicating either too much or too little with each other. The following is a case example:

As previously described, Roger was 32 years of age. In his school years he was placed in special education to teach him to read but he remained illiterate. His mother had also been illiterate. He was unable to decipher most signs. He could not read a grade one level book. He had seasonal employment caring for horses at the track and the Horseman's Benevolent Society kindly funded his training.

Logically, intervention was based on basic neurophysiology and knowledge of brain function. His sight was excellent and his speech good. He could understand verbal communication and things that were read to him. He was having difficulty deciphering the words and could not make sense of sound-symbol correspondence. (For example, he did not link the letter 'B' with the sound 'buh'.) He had no difficulty understanding when it was read to him. We postulated that the cortical area involved might include the insula on the left side and perhaps the Angular Gyrus at the occipital-parietal-temporal lobe junction since activity there affects the visual-spatial-language skills involved in visual word recognition. When he was figuring out a problem, we could observe a clear cut rise in 17 Hz activity and a corresponding drop in 5 Hz activity. We, therefore, operantly conditioned an increase in beta (16 –19 Hz) and a decrease in theta (4-7 Hz) with the active electrode in a location approximately over Werniche's area (about the middle of a triangle formed by C3, T7 & P3). We classically conditioned (paired) reading with this mental state. Throughout the coursed of his neurofeedback training he experienced success. Milestones he related to us included writing his first letter (to his old teacher in Nova Scotia) and reading the cards he received on his birthday. After 60 sessions he was reading short stories and simple novels at about a fifth grade level. He had achieved functional literacy.

ii. Anatomical Areas Involved

(1.) Wernicke's area
This area is known to be important for **understanding** speech. Understanding involves the inferior parietal lobe and the auditory association area of the superior temporal gyrus. If there is damage to this area, speech will still be fluent. Grammar will be good, but the person will **speak nonsense.** They speak a kind of jargon in which (without understanding what they are saying) they substitute inappropriate or the wrong words to the extent that they are unable to understand their own speech. These people have similar difficulties with reading and writing.

(2.) Near Wernicke's
A lesion **near Wernicke's** area at the back of the left temporal lobe leaves the individual with inability to analyze word meanings.

(3.) Local Connections
Damage to the connections between the **auditory cortex** and **Wernicke's area results in** the person being able to hear sounds but they are **word deaf.** They cannot understand the meaning of *spoken* words yet they are able to read, write and speak normally.

(4.) Inter-Lobe Connections
Damage to connections between **Wernicke's** and **Broca's** areas leave the individual **unable to repeat** what is said to them if it is more complex than a single word or phrase. That is, unless it has meaning which can be recognized in some other way. *(This may involve the Superior Longitudinal Fasciculus, a band of very long association fibers running anteroposteriorly in each cerebral hemisphere. These fibers run from the frontal lobe through the parietal lobe above and below the insula (around the end of the lateral sulcus). It has branches to the temporal lobe, and branches that run all the way posterior to the occipital lobe. (Clearly, in the left hemisphere, this communication link is essential for speech.)* It is particularly helpful if these individuals can visualize what is being talked about. They are not able to repeat, for example, a short series of unrelated words. They do, however, understand what is said, can speak well and can intelligently answer a question.

In contrast, in some individuals, the opposite problem can occur. An *overactive* connection between **Wernicke's** and **Broca's** areas may result in the involuntary repeating of words or phrases (*echolalia*).

(5.) Broca's Area
Damage to **Broca's area** interferes with the individual's ability to instruct the motor cortex and results in defects in the articulation of speech. Damage to Broca's area and its **association areas** may result in a condition where the person is able to understand what has been said to him and be conscious of what he wants to say, but not be able to say it. This person may substitute staccato nouns and verbs so that the flow of his speech is lost and it sounds like a telegram. Ungrammatical speech and writing errors may be observed. In some instances these persons may also fail to understand spoken or written grammar.

(6.) Connections between Speech Areas and Surrounding Cortex
Damage to the connections to **speech areas** from their **surrounding cortex** may result in the person being unable to **understand speech.** However they can repeat words or finish well known phrases (e.g., *roses are red …*)

(7.) Angular Gyrus
This is the region of the parietal lobe that sits at the *occipal-parietal-temporal* junction behind (posterior to) the lateral fissure. It involves *visual-spatial-language* skills and therefore **visual word recognition.** The left hemisphere angular gyrus is required for reading. Damage to this area can result in **alexia** (inability to read) and in **agraphia** (inability to write).

(8.) Disconnection of the angular gyrus from the left visual cortex
This means that words cannot be recognized in the normal fashion. However, an intact right visual cortex can still recognize letters and convey that information via the corpus callosum to the left hemisphere speech and language areas. The letters may, therefore, be named. As the patient says the sequence of letters out loud the word can be recognized through auditory input. Sub-vocalizing can also work. Although the client cannot read silently he may be able to read slowly out loud and understand what he is reading. He can also write sentences or copy words from a page.

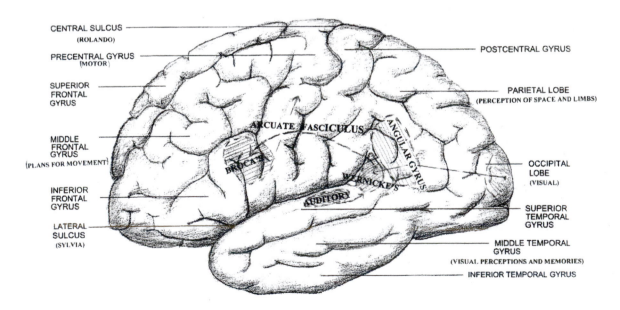

Lateral View of the Left Cerebral Hemisphere to show Broca's and Wernicke's Areas (after Smith, 1962; Carlson, 1986)

iii. Neurologically Based Disorders

(1.) Reading Disorders

At the most severe extreme, the complete inability to recognize a written word (alexia), may be associated with lesions of the left and right occipital lobes. The damage to the left occipital cortex would disconnect the angular gyrus from all right visual field visual input. If this damage was accompanied by a lesion in the right visual cortex, then no information would be available from the left visual field and reading would be impossible. Even without damage to the right occipital cortex, if there was damage to the connection between the right visual cortex and the left hemisphere via the posterior portion of the corpus callosum then information from the left visual field could not be transferred and thus would not be available to be analyzed by the posterior left hemisphere.

Dyslexia ('dys' means poor or faulty) One type of dyslexia appears to be, 'a disconnection syndrome' in which language areas fail to work in concert. The *connections between some of these areas* are not functioning properly. Reading subsumes two basic ways of 'reading'. The first is chiefly **phonological**. Phonology refers to the sounds letters represent. The second is, in a sense, **morphological**: we perceive the shape of the word. Most reading combines both processes (sounding it out and recognizing sight words that are memorized).

An individual with *phonological* difficulties would have trouble decoding non-words, whereas they would immediately recognize a meaningful whole word. On the other hand, a person with a *morphological* problem has difficulty recognizing sight words. This person might sound out the word 'Peugeot' as pu –gee-ot or read 'yacht' as ya –chet even though they knew both these words orally. Those who have trouble recognizing the 'whole word' may also have difficulties in spelling since good spellers know when a word looks right.

Two types of dyslexia - *disphonetic* (trouble sounding out) and *diseidetic* (trouble with visual processing of the letters) - are approached differently in NFB. Lubar has suggested that for disphonetic dyslexia you place the active electrode at F3 or F5 (bipolar try F3 – P3 or F7-P7 (T5). For diseidetic dyslexia try P3 or P5 (bipolar again try F3-P3 or F7-P7 (T5). In both cases you would be attempting to increase activation of these areas by increasing fast wave activity (low beta 16-20 Hz) and decreasing the dominant slow wave activity (theta or thalpha). (Reference: Joel Lubar workshop handout of applications supported by peer reviewed journal papers.)

Some people who have a reading difficulty have dysfunction in the insular area of the brain. The *insula* is lateral to the corpus striatum. Think of it as the cortex floor of that large indentation in the lateral aspect of the cortex called the lateral sulcus. The overgrowth of cortex during development forms two 'lids' like thick heavy eyelids which are the parietal lobe above and the temporal lobe below with the supramarginal gyrus at the posterior end of this lateral sulcus. Immediately posterior to the supramarginal gyrus is the angular gyrus. The lateral fissure goes down the center of this region. Recent work using brain imaging techniques has demonstrated that in some students with dyslexia the insula does not activate appropriately and each language area is activated singly and not in unison (Paulesu, 1996). Incoming words appear to get jumbled.

(2.) Agraphia

An individual who has agraphia is unable to write. A number of attributes are important for writing. These include the memory for sounds, and perhaps for symbols which represent sounds. This is located primarily in the left superior temporal gyrus. Visual symbols are in the visual association cortex.

Left-handedness and Difficulties with Reading and Writing

Left-handed people are significantly more likely to have specific learning disorders, including dyslexia. The literature does not distinguish between 'true-lefties', 'partial-lefties', and 'acquired-lefties'. *True-lefties* have brain functions anatomically reversed. (Language is in the right hemisphere.) *Partial-lefties* demonstrate mixed dominance and may be ambidextrous. Brain functions are not reversed anatomically and language areas are in the left cerebral hemisphere. This should not be surprising considering that the right brain controls the left hand but reading and writing are, for the most part, left brain activities. *Acquired-lefties* are those whose left-handedness was not a result of parental genes but was due to some influence during pregnancy or after birth. These are the children may show mixed dominance. They are more prone to learning disability problems. Their hand, eye and foot dominance may differ.

Always remember, however, that statistics are easily misunderstood. While many dyslexics may be left-handed, most left-handers are not dyslexic! It is also true that, in general, areas involved in language tend to be larger in women. Men may tend to be more visual. There are questions as to whether testosterone slows the growth of the left brain. Remember as you read these generalizations that **what is true statistically for the majority may not apply to that single individual with whom you are working.**

e. Hints for Students based on Neurophysiology

As a general rule, we tell students that the human brain consciously does one thing at a time. They will find that they cannot effectively be reading their textbook and writing notes while singing along with their favourite rock star all at the same time. They can alternate their focus but this will waste time and is not the most efficient way to study. On the other hand, it is true that one can do two things at once if they involve separate areas of the cortex. The student could draw a picture and speak or sing at the same time. If this is true, would it sometimes be helpful for a fidgety student to draw a picture especially if he can make the sketch symbolize what the teacher is saying or what he and others are discussing? For some students this can be a helpful strategy. However, the student must recognize that his brain will be moving off and on what the teacher is saying so this strategy must be used judiciously.

Each of us has our own dominance, visual, auditory or kinaesthetic. Some people say that they always 'hear' in their mind a word that they are trying to spell or write. Others say they are quite the opposite. They virtually always look up and visualize the word. Most of us are somewhere in between. Teachers would do well to avoid pushing their personal preference on to the student. Strategies for teaching that utilize both visual and auditory modalities and also add the kinaesthetic modality can work for either extreme and help individual students to use their own dominance to their own benefit. In early grade school years kinaesthetic learners should be encouraged to 'feel' letters. Drawing letters in sand or tracing letters that they have cut out of

sand paper are techniques that can help hands-on learners master the alphabet.

We feel that it is helpful to incorporate learning strategies into our work with NFB. There is ,therefore, a later section in this book on using metacognitive strategies in training sessions. (See also the 'Clinical Corner' comments in the *Journal of Neurotherapy*, 6(4), 2002, by Judy Lubar and by Lynda Thompson on the question of combining on-task activities with neurofeedback.)

f. Brief Summary of Selected Injuries to the Association Cortex

Injury to the **somatosensory association cortex** can result in difficulties perceiving the shapes of objects that cannot be seen. Drawing or even following a map may become difficult. With Injury to the **visual association cortex** the person can still see but will be unable to recognize objects unless they are able to touch them. Injury to the **auditory association cortex** will result in the person being able to hear but not being able to perceive the meaning of speech. Damage to the **junction of the visual, auditory and somatosensory association cortex** where the three posterior lobes meet can result in difficulties in reading and writing.

g. Temporal Lobe Damage

As noted above, the temporal lobe along with adjacent areas in the occipital and parietal lobes and other connected areas in the frontal lobe, is involved in all aspects of speech, language, reading and writing. In particular, Wernicke's area is crucial in the understanding of spoken words. This includes the identification and categorization of objects. It has close connections to the amygdala and the entire limbic system and damage could result in emotional disturbances, including aggressive behaviour. It is also crucial in laying down and retrieving memories. Of interest to our work with students is the fact that visual memory decay time is about 500 msec whereas auditory decay is closer to 10 seconds. This explains how you can repeat back the last few words your wife said in order to refute her complaint that you were not listening to her. The temporal lobes are important in selective attention. Damage to the temporal lobe can result in what is called prosopagnosia, mentioned previously under left hemisphere damage, and visual agnosias. In normal people the fusiform gyrus specializes in the recognition of human faces. Studies of children with autistic spectrum disorders indicate different activation of the fusiform gyrus when trying to identify emotions. This fusiform gyrus lies on the medial aspect of the temporal lobe between the parahippocampal gyrus above, and the inferior temporal gyrus below.

[You may recall that at its anterior end the parahippocampal gyrus curls around the end of the hippocampal sulcus to form the uncus which is continuous with the amygdaloid nucleus. At this bend is the olfactory sensory area. At its posterior end the parahippocampal gyrus forks with the superior end being continuous with the gyrus cinguli which turns and runs anterior and superior to the corpus callosum. The inferior end is continuous with the lingual gyrus which runs posterior below the calcarine sulcus to the occipital pole. The visual sensory area is on the medial aspect of the occipital lobe at the posterior tip of the lingual gyrus. The counterpart to the hippocampal gyrus on the medial aspect of the temporal lobe is the superior temporal gyrus which lies on the lateral aspect of the temporal lobe and contains the auditory sensory area.]

h. Occipital Lobe Damage

Damage to the occipital lobes can result in a variety of problems related to vision. Damage to one side will cause loss of vision to the opposite visual field. Thus the deficits range from defects in vision, difficulty identifying colours, difficulty recognizing words, drawn objects, movement of objects, to having illusions and hallucinations. Damage more anteriorly in the left occipital lobe near the parietal temporal junction, may result in difficulties in reading and writing. The functions of the visual cortex are anatomically very specific and a great deal of research has gone into delineating discrete areas and their functions.

F. The Limbic System
1. General Description

This system is involved in emotions, learning and motivation. Large portions of this system lie beneath the corpus callosum. In the 3-tiered brain model (reptilian, emotional and neocortical) this is the middle layer. In simple terms, you can think of the area above the corpus callosum as being the conscious brain while below it is the unconscious brain. The limbic system consists of a system or network of interconnected neuron groups. In the diagram below you can see the limbic cortex, hippocampus, amygdala, septum, anterior thalamic nuclei and the mammillary body. As noted in the section on anatomy, the *fornix* or 'arch' connects the hippocampus with the anterior thalamic nuclei and the mammillary body. As noted, when discussing the development of the cerebral hemispheres, the limbic cortex is a C-shaped region on the medial surface of the cerebral hemisphere. It includes: the cingulate gyrus, parahippocampal gyrus, hippocampus and the parolfactory area. It has connections with the frontal, parietal, and temporal lobes connecting to them through the cingulum. The cingulum comprises a bundle of long association fibers that lie within the cingulate and parahippocampal gyri. It is at the core of the limbic lobe. It is involved, therefore, in the conscious perception of emotions. (A surgical procedure to remove tissue (*cingulotomy*) could tame a wild animal. In humans cutting certain fibers in this area (*cingulectomy*) has been used to treat depression, anxiety and obsessive behaviour.

Although these groups of neurons are involved in the limbic system, they also have many other functions. Animals with damage to the septal hippocampal area have trouble finding their way around their environment. Mice with this kind of damage do not build nests. (see Carlson, 1984, p.416) The hippocampus has a central role in laying down memories. In the amygdala negative emotions are generated and links to negative memories are stored.

The amygdala is inhibited during hard work on relatively non-emotional tasks. It seems the Romans had it right with their adage: *Labor callum dolori obducit.* (Hard work removes the sting of pain.) Getting dysphoric clients to working on a project is often helpful. This might also tie in with happiness being associated with activation in the left hemisphere.

The anterior nuclei and the dorsomedial nuclei of the thalamus are part of the limbic system. Destruction of these nuclei can leave a person able to perceive sensation and pain without being bothered by the pain. (Carlson, p.268) The limbic system has extensive connections to the cortex above it and the hypothalamus and pituitary below it. The hypothalamus is located beneath the thalamus. It is particularly important as it controls the autonomic nervous system (sympathetic and parasympathetic) and the endocrine system as previously noted. It controls the behaviours necessary for survival: fight and flight, feeding, drinking, sleeping and sexual behaviours.

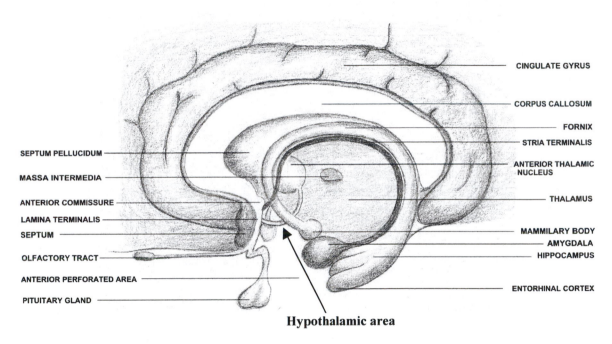

Hypothalamic area

Schematic diagram of a Mid Sagittal Section of the Telencephalon and the Diencephalon (after Carlson, 1986 and Smith, 1962)

2. Learning – Relationship to the Limbic System

We have described classical and operant conditioning in Section I. We will briefly review it here in order to lead into a discussion of the neurophysiological connections that may be involved in learning.

If you accidentally picked up a hot kettle and burned your hand, then you would be cautious and carefully test the heat of a Kettle's handle from that time on. Pain is an *unconditioned stimulus* and your withdrawal of your hand is the *unconditioned response*, that is, a reflex. From that time on, whenever you approached a boiling kettle (now a *conditioned stimulus*), you would hesitantly touch the handle and withdraw your fingers (*conditioned response)* testing the degree of heat. This is **classical** conditioning. The conditioned stimulus *automatically elicits* a conditioned response once it has been paired with an unconditioned stimulus that automatically elicits an almost identical response.

In **operant** (*instrumental*) conditioning a stimulus situation is more likely to elicit a particular behaviour (a response) if that behaviour has been rewarded in the past. In

NFB work we use rewards of visual and auditory feedback concerning success to reinforce the individual for putting their brain in the desired mental state. Then we pair that mental state with doing academic work. Soon the academic work (*conditioned stimulus*) will elicit the appropriate mental state (*conditioned response*).

Neurologically, it is of interest to know what pathway is involved in linking a *discriminative stimulus* with the behavioural response. (If a bar press activates a reward only when a red light comes on, the red light is the discriminative stimulus.) The ***reward*** system appears to involve the *medial forebrain bundle* of axons that run anterior-posterior from the midbrain (ventral tegmental area) to the rostral basal forebrain. This bundle passes through the lateral hypothalamus. The tectum is dorsal to the aqueduct and the tegmentum is ventral to it. The tegmentum contains the red nucleus. The midbrain is like a 'stalk' holding up and entering the forebrain. (The forebrain, remember, consists of the two cerebral hemispheres and the diencephalons – these together are called the cerebrum.) The midbrain has a thick layer of *central gray matter* surrounding the aqueduct. This bundle passes through the lateral hypothalamus.

Stimulation of the **dorsal hypothalamus may cause defensive or flight responses**. Stimulation of the **medial hypothalamus can produce irritability and aggression** (Carlson, p.516).

Extensive studies have revealed many areas which appear to **reinforce behaviour** if electrically stimulated. These reward areas include the medial forebrain bundle, the prefrontal cortex, caudate, putamen, nucleus accumbens, amygdala, substantia nigra, locus coeruleus, various thalamic nuclei and the ventral tegmental area (Carlson). It is a reasonable summary to say that connections among the limbic system, the ventral tegmental area of the mid brain, the ***nucleus accumbens*** and the cortex are involved in the experience of pleasure (reward). (The nucleus accumbens is a region of the basal forebrain adjacent to the septum and anterior to the preoptic area. It is adjacent to the medial and ventral surface of the caudate. It is important in paying attention to a stimulus and in responding to reward.) A rush of the neurotransmitter dopamine in the reward system is associated with pleasure. Dopamine is produced in the substantia nigra and in the

ventral tegmental area. Connections go from the ventral tegmental area to the nucleus accumbens, septum, caudate and the prefrontal cortex. Blocking this pathway to the nucleus accumbens blocks the reinforcing effects of cocaine (Carlson, p.527).

The **medial forebrain bundle (MFB)** is the connecting link (ascending and descending) between the midbrain and the rostral basal forebrain. This *medial forebrain bundle* passes through the hypothalamus. The major catecholaminergic pathways pass through the MFB. (Recall that the locus coeruleus produces norepinephrine.) It also contains serotonergic axons reaching from the brain stem to the diencephalon and telencephalon. Dopaminergic pathways from the substantia nigra and the ventral tegmental area to the nucleus accumbens, septum, prefrontal cortex and the caudate are also involved and stimulation of these pathways may also be reinforcing. Electrical stimulation of this bundle has been used as an experimental model of reward in animal research for the past fifty years. (Olds, Milner, 1954). The release of endorphins is also an important component of the pleasure response. Both dopamine and endorphins work within this system. In addition, serotonin producing cells in the ventromedial area of the prefrontal cortex are involved in feelings of well being as well as in euphoria and mania. In broad terms, **activation of the frontal portion of the right hemisphere is more involved with negative emotions whereas on the left the connection is with positive emotions** (Davidson, 1995). This latter finding is important in NFB because studies have demonstrated that increasing alpha activity in the right frontal cortex compared to the left, the so-called alpha asymmetry protocol, has a positive effect on depression (Rosenfeld, 1997). In this approach the alpha is used as an inverse indicator of activation, so the goal is to activate the left frontal area where positive thoughts and approach behaviour seems to reside. (Davidson, 1995)

G. Basal Ganglia

As previously noted, the basal ganglia comprise the globus pallidus, caudate nucleus and the putamen. This system is involved in movement disorders such as Parkinson's disease. Some of these nuclei have also been implicated in ADD. They are, therefore, important in our understanding of how we may be influencing the brain with NFB training. Lesions in the caudate nucleus may cause **abulia.** This is a syndrome that includes apathy and loss of initiative and of emotional responses (Bhatia and Marsden, 1994). Lesions in the basal ganglia may also result in slowing of information processing, inability to sustain attention, memory defects, and impairment in verbal fluency and motor planning. Difficulty shifting set is observed which can result in perseveration. Like parietal lobe lesions, there may also be neglect of the side contralateral to the lesion (Koropotov, 1999 after Heilman et al., 1994).

Decreased dopamine production in the substantia nigra is the core problem in Parkinson's. The substantia nigra is directly connected to the ventral tegmental area of the midbrain. When the ventral tegmental area (noted above in the discussion of reward systems) is activated, dopaminergic pathways along the MFB inhibit the nucleus accumbens which reduces the inhibitory effect of that nucleus (GABA mediated) on the globus pallidus which results in increased activity of these neurons. This is, in turn, associated with increased locomotion. It is postulated that when the opposite occurs, namely decreased dopaminergic activity, it results in decreased voluntary movement. A major symptom of Parkinson's is, not surprisingly, poverty of movement and freezing, that is, being unable to voluntarily move your muscles.

The caudate nucleus, which is a part of the *striatum,* appears to be involved in the suppression of involuntary movements. The major neurotransmitter in this system is, once again, dopamine. Obvious examples of disruption in this system include ADHD, Parkinson's disease and dystonia. In these latter disorders (which are often seen together) the substantia nigra's decreased production of dopamine throws the system of excitation and inhibition between the nuclei and the various neurotransmitters involved in this system out of balance. The relative influence of acetylcholine, for example, becomes too great when there is insufficient dopamine. The result behaviourally is episodes of rigidity, tremor, and involuntary movements typical of dystonia. These unwanted symptoms may be dramatically increased if the patient is mistakenly given adrenaline (such as during a dental procedure) or if they become excited.

Damage just to the substantia nigra produces a decrease in activity but no tremors. The ventral thalamus – cortical loops appear to be involved in tremors.

In *Huntington's chorea* (chorea is from the Greek word to dance and the movements are fast and jerky) the caudate and putamen degenerate. Interactions between these components of the basal ganglia are required for smooth, stable movements. Damage to the globus pallidus or the ventral thalamus causes deficiency of movement (akinesia). It may also result in a kind of mutism due to an inability to use the muscles necessary for speech. Thus the globus pallidus and the ventral thalamus appear generally to be excitatory, whereas the caudate and the putamen appear to have inhibitory functions (Carlson, p.313).

H. Blood Supply to the Brain

1. Overview
As noted in the introduction to this section, the brain receives more than 20% of cardiac output. The **internal carotid arteries** supply the rostral portion and the **vertebral arteries** the posterior or caudal portion of the brain.

There are connections between these two great arterial supplies. The anterior cerebral artery courses anterior off the internal carotid artery. The medial cerebral arteries run laterally off the internal carotid artery.

The **internal carotid arteries** enter the skull on the lateral aspects of the pharynx. Each carotid artery enters the skull, takes a rather tortuous route, and finally arrives immediately lateral to the optic chiasma where it ascends to the *anterior perforated area.* Here it divides into the **anterior** and **middle cerebral arteries.**

2. Cerebral Arteries
a. Anterior Cerebral
The *anterior cerebral artery* courses anterior and medial above the optic nerve to the front of the *lamina terminalis.* Just anterior to this point the right and left anterior cerebral arteries are within 1 to 2 mm of each other. Here they are joined by a short *anterior communicating artery.* The

anterior cerebral artery arrives at the genu of the corpus callosum and then courses posterior along the corpus callosum to the splenium. The branches of this artery supply the medial surface of the hemisphere almost as far posterior as the junction of the occipital and parietal lobe (fissure). They course over the margin of the hemisphere to supply a portion of the lateral surface. Through the anterior perforated area, the anterior cerebral artery supplies the head of the caudate, anterior pole of the lentiform nucleus and the anterior limb and genu of the internal capsule. It supplies the septum pellucidum and the septal area. Thus it supplies a portion of the motor area that controls the lower limbs. Its pathways in the internal capsule affect the motor supply to the head and arm. The septal region governs consciousness; interruptions of blood supply to the corpus callosum may result in apraxia.

b. Middle Cerebral

The *middle cerebral artery courses* from just lateral to the optic chiasma, posterior and laterally into the *insula* and on to the lateral fissure. It supplies the inferior portion of the lateral aspect of the frontal lobe and much of the temporal lobe but not the uncus, which is supplied by branches of the anterior cerebral artery. Coursing through the central sulcus it supplies motor and sensory areas for the upper half of the body. Vessels entering the lateral aspect of the *anterior perforated area* supply the external capsule, putamen, caudate, lateral globus pallidus and much of the internal capsule.

The vertebral arteries enter the skull through the foramen magnum and ascend along the inferior surface of the medulla to join each other at the junction of the medulla and pons. Here they form one vessel, the **basilar artery.** At the end of the pons segment the basilar divides into right and left **stems of the posterior cerebral arteries** on the midbrain. These ascend to the diencephalon where they give off the **posterior communicating artery** which courses along the base of the diencephalon to join with the internal carotid. This is very important because it means that the two systems, vertebral and carotid, are connected. It means that if, for example, the vertebral blood supply was compromised, some arterial supply could come from the internal carotid.

c. Posterior Cerebral

The *posterior cerebral artery* lies between the parahippocampal gyrus and the brain stem coursing to the splenium where it enters the calcarine sulcus. It therefore supplies the hippocampal formation, including the hippocampus and the dentate nucleus, and the inferior temporal gyrus on the one hand and the visual area of the cortex on the other. It supplies the lateral aspect of the occipital lobe. It supplies the inferior temporal area. Importantly, this artery also supplies the choroids plexus of the midbrain (red nucleus, most cranial nerves), diencephalon, third ventricle and the lateral ventricles. It also supplies the thalamus and subthalamus.

3. Anterior Choroidal Artery

There is another, smaller, artery that should be mentioned. It is the **anterior choroidal.** It arises from the internal carotid lateral to the optic chiasma coursing to the choroid plexus of the inferior horn of the ventricle. It supplies the optic tract, the optic radiation in the sublenticular part of the internal capsule, the posterior limb of the internal capsule, the globus pallidus, the subthalamic nucleus, uncus and part of the hippocampal formation.

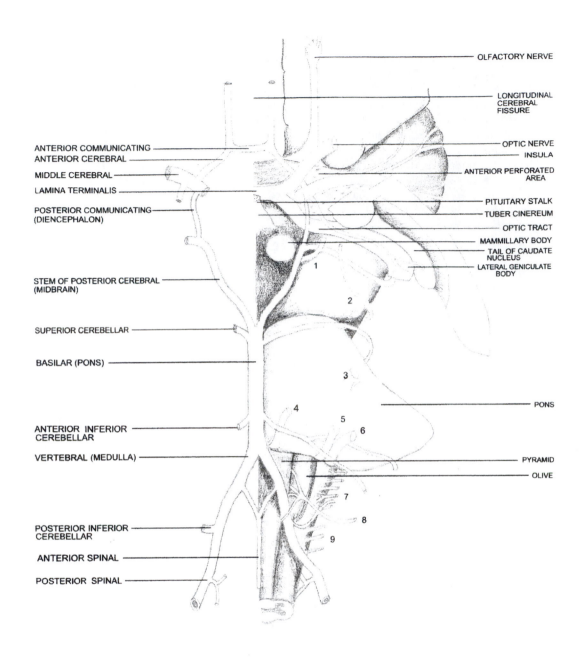

ANTERIOR COMMUNICATING
ANTERIOR CEREBRAL
MIDDLE CEREBRAL
LAMINA TERMINALIS
POSTERIOR COMMUNICATING
(DIENCEPHALON)

STEM OF POSTERIOR CEREBRAL
(MIDBRAIN)

SUPERIOR CEREBELLAR

BASILAR (PONS)

ANTERIOR INFERIOR
CEREBELLAR

VERTEBRAL (MEDULLA)

POSTERIOR INFERIOR
CEREBELLAR

ANTERIOR SPINAL

POSTERIOR SPINAL

OLFACTORY NERVE

LONGITUDINAL
CEREBRAL
FISSURE

OPTIC NERVE
INSULA
ANTERIOR PERFORATED
AREA

PITUITARY STALK
TUBER CINEREUM
OPTIC TRACT
MAMMILLARY BODY
TAIL OF CAUDATE
NUCLEUS
LATERAL GENICULATE
BODY

PONS

PYRAMID
OLIVE

Blood Supply to the Base of the Brain (Numbers refer to Cranial Nerves) (After Smith, 1962)

4. Brief Summary

If you have followed this description, you may note at this juncture that the arterial supply from the vertebral basilar system is linked with the internal carotid system in a circle at the base of the midbrain and diencephalon: basilar artery – stem of the posterior cerebral – posterior communicating artery – internal carotid – anterior carotid – anterior communicating – anterior carotid – internal carotid – posterior communicating – posterior cerebral – basilar.

I. The Autonomic Nervous System
1. Overview

The ANS is part of the motor system. In the viscera this system is distinguished by the fact that ANS motor nerves are paired: excitatory and inhibitory. You may think of the excitatory portion being, for the most part, sympathetic, while the inhibitory is parasympathetic. The ANS controls the activity of smooth muscle, cardiac muscle and glands. It controls musculature in the digestive system, gall bladder, urinary bladder, eyes, blood vessels, respiratory system and in hair follicles. All the sphincters in the digestive and urinary systems are controlled by smooth muscles. The glands include the adrenal, salivary glands, lacrimal glands, and sweat glands. The ANS influences the digestive system including the pancreas, the respiratory system, the urinary system, the cardiovascular system and aspects of the reproductive system and glandular system.

2. Sympathetic Division

For the most part you can think of the sympathetic nervous system (SNS) as being involved in processes that activate and expend energy (catabolic). The cell bodies of the SNS are located in the thoracic and lumbar regions of the spinal cord. The axons exit through the ventral roots of the spinal cord. The majority of these preganglionic fibers synapse in ganglia in the sympathetic chain or trunk or in ganglia of the prevertibral plexus. This is in contrast to the parasympathetic system where the ganglia are all close to the organ being innervated. The nerves of the SNS are motor nerves but the fibers do contain some sensory nerves from the organs.

The synapses within the sympathetic ganglia are acetylcholinergic. However, the terminal *buttons* on the target organs are noradrenergic. An exception to this, which you might predict, is the innervation of the sweat glands which is acetylcholinergic. The endings in the adrenal medulla are acetylcholinergic because it is innervated directly by preganglionic fibers. The output of the medulla is adrenergic (epinephrine and norepinephrine). This is important because these hormones, apart from acting like the sympathetic system (for example, increasing heart rate) also act to stimulate the production of glucose (for energy) from glycogen in muscle cells. The adrenal cortex, on the other hand, is not under direct nerve control but is stimulated by adrenocorticotropic hormone (ACTH) from the anterior pituitary to secrete cortisone.The anterior pituitary is, in turn, controlled by hormones released by the hypothalamus. These hormones enter arterioles which feed small veins in a specialized vascular system that feeds the anterior pituitary.

In our work we are able to measure sympathetic stimulation with respect to its effects on increasing heart rate, peripheral vasoconstriction (which is observed in a decrease in finger - peripheral - skin temperature), and in increasing palm and finger sweating (electrodermal response). It has also been found that there is sympathetic innervation of the muscle spindles in the skeletal muscle system.

3. Parasympathetic Division

For the most part you can think of the parasympathetic nervous system (PSNS) as being involved in processes that inhibit and those that produce or conserve energy (anabolic). It increases the secretion of digestive juices and the blood flow to the gastrointestinal system. It affects salivation and intestinal motility. In contrast to the SNS, the nerves of the PSNS leave the CNS in cranial nerves 3, 7, 9, & 10 and in sacral nerves 2, 3, & 4. The cell bodies or ganglia of the PSNS are located close to the organs which they supply. Therefore, compared to the SNS the postganglionic fibers are relatively short. Although these are motor nerves, they do carry sensory afferents from some organs, such as the chemoreceptors in the mouth, stretch receptors in the lung and receptors in the carotid body. The terminal buttons of both the pre and postganglionic fibers of the PSNS are acetylcholinergic.

In our work we are able to observe the effects of the PSNS with respect to its effect on slowing heart rate with respiratory expiration.

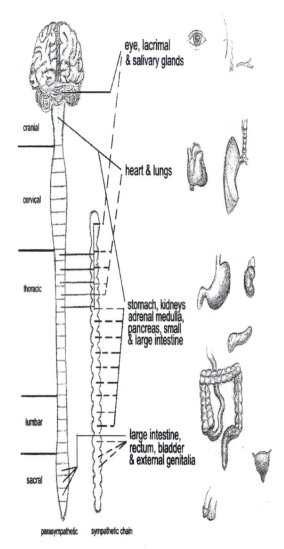

eye, lacrimal & salivary glands

cranial

heart & lungs

cervical

thoracic

stomach, kidneys adrenal medulla, pancreas, small & large intestine

large intestine, rectum, bladder & external genitalia

lumbar

sacral

parasympathetic   sympathetic chain

Schematic Diagram of the Autonomic Nervous System

J. Brief Overview of the Neurophysiology of the Stress Response

The stress response is an adaptive biological mechanism that was important for survival of the human species. As previously noted, we explain to children that when our ancestors were in great danger they had to fight or flee to survive. Children enjoy imagining a tiger jumping out of the forest and figuring out how the early caveman would handle this emergency in order to survive. He would need to have maximum

energy (oxygen and nutrition) in the large muscles of his shoulders and legs. This would require an immediate increase in blood flow to these areas. He did not need to be digesting food or even have much blood flow to his hands and feet. This is why heart rate increases and the finger tips are cool when someone is anxious. Also, the caveman had to be sure his spear would not slip in his hand, so the hand becomes moist when we are under stress. The sympathetic nervous system is responsible for these reactions. This sympathetic system also has another protective function. It prevents extensive bleeding and tissue damage in the acute phase of stress. *Homeostasis* is maintained despite the stressors.

The stress response is controlled by interaction along a brain stem (locus coeruleus)-amygdala-hypothalamus (sympathetic system)-pituitary-adrenal axis (AHPA) with the frontal lobes and hippocampus having a major influence through connections to the amygdala and hypothalamus. The best overview of this that we have read is a paper entitled "The Hypothalamic-Pituitary Adrenal Axis" written by Carolyn Smith-Pellettier, of York University, Toronto, Canada and presented at the annual meeting of the Canadian Medical Association (2003). Hopefully this will eventually be published. Some of it will be briefly summarized here.

When over-stressed this AHPA system can fail. When this AHPA axis becomes dysregulated a number of disorders may be observed. Hypoactivity may result in symptoms of anxiety, fibromyalgia and chronic pain. (A factor in this is that hypothalamic, corticotrophin-releasing-hormone (CRH) has analgesic actions and lower levels could contribute to pain). These are disorders for which we have traditionally used biofeedback (see Section VII, Autonomic Nervous System). Hyperactivity of this AHPA axis, on the other hand, has been implicated in depression.

Biochemically, the normal response to stress involves a sequence of events. A simplified version of what occurs is as follows. The thalamus and amygdala signal the locus coeruleus (LC) in the brain stem to release norepinephrine (NE). This has the effect of increasing selective attention to new stimuli and arousing the sympathetic division of the autonomic system (blood pressure, heart rate, sweating). The effect of increased NE in the

AHPA axis is to increase hypothalamic output of adreno-corticotrophin hormone (ACTH) which stimulates the adrenal glands to produce glucocorticoids (GC). Cortisol counteracts the effects of increased norepinephrine and epinephrine. GC *down-regulates* the CRH producing cells, which in turn, decreases the CRH stimulation of the locus coeruleus to produce NE. The overall effect is to reinstitute homeostasis. Endogenous opiates are also released. These increase the pain threshold.

In addition, in the normal stress response the central nucleus of the amygdala stimulates the hypothalamic production of corticotrophin-releasing hormone (CRH) and argenine vasopressin (AVP). These act to increase AHPA axis activity. Serotonin can also increase the AHPA axis activity. NE and CRH are both involved in the affective responses to stress including: fear, constricted affect, and even stereotypical thinking.

When the brain senses that the full stress response is no longer essential, the AHPA axis is dampened by frontal and hippocampal input. This results in a decrease in ACTH production and a return of the system to its resting state.

The stress response is designed as a short-lived protective mechanism which can improve the chances for survival in a fight or flight situation. Acute improvements in arousal level, memory, focus, and in the immune system occur. However, when stress becomes chronic, abnormal alterations in the system can occur. Corticotrophin releasing hormone (CRH) from the hypothalamus may remain very high despite the high levels of GC. This actually stimulates further output of NE from the locus coeruleus. The increased NE will cause additional increases in the central nucleus of the amygdala activity and this will cause an increase in CRH production from the hypothalamus. It becomes a vicious circle. In unpredictable chronic stress high CRH and high NE will decrease serotonin (5HT) levels. This may result in symptoms of anxiety and depression.

In chronic anxiety and stress CRH and NE levels are held high and the CRH stimulation from the central nucleus of the amygdala will over-ride the modulating effects of GC feedback and continue to activate the CRH production. The decrease in serotonin seen in chronic stress will initially still allow AVP to stimulate the AHPA axis when a new acute stress occurs which, allbeit perhaps temporary, is a good factor. However, this lowered serotonin level will also have the effect of decreasing the modulating effects of the hippocampus on the AHPA axis. Further anxiety will then begin to result in dysregulation of the AHPA axis. The production of CRH will then decrease under this chronic on-going stress. GC levels will then fall, with the result that the modulating influence of GC feedback (to lower the production of NE from the locus coeruleus) is impaired. There is an increase in NE levels and a less adaptive reaction to new stressors. This is what is seen in disorders such as fibromyalgia and chronic pain (Pacak, 1995)

Thus hyperactivity of the AHPA axis with resultant increased CRH increases response-sensitivity to noxious stimuli and depletes the immune system, while hypoactivity can result in chronic pain. The symptoms of over-activity in the AHPA axis are familiar to anyone in the mental health field. These clients exhibit a narrowing of their perspective, producing a focus on their own preoccupations with ruminative thinking and poor cognitive performance. Their sleep is impaired which further compounds their difficulties.

Stress interferes with sleep. There are many biochemical substances involved in this complex process. Only a few of them will be mentioned in this very brief overview. GABA is important in the initiation of sleep. GABA is activated by cholinergic pathways from the brain stem to the thalamus and to the forebrain. GABA decreases the blood flow to the thalamus. It is the shutting down of the thalamus that is responsible for the loss of consciousness in sleep. GABA also dampens the NE output of the locus coeruleus. However, as we have noted above, anxiety increases NE production. If this cannot be reduced, then sleep onset will not occur. GABA also acts to decrease basal ganglia functions causing muscle 'paralysis' (except for breathing) early in sleep. With high anxiety this transitory phenomena may still occur momentarily but sleep does not occur.

In normal sleep, in very general terms, the biochemistry is different in the first and second halves of the process. During the first half of the night growth hormone (GH) is produced and GC are reduced. Slow wave sleep is initiated, in part, by a decrease in ACTH and GC caused by hippocampal influences which decrease the AHPA axis activity during this first half of sleep.

An increase in AHPA axis activity is therefore associated with insomnia. Thus, in chronic stress or chronic pain or fibromyalgia the client will be likely also to suffer from insomnia.

During the second half of the night most people have a more shallow sleep. This is caused by a decrease in GH and increased GC and a rise in CRH. Increased CRH increases ACTH and GC and these substances will reduce slow wave sleep. CRH can induce awakening. (CRH in the central nucleus of the amygdala is also involved in the induction of hyperarousal and fear-related behaviours.)

There are male / female differences in this process but these will not be covered here. In general, the AHPA axis and CRH activity is higher in females. This might make females more susceptible to insomnia with stress. Aging decreases growth hormone releasing hormone (GHRH) and thus GH. This results in a decrease in deep or slow wave sleep with a concomitant decrease in immune regeneration and a reduction in the pain threshold. The increased influence of CRH results in frequent awakening.

The immune response is dampened by glucocorticoids (GC). As we noted earlier, chronic stress initially increases GC and will suppress the immune response and even lead to a reduction in the size of the thymus and a reduction in circulating lymphocytes.

Chronic stress is clearly a very dangerous phenomenon that can have a number of untoward effects. Biofeedback has been demonstrated to be somewhat effective in helping to decrease the symptoms caused by stress. We feel that it is likely that future work will demonstrate that the combination of neurofeedback and biofeedback may assist clients to even more effectively self regulate their responses to stress in their daily lives.

K. Linking Neurophysiology to Disorders That May be Amenable to Neurofeedback Interventions

Now that we have had a brief overview of neuroanatomy, we can hypothesize about how the various structures may work together in selected conditions in which NFB is used. These disorders involve links between the cortex, basal ganglia and the thalamus. These disorders include:

1. Memory problems
2. Obsessive Compulsive Disorder
3. Tourette's Syndrome
4. Reward Deficiency Syndrome
5. Attention Deficit Disorder (ADHD)
6. Movement disorders: Dystonia, Parkinson's Disease
7. Asperger's Syndrome

1. Disorders involving Memory

Memory may be understood in terms of a specific group of neurons which have come to fire in the same pattern each time they are activated. Memory is laid down by *long-term potentiation* (LTP). This is a process wherein each time the neuron-sequence is fired the links between the neurons are strengthened. This follows from Hebb's rule of learning which states: "When an axon of cell A … excites cell B and repeatedly or persistently takes part in firing it, some growth takes place in one or both cells so that A's efficiency as one of the cells firing B is increased (Hebb, 1949). An example is motor memory when a person learns key-boarding; the fingers seem to remember where to find the letters once the person has practiced enough.

When doing NFB, you can teach students to facilitate this process of repetition and LTP. For an example, see the case of Jane in Section XII.

a. Types of Memory
i. Procedural Memory

Memories for procedures, such as the ability to play a card game like bridge, are stored in the cerebellum and putamen. Instincts, on the other hand, which are genetically encoded memories, are stored in the caudate nucleus. Memories associated with fear, such as phobias and flashbacks, are stored in (or triggered by) the amygdala

ii. Episodic Memory

Memory of a recent happening is best remembered if associated with emotions. These conscious memories are stored like 'films', encoded and held for about 2 to 3 years in the hippocampus. (The hippocampus is part of the limbic system as outlined above. It is situated in the medial temporal lobe.) Profound stress has been shown to have a detrimental effect on the hippocampus. Hippocampal memory includes **working memory.** Working memory involves keeping information in mind while performing some operation; for example, doing a 2-step math problem in your head. Memories may return to consciousness during dreaming. It is easiest to recall them when the individual is in the same state of mind (emotionally and chemically) that they were in when that memory was laid down. The inability of a person who drank too much one night to recall things he did or said when he awakens the next morning is an example of state dependant memory. Here are two examples.

Michael, age 21, was a university student. One night he returned home after studying at a friend's house while his parents had a party. The next morning he awoke early to go to his final exam. He drank some of the tomato juice that his parents had left in the refrigerator with his breakfast and left for the exam. He was unable to recall any of the material which he had been able to recall easily with his friends the night before the exam. The tomato juice had really been a Bloody Mary mix. Although not obviously inebriated, his brain was in a different chemical state from when his learning had taken place. Fortunately, the professor sympathized with his situation and he was able to successfully rewrite the exam later in the day and he did very well.

James had thoroughly reviewed material for his final 3-hour examination and had been teaching some of his classmates the material the night before the exam. He was a bright, laid back student who preferred studying with friends in a relaxed environment. The next day he felt extremely tense at the start of the exam. He said later that he went 'blank' when he read the first question. He couldn't remember a thing. After almost an hour of feeling panic and frustration, he decided to give up and then felt very relieved and relaxed as he got ready to leave the exam hall –' the heck with this nonsense' he was saying to himself. Suddenly he recalled everything. He returned to his desk, started writing furiously and got one of the top marks in the class.

In the first example it was a chemical change of state and in the second it was an emotional change of state. Memory and recall can be state dependent. It is helpful for students to have control over their state of mind when studying, going to lectures and taking exams. We use biofeedback to help them learn to relax and self regulate.

iii. Long Term Memory

Hippocampal memories gradually become stored as what we call *long-term memory* in the cortex of the temporal lobe. Episodic memories can take as long as two years to be laid down in the cortex so that they become linked together independently of the hippocampus. Recalling formal memories activates areas of the temporal lobe as well as areas in the frontal lobe. It may be that the frontal lobe involvement is necessary to bring the memory to consciousness.

iv. Semantic Memory:

The meaning of information, the facts, are registered and stored in the cortex of the temporal lobe independent of the personal memories of where you were or how you felt when you learned the fact. The latter details are part of episodic memory. Facts are encoded in the temporal lobe and retrieved by frontal lobe activity. In **Semantic Dementia** there is a loss of semantic or factual memory. The patient tends to forget the names of objects and what they are for. A recent study at the Imperial College of Medicine and reported at the annual meeting of the AAPB 2003 demonstrated improvement in semantic memory with SMR training.

v. Other
(1.) Memory Retrieval
Although the hippocampus and the temporal cortex are most often highlighted in discussions of memory, it is important to keep in mind that the frontal cortex is always involved in retrieval of any memory.

(2.) Memories are constantly changing
Memories are not just recalled, but also reconstructed. Memories are constantly undergoing changes. Errors in and distortions of recall are inevitable. Fragments of events are remembered. When the fragments are recalled, our brain works to make sense of them. Even a little suggestion in one direction may change the 'meaning' of the facts compared to a suggestion made in another direction. This 'new' or revised memory is then stored and so the process proceeds (Carter, p.170). This is an important consideration when discussing emotionally laden events with clients. It is particularly important if the therapist is doing alpha theta therapy. Here, the client is encouraged to enter a mental state in which they are supremely susceptible to recalling fragments of both memory and fantasy. This susceptibility extends to linking the two when laying down 'new' memories which may actually be *false memories.*

(3.) Memory and Emotion
The association cortex connects with the entorhinal cortex which impinges on the dentate gyrus. This connects to the hippocampus which connects via the fornix to the mammillary bodies and so to the limbic system and the thalamus and hence to the cortex. These connections are all two-way. Memory involves this system. Emotions and memory are inextricably entwined in this system which connects the cortex, involved in the laying down of memories and the limbic system.

b. Problems with Memory
i. Korsakoff's Syndrome
Alcoholics affected with this syndrome are unable to form new memories (*anterograde amnesia).* The person can still recall old, long term memories. It is associated with deterioration of the mammillary bodies, and in the dorsomedial nuclei of the thalamus.

ii. Anterograde Amnesia
The same picture of anterograde amnesia may be observed with bilateral damage or removal of the hippocampus. The patient remains forever in the past. Such a patient can still learn procedures through repetition. However, even as they get better at the procedure, they have no memory of having practiced it before! (Carter, p.172)

iii. Alzheimer's Dementia
This illness is due to deterioration of the hippocampus. Recent memory is gone and these patients often can't find their way around and frequently get lost.

iv. Senile Dementia
This is a similar process to Alzheimer's and has the same results but it comes on at a later age.

2. Obsessive Compulsive Disorders (OCD)
This disorder affects about three percent of the population. The pathophysiology involves an overactive loop of neural activity between the **orbital prefrontal cortex,** which is involved in feeling that something is wrong, to the **caudate nucleus,** which gives the urge to act on personal memories or on instincts such as cleaning or grooming, to the **cingulate,** which is important in registering conscious emotion and which can keep focus or attention fixed on the feeling of unease. The client's error detection system is stuck on alert. The caudate nucleus is involved in automatic thinking; for example when you check that you closed the fridge, turned off the stove, locked the door. Over-activity of this circuit means constantly checking and rechecking. Brain scans show that when a person with OCD is asked to imagine something related to their compulsion (such as dirt if it is someone who must compulsively clean) their caudate and prefrontal cortex light up. In NFB we tend to work to reduce this over-activity. We have found this over-activity during the EEG assessment at a number of different sites. Although it is usually found frontally (F3, Fz, or F4) it may also be found centrally and even at Pz.. The assessment guides the placement of the electrode for neurofeedback. The task is to decrease very high amplitude beta where this has been observed in the QEEG assessment. Alternatively, one may work on the right side

and decrease beta while increasing high alpha, a suggestion that has been made by Lubar. We have decreased high beta activity (21-34 Hz) at a mid point between FZ and CZ. Although not published, some clinicians have experienced some success by using regular biofeedback to decrease anxiety (discussed later under Adjunctive Techniques) while also doing neurofeedback, increasing 11-15 Hz activity at C4 and P4. What is in common to these suggestions is decreasing very high amplitude bursts of beta at sites where this has been observed on the QEEG and decreasing anxiety and tension using biofeedback and neurofeedback.

3. Tourette's Syndrome

In Tourette's Syndrome the **putamen** is overactive. The putamen is related to the *urge to do fragments of preprogrammed motor skills.* The putamen is linked to the **premotor cortex** which governs the production of the actual movements. Instead of the relatively complete procedures seen with compulsions, the motor and vocal tics appear in Tourette's Syndrome as fragments of known actions. Oliver Sacks has written a superb description of a surgeon with this disorder in his 1995 book *An Anthropologist on Mars.* In NFB work we tend to encourage the increase of SMR (usually between 13-15 Hz.) and decrease theta at C4. There have been studies using C3 and Cz placements as well. We also decrease sympathetic drive using biofeedback concerning respiration. The rationale for these procedures is given below under movement disorders and dystonia and has been published (Thompson & Thompson, 2002).

4. Reward Deficiency Syndrome

This is similar to OCD but the compulsive behaviour revolves around a pleasurable activity. The person can never get enough of that which they feel they need, such as food, drugs, or gambling (Blum, 1996). In these disorders the cortex is stimulated by something internal (such as hunger) or external (news report on dog races that relates to that person's gambling compulsion). The limbic system is associated with a strong *urge* or desire. When the activity is carried out, the limbic system causes the release of opioid-like substances which result in a dopamine surge and a feeling of satisfaction. At the time of writing we do not have evidence of the efficacy of neurofeedback for this difficult syndrome. We suggest that you follow the assessment findings and the procedure outlined under OCD above. You must discuss the experimental nature of this work with you client and only proceed with their consent.

5. Attention Deficit Disorder
a. Introduction
There are a number of different theories and findings which attempt to delineate the areas of the brain which are primarily involved in attention. Needless to say, one theory doesn't always link cleanly to another. This section will thus present a few different perspectives. Perhaps one of the most elegant formulations was proposed by Molly Malone and her colleagues in 1994. It will be outlined first. Since theta is considered a biological *marker* for the majority of people with Attention Deficit Disorder (ADD) and this is highly relevant to NFB, we will attempt to paraphrase Sterman's thoughts on its production. This will be followed by a short summary of the essence of a number of other suggestions concerning attention.

b. Background to Themes about ADD
In general the left and right cerebral hemispheres are involved in different aspects of attention as follows:

i. The Left Cerebral Hemisphere
This hemisphere is involved in focused, selective attention which favours contralateral space. It is involved in information processing which requires foveal vision, object identification and what Malone refers to as the ventral/anterior system. The principle neurotransmitter for sustained attentional activity and information processing in this hemisphere is dopamine.

It is postulated that in ADD there is reduced dopamine in the fronto-mesolimbic system in the left hemisphere. The type of cognitive processing which is affected and deficient is that which requires slow, serial effort. This type of processing is called *tonic*. The left hemisphere is biased in the direction of carrying out routine and repetitive activities. It is this kind of processing that may be improved with stimulant medication. With the EEG one can observe that as the task becomes boring, the person with ADD will drift off the task. There is an increase in slow wave activity. This is similar to the slowing of electrical activity as we become drowsy. In ADD it is really a modulation of functions that is the primary problem. On the one hand, arousal may increase and actions without reflection may occur; on the other hand, the tolerance for routine, boring activities is low in these individuals and their arousal may suddenly drop rapidly. These characteristics may be improved by stimulant medications and, also, by NFB. Often generalizations about arousal are fueled by older beliefs that the majority of people with ADD were hyperactive. Arousal is an issue but a complex one. Most people with ADD have extremes of arousal, in both directions, which are not always appropriate to the situation in which they find themselves. They may be impulsive on the one hand and literally fall asleep in a classroom on the other hand. Stimulants may help them to better modulate arousal while the drug is in the body at the proper dose. Biofeedback using skin conductance (electrodermal response) combined with NFB can have the same modulating effect - and give a long-term result.

Theoretically, many of the foregoing symptoms may be due to under activation of dopaminergic activity in the left hemisphere. Dopaminergic over-activity, on the other hand, is thought to be associated with blunting of affect, excessive intellectual ideation and introversion. Pathologically, it may underlie other disorders including: paranoid states, anxiety, obsessive compulsive disorder (OCD) and schizophrenia.

ii. The Right Cerebral Hemisphere

This hemisphere is involved in the general maintenance of attention and arousal which is wide to extra-personal space. It regulates information processing which requires peripheral vision, spatial location, rapid shifts in attention. These aspects of attention appear to involve the noradrenergic system.

The noradrenergic system is thus more involved in initial attention plus arousal and wakefulness. It appears to be related to alertness and to responses to change and to new stimuli.

In Attention Deficit Disorder there might be excessive locus coeruleus norepinephrine production and excess noradrenergic stimulation to the right cerebral hemisphere. This represents minor brain stem involvement in arousal (usually arousal is discussed in terms of the involvement of the pontine reticular system). This excessive norepinehrine production has been suggested because Clonidine affects α_2 inhibitory receptors in the locus coeruleus and has been observed to reduce ADD symptoms possibly because it dampens activity in this area.

People with ADD seem to have automatic processing which is fast and simultaneous. These are called 'phasic' attentional abilities. This style of attention is biased towards novelty and change. It has also been noted that overactivation of the noradrenergic system in the right hemisphere is associated with extroversion, histrionic behaviour, impulsivity and manic behaviours (Tucker, 1984).

iii. Brief Summary of Dopaminergic & Noradrenergic Theory (Malone)

According to an excellent paper by Molly Malone and a number of other ADD experts, ADD is characterized by a relative **left hemispheric underactivation.** This involves the left-anterior-ventral-**dopaminergic** system. Combined with this is a **right hemisphere overactivation** or overarousal. This overarousal involves the right-posterior-dorsal-**noradrenergic** system. It could be postulated that this overactivation might be due to a lack of left hemisphere inhibitory control of the right hemisphere. Medications, when appropriately used may correct this imbalance, but high doses may actually reverse this imbalance and produce a different set of problems.

Also discussed in this formulation is the possibility that ADD might be due to left sided dysfunctional dopamine rich frontal-striatal connections with decreased glucose metabolism, plus dysfunctional connections (smaller rostral corpus callosum) adversely affecting regulation of attention between two hemispheres

(Castellanos, p. 246). As an aside, females have a larger corpus callosum (more connections between the two hemispheres). Rates of diagnosis of ADD are much higher in boys – at least 6:1. It may be posited that the right hemisphere functions are being modulated less by the left hemisphere in boys.

In addition, a question is raised as to whether in the ADD inattentive type, there may be right frontal dysfunction. This group demonstrates a tendency for hemispatial neglect of left side. (This is condition is found with brain lesions on the right.) Further, there is the possibility that this right frontal dysfunction might be responsible for a decreased inhibition of right posterior areas which would explain the high distractibility to external stimuli in these individuals.

This theoretical framework is supported, in part, by the observed actions of stimulant medications. These may be listed as follows (Malone, 1994):

- Stimulants in animal studies block uptake of norepinephrine (NEP) and dopamine in the striatum, hypothalamus and the cortex.
- Stimulants facilitate release of dopamine (but not NEP) from the striatum (which includes the caudate.) – It has been observed that the left caudate is small in individuals with ADD. However, stimulants will increase activity in the left striatum (increase blood flow).
- Stimulants dampen activity in the locus coeruleus.
- Stimulants increase Left Hemisphere processing speed.
- Stimulants decrease Right Hemisphere processing speed.

c. Sterman's Hypothesis Concerning the Production of Theta

i. Cortex-Putamen-(Globus Pallidus)-Substantia Nigra-Thalamus

This model is based on M. Barry Sterman's hypothetical framework. Decreased blood flow to, and metabolic activity in, the cells in the frontal / prefrontal areas (including the motor **cortex**) may *lead to r*educed excitation by the motor cortex (layer VI) of the inhibitory cells in the **putamen.** This may result in thalamic relay cells producing bursts of activity at slow frequencies, and then by projection, to the anterior association cortex (layer IV). This results in theta activity being produced which we pick up in the EEG. Two parallel pathways for this origin of theta are proposed: the first involves a direct effect of the putamen on the substantia nigra, while the second is a more indirect route involving an external globus pallidus – subthalamus – (internal globus pallidus) -- substantia nigra pathway. Either way, the substantia nigra would increase its inhibition of areas of the thalamus resulting in the thalamic production of rhythmic bursts at frequencies in the theta range.

To recapitulate this hypothesis, there may be direct reduction in the inhibition by the putamen of the inhibitory cells in the **substantia nigra** which would result in the substantia nigra *being* released to increase its inhibition of the **thalamus.**

There may also be a longer chain of events. The reduced influence of the cortex on the putamen may result in the putamen producing increased inhibition of the external globus pallidus. (Then the external globus pallidus will not be inhibiting the subthalamus.) This would release the excitatory effects of the subthalamic nucleus on the internal globus pallidus and the substantia nigra. This would also result in an increased inhibition of the thalamus.

The net result of both pathways is increased inhibition of the ventral lateral (VL), ventral anterior (VA) and the centromedian (CM) nuclei of the thalamus. This would then result in hyper-polarization of the thalamic cells. These cells would depolarize then repolarize in a slow rhythmic manner. This would begin an oscillatory process that would be conveyed to the cortex. The end result of this cycle would be **theta in the EEG.** (Sterman 2000, DeLong 1990)

ii. Other Sources of Theta

Another postulated source of theta comes from animal (rat) studies. Theta is said to be paced by cholonergic pathways that project from the septal nuclei to the hippocampus. This would correspond to the observed involvement of theta in memory retrieval. Recall of words corresponds to synchronization of theta. This is thought to represent hippocampal theta (Klimesch et al., 1999). The question of whether hippocampal theta is only a rat phenomenon or whether it also occurs in humans is still under investigation. Future studies will probably help our understanding of a number of different mechanisms involved in theta production. Different kinds of theta, possibly from different *generators*, may be found to correspond to different mental states.

iii. Movement May Help Children With ADD

A theoretical model, such as Sterman's, can lead both to an understanding of observed behaviour and to changes in training strategies. Those with ADD are often observed to be much more active than their counterparts in situations where this may not be considered appropriate, such as in lectures or when listening to others in a social context. Most persons who work with children who have ADHD try to have them stop these seemingly non-productive movements. On the one hand, this need for physical activity makes sense. The brain can only consciously consider one thing at one time. Therefore, we don't want the child to be consciously thinking of twirling his pencil when he is supposed to be listening to a history lecture. On the other hand, Sterman's formulation makes us recognize that if the child doesn't maintain activity in the cortex, then the result will be inhibition of thalamic production of theta activity, less active processing in the frontal cortex and a drop in alertness.

We teach all our students the importance of maintaining focus on the cognitive activity they are supposed to be doing. This requires that they not focus on fidgeting types of activity. On the other hand we recognize that, with some individuals, if they don't move, their alertness may drop off rapidly. Think of Greeks manipulating their worry beads while thinking something through. We suggest they find a means of remaining 'active' which will increase (and not decrease) their attention to the problem at hand. Movement during a lecture might involve drawing something that would relate to the lecture content or it could involve note taking. Drawing would theoretically involve a different area of the brain and not compete and interfere with the left hemisphere problem solving cognitive work. However, the student must be careful not to let their focus linger on the drawing task.

With the advent of note-book computers one can type notes as a motor activity. For those ADD types who like to *multi-task*, there is the possibility of running two computer programs at once. The first records the lecture while the second incorporates the key points from the lecture into another document for a paper or for teaching.

In Sterman's proposal the sequence may involve:
1. The individual **moves around** to activate the cortex and counteract an increase of theta.
2. The individual feels more **alert**.
3. The individual reduces motor activity in order to read material and **learn**.
4. This experience fits a model of **reciprocity** between motor activity and visual attention.- *beta up at one site, down at the other.*
5. Very soon, however, the increased activation of the cortex decreases as the person is sitting still so theta starts to increase again.
6. The inhibition of the thalamus takes over again and theta increases.
7. The individual moves to activate the cortex again … and so on.

This is just a way of trying to understand how theta may be produced when we are not actively using our cortex. Remember, brain waves don't cause anything. Brain waves merely are like a flag. A flag tells us if there is wind and what direction the wind is coming from and perhaps a little about the strength of the wind. Brain waves merely signal that something is going on or not going on and with what intensity. They tell us a little about the person's mental state and how it is changing, or remaining stable, over time.

d. The Three Element Theory of Attention: Arousal, Orientation, Focus

Arousal

Arousal involves reticular activating system (RAS) activity. The nerve fibers from this system stretch as far as frontal cortex. They control consciousness, sleep/wake cycles, and the level of activity in the brain. The axons activating the prefrontal lobe release dopamine and noradrenaline and beta activity is observed.

Orientation

Orientation involves the Superior Colliculus (to turn the eyes) and parietal neuronal activity to disengage attention from the current stimulus.

Focus

The Lateral Pulvinar nucleus in the thalamus operates like a spotlight shining on the stimulus, locking on, shunting information about the target to the frontal lobes which then lock on and maintain attention.

Francis Crick, the co-winner of the Nobel Prize in 1962 for his work on DNA, is now studying the question of consciousness (the relationship between mind and brain) by looking at the visual process in humans. He notes that if we don't pay attention to some aspect of the visual scene, our memory of it is very transient and can be overwritten by a subsequent visual stimulus (Carter, p.205).

e. Other Findings concerning Areas involved in Attention

i. Orbito-frontal cortex

This area of the cortex and the prefrontal cortex are said to be involved in inhibiting inappropriate action. Decreased functional activity seems to be greatest in the left frontal area during tests of intellectual or attentional functions. (Sterman, 2000). Amen demonstrated a decrease in blood flow to the prefrontal cortex during a continuous performance task in 65% of his ADD subjects compared to 5% of the controls (Amen et al, 1997).

ii. Left Frontal and Prefrontal Cortex

Decreased activity in this area is not only implicated in ADD, but also in studies of affective disorders (Davidson, 1999).

iii. Anterior Cingulate Cortex (ACC)

This cortex focuses attention and facilitates tuning inwards to one's own thoughts. Increased blood flow on the **right** side of the ACC suggests that attention is focused on **internal events**. The ACC **distinguishes** between **internal and external** events and is under-active in schizophrenia where the subject is unable to distinguish their own thoughts from outside voices.

iv. Ventromedial Cortex

In this area of the cortex **emotions** are experienced and **meaning** is bestowed on perceptions.

v. Dorso-lateral Prefrontal Cortex:

This area is involved when you **hold** a thought in mind, **select** thoughts and perceptions to attend to, **inhibit** other thoughts and perceptions, **bind** the perceptions into a unified whole, endow them with **meaning**, **conceptualize, plan** and **choose**.

In her excellent book, *Mapping the Mind,* Rita Carter describes a *self-will experiment*. In this experiment it was found that lifting a finger will only involve activation of the prefrontal cortex when the subject is not told which finger to lift but must decide on their own. It seems that following an order does not bring an individual's the prefrontal cortex into play, but making a choice does.

vi. Neurotransmitters, Metabolic and Structural Differences

In ADD there appear to be genetic differences as compared to non-ADD controls with respect to dopamine receptors. These differences may lead to reduced dopaminergic activity (LaHoste et al, 1996). Deficiency in dopamine related functions in the frontal-striatal system is the basis of some theories as to the emergence of ADHD symptoms. (Charcot et al, 1996; Malone et al, 1994; Sterman, 2000).

ADD is primarily a frontal lobe dysfunction. The information from various measuring techniques converges to indicate decreased frontal activation. The EEG shows increased theta, Dan Amen's SPECT studies show decreased perfusion and Zametkin's PET studies show decreased glucose metabolism.

In addition to these findings in the frontal lobes, in ADD the blood perfusion and metabolic activity in the caudate may be decreased (Hynd, 1993; Zametkin, 1990). Magnetic resonance imaging (MRI) studies have shown decreased tissue volume in the frontal, premotor, sensorimotor cortex and in the caudate of ADD subjects (Hynd, 1993; Filipek, 1997) as reported in Sterman's review (2000).

vii. Reticular Formation
The reticular activating system is only fully myelinated after puberty. This may partially explain for why younger children have a short attention span. The RAS plays a major role in maintaining attention. A threat causes **activation** (a rush of adrenaline) which **closes down all unnecessary activity** leaving an alert brain which appears on a brain scanner as quiet. It also inhibits body activity. Breathing is shallow and quiet and heart rate slow. In this state, however, **activity remains** in the **superior colliculus** and the **lateral pulvinar nucleus** of the thalamus and in the **parietal cortex.** These areas are involved in **orienting and focusing.**

viii. Right Hemisphere Deficiencies in ADD
Imaging studies demonstrate decreased activity in the right hemisphere in the following areas: the **anterior cingulate** (fixing attention on a given stimulus), the **prefrontal cortex** (planning actions and controlling impulses, which also involves the orbito-frontal cortex) (Arnsten, p.186, Castellanos, p.251,) and the **upper auditory cortex** (integration of stimuli from several different sources.) Perhaps a lack of activity here prevents the child from grasping the whole picture and, instead, he views the world in fragments with one stimulus after another vying for attention.

Neuroimaging studies have also demonstrated differences between children who have ADHD and controls. Smaller volume in the right prefrontal brain regions, caudate nucleus, globus pallidus and a subregion of the cerebellar vermis have all been demonstrated. (Castellanos, 2001)

ix. Hippocampus – Septal Nuclei – Prefrontal Cortex Circuit
The diagram below illustrates one set of connections involved in focused attention

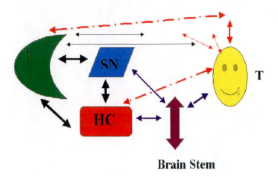

Brain Stem

Fundamental Links to Modulate Attention

BS = Brain Stem, T = Thalamus, SN = Septal Nuclei, HC = Hippocampus, PFC = Prefrontal Cortex

The hippocampus is important in selective inhibition of attention to things that might distract one's focus from the central problem. It also is a part of the brain's system for arousal, alertness, awareness, and orientation in the process of **focusing** attention on one set of environmental signals while excluding others. (In animals retrieval of memories in this process appears to be associated with the production of theta waves.) The hippocampus is also involved in laying down a conscious memory of events.

The prefrontal cortex processes incoming information about an event or a problem and then organizes a response. In this process it signals septal nuclei. (This takes about 300 msec and may be related to the P300 seen in ERP research. (Sieb, 1990) These nuclei then feedback to the hiuppocampus, thus completing the circuit. Inputs to all parts of this circuit come from the brainstem and the thalamus.

f. Stimulant Treatment and Neurofeedback Treatment for ADHD
i. The Stimulant Medications
In children younger than six and in adults, the response to stimulant medication is positive in only about 50% of cases. In school age children

there is about a 75% positive response rate to a trial of a stimulant drug.

Amphetamines raise excitatory neurotransmitters which stimulate the areas that are under-active in ADD. There are numerous studies that demonstrate performance improvements both in persons who have ADHD and in normal controls. The reader is referred to the chapter in *Stimulant Drugs and ADHD* titled, "Comparative Psychopharmacology of Methylphenidate and Related Drugs in Human Volunteers, Patients with ADHD and Experimental Animals" (Mehta et al. in Solanto et al., 2001 p.303-331). Stimulant medications have been shown to increase blood flow in the dorsolateral prefrontal cortex and posterior parietal cortex during tests of spatial working memory (Mehta et al., 2000). Complex working memory tasks and sustained attention may also improve with stimulant medication (Mehta et al., 2001 after Elliot, 1997; Koelega, 1993). Tests of cognitive flexibility in normal volunteers have shown that methylphenidate (40mg) can facilitate the shifting of attention toward newly relevant stimuli, but mean response latencies were increased (Mehta et al., 2001). Stimulant medications reduce the rate of both omission and commission errors on continuous performance tests. (Losier et al., 1996).

Both neurofeedback and the stimulant medications improve the symptoms of ADHD (inattention, distractibility, hyperactivity and impulsivity) in a reasonable percentage of children who have this disorder. There may be some similarities in their actions. However, the goal of NFB is to effect a lasting change in the system through learning, while the goal of stimulant medication is to produce a temporary shift while the drug action persists. Theoretically, the cortical activity stimulants produce has inhibitory effects on the limbic system and thus help to substitute thought for action and produce a more controlled and focused behaviour. It has been found that some people who have ADD may have a genetic alteration in the D4 dopamine receptors (Solanto, 2001, p.356). Ritalin blocks the re-uptake of dopamine, particularly in the striatum. Frontal – striatal circuits that also involve the globus pallidus and the thalamic nuclei may be implicated in ADHD. The frontal areas appear to be important in selection of appropriate stimuli, suppression of irrelevant stimuli and suppression of inappropriate actions. These are the three cardinal symptoms of ADD: inattention, distractibility and impulsivity. Theoretically, the same circuits may account for the observed increase in theta seen in the EEG in children with ADD. As explained above, in ADD the striatum may exert too little inhibition on the globus pallidus. The globus pallidus then inhibits certain thalamic nuclei. These neurons become hyperpolarized and fire in a specific rhythm in the theta range. This activity is conveyed to the cortex and detected in the EEG. (Kropotov, 1997; Sterman, 2000).

EEG differences between children with ADHD and normals (higher theta/beta ratios) have been shown in a number of studies (Mann 1992; Janzen 1995; Monastra, 1999; Clarke 2001). Interestingly, stimulants do not appear to lower the theta / beta ratios significantly but neurofeedback training has been shown to have this effect. This work was originally done by Joel Lubar and has since been replicated by others. EEG studies are beginning to demonstrate different subtypes of ADHD clients according to different patterns found on brain maps (Chabot, 1996; Sterman, 2000). Three groups are clear in Sterman's work: excess theta in the prefrontal cortex, generalized excess of theta in frontal and central leads, an excess of alpha activity at C3, C4 and frontally. Other researchers (Chabot, 2001 ; Clarke, 2001) have noted a group of ADHD subjects who have high amplitudes of beta. (In our experience many clients with ADHD symptoms who demonstrate high amplitude beta (and a low theta / beta ratio at F5 and F6) or high amplitude spindling beta at F3 and Fz and / or F4 also have high theta / beta ratios at Cz). This high amplitude beta, in our experience, is most often directly associated with other disorders, including depression with ruminations, obsessive compulsive disorder, and so on. This high beta has also been observed when one client with a diagnosis of schizophrenia kept tuning out and attending to repetitive delusional thoughts. (This observation will have to be replicated in other centres.). Further, we usually find that this high amplitude beta is often between 23 and 34 Hz. If anxiety is a component of their difficulties then high amplitude bursts of 20 –22 Hz activity may also be observed.

One exception to the above rule-of-thumb are those individuals who lapse into intense cognitive activity during testing and produce high amplitude bursts of beta between 14 and 19 Hz. Some of these clients also tune out and show bursts of high amplitude theta or alpha. Their overall theta / beta ratio is low. Their problem is, however, not an inability to focus when they want to, but rather variability and tuning out in high thalpha when they feel they should have been attentive to someone speaking or to what they were reading. The lesson to be learned from this description is that power averages and post-hoc EEG analysis do not tell the whole story. The clinician must revert to old-fashioned 'know-thy-patient' clinical observation and skills. **In order to correctly interpret the EEG for a particular client, the clinician must, initially, repeatedly pause the recording and enquire about what was going on in the client's mind with each EEG shift. This will allow the clinician and the client to better understand how those shifts in the EEG correspond to shifts in that client's mental state.**

Brief Summary

Research on the fine points of how stimulants may act or on how theta rhythms may be produced does not tell the whole story. For clinicians who have treated thousands of children using medications, behaviour modification, educational approaches and now using NFB, it is apparent that all of these approaches can be beneficial. The medications give the quickest response and are most useful in acute, *urgent* situations. Medications, behaviour modification and remedial educational approaches all give good *short-term* outcomes to many children. For a *long-term* change NFB may prove to the treatment of choice. Neurofeedback is based, for the most part, on two premises: first, increased theta activity does correspond to decreased attention to external stimuli (and less retention of material that the child is either reading or being taught) and, second, on the observation that increasing SMR corresponds to a decrease in both hyperactivity and impulsivity. NFB takes time (often 40 or more sessions) to take effect but the effects appear to be long lasting. Lubar has done one 10 year follow-up (Lubar, 1995) showing that results lasted. We know that stimulants improve the performance of many of these children who have ADHD. On the other hand the precise reason for these observed improvements, although well researched as noted above, remains somewhat confusing and at times contradictory. The stimulant medications may affect these circuits as previously noted. However, the effect on the EEG is minimal (Lubar, 1999), whereas one would have expected

to see marked changes in the EEG. In addition, some observant parents report that their children's eyes *glaze over* (go out of focus) just as frequently on the medications as off them. These same parents will comment that, although their child seems to still go out of focus frequently, they do stay with the task longer and perform better on stimulants than off. Certainly there is reasonable agreement that stimulants, used in children who have ADHD, are excellent chemical restraints and do have a marked effect on impulsivity and hyperactivity and, thus, do fairly uniformly have a secondary positive effect on focus, sustaining concentration and work completion. However, they are drugs and they can have unwanted effects which may prove to be long term although there are no controlled studies to help with this question. Indeed, as one neuropharmacologist succinctly characterized it in a professional lecture, the child on a high dose of Ritalin may look like a deer caught in the headlights of car. Further research is needed and it would be helpful if this included a neurologically and functionally valid operational definition of attention in the classroom situation.

In summary, stimulants are effective for the short-term management of behavioural symptoms. Neurofeedback produces lasting effects on behaviour, academic achievement and even on IQ scores.

ii. A Case Example – Before the Availability of Neurofeedback

Johnny (fictitious name) was a handful as a preschooler and he was referred to a child psychiatrist once he entered Kindergarten. Ritalin (methylphenidate) in a dose of 10 mg twice a day was prescribed at age 6 when he was in the Spring-term in Senior Kindergarten. Although it was somewhat effective in controlling his impulsivity, it was principally effective in decreasing the hyperactivity and decreasing his distractibility to external stimuli. Nevertheless, there remained a 'roller coaster' effect due to its short duration of action. Additionally, there was rebound hyperactivity and increased emotionality as the drug effects wore off each day. He also had no appetite while on the drug and was not gaining weight.

Therefore a trial of Dexedrine (dextro-amphetamine) was attempted using 5 mg twice a day. It was more effective than Ritalin had been. Nevertheless, on reviewing the total symptom picture in the Fall of the school year it was clear that Johnny had become very discouraged, frustrated and depressed. He was crying over the slightest occurrence and seemed very irritable; he couldn't be comforted or calmed when he was upset. He demonstrated some 'regressive' behaviour, such as hiding under the dining room table when he didn't want to do something. He was very sensitive to any comments that he perceived as being critical so it was hard to correct or discipline him. He became obsessive in the sense of being fixated upon and unable to 'let go of' any idea he had his mind set on, such as a toy he wanted. He was becoming very, very difficult for his parents to handle.

The next year, in December in Grade One, the diagnosis of depression was considered and the psychiatrist decided to place him on an antidepressant. Desipramine (a tricyclic anti-depressant) was chosen as it can be effective in ADHD and it may have less anticholinergic effects as compared to medications such as imipramine. Within 3 weeks there was a very marked beneficial effect. The temper tantrums stopped and he was able to control his anger and calm himself down. He wasn't nearly as 'fragile' and irritable as he had been. In play therapy sessions it was clear that he could focus and be creative with the materials and he became much more patient when his parents and the psychiatrist were talking. He would find things to occupy himself at home which mother describes as an 'all time first'.

However, by the end of January, some of the beneficial effects were wearing off and he became increasingly impulsive. Dexedrine was reintroduced in order to better control impulsivity and increase his attention span in school. This seemed to be effective at doses of 10 mg at 8 am and 5 mg at noon. It was necessary to be careful and do regular checks on tricyclic blood levels due to the possibility or an adverse drug interaction (each of the medications could increase the level of the other one).

In March the good effects noted above for the desipramine seemed to be wearing off. This can happen and when it does, one normally merely raises the dose by a small increment. One hopes this will only have to be done once or twice. However, Johnny was already at a dose of 150 mg which can be considered at the high end of an effective adult dose of this medication. A

blood level was done and it was found to be in the therapeutic range. Rather than raising the dose further, a different tricyclic was tried in the hope that it might be as effective but at a lower dose level.

A trial with amitriptyline (Elavil) was begun. On bringing down the dose of desipramine Johnny became quite emotionally fragile or brittle and was quite depressed and very difficult to handle. He was completely unable to occupy himself. He seemed to feel badly about his behaviour but unable to control it. On a dose of 100 mg Elavil he stabilized and was behaving as he had on the much higher dose of desipramine. The improvement didn't last.

Every medication used and every combination had initially had dramatically good effects. These initial good effects, however, were not sustained and the parents and psychiatrist were left wondering if he were worse off now when off medications than he had been before medication treatment was started.

The story of Johnny underscores why it is such a boon to have neurofeedback as an alternative to using drugs. Among the most motivated users of neurofeedback services are the parents of children who have had unacceptable side effects when stimulant drugs were prescribed. Another even larger group are the parents who are reluctant to use drugs in the first place. Now the serotonin selective reuptake inhibitors (SSRI) medications are available and are being used with children. Some children are being prescribed combinations of these and other medications for which there is no substantial research. No matter what the drug or the combination of drugs, the stories for many children in the twenty-first century are not very different than what we observed with Johnny in the 1970's.

iii. A Case Example – ADD Symptoms Treated with NFB

With his freckles and red hair, love of the outdoors and disinterest in school, Jason was a veritable Huck Finn. Though bright, he was restless, poorly organized, and could not get down to homework. Written assignments were a particular problem. Medications had been effective in keeping him in his seat but there was still gross underachievement in school and his grade seven year was in jeopardy. His parents felt that the medications took away his exuberance and they were also concerned about the appetite suppression and the effects on growth as he approached puberty. Neurofeedback training was focused on reducing 4-8 Hz activity and increasing 12 to 15 Hz with placement at Cz referenced to the right ear. After 40 one-hour sessions, done twice a week, he demonstrated improvements in most areas. He was off stimulant medications, parent questionnaires were no longer in the clinically significant range though they were still somewhat elevated for task completion and distractibility. His TOVA and IVA scores had improved but impulsivity / response control scores were still outside the normal range. A further 20 sessions of training were done on a once a week basis and the NFB training was combined with the teaching of metacognitive strategies. Initially these had focused on filling in skill gaps in math and strategies for reading comprehension. The focus then shifted to time management (rewarding him for using his agenda) and written work (see the "hamburger method" in Section XII). After 60 sessions ,retesting demonstrated normalization of attentional variables on both computerized tests and a theta / beta ratio that was no longer extreme. IQ testing revealed a 17 point gain and basic academic skills on the Wide Range Achievement Test were above grade expectations. Parents remarked that he had "grown up a lot". At graduation, being presented with his official ADD Centre mug, he grinned proudly from ear to ear.

6. Movement Disorders
Hypothesis Concerning Involuntary Motor Movement

Dystonia is a good example of how a theoretical hypothesis can lead to a training regimen. When asked by a woman with Parkinson's disease and dystonia if neurofeedback might help her regulate certain disabling symptoms, it was necessary to come up with a rationale as to why it might be worth trying. Her EEG showed a marked decrease of activity in the SMR range. This was not surprising considering the amount of tremor and unwanted dystonic movement.

Shortly after meeting her, she asked if we would do a quick EEG (single channel at Cz) at a group gathering and explain what she was

experimentally attempting with us. Measurements were done on 14 other patients who had Parkinson's. About 1/3 of the patients were not on medication at the time. There was no obvious difference in the EEG between those on and off medications. All demonstrated very low SMR, 13-15 Hz activity.

It was hypothesized that a two-pronged approach to the neurological control of muscle tone through the muscle spindles, might have a beneficial effect. The rational for such a hypothesis is based on the following knowledge. Muscle spindles, which are involved in muscle movement and tone, have double innervations, cholinergic and sympathetic. Both of these systems can be operantly conditioned. The patient can consciously control sympathetic / parasympathetic balance even in difficult situations through diaphragmatic breathing. This could be paired with raising SMR. The combination might have a direct effect on the control of involuntary movements.

The theoretical background to this hypothesis arises from the following knowledge. Gamma efferent fibers from ventral horn of the spinal cord to the contractile ends of the intrafusal muscle fibers receive input from supra-spinal efferents which can arise from the red nucleus. The muscle spindle, in turn, sends somatic afferent fibers back to the red nucleus. This results in a feedback pathway from the muscle spindle which influences the activity of the red nucleus in the midbrain. The red nucleus has been shown to decrease firing when the thalamus is producing the spindle rhythm that Sterman named Sensorimotor Rhythm (SMR) (Sterman, 2000). Sterman demonstrated that SMR can be trained by means of operant conditioning. Theoretically, training to increase SMR could decrease muscle tone and, perhaps, unwanted movements. Simultaneously training for calm relaxed sympathetic / parasympathetic balance in autonomic nervous system functioning might also have a direct beneficial effect on muscle tone by means of the sympathetic influence (Grassi, 1986, Banks, 1998) on muscle spindle activity. To attain this balance in the autonomic nervous system the client is taught: (1) diaphragmatic breathing and (2) to increase the amplitude and quality of RSA (respiratory sinus arrhythmia), also termed heart rate variability entrainment. (Thompson & Thompson, 2002). Since breathing is paired with raising SMR the patient instructed to consciously begin diaphragmatic breathing at a rate of about 6 breaths per minute in order to initiate the beneficial effects. The application of this theoretical formulation to the actual case is described later in this text.

7. Understanding Asperger's Syndrome

a. Introduction: Symptoms & Neuroanatomical Considerations

Autistic spectrum disorders have core symptoms "characterized by the triad of impairments of social interaction, communication, and imagination associated with a narrow range of repetitive activities." (Wing, 2001, p. xiv). Relevant DSM-IV diagnostic codes are Pervasive Developmental Disorder (PDD) and Asperger's Syndrome (AS). Incidence is on the rise and currently estimates are that 1 child in 150 is affected. Brain differences include: smaller cells in the limbic system (Bauman, 2001); larger brains due to more growth in grey and white matter during the first three years of life (Courchesne, 2001); fewer Purkinje cells in the cerebellum (Courchesne, 2001); different activation of the fusiform gyrus for facial recognition (Pierce, 2001); abnormal interaction between frontal and parietal brain areas (Pavlakis, 2001). With respect to Asperger's syndrome a major difference as compared to PDD is that delayed language is not characteristic of AS. They want to have social interactions but lack the social graces to do it appropriately. They often present like little professors with extensive knowledge in their area of interest. Symptoms overlap with Attention Deficit Disorder.

EEG brain maps show less activation in the areas of the right hemisphere that process emotional information ((Thompson, Citation paper, proceedings, AAPB 2003). The amygdala, orbital and medial prefrontal cortex, medial and temporal areas and the thalamus are all involved in the process of attaching emotional significance to stimuli and are most likely of central importance in understanding the autistic spectrum disorders (Schulz, 2000). Temporal lobe dysfunction has been found (Boddaert, 2002). See also Section V, Neuroanatomical Structures, D.1. iii. d.

Neurophysiologically, the medial and basal zones of the cerebral hemispheres are critical in the emotional aspects of social interactions. The ventromedial prefrontal region is important in learning concerning social interactions and the lateral nucleus of the amygdala is critical in assigning emotional valance to events. The central nuclei of the amygdala are more involved in emotional expressions including flight or fight responses. Dysfunction in the interconnections between the orbital and medial wall of the prefrontal cortex and the amygdala and/or dysfunction in the lateral and central nuclei of the amygdala may therefore lie at the root of some of the difficulties encountered in the autistic spectrum disorders.

Are children with Asperger's more right brained or left brained? As discussed in Section V, D. Functional Significance of the Lobes of the Brain, it was concluded that AS is clearly a disorder where the right hemisphere is not doing its job whereas left hemisphere functions (language, scoring well on IQ tests, following routines) are not so problematic. Emotional understanding and expression depends on right hemisphere activation and is deficient.

*Areas exactly corresponding to the speech areas in the left hemisphere exist for the emotional aspects of speech and language in the right hemisphere. Aprosodia refers to deficiencies in this aspect of language ('Prosody' refers to emphasis. intonation, variability of voice and melody.) With **motor aprosodia** the client speaks in a flat monotone without variation even when describing personally emotionally charged events. (However there may still be inappropriate and uncontrollable emotional outbursts such as laughing or crying.) This symptom may be caused by a supra-Sylvian infarction in a frontal area in the right hemisphere, as area that corresponds to Broca's area in the left hemisphere. Broca's aphasia is characterized by nonfluent speech but good comprehension. With **sensory aprosodia** the client does not correctly interpret social innuendo and cannot easily copy emotional tones which express indifference, anger, sadness, or happiness. This may result from right posterosuperior-temporal-lobe and posteroinferior-parietal-lobe infarctions. This area corresponds to Wernicke's area in the left hemisphere. Wernicke's aphasia is characterized by fluent speech, poor repetition, poor comprehension of both written and spoken propositional language. The loss of understanding of written communications corresponds to the loss of an ability to interpret gestures in the right hemisphere. The ability to interpret gestures may be retained in some cases where the connections, occipital to parietal areas are spared. In **global aprosodia** the client shows both motor and sensory aprosodias. (Ross, 1981)*

b. Early Child Development
i. A Very Brief Theoretical Review
(Reference: Thompson & Patterson, 1986)
The key principles underlying normal development are:

1. The child's earliest interactions **evoke reactions** from the environment, and from these interactions and feedback the child forms **basic underlying assumptions** about self and self-in-relation-to-the-world.

2. The infant and then toddler will begin to **interact** in a manner which tends to elicit feedback from the environment which **reaffirms** these assumptions and thus **allows a psychic homeostasis** or equilibrium to be maintained.

3. In the first 3 years of life the infant – toddler normally moves through a **predictable sequence** of behaviour. First there is movement **towards** the mothering figure to satisfy **homonomous** (in-born social) needs. This is followed by movement **away** from the mothering figure to satisfy **autonomous** needs.

If the environment flows with the child, welcoming the closeness and clinging (7 to 11 months and again around 18 months) in the first stage, then greeting the curiosity, exploration and needs for autonomy of the second stage (approximately 14 to 16 months and again at about 22 months), then it is likely that the child will **develop assumptions** of being acceptable and will exude a **confidence** that the **world will meet a basic modicum of his/her needs**.

ii. Temperament and Stages of Development
The normal child goes through a **well defined progression** of steps or **stages** of development in the first few years of life in each of the following areas: motor, cognitive, speech, and social development. In addition, each child is born with a **unique** *temperament*. Extremes in certain aspects of temperament can lead to disorders such as ADHD. Behaviour disorders, on the other hand, tend to arise from *negative* and/or *conditional messages* during the early years when the mothering figure is, for the most part, the *universe* to the infant/toddler.

iii. Inborn Deficits
Note: Although usually inborn, there are many cases where parents report a sudden onset of these deficits that may be due to a reaction to a toxic substance.

In-born deficits/delays in normal development can occur in each of the *staged developmental lines:* motor, cognitive, speech, and social. Delays in cognitive development result in general learning disabilities (slow learners) or specific learning disabilities. Delays in social development may result in autistic spectrum disorders: autism and Asperger's syndrome. An inborn temperament difference, such as is seen in ADHD, is highly correlated with other developmental delays in both cognitive and speech development (Love & Thompson, 1988). In conditions such as ADHD, LD, and Asperger's, the **differences** in these children as compared to the average child would tend to **alter** and even govern the way each of these children initially, and during the first few years of life, began to **view self** and self in relation to the world. In response, the **autistic child** or the child with **Asperger's** may have defensively withdrawn (autistic withdrawal) due to primary deficiencies in their:
- Ability to **socialize**
- Ability to sooth themselves and remain calm (**anxiety** is high)
- Connative (cognitive / emotional) understanding of social nuances / **innuendo**
- Ability to *infer meaning* (later called abstraction)

They may later develop ritualistic, **compulsive** behaviour patterns which can have the effect of helping them at least maintain a primitive known psychological equilibrium (Thompson & Havelkova, 1983; Thompson & Patterson, 1986). These children are hard to socialize and seem to be stuck at a primitive level of ego-centricity and omnipotence usually seen at an earlier stage of the toddler's development.

iv. ADD and LD Children may need to use Behaviour to make their Environment Predictable
The children with ADD or, even more clearly, those with hyperactivity, in many circumstances will **cause the environment to react** in a controlling manner. This reaction **runs counter to the child's autonomous** strivings and it may be perceived as negative feedback about self. Children who feel negative about themselves tend to demonstrate negative behaviours. These behaviors guarantee that their environment will react predictably, albeit negatively, towards them. This establishes a kind of predictable equilibrium in which the child has a kind of control. It is a vicious cycle.

The child with learning disabilities may unconsciously **need to sustain a more positive** sense of self **by withdrawing effort** from that which appears futile and/or **obtaining attention** from peers through behaviours that receive negative adult feedback – the class clown, the instigator, and so on. Again, these behaviours establish a kind of predictable equilibrium in which the child has a kind of control over his environment.

c. Asperger's Syndrome Treatment Requires a Multimodal Approach

Neurofeedback has dramatically changed the outcome for our clients with high functioning Autism and for those with Asperger's syndrome both in terms of speed of change and the quality and amount of change. It is certainly not a quick fix, but at least in many cases it may no longer require a lifetime of careful management. For these clients NFB is only one part of a multimodal approach. There are just starting to be reports at this time to demonstrate the effectiveness of NFB (Sichel, Fehmi, & Goldstein, 1995; Jarusiewicz, 2002; Thompson, 1995, 2003). Thus the approaches suggested here should be presented to the client and family as purely experimental and based on outcome studies, a pilot study with a waiting list control group, and anecdotal evidence.

i. Practical Pointers when Working with a Young Child:

If you want the young child who has behaviours which place them on the autistic spectrum to do an activity with you, then it is quite effective if you begin by *'joining'* with the child in whatever activity they are doing. It may be an activity that fits their obsessional interest. Then very gradually *'redirect'* the child into a more appropriate activity / behaviour or the activity that you want them to partake in. Initially, if possible, do not speak. Use hand and body posture signals. If you must talk, use as few words as possible. The following example is one showing how the author (M.T.) has handled young, fairly bright, high functioning autistic children.

Jason, age 5, was screeching and running around the waiting room. The words he used were not related to the situation he was in and were repeated incessantly. He was dancing around the waiting room flailing his arms in the air. His mother was talking at him without stopping, explaining over and over how he must stop what he is doing and go with the therapist. The therapist was also attempting to explain why he should come with her and the reward he would get when he came. The author came into the room and signalled with his hand to mother and the therapist to stop talking and sit down. The author noted that Jason had come with his favourite cars and blocks. The author took several blocks and a car and sat on the floor on the opposite side of the room from Jason, who had now stopped screeching and running and was rocking back and forth near his toys. He did not look at Jason but sat very still and thought about how Jason would come and join him in play. After a couple of minutes the author moved three blocks slowly to make a crude bridge. Then he held out a block in Jason's direction, still without looking at Jason. Jason took the block and put it near the bridge. The author took another block and placed it on top of Jason's. He then offered Jason a second block. This interaction proceeded for a short time. Then the author got up on one knee and, still without looking directly at Jason, offered Jason his hand. Jason took it and went quietly to the next room to do his NFB session.

As sessions proceeded Jason was taught to calm down whenever a downward motion of the trainer's hand was used. When Jason calmed, his SMR (13-15 Hz) rose and activity began on the screen. The hand signal worked when they went to the waiting room at the end of the session. Mom was asked to say nothing and use this simple hand signal. When Jason calmed she was to give him a simple reward (quiet, short, praise is usually sufficient).

The above example is not unique but is based on over 25 years of experience. If you must intervene verbally, do so using very short, firm, direct commands. One to three words is far more effective than a sentence. An explanation at this juncture will be ignored. Explanations are done later through Socratic questioning that helps the child develop a rationale for appropriate behaviour. Play acting the new behaviour helps to make it more available to the child the next time this situation occurs. Remember, initially these children will not generalize. Each learned behaviour must be taught and be repeated in different environmental settings and with different people. Fortunately, the children who now get NFB training appear to generalize much more easily than children who did not receive this therapeutic modality in past years. Gradually, more verbal communication becomes possible and language use is more appropriate. At this juncture telling stories becomes a very effective way of teaching appropriate social behaviour and helping the child to assimilate rules.

ii. Practical Pointers when Working with an Adolescent:

The following procedure can be important when you and others are working with adolescents diagnosed with Asperger's syndrome. As a general principle, try using as <u>few</u> words as possible when you are explaining a situation or making a request. Many of these individuals will mentally drift off and stop registering what you are explaining if you make more than one point at one time. It is important that you avoid the use of indefinite terms such as: 'probably', 'usually', 'try', 'sometimes' and so on. Remember they tend to be literal and concrete in their thinking, even when they have very high verbal IQ's. Saying, "Would you like to do Math now?" will be interpreted as a choice, not a command.

With older adolescents and young adults it can be quite helpful to work out a **memory trick** which fits *their interest area* in order for them to do following the sequence before taking action:
1st STOP. 2nd REFLECT . 3rd DECIDE on correct behaviour . 4th Now act.
If the adolescent has acted in a manner that is socially inappropriate, make sure that you first define the difficult situation precisely. Second, ask them what the effect was on each of the other persons. Then state simply and clearly your impression of the reactions of others to what they did. Third, ask them what they will do next time this happens. Then state concretely and briefly exactly what you would suggest they should do next time. Now ask them to enact with you the whole situation. You will try to portray the other people and they will act the way that they think might be appropriate. Now change roles with them and play-act it again. Be sure that the play-acting is concrete. Help them decide what to say. You may actually have to write down and give them a list of phrases that they can use. Ask the adolescent who they feel is a good example socially. Then specifically identify the behaviours that make that person a good example. Write these down. Suggest that they try

to copy how that person behaves. Ask them if they could listen carefully and watch that individual and try copying a few of their behaviours. These should be behaviours that they have first discussed with you. Always be careful to model appropriate behaviour. Jokes are not usually understood. However, as NFB begins to take effect, you will notice that the adolescent begins to smile more often at the right times and begins to demonstrate a sense of humour. Other helpful advice is to tell them to limit talk about their own interest area. They may mention it, however, if asked about it.

With the young adolescent you might suggest that the parents use the *set-up-for-success* principle by having another child share an event that does not require too much interaction. The parents should supervise to make sure it all goes well. Going to a movie or sports event, a place with rides, a science centre, museum and so on, where adults can stay between kids, can turn out to be lots of fun for the potential new friend. No matter what the age or the extreme of the behaviour, you must always model being calm and reflective. Do NOT mirror the child's impulsiveness – model reflective thoughtfulness. Anxiety may be at the root of the child's impulsive or unusual behaviour. Regardless of how hard you try to cover up tension, these children will always sense it. You must be genuinely calm. If you cannot be, arrange for someone else to work with the child.

Finally, remember that this condition **is a developmental deficiency** (in-born) or a deficit possibly caused by exposure to a toxic substance, such as mercury. *There is a hypothesis with considerable documentation that the incidence of autistic spectrum disorders has risen recently and corresponds to the use of vaccination where the preservative for multi-dose serum apparently contains a mercury related compound (Thimerosal). Most children are able to eliminate toxic substances, including mercury, with no untoward effects. However, some children cannot handle the toxic burden due to differences in their digestive systems. It is hypothesized that this "leaky gut" problem makes them vulnerable. In such children there may be the onset of autistic symptomatology in the second year of life after early development was normal.* Whether inborn or acquired, it **is not learned** bad behaviour so insistence on appropriate social behaviour is like asking a visually impaired child to read the blackboard. Kind, understanding but firm assistance and **close supervision** may be needed in social situations for a number of years.

d. Results of Neurofeedback Training

In the children that we have trained over the past ten years with neurofeedback, the EEG patterns at Cz initially resembled those of children with ADD. However the high amplitudes of the slow waves and the dip in the SMR frequency band tended to be more extreme. Excess slow wave activity in either the delta through theta range or excess alpha activity was found. Peaks at 7 Hz. had the morphology of paediatric alpha. Full cap assessments showed slowing (theta or excessive theta or low alpha, 8 to 10 Hz.) in the right parietal region (P4) and some slowing at T6. There was high amplitude theta at FP1, F3, Fz and Cz. There were also differences in coherence and comodulation.

Sufficient training (sometimes more than 100 sessions) consistently produced a decrease in theta / beta ratio with the clearest change being an increase in SMR. IQ increases of about 10 points were found. With respect to the TOVA (Test Of Variables of Attention), on initial assessment some of the autistic children could not complete the test. At the other extreme, children with Asperger's syndrome often scored well even prior to training. TOVA data showed that variability was the weakest score and the majority of subjects with Asperger's syndrome were in the normal range for impulsivity and attention span. Part of the reason for these good scores may have been that the children with Asperger's syndrome were anxious and, in general, wanted to please the examiner and follow the rules. All the client's TOVA scores improved with training. Academic testing using the WRAT (Wide Range Achievement Test) also demonstrated consistent improvements with training. Perhaps the most clear-cut positive change, however, was in the social functioning of all of these clients. Parents noted improved social interactions: children went from having no friends to initiating and maintaining some peer friendships. The largest improvements were in those who received > 80 sessions. Autistic clients were all difficult to work with. Those with AS were easier to work with once they knew the routines Thompson, 1994, 2003).

An example of one severe Asperger's syndrome child's improvement when he was requested to "draw-a-person" is shown below. (For a discussion of this case see 'Steven', age 12, under the section on 'Intervention'.)

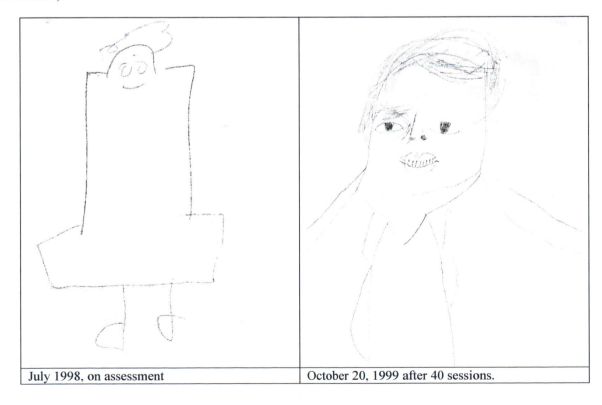

| July 1998, on assessment | October 20, 1999 after 40 sessions. |

e. Discussion

EEG differences observed in autistic spectrum disorders provide a rationale for using neurofeedback. Excess slow wave activity corresponds to being more in their own world; low SMR is consistent with fidgety and impulsive behaviour and also with the tactile sensitivity exhibited by many; high left prefrontal and frontal slow wave activity is consistent with lack of appropriate inhibition; high slow wave activity in right parietal-temporal area is consistent with inability to interpret social cues and emotions. Improved social interaction found in conjunction with EEG shifts makes sense: more activation means more alert to the outside world and thus better able to benefit from socialization efforts. The positive results support neurofeedback as an intervention in autistic spectrum disorders, particularly Asperger's syndrome. Further research could build on these observational data.

Glossary of Some Terms That Also Appear in the Foregoing Text:

Abulia: loss of interactional spontaneity.

Agraphia: inability to write due to word finding difficulties

Alexia: inability to read

Anomia: inability to name objects

Apraxia: lack of awareness, and neglect, of body parts and surrounding space

    Constructional apraxia: inability to correctly construct objects

    Gertsmann's syndrome: left parietal lobe damage with resulting left / right confusion

    Ocular apraxia: inability to control gaze.

Acalculia: inability to calculate

Aphasia: inability to talk

Agnosia: lack of ability to know or understand.

    Anosognosia: denial of deficits.

        Simultagnosia: inability to integrate components of a visual scene

        Optic ataxia: inability to accurately reach for an object with visual guidance.

Dyscalculia: difficulty with mathematics

Dyslexia: difficulty with reading

Perseveration: loss of flexibility in thinking, persistence of a single thought. It is related to organic brain damage.

PART TWO

ASSESSMENT AND INTERVENTION

This portion of the book begins with case examples showing a variety of clients. In each case the assessment led to appropriate procedures being applied. It becomes clear from these illustrations that one-size-fits-all does not apply when doing neurofeedback. Even practitioners whose software is set for particular protocols will tell you, if asked, that they make adjustments to individualize the feedback. The rationale for basing intervention on an objective assessment is presented. This will include setting goals plus enabling objectives with the client. The text will then discuss how to carry out EEG assessments which lead to decisions regarding neurofeedback (NFB) training. This is followed by a section on the physiological variables used in general biofeedback and a description of how to carry out a brief psychophysiological stress assessment. The next section is on intervention, first neurofeedback and then how to add biofeedback (BFB) to the NFB training. Finally, there is a section on metacognition, those executive strategies that guide our thinking and planning. Our approach to training using NFB is that it is not a stand-alone intervention. Weaving some meta-cognitive strategies into the training once the client is in a receptive mental state provides added value.

Even by the time this book is published, new and better assessment and neurofeedback / biofeedback training programs will be on the market. Better statistical analysis of assessment data and more immediate feedback of statistics and trends will be one improvement. More versatility in display screens and more ability to adjust the displays to the unique needs of each client will likely also be available in the next generation of programs.

However, the principles outlined here will, for the most part, not change. Most of our present NFB and BFB display screens will still work very well for our clients.

SECTION VI
The Basics of Assessment

A. Why You Do an Assessment

We recommend that if you are going to use any biofeedback procedure, it is imperative that you first do an assessment to look at the person's baseline functioning. This assessment should ideally include all of the physiological measures that are relevant and that might be used in training. Careful history taking, discussion of current functioning plus future goals, as well as objective physiological measures all have bearing on how you design a training program for your student/client. There is a very basic principle in **systems theory**. You alter any component in a system and all the other elements in the system will shift their functions in order to accomplish the goal or function of that system. In keeping with this principle, we often find on reassessment that functions that were not directly physiologically targeted have improved. A good example is social appropriateness improving in clients with ADD and those with Asperger's syndrome when the main intervention has been to encourage a calm state while maintaining attention to the outside world.

This systems theory principle applies to how we use NFB and BFB with clients. Differences between people and/or new knowledge mean that we must shift how we deal with similar appearing clinical "entities". How a specific individual responds to different types of measurement and to different biofeedback presentations will help determine the best approach for that client. Therefore, we do not use specific protocols in the usual way that that term is used. Instead, we use an overall model for decision making which is based on the premise that our knowledge base is continually changing and that each client is unique in their responses both to our measurements and to our feedback techniques. Our assessment measurements are a tool which **help us decide which feedback modalities** to use and **how and where** to do feedback. The model below also allows for change in the way we practice over the years as we learn more about neurophysiology and as our biofeedback instruments improve. The *Decision Pyramid* model we use is diagrammed in the figure below.

1. The Decision Pyramid

Decisions concerning placement of electrodes and the frequency bands to enhance or inhibit should be based on rational considerations and, where possible, research. One should avoid hearsay or belief unless you are being 'intuitive' and then you should discuss with the client / parents the placement as being experimental. Research may be based on clinical experience and consist of a case series. These studies should have a large number of clients, appropriate diagnostic criteria which can be replicated, a good description of what was done, pre and post objective testing, and perhaps a discussion of deviations from the general findings for specific cases.

Rational decisions should include consideration of our present knowledge about the functional significance of different areas of the brain and the correlations of mental states to the activation of different EEG frequency bandwidths.

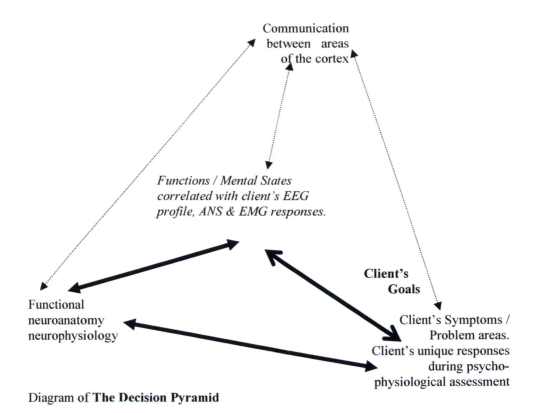

Diagram of **The Decision Pyramid**

The decision pyramid covers the components of an assessment. These include client goals and the assessment of EEG amplitudes at different frequencies. It suggests that with some clients you may additionally wish to do a *psychophysiological stress profile* for information about the autonomic nervous system and electromyogram changes with stress. It requires that we use the assessment information in conjunction with knowledge of neurophysiology and anatomy in order to derive appropriate placements of sensors for training. The top of the pyramid regarding communication between areas of the cortex is relevant when 19 lead assessments are done. The base of the pyramid applies to all neurofeedback work.

Rational decisions concerning what and where to train should include consideration of our present knowledge about the functional significance of different areas of the brain and the correlations of mental states to EEG frequency bandwidths.

2. Candidates for Assessment and Training

a. An Overview

Who is a reasonable candidate to assess and train, given the present literature and professional experience? The first group are those who have a known disorder and wish to improve functioning or quality of life. This group can be subdivided according to present experience using NFB. Conditions where there is a solid research literature include ADHD and seizure disorders. Other conditions where research literature is building include learning disabilities, depression (dysphoria), anxiety and tension, alcohol and substance abuse, headaches and migraine, obsessive compulsive disorder, and closed head injury. (Migraine requires a combination of biofeedback for relaxation and neurofeedback to decrease high beta (21-34 Hz ad increase SMR (13-15 Hz).

Other conditions which are supported by anecdotal experience and presentations at professional meetings include mood disorders, Asperger's syndrome, Tourette's syndrome and other movement disorders (dystonia, Parkinson's disease), Pervasive Developmental Disorder (especially high functioning autism), facilitation of psychotherapy, chronic fatigue, fibromyalgia and stroke rehabilitation.

The second group includes people who wish to optimize their performance. These are usually students, academics, athletes, or professionals in business, law, medicine or skilled trades. Although there is not a lot of published literature, there is some with respect to athletes, such as Lander's work with archers published in 1991. Recently John Gruzelier did a two year pilot study at the Royal Conservatoire of music in London, England. Results were impressive enough that neurofeedback became part of the curriculum at the Conservatory starting in Fall 2002. These elite students showed improvements, in particular with respect to interpretive and emotive aspects of their musical performance after neurofeedback training which encouraged increased theta.

There has been a joint publication by the Association of Applied Psychophysiology and Biofeedback (AAPB) and the Society for Neuronal Regulation (SNR) concerning standards for judging research in our field. Other helpful bibliographies are Ralph Byers *Neurotherapy Reference Handbook* available from the AAPB and Cory Hammond's more selective Bibliography published in the Journal of Neurotherapy (2002) which cites the research for each condition for which neurotherapy has been used.

b. The Common Factors

Given the growing number of disorders where favourable results are being observed, it is of interest to discuss what some of these disorders have in common that neurofeedback is favourably influencing. They are, in the main, conditions for which traditional medical approaches do not yield consistent or complete control.

i. Attention to External Stimuli

Attention has been found to be improved by decreasing the dominant slow wave amplitude. In children this is usually in the theta range, 4-8 Hz. In adults it may be in the low alpha range, 9-

10 Hz., or the range Lubar calls "thalpha", 6-10 Hz.

Excess theta is a key difficulty in Attention Deficit Disorder (ADD / ADHD) and in perhaps the majority of children with Learning Disabilities (LD). This is also a key difficulty observed in many clients who have had a closed head injury and in some who have suffered a stroke. It is an important component of the profile in both Autistic Spectrum Disorders, both Asperger's syndrome (AS) and Pervasive Developmental Disorders (PDD or Autism).

In Asperger's syndrome the high slow wave amplitude is found in the central and frontal and pre frontal areas (Cz and Fz) as it may be in ADHD. It may also be seen at P4 and T6 if a 19-lead assessment is done. (One must be careful here and be sure that that high amplitude alpha is also present in the eyes open condition.) Both hyper and hypo coherence and comodulation is observed depending on sites and frequencies. (This will need to be clarified by future research. For your work it is best to take each case as unique and work to 'normalize' the EEG.) We seem to be finding right hemisphere, high amplitude, low frequency, alpha rhythm (eyes open) as a sign that parts of the brain are 'idling' more often in these clients. This right hemisphere 'idling' combined with prefrontal slow wave activity correlates with the difficulty these clients have with interpretation and expression of social communication. Deficits in the ability to sustain attention are also found in the elderly and in people who are depressed.

ii. Prevention of the Spread of Epileptiform Activity

Decreasing the frequency, duration and intensity of seizure activity has been observed as a result of increasing SMR (13-15 Hz) training. The literature on this is reviewed by Barry Sterman the original investigator in this field (Sterman, 2000) in the special issue of *Clinical EEG* devoted to neurofeedback. It is perhaps not only those with diagnosed epilepsy who can benefit, but also those with undiagnosed sub-clinical seizure activity. This is thought to occur in almost 10% of children diagnosed with ADHD.

iii. Stability

Here there are probably a number of inhibitory mechanisms involved which will be gradually elucidated by research in the years to come. **Instability** in terms of mood appears to be favourably stabilized by increasing high-alpha and SMR, 11-15 Hz. Both adults and children appear to become calm, less impulsive and able to reflect more before speaking or acting (Thompson &Thompson, 1998). We also find that anxious clients become more self-assured with less fluctuation in mood. Some clients with bipolar disorder appear to become less extreme in the manic phases of their mood swings. However, these observations concerning mood still require more case reports and research.

Stabilizing the extrapyramidal system and, specifically, the muscle spindle gamma motor and sympathetic input may be the reason for successes that are beginning to be seen with clients who have movement disorders.

iv. Normalizing of the EEG in Areas that are Over-active or Under-active and/or Normalizing Communication Between Areas of the Cortex.

Activation of an area of the brain which is relatively inactive ('idling') is a logical approach for certain conditions. *Dysphoria* (mild to moderate depression) appears to be improved in a proportion of clients when they practice activating their relatively less active left frontal lobe. Movement disorders may improve when the client is encouraged to control and sustain a higher amplitude of 13-15 Hz, SMR. Sustained activation of areas in the left hemisphere associated with language functions may be what is assisting learning disabled clients to improve their academic performance. (A caution here, Tom Budzynski has stated that you should not do beta training on the left side with children who have Reactive Attachment Disorder. He says RAD children will show a worsening of behaviour with increased left side activation.)

One has to question whether activation may also be a key factor in the improvement of social functioning in clients where the principle difficulty relates to interpretation and expression of emotion. These are primarily functions of the right cerebral hemisphere which include expressing emotions and interpreting nonverbal social cues (These problems are found in children with non-verbal learning disabilities and also in Asperger's syndrome). It may be, in those cases where these symptoms improve, that the improvement is related to activation of the right cerebral hemisphere through decreasing the dominant slow wave and increasing low beta (12-15 Hz).

Encouraging the client to decrease an over-active area may also be helpful in some clients. For example, when extremely high amplitude hi-beta or beta-spindling is observed (usually in central and right frontal locations), encouraging a decrease in hi-beta (24-34 Hz) can correlate with a decrease in depressive ruminations and/or obsessions and compulsions.

The foregoing are all examples of normalizing the EEG. Obviously, the oldest and best example comes from Sterman's work with seizure disorders. He always works from a 19 channel assessment with brain maps and takes a two-pronged approach: reducing slow wave activity at the site of the eplileptiform activity and increasing the protective SMR activity across the sensorimotor strip.

Improving communication between areas of the brain is an emerging field. Numerous excellent reports are being given at professional meetings regarding coherence training. More work on this area and on comodulation training will come as newer instruments come onto the market that allow practitioners to do this type of training. Currently, the LEXICOR equipment is the mainstay for both data collection to produce brain maps and to do coherence training. A relatively new instrument, the Neuronavigator, is designed to do 19 channel data collections (22 leads) and comodulation training. There have also been new instruments recently introduced from Czechoslovakia and from St. Petersburg, Russia.

v. Brief Summary

Both NFB and the combination of NFB with traditional BFB are powerful tools that a client may use to overcome a few symptoms, or symptom patterns, which are common to a number of conditions. Some very general and important neural circuits are being changed. It may be that when one or two key symptoms are removed and/or key neural circuits are changed, that the individual is able to self regulate. These people begin to be able to manage their symptoms and then to compensate for their remaining problems. You are training for mental flexibility and for control.

3. Case Examples

In the following case examples, history and assessment findings were found to correlate. Names have been changed to protect confidentiality. These cases demonstrate that it is possible to set realistic feedback goals. For a few of these cases we have summarized the training program and given the results in order that the reader can refer back to this list for a quick reminder of some typical training parameters. We have not attempted to list all the disorders that may be helped. The underlying difficulties that are being addressed with neurofeedback are often similar for more than one disorder. For example, under the title 'Movement Disorders' the example is of Dystonia but Tourette's Syndrome responds to the same approach. Later in this section we will describe how to set up appropriate feedback screens for the combined NFB and BFB training mentioned in these examples. When electrode placements are mentioned (CZ, P3, etc.) you can check the location in the diagram of the 10-20 electrode placement system found later in this chapter.

a. Optimizing Performance in Adults

Case #1: *Jane, age 39, a bright, successful business woman, felt she could be more productive if she could be relaxed and calm when dealing with her employees and her peers. She was somewhat tense and anxious. When assessed, it was found that her peripheral skin temperature was 85 degrees and it dropped rapidly to 79 degrees when she was asked to imagine a difficult business situation. She had practiced yoga for some years and easily demonstrated diaphragmatic breathing with excellent synchrony between respiration and heart rate variability (RSA). However, she had not applied this ability to work situations. She was able to relax her shoulders, but during the stress test she unconsciously tensed her shoulder and neck muscles (trapezius and occipitalus).*

Case #2: *John, age 47, complained of similar symptoms of tension at work. Compared to Jane, he was less anxious but he complained more of muscle tension. His peripheral skin temperature was 95 degrees. It changed very little when he was asked to imagine a very difficult situation at work. On the other hand, during his stress test his respiration changed markedly becoming very shallow, rapid and irregular. His EMG reading from his trapezius (shoulder) muscles was quite high. John had a second area of concern. He had always been extremely creative and his IQ was in the very superior range. Nevertheless, his school performance had been highly variable. He had gotten over 90% in subjects he liked and with teachers he respected, but earned only 60's and 70's when he didn't like the teacher.*

You might decide that maintaining a relaxed mental state while under stress, as reflected by an increase in skin temperature, could be a useful exercise for Jane, but would be less important for John. On the other hand, learning diaphragmatic breathing while monitoring the pulse rate for respiratory sinus arrhythmia (RSA) might be the most helpful relaxation technique and feedback for John. Jane did not need to learn this technique. However, she did need to use a simple heart rate monitor while doing stressful phone calls in order to apply her ability to attain excellent balance between sympathetic and parasympathetic activity to stressful situations. Both of these clients could benefit from EMG feedback to help them learn to relax their muscles.

Both John and Jane complained of constantly going over and over both business and personal problems in their mind. Both would awake at night and ruminate. John and Jane both demonstrated a dip in SMR at 13-14 Hz when stressed. Both of them also demonstrated high 27 –32 Hz activity. Jane also demonstrated relatively high average amplitude 21-23 Hz. Often this corresponds to anxiety.

In addition to his difficulty handling stress, John showed very high 6-10 Hz activity when doing math tasks and when reading boring material.

Given these findings on the EEG it could be helpful to both of these clients if they learned to raise high alpha and SMR (12-15 Hz) and lower high beta (approximately 22 –34 Hz). John would benefit from lowering thalpha (6-10 Hz) activity when doing boring academic-like tasks.

b. Attention Deficit / Hyperactivity Disorder

Case #3: *Jason, age 8, was very active, impulsive and could not seem to attend for more than a few minutes during class at school. He was very bright and tremendously creative. His doctor felt he had a problem with short-term memory and, when tested, it was also thought that he had a central auditory processing (CAP) problem. He loved to draw and build. His EEG demonstrated extremely high 3 to 6 Hz activity and slightly lower SMR than beta. His Theta / Beta power ratio (4 – 8Hz) / (13 – 21 Hz) was high (14).*

Jason was a very straight-forward and uncomplicated case of ADHD. He had supportive parents and was not a behaviour problem though he was underachieving at school. We used the assessment to set the bandwidths and locations for training. We worked at both Cz and C4 locations and encouraged an SMR increase and a decrease in theta. After 50 sessions both bands had altered appropriately on retesting. His impulsivity and hyperactivity had decreased, his attention span had increased, his measured IQ came up by 16 points and he was achieving in the top half of his class academically. He did not have any problem with memory and his functioning was such that there was no reason to re-do the CAP testing.

c. Learning Disability

Case #4: *Sam, age 11, presented with severe learning disabilities in addition to ADD symptoms. He was entering grade 6, but his reading and math were at late grade 1 and early grade 2 levels despite intensive special tutoring both at school and home. His parents were both teachers. He had optimal support in a wonderful family and extended family. Despite his academic subject difficulties, he gave the appearance of being a bright articulate boy. Delta activity was observed in the EEG and somewhat high theta activity. Training was begun in August. Sam was functioning at a fifth grade level in all subjects within 4 1/2 months (retested by his school) and was in the top half of his grade 6 class at the end of the year. He has remained an A level student into high school. Training included decreasing his dominant slow wave while (a.)increasing SMR, 13-15 Hz, at C3*

and (b.) increasing beta 15-18 Hz at P3 while doing reading exercises.

Sam is used as an example because we have a 7 year follow-up history at the time of writing. When he graduated his father made the observation that the training had saved his son. His assessment was more difficult than more recent cases of children with learning disabilities both because he had a reasonable attention span despite being physically restless and because we did not have full-cap capabilities when he was seen. With more recent cases we are able to pinpoint to a greater extent where delta and theta activity are seen. In students like Sam it is often between the T3 and P3 area or in the middle of the triangle formed by C3, T3 and P3. There may also be comodulation differences. These can involve this general area. (Both these observations require research.) Because reading difficulties are thought to involve the insula cortex and its connections, we usually decrease slow wave activity over P3, C3, and F3 and encourage activation with beta activity (15-18 Hz) when reading (*operant conditioning*). We teach strategies for handling academics while the child receives feedback (*classical conditioning* that pairs the calm, alert mental state with academic tasks). These strategies are described in Section XII, Metacognitive Strategies.

d. Movement Disorders: Example of Parkinson's with Dystonia

Case #5: *Mary, age 47, has both Parkinson's disease and severe dystonia. She has had most medications that are used for these disorders and has even partaken in experimental surgery. Prior to doing NFB & BFB walking was extremely difficult and she was still unable to control the sudden onset of gross motor movements or the sudden inability to turn when standing or even to get up when lying down ("freezing"). An EEG assessment at Cz showed very low SMR (13 & 14 Hz) activity and high alpha (9 & 10 Hz) activity. A 'stress-test' looking at traditional biofeedback measurements demonstrated low peripheral temperature, high EDR, shallow, rapid, irregular breathing with no synchrony to heart rate variations (RSA).*

Medications help Mary and she has used a variety of drug combinations during the 14 years that she has had Parkinson's disease. Increases and decreases in dopamine may be part of a biochemical understanding of the problem and of a medical approach to it, but they do not answer the important question of how to control her sudden, precipitous onset of gross dystonic movements. In dystonia a noradrenergic predominance has been proposed (Guberman, A. 1994). It stands to reason that our traditional drug approach is necessary but not sufficient. In Mary's case one obvious factor in precipitating worsening of symptoms is stress. Increased sympathetic drive is a factor. Noradrenalin is also a factor. One iatrogenic precipitator of a major dystonic episode can be the injection of even a very small dose of adrenalin as might occur in a dental procedure.

If an increase in SMR is associated with decreasing spinothalamic tract activity and a decrease in the firing rate of the red nucleus (which has gamma motor system efferents to the muscle spindles), then it would appear sensible to see whether raising this rhythm would correspond to a decrease in undesirable muscle tension, jerks and 'spasms'. Raising this rhythm has also been observed to be associated with a feeling of *calm*. Muscle spindles are involved in reflexes and in governing muscle tone. They are innervated both by the motor/sensory pathways to the spinal cord, red nucleus and basal ganglia and by the sympathetic nervous system. We might have some constructive influence on the first half of this innervation by raising SMR. Indeed, Sterman demonstrated in his early research with cats that the red nucleus stopped firing when the thalamus started to fire producing SMR rhythm. Perhaps training Mary to relax would affect the second (sympathetic) part of this spindle in a helpful manner.

We trained Mary to get diaphragmatic breathing at 6 breaths per minute in synchrony with variations in heart rate (that is, to achieve good quality *respiratory sinus arrhythmia*, or RAS) and to associate this breathing style with increasing her SMR using NFB. She is now able, for the most part, to bring both 'freezing' and gross unwanted dystonic movements under her voluntary control. Day time alertness is also a problem with Mary and most people with Parkinson's disease. Bringing her alpha (9 & 10 Hz), which had been too high, a little more under her control is helping with this. Mary was formerly an avid reader. For 5 years she had not been able to read a novel. Now she is again able to finish a book and she enjoys reading. The

improved focus for reading was achieved after about 20 training sessions. The improved motor control and a reduction in medications was consolidated after about 40 sessions. She has also resumed her work doing crafts and writing and illustrating small books.

e. Professional Athletes

Case #6: *Joan, age 28, is a golf professional. Her dream was to play well enough to make the woman's tour. She felt her game could be improved, but had no idea how to do this other than practice. She was also frustrated that some of her golf students did not seem able to improve despite many lessons over an extended period of time. The EEG showed higher than expected 5 – 9 Hz activity. When specifically asked, it turned out that Joan had been a bright student, but had found it difficult to remain focused in classes. So this ADD pattern was not too surprising. She was outwardly calm and certainly not at all anxious, but, when assessed, her breathing rate was irregular, shallow and rapid. Her skin temperature was 88 degrees. Her shoulders (trapezius) became tense with the math stress test. When we discussed what occurred mentally during her approach to the ball and in the back-swing, she realized that she was ruminating and worrying about the outcome of the shot. This corresponded to increases in her 23-34 Hz activity and to an increased breathing rate and increased muscle tension in her face, shoulders and forearm. She then talked about being a very out-going person, but said that this covered up the fact that she was often quite tense and anxious and a great worrier. Training involved a stepwise progression through different mental states. This will be described later.*

Case #7: *John, age 21, is a professional racing car driver. He was quite aware that he had been inattentive and impulsive as a student. He was happy to be finished with high school and following his passion for driving. His EEG demonstrated numerous bursts of slow wave activity, 4 –7 Hz and 9 - 10 Hz. His breathing was rapid and shallow. His shoulder muscles became tense with stress.*

The goal for John will be mental flexibility since he will not be sustaining intense beta throughout the time a car race takes. He will be going in and out of beta problem solving depending on the situation. He is very good at that. He does extremely well during races when he "locks-on" to the car ahead that he is trying to pass, but does not do as well without other cars around him on the track. His qualifying times are not as good as they should be and he wanted to do training so that he could stay focused and be more consistent during qualifying laps. John does not want to mentally 'rest' in a mental state where he is at all tuned out. For him, tuning out appears to correspond to EEG frequencies below 10 Hz. He is rightly concerned that if this happened on the track, his reflexes to handle a sudden situation change could be too slow and this could result in a poor standing or, even, in injury. He wants to *rest* in a *readiness* state where his reflexes both mentally and physically are optimal. This requires that he turn on low beta instantly to solve problems, then reflect in a state where he is aware of every aspect of the track conditions and all cars around him. This desirable mental state is generally between 11 to 15 Hz. This state is also associated with a sense of calm, but alert relaxation. This mental state can also be reflected by biofeedback measurements. He wants his muscle tone to reflect relaxation in muscle groups not in use and an appropriate tone (not overly tense) in groups which are necessary for continuous shifting, braking and steering. This state is also reflected in the presence of synchrony between heart rate and respiration, a responsive level of EDR (alert, but not over-aroused), and a peripheral skin temperature in the 90's.

The EEG assessment using both EEG and biofeedback modalities with both Joan and John led to the design of a combined NFB and BFB program which rapidly produced changes in how they performed athletically. In Joan's case, she now taught her golf students how to breathe and relax their shoulders and in 2 weeks had greatly improved all of their games. One man who had been with her 2 years went from getting 50 to 80 yard drives to driving over 200 yards. All her students increased the distance they could hit, usually almost doubling their driving distance. She now wants to set up feedback training at her golf club.

f. Hunter Mind Traits

Case #8: *Allison, age 12, is a good example of the type of interesting students and professionals who come for NFB training. Allison is used as an example because she also represents an* *important problem in research studies - choosing a control group. Allison was to be included as a 'normal' control in a study looking at EEG theta / beta ratios in Chinese children with ADHD in Canada, Hong Kong, and mainland China. Allison was the older sister of an ADHD boy who was doing NFB training. Her continuous performance test, (TOVA), was normal. Questionnaires done by her parents were well within the normal range. She stood near the top of her class in school. She was an obedient, polite, well-behaved child. She agreed to do an extra EEG assessment to validate the ratio obtained by the researcher doing the study. Using a procomp[+] the researcher had obtained microvolt ratios for 4-8 Hz/16-20 Hz of 2.9 and 2.7 for eyes open and a math task respectively.* **(As a rough measure, ratios above 2.5 in children are usually associated with ADHD diagnosis.)** *A different machine, (A620), yielded ratios for eyes open baseline and a math task of 3.3 and 2.2 respectively. She agreed to do a third EEG on a different A620 instrument. A Math task was done and the ratio was 2.8. Allison was asked if anything was different between the tests. She responded, a little embarrassed, saying that she had drifted off in the first test where she was just staring at a dot. She loved math and on the second test she said her mind had not wandered very much. On the third evaluation using a math task she said that she had become a little bored and drifted off. She noted that this was somewhat like her original test with the other doctor. Her EEG ratios reflected her mental states during each test. When asked, she said that she did drift off in school, but it wasn't a problem because school was "so easy". Allison had a superior range IQ. She had a positive attitude towards school. She was a very pleasant girl who would strive to do what was asked of her. Allison has "hunter mind" characteristics. Her EEG ratios were a little high and often in the range associated with ADHD. She was very bright, intelligent and energetic. Thom Hartman's analogy of a Hunter Mind would apply because she could both scan and then hyperfocus on something of interest. She survived, indeed thrived, in the Farmer's world of school because of her high IQ and desire to please parents and teachers. She does not have ADHD. Although she does have most of the traits, she is not impaired to a clinically significant degree by them. However, she does have a "hunter mind" and she probably should not be in the "normal control" group of a study* *that compares EEGs in ADHD children and normals.*

The Edison Syndrome

Perhaps the easiest way to resolve the over-diagnosis of ADHD and the confusion of ADHD with oppositional defiant disorder and conduct disorder and also resolve some of the difficulty in properly 'diagnosing' a control group for studies, would be to remove ADHD from the DSM altogether. It could be replaced with a diagnostic category that recognized 'incapacitating hyperactivity' and/or inattention. On the other hand, one could leave the ADHD diagnosis in the manual but insist that the present diagnostic category be properly used. If this was done, ADHD would include those persons where the symptoms (and not those of associated disorders) significantly impaired functioning. If this were the case then a new term could be introduced for those without impairment but with a degree of underachievement.

Such a new term would not be a diagnostic category in the manual of medical disorders. It would give a positive frame of reference and include all the very bright, capable, creative individuals who have that cognitive style so well exemplified by productive historical figures such as Thomas Edison and Mozart. The term "Edison Syndrome" has been proposed for this group. They fit the diagnostic criteria of inattention, distractibility, impulsivity (spontaneity) and, at times, hyperactivity and they do get bored in school. Their performance is often quite variable. Academically, they may hyperfocus and do extremely well on subjects that catch their interest but underachieve on subjects where they don't find the teacher interesting. These children, using neurofeedback, can learn to sustain focus even in boring situations. They decrease the variability in their performance. This is a group where NFB can be extremely effective.

Diagram: The Hunters & The Farmers

Edison Syndrome (Hunter Mind)
These are the bright, capable, creative individuals who fit the diagnostic criteria of inattention, distractibility, impulsivity (spontaneity) and, at times, hyperactivity but who do not fit the category of being "impaired to a clinically significant degree. They are often very good at developing new organizations but tend to move on to new challenges rather than staying on to maintain and administrate them.

Attention Deficit <u>Disorder</u> (Hunter Mind).
These are the individuals who exhibit all the symptoms of ADHD and are significantly impaired by these symptoms. (Not just by the symptoms of associated disorders such as oppositional defiant disorder.)

Farmer Mind (normal in the sense of most common)
This style is found in the majority of the population. They do not exhibit the symptoms of ADHD. They tend to be comfortable with daily routines and "maintaining" organizations rather than creating them.

A caution using ADD as an example: Control group studies (Ritalin versus NFB or cognitive behaviour therapy versus NFB) should demonstrate a reasonably objective diagnostic workup to prove a clear difference, with respect to the primary targeted symptoms (attention span, distractibility and impulsivity), between the control group and the subjects. Studies on A.D.D. are a clear example of problems in this area. Control groups should not contain successful, non-problematic (to others) "hunters"(term introduced by Thom Hartmann). The control group should have persons who fit Tom Hartmann's 'Farmer' Mind classification (non-A.D.D and non Hunter mind). The A.D.D. group should be the 'Hunter' mind subjects whose functioning is impaired by the symptoms. If some individuals have behaviour problems then this should be part of the matching process between groups.

Case # 9: Mike, age 29, wanted to return to university to do an MBA. He had an engineering degree and said he had had to work much harder than his fellow students even to get just passing grades at university. He was extremely anxious, particularly in performance situations. He would wake up at night worrying about his work and his social relationships. He had to succeed in the GMATs (graduate achievement tests) yet he could not get-down to studying. They are an incredibly stress producing exam. When asked during the assessment to do even simple math, he stumbled over it and began to make silly errors. His respiration rate rose to 40 breaths per minute (BrPM) and was shallow and irregular. His heart rate rose and was completely out of synchrony with his breathing. His skin temperature dropped, electrodermal response rose markedly and his muscles tensed. The electroencephalogram with placement at Cz showed high thalpha, 6 - 10 Hz, low SMR, 13 - 15 Hz, and high beta with peaks at 21 Hz and 27 Hz .

Training, therefore, emphasized learning how to remain relaxed (breathing at 6 breaths per minute, skin temperature up, forehead EMG down, and SMR up), but alert (EDR remaining high but not extreme), focused (decreased thalpha), not anxious or ruminating (decreased 20 – 23 Hz and 24 - 32 Hz). We taught him metacognitive strategies that focused on test taking skills and reading comprehension. He sent us an e-mail immediately after getting his results. He had attained an almost unbelievable result - 94th percentile rank. He attributed his success to the accuracy of the training in pinpointing his problems (assessment) and helping him to overcome them (training). Best of all, being able to produce a relaxed, yet alert state even during a stressful situation like an exam, is a skill he should retain for the rest of this life.

g. Depression / Ruminations

Case # 10: Lorraine was 63 years of age when she started NFB training. She was extremely bright and active. She had been under unremitting stress for some time. She complained of depression and was constantly ruminating (negative thoughts). For more than 35 years she had been treated for severe bipolar disorder. She had been on virtually all appropriate and available medications during the course of this time. Her childhood history demonstrated clear ADHD symptoms, but she was an exceptionally bright student. Her EEG and stress test is discussed as a detailed example in the intervention section (Section VII) of this text. Neurofeedback combined with biofeedback was carried out. In a subsequent follow-up session three years later, it was found that she had remained off medications and has been functioning reasonably normally without medication for the entire time. Note: the authors wish to emphasize that this is a single case. Other cases have also improved. For case examples of depression the reader is referred to work by Elsa Baehr in her discussion of NFB techniques and results (Baehr et al., 1999).

h. Autism

Case # 11: (Also cited in Section V, Neuroanatomy) Troy, age 13, was completely oblivious to the meaning of expressed emotions of others. He appeared baffled, rather than angry, worried or saddened by loudly expressed anger towards himself or other people. He appeared flat, or merely overly excited, even with events that would be expected to evoke emotions. He did not express emotions appropriately either verbally or non verbally. His behaviour was impulsive and, as with many autistic children, it could be best understood if one assumed an underlying anxiety. During his sessions he would sometimes start to flap his hands or laugh suddenly with no external stimulation producing those behaviours. At school he was in a general learning disability class for very low functioning children. He had no friends and no interest in other people. Troy had been diagnosed as autistic both at the local children's hospital and, independently, by two other senior psychiatrists. Parents were told by a psychiatrist that the only help available was counseling to help them accept their son's permanent disability.

The right hemisphere's involvement in the expression of emotion (anterior area) and understanding of emotional communications *(parietal-temporal areas)* has been known for many years. The underlying major symptom of anxiety, coupled often with inexplicable impulsive outbursts and/or actions, are well known in individuals who have autistic spectrum disorders or Asperger's syndrome. The calming effect of right sided (C2, C4) SMR training in anxious and impulsive individuals has also been demonstrated. Therefore, augmenting 13-15 Hz and decreasing in the 'tuning out' dominant slow wave activity (3-10 Hz) made good sense, both neurologically and from experience.

During his grade eight year and the summer thereafter Troy took 80 NFB sessions. He was placed in a regular classroom for high school and took advanced courses in Math in 10th grade after having been in special education since kindergarten. He was socializing and made friends in his class and ate lunch with them. Of course, he was still recognizably different. He did not go in for sports, but otherwise he was able to fit into the regular activities of the school to a reasonable degree.

Eight years later, in a telephone follow-up, Troy's father indicated that Troy was too busy to take time to come in to do the retesting at this time. (He lives a long distance from the center.) His parents said that they thought his reluctance was also because he didn't want to recall that anything was ever wrong with him. He is doing well both socially and academically and he is in university.

The degree of the positive result with Troy, however, was not expected. We wish to be very cautious in making too much of his success (and the successful out-comes with a small number of other children) at least until there is a large case series to replicate our work.

We have previously noted that in autism and in Asperger's syndrome high slow wave amplitudes may be found in the central and frontal and pre frontal areas (Cz and Fz), similar to ADHD patterns. However, slowing may also be seen at T6 and, occasionally, very high amplitude of theta or low frequency alpha may be observed at P4. Right hemisphere, high amplitude, low frequency (7-8 Hz), activity that has the morphology of sinusoidal alpha waves is a kind of 'idling'. This right hemisphere 'idling', combined with prefrontal slow wave activity, may be a reflection of the difficulty these clients

have with expressing themselves appropriately socially, expressing affect, and interpreting social communication. In particular, they have an inability to interpret abstract references, inferences and innuendo and to understand non-verbal communication. We are finding improvements in social functioning in our Asperger's clients when we use P4, T6 low beta (13-15 Hz) training, in addition to decreasing the high amplitude low frequency (7-8 Hz) alpha (or theta when this is elevated) in this region. We combine this with decreasing left prefrontal and frontal high amplitude, slow wave activity and increasing SMR (12-15 Hz) in the right central region (C4).

i. Asperger's Syndrome
i. Mild Asperger's Symptoms
Case # 12, Brad, age 20. Brad had failed in his first year in a community college. He came for assessment and training largely because of difficulties with attention span and concentration in class and when doing assignments. However, his parents had another concern. Brad had never had friends in his own peer group. Exploring his history, symptom picture and, especially, his style of social interacting suggested mild Asperger's syndrome, rather that ADHD, Inattentive Type. His expression of affect was different. He would laugh suddenly when he thought he should, but it was often at an inappropriate time. The laugh did not sound genuine. His emotions and expressions were flat. He had limited comprehension of non-verbal communication and innuendo. Despite the obviously flat emotional appearance, Brad demonstrated physiological signs of anxiety that were confirmed with a psychophysiological stress assessment. This type of assessment involves measurement of pulse, heart rate variability, respiration, peripheral skin temperature, electrodermal response and electromyography activity in different states; for example, under the stress of doing difficult mental math and then while learning to relax..

The 19 channel EEG demonstrated high theta frontally and centrally and high amplitude low frequency activity (7 Hz & 9 Hz) that had the morphology of alpha at P4 & T6. This P4 & T6 slow wave activity can be seen in the eyes open segment of the EEG shown below.

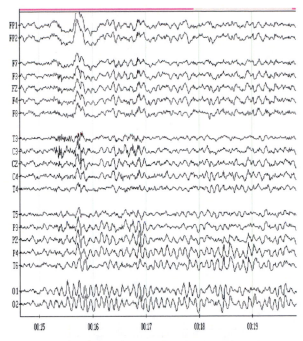

ii. Severe Asperger's Symptoms with a Low IQ

Case # 13. Ben, a 15 year old boy, has had well over 100 training sessions. Ben had hydrocephalus as an infant and, though treated, he remained a child with some cognitive deficits and a lower I.Q (1st percentile rank). When he presented at the center, he demonstrated extreme hyperactivity and impulsivity. His attention span was very short. He would burst into one office after another regardless of what the practitioner in that office was doing. He asked incessant questions in a loud voice but did not always wait for an answer before his next question. He irritated everyone. He ignored the fact that you were working with another person. Often his questions were personal and inappropriate and they could be about the person you were working with at the time. His conversations were entirely one-sided. He was overly formal, pedantic, precise, and his vocal tone was rather flat. He was completely oblivious to his effect on others – he couldn't "read" their reactions to him. Intellectual assessment showed him to be developmentally delayed but his problems went far beyond being a slow learner.

In addition high frequency (23-30 Hz) spindling beta was observed frontally. Initially training was to enhance 12-15 Hz activity and decrease theta (3-7 Hz) at Cz. Then he suppressed high beta (23-30 Hz) activity at F3 and Fz. Later, training also included enhancing low beta (13-15 Hz) and decreasing the high amplitude low frequency (7-9 Hz) at P4 and T6. This was followed by 2 channel training that combined decreasing left frontal high amplitude slow wave activity and increasing SMR in the right central region (C4) where there was a dip in SMR at 12-13 Hz. Concurrently, Brad practiced rhythmic diaphragmatic breathing at 6 breaths per minute in order to relax while remaining alert and learning cognitive strategies for school. Brad was easy to work with as he liked routines and was anxious to please.

Socially, he would only play with much younger children or just want to interact with adults. He had to control the interactions. His special interest was cars. He knows all the makes and likes to ask people what kind of car they drive.

He demonstrated very high theta and low SMR (13-14 Hz) activity at Cz. After 40 NFB training sessions (to decrease theta and increase SMR) he would walk calmly into the centre and wait for his trainer. If he wanted to ask a question, he would wait outside the room and not speak until you indicated he might. He could ask a sensible question and wait for an answer. He has learned that some questions are not OK to ask someone outside of his family. For example, he asked one of the staff if it is OK to ask people how old they are or how much money they earn. He is learning through observation and copying how to behave appropriately. One of the most dramatic examples of change in Ben was his response, upon retesting, to being asked to draw-a-person. His pictures at the time of initial assessment and after 40 sessions were shown earlier at the end of the last section on neuroanatomy. His brain maps are shown below, derived from the SKIL program (Sterman-Kaiser Imaging Labs).

After 40 sessions his parents are finding him more sociable. His listening has improved and he is managing much better at his part time job at a fast-food outlet. He can now take orders and do cash, whereas before he was only in the back doing routine food preparation. He has returned to college and is now passing his courses except in the case of not doing a group project because he did not have a group. Even more remarkable given his initial presentation and history, he is understanding jokes and he is able to appropriately carry on conversations with good eye contact.

In 2002 Ben was continuing to improve so he continued training once week. He is behaving in a more mature manner and is far less egocentric. He is still of below average intelligence but he communicates well now with both staff and students. When the school psychologist did a reassessment, the report stated she would not support the previous diagnosis of Asperger's syndrome because he made good eye contact ad was appropriate in conversation with adults. He is entirely bilingual, Cantonese and English, and translates for his parents. Ben has become a model for what neurofeedback can do in terms of increased calmness and social awareness. Parents in his community have noticed the improvement in Ben and have brought their own children for assessment and training.

This case is given not only because of the complex symptom picture, but also to demonstrate that children in a lower IQ range, the 1st % ile, may benefit from NFB training, though it will take longer and goals will be more modest. Also, due to the length of time necessary for training a child with severe Asperger's, some of these children are given a partial scholarship.

Brain maps done with Ben using SKIL (severe Asperger's Syndrome symptoms with low IQ).
 Eyes Closed Data:

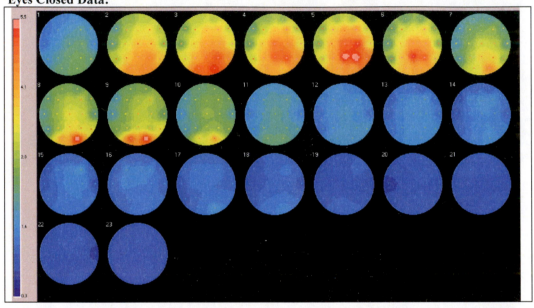

Eyes Open   Red = 4.4 μV   Light Blue = 1.1 μV

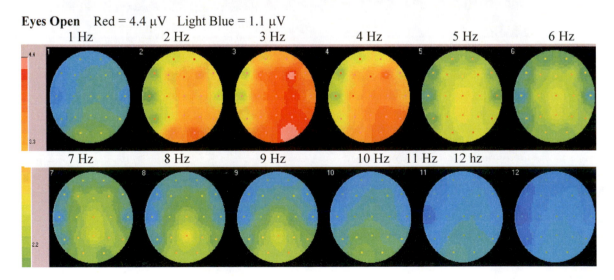

Note that eyes open data show slowing in the right hemisphere. Note also that they are similar but not quite the same as the eyes closed data shown earlier.

Figure Below: **Brain Map,** eyes open, comparison with **database** with a time-of-day correction on. Red = 1.5 SD above the da,ta base mean. Note the slowing in the right temporal region.

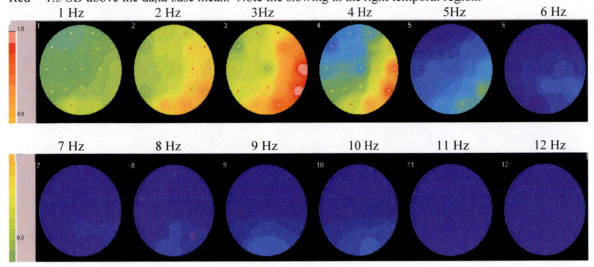

Figure Below: Brain Map, eyes open, showing comodulation of the dominant frequency range, 3-5 Hz, compared to the statistical database with a time of day correction on.

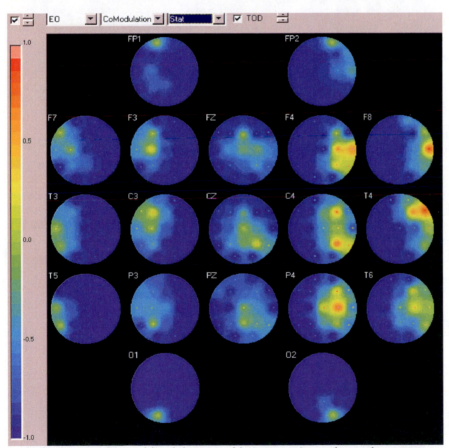

In the brain map above, this adolescent with Asperger's syndrome demonstrates a right to left disconnect (presumably not communicating at an expected level compared to the SKIL database) and some evidence of hyper comodulation ('spectral correlation") within the right hemisphere particularly between F4, C4 and P4. Social contextual functions would be expected to be degraded by this local disturbance in function.

These EEG findings and results of NFB in children who exhibit the symptoms of either high functioning autism or Asperger's syndrome are particularly interesting in light of recent imaging study findings and the findings on autopsy of individuals diagnosed with autism. For example, Dr. John Sweeney, a University of Illinois psychologist, found that activity in the prefrontal and parietal cortex is far below normal in autistic adults when they perform tasks that involve spatial memory. Functional imaging has demonstrated temporal lobe abnormalities and abnormal interaction between frontal and parietal brain areas (Pavlakis, 2001). As noted in the section on functional neuroanatomy, these areas of the brain are involved in planning and problem solving. They are important for keeping an ever-changing spatial map in our working memory. Sweeney used an experiment in which the subject must keep track of the locations of a blinking light. Nancy Minshew, a neurologist at the University of Pittsburgh, has collaborated with Sweeney and has suggested that connections between these areas of the brain are not functioning properly in autistic children (Minshew, Luna, Sweeney, 1999). This kind of finding suggests that in our work with the EEG, we should look carefully at *coherence* and *comodulation* between these and other areas of the brain in children who are diagnosed with autistic spectrum disorders. Perhaps training to improve deficiencies in communication and/or lack of appropriate discrimination in function between areas of the brain might be helpful.

Also of interest to NFB practitioners are the findings of Margaret Bauman, a pediatric neurologist at Harvard Medical School. She reported that on postmortem examination of subjects who had been diagnosed autistic, there were abnormalities in the limbic system. The cells in the area that includes the amygdala and the hippocampus were found to be atypically small and tightly packed together compared with the cells in normal subjects. Edwin Cook, University of Chicago, suggested that they look immature.

Neuroimaging studies carried out by Karen Pierce, a neuroscientist at the University of California at San Diego, demonstrated that the fusiform gyrus in people with autistic spectrum disorders did not react when they were presented with photographs of strangers but lit up when shown photographs of parents. Emotional responses thus seem to register in their brains even if persons who have symptoms in the autistic spectrum do not express the emotion outwardly. (Pierce, 2001). This finding of decreased activity extended to other areas of the brain that normally are expected to respond to emotional events. In normal people the fusiform gyrus specializes in the recognition of human faces. This fusiform gyrus lies on the medial aspect of the temporal lobe between the parahippocampal gyrus above and the inferior temporal gyrus below.

[You may recall that at its anterior end the parahippocampal gyrus curls around the end of the hippocampal sulcus to form the uncus which is continuous with the amygdaloid nucleus. At this bend is the olfactory sensory area. At its posterior end the parahippocampal gyrus forks with the superior end being continuous with the gyrus cinguli which turns around the splenium (posterior end of the corpus callosum) and runs anterior and superior to the corpus callosum. The inferior end is continuous with the lingual gyrus which runs posterior below the calcarine sulcus to the occipital pole. The visual sensory area is on the medial aspect of the occipital lobe at the posterior tip of the lingual gyrus. The counterpart to the hippocampal gyrus on the medial aspect of the temporal lobe is the superior temporal gyrus which lies on the lateral aspect of the temporal lobe and contains the auditory sensory area.]

Another finding, one which we cannot directly examine with the EEG, is that of Eric Courchesne. He has found that there are a smaller number of Purkinje cells in the cerebellum of autistic persons. Purkinje cells are an integral part of the brain's system for integrating sensory information with other areas of the brain. One could speculate that the work done by NFB practitioners to decrease slow wave activity and increase low beta and SMR in the 12-15 Hz range may have some beneficial effect on this system. This might, in part, account for some of the good results observed with clients who have autistic spectrum disorders.

Courchesne also has reported from brain imaging studies that the brain in autistic subjects is normal at birth but is larger than normal by age three (Courchesne, 2001). MRI-imaging demonstrated increases in both gray and white matter of the cerebral cortex. These differences are most likely genetic. Other theories abound including concerns about environmental pollutants and vaccinations for measles-mumps-rubella (MMR) One hypothesis regarding MMR is that it its not the vaccine itself but the fact that some batches have been preserved with thimersol, a substance containing mercury which could be toxic to the immature immune system. There are suggestions that there may be an increased genetic sensitivity to mercury due to other factors that might be encountered in the earliest years of life, such as the infant body's ability to eliminate such toxins.

We have found that the children and adults with Asperger's symptoms have characteristics which overlap with other disorders including: ADHD, obsessive compulsive disorder (OCD), anxiety and depression, subclinical seizure disorder, allergies, sensory disturbances. The symptom picture and treatments in the majority of traditional centres working with these clients differs little from that which has been carried out for decades (Thompson, 1983; Attwood, 1997; Wing, 2001).

We have found that constructive change can be considerably accelerated in some children and adults by the addition of NFB to the traditional approaches. It was encouraging that at scientific meetings in early 2003 there were independent reports of improvement in clients with Aspergr's syndrome (AS) from three different practices: Michael Linden in California, Betty Jarusiewicz in Massachusetts, and the authors in Toronto, Canada. Going beyond clinical anecdotes to controlled research will require research money and clinical trials.

iii. High Functioning Asperger's Syndrome

Case #14: Peter was an extremely bright but rather eccentric man in his early 50's. He came for neurofeedback training because he wanted to improve his attention when teaching bridge and when playing bridge competitively. Taking his history it became obvious that Peter's symptom picture was indicative of Asperger's syndrome rather than attentional problems. He was highly intelligent and had an IQ in the gifted range around 130 but, despite a university education, he had never had regular employment. He gave a detailed clinical history in a detached manner with a monotone voice. He described being seen by a number of child psychiatrists and psychologists in his youth and noted, "Nobody knew what to make of me but they said I was not

schizophrenic." His best adjustment was at university where he says being eccentric was all right. For a time he worked in a stamp and coin business (collecting was among his intense interests). In his 30's he had decided that he needed to change his behaviour and so he began to copy his stepfather. He even got married to a woman older than he; he chose for a wife because she had no faults and he could relate to her as his stepfather had related to his mother. Peter's EEG was characterized by an extremely high alpha amplitude at 11 Hz. He reported that he did often tune out; indeed, he did not drive because he said it would be unsafe due to what he termed his "white-outs".

With training he learned how to control his excess alpha and he also became calmer (less anxious) and more organized with SMR up-training. His IQ tested at 140 after training. He had increased the number of bridge classes he was teaching. About two years after finishing training he dropped in, looking very well turned out in blazer, tie and flannels This was in contrast to his previous style of dressing which had been based on comfort ahead of fashion. (In his first interview, for example, he had come with his trousers belted around his chest.) He had been in the area and wanted to share a copy of a glossy bridge magazine which featured an article he had written, "The Psychology of Bridge". Not only had his ability to organize his thoughts and get them down on paper improved, he now had something to say about how to navigate the social scene and get invited back to play again. He reflected that NFB training had had its greatest effect in the social domain.

Similar EEG and Symptom Findings Post-Encephalitis

The brain map below shows 9-10 Hz eyes closed comodulation comparison with the SKIL database. The subject is a very bright 44 year old woman who suffered from encephalitis when she was 22 years of age. At that time she had profound memory loss, speech impediment, disorientation. She stumbled into objects and the left side of her face drooped. She lost all ability to think in abstract terms. Before becoming ill she was superb at visualizing things. Even now she still must have everything presented concretely. Perhaps the anterior/posterior disconnect seen in the brain map below may correspond to her post-encephalitis loss of ability to visualize or even to interpret visual information or infer the abstract meaning of written material. She still has great difficulty correctly understanding social innuendo and the non-verbal aspects of social communication. Below the brain map is a sample of the eyes closed EEG from the same recording. (The same findings were present at 2 SD from the mean but the figure is presented here at 1 SD in order to be distinct for printing purposes.) Similar findings were found in the eyes open conditions doing reading and math.

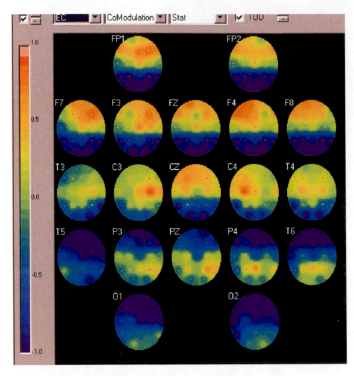

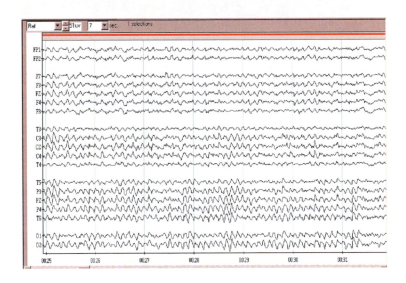

j. Brief Summary

The EEG assessment, which is often combined with a stress assessment for autonomic nervous system and EMG measures, leads to the design of an individualized, and therefore appropriate, combined NFB and BFB program. This careful assessment allows the practitioner to use these same measures to **assess physiological progress as training proceeds**. In our experience physiological shifts appear to correspond to long-term changes in both productivity and quality of life. In addition to doing NFB and

BFB, it is a good idea to complement this work with other stress reduction strategies, cognitive strategies, appropriate educational or work settings, and social support.

Careful assessment in each of the foregoing case examples led to more precise biofeedback. The assessment also enabled the client and the practitioner to evaluate physiological changes and correlate these with progress experienced subjectively by the client as training proceeded. Although it is a diverse group of clients, the four *common factors* suggested at the beginning of this section (attention, epileptiform activity, stability, and normalization of EEG patterns) encompass all of the difficulties presented by these clients. Depending on the client's symptom picture, the goal is either normalization or just self-regulation. Normalization is the goal if there is a disorder. Self-regulation, that is, increased control of mental states, is the primary goal if there is no disorder or if the client has not come to correct a disorder. This was true in the examples of an engineer applying to do postgraduate studies and the professional golfer who wanted to improve her golf.

B. How Assessment Relates to Goal Setting

1. Rationale for doing an Assessment
a. EEG Assessment
An EEG assessment is useful if you agree that:
1. There are differences in the EEG patterns between different mental states.
2. These differences can be detected by the EEG.
3. These EEG findings relate directly to what we should encourage with feedback; that is, training the right parameters allows a person to self regulate their mental state and, over time, normalize or shift their EEG pattern.

b. ANS and EMG Assessment
An assessment of the ANS (autonomic nervous system functions) and EMG (muscle tension) is useful if you agree that:
1. There are differences in the ANS patterns between relaxed and tense mental states.

2. These differences can be detected by the psychophysiological measurements used.
3. The findings relate directly to what we should encourage with biofeedback.

c. Before You Commence Training:
In our experience the EEG and ANS / EMG findings accurately reflect the histories given by students and clients. However, if you do encounter a discrepancy between the client's history and your findings, then this must be clarified and understood before commencing neurofeedback (NFB) and/or biofeedback (BFB). You must also set realistic goals with your client and then delineate enabling objectives with clear steps for reaching each of these goals. In this manner objectives are linked to procedures that you can do with your NFB and BFB equipment.

The case examples presented here clearly demonstrate that history and EEG findings do correlate and that it is possible to set realistic feedback goals.

2. Goal Setting
a. Most Common Client Goal: To Optimize Performance

i. Overview
Whatever the specifics of their original reason for coming, most clients want to optimize conscious, task-oriented performance. The goal to optimize performance can be expanded as follows:

To help a student/client achieve self-regulation of their mental state; in particular, the ability to have mental flexibility and to be able to produce a self-defined optimal mental state. This is usually a state of relaxed, alert, aware, calm, focused, problem-solving concentration, though different aspects will be emphasized with different clients and at different times with individual clients.

Each of these states, such as being relaxed or alert and so on, can be reworded as an *enabling objective.* To achieve each *enabling* objective you can use one or more biofeedback procedures which are designed to assist the student / client in learning self-regulation. The following is a brief overview of these enabling objectives and some of the biofeedback methods that can be used to improve them.

ii. To achieve a *relaxed* mental and physical state.

To achieve a relaxed state we will most often have the client increase EEG activity between 11-15 Hz and teach them to breathe diaphragmatically at a rate of about 6 breaths per minute (BrPM). For most adult clients this rate, 6 BrPM, will result in their breathing being in synchrony with their heart rate. In children the respiration rate will be a little faster than in adults. The heart rate will increase with inspiration and decrease with expiration (RSA). At the same time the client is taught to warm their hands and relax their muscles. The client is taught to gradually relax their forehead followed by their neck, shoulders, arms and hands. Relaxing often corresponds to a decrease in anxiety when this pattern is present. Anxiety may correlate with a high or labile electrodermal response (EDR). Chronic stress, on the other hand, may result in an abnormal response to a new stress. The EDR will go flat rather than showing an increase and finger temperature may actually increase rather than decrease.

Anxiety may also be reflected in the EEG. In the EEG it usually corresponds to an increase in 19-23 Hz activity relative to 15-18 Hz beta. A relaxed frame of mind implies that the individual is not negatively ruminating and worrying about aspects of their life. This type of unproductive mental activity may be found in conjunction with an increase in the amplitude of the EEG somewhere between 24 and 33 Hz as compared to beta activity immediately above and below that band-width.

Note that you adjust these general guidelines for individual clients. Depending on the EEG findings in assessment one may, for example, train 12-15 or 13 to 15 Hz.

iii. To achieve an *alert* mental state.

To accomplish this objective we encourage the student to maintain their electrodermal response (EDR) at a level which corresponds to alertness;

It should, however, not be as extreme as it could be with anxiety (too high) or with a drop in mental alertness (too low). EDR is measured between 2 electrodes placed across the palm or on 2 fingers. The EDR corresponds to sweat gland activity which is controlled by the sympathetic nervous system. For most young children being alert corresponds to a level between 12 –16 micromho (μMhos), adolescents 10 –15 μMhos, middle aged adults 8-12 μMhos, and as low as 3 –7 μMhos in older clients. (As always there are exceptions to this general outline.) It is usually desirable to see the student's /client's EDR constantly shifting but not fluctuating wildly between extremes.

Note: *You may encounter the term galvanic skin response (GSR) in your reading. This is the old unit of measurement of skin conductivity or* **'resistance'**. *It is measured in* **'ohms'**. *This was changed to its inverse (1/GSR) and called* **'conductivity'** *or electrodermal response (EDR). EDR is more intuitively obvious because it rises with alertness and excitement. The unit of measurement is just 'ohm' spelled backwards,* **'mho'**.

iv. To be *aware* of the environment.

In athletics this corresponds to the ability to respond rapidly to changing conditions. For example, a goalie in hockey must be aware of every player's position around the net. In this mental state the EEG will show a clear increase in 11 to 13 Hz. The athlete moves rapidly in and out of this state depending on the task. For example, an archer will be in *narrow focus* (beta, 16-18 Hz activity) when judging the wind and the distance. The archer will then move to this state of calm, *open awareness* (11-13 Hz) just prior to the release of the arrow (Landers, 1991).

Flexibility is important in terms of moving appropriately between different states (small changes between different ranges within alpha appears to be important in performance). As implied above, the alpha rhythm appears to be associated with a number of functional states. Some authors have said that low alpha (approximately 8-10 Hz) is associated with general or global attention. We find this is more often global in the sense of internal rather than external attention. People with good (versus poor) memories desynchronize (show desynchronized beta activity) and low alpha drops in amplitude during the encoding and retrieval of memory (Klimesch, 1999). A high alpha band (approximately 11-13 Hz) is associated with task specific attention. (Klimesch, Pfurtscheller and Schilmke, 1992; Cory Hammond and Barry Sterman, personal communication). A rise in alpha amplitude is seen in this range in high performing athletes (Landers, 1991). In this case the words 'task specific' may actually refer to what we term *broad total awareness*, which is a state of intense focus and readiness, without tension that is seen in the athlete.

v. To be appropriately *reflective*

This mental state usually corresponds to a temporary increase in the amplitude of high alpha, around 10-13 Hz. A task such as scanning text, organizing the important facts and registering them in one's memory, requires that a student move from narrow external focus on the material to internal reflection. Moving flexibly and continually between states is characteristic of effective learning.

vi. To remain *calm* even under stress

This mental state is also associated with being both *aware* and *reflective*. It may be attained by increasing 11-15 Hz and by decreasing 24 - 35 Hz. The 11 to 15 Hz band corresponds to the production of high alpha for reflection and sensorimotor rhythm for a sense of *calm*. As discussed above, increases in 21-35 Hz are often found to correspond to moments when a person is anxious and worrying or ruminating (usually negatively). This kind of ruminating mental state is the opposite of being calm. It is not conducive to efficient action or to the breadth of associations that would be necessary for creative thinking. In a calm mental state a person may also be physically relaxed. This state may, therefore, be associated with diaphragmatic breathing, good RSA, warm hands and relaxed musculature. One can also be calm mentally while carrying out a physically strenuous task. In this instance breathing and muscle tension would vary with the task.

vii. To be capable of sustaining a *narrow focus*

Being capable of sustaining a *narrow focus* for the required length of time for a specific task is a key to efficient academics and to optimal athletic performance. The student who is continually distracted by either internal or external stimuli will not achieve at the level of their intellectual potential. The athlete who loses focus in the middle of a golf swing will not win that round. Most of us produce bursts of waves either in the theta or the alpha range (somewhere between 3-10 Hz) when we are *internally* distracted.

viii. To be able to turn on and remain in a state of *problem-solving concentration*

Clients need to be able to turn on and remain in a state of *problem-solving concentration* until a task is complete or a problem is solved. This sustaining of focused concentration is a key to success both in school and in business. This state is usually associated with 16-18 Hz activity. It is also said to be associated with activity in the 39-41 Hz range known as Sheer rhythm.

However, one should also note that cognitive tasks require both memory retrieval (episodic memories) and semantic processing. Theta may be associated with tuning out from the external environment but it is also apparently necessary for *memory recall*. By asking the student to recall information, you can observe the frequency of theta and the wave-form produced for that individual. It will be different than the theta produced when that student is in a rather dreamy, *tuned out* state. Often more synchronous theta is evident in the tuned out state. Alpha-theta training in very accomplished music students (people who probably quite readily produced a lot of beta) was found to enhance aspects of their musical performance (Gruzelier 2003). In addition, semantic processing with eyes open has been observed to be associated with a decrease in synchronous high alpha, (Klimesch, 1999). Clearly one does not just shift into high amplitude beta and stay there to solve problems. There is a constant shifting between frequencies as one actively receives and processes information.

ix. Brief Summary

When working, studying or being involved in an athletic event the efficient individual is constantly fluctuating between the beta of narrow problem solving focus, high amplitude alpha for reflection and theta memory retrieval. Sterman has also noted that there is a brief burst of alpha activity after successful completion of a task that required sustained concentration. In the research he conducted with top gun pilots an alpha burst was observed when the wheels touched down during landing. These bursts may be called *event-related-synchronization*. This seems to be a way in which the brain rewards itself.

When one is working on optimizing performance it is usually beneficial to use various combinations of neurofeedback and traditional biofeedback. If you have an instrument which does only one of these, you may wish to expand some time in the future. Most clients require a combined approach. You can get good results with either, but our view is that the combination is more powerful. (This would make a good thesis topic to do efficacy comparisons.)

b. Normalization of the EEG:

Some clients have specific disorders and needs where the goal of training is related to reducing a defined symptom or problem, such as a learning disability, seizure disorder, movement disorder, stroke, speech disorder, depression, Autism, Asperger's and so on. In these clients it is appropriate to refer to *normalization of the EEG*. Normalization includes such factors as bringing the amplitudes of frequency bands and the communication (coherence or comodulation depending on what instrument and database you are using) between areas of the brain into the ranges found in normal databases. This kind of work is facilitated by a full-cap ($\geq$ 19 leads) assessment. This is more advanced work. Usually one is working on variations of normal brainwaves, such as excess theta in the majority of children with ADHD, rather than abnormal waves. Epilepsy is the obvious example where normalization, in the sense of having less epileptiform activity, is clearly the goal.

C. The EEG Assessment (QEEG)

1. An Overview from Assessment to Training
a. Steps to Optimize Performance

1. Decide on which mental state the client/student wishes to encourage and / or discourage. This investigation is facilitated by the intake interview and history taking. Goals may be clarified by psychological and performance testing as is appropriate for your student/client. Goals should be realistic and put in writing. After the EEG, ANS (autonomic nervous system) and EMG (electromyogram) assessments these goals will be linked to specific objectives for neurofeedback combined with biofeedback.

2. Assess the client's central nervous system (CNS) state by means of the EEG. Delineate how the client's quantitative electroencephalogram (QEEG) differs from expected age values. If you are not using a database, you can look at the pattern, both watching the dynamic EEG and looking at average values in different frequency ranges for the time period. Some programs produce a histogram and statistics, other provide values from which you can create your own graph. *Recall how Jane and John demonstrated differences from normally expected values in their EEG assessments and how these differences did correspond to the problems they were experiencing at work.* (Case examples #1 and #2 in part B of this section.)

3. Place electrodes at the sites you decide on based on EEG data, client's goals and history and your knowledge of neuroanatomy and brain function (see Decision Making Pyramid at the very beginning of part A of this section.) You want to inhibit the frequencies prone to EMG artifact in order to provide accurate feedback. Encourage the client to decrease the appropriate slow wave frequency band(s) while simultaneously increasing the appropriate fast wave frequency band. (Appropriate, here, means appropriate for that client's EEG pattern, symptom picture and goals.) Remember, **the EEG acts like a '*flag*' which reflects brain functioning. You can infer from a flag's activity the wind's velocity (amplitude) and direction. You make inferences about the brain's activity by reading the EEG.** You are now ready to set up display screen instruments to assist the client to self-regulate their mental state using EEG biofeedback or neurofeedback.

4. Decide on the training screen you wish to use. The selection will depend on the EEG equipment you are using. Some allow you to customize the visual feedback and audio feedback and nearly all instruments offer a range

of feedback screens. It is helpful if there are methods for measuring achievement. These may include percentage-of-time over or under threshold and a measurement that gives the client a sense of how often they are able to hold a mental state for 1 or more seconds (*decrease variability*). It is also helpful if the raw EEG is available for viewing. Children, in particular, become very good at *pattern-recognition* quite quickly.

5. Assess the *flags* which reflect information concerning the client's autonomic nervous system (ANS) such as: peripheral skin temperature, electrodermal responses, respiration, pulse rate, heart rate variability with inspiration and expiration (termed *respiratory sinus arrhythmia* or RSA), and musculo-skeletal nervous system (MSNS) activity in terms of muscle tension (EMG).

6. Assist those clients who demonstrate anxiety and tension to relax in order to facilitate their work on self-regulation of their mental state. Both you and the client can see how they are doing if you set up feedback for autonomic nervous system/electromyogram (ANS/EMG) feedback. If you do not have general biofeedback capabilities, you can still work on diaphragmatic breathing, imagery, and other relaxation techniques. Remember, however, that you are usually not trying to achieve the kind of relaxation associated with being in a hammock. **You want to maintain mental alertness but be free of tension.** Use the example of the top gun pilots to epitomize being alert yet physically relaxed (not tense).

7. Do the training until the client has mastered an appropriate degree of self-regulation and achieved the goals that were set out initially.

Note: *In the following though the specific examples will often involve applications to ADHD and/or to optimizing performance, the principles apply to the general use of neurofeedback and biofeedback. At the time of writing applications of EEG biofeedback other than for ADHD and seizure disorders would be considered experimental. This may rapidly change as more papers are published.*

2. Doing the EEG Assessment (QEEG)
a. Overview
When we speak of assessment remember that we are assessing the client's suitability for neurofeedback. We are not assessing this EEG in order to make a diagnosis.

This section outlines how to make decisions concerning the type of EEG assessment to carry out, the electrode sites to use, the preparation of the sites and the importance of measuring impedances between each pair of electrodes. Different *filtering* (FIR, IIR, FFT) will affect your data. This will be noted, though much of the equipment currently available on the market does not offer you a choice; you use the filter that the manufacturer decided was best. This is followed by a consideration of *conditions* under which the recording is made (eyes open or closed, with or without tasks), types of artifacts that may affect the recording and how these artifacts are recognized and removed. This section will conclude with a short summary of some of the different EEG patterns you are likely to encounter.

i. A Note about Disorders appropriate for Neurofeedback Intervention
It is important to communicate clearly to your client that you are only interested in variations in the distribution and amplitudes of NORMAL brain waves. (The exceptions would be work with epilepsy or closed head injury.) Doing QEEG assessment as a preparatory step before working with clients to help them learn self-regulation is a totally different process than that carried out by the neurologist when he does an EEG assessment. Let us underscore again that the neurologist is looking for abnormalities, whereas we are looking, by and large, at variations on normal. As well, we are not doing a diagnosis. We are looking for patterns that indicate whether a person is an appropriate candidate for neurofeedback intervention.

An EEG is defined as 'normal' if it does not contain 'abnormal' waves or patterns "which are known to be associated with clinical disorders" (Fisch, p. 141). In this definition clinical disorders are understood to refer to medical illnesses, such as: seizure disorders, dementias, conditions causing encephalopathies and space occupying lesions such as tumors, subdural haematomas and aneurysms. We do not usually interpret the term "clinical disorders" (when it is used referring to neurological conditions) to include mild to moderate changes in mood, movement, impulsivity, attention or focus. These are not, in themselves, the usual reasons a physician would refer a patient to a neurologist for an EEG assessment. In this regard a traditional EEG read by a neurologist is not helpful when diagnosing ADD, but a QEEG is invaluable when planning a neurofeedback intervention for this disorder. Norms for theta/beta ratio measured at CZ have been published and they discriminate ADHD from controls with 98% accuracy (Monastra et al., 1999).

Where symptoms are due to a serious, significantly incapacitating medical illness, then that individual must first be assessed by a physician before you begin your work. A child with difficulties in school but no physical symptoms would usually not fit into this category. This being said, some people use the term disorder (as in Attention-Deficit/Hyperactivity Disorder) incorrectly for children who are having difficulties, such as being restless or daydreaming or underachieving. ADHD should be reserved for those who are "impaired to a clinically significantly degree"(DSM IV) by difficulties with attention span, distractibility and impulsivity.(Note, this does not refer to symptoms from other, comorbid disorders such as oppositional defiant disorder.)

It is important in ADHD to be clear concerning severity of the primary symptoms. There are a small percentage of children who do, for example, fit the diagnostic label of attention deficit DISORDER. These are the children who usually cannot attend regular school programs due to the severity of the impulsive and hyperactive symptoms. These children require medications and should be first seen by a physician. They may then attend NFB sessions and it is likely that over time their need for medication will lesson. Many of these children may later be able to come off medications altogether as they learn to self regulate and manage their symptoms. In one clinical study 80% of the children who were taking Ritalin when they started neurofeedback training were off the stimulant drug by the time they had done

40 sessions of training (Thompson & Thompson, 1998).

ii. The Principle of Parsimony

In general we should follow the medical motto, "do no harm" and also follow the principal of parsimony. Being parsimonious suggests that we first try the least invasive, least disruptive intervention which has a chance of being effective. (The late Naomi Rae-Grant, a very wise and practical professor of child psychiatry, always stressed this principle, especially when she was the Director of Children's Mental Health Services for the Province of Ontario in Canada.) We should all keep these basic tenets in mind as we work with clients. If a child is impaired to a significant degree, then that child may have to be referred to a physician for a treatment which will allow the child to attend school, such as stimulant medication for a very hyperactive child. This, however, is *invasive* and ideally should only be used for a short time until the child can learn self-regulation. Self-regulation to manage ADHD symptoms can be accomplished using neurofeedback. Joel Lubar has worked in this field for more than 25 years and has tracked his clients' outcomes. He reports a 90% success rate using neurofeedback with children who have ADHD.

On the other hand, the term "clinical disorder" is appropriately applied to some conditions which should always be seen first by a physician but which can also be helped with neurofeedback training as an adjunct to medical management. This list includes disorders such as: seizure disorders (Sterman, 2000) where there is good research (i.e., good controlled studies that have been replicated), depressive disorders where there is just a little research (Rosenfeld, 1997; Baehr, 1999), and Parkinson's Disease where work is just beginning (Thompson & Thompson, 2002). There is also a small base of literature on closed head injury and the state of Texas passed legislation in 2002 that ruled that neurofeedback as an intervention should be reimbursed when used in the treatment of brain injured patients. (Lynda Kirk, personal communication)

b. Goal of the Assessment
i. Goal

One goal for assessment is to ascertain what is different from usual patterns in your client's EEG so that you may decide on an EEG normalization training program. You must first compare a number of variables, such as the power of the EEG in different frequency bands, as compared to expected age norms. Database norms for children doing active tasks, such as reading and math, are very limited. Norms for persons doing activities with their eyes both open and closed have been gathered by Sterman and are contained in the SKIL program for analyzing 19 lead EEG data. Large databases are available for EEGs with eyes closed from several sources, such as those from Frank Duffy, E. Roy John, Robert Thatcher or William Hudspeth (Duffy, 1989). (However, you may have difficulty comparing your data to a particular database (see Congedo et al, 2002).)

For a one or two channel assessment we suggest the following brief list of objectives. Usually one is trying to assist the student to achieve self-regulation of mental states that are reflected in the EEG, so keep that in mind as the purpose of collecting data.

ii. Objectives:
(1.) To be able to graph amplitude (either microvolts or picawatts) versus frequency (1 to 61 Hz) to show a pattern typical for the individual client.

(2.) To ascertain the dominant slow wave frequencies within the 3-10 Hz frequency range since these are the frequencies one will likely wish to inhibit.

(3.) To be able to examine the relative power in different fast wave frequency bands from 12 to 61 Hz. These can be relatively wide bands such as: high alpha 11-13 Hz, SMR 13-15 Hz, low beta 16-20 Hz, high Beta 21-24 Hz, 25-36 Hz (particularly 27-32 Hz for some clients), 39-41 Hz (Sheer Rhythm), 45-58 Hz (which can reflect muscle activity) and 49-51 Hz in Asia, Australia and Europe (which may warn you that your electrode connections should be redone or that there is external ambient electrical activity which you may need to reduce). Rather than the foregoing wide bandwidths, it is preferable for some purposes to do 1Hz band topographs as can be seen, for example, in 19 channel assessments using the SKIL program. However, overlapping 2 Hz bands as can be used in single channel assessments with instruments such as the ProComp+/BioGraph. The Autogen A620 program also does a very well thought out assessment that is particularly useful for ADHD when used in conjunction with the norms for theta/beta power ratios (4-8/13-21Hz) from a multi-site study. (Monastra, Lubar et al, 1999)

(3.) To be able to calculate the ratios of slow (theta and alpha) frequency bands to fast wave (SMR and low beta) frequency bands.

c. EEG Assessment - Outline
To fulfill objectives for either optimizing performance or normalizing an EEG pattern it is helpful to have an *EEG assessment profile presented as a histogram or graph.* Some instruments do this for you. With others you can collect the necessary data to plot amplitude (in microvolts) on the vertical or 'y' axis against frequency (in Hertz) on the horizontal or 'x' axis. This will enable you to distinguish EEG frequency patterns and design an EEG feedback program. In the future we hope that most EEG instruments will do this for you as part of their software. However, at the time of writing only three out of seven different manufacturers' instruments at our centre either do this or allow you to collect the necessary data to do this for yourself on a summary graph sheet.

We, therefore, recommend that, regardless of which instrument you choose to use for neurofeedback, you should also have one instrument that will enable you to do a careful assessment. There are some instruments that do both data collection for assessment purposes and feedback.

d. EEG Assessment - Method
i. Overview of Electrode Site Locations
An electrode or *sensor* is usually a tiny gold or tin cup. Whatever material you use, all your sensors must be of the same metal. The first thing you want to know is where to place these electrodes on the scalp. This is done in a world-wide standardized and systematic way. It is called the international 10-20 system (Jasper, 1958). This system is reviewed in the diagram below. The name is descriptive. You will note on the diagram moving from the front of the head (face), which is called *anterior,* to the back of the head, called *posterior,* that the 10 and the 20 of '10-20' refer to 10% and 20% of the distance between the *nasion* (anterior) and the *inion* (posterior). You can easily feel both of these

bony protuberances. The nasion is the little notch above (*superior to*) your nose and below your forehead. The inion is the little bump or ridge at the base of your *occiput* (back of your skull) and above your neck. You measure the distance between these two points with a measuring tape, preferably one in centimeters to give more accurate readings. A typical measurement is 36 cm. 10% of this distance above the nasion gives a midpoint between two prefrontal lobe sites called FP1 and FP2. 20% of the distance between nasion and inion takes you to the next point on the diagram, Fz. The next 20%, moving from front to back, takes you to Cz, which is the half-way point between nasion and inion.

Odd numbers always refer to electrode placements on the left side of the head. Even numbers refer to electrode placements on the right side of the head. The letter 'z' is used to denote any point along the central or midline between nasion (Nz) and inion (Iz).

The letters F, C, P, O, and T refer to areas of the brain: Frontal, Central, Parietal, Occipital and Temporal.

In a similar fashion you measure transversely from the *pre-auricular notch* on the left side to the same notch on the right side of the head. The pre-auricular notch is an indentation you can feel just in front of the ear canal. It is most easily felt if you open and close your jaw. Measuring from the pre-auricular notch on the left side to the pre-auricular notch on the right side, 10% of the total distance brings you to a point above the left pre-auricular notch called T3. The next 20% measured from T3 brings you to C3 and the next 20% to the central point Cz. Frontal, central and parietal sites used in the 19 channel full-cap assessments are the main locations for most of our work with neurofeedback.

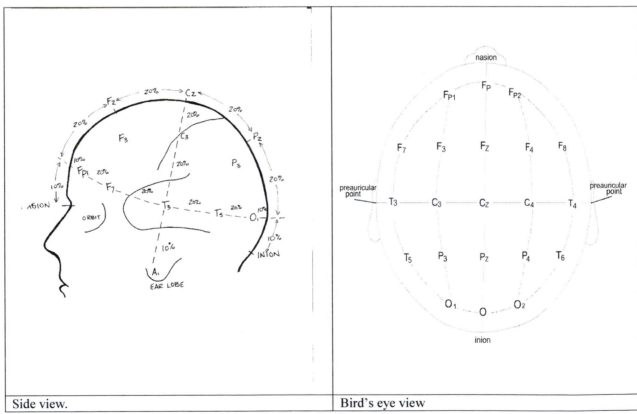

| Side view. | Bird's eye view |

Diagram of the International 10-20 Electrode Placement System

The neurologist is often looking for seizure activity. We are not usually doing that but you should be aware that interictal epileptiform activity (that which occurs *between seizures*, as contrasted to activity during a seizure) is most often detected in the anterior temporal region.

An electrode to detect this activity may be placed 1 cm above a point on the line between the lateral canthus of the eye and the external ear canal that is a third of the distance from the ear canal.

A styrofoam 'head' from a hairdressing supply house, though not anatomically correct and lacking a proper inion, is useful to help you practice marking these points on a model head so you can visualize them more easily. It is not as easy as it sounds if you want to be precise about placements. Fortunately a cap, available in different sizes, is available that has the electrodes built in for the 19 sites on the scalp that are used for standard EEG recordings. It looks rather like a bathing cap. A neurologist or an EEG technician, however, may measure for each location rather than using a cap. To obtain sites encircling the head they measure the circumference. This is done by beginning the measurement from the midpoint between O1 and O2, ('O' for occiput) which is 10 % above the inion on the anterior-posterior midline of the head. Alternatively, one can begin from a point which we call Fpz that is 10% of the anterior – posterior distance but above the nasion. The measurement for the circumference then goes through Fp1 (frontal pole on the left) approximately above the middle of the eyebrow, which is 5% of the distance around the circumference to the left from FPz, then F7, T3, T5, 01, 02, T6, T4, F8, FP2 that are all 10% of the total circumference from each other. The diagram above indicates measurements for just one side, from FPz to midway between O1 and O2, so the percents are 10% and 20% of half circumference.

Don't be confused if you see designations that differ from the above! Renaming of sites has occurred in the last decade and in some literature you may find the *Expanded 10-20 System* is being used. In that case T3 and T4 are now T7 and T8 while T5 and T6 are now P7 and P8. This is according to a modified and expanded 10-20 system proposed by the American Clinical Neurophysiology Society. (See Appendix II in Fisch, 1999 for the details and a diagram and also Jasper, 1958.) Some labs are using 128 leads and there is even research being conducted using more than 200 leads so that maximum spatial resolution is achieved. The highest number of channels used by neurofeedback practitioners is typically 22 leads, 19 on the scalp, a ground, and the two ears for reference.

ii. Choosing Electrode Placements for Assessment

Now you must decide how many channels you will use for your initial assessment. Think of a *channel* as the gateway where you plug the wire from your electrodes into the encoder which sits on the desk and is attached to the computer. Three leads go into a preamplifier which is closer to the electrodes (on the scalp in the very sophisticated research done with pilots or clipped to the persons shirt near the shoulder). These three leads are the *active* and *reference* electrodes and the *ground* wire. One lead comes out of the preamplifier and goes to a single channel or entrance point on an encoder which sits on the desk or is attached to the client's belt. In some equipment the preamplifier and the encoder are in a single box on the desk. The encoder may have more than one entrance or channel for sets of wires. For most people the choice is between 1 and 2 channels. For more complex cases a full-cap (19 channels) is preferable. The encoder may have other channel inputs for other biosignals used in regular biofeedback, such as temperature, EDR, EMG, pulse and respiration.

The most common placement for a single channel recording is Cz. This site is less influenced by artifact because it is far from the eyes (eye blink and eye movement artifacts) and from the jaws (a common source of muscle artifact). Cz is also far from the ear reference so that there is less common mode rejection and you record a higher amplitude activity than you would at sites closer to the ear lobe. It provides information about activation (or lack of it) in the central region and across the sensorimotor strip. The most common type of ADHD characterized by theta in frontal and central regions can be readily seen at the Cz location. For adults, move the electrode slightly forward to FCz (half way between Fz and Cz) for an ADD assessment.

3. Types of Single Channel QEEG Assessment

A minimum of three leads are necessary to record the EEG. It is analogous to getting electricity from a 3-prong wall electrical outlet.

These leads are: an active electrode (+ve) and a reference electrode (-ve) and a *ground*. Electrical activity is measured as the potential difference between two sites, that is between your positive and negative leads. In what is called a *referential* recording, you will usually initially place an active electrode at Cz with a reference electrode attached to the left ear or placed over the mastoid. A sequential placement (in older terminology *bipolar*) also uses three electrodes. In this case, however, you are measuring the potential difference between 2 electrodes which are both "active" in the sense of being over an area of the brain where cortical electrical activity is produced. More on this shortly.

a. Types of Single Channel EEG Assessments

i. The 3 Electrode Referential Placement

For most clients we use a *referential* placement. As explained earlier, *Referential placement* means that you place an *active* (+ve) electrode at one site, for example, Cz, and a *reference* (-ve) electrode on the left (or right) ear lobe or over the mastoid bone. The word *active* means that you presume most of the EEG electrical activity that you are recording, comes from this site. *Reference* means that you presume that this site is relatively inactive. The ear lobe has been found to have less than 15% of the electrical activity of other sites on the scalp. A third electrode is called a *ground*. This wire is not actually connected to ground. It goes to the amplifier and does what could be termed *electrical housekeeping*. In some instruments, such as the F1000, you can demonstrate a good quality EEG without this wire if the client remains motionless and there is no movement in the environment. In practice, however, you must be as careful about the attachment of the ground electrode as you are about the two that produce the voltage difference you are measuring.

Where should I place the electrodes when the results at Cz do not parallel the clinical history?
Using ADHD as the example, if you look at the assessment of a person who has all the symptoms of ADHD and you do not see any deviation in the EEG from what you would expect in an individual who does not exhibit this cognitive style, then you should look a little further. Try placing your active (+ve) electrode on Fz. You may then measure the high amplitude slow wave (theta or alpha) that was not seen at Cz. There are different EEG patterns for ADD and you will pick up most of them by placing your electrode at Cz and then trying Fz to get a clear picture of high slow wave activity relative to beta. In some clients you may find that theta is higher at C3 or C4 than at Cz. Thus, if you are not able to do a full-cap and your client's EEG does not appear to match the clinical history, move the active electrode to different sites. *High beta ADD* may show more in the frontal sites. (In our experience, *high beta ADD* is usually associated with other difficulties. The clients do drift off focus on what is being said to them or what they are reading but they note that this is because their mind is 'racing' on about other matters. Usually these 'other matters' are personal problems that they ruminate about repeatedly. Most often the high beta is above 23 Hz but some clients also have very high amplitude bursts between 15 and 20 Hz and even occasionally between 13 and 15 Hz. If you take the time to watch the EEG and pause it at these points of increased beta amplitude, your client may be able to tell you exactly how their mental state changed and what they were thinking about. The majority of these clients will complain of dysphoria if not depression.

For some clients, where the symptom picture is clear but the Cz site and other sites referenced to the left ear do not show ratios significantly different from expected values, we will do one or more of the following:
- A bipolar assessment
- A 2 channel assessment
- A full-cap assessment

ii. Sequential (bipolar) QEEG Assessment:

When you use a sequential placement, you have 2 active electrodes in sequence on the surface of the scalp. Since all measurements are *bipolar* because you are always measuring the potential difference between two sites, use of the term bipolar to refer to measurements where there was cortical activity at both sites has fallen out of favour and been replaced with the term *sequential*. This is in contrast to a referential placement where one electrode is considered to be relatively inactive (ear lobe or mastoid bone). The sequential montage may measure activity between electrodes placed either longitudinal (anterior-posterior *lateral*) or *transverse*, (right-left *lateral*). Thus both these placements may be referred to as *lateral*. The activity measured is coming from dipoles between the electrodes. It is a difference between two points in the cortex. This is a different measurement than the referential placement which measures almost vertical to the surface of the cortex and may be referred to as a *radial* measurement.

For an initial assessment of a child thought to have ADHD, the sequential placement will place the positive (+ve) electrode at FCz (10% anterior to Cz which is half way between Fz and Cz) and the negative (-ve) at PCz (10% posterior to Cz - where % refers to % of the distance between the nasion and inion). To assess an older adolescent (age ≥16) or adult we will place the electrodes slightly more anterior at Fz and Cz. Usually a sequential placement will give lower amplitude readings due to *common mode rejection*. (There will be more activity in common between Fz and Cz than between Cz and the ear.) Occasionally, we will observe a much higher theta/beta ratio with the sequential placement than we do with a referential placement. Lubar suggests that you train using the placement that gives the highest ratio.

With the *referential* placement one can reasonably assume that any electrical changes being measured are from the site under the electrode on the scalp.

With the *bipolar* placement you cannot be sure what the electrical measurements represent. For example, a Fz–Cz sequential placement indicating that theta was high amplitude could mean it was high at Fz (relative to Cz) or that it was high at Cz (compared to Fz). It could also be a phase difference, that the wave at Cz was *out-of-phase* with the wave at Fz. With waves 180° *out-of-phase* one would register a higher amplitude of that frequency compared to waves which were *in-phase*.

To make it more complicated, if you were trying to measure changes over time, it is conceivable that you could have a situation where you might conclude, after training using a sequential placement, that no electrical change had take place using a referential montage and yet see a significant change using a sequential montage. This is diagramed below. In this figure the beginning higher amplitude (amplitude is the y axis) is theta and the lower amplitude at the starting point (time is the x axis) is beta or SMR. **This is a hypothetical example.**

Inhibit & Reward Frequencies *Changes over time with training:*
(Adapted from Discussion With Professor Joel Lubar)

Below is a diagram representing sequential measurements done at:
Fz-Cz

Below is a diagram representing referential measurements done at:
Fz

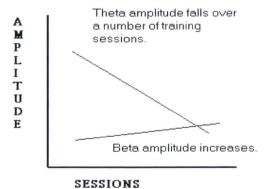

Bipolar Measurement Done.

Theta amplitude falls over a number of training sessions.

Beta amplitude increases.

SESSIONS

Theta & beta amplitude apparently remained the same when measured referentially.

Measurements are with sequential placement.

Measurements with referential placement.

In both the above diagrams and the diagram shown below, the 'y' axis is amplitude in microvolts and the 'x' axis is the number of sessions from pre-training assessment to post-training reassessment.

Below is a diagram representing referential measurements done at **Cz**

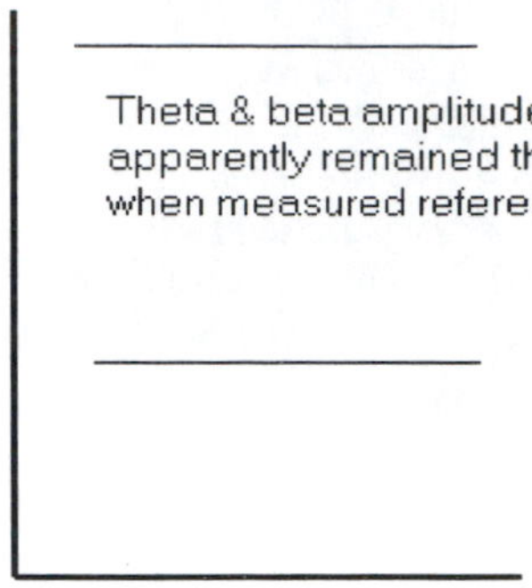

Explanation

Y axis = amplitude (uv)

X axis = time (treatment)

Referential: apparently **no** change.

Bipolar: large change due either to *phase* alteration or to do with the fact that a different axis of activity (lateral versus radial) is being measured.

Theta & beta amplitude apparently remained the same when measured referentially.

One other possible explanation of this is that the rate of transmission of information between the two sites (Fz & Cz) may have changed (not the true amplitude). This could change the phase relationship which would appear as a change in amplitude. Lubar has remarked that using a sequential placement, though it has the disadvantage of not knowing at which site change has taken place, may have the advantage that it gives the brain more possible ways to learn the task of changing the theta/beta ratio.

b. Interpretation of Findings from Your One Channel Assessment Bandwidths

ADD is a good example for EEG assessment. It is relatively simple to do but it demonstrates the care that must be taken in interpreting the EEG findings. For example, the clinician must consider other factors which may affect the ratio of theta / beta activity. These include anxiety and/or alcohol problems that may increases beta, especially above 20 Hz. This may lower the theta / beta ratio. If one doesn't carefully remove artifacts the data may be distorted in a way that makes theta appear high. For example 4-8 Hz activity may be high due to electrode movement, eye movement or eye blinks. This may give a false impression of a high theta / beta ratio. Beta activity may appear high due to muscle tension giving a false impression of a low theta / beta ratio.

The ratio, itself, may not reflect what is going on due to measurement factors. For example, if you use 4-8 Hz for theta but the client's high activity is 7-9 Hz then your theta / beta ratio may look fine as it does not reflect this client's tuning out in what we call *thalpha*. If a power ratio 4 –8 /13 – 21 Hz is used, but alpha is very high spilling over into 13 and 14 Hz range, then a person with clear ADD symptoms might be reported as having a ratio within the normal range. Another problem is that not just artifact, but real cortical activity, such as a brief absence seizure, will affect the ratio by producing a short burst of extraordinarily high slow wave activity. There is simply no substitute for a careful analysis of the raw, dynamic EEG. Being able to see an FFT derived spectrum of 1 Hz bins of activity for each one second epoch of EEG activity is extremely helpful as well. This is shown in our assessment screen below.

The diagrams below represent a range of clients measured on different instruments. They demonstrate how EEG patterns differ among clients with different symptom pictures. They also demonstrate different ways of looking at the data from a one channel assessment.

i. Case Example: Philip, age 10, ADD without Hyperactivity.

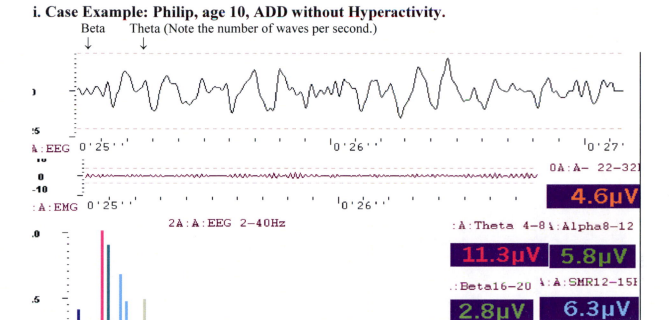

The above figure is an example of a one channel EEG assessment screen created using Procomp+/Biograph from Thought Technology. The screen shows a 2 second EEG sample and a spectrum that relates information about the first second shown at the top. The student, Philip M. is a 10 year old boy. He demonstrates all the symptoms associated with Attention Deficit Disorder. When Philip's mind wanders off topic, his EEG demonstrates an increase in amplitude at 6-7 Hz. In the figure above the theta/beta ratio (4-8 / 16-20) is 4. Microvolt ratios above 3 are fairly typical of young children who have ADD symptoms. Children without ADD symptoms are usually below 2.5. Philip is not an impulsive child. He has been diagnosed with ADHD Inattentive Type (DSM-IV 314.00) and his SMR activity is consistently higher than beta. There is virtually no effect of muscle activity on this EEG (45-58 Hz is very low) as shown in the "EMG" line below the EEG line. This 2-second sample was consistent with the statistics for an artifacted 3-minute sample done eyes open.

ii. Case Example: Mike, age 29, ADHD and Anxiety.

In the figure below Mike, case example # 9, said he had tuned out and could not recall what I was saying to him.

In the figure opposite, alpha wave is seen. Compare its repeated sinusoidal nature to most theta and beta waves.

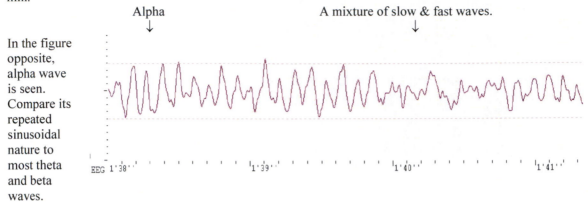

iii. Example: Barry, teenager, non-ADD.

In the figure below, a Fast Fourier Transform (FFT) power spectral array from the A620 (Stoelting Autogenics) program shows the EEG from a referential assessment (Cz to the left ear lobe). This EEG was taken from a client who reported **no** ADD symptoms. Note the reasonably high level of activity through the beta range to 18 Hz.

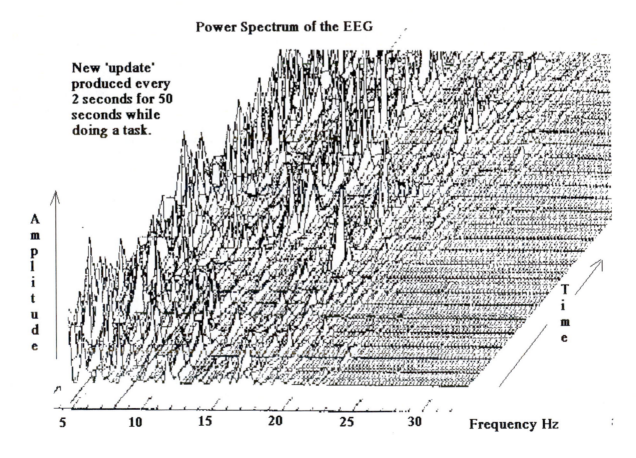

iv. Case Example: John, 10 years of age, ADHD, Combined Type.

The figure below is another Fast Fourier Transform (FFT) power spectral array from the A620 (Stoelting Autogenics) program showing the EEG from a referential Cz to the left ear lobe assessment. This EEG was taken from a client who demonstrated moderately severe symptoms of ADHD. Note the striking lack of activity through the beta range compared to relatively high activity in theta.

Although the power spectrum showing the ADHD pattern is at a slightly lower magnification than the one in the foregoing diagram, the differences are clear. (The magnification is usually increased for older clients since amplitude decreases with age, in part due to the adult's thicker skull.) Numerically, in the non-ADD example above, the theta / beta (4-8 / 16-20) µV ratio was 1.2 whereas the same ratio in the second, ADD example, was 3.2. These two samples demonstrate a very clear difference in the amount of slow wave as compared to fast wave activity. While teaching in Basel Switzerland, we used the analogy that the activity between 2 and 20 Hz is like Canadian geography for the person with ADHD, with the western mountains (lower frequencies) and the plains of the prairie provinces (higher frequencies), whereas the non-ADHD pattern is like Swiss geography with mountains and valleys across the whole range.

Power Spectrum of the EEG

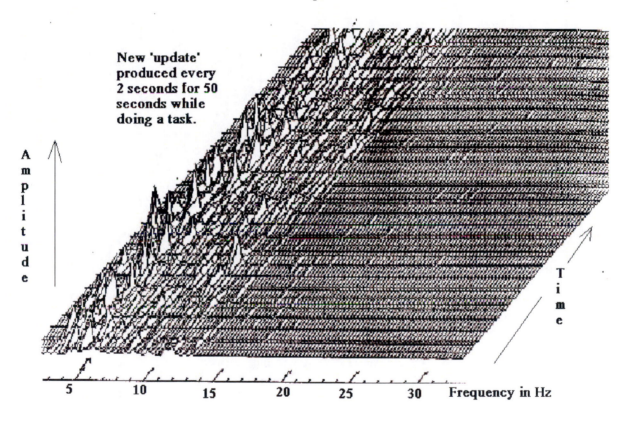

New 'update' produced every 2 seconds for 50 seconds while doing a task.

v. Case Example: Mary, age 47, Parkinson's Disease plus Dystonia.

Note: We find the same pattern (though less extreme) in *Tourette's* and the same treatment regimen has been successful in the clients who present with Tourette's disorder.

The next figure constitutes a histogram. It was drawn from a 3 minute artifacted collection of

EEG data which had been taken using a sequential recording at Fz-Cz. A sequential placement ("bipolar" using older terminology) was used to try to reduce the movement artifact. Unwanted movement, both tremor and dystonic movements, were not within this client's control at the time of assessment.

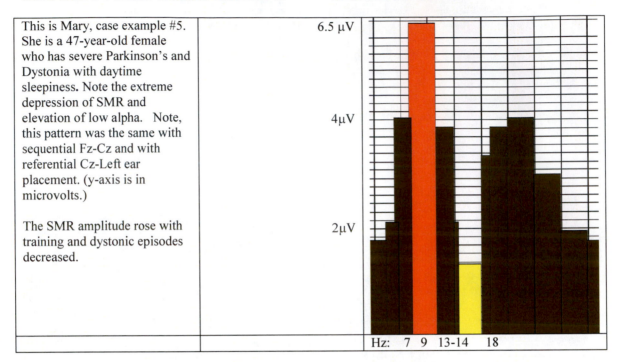

This is Mary, case example #5. She is a 47-year-old female who has severe Parkinson's and Dystonia with daytime sleepiness. Note the extreme depression of SMR and elevation of low alpha. Note, this pattern was the same with sequential Fz-Cz and with referential Cz-Left ear placement. (y-axis is in microvolts.)

The SMR amplitude rose with training and dystonic episodes decreased.

As you can see, it is very helpful to graph your data. It also allows comparisons of frequency band amplitudes over time as training progresses.

vi. Case Example: Joan, age 28, a professional golfer with ADHD.

Joan came to the ADD Centre to add to her concentration skills and to improve her performance in golf. However, on taking her history it became evident that she had had some difficulty staying focused in school and had many symptoms of ADHD. In addition, she worried about her performance constantly while playing in competition. When she worried, 29-32 Hz beta activity increased and SMR (13-15 Hz) activity decreased. This kind of pattern is also seen in clients who are depressed and tend to ruminate. The client's mind is likened to a car engine. The accelerator has been pressed to the

floor and the engine is on maximum revolutions. However, the car is in first gear and effectively going nowhere!

Below is another method of graphing the results of an assessment. In this example Joan's data has been exported to a spreadsheet. The spreadsheet below is a relatively simple one from Microsoft Works. This kind of spreadsheet allows one to overlay reassessments over a period of time in order to follow changes in frequency amplitudes with training.

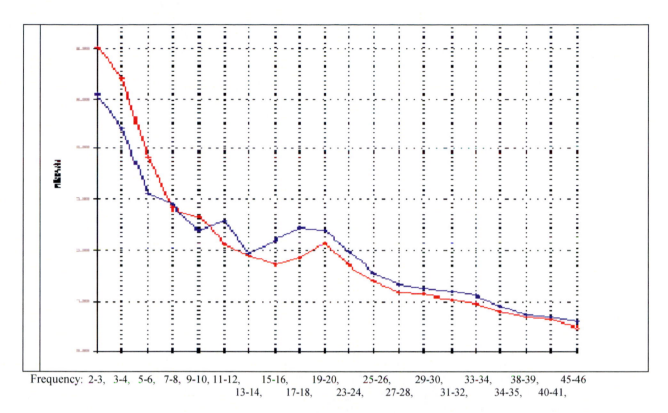

Frequency: 2-3, 3-4, 5-6, 7-8, 9-10, 11-12, 15-16, 19-20, 25-26, 29-30, 33-34, 38-39, 45-46
                                    13-14,   17-18,   23-24,   27-28,   31-32,   34-35,   40-41,

The above graph is enlarged below so as to better look at the 4 to 28 Hz range.

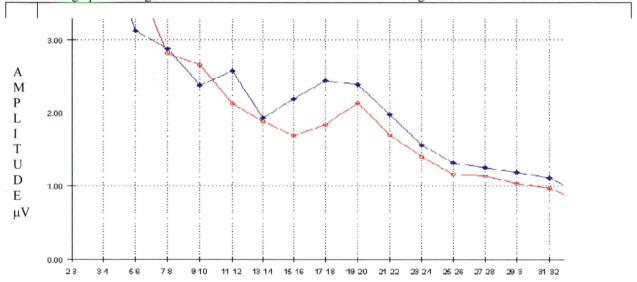

In this example a referential Cz – left ear lobe recording from a 3-minute artifacted sample is diagrammed. Open circles (red) show the pre-training record. Note the high theta compared to SMR and beta activity. The line of filled circles (blue) shows that after five training sessions slow waves (< 7 Hz) and low alpha (9-10 Hz) have dropped while high alpha (11-12 Hz), which she had been training up, has increased. Low beta (15-18 Hz) has also increased as she focuses more on analyzing the terrain for her next putt.

The x-axis is in 2 Hz bins. After being shown this progress report, she then worked on being very calm and raising 13-15 Hz (SMR) activity and not being anxious and worrying when performing. When she learned to do this, higher beta frequencies (20-34 Hz) dropped well below her initial assessment levels and her golf performance improved further.

vii. Case Example: Lorraine, Age 63, (case #10 above) Bipolar Disorder and a History of ADHD.

One second of EEG activity and its corresponding spectral analysis is represented in the figure opposite. The average spectral analysis of a 3 minute artifacted specimen of eyes open EEG showed much the same pattern.

Lorraine, a female client is 63 years of age. She is extremely bright and active. She has been under unremitting stress for some time. She complains of depression and is constantly ruminating (negative thoughts). A stress profile was done during which she was asked to imagine a very stressful situation. When she did so her breathing became rapid, irregular and shallow and her heart rate increased. Her skin temperature increased (rather than the expected decrease) and her EDR was flat. This corresponds to other clients who have experienced long-term chronic stress. It was in keeping with the chronic nature of the stress she was re-experiencing. The EEG at FCz (half way between Fz and Cz) looked like the pattern opposite with very low SMR and high 29-32 Hz activity. The same pattern could be seen at Cz and frontally with F4 > F3 for the 31 Hz activity.

In contrast, when she began a mental math task, which usually puts subjects under tremendous stress, her breathing became regular and its rate decreased, as did her heart rate. Her temperature and EDR both decreased slightly. Her 29-32 Hz activity dropped off to a very low level and 16-18 Hz activity increased. She explained that doing even extremely difficult math was a tremendous relief compared to just sitting and trying to relax. She said that while doing math she didn't have circular negative thoughts going through her head.

Example of high amplitude, High-beta

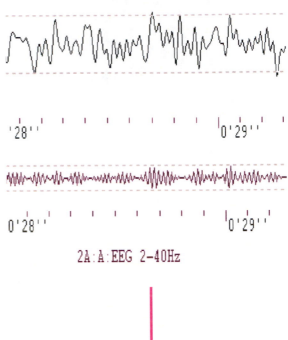

2A:A:EEG 2-40Hz

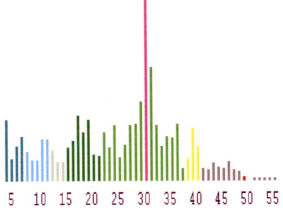

(Remember neurophysiology: The amygdala holds unconscious negative memories and relates them to the physiological state which corresponds to those thoughts or that incident. This aspect of the amygdala's functioning seems to (relatively) turn off when you are intensely involved in a cognitive problem solving task or creative operation.)

In the sessions Lorraine was encouraged to relax, externally focus and 'empty her mind' while remaining very calm. To help her do this Lorraine chose a complex screen with multiple feedbacks. She said that she could then choose what she would focus on and the steps she would take to meet her objectives. The training program for Lorraine included simultaneous feedback of respiration and pulse for RSA, together with forehead and/or trapezius EMG. Two channel neurofeedback was used. A Cz channel to encourage a decrease in 28-33 Hz / 13-15 Hz ratio and an F3 channel to encourage a decrease in 6-10 Hz activity and an increase in 15-18 Hz to activate the left frontal lobe. *When follow up was carried out it was found that she had remained off medications and has been functioning reasonably normally for the past 3 years.*

viii. Case Example: Brad, age 19, Asperger's Syndrome (Case #12 above).
High Beta – Beta Spindling

Brad demonstrated a lack of ability to interpret innuendo and to make inferences about the meaning of written communication. He was inappropriate in social communication. He would smile or laugh at incorrect times during a conversation. He had very poor attention span except in his own area of intense special interest. He demonstrated extremely high Cz theta, T6 idling in low alpha and high amplitude bursts of beta spindling in the frontal region. This kind of beta activity may be seen in some cases of ADD. The lack of activation in the right temporal area is a pattern we have observed with Asperger's Syndrome though there is not yet any publication of this finding. The figure below shows an example of this pattern. It is a relatively high amplitude beta.

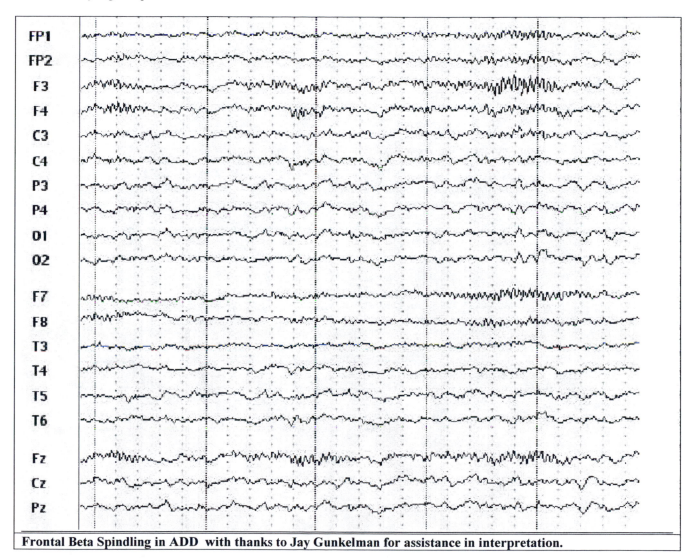

Frontal Beta Spindling in ADD with thanks to Jay Gunkelman for assistance in interpretation.

ix. Case Example of Asperger's Syndrome, Age 58.
High Slow Wave Activity at T6

An eyes closed example of a segment of EEG in a 62 year old male who has mild to moderate Asperger's syndrome is shown below to give an example of high slow wave activity in the T6 area. T6 is oriented for spatial and emotional contextual comprehension, and non-verbal memory.

This man has never been able to visualize. His emotions have always been flat. He has experienced high anxiety throughout his life and has only recently stopped taking anxiolytics.

When talking to an old friend, he has a sense that he is just talking to himself – not really connecting. He doesn't have the feeling or the sense that the other individual (e.g., giving feedback to a client) is hearing or understanding what he is trying to put across. He has done psychological testing with clients and given feedback on their results for about 20 years but he feels that this has become more difficult to do in the last two or three years. In addition, he feels his ability to sustain attention and complete tasks has deteriorated. He has had a full medical and neurological work up but nothing abnormal has been detected.

He has always 'craved isolation' and feels this has also become more extreme. He dreads going out and being with people. He says that it is more peaceful just being by himself.

Recently, he has been feeling mildly depressed and this appears to correspond to high slow wave activity at F3 which was more easily seen in eyes open recordings. In the eyes-closed recording shown in the figures below (also observed with eyes open), note in particular the high amplitude slow wave activity at T6.

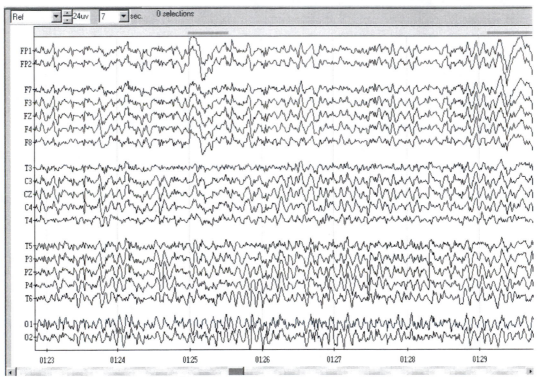

Eyes closed referenced to linked ears.

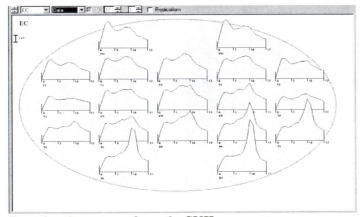

Eyes closed spectrum from the SKIL program.

INTERVENTION

When the total record was reviewed, it was found that the eyes open math task demonstrated, in addition to the P4 and T6 findings shown above, high slow wave activity at F3 and Fz. Therefore, in the initial sessions, this man was encouraged to increase frontal beta (15-18) Hz and decrease 4-10 Hz activity at F3 referenced to linked ears or to the right ear. Activation of this site tends to counter depressive affect.

He also demonstrated high thalpha (6-10 Hz) at Fz, perhaps associated with inattention. High amplitude beta spindling at 30 Hz was also noted at Fz. This might represent cingulate activity, corresponding to mild compulsive tendencies and severe ruminating. Training, therefore, encouraged a decrease in thalpha and in high beta frequency (28 - 32 Hz) activity at Fz.

For calming and stabilization and to help him control anxiety, respiration and EMG biofeedback was combined with neurofeedback. CPz (half way between Cz and PZ) and Pz training was done to enhance 11-14 Hz and to suppress 4 - 10 Hz.

To improve his ability to visualize objects and events T6 training was done. He has never been able to use visual imagery. Hopefully work at T6 might also improve his non-verbal memory. In addition this area is involved in emotional contextual comprehension. The hope is that activating this area and 'normalizing the EEG' will result in a better ability to understand and respond to social nuances, decrease the flatness of his affect and decrease his anxiety during social interactions.

To achieve these goals T6 was referenced to the left ear (referencing to the contralateral ear reduces common mode rejection) and he was instructed to enhance 13 – 16 Hz and suppress 4 – 10 Hz. This was coupled with respiration and EMG biofeedback and having him attempt to visualize a pleasant object (a flower) or a scene.

c. Units of Measurement

In most of the foregoing discussion, the units used for relating the amplitude of the waves have been microvolts. However, some of the literature is reported in power units called picowatts. A *picowatt* ≈ 6.14 x μV^2. It is important that the reader know what units are being used when reading the literature.

Units: Picowatts or Microvolts

Not only do the frequency bands used in various research studies often differ from the ones most of us use when doing neurofeedback, but the units are also different. Take for example the landmark multi-site study regarding theta/beta ratios in ADHD (Monastra, Lubar et al, 1999) entitled Assessing Attention Deficit Hyperactivity Disorder via Quantitative Electro-encephalography: An Initial Validation Study, (Neuropsychology, Vol. 13, No. 3, 424-433). They report mean theta/beta ratios 4-8 / 13-21 Hz in picowatts. The A620 assessment program will do this calculation either for amplitude (measured in uV) or for power (measured in picowatts) . However, most NFB instruments record only amplitudes in microvolts. This presents a small challenge if you want to compare your data with the Monastra norms and you are not using an A620.

What is the relationship between microvolts and picowatts? Recall that In mathematical terms the relationship between amplitude and power is: (microvolts)^2 x 6.14 = picowatts. However, we are usually just trying to relate the published literature findings for ratios in picowatts to the microvolts that we are measuring on a daily basis with our students. A simple approximation used by some practitioners is that the (ratio in microvolts)^2 is similar to the ratio in picowatts. However, this simpler calculation mainly holds true if there is little variability in the sample amplitudes.

Jon Breslaw, an economist and a statistician in Montreal Canada, kindly gave us the following example to consider:
Two data sets:
Data Set 1: Theta in microvolts: 20 20 20 20 20
Beta in microvolts: 10 10 10 10 10

Data set 2: Theta in microvolts: 40 5 5 40 10
Beta in microvolts 10 10 10 10 10

Means: Data set 1: theta 20, beta 10. beta/theta = 2
Data set 2: theta 20, beta 10 beta/theta = 2

If this had been done in picowatts, and leaving out the factor of 6.14
Data Set 1: Theta in picowatts: 400 400 400 400 400
Beta in picowatts: 100 100 100 100 100

Data Set 2: Theta in picowatts: 1600 25 25 1600 100

Beta in picowatts: 100 100 100 100 100

Means: Data set 1: theta 400, beta 100, beta/theta = 4
*   Data set 2: theta 670, beta 100, beta/theta = 6.7*

He then noted that, *"Squaring the beta/theta ratio to make comparisons to the Lubar studies reported in picowatts is not valid if there is any degree of variability. The mean of the squares is not the square of the mean."*

He suggests that, *"To replicate the Lubar results, one can take the microvolt reading, and create a data channel equal to the square of the microvolt reading using compute and multiply the original channel with itself."*

d. Theta/beta Ratios in ADHD

Where this discussion is important at the present time is in working with ADHD. The most comprehensive published work cited above (Monastra et al, 1999), reports ADHD ratios 4-8 / 13-21 Hz in picowatts. Many people, however, will be using microvolt ratios and often programs will calculate a theta / beta ratio that is 4-8 / 16-20 Hz since these frequency bands are often used in training.   Here are our clinical observations, using microvolts, which provide a less precise guideline. In general, most children between 7 and 11 will have a microvolt ratio (4-8/16-20) less than 2.4 unless they are observed to be having problems with attention span in school. The majority of children we see in this age group who are definitely having attention difficulties in school will have μV ratios >2.8 and often >3. The ratio decreases in older age groups. In general, however, our conservative estimate is that the majority of adolescents and adults have ratios below 2.1 unless they are reporting difficulties with attention span. (We gave an SNR presentation of an unpublished study comparing adults with and without an ADD history that found a cut off at 1.8) The majority of our adolescent population who have difficulty with attention span at school and when doing homework have ratios above 2.4 before training.   As a rough guideline, one should suspect ADD if the 4-8/16-20 theta/beta microvolt ratio is > 2.5 in children above age 7 and if it is > 2 in older adolescents and adults.

4. Two Channel QEEG Assessments

a. Rationale
As mentioned earlier, some equipment allows 2 channels of EEG biofeedback where *2-channels* refers to 2 sites being monitored with the use of 2 separate preamplifiers (and, in some equipment, 2 input jacks into the encoder). Each of these channels have 3 electrodes: active, reference and ground. This is a different set up than that used when doing a 19 or more channel full-cap assessment. In the *full-cap assessment* you have a common ground lead and a common reference (usually linked ears). You can also get electrodes for 2 channels that have a common reference and a common ground. This helps ensure more accurate comparisons between activity at the two active sites.

i. Why Use a 2 Channel EEG Assessment
A two channel assessment is carried out in order to compare the relative amplitudes of different frequency bands at two different sites. This can be very useful. We suggested above that if a client had all the expected symptoms of ADD, but your Cz placement did not show any frequency bands that were outside of the expected range given the overall amplitude of that client's EEG, then you should redo the assessment with the active electrode placed at a different site such as Fz. Similarly, you could assess 2 sites individually to compare different bandwidth amplitudes in the two hemispheres. In both instances the two assessments could be done at different times. (You use the same electrode and move it to a new site.) However, in this instance the results may be reasonable for planning training but they are not truly comparable.

A two-channel instrument allows you to get around this problem since you can compare, for example, F3 with F4 at the same moment in time. It is also more time efficient than having to move the active electrode and take additional EEG samples.   This is an important consideration since fatigue will affect the EEG. (Drowsiness = increased theta.)

b. How to Set Up Two Channels
i. Electrode Placement
With the one channel referential assessment described above, the first assessment is typically done with the active electrode at Cz referenced either to the left or to the right ear or mastoid. Cz is chosen as it is less prone to eye movement and muscle artifact and gives the highest amplitudes for most frequencies since it is farther from the ear reference. (Less common mode rejection means higher amplitudes.) In some EEG instruments there are two or more channels available for EEG. This opens up a number of possibilities for electrode placements and referencing.

(1.) Comparing 2 Central Locations
A client with ADD may be assessed with Channel 1 (A) active electrode at Fz (or F3) and Channel 2 (B) active electrode at Cz. This usually allows you quickly to identify the appropriate area for your inhibit frequency. Some people with ADD symptoms of inattention and distractibility have a very high amplitude at a particular slow wave frequency when they 'tune out' that appears frontally and not centrally. In these cases it may be better to place your reward frequency active electrode at a different site than this frontal electrode which is being used to inhibit the dominant slow wave. An electrode to reward the production of SMR, for example, should be placed over the sensori-motor strip. A reward in beta for improving speech, verbal memory or reading would be placed at an appropriate site on the left hemisphere. This type of feedback requires two channels if you are to do it simultaneously, though it could be done with one channel if you train one aspect first (for example, decrease 7-9 Hz at F3) and then the other (increase 12-15 Hz at Cz) later. The sites could be alternated within each session or every other session. Alternatively, you could train at one site till the associated symptoms for one site are under control and then change to the second site. If being hyperactive and/or impulsive was the biggest problem, one would do SMR training first. If tuning out, being in his own world, was the main complaint you would decrease the frontal slow wave activity first.

(2.) Assessing Differences Between Hemispheres
In some clients you may wish to compare activity in the two hemispheres. We find this useful for clients who complain of ruminating and becoming internally distracted by concerns over matters not relevant to the task at hand - in other words, the worriers. In these clients you can compare a site in the left hemisphere with a similarly positioned site in the right hemisphere, such as F3 and F4 both referenced to Cz (or reference them to their ipsilateral ear lobe or mastoid). You can purchase electrodes where the two ear electrodes are attached to each other. Two leads come off this common wire between the two ear electrodes and these go to channel A and Channel B respectively. This results in a common reference for the 2 channels of EEG. You can also purchase a ground electrode that has 2 leads that go to channels A and B respectively giving a common ground for both channels. (See IMA in the Resources section to order these electrodes.) This type of assessment may be particularly useful for a client with dysphoria or mild to moderate depression. (Clients with severe depression should of course be under medical care).

When you are comparing the EEG in two channels, it is essential that you have good impedance readings that are virtually the same for both channels.

Now that you have your electrodes in place, compare the activity at the 2 sites for different frequency ranges. For catching the worriers one of these should be within the 22-34 Hz range. The precise bandwidth(s) for comparisons will depend on your equipment and your hypotheses about your client and the EEG patterns that would mirror their symptoms. In the assessment you might observe single Hz or overlapping two Hz bins depending on the constraints of your programs. We are finding that, when clients think negative thoughts, 23-34 Hz activity measured either in microvolts or as %-time-over-threshold (which you can put on your screen with some instruments) tends to be higher in the right frontal region. When the same client thinks positive thoughts it may tend to be higher on the left. (This observation requires replication in other centers and is not true in every case.) We also find that when the client relaxes and becomes externally, openly aware that activity in this frequency band (23-34 Hz) drops in both hemispheres and the 11-15 Hz range shows an increase. We are not finding large overall differences in 9-10 Hz or in 11-15 Hz comparing right and left hemispheres although there are reports in the literature concerning higher frontal alpha in the left hemisphere than the right in depressed persons (Baehr, 1999). The higher left hemisphere alpha is taken as an indicator that the left frontal area is resting; that is, there is a lack of activation in the area. This may be associated with depression. On the other hand, Davidson has found left hemisphere activation to be associated with approach tendencies (being engaged in the world, not withdrawing) and positive affect (Davidson, 1998). This just underlines again the necessity for respecting individual differences and doing careful assessments and progress testing to ascertain the precise frequency bands (and locations) that correspond to the mental states that concern each individual client.

ii. Clinical Tip:
If you have symptoms of both tuning out and dysphoria, here is a suggested method to make electrode placement relatively quick and simple.

(1.) With Electrodes that are Not Linked:
In your first assessment do: channel 1, F3-Left ear and channel 2, Cz-Right ear. Then you only need to move the channel 2 active electrode to F4 in order to do a second assessment comparing the activity at similar sites over the 2 frontal lobes.

(2.) With Linked Electrodes: (Preferable)
In the diagram below note that there are linked ear reference electrodes. In addition, the ground is linked and goes to both preamps **(channel A and channel B).** This arrangement makes it very simple to check impedances. It assures that the impedances are the same for reference and ground electrodes at the two sites so that comparisons between the two active sites are valid. The ground can go anywhere. It is shown here in a frontal location.

iii. Diagram of Linked Ear Reference and Common Ground Set-Up

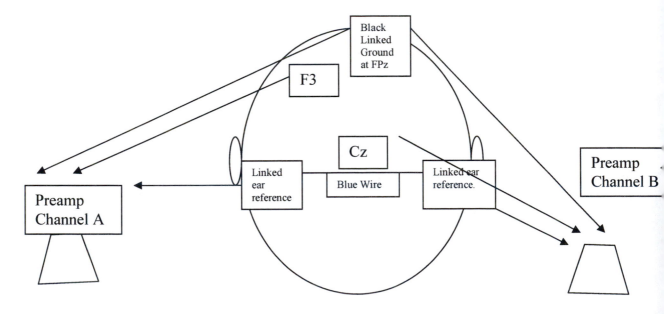

iv. An Example of a Two Channel Assessment
John was a client who complained of dysphoria (mild depression) and anxiety.

John is a 25 year old university student who complained of lack of focus and a disorganized approach to his academic work. He finds himself ruminating about small problems in life when he

should be attending in class or studying. When a 2 channel assessment was done with active electrodes at F3-left ear and F4-right ear, it demonstrated that, when he thought about negative things in his life, %-time- over-threshold for 23-34 Hz rose much higher on the right than the left. The reverse was true when he thought about pleasant things in his life. Both %-over-threshold readings dropped dramatically when he was calm, relaxed, and highly focused on the trainer describing a metacognitive reading strategy for his university science subjects.

The most important finding here is not so much that the high beta is on one side or the other but that the client's mental activity related to worrying and ruminating seems to correspond to high amplitude, high beta activity. This may be a subtype of ADD in that the client is internally distracted by these thoughts and not attending to external stimulation. When the client becomes calm and focused, this excess high beta activity decreases.

John's 2 Channel EEG Assessment

The figure below is a brief 4 second sample of John's EEG at F3 (Channel A) and F4 (Channel B). Both are referenced to their ipsilateral ear. Impedances were below 5 Kohms and within 1 Kohm for each pairing of electrodes. Note the high high-beta activity on the right side. This pattern was consistent with findings from a 3-minute artifacted sample of his EEG.

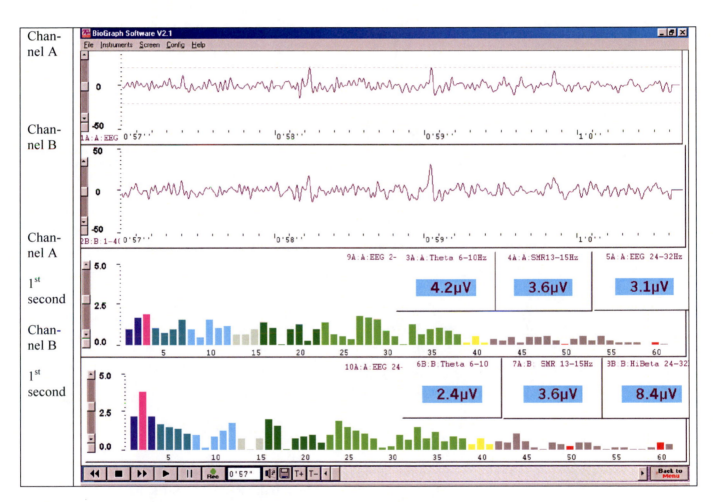

When this assessment was done, John was feeling somewhat discouraged and dysphoric. The spectrums and the figures refer only to the first second (57'-58') for each EEG channel. Note the high slow wave activity on the left side (channel A) and the high high-beta, 24-32 Hz, in the right frontal area. Note artifacts at 58.2 and 59.0 seconds. These would be excluded from a statistical analysis.

When you do these 2 channel assessments, you should do the statistics in one or two Hz bandwidths. Then graph it using a spreadsheet program such as Microsoft Works. These spreadsheet programs allow you to superimpose the two graphs or histograms (one for each channel). This will make it easy to visually compare the amplitude of different frequency bands in the 2 hemispheres. This comparison will make it relatively simple to choose appropriate inhibit and reward frequency bandwidths for each hemisphere for training. The most common meaningful comparison deals with activity in the frontal lobes at F3 and F4. The spreadsheet allows one to automatically graph and superimpose progress assessment results in different colours on to the original assessment graph in order to assess progress.

To decrease dysphoric ruminating and increase a sense of calm, John was successfully trained using a 2 channel placement (channel A at F3 and channel B at F4) to decrease 23-34 Hz at F4 (compared to F3). Then he was trained to decrease 23-34 Hz overall with channel A at Fz while increasing 11-15 Hz with channel B at C4. When only one channel was used the active electrode was placed at FCz.

The focus of training for John was then changed to emphasize a decrease in distractibility and an increase in concentration when carrying out a cognitive task. He was asked to maintain his calm mental state while keeping his dominant slow wave very low (5Hz and 9Hz peaks were evident initially in John's case) and raise 15-18 Hz when problem solving or analyzing a chapter in a text-book. (On assessment it had been found that he increased 17 Hz when problem solving.) This training was combined with teaching metacognitive strategies and practicing holding the appropriate mental state while carrying out academic tasks.

To do this training a different two channel placement was used. Channel A was used to decrease his "thalpha" (5-9Hz) / low-beta (15-!8 Hz) ratio of activity with the active electrode between F3 and C3 referenced to the right ear lobe. Channel B training had the active electrode just anterior to C4. It was used for decreasing the relatively high 23-34 Hz activity in the right hemisphere while at the same time encouraging an increase in 13-15 Hz activity. He was also receiving biofeedback concerning respiration and forehead EMG during these sessions. At the end of training he felt he was able to control his mental states and stop his negative ruminations.

Conclusion
The real point in doing a careful assessment is to find out what is true on the EEG for your client. Then respond to these findings by placing your active electrode over the relevant area and increase and/or decrease the appropriate frequency band-widths. In the future coherence and/or comodulation training may make this a more efficient process, though we do not yet have much published data regarding outcomes for different groups/different coherence patterns using coherence training.

v. Importance of Impedance in the 2 - Channel Approach
When you are comparing EEG frequency bands in two channels the impedances must be virtually the same. If they are not almost identical then any apparent differences between the hemispheres may just be due to the different electrode connections (Hammond & Gunkelman, 2001). You might then come to incorrect conclusions about the activity in the two hemispheres.

Theoretically, using high resistance amplifiers, impedance differences should not present a problem. However, try experimenting and you will find (as we have) that it does make a difference. It makes a huge difference if the client should move their head even a small amount! Impedance should be between 100 and 5000 Ω. Measures for each pair of electrodes should be within 1 Kohm of each other. Electrodes with much higher impedance may cause 60 Hz artifact and attenuate the recording (Fisch, B., 1999).

Impedance will be further discussed under "Site Preparation".

5. A 19 Channel (Full-Cap) QEEG Assessment

a. Advantages of the 19 Channel – Full-cap Assessment
Nineteen active leads plus a ground and reference electrodes on the ears are typically used in what is called a *full-cap* assessment. (In research labs the number of leads can multiply to over 200 to attempt to get better spatial resolution.) This type of quantitative EEG allows one to collect data at Standard 10-20 sites around the scalp. Each of these sites is referenced to linked ears. The data which are collected, however, can be analyzed in various ways using

different *montages* other than linked ears (see below). The information can be used to produce brain maps which plot the activity at the 19 sites and interpolate the data for the spaces between the electrode locations. As noted previously, the term 'full-cap' is apt since this type of assessment usually utilizes a soft, thin, cloth cap which looks very like a swimmer's bathing cap. (If the client is a male child who does not like the idea of putting a cap on, compare the cap to what water polo players wear.) The cap has 19 tiny electrodes built into it. The wires from these are sewn into the cap and are joined into a cord that hangs like a queue at the nape of the client's neck. This cord has a plug at the end that fits into the EEG machine.

In our field it has traditionally been an EEG recording system developed by LEXICOR, Inc. (Golden, Colorado) This company has also contributed to teaching full-cap EEG recording methods. LEXICOR is also one of the companies that will provide interpretations after the clinician has collected the data. In 2003 there is a new instrument called the NeuroNavigator which provides an advanced option for both QEEG and neurofeedback. It is available through Thought Technology. Courses on the use of this equipment, are taught by M. Barry Sterman who developed the NeuroNavigator in conjunction with Jan Hoover at J & J Engineering. Other newly available options (although at the time of writing without FDA approval) include the DeyMed from Czechoslovakia and the Mitsar from Yuri Kroptovos group in St. Petersburg Russia.

b. Montages

In a full-cap assessment various *montages* may be used. This does not affect the collection of data as it is something that is done at the interpretation stage using computer software. The data that are collected using a linked ear reference may be *remontaged* using computer programs which are designed for analyzing the results of the EEG recording.

i. Linked Ear Referential Montage

Recordings are usually carried out using a linked ear reference and a forehead ground. In the computer programs for interpreting the results of the EEG assessment you may use this montage to interpret the data. Neurofeedback practitioners often look at this montage first when artifacting the data. Other montages may then be used to

help bring out any abnormalities in the record or to help clarify what might be artifact.

ii. Sequential (Bipolar) Montages

Sequential (bipolar) montages compare adjacent pairs of electrodes in the 10-20 placement system. These may be either *longitudinal* pairs (such as F3-C3) or *transverse* pairs going across the head (such as C3-CZ). The term bipolar refers to the amplifier. There used to be both bipolar (also called *differential* or *push-pull* amplifiers, using an active, a reference and a ground electrode) and monopolar (single ended, using active and ground electrodes) amplifiers. Nowadays there are only differential amplifiers (Notes from correspondence with Jay Gunkelman). Recording should always be done referentially so that the remontaging can be done. It would be best according to some electroencephalographers if the recording were done using a single ear montage. A single ear reference avoids what is called *shunting*. Shunting occurs as a result of an impedance imbalance between the ear electrodes. Shunting produces a skewing of the topographic maps towards (or away from) one side, due to the impedance mismatch. The shifting follows the path of least resistance. In practice most of us are using instruments where the linked ear reference is built into the hardware and there is no choice concerning how the recording is carried out. We must, therefore, be careful to check that the impedances are the same in the two ear electrodes..

iii. 'Global Average' Laplacian Montage

An active reference montage using common average reference (CAR) will reference an active electrode to an average of all the other electrodes. This means that all of the 10-20 electrodes are added together in Input 2 of every amplifier. This then serves as a reference for each of the electrodes in Input 1 (the 'active' electrode). Thus each of the 19 will contribute 1/19th of the total activity in input 2. Strictly speaking, this should be called a *"global average" Laplacian technique,* where weighting factors are added to correct for inter-electrode distances. Laplacios was a mathematician and physicist. The name Laplacian refers to an application of his mathematics to the EEG by Hjorth (Hjorth, 1980).

iv. 'Local Average' Laplacian or Hjorth Montage

A *'Local Average' Laplacian or Hjorth Montage* will reference to the average of the electrodes immediately surrounding each active electrode (Fisch). Strictly speaking this Laplacian montage is termed the *local average*, or *Hjorth* montage.

v. Brief Discussion Concerning Full-cap Assessments and Montages

Each *montage* is a mathematical reworking of the data which can be done rapidly by the computer. Each of these different ways of looking at the data will have advantages and disadvantages. As with many aspects of instrumentation, there are trade-offs when it comes to choosing a montage. As noted earlier in this text, the *sequential (bipolar)* and *Laplacian (Hjorth)* montages are good for viewing highly localized activity. This would be of great value to neurologists looking for abnormalities. The *common average reference montage (global average Lapacian technique),* on the other hand, is excellent for detection of widely distributed currents and for analyzing asymmetry. It is also very good for the detection of artifacts. It is not so useful for viewing localized activity.

Regardless of the montage, one must always pay attention to strict removal of artifacts from the EEG before analyzing it to produce brain maps. This process will remove *transients.* (As previously mentioned, a *transient* wave is one that stands out as different against the background EEG.) These transients may include clinically important data (e.g., an epileptiform burst). Always remember, the morphology of the EEG is diagnostically important. You can only see waveforms (*morphology*) by looking at the raw EEG. You do not want to miss waves such as triphasic waveforms that could indicate a toxic/metabolic encephalopathy, or periodic discharges such as may be seen in other encephalopathies, or epileptiform bursts. These discharges would alert you immediately to the need to have the record read by experts and to refer your client to the appropriate medical specialist, usually a neurologist.

Instructions for placing the 'cap' on the client's head are given in detail with the cap when you purchase it and are, therefore, not repeated here. You will have to have individual supervision in order to learn how to properly put a cap onto a client and make sure that the cap is giving accurate information to the computer. This will require that you learn how to bring the impedances for all the electrode pairs to <5 KΩ and within 1 KΩ of each other.

The full-cap assessment has the advantage of doing all sites at the same instant in time. EEG has wonderful temporal resolution. You can record under different conditions such as: eyes closed, eyes open (looking at a single point to minimize eye movement artifact), reading and math. This type of assessment allows for a conventional investigation of amplitude differences between sites at different frequencies under different conditions. Additionally, it allows for an analysis of communication between different sites. This is traditionally called *coherence* which is calculated using a cross-correlation co-efficient concerning the waveforms at two different sites.

c. Definitions of Common Terms

Terms that arise in discussion about how different areas of the cortex are communicating with one another include: *phase, coherence, synchrony* and *comodulation.*

i. Phase

Covariance in time is called **phase.** When waves that are morphologically the same occur at the same time at two different sites these waves are said to be *in-phase. Conducted phase* refers to time delays between two sites. With a time delay the waves will be said to be *out-of-phase.* This is measured in terms of degrees, 0-180°.

Propagated phase refers to a *focal phase reversal.* This type of phase reversal is best seen in sequential recordings between adjacent pairs of electrodes. A phase reversal in this case may point to the source of an EEG phenomenon.

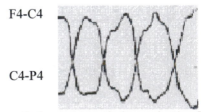

The type of phase reversal shown in the figure above could appear in the EEG of a person who had seizures. The origin of the seizures in this instance is likely at C4.

ii. Coherence

(Special thanks to Dr. M. B. Sterman for his help with the following three sections.)

Coherence refers to a cross correlation between frequencies. It indicates the degree of shared activity between sites. Coherent waves have the same morphology. The amplitude of the waves is not a factor. Being *in-phase* is not a factor. There could be shifting in-phase or out-of-phase as long as the morphology of the waves is the same. Time is also not taken into account as it is when calculating comodulation.

Calculations for coherence compare the waveform at two sites and then do an FFT spectral analysis. Comodulation calculations (described below) do the spectral analysis first and then compare the rise and fall of the amplitude of a specified waveform.

Coherence is expressed as the square of the correlation coefficient ($[r]^2$). Correlation coefficients range from -1 to $+1$. Since coherence is the square of the correlation coefficient, it will therefore range from 0 to 1. It is a measure of the linear association between two variables, in our case the EEG waveforms recorded from two different scalp locations, independent of the EEG amplitude at either location.

Coherence is calculated as the *Fast Fourier Transform* of the cross correlation between sites across the frequency spectrum. It discloses the frequencies with the most shared activity between any given pair of sites across a sample of data. Thus, the specific timing of coherent activity is not a factor. The waveform morphology and phase are compared between sites, independently of amplitude. Coherent waves have the same morphology and therefore frequency. There can be a shifting in phase as long as the morphology/frequency of the waves is the same. As long as the morphology is the same you have the same kid of activity (say theta or alpha) at the two sites and there is coherence. Phase relationships can be derived from this measure separately.

Clinically, coherence represents the degree to which two sites have similar waveforms (vary together) and may imply that the two sites are getting input from a common generator. As a child matures, coherence will increase between central and temporal and parietal regions in all bands. However, with maturation coherence will decrease between the frontal lobes. This implies that with maturation there is greater cortical differentiation in the frontal regions of the brain (Thatcher, 1986). Learning disabled children, on the other hand, demonstrate increasing frontal coherence in theta, alpha and beta bands (Marosi, 1992).

Why Use a Coherence Measure?

The EEG measures summations of extracellular electrical changes produce by radially generated activity within pyramidal cells which lie perpendicular to the surface of the cortex. It measures the extracellular summation of EPSPs and IPSPs as discussed earlier. The EEG is *blind* to about 2/3 of the cortex's electrical activity. It doesn't measure *lateral* current flow or intracellular activity. A magnetoencephalogram (MEG) measures magnetic activity in the brain. This may be thought of as *lateral* current flow or intracellular activity. The MEG, however, is blind to the extracellular potentials measured by the EEG.

The EEG amplitudes are also *blind* to the longitudinal myelinated fiber tracts. These tracts connect different areas of the brain. These are the intra-hemispheric fasciculi and the inter-hemispheric commissures discussed in the neuroanatomy section of this book.

Coherence and phase measurements allow us to infer the *connectivity* between areas of the brain. When differences from databases of normals are observed this can lead to a NFB program which attempts to 'normalize' our measurements of these connections with the objective of seeing a corresponding 'normalization' of cognition and behaviour.

iii. Comodulation

Dr. M. Barry Sterman has often been referred to as the "grandfather" of the NFB field because he was the first researcher to establish that operant conditioning of brainwaves was possible. He has produced a database that is included with the SKIL software. Using SKIL (from Sterman Kaiser Imaging Labs) one can produce brain maps and topographic displays. This software has been helpful in introducing many clinicians to the complex world of 19 channel EEG assessments. In this software, SKIL has introduced a new measurement of the integration between different areas in the cerebral hemispheres, termed *comodulation*. Simply put, comodulation assesses the degree to which a given frequency is increased and decreased in its spectral magnitude simultaneously at two different sites over time. Comodulation refers to a spectral correlation; that is, a correlation between shared spectral content across time. In contrast to coherence, comodulation assess the degree to which waves of the same frequency are moving together over time. It is a measure of collective integration rather than connectivity. As previously noted, these calculations require that the FFT be done first for a given frequency band and then the cross-correlation between sites is compared over time. Any frequency band can be selected for this comparison, and it can reflect either the subject's own unique integration or be compared statistically with a normative database. Comodulation, accordingly, stresses changes over time, a focus not provided in coherence analysis. However, like coherence, amplitude at the two sites does not matter.

Thus comodulation estimates are time locked. Comodulation is a stepwise calculation; for example, it may be done each quarter second. In this case the waves must stay lock-stepped together for that ¼ sec to be registered as comodulating. Comodulation is a new term that will not be familiar to neurologists (they may refer to it as spectral correlation) but people doing neurofeedback will likely hear more about it in the future. Remember that sensorimotor rhythm (SMR) was also a term coined by Sterman and it has become part of the basic jargon in our field.

Why are Coherence and Comodulation Important in NFB

Measures of coherence or comodulation lead directly into a different way of training. In order to normalize the EEG the client may be trained to either increase or decrease communication or functional coordination between two or more sites on the scalp. At the time of writing only Lexicor equipment permits coherence training while the NeuroNavigator has the capacity to do comodulation training.

v. Synchrony

Synchrony is a term used in Lexicor programs. It refers to a mathematical calculation that considers phase and coherence in a single calculation. The waves are, therefore, the same shape (morphology) waves and are in-phase (going up and down at the same time) at the two sites to be considered synchronous.

v. Spectral Density

It is important to remember that all frequency analysis methods must estimate amplitude over time and thus include *incidence*. Simple amplitude cannot be assessed. Thus, *Spectral Density* refers to the incidence and amplitude of a particular frequency band. For example, 50 μV of 6 Hz activity for ½ second would have the same spectral density as 25 μV for 1 second. This metric is also sometimes called *spectral magnitude*.

d. 19 Channel Assessment - Case Examples

The following 19 Channel EEG data samples are interpreted using the SKIL program from Sterman Kaiser Imaging Labs. Similar analyses may be carried out with other programs and other databases. A number of these examples have been provided by Dr. Sterman and we gratefully acknowledge their provision. These examples show:
(1.) Amplitude in 1 Hz frequency bands
(2.) Amplitude of particular frequency bands compared to the SKIL normative database
(3.) Comodulation, for a chosen frequency range (usually the dominant frequency), of each of the 19 sites with all other sites.

i. Goal of this Section:

In this book on 'fundamentals of neurofeedback' we will not describe how to do a full-cap assessment since that involves hands-on training. It is an art to inject the gel and abrade the surface of the scalp enough to get good impedance readings but without breaking the skin, and do all this quickly. The basic principles regarding preparation and impedance checking are analogous to what is done with three electrode assessments. The objective here is to demonstrate, first, how information from a full-cap assessment may extend your understanding of a client's difficulties and, second, how this information may suggest additional training interventions.

A full-cap assessment can elucidate many features that cannot be seen in a single channel assessment. However, nothing is perfect. (Remember those trade offs). The full-cap does not, for example, give valuable information concerning frequencies above the mid-20's. It also gives no information about the autonomic nervous system or about muscle tension (EMG). These pieces of information are also helpful, both in assessment and training, particularly with adolescent and adult clients.

In order to meet the above two objectives case examples will be given. The first case is Sean, a man with ADD and the co-morbidities of learning differences and mild depression. He was initially assessed and trained based on assessments using a single channel EEG and a stress test. He was showing significant improvement concerning management of ADD symptoms. The full-cap was done to provide a more detailed assessment that might guide training to address the LD and depressive problems. A second client, Betty, had a closed head injury. Her training was not initiated until a full-cap assessment had been carried out.

ii. Case Example #1 Sean, A 34-year-old man with ADD, LD and depressive problems.

Sean, 34 years of age, was married with two young children. He was employed as manager of a large commercial greenhouse. He had dropped out of high-school due to frustration associated with undiagnosed learning difficulties and inattention. He came to the centre after testing by his company identified personality variables that were affecting his job performance; in particular, his communication style with staff (which could be abrupt) and his weak organizational skills. He also reported tensions in his marriage, anger management problems, and symptoms of depression. At work he was having difficulty maintaining his focus on the task at hand. He "had a short fuse" and could become rapidly upset and angry.

Cognitively, he had some difficulty explaining things in a sequenced, organized fashion. He might say things impulsively. He had poor listening skills. These characteristics were frustrating for his employees. Nevertheless, his creative problem solving, high energy, excellent hands-on skills and ability to hyperfocus and get a job done meant that the greenhouse he managed was the top producer among the many sites owned by a large corporation.

IQ testing revealed that he was bright with an overall IQ just above the 75th percentile rank. However, his performance IQ was lower than his verbal IQ. Attention to visual detail was far below his other abilities and he was very slow at reproducing visual symbols and had difficulty constructing whole objects from their components. Being impatient, having a disorganized approach rather than applying strategies, together with difficulty sustaining attention were associated with these weak scores.

The initial assessment demonstrated high amplitude 4 – 9 Hz activity and a dip in the SMR range at 13-15 Hz measured at Cz referenced to the left ear lobe. 27-31 Hz activity was high. The stress test showed how he became rapidly frustrated with math. During this part of the test peripheral skin temperature dropped, EDR, respiration rate, heart rate and EMG forehead readings all rose. Training was initially focused on improving attention span (decrease 4-9 Hz activity), becoming calm and reflective (increase 13-15 Hz activity) and focusing his thoughts on a task at hand rather than ruminating about work and home (decrease 27-31 Hz activity). He was also taught to relax and breathe at six breaths per minute. Excellent progress was made in each of these areas during the first 25 sessions.

We had several hypotheses when doing the full-cap assessment. First, that his mild depression might be reflected in *hypercomodulation* frontally. Second, that his learning difficulties might correlate with inappropriate 'idling' in areas of the brain that are involved in synthesis and integration of visual, perceptual, verbal and reading tasks. These patterns would be expected to emerge because he was engaged in a cognitive task for part of the assessment, namely, the silent reading and mental math conditions. Third, that the learning difficulties might also be associated with a lack of differentiation (hypercomodulation between areas of the brain) and/or *disconnects* (hypocomodulation) between areas of the cerebral cortex. Note that we like to have a rationale to justify the extra cost of a full-cap assessment. With simple ADD a single channel assessment will often suffice since problems are evident at the central location and training is also done there. Here are Sean's results:

1st Amplitudes using 1 Hz Frequency Bins

In the following brain maps, red is high amplitude and blue is low amplitude, green and yellow are in the middle range. These data are from Sean, age 34, a 3-minute sample of EEG done with eyes open doing math.

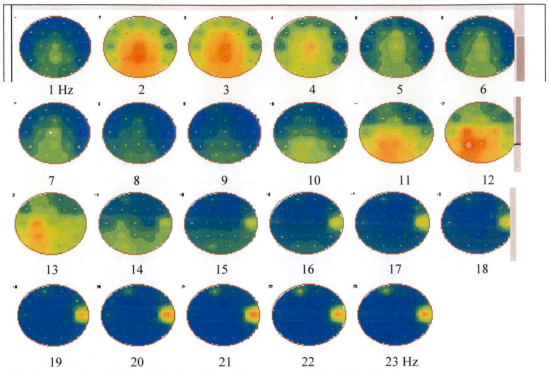

Brain maps showing amplitudes of each frequency while doing Math

The above display is called a **topographic map**. In each circle the front of the head is towards the top of the page and the back of the head (occiput) is towards the bottom of the page. This brain map displays information about activity in terms of raw data concerning amplitude of single Hertz frequencies. It was generated from the SKIL program. EMG activity was high throughout the record at T4. This accounts for the higher amplitude seen at T4 on the maps from 14 Hz. through to 23 Hz.

He had unusually high amplitude low frequency activity (delta through low theta) activity at Cz and Pz compared to other sites. In addition, he had high amplitude alpha at 11 and 12 Hz at P3 and alpha was somewhat elevated at C3 and Pz compared to alpha at other sites. These findings relate to the second and third hypotheses outlined above concerning problems with synthesis and integration of information. Although we had picked up the high amplitude slow wave activity at Cz on the initial one channel assessment, the full-cap allowed us to observe the alpha at P3 and plan an intervention to address the learning problems.

(Note: The above image was done after 25 sessions of training at Cz which was aimed at decreasing 4-9 Hz and increasing 13-15 Hz activity.)

Sean's early data had appeared to fit a *beta minima* pattern at F8 in eyes closed recordings but it was not so evident in this recording while doing mental math. This low amplitude right frontal beta may sometimes be seen in persons who lack impulse control and this was a problem that manifested itself as sudden angry outbursts in Sean's case.

2nd Amplitude of particular frequency bands compared to the SKIL database

Sean demonstrated an unusual pattern in his dominant frequency, the 10-11 Hz range, when doing mental math. (His dominant alpha frequency had been determined from eyes closed data which is not shown.) This could be seen on a *topometric analysis* which allows a comparison of the client's data with a normal database. It displays the amplitude of a chosen frequency band at each of the electrode sites. Sean's results are in red, the line joining solid circles. The average for the normal database is the dark black line, the line joining squares. Light gray lines above and below represent + 2 SD (standard deviations) and – 2 SD respectively. 95% of the population is within 2 SD of the mean. Sean is outside the normal limits at C3 and P3.

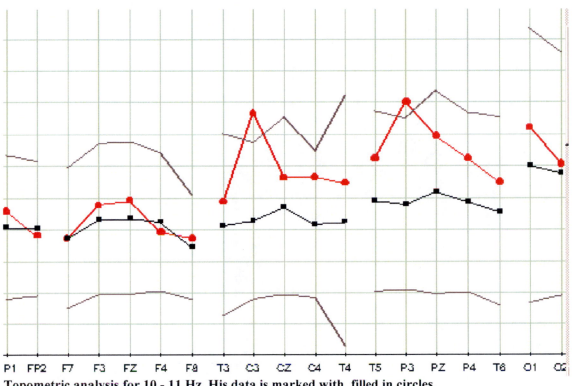

Topometric analysis for 10 - 11 Hz. His data is marked with filled in circles.

3rd Comodulation of each of the 19 sites with all other sites

The 19 lead assessment also permits you to observe communication links among different areas of the brain. The electrode site will, of course, communicate (comodulate) with itself perfectly (+1). The display below is a statistical comparison of each site with all other sites compared to the SKIL normal database for similarly aged men doing a math task with eyes open. This program also allows one to compare the client with a normal database for eyes closed, eyes open, and a reading task.

The colour at the active site is usually yellow surrounded by light green. If that site comodulates too much (≥ 2SD above the mean)

with another site then the other area will be an orange to red colour. If it comodulates too little with another site (≥ 2SD below the mean) then that area will be a blue colour.

IMPORTANT: All of the following is discussed only to show the kind of decision making processes which may evolve in the next few years. At the time of writing, relating 19 lead assessment findings with respect to comodulation to clinical observations must be considered only as a way to generate interesting hypotheses. There is no solid published research base at this time as the technique is quite new.

Comodulation With Eyes Open Doing Math

A comodulation analysis, according to Sterman, is best done using the client's dominant frequency. For most adult clients this is usually in the alpha range. It can be a very narrow band, even a single Hz, or a 2 Hz or a 3 Hz. range; for example, 9 Hz. or 9-10 Hz. If there is hyper or hypo comodulation it will stand out best using the dominant frequencies but might not show up if a broad range such as 8-12 Hz was used. In Sean's case there was a bimodal distribution with two peak frequency bands. The first figure shows the dominant alpha between 10 –11 Hz. The second shows in the 3-5 Hz range.

The figure below shows comodulation in the dominant alpha frequencies while doing a math task. (statistical comparison with normal SKIL database at 2 SD)

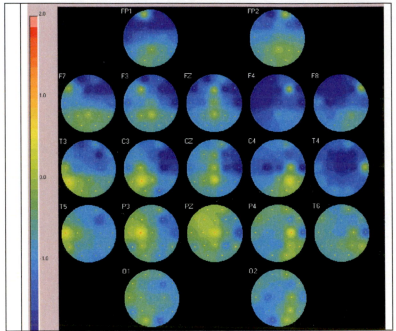

Comodulation in the dominant alpha frequencies while doing at math task. (Statistical comparison with normal SKIL database at 2 SD.)
(On the raw EEG for this case example, there was some muscle artifact at T4. Therefore, NO comodulation interpretations are made concerning the comodulation of T4 with other sites.)

In the foregoing figure 10-11 Hz activity is used as it is Sean's dominant frequency. He was doing a math task. Here comodulation between sites is compared against the SKIL database. Dark blue is – 2 SD from the mean of the database. In this figure we see a suggestion of hyper-comodulation between central and parietal regions particularly between C3 and P3 (possibly indicating a lack of discrimination of function). We also note hypo-comodulation – disconnect – between sites on the left and the right frontal & central region. Clinically, we hypothesized that there was a possibility that this disconnect(s) could relate to some of Sean's difficulties with synthesis and integration in learning. Training could include encouraging comodulation between C3 and F4, C4, and also between F4 and FP1, F3.

In the figure below a comodulation comparison with the SKIL database shows hyper-comodulation between the central and parietal leads in the 3-5 Hz frequency range. The data are with eyes open, doing a math task. The prefrontal area and F7 and F8 appear to be hypocomodulating with other frontal and temporal areas. This could be artifactual and due to eye movement although careful artifacting had been done. It might also be postulated that, since the prefrontal areas are involved in impulse control, this finding might relate to his difficulties with anger management.

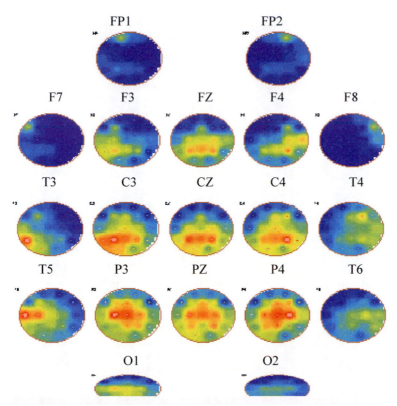

Brain map showing comodulation during a math task. (Statistical comparison with normal SKIL database, 3-5 Hz band.)

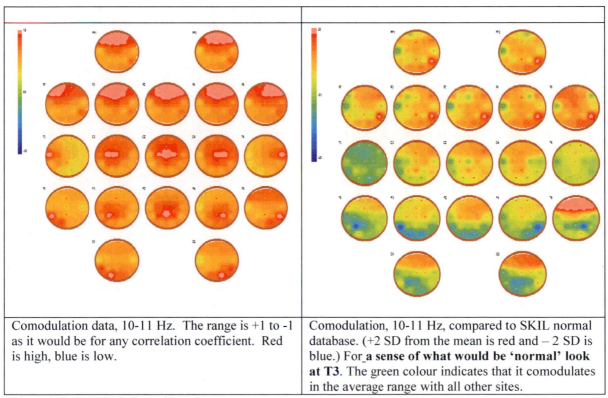

Comodulation data, 10-11 Hz. The range is +1 to -1 as it would be for any correlation coefficient. Red is high, blue is low.	Comodulation, 10-11 Hz, compared to SKIL normal database. (+2 SD from the mean is red and – 2 SD is blue.) For **a sense of what would be 'normal' look at T3**. The green colour indicates that it comodulates in the average range with all other sites.

Comodulation With Eyes Closed

Concerning the above figures: We wondered if eyes closed might give a different picture than the math above. Indeed, when this was analyzed, it gave 2 clear pictures which had not been seen when he was struggling with the math task. **Comodulation With Eyes Closed** used the dominant frequency range which for Sean was in alpha at 10-11 Hz. Thanks are given to Maurice Barry Sterman for his assistance in interpreting these comodulation figures.

Sean, as noted above, was age 34 and was mildly to moderately depressed. The figure on the left, above, shows raw data. It demonstrates hyper-comodulation in the frontal area with eyes closed. This pattern has been frequently observed by Sterman in depressed persons.

The figure on the right above shows a comparison of cross-correlation coefficients with the SKIL comodulation database. It indicates clear disturbance in communication / coordination between the frontal and pre-frontal cortex and the right posterior temporal cortex. This is an example of 'hyper-comodulation'. One could postulate that discrimination of functioning was impaired.

We questioned whether this might be related to Sean's difficulties with anger control and with understanding and responding appropriately to non-verbal communication at home and with his subordinates at work. It might also be another finding that related to his learning difficulties.

Suggestions For Training Arising From Comodulation Findings

The eyes closed assessment led to two objectives for training. The first objective was to decrease comodulation in the frontal area. The second objective was to decrease comodulation between F3, Fz, F4 and T6. Since direct training of comodulation is not yet possible, another strategy would be training to activate the left frontal area (F3). This area's functioning would then become more independent from activity at the other sites.

Important Cautions

As is true of all cutting-edge science, little is known about comodulation. The comodulation differences that are 2 standard deviations from a normal database may be taken as a concrete finding, a difference from the norms. However, all interpretations of what this may signify and suggestions as to which of the client's symptoms these differences from the normal database might relate to, **are only hypotheses.** At the time of writing there is no published research concerning whether these deviations from the norm relate to specific symptom pictures. Nor is there research to show that training to increase or decrease comodulation has an effect on the symptom picture. As equipment which allows this kind of training is developed we can look forward to its clinical application and await the results.

A second caution is that no comodulation conclusions can be drawn in any channel in a frequency range affected by an artifact such as muscle activity. In Sean's case this means that we can not look at comodulation related to T4 in the beta frequency range.

For Sean, a 1 Channel or 19 Channels Assessment - Which Should We Have Done?

In Sean's case the single channel (Cz), three lead assessment, using the decision pyramid, led to informative results. It demonstrated very high slow wave activity at 3-5 Hz and high 27-31 Hz activity. Because he had high 11-13 Hz alpha, it was difficult to say definitely if SMR was low. However, given his history of impulsivity and the fact that we found 14-15 Hz activity was approximately the same as 15-16 Hz we could conclude that encouraging him to decrease slow wave activity 3-9 Hz, and also decreasing 27–31 Hz while increasing SMR 14-15 Hz, might be an appropriate starting point. The initial results, based on this single channel assessment, were good. Nevertheless, without the full-cap we would have missed the parietal location of very high 12 Hz activity. We would also not have been aware of a possible frontal-central disconnect and a possible relative lack of left to right frontal communication when doing a math task and the hypercomodulation noted in the eyes closed condition. Acting on these additional findings might help his mild learning difficulties. This additional work would be based both on a knowledge of neurophysiology and brain function and on a comparison of his EEG with a normal database. The recommendations for further training were based on 'normalizing' the EEG. However, Colin was quite satisfied with his results following our initial training based on the single channel assessment and he opted not to do further training. Since his job did not require new learning to any appreciable extent, the learning difficulties were not posing a problem.

Note Regarding Equipment.

The NeuroNavigator will have software for training comodulation. Lexicor equipment can be used for coherence training. Remember that coherence and comodulation are related – both involve the calculation of cross-correlation coefficients; but comodulation adds in a time dimension. With comodulation the question is whether you have the same kind of activity (same morphology of the waves) going up and together over time. With comodulation the correlation is done after the FFT analysis. (Comodulation is also called *spectral correlation*.)

Importance of this Example

It is important for the reader to understand that this example was chosen, in part, because it was not a medical illness that the client demonstrated. A full-cap was not necessary. Perfectly adequate learning did take place before the full-cap was done. In most cases where the client presents with just ADD the full-cap may **not give additional information which changes your intervention**. However, Colin's case was one where we did not understand the unevenness of his subtest scores on the IQ testing. He could afford the full-cap and it did give additional information. Nevertheless, he decided that he had accomplished his objectives without acting on this further information. What to recommend

concerning both assessment and training is a judgment call that must be made with the client in the light of all factors, including the client's main objectives and finances. This concept will be developed further in examples that follow.

iii. Case Example #2 – Dawn, 48 year old woman after several Closed Head Injuries.

Use a Full-cap Assessment if there is a Medical Problem

Clients who have more complex histories (for example, head injury, seizure disorder, depression, and so on) can be expected to show differences from the general population. They will often have major difficulties with attention span, concentration and recall. You must use a Full-cap assessment to adequately assess these individuals and plan a neurofeedback intervention to complement their total treatment program.

Having done the full-cap, Dawn's EEG, below, is an example of one instance when you would decide that a full-cap should be interpreted by an expert. Although this may be interpreted as within normal limits, you can see paroxysms of high amplitude waves through much of the record. This may represent more than just a slight variation from expected normal frequency distributions.

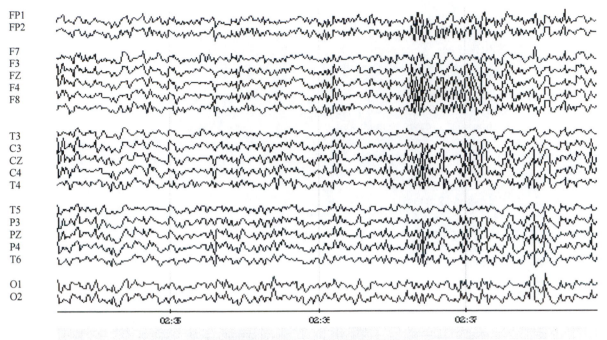

FP1
FP2

F7
F3
FZ
F4
F8

T3
C3
CZ
C4
T4

T5
P3
PZ
P4
T6

O1
O2

02:35   02:36   02:37

4 seconds of eyes open baseline data (no task)

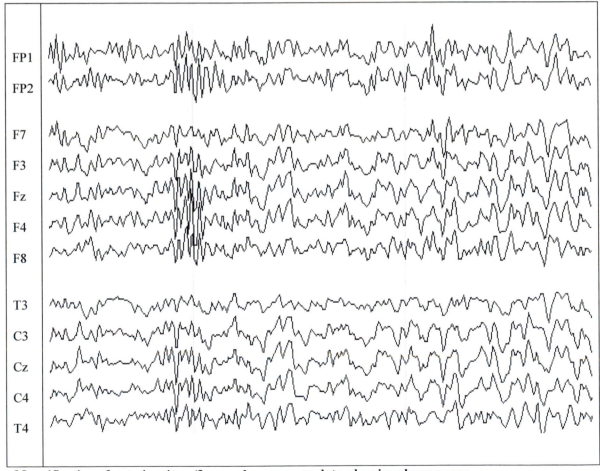

FP1

FP2

F7

F3

Fz

F4

F8

T3

C3

Cz

C4

T4

Magnification of anterior sites, (2 seconds, eyes open data, showing sharp waves.

This client, Dawn, age 48, had been in 3 minor car accidents without hospitalization. In one of these there was a whiplash type of injury. She was previously an articulate, intelligent lady. Now she has extreme problems with memory. She often has to close her eyes to attempt to recall a series of things in order to compose a sentence. She used to be able to rapidly read and synthesize information. She cannot do this now. She is not even able to help her teenage children with their homework though she tries. Previously she was an excellent source when they wrote essays. Focusing and concentrating is difficult. Standard neuropsychological testing at a large hospital centre did not show her deficits. When a 3 lead EEG was done at Cz referenced to the left ear, it demonstrated repeated bursts of what appeared to be sharp waves. Because of this finding and her history of injuries and her symptom picture it was recommended to Dawn

that a full-cap be done and sent to Q-Metrx for specialized evaluation. A sample from the full-cap is shown above, with an enlargement of the anterior leads shown in the second figure. These bursts were seen throughout the record. Her brain map showed a clear disconnect between right and left frontal lobes when comodulation statistical comparisons to the normal database were done for 4-7 Hz and for 13-18 Hz.

This analysis also demonstrates a mild (above 1SD) hypercomodulation between central (C3, Cz, C4) areas and parietal and posterior temporal areas (P3, Pz, P4 & T5, T6). This may point to a lack of discriminatory functioning; that is, more of the brain is being recruited to process information than would usually be required. The second objective for comodulation training might be to encourage her to decrease comodulation between these areas.

As noted above, this 48 year old woman had 3 car accidents. At the time this EEG was done she was having significant difficulty with memory recall. She would close her eyes and write with one hand on the palm of the other to help her recall information.

4-7 Hz comodulation is compared to the SKIL database. The result demonstrates a right to left frontal lobe disconnect. The objective for comodulation training would be to increase left to right frontal communication .

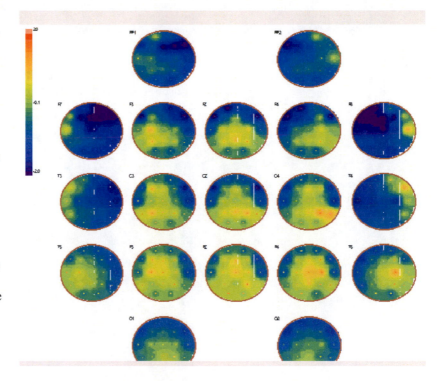

iv. Case Example # 3 – Christian, 18 years of age, Severe Learning Disability, Social Awkwardness, Dysphoria

Christian is 18 years of age. This example is used only to show how a QEEG with topographic displays can reflect the symptom picture and suggest a focus for neurofeedback intervention.

Christian has been in special education throughout his school years. Reading is at a grade 5 level. He is well motivated and parents are supportive. The first topometric display is eyes closed raw data. The posterior, occipital alpha is appropriately the dominant frequency. However, the peak alpha at 9 Hz at Fz and Cz is not the expected pattern. It corresponds to his ADD inattentive symptoms.

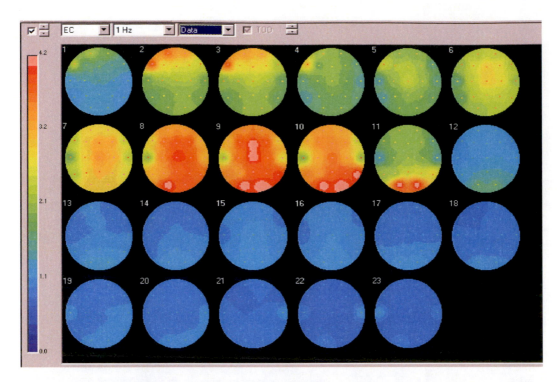

The next topometric display (shown below) indicates comodulation at his dominant frequency range 8-10 Hz (eyes closed). The lack of comodulation T5 to the left central and frontal areas and to P4 corresponds to his difficulties with language and expressing himself. It also corresponds to his language based learning disabilities. The hypercomodulation observed between C4 and Fz and C4 and F2 may correspond to difficulties in emotional expression.

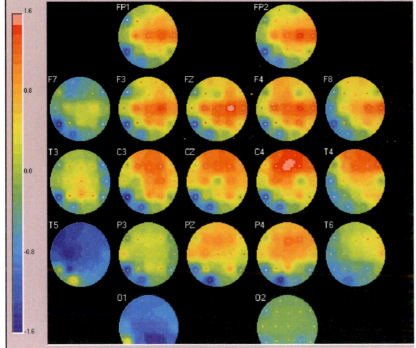

On a topometric map for comodulation data at 8-11 Hz (not shown) he demonstrated hypercomodulation in the frontal areas corresponding to his dysphoric symptoms.

In addition, Christian displayed abnormal jerking movements and twitching. SMR demonstrated a dip in the 13-15 Hz range at C3, Cz, and C4.

The neurofeedback training program for Christian should initially emphasize increasing SMR at Cz in channel A. At the same time, he will be encouraged to increase activity in channel B (decreasing the dominant slow wave activity and increasing 14-17 Hz beta) at T5 then at F3 while reading. Later, comodulation training may be attempted.

v. Case Example #4 – Jane, age 8 years old, Reading Disability

Jane was an 8-year-old girl who was not even reading at a beginning grade one level. This is a specific learning disability in a girl with normal intelligence. She also exhibited all the symptoms of ADHD, some difficulties with geometric shapes and mild social inappropriateness (slightly behind age level). In the record below taken while she was reading the raw EEG shows some slow activity on the left side. Note large burst of slow activity at P3 and Pz and at C3. The slow activity seen at PZ, P4 and T6 may correspond to her not always being appropriate with older professional people and acting younger than her age (This can only be a hypothesis). This slowing could also correspond to visual spatial comprehension difficulties and her difficulty understanding geometric forms. Her ophthalmologist has also noted that she has problems with geometric shapes and trying to reverse them.

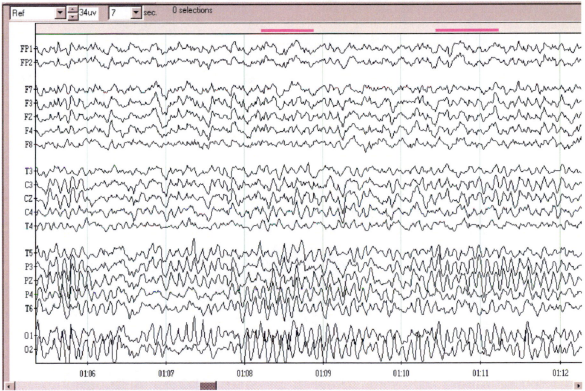

EEG, linked ears reference, while reading.

In the brain map, with eyes closed, there is also some slowing. The amplitude of 3-5 Hz activity is compared with the SKIL database. This database does not yet include children, therefore, the only usefulness of the information is the comparison of the left and right side in the temporal – parietal region and seeing if this corresponds to what is observed on the raw EEG.

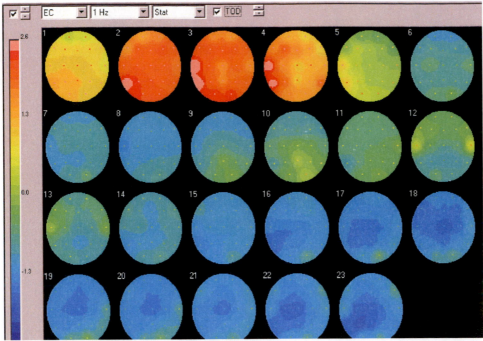

Brain map, eyes closed, referenced to linked ears.

Hopefully there will be good database information for children and more publications on findings with learning disabilities in the near future. At this time, one can only cautiously make hypotheses about areas that are affected based non neuroanatomical knowledge and see if these correspond to expected findings on the EEG. In this case we would expect slowing in areas that correspond to known brain areas for reading on the left and for visual spatial manipulation on the right. The above EEG findings do correspond and therefore lead to suggestions for neurofeedback training. Jane was asked to decrease dominant slow wave activity in areas where it was observed. This is discussed further under interventions.

v. Artifacts in 19 Channel Assessment
Example of Muscle Artifact and Left-Right Asymmetry

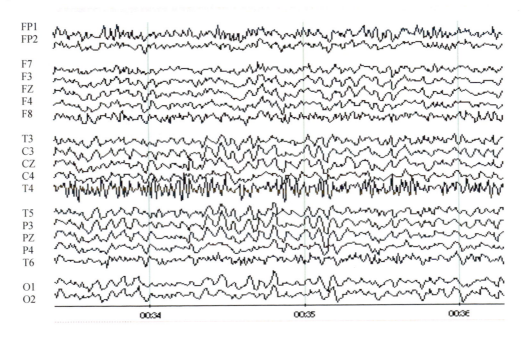

The above example of a 19 lead EEG (eyes open) assessment demonstrates several points. First, it is sometimes difficult to obtain a clean record without artifact. This client had a mild injury to the right side of his jaw. The muscle artifact at T4 and a bit at F8 and T6 is consistent throughout the record. There is also muscle artifact in the left prefrontal lead. An additional observation is that there is a consistent difference throughout the record between the left and right cerebral hemispheres that is independent of the differences due to EMG artifact. The left side demonstrates more slow wave activity in the central and parietal regions.

e. 19 Channel Assessment Examples Provided by M. B. Sterman (SKIL Program – Sterman & Kaiser) to Illustrate How a 19 Channel Assessment May Give Valuable Additional Information.

There are a number of databases in use such as those by Frank Duffy, Robert Thatcher, William Hudspeth and E.Roy John's group at N.Y.U. The figures for the following examples came from the training manual for the SKIL program. The comments are a précis of Sterman's remarks plus some additional observations. SKIL provides a method of artifacting and interpreting 19-lead assessment data that has been collected with a 2 Hz high pass filter on for the data collecton. Comparisons with Sterman's database are also utilized by the program. Numbers, such as #14, refer to the figures in the SKIL manual published in 1999.

i. ADHD – Comparison of Data: EC, EO, Reading And Math

State comparisons

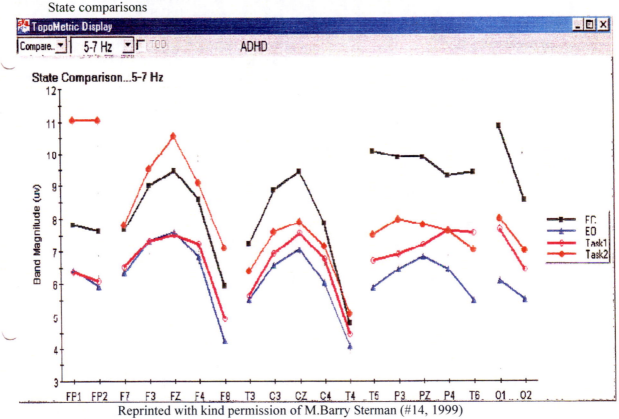

Reprinted with kind permission of M.Barry Sterman (#14, 1999)

State comparison plot from the SKIL program. The client is 16 years of age and has ADHD and affective symptoms. This pattern of high amplitude frontal 5-7 Hz activity was only seen during a math task and not on the eyes closed, eyes open and reading conditions. Black with squares is eyes closed. Blue with stars is eyes open. Pink, task 1, with open circles is reading. Red, task 2, with filled in circles is doing math. This state comparison also illustrates that the state change from eyes closed to eyes open produces the biggest change in theta activity.

ii. ADHD and Math Task – Comparison to Database

Figure_: Increased frontal theta during a math task.

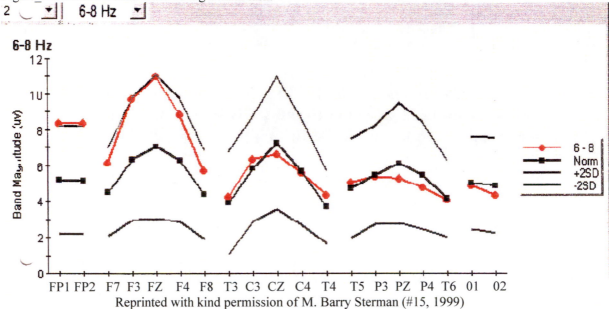

Reprinted with kind permission of M. Barry Sterman (#15, 1999)

The client is 23 years of age and has ADHD symptoms. This pattern of high prefrontal and frontal 6-8 Hz activity was recorded during a math task. The red line with filled in circles is this client's data, heavy black is the database, and the gray lines represent +/- 2 SD from the norms. Note that in both of these examples FZ is a better site for seeing the excess theta than CZ. This is in line with Lubar's suggestion that you use CZ for children with ADHD and move more frontally with older adolescents and adults.

iii. Head Injury

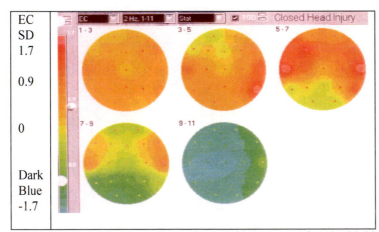

Brain maps (comparative data) after head injury. Reprinted with kind permission of M. Barry Sterman (#19, 1999)

Topographic map (SKIL program) comparison with normal database: This 28-year-old female client, in a car accident, suffered a blow to the left frontal-temporal region. Note the high amplitude 5-7 Hz activity at T3 and F3. Note also the 'contra-coup' focus of high amplitude 5- 7 Hz activity at T4 and T6. Since the accident, her IQ dropped (126 TO 96) and she had symptoms which include episodes of confusion, word aphasia, memory deficits, and short attention span. NFB training would suppress 5-7 Hz at F3, T3, T4 and T6.

Head Injury With and Without Time of Day Corrections

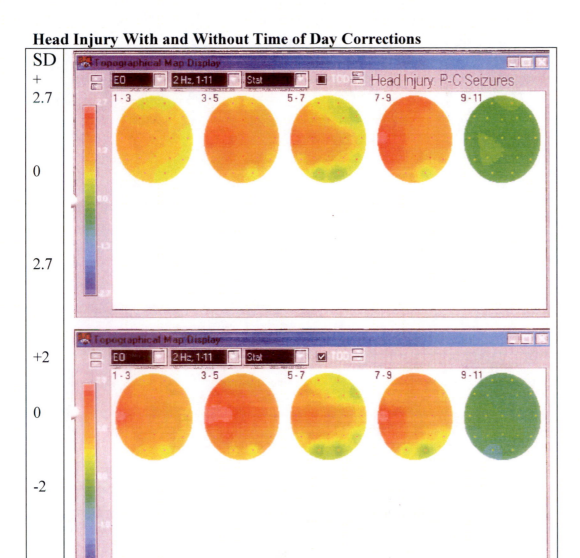

The above brain maps after head injury with and without time of day correction are reprinted with kind permission of M. Barry Sterman (#20, 1999). It shows a Topographic Map after head injury in a 42-year-old male: This figure demonstrates the importance of a time-of-day correction. Both figures demonstrate a significant increase in amplitude of 7-9 Hz activity at T3. The bottom figure is time-of-day corrected, however, and shows a clear 3-5 Hz focus at T3 and C3 and a 1-3 Hz band focus at T3 which are not seen in the top figure. Training would decrease these high amplitude bands. The reference electrodes would be placed on the contra-lateral (right) ear to decrease suppression of signal strength due to common mode rejection.

iv. ADHD (Child)

Owl or Monkey pattern in the brain map of a child with ADHD.

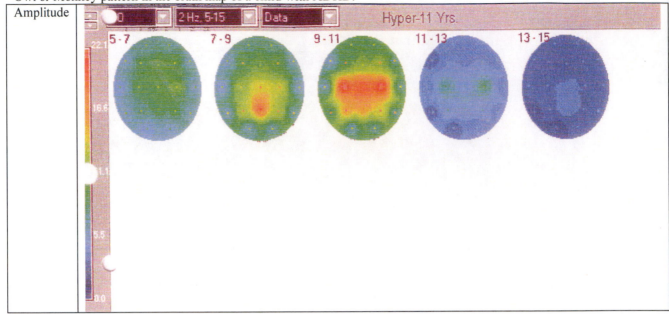

Reprinted with kind permission of M.Barry Sterman (#21, 1999)

Topographic map, 11-year-old male diagnosed with ADHD: This figure demonstrates Sterman's *owl* or *monkey* pattern. Sterman suggests that this is an EEG subtype of ADHD. Note the high 9-11 Hz activity at C3 and C4. The child is too young to compare to the normal database. On the raw EEG the waveform was not the wicket pattern seen with a Mu rhythm. One must always distinguish this from alpha as previously explained. NFB would suppress 7-9 or 7-10 Hz activity and increase SMR 13-15 Hz. One avoids suppressing 11 Hz activity due to its proximity to the SMR activity that one is attempting to increase.

v. Seizure Disorder

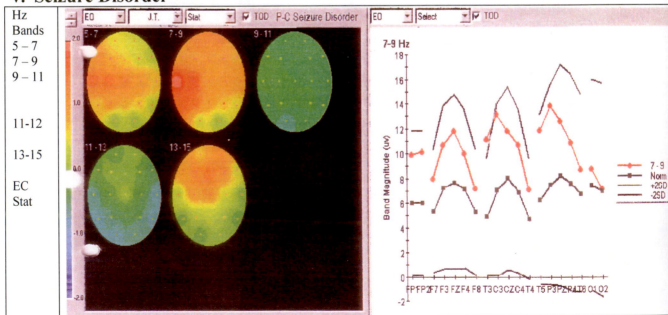

Figure_: Brain map and topographic display (comparative data) in a client with seizures. Reprinted with kind permission of M.Barry Sterman (#24, 1999)

Convergent analysis, using the SKIL program, in a client who has partial-complex seizures. 7-9 Hz activity is raised at the anterior temporal seizure focus. The topographic maps compare amplitudes of different frequency bands to the normal database. The topometric plot on the right gives details concerning the spectral distribution of the 7-9 Hz band.

vi Comodulation in Depression – Comparison with Database

Hypercomodulation in the frontal regions in depression (comparative data)

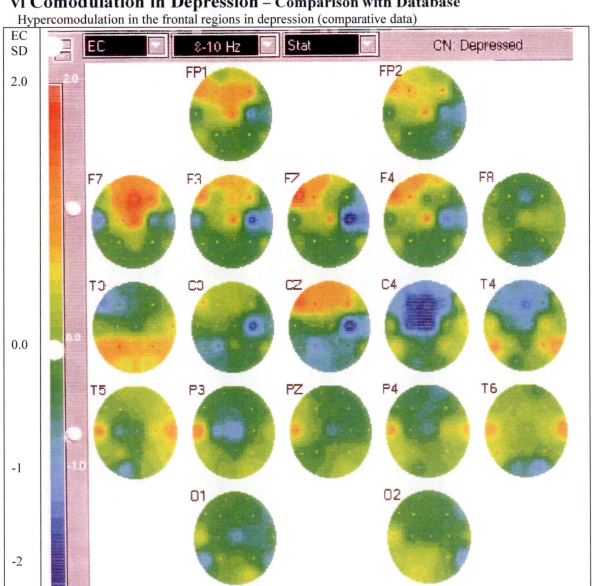

Reprinted with kind permission of M.Barry Sterman (#27, 1999)

This is a statistical comparison, using the normal database on the SKIL program, in the eyes closed condition, of the comodulation of 8-10 Hz activity in a depressed female in her early forties. Note the hyper-comodulation between F7 and Fz at 2 SD from the mean for the normal database. Sterman suggests that this hypercomodulation may represent a lack of differentiation between these sites and in thalamocortical regulation. He notes that this hyper-comodulation is more likely to be due to a change in thalamocortical than intracortical connections because severing intracortical connections has been shown not to abolish covariation between cortical sites (Contreras 1997, Sterman 1998). Note also the hypo-comodulation between C4 and Cz and Fz.

vii. Frontal – Central Disconnect Pattern

Figure: Frontal central disconnect pattern: statistical comparison.
Reprinted with kind permission of M.Barry Sterman (#30, 1999)

Comodulation comparison with normal database for a 23-year-old male. Note the hypo-comodulation in the 7-9 Hz band between frontal and central cortical sites. Sterman has termed this type of pattern a *frontal-central disconnect* or *dissociation*. In this example Sterman postulates that a lack of shared activity between these areas might result in impairments in reciprocal interactions and the individual's ability to regulate sensory input and motor output. In this particular patient Sterman observed facial tics, stuttering, insomnia and attentional problems.

viii. A Note on Pre - Post EEG Comparisons

It is important for clients to be shown clear pre and post NFB treatment comparisons of the frequency ranges that they have been working on. This can be easily done in single channel work (Thompson & Thompson, 1998). It is also possible to plot this type of comparison data for 19 channel assessments. It is always gratifying for a client to see that their behavioural changes correspond to electrical changes.

A caution, however, is needed. Training, for client who has a specific disorder, such as ADHD, involves 'normalizing' the EEG. In this type of work you would expect to see an overall EEG change. For ADHD this often includes a decrease in theta and/or low alpha and an increase in SMR. For an executive or professional athlete training does not usually involve normalization of the EEG; rather it emphasizes self-regulation where the client learns to control mental states. Thus, with these clients, post testing should demonstrate

their ability to consciously enter a specific state. Measurements would, therefore, have to be made when they were in, and then out of, the desired state. The EEG should demonstrate a shift. For example, a professional golfer (see later example) may want to block out all inner thoughts, concerns, and worries. When she does this the amplitude of a 27-31 Hz band decreases. Post testing should demonstrate her ability to do this. You are training for a more flexible brain.

f. Single Channel or 19 Channel Assessments – When is Each Appropriate?

Here are three important considerations to open the discussion on EEG assessment. First, who are you in terms of professional qualifications and experience in reading the EEG? Are you an educator, coach, trainer, therapist or a neurologist? Second, what is the purpose of your EEG? Third, what do you plan to do with the results of the EEG assessment?

i. The Advantages of Doing a Full-cap Assessment

The 'gold standard' is the 19-channel EEG assessment. This is also frequently referred to as a *full-cap assessment*. It allows you to view what is happening at each frequency at all 19 of the standard sites in the 10-20 electrode system. As noted above, when done before and after neurofeedback training, you can see what has changed in terms of brain wave activity not only at the site(s) where training was done, but at all sites. Certainly you would use this for any client who had a history of a head injury or a seizure disorder since it would indicate the best site(s) for training. You must use it if you are going to do coherence or comodulation feedback. You would also want to use it for any research study in which the EEG brain map was helpful for differentiating between different diagnostic categories; for example, differentiating between different EEG subtypes of ADD.

ii. The Drawbacks of a Full-cap Assessment

This ideal kind of assessment has some drawbacks. It is expensive, takes a great deal more background and training to analyze, and it does not look at the spectrum up to 62 Hz. It is important for our work with NFB to be able to assess and monitor the frequencies not only up to 23 Hz but also above the mid-20's up to 62 Hz in some cases, particularly if you are concerned with anxiety and ruminations you want to look at the hi-beta frequencies. At the time of writing this kind of assessment was not available using the 19 channel instruments commonly used by neurofeedback practitioners.

It is expensive because of the initial cost of acquiring an instrument capable of 19 lead assessments. Also be aware that it takes a little more time to set up and collect information. In addition, it takes a great deal more time and expertise to read and interpret the data once it is collected. Families and individuals usually only have a certain amount of money that they are willing or able to spend. You must decide whether it is absolutely necessary to advise the family that this must be done when it may mean that they would only be able to afford an inadequate number of sessions of training. Of course, the data is of great interest but in many cases this may be mainly academically interesting and not influence what and where you train. Your interest in having data, however, must not over-ride common sense considerations with respect to helping the family.

If you are likely to be able to obtain clear information as to the probability of a condition and good-enough training parameters to help that condition from a simple single channel, 3-lead assessment, then you should probably follow the Principle of Parsimony: do the least intrusive and least expensive intervention that has a probability of success. In the case of neurofeedback interventions this would become: do the simplest and least invasive and disruptive intervention first. Therefore, if a 3-lead assessment can give sufficient information to set parameters and carry out a successful training program, you may be justified in doing that rather than the full 19 channels. Always ask yourself, "How can I provide the best service?" and, "What is realistic for this family in this situation?"

A practical consideration is rapport with your client. On the one hand, it is impressive if you do 19 channels. On the other hand, a single channel assessment can be a quick and painless hookup whereas a full-cap assessment takes more time and can be uncomfortable for some clients.

Another practical consideration is experience and training. Most biofeedback practitioners have one or two channel instruments. Most of these individuals can do an adequate job of reading the EEG produced with their equipment. These people are not electroencephalographers and do not have the training or experience to read a full-cap assessment. They should not pretend that they do. If they decide to do a full-cap they must either out-source the job to a trained practitioner or undertake extensive training so that they can interpret the full-cap assessment themselves. Interpreting the data from a 19-lead assessment involves both art and science. Different databases and different montages may give different results and, as shown at the SNR annual meeting each year when a panel is given the same EEG data on a selected case to interpret, even the experts may disagree on some points of interpretation. It is the gold standard for neurofeedback assessments but it is not entirely objective. We need more validity and reliability data concerning this procedure. Of course, neurologists reading EEG's are also not entirely objective. Sterman quotes a statistic that the correlation co-efficient for different neurologists reading the same record is only .56 and the correlation for the same neurologist doing it at two different points in time is about the same. Here is an excellent thesis topic for an enterprising student: investigate the correlation in findings from 19-lead assessments done for the purpose of designing neurofeedback interventions both across different practitioners and with same the practitioner over time.

In summary, full-cap assessment is excellent and necessary for certain purposes, however, most software programs for doing the full-cap, at the time of writing, are not looking at the spectrum of activity to 62 Hz. Secondly, people getting started in neurofeedback will not yet be doing full-cap assessments on a regular basis and are not yet comfortable with reading the output. Thirdly, a full-cap assessment is much more expensive, particularly if the information is sent away to be read elsewhere. It may use up funds that clients might otherwise have been able to use for training. Finally, the cost may reduce the number of clients who are able or willing to pay for post-training EEG assessment.

iii. General Discussion: When Do We Recommend a Full-Cap Assessment?

In this section we are stating a personal bias. There are centres that do a full-cap assessment on every client both pre and post training and they might say it is the only way to know what changes you have made in the brain's functioning. Personally, our view is that it is hard to justify the extra cost of $1,000-$1,500 in every case particularly if training can proceed with the information from a single channel assessment or from repeated single channel data collection. Collect data at Cz, move electrode to Fz, collect data again, and repeat for as many locations as are appropriate to provide the data needed in order to proceed with a particular client. Paul Swingle, a psychologist with a large neurofeedback practice in Vancouver, has a system for doing this that he calls a 'mini-Q'.

We recommend 19 lead full-cap assessment for clients who have more complex symptom pictures. This includes all clients who have a history of head injury or a seizure disorder. It includes clients who have a complex array of symptoms such as may be found in Asperger's syndrome or in clients who have a combination of problems, such as depression and anger management. At the ADD Centre / Biofeedback Institute of Toronto this has been done using Lexicor equipment and we look forward to augmenting this with the NeuroNavigator instrument. (The NeuroNavigator is an instrument built by Jan Hoover at J & J Instruments according to the specifications of M. Barry Sterman. It is distributed through Thought Technology.) To analyse the data we are using the SKIL program, the creation of Barry Sterman and David Kaiser (Sterman-Kaiser Imaging Labs) and, in addition, we suggest to our clients that they pay an extra fee so that we obtain a second professional opinion. Data can be sent by CD or via the internet to companies that provide interpretations, such as Lexicor, SKIL or Q-Metrx or to knowledgeable individuals such as a network co-ordinated by Bill Hudspith. The Q-Metrx services, for example, include having a neurologist, who specializes in EEG, write a report on the data. In addition, there is also a report or summary written by an EEG specialist (usually not a neurologist) who is capable of advising on the best neurofeedback training program to carry out. Experienced individuals can both read the EEG and give valuable advice on appropriate neurofeedback parameters for training that are specific to the client's EEG findings. Unless one is doing large numbers of QEEG assessments and has invested in purchasing the normative databases, it makes economic sense to out-source the interpretation.

Use the services of those who have looked at thousands of EEGs, who have purchased or created normative databases for comparison purposes, who know the intricacies of re-montaging the data to yield the most helpful information, and who have knowledge of neurofeedback.

It is a wonderful learning experience to get intimate with the EEG data yourself and come up with hypotheses as to what it all means but it takes time to become an expert. Our view, as noted above, is that there is a great deal of art as well as science in quantitative EEG analysis. As in much of our field, the adage "A little knowledge is a dangerous thing." should be kept in mind by those starting to do 19 channel QEEG work. People who have just taken a few week-end workshops are not ready to do a 19 lead QEEG interpretation solo any more than an aspiring pilot is ready to take over the controls without his flight instructor beside him.

There are exceptions to every rule. People with extensive training in neurophysiology, anatomy and pathology who have had previous clinical training and experience in this area may learn more rapidly than others how to run this kind of equipment and interpret the results.

If there is any concern about a primary medical condition, such as a seizure disorder, head injury, and so on, your client MUST be seen and assessed by the appropriate medical practitioners before undertaking EEG biofeedback. The QEEG which you are doing is being done to look at data concerning *normal* brain waves. **You make no claim regarding assessing, training or even recognition of abnormal waveforms or patterns.** This is the task of a specially trained neurologist in conjunction with an EEG technician.

iv. Effect on NFB Results
At the time of writing, we are not aware of any studies that investigate the question of whether there would be a difference in outcome if a full-cap had been done as compared to a single channel, three lead assessment. Most of our students want to improve focus and attention span and, at times, decrease tension. There is good evidence in the literature that a single channel assessment at Cz works very well for recognizing patterns seen in ADD (Monastra; Linden; Lubar; Thompson & Thompson). We do

obtain a great deal of useful information concerning the higher range of beta (above 28 Hz) activity using a single or two channel instrument. For this reason we would always have to do this whether or not a full-cap was also done. The multisite study headed by Monastra and Lubar showed good reliability and validity data using the single channel assessment at Cz. Nevertheless, as pointed out above, there are cases with additional problems where a full-cap may be very helpful and the cost is justified.

g. Overview of Interpretation of Findings Using Different Types of Assessment

i. Single Channel Findings
With a *referential* montage with the active electrode placed at Cz you can be reasonably certain that the electrical activity recorded reflects the cortical activity under the active electrode. It is unlikely that you will have a false positive result. On the other hand, you may have a false negative. We have already discussed a good example regarding ADD. A Cz assessment may not show high slow wave relative to fast wave activity when the client is tuning out but a second assessment using a frontal placement may pick up the problem and show the ADD symptom picture.

With a *bipolar* montage you will not know which of the two electrodes has the higher amplitude electrical activity under it. Perhaps there is no difference between the two waves at the two sites in terms of type of activity but a potential difference (voltage) is being recorded because they are *out-of-phase*.

ii. Two Channel Findings
Two channel results may clarify differences between two different areas of the brain. However, special caution must be exerted to assure that impedances were the same for all electrode placements before findings at different sites are compared. Again, many areas of the brain are ignored and findings are therefore still quite limited. Another caution is to be sure that the influence of muscle tension artifact is approximately the same for both sites. This can be very subtle and can make beta activity for the site where there is more EMG influence appear

(falsely) high compared to the other site. It is easier and better to compare two sites using two channels with a common reference or a 19-channel assessment where the whole picture can be seen.

iii. Full-cap Findings

These findings are obviously more complete. Different sites may be compared and communication between areas of the brain elucidated. However, as previously noted, it takes many years of experience to interpret accurately the findings. Each way of referencing the electrodes will yield different information. In the standard, linked ears reference the electrode sites close to the ears will show low amplitudes compared to more central sites due to amplifier common mode rejection. The topometric graphs from Sterman's SKIL program allows the clinician to visualize this. False impressions of frontal and/or prefrontal high slow wave activity (due to high temporal slow wave amplitudes which have contaminated the ear references) may be quickly clarified by switching to a sequential montage. This is just a key stroke during an analysis of the data and does not require a different type of electrode placement as it would when only using a one or two channel instrument. Unusual sites of high or low amplitude activity at different frequencies can be distinguished. Hyper or hypocommunication between areas of the brain can be evaluated and compared to normal databases. All of these findings will provide additional suggestions for NFB training.

iv. Advantages of Also Doing Single Channel Assessments to 62 Hz

For some clients, doing an additional assessment on an instrument that shows the spectrum to 62 Hz may have some advantages. For example, we find that negative ruminating may be reflected in high amplitude activity between 23 and 27 Hz or 28 and 34 Hz. This high frequency, high amplitude beta is sometimes called a type of ADD. Certainly it is a form of tuning out and these individuals do have difficulty sustaining attention to other things. However, we feel it is more often a clear reflection of internal ruminations which are often associated with depressive affect. (Of course, ADD plus depression and or anxiety is a common co-morbidity in adults.) Constructive cognitive activity and attention, on the other hand, may be

reflected in activity in the 38 to 42 Hz range, the so-called Sheer Rhythm. The influence of muscle can usually be distinguished from these high frequency beta (also called gamma) bursts by examining the effect of EMG on the activity above 43 Hz. If activity above 43 Hz is consistently low compared to frequencies below 42 Hz then it is reasonably likely that the activity you are observing below 42 Hz is not a reflection of muscle tension.

Ambient electrical activity may raise 50 Hz activity in Europe and Australia or 60 Hz in America. Observing a higher amplitude of these frequencies compared to 48 and 52 Hz in Europe, Asia and Australia or 58 and 62 Hz in America may be a reflection of a difference in impedances between the electrode sites. You should attempt to correct this by re-prepping the electrode sites and checking impedances again. All of these observations are useful not only during an assessment but also during the actual NFB sessions. Not only will the client change mental activity and muscle tension during the session, but they may move and loosen an electrode, thus changing its impedance.

6. Quality Data Collection

The following tips apply to data acquisition whether it is one-channel or nineteen channels. They also apply whether one is doing an assessment or running a training session. One is naturally going to be very fussy about things like low and equal impedance readings when collecting data for a 19-channel assessment because you are basing important decisions on the interpretation of this data. Yet training outcomes are also going to be influenced by the quality of the feedback, which depends first and foremost on the quality of the EEG information. The saying among computer users of "garbage in – garbage out" is very much true when dealing with EEG data. If you are going to be spending the next hour with a client, giving them support while they try to make EEG changes and exercise their brain, you want to be using the best feedback information you can obtain. So make it a habit to be careful about the following things all the time.

a. Site Preparation

Having decided on which sites you are going to use for assessment you now must prepare the site for accurate recording. The first step is to clean the site and test for *impedance*. Impedance is the resistance to the flow of an alternating current (AC). However, in order to understand impedance we should first review two terms, *voltage* and *differential amplifier*.

i. Measurements – Voltage and Amplification

When measuring the EEG, we are measuring tiny amounts of electricity. Remember that a microvolt is a millionth of a volt. You are always measuring the potential differences between two sites for the different EEG frequencies. EEG is an alternating current and most instruments measure *peak-to-peak* voltage differences. Occasionally you will use equipment or read a report where *root-mean-square* (RMS) is the measurement used. The values are smaller because the relationship is that RMS = 0.707 x peak-to-peak values. Occasionally you might see the value expressed as *Peak* value. Peak-to-peak = 2 x Peak value.

Differential Amplifier *(Also covered in the earlier section on 'Electrical Artifact'.)*

The original concept for this type of amplifier came from the work of Thomas Edison. The actual amplifier, however, was not developed until the 1930s. In simplest terms just think of the electrode at one site going to the preamp. There is a potential difference between the site on the scalp and a 'comparison' within the amplifier that involves your third electrode which is called a '*ground*. Many years ago the comparison actually was with ground. Now there is not a direct connection of your client to ground. The measurement and calculations are done differently within the amplifier. The wire from the second site enters at another point in the preamplifier. As previously explained (in Section IV), think of the first site being positive and the second negative. Often a positive (+ve) sign is seen on the electrode that you use as your *active* electrode and a negative (–ve) sign is on the other (*reference*) electrode. Now these two potential differences, the active site to the amplifier (+ve) and the reference site to the amplifier (-ve) are compared. Any induced current from another source, such as a nearby lamp (60 Hz), should be the same and *in-phase* on both inputs. The +ve wire from the active electrode will, in this case, be the mirror image

of the -ve wire from the reference site with respect to 60 Hz current and the two will cancel out and, therefore NOT be amplified. The EEG voltages, on the other hand, will be different as recorded from each of these wires and, therefore, will not cancel out and will be amplified. Thus the difference between the two EEG voltages that have simultaneous input to the amplifier will be amplified. This is the unique function of a *differential amplifier*.

The importance of having almost the same impedance at all electrode sites can now be better understood. If the impedances were very different, then the induced voltage from a common electrical source would not appear the same when the *differential* amplifier compared the active and reference inputs. Therefore it would not cancel out and might be amplified. This would result in a large artifact in the recording. The *common mode rejection* feature only works well if you have low and equal impedance readings.

ii. Preparing the Electrode Site

The first step before preparing the electrode site is to prepare your client by telling your client exactly what you are going to do. You thus get permission for you to attach electrodes to their head and ear lobes. Reassure them that the paste used will be easily removed with alcohol at the end of the session and that they will leave with their hair looking as it did when they arrived. After you have measured the head to accurately find the site that you want to use (such as Cz) according to the 10-20 electrode system, mark it with a felt tip pen. (A practical suggestion: do not mark it with a red pen as that may look like blood when you rub it off.) Then part the hair so that you have a flat base and scalp showing. To obtain a good connection between the scalp and the electrode (good connection = a low impedance) you may begin by cleaning each site with an alcohol swab to remove sweat and skin oils. It is then essential to rub the site vigorously with a non-allergenic prep such as omni-prep or nu-prep to remove dead skin cells and anything else that might act as an insulator. (Hairspray, for example, is a good insulator). Nu-Prep is slightly less abrasive and is now used at our centres. It is imperative, however, that you do **not** break the surface of the skin. Now carefully put some 10-20 EEG paste on the site and press it into the skin. Q-Tips are handy for applying both Nu-Prep and 10-20 paste. Put more EEG conductive paste (e.g., "10-20") in the electrode cup, leaving a small mound where it will touch the skin. Place the electrodes on to the prepared sites. Do **not** allow any bare electrode metal to touch the skin, as metal to skin would have different conductance than metal-electrode paste-skin. Jan Hoover, whose company (J&J) is a manufacturer of equipment and electrodes says, "A good daub of conductive paste is the best way to ensure good electrical conductivity." This is, of course, why many electrodes are designed with little cups that hold gel. Flat gold electrodes, available from IMA in Florida, are easier to clean but you have to be more careful about ensuring a cushion of paste between electrode and skin.

At this juncture you must check the impedance between each pair of electrodes. For a one channel referential assessment this means three checks: active to reference, active to ground, and reference to ground.

iii. Impedance – Definition and Measurement

As explained briefly under Section IV Measuring the EEG, electrode *impedance* may be defined as the resistance to the flow of an alternating electrical current. You must distinguish this from the electrical term, '*resistance*'. Resistance is the inability of a part of an electrical circuit to allow the passage of a *direct* (constant voltage) current (Fisch p.44). You should always check impedance for each electrode site using a specially constructed impedance meter that passes a weak alternating current from the selected electrode through the scalp to all other electrodes connected to the meter. The mild current should alternate at 10 Hz to approximate a common EEG frequency. Ohm's law for a direct current is V=IR (voltage = current x resistance). However, for an alternating current this becomes v=iz where z is the impedance of the circuit. This is what we are dealing with because electrical activity in the brain is AC not DC. Both resistance (R) and impedance (z) are measured in ohms. In a *DC circuit*, when a potential difference occurs between two points, then instantly a current flows and will flow as long as that potential difference remains. In an *AC circuit* the current will instantly flow but will not remain flowing.

Mathematically:

$$Impedance(z) = \sqrt{(square\ root\ of)}[\ R^2 + (10^6 / 2\pi fC)^2]$$

where π is 3.14, f is the frequency of the alternating current in Hz, and C is the capacitance. You are not expected to be an expert in electronics. However, there are a couple of points to be learned by looking at this formula. First, C(capacitance), which is measured in 'microfarads (μF)', refers to the storage of electrons. A capacitor consists of two conductors separated by a resistance. It introduces a time factor because current will rise instantly, then the capacitor stores electrons with the result that the current will gradually decrease over time. Thus DC current is stopped and only AC current can pass. Cell walls act as 'capacitors'. So do the electric wires that run from the client to the preamp.

If C and f were held constant (as they would be in a DC circuit), then the z would vary directly with R. However, this is not the case in an AC circuit. The formula shows that z will go up as C goes down. z also varies inversely with frequency. Thus as frequency increases, the measured impedance will decrease. For this reason a standard measurement was introduced so that we are all talking in equivalent terms. The standard is to use a 10 Hz frequency (AC) when measuring impedances for our electrode sites. This frequency was chosen as it is the most common dominant frequency found when adult EEG activity is measured with eyes closed.

Notes Regarding Measuring Impedance

You must have an impedance meter unless you have exceptional equipment that either checks impedance (like the new EEG-Z preamp available for the Procomp+ and Infinity) or has such high input impedance that you can just check your raw EEG signal and 60 Hz in the spectral display to ensure you have good connections (F1000 equipment). An *impedance meter* is not an ordinary meter for measuring resistance purchased at an electrical outlet store. As noted above, it is an instrument specifically constructed for EEG work. The specially constructed impedance meter passes a weak alternating current (that mimics an EEG frequency) from the selected electrode through the scalp to all other electrodes connected to the meter. The current is at a 10 Hz frequency to approximate a common EEG frequency. It is essential that you have good impedances for all channels. Otherwise, the EEG will be recording differences which may be, in part, due to differences in your connections. This is particularly important when you do a *two-channel assessment* where impedances must be virtually exactly the same in order to compare frequency bands in two hemispheres. As noted above, theoretically, with high resistance amplifiers, this should not be a great problem. However, try experimenting and you may find that it does make a difference. (It can make a large difference if the client should move their head even a small amount!). Impedances should be between 100 and 5000 Ω. Electrodes with much higher impedance may produce 60 Hz artifact and attenuate the recording. Impedance less than 100 Ω is an indication of an abnormal *shunt,* or short circuit, between electrodes (Fisch, B., 1999). This could be caused, for example, by electrode paste connecting and creating a bridge between two adjacent electrodes.

Electrode polarization may occur if a direct current is used to measure impedance. This would then encourage current flow in one direction and resist flow in the other direction. This would distort recordings and is another reason for using an alternating current for checking impedances. Direct current is appropriate for measuring resistance but not impedance, as explained above. So you cannot use an inexpensive meter from your local hardware. You must go to the expense of purchasing an impedance meter or use equipment that has a built-in impedance check. (Note: Electrode connections that use saline rather than conductive paste are prone to poor impedance.)

The most common indicator of unequal impedances is the appearance on the output recording of 60 Hz electrical artifact from alternating current sources in the recording area (or 50 Hz in countries where that is the standard electrical current). The amplitude of this artifact will be proportional to the inequality in impedances and the strength of the signal. In full-cap assessments the ground is usually placed at FPz. (The result when an electrode detaches from the scalp is that the other input is compared to the ground giving a clear reading of eye movements which are easily recognized.)

You are doing an excellent job if impedance is <5 Kohms and the pairs are within 1 Kohm of each other. As previously noted, impedance should be between 100 and 5000 Ω. Electrodes with much higher impedance may cause 60 Hz artifact and attenuate the recording (Fisch, 1999).

Note: For most of our neurofeedback work, the most important factor is that the impedance readings for each pair of electrodes all be very close to one another. If all three were between 8 and 9 this would be more acceptable than 2 being at 8 and one at 2. If you have equal impedance readings, movement artifact and externally induced electrical artifact will be minimized. Induced artifact will be discussed further under artifacts and filters.

What if the Impedance Readings are Higher than 5 Kohms?

The answer depends to a great extent on which instrument you are using. Instruments differ in characteristics such as input impedance of the amplifier (which is an independent issue from the question of the impedance readings you get from your electrodes.) In our experience instruments such as the A620 (Stoelting Autogenics) and Lexicor require a strict adherence to the above recommendations for impedance to ensure good EEG readings. We redo the preparation of the electrode site with alcohol cleansing, gentle abrading with NuPrep and then spreading 10-20 conductive EEG paste until we get those impedances down. We may let the client rub their own ear lobes as they know what the goal is and often tend to be more vigorous in the rubbing than the trainer would be. Children love to hold the impedance metre and are quite willing to tolerate a little squeeze on the ear electrode if they can watch the result of the reading getting down to the magic < 5 Kohm range. With good impedances one will see a good consistent EEG on these instruments.

Instruments such as the F1000 (Focused Technology) or the ProComp+ or Infiniity (Thought Technology), where the input impedance of the amplifier is high and work has gone into protecting the wires from the electrode site to the pre-amp, may be more forgiving of impedance readings that do not meet research criteria. (Research criteria, as you know by now, are that all pairs be below 5000 ohms and within 1000 ohms of each other.) Frank Diets, manufacturer of the F1000, does not even recommend the need to check impedances with his equipment. You just check the EEG spectral display before proceeding with feedback to ensure that it looks like good EEG and that 60 Hz. is not too high. (It also indicates clearly if you forgot to turn the instrument on, which will happen occasionally!) We have experimented with the Thought Technology instrument and could see very little difference in the EEG tracings with higher impedances, if they were all close to one another (for example, all three readings around 14 Kohms). There were two exceptions to this. The first was found when we moved the electrode a little bit by pulling on the skin or wiggling the ear such as might occur during feedback sessions. When there were good impedances, it took a great deal more movement of the skin to affect the EEG readings. The second exception was when the client turned their head. With poor impedance and a difference in impedances between the electrode pairs, even a small movement of the head (30 degrees) to look at the trainer, caused a large artifact in the EEG. With reasonable but not great impedance readings (< 18 Kohms) but almost no difference between pairs of electrodes, there was little discernable difference in the EEG. These observations need to be replicated. Poor impedances do lead to a lower amplitude EEG. This will affect comparisons between sessions and pre-post neurofeedback training assessments.

Impedance: Client's Perspective

Consistent impedance readings from session to session mean that data comparisons are more meaningful; that is, more likely to represent changes the client is making in their EEG rather than differences in electrode contacts with the scalp that affect the measurement of the EEG. We have observed that the total amplitude of the EEG is lower when there are high impedance readings. This makes a big difference to clients when they are trying to equal, or improve on, yesterday's %-over-threshold scores or point score when doing feedback training.

This might also be of interest from the standpoint that lowering total amplitude is being put forth, in some quarters, as being useful for optimizing performance. This is sometimes referred to as a frontal 'squash' protocol. Certainly, an overall decrease in amplitude of the EEG would have one assume that theta and alpha were lower and that there were no major artifacts in either slow

frequencies (due to eye movement) or faster frequencies (due to muscle activity). It could imply that greater desynchronized activity was taking place. The normal adult, eyes open EEG displays low voltage and is fairly flat. There are also some good anecdotal reports of its usefulness.

However, for optimal performance we emphasize a rise in certain bandwidths such as 11-13 Hz. We also emphasize mental flexibility, that is, being able to change quickly from one state to another as appropriate for task conditions. Thus lowering of the total EEG amplitude would not usually be the sole objective.

Last, but by no means least, equal impedances between each of the electrode pairs may help to minimize cardiac artifact during NFB training. The heart produces about ten times the electrical output of the brain and EKG artifact due to volume conduction is sometimes a problem. (An example is given in the section on artifacts.)

If you are going to sit with a client for an hour, you want them to have valid, reliable feedback. Taking a few minutes to get good impedance readings is the first step in providing quality neurofeedback.

Offset

The hand held impedance meter also allows you to check the offset of the wires. High offset (above 50, and certainly above 100) may be your first warning that a wire is breaking or that your gold electrode cup is deteriorating. Deterioration will occur rapidly if you do not immediately clean your electrodes after each session. It will cause a little 'battery-like' effect at the site. Another indicator of a faulty wire may be the occasional flattening of the EEG.

Site Preparation – A Caution

You must be careful that you do not allow the Nu-Prep or the 10-20 EEG paste (or other electrode gel) to cover the space between any two electrodes. If it does, this bridge will cause a short circuit. If you aren't careful, it is possible that you might miss this when reading the EEG quickly before you record data. This could mean that you would have to redo your recording at another time. An example of this problem is given below.

A salt bridge is not the only possible cause when you see two sites with identical recordings. On one occasion we sent back a new EEG instrument because it had an internal fault that linked the two electrodes.

With Full-cap Be Careful That Gel Doesn't "Bridge" Between Electrodes

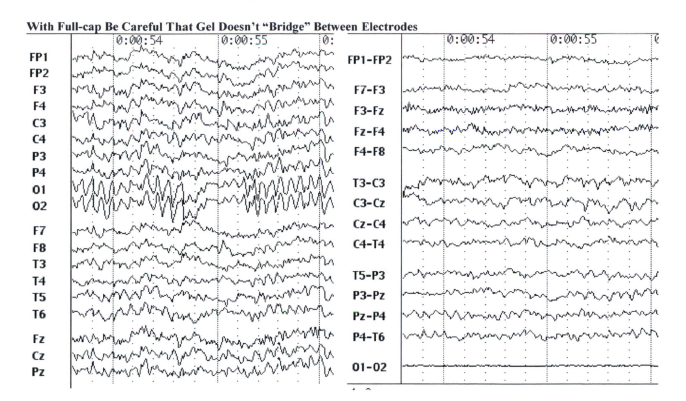

Referential montage (linked ears)
Note how O1 and O2 are exactly alike. This may be due to what is termed a "bridge". In the above example it is a **salt bridge due to** excessive electrode gel which bridged between the two electrodes.

Gunkelman notes that a cap requires 3.5 to 4.0 cc's of gel but many people use over 5. Movement of the cap (or even having it pressed against a recliner without a neck support to elevate the cap) can smear gel too.

Sequential Montage (old term "bipolar")
Common mode rejection makes it appear as if there is no signal at O1-O2 because the signal was identical at the two sites. Gunkelman points out that this is a good example of how a different **montage** would instantly clarify the problem. Note the flat line O1-O2. The 'salt' bridge is caused by the salts in the gel (stannous chloride). This causes a 'short'.

Thanks extended to Jay Gunkelman for this example.

b. Collecting Data
Introduction
It is helpful to collect data using a screen which has been made for the specific purpose of doing an assessment. This screen should have a means for artifacting the data once it is collected. Shading segments, for later inclusion or exclusion when calculating statistics, is the method used both in the BioGraph program and the SKIL program. In the A620 or the Lexicor programs, screens that show 2 seconds worth of data are either accepted or rejected. It is also helpful if this assessment display screen has some secondary means for clarifying the frequency spectrum and amplitudes of the waves for each frequency from 2 to above 60 Hz and for showing when EMG activity is particularly high. An example of this type of screen is shown under section c. below: "Assessment, Artifacting and Teaching Screen" with permission of Thought Technology.

Become Familiar with Your Client's Typical Artifacts

Your first task is to look at your client's raw EEG to differentiate different types of artifact before you begin data collection. Artifacts may have different appearances from one student/client to the next. Eye blinks, for example, though they all have a similar triangular form, will look different and affect slightly different frequency ranges depending on things like the individual's eye shape and how quickly they blink. You must, therefore, have the student/client do things which produce artifacts while you observe and make a mental note of what that person's artifacts look like. In this way you will recognize them if they occur later in the EEG sample you use for your assessment statistics.

Ask your client to blink, roll their eyes, look left then right, up then down. Have your client clench their jaws vigorously then very gently. Ask them to wiggle their ears (people who can do this like to show off their talent), furrow their brow, tense their neck and shoulder muscles, lean their head forward then left, right and backwards. Watch to see which movements produce artifacts and what the artifacts look like. You are going to have to recognize these artifacts when you review the assessment EEG. If you notice a regular, approximately once-per-second waveform it may be the electrical activity of the heart, referred to as a *cardioballistic* or *EKG artifact*. In some clients, moving your electrodes to a position where they are not over a blood vessel may be helpful. It is important to make absolutely sure that the impedance readings between electrode pairs was the same for each pair. In the worst-case scenario, if you cannot get rid of a consistent artifact when you are using a referential placement, you may have to try a sequential placement in order that the amplifier's *common mode rejection* lessens the artifact. The sequential placement will decrease the artifact at least to the extent that it is affecting the two sites used for this *bi-polar* placement equally, that is, the waveform produced by a non-cortical source is *in-phase* and at about the same amplitude and frequency at the two sites.

You should also watch the client and the EEG during each of the conditions as you record the EEG. You watch the client to observe eyes glazing over and any movements. You glance back and forth to the EEG and get a general impression of how it is changing with the client's changes during the actual recording. (At least, on those instruments where you can see the EEG while it is being recorded, you can look back and forth, if the raw EEG is not visible then note the time when an event occurs, such as 'eye blink at 38 seconds').

iii. Conditions for Data Collection

Conditions are usually eyes closed (ec), eyes open (eo), reading (r) and math (m). You do different conditions because clients may show patterns that are outside the range of usual values more, or even exclusively, in one condition and not in others. *Eyes-closed* is the condition used by neurologists and most databases have been collected only in this condition. Eyes closed may make it easier to differentiate high delta and low theta activity in a client who has frequent and high amplitude eye blink artifact. (Though you still get eye movements with eyes closed.) On the other hand, keeping one's eyes closed in business or school is frowned upon, so it is usually of major interest to us to see what is happening in the EEG when the client must just look to the front and remain quiet for a few minutes, or, when they silently read a passage or do mental math calculations. Do they tune out? Do they become tense, anxious and ruminate? We, therefore, recommend that you do the EEG assessment using more than one condition. It is essential in our work with ADD to do a minimum of at least one *active* condition - a reading or mental math task since that academic work will elicit the tuning out in most clients who have ADD.

If you are doing a 19-lead assessment, be aware of what high pass filter to use. The SKIL program and Sterman's database requires the use of a 2-Hz high pass filter. Most other databases use no high pass filter so you just let pass the frequencies selected by the equipment manufacturer. These might start at 0.5 Hz. (For feedback, as contrasted with assessment, the frequencies sampled usually start at 2 or 3 Hz. to avoid the very slow frequencies that make your EEG recording appear to sway.) It is more expensive to produce instruments that sample down to 0.1 or 0.5 Hz. so that is another factor that manufacturers keep in mind. As an aside, you must be able to sample those very slow frequencies when you work with *event related potentials*. For ERP's the same electrodes are used and some of the same EEG hardware, but the data collection procedures and the software for analysis are entirely different.

iv. Remember to Minimize Artifact During Recording

Some researchers (for example, Sterman) have reported that, with clients who have ADD, the math task is the best condition to clearly bring out the QEEG differences as compared to age norms. Lubar, who designed the assessment program for the Autogen A620 over a decade ago, has always advocated at least a 3-minute sample that includes 1 minute eyes open baseline and 2 minutes of silent reading. If it is possible, you should do all 4 tasks: eyes closed, eyes open, reading and mental math. Each of these conditions should be done for about 3 minutes. It is always a good procedure to ask your client to blink several times before recording in order to minimize eye blink artifact during data collection. During the *eyes open* condition, cover the screen and have the client look at a single dot on a piece of paper that is placed in front of the monitor screen. This will help to minimize eye movement artifact. During the reading task, place the material to be read on a stand so that the client does not have to turn their head or bend their neck to read.

The best data is usually recorded between 30 seconds and 3 minutes. The first 30 seconds can reflect EEG activity related to a change of state (such as from eyes open to eyes closed) and after 2 ½ to 3 minutes the client may become drowsy.

v. Math Tasks

Sterman has standard math tasks which can be downloaded from the SKIL website (www.skiltopo.com). Alternatively, use *serial seven's*. In this task the client keeps subtracting 7 (in his head, not aloud) from a large number, say 200 for children and 900 for adults. The sequence goes 200…193… 186…179, and so on. When the data collection is finished he must tell you the number he got to. This instruction ensures that they try to stay at the task. The advantage of this task is that the subject can do the task silently without moving or looking around. In the serial sevens task, we usually ask the client to look at the paper in front of them or at the dot in front of the monitor screen while doing the math task. This will minimize eye movement artifact. A third possible task requires that they write down the number that is the sum of the last two numbers spoken by the tester. This they can usually do with very little movement if they sit in a comfortable position and just look at their pen and the paper they are writing on. This minimizes eye movement artifact. The examiner starts by giving 2 numbers (say 2, 3). The client writes 5. The examiner gives another number, perhaps 7. The client must add this number to the last number the examiner said, which in this example was 3. The client writes down 10. The examiner might then say 9. The client would have to recall that 7 was the last number the examiner said, add to it 9 and write down 16. The examiner continues saying numbers, making it difficult enough to challenge the client. The advantage of this task, for the population we work with, is that it involves working memory, which tends to be a weak area in clients with ADD. Therefore, it is likely to show up the person's tendency to drift off and forget what they heard a moment ago.

vi. Time of Day Effects

When saving data note the type of task used and the time of day. Time of day will affect the EEG. Sleep latency studies indicate that there are certain times of day when people are naturally sleepier, independent of other factors such as whether they have just eaten a meal. When sleepy there is higher theta. This occurs usually around 11 a.m. and again, to an even greater extent, in the early afternoon around 1 to 2 p.m. This EEG finding confirms what some societies already respect through their customs, such as having a siesta after lunch or having school go from 8 a.m. to 12:30 or 1:00 p.m. When we are working with people at this time of day, we often use an EDR monitor and train them to control their alertness level. (Good posture helps.)

vii. Purpose of a Special Assessment and Artifacting Screen

We do the initial data collection on a specific screen for three purposes. First, it is done in order to remove artifacts which could distort the data and thus the interpretations you make from the data. Second, this screen is used to help you interpret the EEG data by assessing the amplitude of various frequency bands. Third, this display screen is used to teach the client / student (and parents in the case of children) about the EEG and the manner in which it corresponds mental states.

The example used below is from Procomp+/Biograph. It shows an assessment done at Cz. We also use the Autogenics (A620) assessment with all clients since we started our database with that instrument. In selected cases we will do a 19 channel assessment using LEXICOR equipment. In future we will add the NeuroNavigator to the assessment equipment. We are not endorsing a particular brand of instrument but we are recommending that you do some form of assessment with whatever instrument you have. It does not matter which instrument you use as long as you are consistent and can do pre-post evaluations.

c. Assessment, Artifacting & Teaching Screen

i. Introduction

It is important that one of your EEG instruments have a screen that shows about 2 or 3 seconds of the raw EEG. Since the EEG of an older person will be of a much lower amplitude than the EEG of a child, it is important that you are able to adjust the display range on this screen to make it easy to read. On the screen shown below, the spectrum and the boxes that display the amplitude, in microvolts, for a particular bandwidth refer to the first second of the raw EEG. You may notice that the display items that require mathematical calculations by your computer may show a slight lag behind your 'raw' EEG.

An assessment screen created using the ProComp+/Biograph instrument.

ii. The Screen

It is essential that you be able to view the raw EEG signal. It is helpful if the screen automatically adjusts the y-axis scale or if you can manually change the amplitude of the display because adults will usually have a lower amplitude EEG record as compared with children. (It is most likely that this is due, for the most part, to the tissue between the electrode and the brain and not the actual neuronal activity; that is, factors like a thicker skull in adults and more fluid as the brain shrinks a bit with age.) We also find that a display showing more than 4 seconds of EEG sometimes obscures the waveforms to a degree that makes it a little harder to recognize the morphology (shape) when we are only artifacting 1 or 2 channels. (On the other hand, when we artifact 19 leads we use 5 to 7 second segments.) It is helpful to be able to view a line-graph under the EEG which reflects muscle and ambient electrical activity. In North America we use 45-58 Hz to show the effect of muscle activity on the EEG. In Europe and Australia we use 53-62 Hz. Alternatively, we may use 45-70 Hz. In the latter case the combination of this EMG indicator, plus the EEG spectrum, helps us to differentiate activity that may be due to electrical interference (60 Hz in North America, 50 Hz in Europe and Australia) and/or muscle as compared to actual brain wave activity. It is very useful to simultaneously see the raw EEG and the spectrum. (The spectrum in the above example corresponds to the first second of the EEG above it.) It can be quite a challenge to distinguish true delta wave activity (which is not artifact due to movement or eye blink that imitates delta) on a one-channel assessment from low frequency theta when you just observe the raw EEG. The spectrum will show you more accurately where the highest amplitudes are. The pink bar indicates the highest amplitude when you use biograph software. Another helpful feature is that frequency ranges (theta, alpha, etc.) are colour coded. In addition, it is useful to be able to see the relationship between commonly used frequency bandwidths as you move through the EEG. We often (though not in this example) put a theta / beta ratio box as one of the boxes which you can see on the right hand side of this figure because this ratio is helpful in distinguishing the most common type of ADHD in children.

Note regarding equipment:

The Procomp+/Biograph is used for illustrative purposes as it is equipment that is currently in common use and is still available. There are other instruments that also allow for quantitative assessments that are not full-cap, 19-channel. The Autogen A620 assessment program developed by Lubar is excellent and is the one which we have used with nearly every client since starting our ADD Centre, to generate pre and post training statistics and profiles. The original DOS-based program has not been available for a couple of years but it may re-emerge with updated windows software. We have done more than 2,000 such assessments. The assessments are then repeated after 40 sessions of neurofeedback to assess progress in

training. Monastra, Lubar et al. have published norms from a multi-site study for mean theta/beta ratios for ADHD and control subjects using this instrument These norms are very helpful in working with clients who present with attentional problems.

It is also possible to select a portion of good EEG data and calculate your own theta/beta ratios (or any other ratios you wish) using the F1000 equipment from Focused Technology. The F1000 regrettably went out of production in 2002 though there is still support for equipment already sold. The F1000 has always been a favourite of ours because the electronics are so good. There are analog as well as digital filters for some screens. You also have the option of simultaneously monitoring temperature and EDR. We wish Frank and Mary Dietz a happy and healthy retirement from the equipment manufacturing side of the neurofeedback business, but look forward to their continuing contributions to the field.

Some other instruments are designed for doing feedback and cannot be easily adapted to do an assessment. On-the-other-hand software such as that used with the popular Brainmaster and with EEG Spectrum's Neurocybernetics system can be very useful for neurofeedback training. On some instruments that are designed primarily for training you may want to do an assessment on another instrument first to ensure that you are using appropriate parameters for your client. In addition, you may wish to have other equipment available to do biofeedback at the same time as you are doing neurofeedback with instruments that do not have the combination. The Roshi system works on different principles and does some entrainment as well as feedback. It has shown promise for some applications, particularly optimal performance, for example, Dan Chartier's research with golfers. Clinicians report high client satisfaction with the Roshi. The Peak Achievement Trainer (PAT) has also been marketed for use with athletes. It uses a sensor on a headband and the protocol calls for reducing the amplitude for a very wide frequency range from delta through beta. This set-up would seem to leave the EEG data prone to artifact so you would certainly want to ensure good connections (low impedance readings) and try to minimize eye movements. The goal of reducing the wide range of EEG activity would, in practice, reduce slower frequencies more since they have the higher amplitudes to begin with.

(Recall that the skull attenuates the higher frequencies more than the slower ones.) This might be helpful for improving attention. Since we have not used the Roshi or the PAT, we cannot comment further.

Important: The foregoing discussion is meant to show that there are a broad range of instruments available. Our discussion is not inclusive. We are only able to give examples in this book from equipment and software that we presently use. There are many other instruments and software systems. You may find it helpful to discuss the advantages of each instrument and software with manufacturers who exhibit at conferences such as those given by AAPB (Association of Applied Psychophysiology), BFE (Biofeedback Foundation of Europe), Future Health, and iSNR (International Society for Neuronal Regulation).

iii. Purposes of The Above Assessment Screen

This screen is used both when the client is first seen and at the beginning of each neurofeedback training session done with this equipment. Initially it is used to obtain an EEG profile. This profile helps in decision making concerning where electrodes should be placed and the frequency bands which should be enhanced or decreased. It is also used at the beginning of each training session to check that you have a good EEG signal and to remind the client of the purpose(s) of the NFB training session. In each instance the clinician is using the screen for three purposes: assessment, artifacting and teaching.

Assessment

To assure that sufficient data without artifact is collected during the initial assessment, the trainer/clinician can watch this screen while the client is carrying out each of the data collection conditions. The trainer can also observe what the artifact looks like on the EEG when the client blinks or moves. The trainer can also mark down, or place a marker (by hitting the space bar), for each change of condition (EO, EC, reading, math) so that statistics can be done separately for each condition. Alternatively, the clinician may pause or restart for each new condition. At the beginning of each training session the clinician will usually only do a brief reassessment using whichever task seems to give the best profile. (Use the same condition each time.) As noted previously, the best data is usually collected after the first 30", which

represents a change of state (for example from eyes open to eyes closed), and before three minutes has elapsed as a subject may start to get drowsy at that point. For daily session recordings, you may find it helpful to start the recording after the client has been doing the task for 30 seconds in order to avoid this problem with change of state. Then record for 30 seconds to a minute, artifact the resulting EEG with your client, print the statistics and discuss the objectives for the session.

Artifacting

While reviewing the data the clinician should mark artifacts that are to be removed when doing statistics. Mark data for artifacts and *exclude* these data when calculating statistics on the report screens. Of course, you should attempt to minimize artifacts in the first place, not just get rid of them later. You do this by asking the client to blink before recording begins (so they need not blink as much during the recording) and to sit comfortably and still while you are recording. Remind them to keep their muscles relaxed, with the mouth slightly open, and the tongue just suspended, not touching teeth or roof of mouth. (These instructions are important because the eye has its own polarity, think of the cornea as positive and the retina as negative. The tongue is also a dipole with the tip negative relative to the base.) If you are doing a recording with the eyes open, have the client look at a dot on a piece of paper covering the screen (if not reading). Most of the record, under these circumstances, should be relatively artifact free. There are circumstances when you would choose to mark data for 'inclusion' rather than 'exclusion'. Examples are when you have a very poor record and you just select the good bits or when you wish to have statistical information on particular kinds of activity, such as paroxysms. You must decide to either include or to exclude data before artifacting so that you get a consistent record when you do your statistics. On the assessment display screen shown above, for example, you would mark, and later exclude, the right half of the EEG (18.5 - 19.6 seconds) due to eye blink and eye movement artifact.

The 45-58 Hz EMG line below the EEG helps you distinguish muscle artifact from high beta activity. (Note: Be careful not to include either here or in the EMG inhibits on your feedback screens, 39 - 41 Hz activity. This bandwidth is sometimes referred to as the Sheer rhythm. It is named after David Sheer who reported in the 70's that the frequencies around 40 Hz were related to certain attentional processes.)

As suggested above, at the beginning of each training session it takes only a few seconds to artifact one or two minutes of data. This time can have a second function of reminding the client about the functional significance of different frequencies and what their training session will emphasize. Clients, especially children, often become very good at pattern recognition and may play an active role in artifacting.

As previously noted, in the example in the figure above showing an assessment screen, an artifact may be highlighted using the mouse. This is the method used in both the ProComp+/Biograph and the SKIL programs. An alternative method is to simply reject any 2-second segment of the EEG that contains an artifact. This method is used in the A620 assessment program (Stoelting Autogenics) and in the Lexicor program.

Teaching

One of the most important objectives of an assessment screen is to help your clients understand the EEG pattern and its possible meaning in terms of mental state changes. It is a useful tool when one explains to parents or to the client how frequency bands correspond to mental states. Having a spectral array and boxes showing the microvolt reading for particular frequency ranges on the assessment screen can help you do this. For example, the clinician might discuss the following in the assessment screen shown above
.

(1.) The dominant slow wave frequency is at 7 Hz. This client may be internally focused and not fully aware of the external environment at this point in time. If we had observed and marked the times when this client appeared to drift off (eyes may seem to 'glaze' over), then this pattern might correlate with these observations. To help the client become aware of this 'change of state' the trainer may pause the EEG when this waveform is observed and then ask the client what their brain was doing a moment ago, just before the screen was paused.

(2.) The amplitude of the EEG is lower in the SMR range 12 - 15 Hz than in the beta range 16-20 Hz. If the low SMR activity is present throughout much of the recording, then it may correspond to this child's hyperactivity and impulsivity. Both SMR and beta are much lower than theta 4-8 Hz activity which is typical of those with ADD. (See the microvolt readings to the right of the spectral array.) We have also repeatedly observed extremely low SMR readings in clients who have Parkinson's Disease. They have difficulty controlling unwanted movements, such as tremor.

(3.) The beta amplitudes between 23 and 36 Hz are usually lower than in the beta range between 15 and 19 Hz which is a normal pattern. When they are higher, check with the client what kind of thoughts were going through their mind during the recording. You may find that this activity corresponds to a combination of anxiety, tension and worrisome ruminations.

You can show your client a section with slow waves and ask them to estimate the number of such waves that could fit into one second. Let them actually count the waves, if they want to do so. Then show a second segment of EEG where they are really tuned in and, perhaps, problem solving. It will contain a large proportion of low voltage, desynchronized fast waves. Have the student estimate how many waves of this sort would fit into one second of time. Usually they estimate between 16 and 20. Some students become so good at pattern recognition that they actually prefer to watch the EEG in feedback sessions rather than a game screen. Motivation for biofeedback training increases profoundly when students understand what it is they are trying to do in terms of learning the task of *self-regulation* of brain wave activity. It also helps recruit their co-operation in keeping EMG artifact to a minimum when they understand that it affects the quality of the feedback they are receiving.

d. Common Artifacts
i. Introduction

Artifacting, as previously discussed, is the process in which you review the EEG recorded from each condition (eyes closed, eyes open, etc.) and look for activity that is likely not of cortical origin. In other words, it is not true EEG that reflects neuronal activity. You usually look at from 2 to 4 seconds at a time. As mentioned above, your assessment program should have a simple means for marking or rejecting data which contains an artifact. Artifacting should be rigorous. If it is not well done, you may have statistics which distort the real picture; for example, thinking you have beta activity when it is really the result of muscle artifact or interpreting eye blinks as if they were delta or theta activity. Distortion may lead to incorrect conclusions about the EEG patterns and might then lead to incorrectly deciding on what frequencies to inhibit or encourage during training. Your training result would then quite possibly be due to that the person learning to inhibit eye blinks when you thought you were actually reducing delta activity.

You wish to exclude from the statistical analysis segments which are contaminated by eye movements, blinking, muscle contractions or cardiovascular activity. Electrode movement and eye movement or blinks usually produce artifact in the low frequency range (1-3 Hz, delta). However, occasionally it may affect the amplitude of waves in the theta range up to 7 Hz. Muscle artifact usually produces changes (increased amplitudes) in the higher frequency range (above 11 Hz, SMR and beta) although it can influence even the alpha range if it is high enough in voltage, as in teeth clenching.

ii. What are Artifacts

An artifact in EEG parlance refers to a segment of unwanted data. When doing an EEG assessment, 'unwanted' refers to data which is not generated by neurons in the brain. Hammond and Gunkelman (2002) state, "An artifact refers to a modification of the EEG tracing that is due to an extracerebral source." This is a good definition as it includes both interfering biosignals produced by the person and also external sources of electrical interference. These segments of unwanted data can be caused by a number of different mechanisms. The most common are:

- movements of the electrodes on the scalp
- movement of wires
- eye movement
- tongue movement
- EKG (heart) activity
- facial, scalp or neck and shoulder muscle tension
- electrical activity near the equipment (lamp, extension cord)
- waves from a strong radio transmitter or other electrical source.

iii. Why Is Artifacting Important

A gross artifact such as that caused by a sudden electrical surge or a movement of the client can make it impossible to read anything in the EEG. More subtle artifacts may be more damaging to our neurofeedback work precisely because they are subtle and may not be detected. Undetected movement artifacts or eye blinks may make it appear that slow wave activity is higher than it really is. Undetected muscle tension artifact may make it appear that there is higher beta or SMR activity than is really taking place. Cardiac artifact is much more difficult to analyze as it affects a number of different frequency bands. Fortunately, it is fairly easy to see in the raw EEG and you can often move the electrodes and minimize or get rid of it. In addition, it is usually constant and, therefore, *changes* in bandwidth amplitudes are more consistent than with other, more transient artifacts. This will be discussed later in more detail.

iv. General Rules for Detecting Most Artifacts

The first rule is simple: a relatively high amplitude potential that occurs only in one channel (at one site) is probably an artifact. The second rule is simple too: repetitive waveforms that appear simultaneously in unrelated head regions are usually artifact. The reason for these two common sense guidelines is that true neuronal activity usually will have a predictable physiological distribution with a maximum potential where the activity originates. Then, there will be a gradual decrease, with increasing distance, at other sites. Abrupt neurological changes do not just 'jump' to a distant site on the head.

v. Artifacts
(1.) Artifact - Electrical Sources
This is discussed extensively under Instrumentation.

(2.) Artifact - Muscle (Reflecting EMG)
EMG stands for electromyography. We use it as a short form when we are talking about the activity in the EEG recording which is not neuronal, but is a reflection of the electrical activity from skeletal muscles. True EMG activity is usually above 60 Hz and, thus, at a much higher frequency than we are measuring with the EEG. However, EMG activity is also usually of much higher voltage. It also may have

harmonics at lower frequencies. It may even be of a high enough amplitude to *overwhelm* the instrument's low pass filter. You can have the student demonstrate this overwhelming of the low pass filter by asking them to clench their teeth. They will observe with a very light clenching of their jaw that only the higher frequencies on the spectrum increase. Slightly more tension will overwhelm all frequency bands. In explaining this to a client a useful analogy is to say it is like a loud noise drowning out a whisper. The EEG signal is like a whisper.

When doing EEG biofeedback have your client understand that they want to learn control of their brain, therefore they must keep muscle tension to a minimum so that they receive quality feedback that truly reflects brain activity. With young children you demonstrate how EMG activity will shut off the point counter. They don't want to do that! Another fact you can

share that will encourage the client to keep the frequencies affected by EMG as low as possible is to explain that work with athletes shows that reaction times are faster if muscles are relaxed rather than tense. You can mimic an elderly person holding a steering wheel with shoulders all hunched up and tense. Contrast this with a top gun pilot who is physically relaxed, yet mentally alert while flying. They want to emulate the pilot, which corresponds to low EMG readings.

During feedback it is very helpful to have a muscle inhibit (or a 45-58 Hz %-over-threshold) on every feedback screen. Otherwise you will not know if an increase in the student's fast wave reward frequency, (for example, SMR 12-15 Hz or beta 16 - 20 Hz), is due to muscle tension or actual brain activity in the 12-15 Hz or 16 to 20 Hz range.

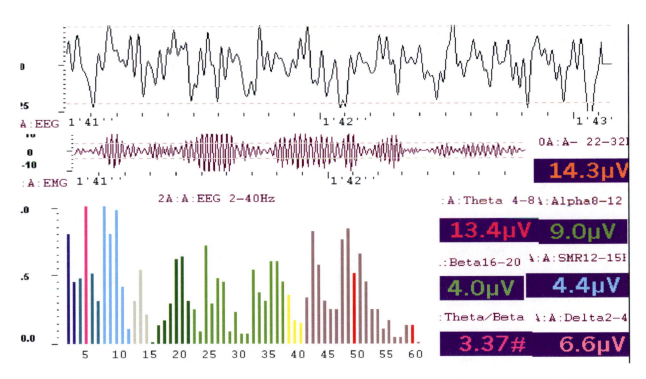

The above figure shows muscle artifact. Compare this with the figure shown in the section above on one-channel EEG assessment. It is the same child in the same session. (A slightly different assessment screen with a box for theta / beta ratio was used for this recording.) You can see that the amplitudes of most bandwidths are grossly increased. In particular, note the differences in the EEG wave (top), and the "EMG" (44-58 Hz) band or 52-60 Hz band in Europe and Asia (center line graph). For NFB

sessions these frequencies are used as an "EMG" inhibit. (On the other hand, you may decide to use an inhibit on 22 – 32 Hz activity during feedback sessions. Using this range as an inhibit discourages EMG as well as anxiety and ruminative activity.) Note the very large increase on the right side of the spectrum (gray, above 43 Hz). This is the area of the spectrum that first shows an increase in amplitude when a child tenses his jaw or his neck muscles.

The raw EEG in this example has used an FIR, Hamming, 2-40 Hz bandpass filter.

EMG activity is fairly easy to distinguish with 19 channels. Unlike the EEG seen in the singe channel recording, it is usually seen affecting only one or two channels. The channels affected are usually seen in the periphery at T3, T4 (jaw tension) and sometimes at O1, O2, (neck tension) or at Fp1, Fp2. (forehead tension)

The figure opposite shows how muscle artifact may appear in one temporal region (T4). More often it is seen bilaterally at T3 and T4.

Helping the client to be aware of tensing their jaw or neck is a first step. Then the trainer will assist the client to find ways to relax these muscle groups. This may involve the use of biofeedback which will be discussed later.

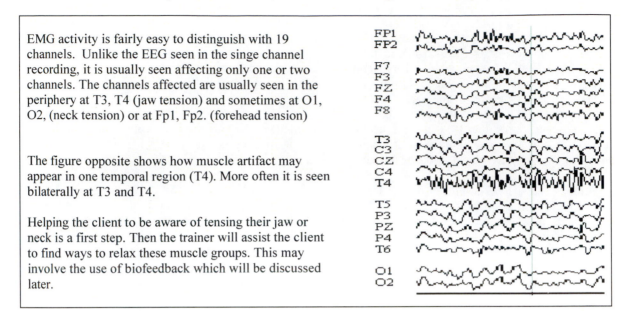

As previously mentioned, when doing NFB to inhibit the influence of muscle you may choose to inhibit 45-58 Hz (in Europe, 44 – 48 Hz or 52 – 60 Hz) frequencies which mainly reflect muscle tension. In addition, you may wish to be warned if there is a sudden increase in electrical interference. You would then use a 45-70 Hz inhibit. This will catch the 60 Hz electrical activity. These inhibits avoid affecting good Sheer rhythm activity in the 38-41 Hz range. Research suggests that Sheer rhythm is associated with attention. (Some clinicians have recommended reinforcing 38-41 Hz with neurofeedback. Sheer's research suggested that this may be effective when working with those who have learning disabilities. However, it is a difficult range to reinforce because amplitudes tend to be very low and muscle artifact may interfere a great deal.)

It is important to be able to distinguish high amplitude beta activity which is due to muscle tension from that which is due to worry and ruminations. A client who is tense and anxious may demonstrate excessive activity somewhere in the 21-35 Hz. range. We find that the anxiety component appears to correspond to a rise in the 19 – 23 Hz range, whereas the constant worrying and ruminating seems to more often correspond to a peak somewhere between 25 and 35 Hz. The peak differs between clients but is consistent for a particular client. When this EEG picture is seen and found to correspond to the client's complaints, then you may choose to train down one or more frequency bands in the 20-35 Hz range. In addition you would place a severe inhibit on activity that corresponds to muscle activity in the 45-58 Hz range. In this manner you allow your client to know which kind of activity is causing an increase in high beta and assure that muscle tension does not influence the EEG feedback.

Despite the forgoing discussion, it is true that many EEG biofeedback instruments presently on the market do not register activity above 32 Hz. These instruments tend to treat all increases in the 24–32 Hz range as muscle artifact. In working with children with ADD this may, for the most part, be true. With anxious and/or worried adult clients it is frequently not true.

On those instruments that do not allow you to differentiate between muscle activity and high beta neuronal activity, you just inhibit 24-30 Hz and thus inhibit muscle influences while, at the same time, discouraging tense ruminative thinking. As previously noted, we feel quite strongly that it is important that you know which factor is responsible for the activity in this range. Then you can make an *informed* decision on how to design your feedback screen and how to advise your client. (If you only know that 24-30 Hz keeps rising and you keep telling a client to relax their jaw and neck, when these muscles are perfectly relaxed, you are not being very helpful and you may, in fact, increase their already elevated anxiety.)

(3.) Artifact - Electrode Movement

V (voltage) = I (current) x R (resistance) according to Ohm's Law. As noted above, since the EEG is alternating current, it is actually impedance, not resistance, that concerns us. However, the principle is the same. Impedance is, in simple terms, resistance to the flow of AC current. So here we will keep it basic and use just Ohm's basic equation. Because the current (I) is so small, any change in resistance (R) or impedance (z) will have a major effect on voltage (V). Even a very small movement of an electrode will massively alter 'R' (or z) and, thus, 'V'. Further it may do so in the frequency range that we are measuring, such as 3 - 6 Hz. This will mean that you might interpret a rise in theta as the client tuning out when, in fact, it is just due to a small movement of the electrode on the skin or a poor connection. This can be very frustrating for your client who cannot relate their genuine attempts to remain highly focused to a decrease in theta!

Electrode movement will usually be different at each electrode site and, therefore, not removed by the amplifier's *common mode rejection* feature. It usually results in a high amplitude slow wave in the delta or low theta range.

There are a few simple procedures that we routinely employ to minimize movement artifacts. We always have the client wear a headband. We purchased hundreds of these at a discount from the local sporting goods store. They can be thrown in a bag after use and washed. Regular clients have their own headband tucked into their training file. It makes the file bulky but follows the principle that nothing that touches one client's head touches another client's head without being cleaned first. You put the head band on and tuck the electrode wires under it. The kids can have flashy colours or their favourite sports company's logo and we tell them they look like a tennis star. Headbands have the added advantage of making it easier to put the electrodes on a child's head because children often do not sit perfectly still. Be consistent and no one will object.

Artifacts from EMG and Electrode Sway

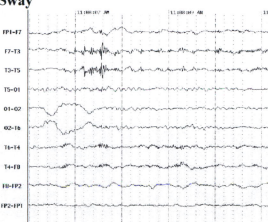

EMG artifact in the temporal regions and Electrode Sway Movement Artifact in the right occipital region With thanks to Jay Gunkelman

(4.) Artifact - Eye Blink

The cornea is 100 mV electropositive with respect to the retina (Fisch 1999, p 108). There is over a 100 millivolts difference between the aqueous and vitreous humor (Hammond 2001). When the client blinks, the eyeball rolls upward (*Bell's phenomenon*). When the eyelid touches the cornea, it is like touching the positive end of a little battery. This increases the positivity in Fp1 and Fp2, whereas F3 and F4 may become relatively more negative (Dyro, 1989). The result is a sudden large amplitude slow wave that is seen on the EEG. Movements of the eye will also result in currents which produce artifact on the EEG, particularly in the frontal leads. It is always higher in amplitude anteriorly and decreases as you view sites that are more posterior. Sections of the EEG with this type of artifact must be rejected during the assessment or you will have a false impression of high slow wave activity when looking at the statistics. The eye blinks and eye movements mimic delta (and sometimes theta) activity. As previously noted, during feedback you may also decide to reject this type of artifact by placing threshold lines above and below the EEG linegraph with an *inhibit-over-threshold* command. By doing this you assure that there will be no auditory or visual feedback during an eye blink. For example, the EEG Spectrum and Biograph programs both allow this. The amplitude of these artifacts is usually much higher than the regular EEG waves so they extend beyond the threshold lines. Below is an example of an eye blink artifact in a single channel EEG with the active electrode at Cz referenced to the left ear. In this example white threshold lines are seen above and below the EEG. The large amplitude eye blink artifact has gone outside these threshold lines.

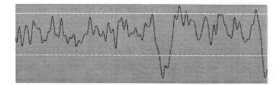

Having threshold lines placed like this is a doubly effective method as the trainer can see both artifact and the EEG. Many clinicians feel you must watch the raw EEG during feedback sessions both to assure that the EEG remains of good quality and to observe the EEG for artifacts.

Note, however, that if your instrument's program still calculates an average amplitude for frequency bins during the time that that wave is being produced, then the threshold lines would only cut out the excess amplitude of that wave but the wave itself would remain in the calculations. The result would be that your data would be skewed to give a falsely high average power for that frequency bin. Some programs deal with this difficulty by stopping all feedback instruments, sound, animations, percent-over-threshold calculations and points, for the 'time' period that any waveform goes outside of threshold boundaries (With thanks to Frederick Arndt, engineer, personal communication).

Eye movement Artifact in a 19-lead recording

Eye movement is one of the most common artifacts.

Two eye blink artifacts are demonstrated in this recording. Note how the primary effect is seen in the frontal electrodes.

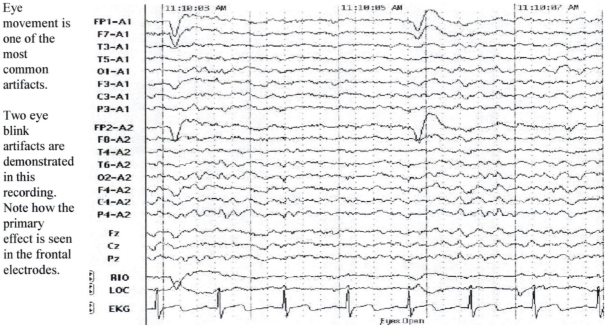

Eye Movement Artifact: With thanks to Jay Gunkelman

(5.) Artifact - Eye Movement
A vertical eye movement may give a downward deflection (positive) of the EEG because the positively charged cornea is moving towards Fp1. A downward movement of the eye would give the opposite deflection. This is most easily seen in a longitudinal sequential montage. It is usually seen frontally (Fp1-F3 and Fp2-F4). A movement to the left may show a positive deflection (downward) in F7 and the opposite deflection in F8. We usually just think of this as the whole EEG seems to move up in one case and down in the other so that, for example, the two EEG lines appear to come closer to each other. A spike preceding this slow wave may just represent EMG activity and should not be

confused with a spike and wave. The 19 channel referential montage shown below demonstrates lateral eye movement.

Lateral eye movement while reading.

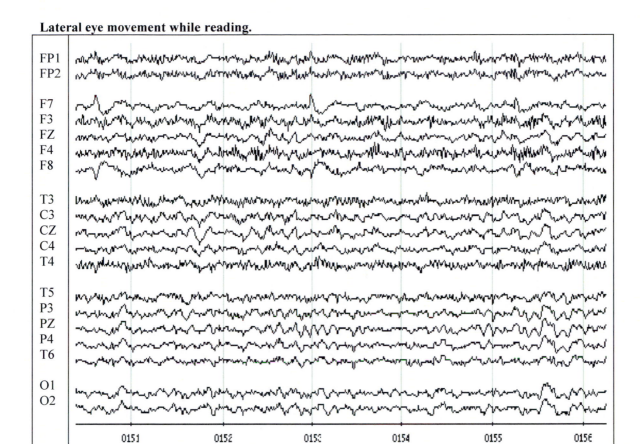

In the above recording, the subject was reading. Note the **lateral eye movement is** seen best in leads F7 and F8 preceding time: 0151 and at 0153.

On this record it is also possible to see a small **evoked potential** at 0155 and an artifact (**transient**), maximal in the occipital leads, just preceding 0156 at the end of this segment. There also appears to be **muscle artifact** at F3, F4, T3 and T4.

A *transient* is best thought of as "a change in kind" from the ongoing activity. Transients may have little effect on averaged bandwidth activity but variability is increased. (Hammond, 2001). You typically remove transients, treating them as artifacts, following the maxim, "When in doubt, leave it out".

Know the Effect of Artifacts on Frequency Bands that are Involved in NFB Training.
The diagram below is a topographic display taken from the SKIL program and thanks are extended to Barry Sterman for artifacting this EEG sample for this figure. This example shows the amplitude of delta wave activity before (blue lines) and after (red lines) artifacting the EEG for eye-blinks. Note how the removal of artifact activity does make a visible difference in the average amplitude of the delta wave activity in the prefrontal and frontal leads. No difference can be observed, in this example, in the central or parietal leads. Thus, with this client, eye-blink would have an effect when the active lead was placed frontally but probably not when a central placement was used. When tested in this way, there are a small number of clients where the eye-blink artifact activity affects the amplitude of frequencies as high as 5 or 6 Hz even at Cz. It is crucial that the neurofeedback practitioner who is setting up a training protocol

know the extent to which this kind of activity is affecting the recordings.

Effects of manual artifact correction are seen in differences between level of frontal and pre-frontal slow activiy.

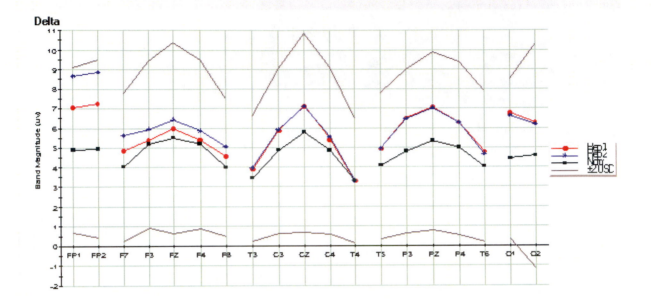

Movement and Muscle in review

Eye blinks, rolling eyes, and other eye movements can give **a false impression of high delta and theta.** Theta is also affected by heart beat (a consistent artifact) or any electrode movement over the skin. Muscle tension can give a **false impression of increased SMR or beta amplitudes**.

(6.) Artifact – Heart

A regular, high amplitude artifact at a rate of approximately once per second is usually not due to movement but, rather, to electrical activity related to the regular contractions of heart muscle. This electrical signal may be carried through arterial connections. It would make sense that this activity may be more pronounced if an electrode is placed over or close to an artery. However, Jay Gunkelman tells us that this "electrical artifact also is picked up as a 'field

effect' that has nothing to do with arterial closeness." He went on to note, "A *pulse artifact* (slow sway due to electrode movement with each heart beat) is from arterial or venous pulsation, unlike the cardioballistic sharp waves." He feels that, "the linking of the ears makes the cardioballistic artifact much less of a problem, since it has reversed polarities in each ear, and tends to cancel... though not in all individuals." We have used linked ear electrodes in the past when doing NFB with the F1000 equipment and found this helpful in eliminating such artifact.

We have seen this phenomenon in a client who was awaiting valve surgery. However, we most often have this problem with people who have very large, short necks. The EEG segment below is from such a client. The recording is from a single channel at Cz referenced to the left ear lobe.

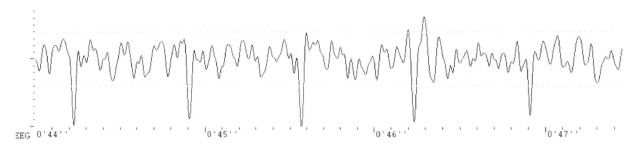

EEG 0'44''   0'45''   0'46''   0'47''

This artifact is usually seen as a regular wave approximately once per second. It does affect your bandwidth calculations. It is quite a frustrating wave to try to analyze. We have found it can differ in different people as to which frequencies it increases. It is a complex waveform and, as such, it always increases frequencies in more than one bandwidth. Quite often it will influence not only delta, but also alpha and beta (Hammond, 2001). Because it is in common to many electrodes, **it will artificially increase coherence or comodulation** (Hammond & Gunkelman, 2001). It is much more prominent in some individuals than in others and is more often seen in adults compared to children. Being a relative constant you may take some consolation in assuming that changes in band wave average amplitudes will not be overly affected during

feedback sessions. Since we are usually looking for changes this is helpful. However, prevention is the easiest solution. During an assessment the first step for prevention is to make sure that impedances are low and exactly the same between the ear electrodes. If doing a 19 channel assessment you may just have to analyze the EEG using a different montage (Laplacian or sequential). For NFB sessions one can often eliminate the problem by moving each of the electrodes in turn until it disappears. If this doesn't work you may find that a sequential (bipolar) montage will eliminate it by means of the amplifier's common mode rejection.

In the figure below the electrodes were moved from the above referential placement to a sequential (bipolar), Fz-Cz, placement. There is some decrease in the cardiac artifact amplitude.

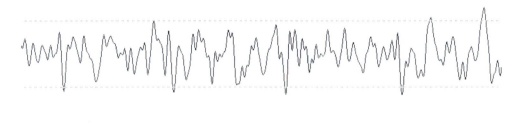

0'7''   0'8''   0'9''

The cardiac artifact is still definitely present but at a lower amplitude relative to the rest of the EEG. This is a good example for another reason: it demonstrates, in the second EEG, how difficult it can be to see the effect of the cardiac influence on the EEG when the waves are not large. It might have been difficult to pick out the cardiac artifact if one had been rapidly moving through just the sample from the sequential placement.

The more consistent the wave, the less may be its overall effect when averaging amplitudes in

different bandwidths. The heart rate effects may be a little more consistent if you train the client to relax and breathe diaphragmatically at 6 breaths per minute (see the section on RSA - respiratory sinus arrhythmia - later in this book). Because the changes that cardiac artifact will make in your recording are fairly consistent over time, you can still do successful feedback. Absolute values will be affected but *average changes* in fast and slow wave amplitudes will be reasonably correct and your client can still learn self-regulation.

(7.) Artifact – Tongue & Swallowing

The base and the tip of the tongue form a dipole with the tip being negative. Movement will mimic delta activity. It is fairly easy to see this artifact as the entire EEG line will move gently up or down in the frontal and temporal areas. This mimics frontal intermittent rhythmic delta activity (FIRDA) which neurologists may associate with a structural lesion of the brain (Fisch p 354). Clients with dystonia may demonstrate this kind of artifact and be unable to control muscle spasms.

(8.) Artifact - Other Eye Movements
Eye Lid Flutter:

Watch your client's eyes during the recording. Unfortunately, an anxious client may flutter their eyelids. This may mimic frontal delta or theta waves in the 2- 4 Hz range (Dyro,1989) or even "thalpha" activity in the 5-10 Hz range. Only careful observation of the client while also observing the EEG will distinguish this kind of artifact from true frontal slow wave activity. The figure below shows this activity at FP1 and FP2.

Eye Lid Flutter Artifact in FP1 and FP2 in an eyes open, linked ear reference recording.

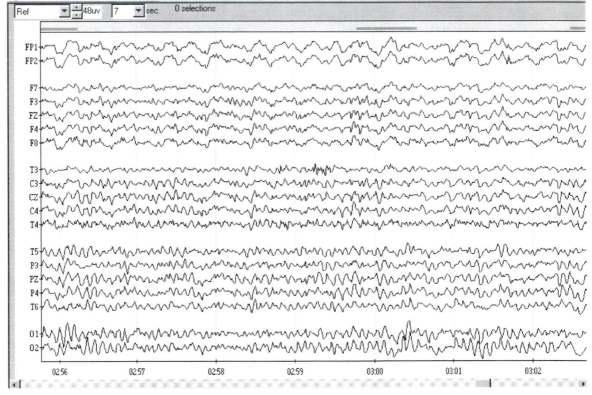

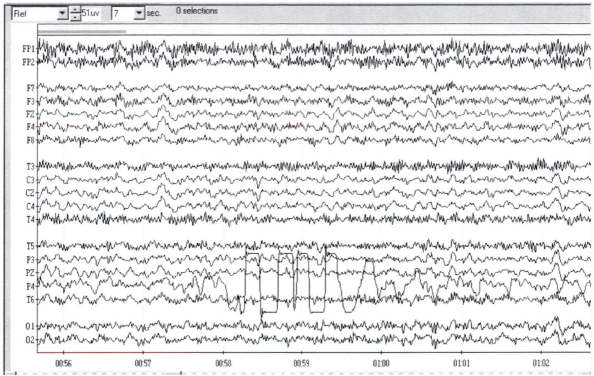

FP1
FP2

F7
F3
FZ
F4
F8

T3
C3
CZ
C4
T4

T5
P3
PZ
P4
T6

O1
O2

00:56   00:57   00:58   00:59   01:00   01:01   01:02

Electrode Pop Artifact at P4

Electrode Pop Artifact:

In the above figure the electrode at P4 lost its connection. The EEG was paused and more electrode gel was put into the site. The artifact disappeared.

Note also the muscle artifact. It is particularly evident at FP1, FP2, F3, T3 and T4. This 12 year old autistic child was grimacing and furrowing his brow.

Drowsiness:

This may produce spike-like activity. More often it just looks like excess theta or thalpha activity in the frontal regions. In the eyes closed condition, as a client becomes drowsy you may observe slow eye movements under their closed eyelids. Sometimes you will observe a fairly sudden drop in occipital alpha activity. You should watch for these signs when doing an eyes closed recording. It is a signal for you to pause the recording and alert the client. These slow movements can mimic theta activity on the EEG. If you just notice it when reading the EEG, then you should reject those epochs. Good examples of this kind of phenomenon are given in the book *The Art of Artifacting* by Hammond and Gunkelman.

e. Effects of Medications on the EEG

A detailed account of the effects of medication is beyond the scope of this text. We will just give a general overview. For a more complete understanding the reader should consult Bauer (1999) the chapter by Bauer and Bauer in Niedermyer & Da Sylva's book, *Electroencephalography* (1999).

i. Benzodiazepines, Barbiturates and Tranquilizers

These medications can significantly increase beta activity – particularly beta over 20 Hz. There may also be a slight decrease in alpha. They also increase sleep spindles (Fisch p. 417). **Neuroleptics,** however, are found to generally increase alpha power and reduce beta power (Hughes & John, 1999)

ii. Marijuana

This drug will increase alpha and you can easily see this the next day. If you know that your patient 'smokes', then ask them to refrain for a few days before the recording. Some of our teenagers actually have requested that we put their appointments mid week in order to minimize this effect. Most, however, have been shocked that there could be such a marked effect on their brain and it changes their recreational use of marijuana. This, coupled with Dan Amen's pictures of SPECT scans of the brains of chronic marijuana users, has been quite effective in encouraging teens to re-evaluate their behaviour. Most quit the habit early in training. (We also had a parent phone confidentially after he sat through his daughter's assessment to reveal that he had been smoking marijuana regularly for 14 years. After learning about the effects on the brain he went through the Employee Assistance Plan at his company and did a six month treatment programme. It was an unexpected example of the power of educating clients about brain functions during the initial assessment.)

iii. Antidepressants
Some Antidepressants may decrease alpha activity. **Tricyclic antidepressants** may produce generalized asynchronous slow waves and spike and wave discharges. Although they decrease alpha and also perhaps low beta, they may increase high beta. They also increase sleep spindles. Selective serotonin reuptake inhibitors **(SSRI's)** increase beta activity and may decrease alpha.

iv. Lithium
Lithium use can result in generalized asynchronous slowing and some slowing of alpha. It may increase theta.

v. Phenothiazines, Haloperidol and Rauwolfia derivatives
These drugs may slow alpha and produce asynchronous slow waves even at non-toxic doses. There may also be increased synchrony.

vi. Alcohol
Alcohol can increase beta (usually above 20 Hz) and decrease "thalpha" and alpha.

vii. Stimulants
These drugs can produce some increase in beta and, possibly, a decrease in theta. The theta decrease may, in part, be secondary due to increasing alertness. However, we usually see minimal, if any, effect in the brainwave patterns of children with ADHD who are training using NFB. Note: Stimulant drugs have major effects on brain neurotransmitter activity. Cocaine and

Ritalin, for example, are taken up by the basal ganglia (Amen, 1998 p 86) and enhance dopamine availability giving a high feeling. Ritalin prescribed in the usual therapeutic doses is slow to produce effects and thus is not considered to be addictive. The cocaine 'reward' effect may be due to its stimulation of the ventral tegmental area (Bozarth, 1987).

viii. Caffeine & Nicotine
These substances will suppress alpha and theta. Withdrawal may result in an increase in alpha and theta frontally. One reason that some people give for being reluctant to quit smoking is that they do not wish to lose the mental sharpness that smoking a cigarette provides. Morning coffee is a way to wake up your brain.

ix. LSD & Cocaine
These drugs both increase fast activity. LSD, however, will decrease alpha whereas Cocaine tends to increase it. **Phencyclidine (PCP)** increases slow activity.

x. Heroin and Morphine
These drugs will increase slow alpha initially but this is followed by a decrease in alpha and an increase in theta and delta.

f. Other Rare Events
(1.) Toxic Materials:
This subject is beyond the scope of this book. Poisons such as lead, aluminum, mercury, various insecticides and chlorinated hydrocarbons will all cause major clinical and EEG changes.

(2.) Withdrawal from medications may have an effect on the EEG. This is especially true if the withdrawal is sudden and after a long period of time on that medication. Generalized epileptiform activity may be seen.

(3.) Encephalopathies
These are beyond the scope of this text. You always ask your client about medical illness. The EEG may be quite confusing to you, showing bisynchronous and asynchronous slow waves and generalized epileptiform discharges. If you do an EEG on a client with any chronic illness, we would strongly advise that you get a second opinion from an expert in reading EEGs. (We use Q-Metrx, Burbank California.)

g. Artifact - Other

(1.) Hyperventilation may cause an increase in frontal theta and delta activity.

(2.) Sweating produces large, slow, up and down movements of the EEG line, like low rollers on the ocean surface. This slow undulation of the EEG may in part be due to a loosening of an electrode's connection to the surface of the scalp. This artifact is most often seen frontally (not maximal at F7, F8 like eye roll) and it does not reverse phase like horizontal eye movements do. It is usually seen in more than one channel. You may also be recording electro dermal responses (EDR) when doing feedback. These sympathetic nervous system cholinergic responses are also seen in the EEG. Usually they give an isolated slow wave pattern, 1 or 2 Hz, lasting only 1 or 2 seconds. They are usually frontal and central. They are most often seen in response to a sudden unexpected stimulus such as a loud noise or a visual stimulus. The distance from the brain to the finger tips is relatively long and the EDR reaction seen in the hand or fingers will, therefore, occur slightly after it is seen in the EEG.

(3.) 'Bridging' between electrodes occurs if you use too much electrode paste or if the client is sweating or has a wet head. It is an electrical short circuit between two electrodes. An example of this is given above under 'Site Preparation'. (There can be rare instances when the bridging is due to a problem with the cap or hardware. We once found that, despite very careful preparation, two adjacent electrode sites kept giving exactly the same EEG recording. The new instrument had a fault and had to be returned to the manufacturer.)

(4.) Electrode Pop, as noted above, refers to an electrode suddenly losing its connection with the skin surface. It is usually seen as a very large abrupt deflection in one or more channels. A more subtle 'popping' of an electrode may be seen as an irregular series of spikes in a single channel (Dyro 1989, p14). If you observe unusual activity of this nature, check your electrode connections and check your impedances. It might also be that you have a faulty wire.

(5.) Evoked Potentials may also be called a 'transient'. These are seen as a single abrupt change in the recording which is usually observed in several channels. As a general rule you will only reject that epoch if it is 50% greater than the background activity. These changes increase the variability and reduce the reliability of the recording but have little effect on averaged data (Hammond, 2001). A visual evoked potential occurs between 80-150 ms after the flash and is positive.

(5.) Parkinson's patients may produce a slow rhythmic theta in the occipital regions due to their head tremor (Westmoreland et al, 1973). It is abrupt, occurs at a single frequency, and presents as a change isolated from the rest of the background activity. We have observed low SMR activity and increased alpha in those with PD.

h. Preventing Artifacts

Before the client comes for their assessment they should be asked to shampoo their hair twice or even three times. They should not use any hair conditioner or hair spray. If it is raining, they must keep their hair dry. You should also request that they go to bed early and get 9 hours sleep if they can. They should refrain from drinking beverages containing caffeine on the day of their assessment. When recording, make sure that no electrical appliances such as table lamps or portable telephones are turned on. The impedances must be below 5 Kohms and within 1 Kohm of each other. It is particularly important that impedances for the two ears compared to the ground be the same for linked ear references (Hammond, D. 2001). It is also very important that homologous (interhemispheric) electrodes be balanced as perfectly as possible because, as you become more sophisticated in your work, you are likely going to be doing types of neurofeedback training that require that you accurately discern differences between homologous sites on the left and right side of the head (Hammond, 2001); Weidmann, (1999); Davidson, 1998); Heller, 1997); Rosenfeld, 1997). Differences in impedances between electrodes can make it falsely appear as if there are differences between cerebral activity in the two hemispheres.

When doing a 19 channel assessment, have the client sit in a comfortable chair. A small towel rolled up behind the neck may assist some clients to relax their neck muscles. This will also assure that the back of the cap is not touching the chair. Infrequently, it may be necessary to gently place a finger over closed eyelids to discourage eye movement. It is helpful for most clients if you present as calm, quiet, and reassuring. Ask the client to relax their shoulders, jaw, neck and tongue. Some clients tend to hold tension in their jaw muscles. Suggesting that they allow their teeth and lips to rest slightly apart, with their tongue floating, may help them relax their jaw musculature.

Clients appreciate knowing as much as possible about the procedure you are doing. They also appreciate the care you are taking to assure an accurate recording of their brain waves. Tell them you need to get familiar with how artifacts look in their EEG. With the equipment running and the EEG visible on the screen ask them, both with eyes open and eyes closed, to move their eyes to the left, right, up and down. With eyes open ask them to blink, move their tongue up, down and sideways and push it against their palate, teeth and cheeks. Now ask the client to say 'lift' and tense their jaw and wrinkle their brow. A short form for entering your observations when the client does each of these actions can be copied from *The Art of Artifacting* (Hammond & Gunkelman, 2001). This book will also give you practice in identifying artifacts. Make sure your client is not chewing gum and with some clients you may need to ask them to remove their dentures or dental appliances. We ask clients who wear contact lenses to also bring their glasses since they may blink more while wearing lenses. Pause the recording after each artifact is produced and discuss it with the client.

Now that you and your client have observed various possible artifacts, you can record and play back a short segment of EEG. Look at this segment of EEG to see if there are any major artifacts which you should try to reduce with the client. With many clients you will find EMG activity in one or other temporal leads. With these clients you will have to find some way to help them relax their jaw so that the EMG activity decreases. Sometimes you will observe occipital EMG due to neck tension. Do the best you can but don't be discouraged, there will always be the occasional person who is just not able to decrease muscle tension. Even with this careful preparation you may have to pause the

recording if you begin to see artifact reappearing. A few clients will begin to fall asleep when you are recording the EEG. As mentioned previously in this section on artifacts, you must watch for this. If it happens, you can have the patient wiggle their fingers, arms and legs from time to time in order to maintain their alertness.

As previously noted, to avoid 'change in state' data affecting your overall statistics you should have your client be in the required state (eyes closed (ec) or eyes open (eo) or activity (reading or math) for at least 30 seconds before you begin recording.

Last, and very rarely encountered, if you see spike and wave activity frontally, ask your client about fillings and possible jaw or facial surgery. Different metals in the oral cavity may cause this kind of artifact.

Always ask your client about medical conditions and medications and record this in your notes. Send EEGs from these clients to a professional electroencephalographer and neurologist to be interpreted.

i. False Impression of Frontal Slow Wave Activity

The following illustration is not an example of an artifact. Rather, it is an example of how the apparent EEG waveforms can be misinterpreted. This example is given, first, as a caution to warn you to make sure that what you see is really what you've got and, second, to demonstrate the value of looking at the raw EEG and being able to remontage it. In the case shown below this was necessary in order to clarify the source of the apparent frontal slow wave (alpha). In this case the ears, which are usually electrically inactive, were contaminated by the alpha activity in the temporal regions. We are always measuring the potential difference between two electrodes. We usually are safe in making the assumption that the linked ear reference electrodes have very little electrical activity compared to the scalp electrode. The example below is a relatively infrequent occurrence where the high amplitude electrical activity in the alpha range was located in the ear electrode as compared to the usual state of affairs where the scalp electrode has the higher electrical activity.

The figure below shows the same data using two different montages.

Sample of EEG with eyes closed using a referential linked ears montage. Note the suggestion of frontal dominant slow wave activity.	This is the same sample of eyes closed EEG but viewed with a transverse sequential montage. Note that the frontal dominant activity is eliminated. This demonstrates that the origin of this 'apparent' frontal slow wave activity is really slow wave activity near the ear reference electrodes. This is termed, "reference corruption". It could be quite misleading both in terms of diagnosis and with respect to prescribed intervention.

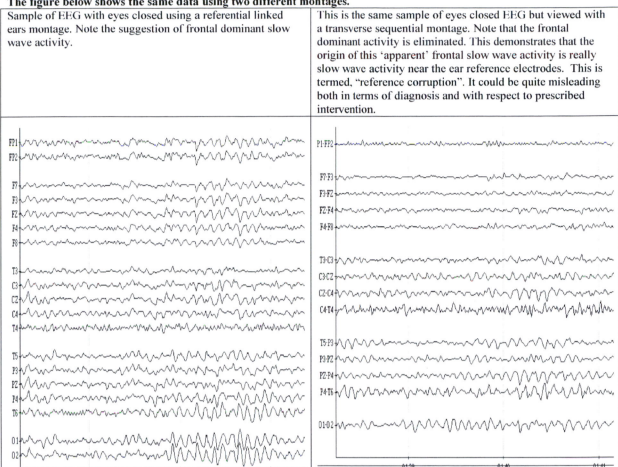

ii. Looking at the EEG Recording

Some programs, such as SKIL, will automatically reject the first 30 seconds of recording. This helps avoid what is called a 'state' change. The clinician should then remove all other visible artifacts before accepting the remainder of the record for analysis. This must be done carefully and severely. With possible artifacts remember the two important adages: "Garbage in means garbage out" and "When in doubt, throw it out".

Some assessment programs have what is termed 'automatic artifacting'. This is mainly helpful in removing frontal eye blink artifact. It is never a substitute for careful artifacting on the part of the practitioner. Automatic artifacting will sometimes eliminate good EEG data. It will also miss artifacts that do not reach a required amplitude. In addition, it may not pick up artifacts that occur in outside of the frontal and central areas.

EMG activity that is consistent throughout the record, and therefore cannot be eliminated, is usually readily identified in 1 Hz topographic maps and in power spectrum diagrams. Identification is relatively easy because this EMG activity will usually be morphologically different from the EEG waves, at a high frequency, and be isolated to specific locations, such as T3 and/or T4.

7. Pathological Activity

a. Absence Seizures

Absence seizures are reasonably easy to distinguish in the figure below. You are not trained to recognize abnormal EEG activity. Nevertheless, it is important that you be able to spot this high amplitude 3 per second spike and wave activity. It is important because these children may be misdiagnosed as being ADD (ADHD, Inattentive Type) and, subsequently, come to you for NFB treatment due to classroom behaviour that is inattentive. They should be seen as soon as possible by a neurologist. There is **no** published research evidence at this time that this type of seizure activity can be helped by using neurofeedback. All the research on using neurofeedback to reduce seizures has been done with patients whose seizures had a motor component. (We have worked with children who had absence seizures combined with ADD. They were under the care of a neurologist and taking medication. Some have demonstrated a decrease in seizure frequency as well as in the ADD symptoms but this may just have been coincidence. Some children with absence seizures develop grand mal or partial complex seizures as they grow older. It is unknown at this time whether SMR training might have a 'protective' influence with respect to this complication.

Absence seizure with spike and wave activity seen at Cz.

Uniform 3 per second spike and wave 'pairs' which are characteristic of an absence (petit mal) seizure. Note very high amplitude (160 µv) of these waves.	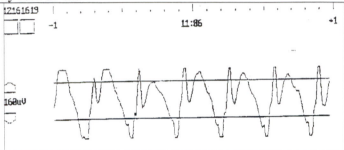

b. Closed Head Injury

Severe closed head injury may show rhythmic delta activity. These clients should always be assessed and treated medically first. Hughes notes that, "There is a broad consensus that increased focal or diffuse theta , decreased alpha, decreased coherence, and increased asymmetry are common EEG indicators of the post concussion syndrome" (Hughes & John, 1999, p.198). If you are going to do NFB you should consider doing a full-cap assessment first. It is likely that the EEG assessment would demonstrate decreased communication between some areas in the brain. This may be helped using coherence or comodulation training.

c. Hypoglycemia

Hypoglycemia may be accompanied by an increase in theta and delta wave activity. This should normalize when blood sugar levels are restored to normal.

d. Grand Mal and Partial Complex Seizures

Grand mal and partial complex seizures both produce bursts of sharp wave activity. These patients must always be first assessed and treated medically. It would be very unusual for you to be the first person to notice this activity. However, you may see clients with subclinical EEG seizure activity in the form of frequent paroxysms of waves in the figure below. You are not qualified to make this kind of diagnosis. If you see bursts of waves you do not understand then immediately have the client obtain a neurologist's opinion before you agree to do NFB work with them. The example below is of a sub-clinical seizure in an eyes closed recording. It shows spike and wave activity in the posterior left frontal lobe from a seizure focus near F3. This client's parents had never observed a seizure. He was brought to the center with a diagnosis of ADHD inattentive type due to difficulties with his attention span in school. He was sent for neurological evaluation and the EEG findings were confirmed.

Sub-clinical seizure activity: Sequential (bipolar) longitudinal montage of a sample of the resting EEG with eyes closed.

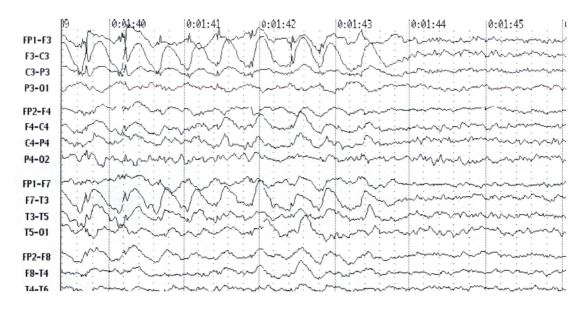

Sub-clinical seizure activity: Linked ear referential montage of a sample of the resting EEG with eyes closed.

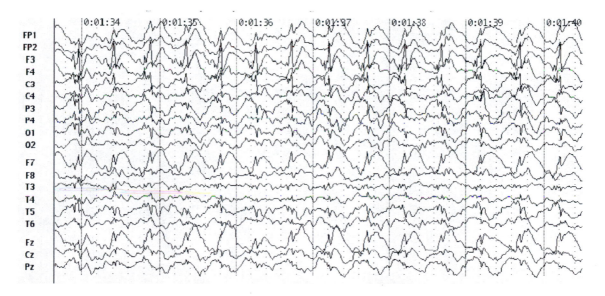

e. Unusual Analyses

i. A separate analysis of transients

Occasionally you may see bursts of unusual activity. These clients should always be under the care of a neurologist in addition to doing neurofeedback. It would be unusual for you to be the first person to see this kind of activity in a client but it has happened at our centre. In one case the paroxysms were bursts of high amplitude slow waves and sharp waves. This teenager turned out to be having myoclonic seizures but he had not mentioned to anyone his occasional sudden collapses in the shower and at home. He tried medications prescribed by a neurologist after he was referred for medical assessment but debated whether the side effects were worse than the symptoms. We insisted that he make all decisions about medications with his neurologist. He also had symptoms of attention deficit disorder. We therefore agreed to work with him to decrease his dominant slow wave and learn metacognitive strategies to use in school. In addition, however, we followed the published recommendations of Sterman and put a special emphasis on also increasing his SMR.

The figure below is a sample of the EEG of a 19 year old man with a history of frequent myoclonic seizures. He came to us because he tuned out frequently and, therefore, couldn't follow arguments the teacher was developing in classes. These bursts were frequent throughout the entire record with eyes closed. This is an example of the type of case where neurological consultation and treatment is essential.

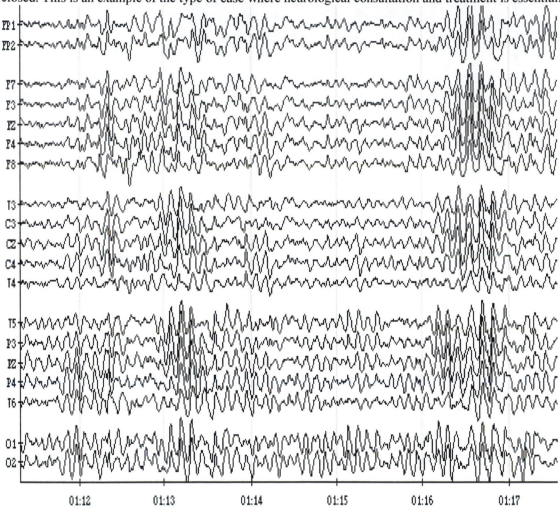

When you do the EEG and see paroxysms of unusual waves it may be helpful to do two separate statistical analyses. First, mark each of these paroxysms as if it were an artifact, omit those segments and do your statistics. If you are doing a full-cap, look at the topographics with these segments eliminated. Second, analyze only these segments. The location and the characteristics of these waves may then clearly stand out.

'Unusual activity' can be waves which represent pathology. On a 19 lead assessment, using a sequential montage, you might occasionally see what is called a *phase reversal*. In these instances the EEG wave on one line (from one pair of electrodes on the scalp) seems to point down to a rise in a wave in the EEG from another pair of electrodes. These waves may, in fact, be pointing to a site of pathology that is the origin of seizure activity. Presumably such a client is already under the care of a neurologist.

If not, require that the client see the appropriate medical practitioners as soon as possible.

ii. Can the EEG distinguish sub-types of some disorders?

Distinuishing sub-types of seizure disorders has been done by neurologists for many years. E. Roy John and Leslie Prichip at New York University (NYU) have specialized in correlating brain mapping data with psychiatric disorders. Their sophisticated neurometrics can, for example, distinguish subtypes of depression and predict medication response. Now it is becoming possible to distinguish a few different EEG subtypes of ADD. In the example of Peter, we saw a distinct subtype of ADD where slow wave activity was not picked up in the central leads but was in the frontal region. A full-cap allows for an even more precise analysis of EEG subtypes and this is outlined in Section X under ADD.

f. Research Using Full-cap Assessments to Distinguish Psychiatric And Neurological Disorders

i. Introduction

This discussion is for a more advanced book concerning research findings and the EEG so it will only be touched upon here. Most of these findings are not yet being utilized by NFB practitioners. Sometimes brain maps are being used to guide psychiatrists as to which medications a patient would most likely respond. This work has been done extensively by E. Roy John and Leslie Prichep at New York University in Manhattan. We refer the interested reader to articles by E. Roy John, Leslie Prichep, Frank Duffy, and Bob Thatcher (Hughes, 1999; John, 1989; John, 1988; Duffy, 1994; Prichep, 1993; Thatcher, 1989).

A brief summary of some recent findings has been reviewed in the article "EEG Findings in Selected Neurological and Psychiatric Conditions" (Hughes, 1999) and what follows is a very brief summary of the highlights.

Various brain imagining techniques have given information concerning structural and functional pathology in mental disorders. These include: QEEG (quantitative elecroencephalogram), MRI (magnetic resonance imaging), PET (positron emission tomography indicating regional cerebral metabolic rate), SPECT (single photon emission computed tomography indicating regional blood flow), MEEG (magneto-encephalography), ERP (event-related-potentials), LORETA (low-resolution electro-magnetic tomography). Hughes and John state that these techniques have "unequivocally established that mental illness has definite correlates with brain dysfunction". They go on to state that, " QEEG and ERP methods afford the psychiatric practitioner a set of non-invasive tools that are capable of quantitatively assessing resting and evoked activity of the brain with sensitivity and temporal resolution superior to those of any other imaging method". A few of the findings in various conditions are summarized below.

ii. Dementia

In *organic delusional states* increased slow-wave activity may be observed over both temporal lobes. In delirium there is slowing of the EEG with increased theta and delta activity.

In *Alzheimer's* there is a diffuse increase in slow wave activity and a decreased mean frequency of the dominant alpha activity. The slowing is proportional to the severity of the dementia. The dominant eyes closed alpha peak in normals is 10 Hz and it may be higher and be seen at 11 or even 12 Hz. In patients whose *mental capacities*, including memory, are *decreasing* the peak frequency is lower. In dementia, in addition to the increased theta and, in more severe cases, increased delta activity there is a decrease in beta. There is also a decrease in occipital alpha power. In *frontotemporal dementia* (*Pick's* disease) the changes are more localized. These EEG change are focal in *multi-infarct dementia*. These EEG changes, however, are not present in *depression* which is an important factor in making an accurate differential diagnosis and distinguishing dementia from depression in the elderly.

iii. Cerebrovascular Disease

Decreased regional cerebral blood flow correlates with EEG slowing.

iv. Mild Head Injury

Increased theta, decreased alpha power and/or decreased coherence and asymmetry are characteristic and examples are given elsewhere in the text.

v. Schizophrenia

There is a relatively low mean alpha frequency and alpha power and an increase in beta activity. An EEG assessment, however, may not demonstrate this if the patient is on neuroleptic medications due to the fact that these medications typically increase alpha power and decrease beta activity. There may also be an increase in frontal theta and delta activity. Not all characteristics are found in all patients. There appear to be subgroups that respond differently to different medications. Other changes include a decrease in stage III, IV, and REM sleep. There is also increased delta in the left anterior temporal region. There is increased interhemispheric coherence which distinguishes patterns in schizophrenia from the findings of decreased coherence in depression. This may be helpful in the differential diagnosis of schizophrenia from bipolar illness.

In work at the ADD centre we have noted that when the client is 'hearing voices' and / or having intense delusional thinking that the EEG shows peaks in the 'high' beta range often somewhere between 21 and 32 Hz. These peaks disappear when the client is assisted to externalize and normalize their thoughts.

Rod, age 20, had been a client of the centre when he was 12 years old. He was diagnosed with ADHD. He did very well, became a straight A student, and went into higher mathematics at University. At age 19 he began having delusional thoughts. He was diagnosed as being schizophrenic. He was no longer able to maintain his focus and concentration on his work and failed his year. Medications helped him stay in touch with reality but he couldn't get motivated and concentrate. With his family's help, he returned to the ADD centre to see if he could improve sufficiently to be able to return to school. He demonstrated high amplitude beta peaks at 21 and 25 Hz. When these occurred a dip was observed in 13 – 15 Hz activity. The author gave him an academic task and asked for his help in critically analysing material the author had written in order to give suggestions

for improvement. Rod did this and as he worked the high beta dropped sharply and 13-15 Hz activity increased. However, at times there would be a sudden reversal, 13-15 would drop and 21 Hz and 25 Hz rose. The trainer intervened and asked what had happened. In every instance the delusional thinking had returned.

vi. Depression

Decreased activation of the left frontal area compared to the right has been used to guide NFB treatment. Studies have shown increased theta and/or alpha power. This may not be observed if the patient is on antidepressants as these medications generally reduce alpha activity. Coherence is decreased between the frontal lobes. 6 per second spike and wave complexes have been reported, particularly in the right hemisphere.

vii. Bipolar Disorder

In contrast to the unipolar depressions described above, alpha appears to be reduced and beta increased.

viii. Anxiety and Panic

There is usually a decrease in alpha activity. In panic disorder, paroxysmal activity may be observed. Temporal lobe abnormalities are also found. (Note, however, in adults with ADHD, anxiety is a common comorbidity. These individuals may have high amplitude alpha.) We have also observed increased beta activity between 19 and 22 Hz though this is not reported in Hugh's paper.

ix. Obsessive Compulsive Disorder (OCD)

There are two groups of patients. In the first group there is an increase in alpha relative power. These patients usually respond (82%) to serotonergic antidepressant (SSRI) interventions. In a second group of OCD patients there is an increase in theta activity and about 80% of these patients do not improve with SSRI medications.

x. Learning Disabilities

Diffuse slowing (theta and/or delta) and decreased alpha and/ or beta activity have been reported. Since there are many different kinds of

LD, it is not surprising that EEG findings are less consistent than in other disorders.

xi. ADHD

As noted in other areas of this text, increased theta and/or low alpha may be seen centrally and/or in frontal locations. In addition there may be hypercoherence and interhemispheric asymmetry.

xii. Alcoholism

Increased beta activity is found. There is a high incidence of comorbidity with ADHD in adults and the typical EEG findings of ADHD may therefore be somewhat masked. The increased beta makes the theta/beta a less accurate guide when there are also problems with addictions.

8. Additional Data Interpretation – LORETA
(Low Resolution Electromagnetic Tomography) – with thanks to Joel Lubar for this description.

Almost 150 years ago two physicists Green and Gauss independently developed a mathematical theorem showing that if there is a distribution of electrical activity or charges on the surface of a 3-dimensional hollow object such as a sphere, then by means of a complex vector analysis it is possible to localize inside the object the generators of the surface distribution of electrical activity. This procedure is known as the inverse solution. In 1994 a researcher and his team in Zurich Switzerland Dr. Roberto Pascual Marqui implemented this inverse solution with some appropriate modifications and updating to provide a methodology known as *low-resolution electromagnetic tomography* or LORETA. Actually, there are an infinite number of inverse solutions for determining the generators of activity inside of a three-dimensional solid with a surface charge distribution. Pascual Marqui wrote several papers in which he described the various inverse solutions and showed that LORETA was the most accurate.

In terms of practical application a three-dimensional object - the head - consists of the skin, skull and the cerebral cortex. These three components provide what is called a three concentric shell model and provides more accurate localization of the internal generators than a single shell model would. LORETA includes the gray matter of the brain which encompasses the cerebral cortex and the hippocampal formation; it also localizes activity in nearby structures such as the parahippocampal gyrus, insular cortex and other internal temporal lobe structures. All of the gray matter that contains dipole generators are part of the LORETA solution space. The gray matter is broken down into 2394, 7X7X7 mm cubes called Voxel's. For each Voxel there is a three-dimensional vector, which is part of the solution in terms of localizing the internal generators of the surface EEG activity. The LORETA technique cannot be used to localize monopole activity such as found in thalamic regions, brain stem and other subcortical nuclear structures.

There are a number of studies that have shown the relationship between LORETA tomography, functional MRI and PET scans. One of the newest developments that Dr. Lubar's laboratory has been developing is the potential for using LORETA for neurofeedback. For example, teaching an individual to change activity in the cingulate gyrus which is known to be a generator of theta activity in the brain. This might be particularly helpful since the anterior cingulate plays a very important role in a number of complex cognitive and emotional functions. LORETA neurofeedback will require considerable research before it can be considered as a potential clinical tool.

The figure below has been copied with the kind permission of Joel Lubar.

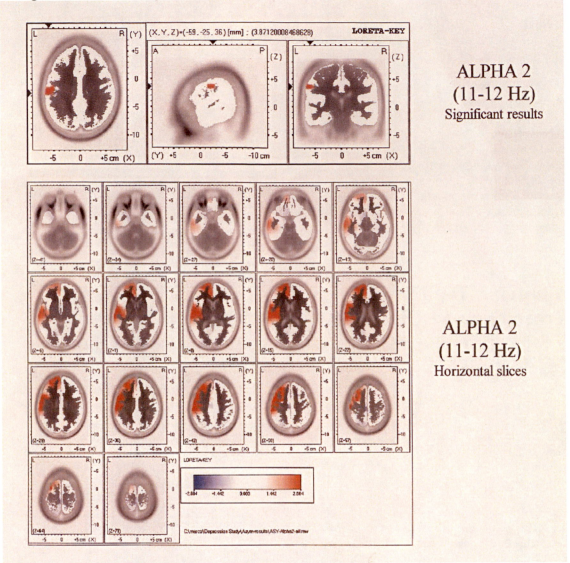

ALPHA 2
(11-12 Hz)
Significant results

ALPHA 2
(11-12 Hz)
Horizontal slices

The diagram above represents the difference between 15 chronically depressed females and age matched controls. The left sided alpha activity is very clear.

This diagram will also be found in a future article by Joel Lubar and published by the *International Journal of Psychophysiology*, Elsevier Science Publications. Acknowledgements are given to Elsevier Science Publications and thanks to Dr. Lubar for permission to use this figure.

9. Training in Assessment Procedures

To learn how to do QEEG with one or two channels you may attend workshops at the annual meetings of AAPB (Association for Applied Psychophysiology and Biofeedback – chapters in North America and Australia), iSNR (International Society for Neuronal Regulation – chapters in North America, Australia and Europe), BFE (Biofeedback Foundation of Europe), and workshops sponsored by manufacturers such as Thought Technology or brokers such as Stens Corporation and American Biotech. You should then obtain personal mentoring from an experienced practitioner. For

QEEG assessment with 19 or more channels, you must attend specific courses and obtain personal instruction.

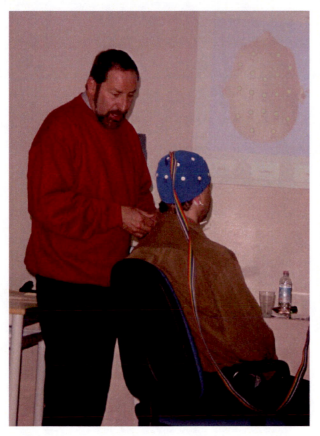

At the time of writing workshops and or training concerning 19 channel QEEG were been given by the following: LEXICOR corporation, Barry Sterman (using his SKIL program), regarding coherence by Joe Horvath, LORETA by Joel Lubar (or Roberto Pasqual-Marquis, or Robert Thatcher), and about reading the full-cap QEEG by Jay Gunkelman.

An invaluable resource for artifacting is the already mentioned SNR publication entitled *The Art of Artifacting* (2001) by D. Corydon Hammond & Jay Gunkelman. The purchase enriches your knowledge and also the field, since the authors have donated all proceeds to the Society for Neuronal Regulation. Check out www.snr-jnt.org. For a basic textbook we recommend *Fisch and Spehlmann's EEG Primer, Basic Principles of Digital and Analog EEG* (Fisch, 1999). For educational opportunities, check www.aapb.org, www.bfe.org, www.thoughttechnology.org, www.snr-jnt.org, www.futurehealth.org and, for certification information, www.bcia.org.

Above, Barry Sterman is demonstrating to a group of psychologists how to put on a full-cap correctly. He will then demonstrate how to use the NeuroNavigator to collect data from 19 channels. (www.skiltopo.com)

SECTION VII:
Autonomic Nervous System (ANS) and Skeletal Muscle Tone (EMG) Assessment

A. Introduction

In this section we will discuss the purpose of measuring physiological responses to stress and tension. The areas which can be easily measured will be listed and the methods for measuring them discussed. This is not a book on autonomic nervous system (ANS) and electromyogram (EMG) biofeedback. There are many excellent texts on this subject, George Fuller wrote a text on the basics which is very easy to read (Fuller, 1984) and still relevant. Mark Schwartz's *Biofeedback A Practitioner's Guide* is a classic reference text. In 2003 Don Moss edited a comprehensive tome on mind-body medicine. Our overview will be brief and specific to combining biofeedback (BFB) with neurofeedback (NFB).

1. What can be measured?

We are able to measure Autonomic Nervous System (ANS) activity, sympathetic and parasympathetic branches, and the skeletal muscle tone as measured by the electromyogram.. The ANS governs a large part of our daily lives. All our internal organs are regulated through this branch of the nervous system.   It functions automatically and unconsciously.   However, it is possible to influence this part of our nervous system consciously through the use of biofeedback. The common measurements that are used are listed below:

a. For the Autonomic Nervous System
- Peripheral skin temperature
- Electrodermal responses (EDR)
- Heart rate (pulse)
- Respiration
- Respiratory Sinus Arrhythmia (RSA)

b. For the Skeletal Muscle System
- Electromyogram (EMG)

c. Notes regarding the Autonomic Nervous System

This has been previously described in the neuroanatomy section of the book. It is reviewed here to give an example of how it may be explained to the client.

The ANS is divided into two divisions: the sympathetic and the parasympathetic systems. The main neurotransmitter for the parasympathetic system is acetylcholine. The main neurotransmitter for the sympathetic nervous system is noradrenaline. The parasympathetic system is generally thought of as acting to restore the body. Its major functions are related to rest and relaxation. The sympathetic system, on the other hand, is involved in expenditure of energy with resulting increases in blood pressure, heart rate and the utilization of energy (glucose metabolism, oxygen). Sympathetic drive is associated with the fight or flight response which was related to survival for our ancestors. This type of response was first described in physiological terms by Walter Cannon in 1915. As previously noted, the release of adrenaline when a person is stressed appears to be related to improved blood clotting, increased EDR and alertness, and a concentration of blood flow to the brain and to large muscle groups that are necessary for fight or flight.

It is important to recognize that every client is different in terms of their physiology. For example, one anxious client may show a peripheral skin temperature of 70 degrees Fahrenheit while a second, very tense client, has a peripheral skin temperature of 93 degrees Fahrenheit. With the second client you may find the tension reflected in other modalities, such as respiration, RSA (respiratory sinus arrhythmia), pulse, or the EMG. Despite these individual differences, it is nearly always very helpful to look carefully during the assessment at the synchrony between respiration and cardiac variability. With most clients it is a good starting point to teach them diaphragmatic breathing and relaxation techniques. The exception is the client who has grand mal or partial complex seizures. With these clients you must be very cautious when teaching diaphragmatic breathing because accidental hyperventilation could precipitate a seizure.

2. Goal of the Assessment

The goal of the assessment is to discover how a particular client responds physiologically to mental stress. These findings may then be used to set up a biofeedback program to help that client self regulate, that is, control their own physiological responses even under stressful circumstances. In addition, practicing this control may produce an automatic, unconscious, beneficial change in that client's response to stress in the future.

This goal is really the same as that which we usually have when doing work with neurofeedback; namely, to produce an optimal state of mental and physiological functioning. In this state the client is both relaxed and alert. This will broaden associative capabilities and perspective, decrease fatigue, allow calm reflection on alternative approaches to tasks and, when combined with high levels of alertness, improve reaction time and increase response accuracy. The individual will be flexible in terms of mental state and resilient in terms of their physiology.

In the first or second interview after EEG parameters have been set we use a structured interview process with the client to fill out a single page questionnaire. This questionnaire, an assessment profile called the TOPS Evaluation, also outlines the variables that we can measure

and use to give feedback. (This form is found below under D., Method.)

It is crucial to remember that seldom are there simple miracle 'cures'. You must gently but firmly help your client to generalize what they learn. The techniques for doing this include attaching a new habit, such as relaxing with diaphragmatic breathing, to old habits. These should be regular daily activities, such as driving or answering the phone. The new learning which combines both NFB and BFB must become an integral part of daily living.

B. Brief Overview of ANS and EMG Measures

1. Peripheral Skin Temperature:

This is perhaps the simplest and yet most useful measurement in biofeedback. A *thermistor* is placed on the pulp of the distal portion of the little finger. When the subject becomes tense, the sympathetic nervous system will cause the arterial blood vessels in the finger to constrict. The result is a cooling of the finger. Most people in a relaxed state demonstrate a temperature of 94 to 95 degrees Fahrenheit.

Even children should be able to learn to raise and lower their peripheral skin temperature. Children enjoy understanding the advantages of the hands becoming cold and wet when a person is tense or afraid. To make it interesting and fun we ask them to imagine what a cave-man would have to do when a saber-toothed tiger jumped out of the woods. To save his own life he had to fight or flee. If his hand was dry, his spear would slip out of it. To fight or flee he needed all his energy conserved for his brain and his large muscle groups. Therefore arteries to these areas dilated while other arteries, to areas which were not immediately so necessary (like the finger tips), would constrict under the influence of the sympathetic nervous system. In addition to helping a client learn to relax, skin temperature feedback has been shown to be useful in decreasing migraine headaches (Andreassi, 1995 p. 327 after: Blanchard, 1978). It is also the first step in the Peniston protocol used in the treatment of alcoholic patients.

2. Electrodermal response (EDR)

This is a measure of skin conduction (SC). It is most easily measured by placing a silver/silver chloride sensor on the distal, ventral (palm) surface of the index and ring fingers. The middle finger prevents the two sensors touching which would cause a short-circuit. The conductance in μMhos of a very small current of electricity is measured between these two sensors. (This measurement is the inverse of GSR, galvanic skin response, measured in Ohms for skin resistance.) Alternatively, the sensors may be placed at two sites on the palm of the hand. Skin conductivity increases when the sweat glands open. Like skin temperature, this is regulated by the sympathetic nervous system. We use the same imaginary story and ask the child to imagine the cave-man fighting the saber-toothed tiger. Early man needed his hands to be moist (a bit sweaty) in order to hold his spear without it slipping. This example is enjoyed, understood and remembered by children.

Extremely high arousal may correlate with high anxiety and tension. A flat unchanging EDR may also correlate with tension (often chronic) in some individuals. You may find that your adolescent and adult ADD clients demonstrate low arousal a short time into a training session. Their alertness level is dropping as they become bored with the activity. In these ADD clients, raising their alertness correlates with increasing their EDR. Teaching these clients to maintain alertness is important if you hope to succeed with neurofeedback training. Research has demonstrated that children with higher levels of arousal and more labile EDR are better able to sustain attention and can perform faster on assigned tasks. Higher EDR is associated with better learning of novel material and improved memory recall. (Andreassi, 1995, after Sakai, et al 1992)

Optimal performance may be associated with increases in heart rate (HR) and skin conduction (SC) which may, in turn, be related to improved attention and short term memory (Andreassi, 1995 after Yuille, 1980).

3. Heart Rate (HR)

We measure HR and blood volume (BV) using a *plethysmograph* with a photoelectric transducer. For BV measurements, the difference in magnitude between the lowest point of a pulse and its peak is expressed as a percentage of the average. A sensor on the thumb is used and it is held in place comfortably with either an elasticized band or skin sensitive tape.

Heart rate increases are greater for stress associated with anger, fear or sadness than increases noted with surprise, happiness and disgust. (Andreassi, 1995 after Ekman, Levenson and Friesen, 1983). We have all experienced heart rate increases with frustration and with a defensive response to and/or rejection of, a stimulus. HR decreases with the orienting response, stimulus acceptance, or being given a reward. One would also expect differences in Type A versus Type B personalities (Friedman, Rosenman, 1974). It has also been found that HR responses are greater when the person is capable of exerting some control over the event (Andreassi, 1995)

4. Respiration

There is a vast literature on the importance of proper breathing and for those interested in this topic, we refer you to Robert Fried's work. Breath work is emphasized in all the martial arts and in Eastern traditions of meditation and yoga. For our purposes the main application of breathing is for relaxation and tension reduction. We tell clients, "If your breathing is relaxed, you are relaxed."

In a training program using BFB, most clients can be rapidly taught to breathe deeply, more slowly and regularly. Older children enjoy pretending they are blowing up a balloon in their tummy while balancing a small ball on their shoulder. In this manner they breathe deeply while keeping their shoulders relaxed and motionless. They easily understand that rate of breathing is controlled by pCO2 (partial pressure of CO2) in the blood stream and that this will be decreased if they blow out all the CO2 from the bottom of their lungs. In this way they lower their breathing rate to a comfortable 5 to 8 breaths per minute. An ideal rate for most adults is 6 breaths per minute. Children breath at a slightly faster rate.

Correct breathing appears to be a particularly helpful adjunct when you are doing SMR training. Producing 12-15 Hz activity across the sensori-motor cortex is associated with being physically calm while maintaining mental alertness. We encourage this in children who are hyperactive and impulsive. We always teach them diaphragmatic breathing as well. The old advice to "Take a deep breath" before responding, especially if you feel angry, is an invaluable technique for the child with ADHD and for their parents, too. The combination of SMR up-training and slow diaphragmatic breathing (about 6 BrPM) has been used successfully in a single case report of treating Tourette's Syndrome (Daly, 2002) and in Parkinson's Disease plus dystonia (Thompson & Thompson, 2002).

5. RSA (Respiratory Sinus Arrhythmia)

When a student/client breathes diaphragmatically and effortlessly at a rate of about 6 breaths per minute, the heart rate will follow a sinusoidal pattern. This pattern correlates with the respiration pattern and is called respiratory sinus arrhythmia (RSA) (Basmajian, 1989 after: Fried, 1987.)

Measurement for respiration is carried out by monitoring the degree of stretch in at least one respiratory band (a kind of lightweight belt with velcro closure). Ideally you would place one sensor band around the chest just below the armpits to measure thoracic breathing. The second sensor would be placed around the abdomen at a level of maximum change during inspiration and expiration. If only one sensor is used, it should be placed around the abdomen. When a single sensor is used, thoracic movement may be detected by using EMG sensors over the trapezius muscle. A second EMG sensor could be placed over the occipitalis muscle group.

As noted previously, the photoplethysmograph (PPG) is usually attached to the thumb or put on a finger (ventral surface). Its light source and photodetector register changes in blood flow and thus heart rate.

With stress the heart rate will increase. Stress may result in the client's breathing becoming shallow and irregular. Some clients may reverse the normal process by moving their diaphragm up with inhalation and down with exhalation. With stress one does not usually observe synchrony between heart rate variations and inspiration and expiration.

At 6 breaths-per-minute most adults will demonstrate synchrony between their breathing and their heart rate. Children breathe at a slightly faster rate. When graphed, a beautiful synchrony is observed. There is an increase in heart rate with inspiration (sympathetic nervous system) and a decrease in heart rate with expiration (released from the sympathetic NS, allowing parasympathetic nervous system influence, which is, in part, regulated by the medullary respiratory center through the vagus). This is said to be the only measure which allows the clinician to influence the activity of the parasympathetic nervous system and, thereby, affect the balance of sympathetic to parasympathetic activity. A simple instrument to follow just heart rate variability is called the Freeze Framer from a company called Heartmath. Biograph is one program that allows one to look at RSA while simultaneously monitoring other modalities, including EEG.

All of us tend to link the way we breathe to different activities in our lives. The objective in training is to have the client take over control of how they breathe even in stressful situations. When breathing is predominantly thoracic, there may be an associated hyper arousal. This is a catabolic state which is thought to predispose the body to pathology. The catabolic state is associated with a decrease in the production of white cells for the immune system, increased salt and water retention, decreased repair and replacement of cells, and a decrease in the synthesis of protein, fat, and carbohydrate. Cardiac output and blood pressure may also increase. However, a positive result of being in a "stressed state" has been identified by recent research which suggests that the release of adrenaline with stress may improve blood clotting and, thus, be a factor in improving survival in some situations (Andreassi, p.29, 1995):

Pepper notes that, "Effortless diaphragmatic breathing reduces sympathetic arousal and promotes an anabolic state, which encourages regeneration" This has been shown to improve a variety of disorders including asthma, coronary heart disease, pain, panic and hypertension. It has also been shown to improve athletic performance (Pepper, 1997). The clinical result of achieving RSA synchrony, which is found in conjunction with effortless breathing, is usually a sense of a release in tension and an increase in physical and mental relaxation.

Note regarding measurement: If your instrument uses a '%' measurement, then this may be confusing for you at first. These *measurements cannot be used to compare one session to another session*. For the respiration sensor '%' means percent of possible tension of the sensor itself. It is not a physiologic measure: 100% means the sensor is stretched to its maximum length, O% means the cable around the abdomen is too slack and there is no tension in it. With the PPG sensor for pulse, '%' is a measure of the percentage of light being reflected. This is useful to see changes during a session, but it may be highly sensitive to a number of artifacts such as the angle of the instrument on the skin or ambient light around the subject's finger. Movement of the finger may grossly disrupt the readings. Thus percent measurements are used for monitoring changes within a session. They are not comparable between sessions or between individuals.

6. Electromyography (EMG)

EMG readings reflect the depolarization and repolarization of muscle fibers. There has been some research which shows that, in clients with ADHD, behavior improves with muscle relaxation, as do their scores on reading and language tests. *Locus of control* is the best predictor of lasting success and it has been shown to move from external to internal with successful EMG feedback (Andreassi, 1995 after: Denkowski, et al, 1984). We postulate that future research will demonstrate this shift in locus of control correlates with success in many modalities of biofeedback and neurofeedback. Logically, locus of control should become more internal as the client learns to self-regulate since internal locus of control means the person feels they or their attributes are responsible for outcomes. (I got a poor grade because I did not study enough.) Those with an external locus of control believe outcomes are dependant on luck,

chance or the behaviour of others who have more power. ("I got a poor mark because the teacher does not like boys.")

It is important to recognize that research has shown that relaxation of one targeted muscle group does not necessarily generalize to adjacent muscles (Andreassi, 1995 after: Fridlund, et al, 1984). Nevertheless, training a client to relax a muscle, such as the frontalis (forehead) or trapezius (shoulder), does help that client to recognize the difference between tension and relaxation. This recognition helps most clients to generalize learning how to relax to other muscle groups.

The raw EMG has both positive and negative signals. This is usually amplified by a factor of >1000 and mathematically changed to root-mean-square (RMS). RMS allows the EMG to be seen as a positive signal. Normal resting muscle activity is usually <4µV. High RMS amplitude indicates muscle tension. To detect muscle tension +ve and −ve electrodes are usually placed 2 cm apart and parallel to the muscle fibers. A third electrode, the 'ground', is placed equidistant from the other 2 electrodes (Sella, 1997). The 'ground' electrode does the electrical housekeeping including filtering out electrical noise. If you want a general measure of total upper body tension, try putting an EMG electrode on each forearm (with the ground further up the forearm on one side). Heart (EKG) artifact may be seen as sharp spikes at 1 second intervals. Absolute values are not that important: the goal is a downward trend in the EMG recording. (Stephen Sideroff, personal communication)

Artifacts may be dealt with in several ways. The EMG amplifier should have a preset *notch* filter, to filter out the prevailing environmental electrical *noise* (50 Hz in Europe and 60 Hz in North America). In addition, one may use a narrow 100-200 Hz filter to filter out the heart muscle signals when using a chest placement near the heart. A constant high signal may indicate that one electrode is not properly attached to the sensor or one electrode is not making contact with the skin. A short burst of high signal may indicate a movement artifact or a low battery.

To learn self-regulation of EMG, the client is asked to tense and then relax the muscle being measured several times. During this exercise the examiner and the client observe the changes in the EMG recording. The client then attempts self-regulation by varying the tension in the muscle group and observing the changes on the meter. To do this the client changes the tension in the muscle being recorded by varying amounts (e.g., 100%, 50%, 25%, 10%, 5% of maximum contraction holding each state for 5 seconds then relaxing). To improve muscle control (as might be desired post-stroke) this would be done on a flexor muscle while the client attempted not to contract the opposing extensor muscle group. Thus a client who is having difficulty flexing a limb would first work on relaxing the opposing extensor muscle group. When the client achieves some success in consciously relaxing the extensor group then work would begin on a combination of relaxation of the extensor while contracting the flexor (Bernie Brooker, Lynda Kirk, personal communications). EMG biofeedback has been applied to rehabilitation with great success by Bernard Brooker's group at the Miami School of Medicine Rehabilitation Department. Indeed, they have been setting up similar centres world wide (Brazil, Germany, India). They are sometimes literally able to make the lame walk. In a dramatic case that illustrates both the success and limitations of training specific muscle groups, Brooker was able to work with a concert pianist to restore function to his hands to a concert pianist after he suffered a severe head injury when he was attacked and robbed when performing in a foreign country. After EMG biofeedback training he was able to return to playing the piano and the concert stage. He was, however, still not able to button his shirt, a motor act that involved a different muscle group than playing piano.

Biofeedback using EMG combined with thermal feedback and relaxation has been shown to decrease both systolic and diastolic pressure (Andreassi, 1995 after Cohen & Sedlacek, 1983). Chronic tension headache may also be treated using EMG feedback. For headache, electrodes are often placed on the forehead. In this case the electrodes may be placed slightly further apart. This can be done in a consistent manner if you use the same 'strip' each time (for example, a velcro band with active electrodes 7 cm apart is is available for use with equipment from Thought Technology). In this placement the ground electrode is between the two active electrodes. In a relaxed state the forehead EMG is $< 2\mu V$. Alternatively, electrodes may be placed over the left and right trapezius muscles and/or on the neck (occipitalis) region (Arena, 1997).

C. Associated Therapeutic Techniques

During all of the above work the client is assisted to learn ways of relaxing and to generalize what they learn in sessions to their everyday life. Below you will find a brief discussion of some of the main therapeutic techniques used with these clients.

1. Imagery

Imagery is often encouraged during biofeedback training sessions especially if stress management is the goal. The client is asked to release all muscle tension while producing images of scenes or events that are personally relaxing. The client may then alternate these relaxing images with images that have the opposite effect on them, that is, images which simulate a crisis. A crisis may be defined as "a personally perceived potential adaptive incompetency" (Thompson, 1979). The client may be asked to imagine an event which fits this definition and then alternate this image with relaxing images while monitoring and gradually gaining control over their physiological responses. Whenever possible, the imagery used by the client should involve all the senses. In other words, imagery is not just about picturing things but also hearing, smelling, feeling and even tasting using your imagination. Dr. Vietta (Sue) Wilson, a sports psychologist at York University in Toronto, Canada, who has worked with elite athletes for decades, gave us an example of working with swimmers. When they practice a race using imagery, she encourages them to see the sequence of scenes in the pool, feel the water on their skin, hear the splashing and the sounds of spectators, smell and taste the chlorine, and finally, visualize themselves finishing ahead of other swimmers. The sequence using imagery should take the same time as the actual race. An interesting aside is that Wilson found when she was doing brain maps with her swimmers that there was a male-female difference in activation during imagery. In females the areas associated with language lit up more, indicating that they did more self-talk, whereas the male swimmers showed more activation in areas associated with visualization.

The name of Jacobson, has been associated with progressive muscle relaxation although similar procedures had been taught by others for many years. Imagery of warmth, heaviness and pleasant tranquil situations may help the client to relax. 'Autogenic training' refers to a specific series of exercises and is discussed below.

2. Autogenic Training

Autogenic training was done prior to 1930 in Germany (Stoyva, 1986). There are 6 standard exercises: limb heaviness, limb warmth, cardiac, respiration (diaphragmatic breathing), solar plexus warmth and forehead cooling. More often only 4 modifications of these exercises are done: heaviness, warmth, respiration and solar plexus warmth (Basmajian, 1989, p170). During this type of relaxation training, the trainer may use suggestive phrases such as: "Your arms and legs feel heavy and warm". In practice, most people who talk about doing autogenic training are not doing the full regimen of exercises.

A simplified version is to teach effortless diaphragmatic breathing which is regular without chest or shoulder muscle tension. The student/client may practice these exercises at home beginning with having each limb first feel heavy, then feel both heavy and warm. Then while maintaining this state of limb relaxation, the student/client pretends that they are gently blowing up, then deflating, a little balloon in their abdomen. After each exhale they briefly 'rest' and increase their feelings of having relaxed muscles and a sense of warmth (hands, arms, legs) before beginning their next inspiration. Soon they may also begin to feel warm in their solar plexus area. Some students/clients may need to precede the relaxation exercises with tensing-then-releasing hand, arm, shoulders neck and jaw muscles in sequence. This helps them feel the difference between tension and relaxation. Some students/clients may augment this with the use of imagery. They may imagine an image which represents, for them, peace and calm and good feelings. Other students/clients find that they can use either a cue word or scene to bring on this state of calm. It is important to note that up to 40% of clients may experience discomfort while doing relaxation and/or autogenic training (Strifel, Workshop on autogenic training, AAPB Annual Meeting 2000)

3. Systematic Desensitization

Systematic desensitization is the next step for some clients. It is a good method to help *transfer* the student's/client's ability to induce a calm mental and physiological state into the real world of stressful situations. To do this the students/clients imagine themselves in progressively more stressful situations. This technique has been shown in controlled studies to be very effective in migraine control (Basmajian, 1989 after: Mitchell & Mitchell, 1971)

4. Shaping

Shaping involves giving the student/client a task which is fairly simple, recording their success and then gradually making it more difficult until you reach the desired behaviour. It entails successive approximations which are recorded. This technique is used during the sessions and in home assignments, as appropriate to the client's present situation and goals.

5. Generalization

Generalization of what they have learned in training sessions to their everyday life is the key to successful training. We use the adage, "Attach a habit to a habit". It is very difficult for any of us to just form a new habit no matter how good we know it would be for us. Thus, if you want a habit, such as diaphragmatic breathing at 6 BrPM, to generalize and become a new habit, ask the student/client to list activities that occur every day. These may include: getting out of bed, sitting down to eat, brushing their teeth, answering the telephone, opening the mail, reading e-mail, driving to and from work and so on. The student/client must then, without exception, relax for 2 or more deep diaphragmatic breaths before beginning each of these tasks throughout the day. We say, "without exception", because we know that any exception will lead to more exceptions and to an eventual failure of this attempt to form a new habit and generalize their relaxation exercises to everyday living. Most students/clients can master this assignment in a very short time. Then we request that they maintain the relaxed breathing exercise that they do in sessions, and at the beginning of each of these daily routines, throughout these regular activities. They are encouraged to make notes in their SMIRB (see below) pocket book on how successful they have been, preferably at a time and place that is already routine, such as when they have dessert at dinner each night or coffee in the morning.

6. Compartmentalizing

Compartmentalizing is another key technique to assist in generalizing relaxed self regulation to everyday living. Compartmentalizing means that each of your problem areas has its own compartment and does not flow over into other areas of your life. For example, when you are at home playing with your children you should not be thinking about work. Doctors have to learn to severely compartmentalize. They cannot be worrying about one patient when they are treating another. Their family life will be a disaster if they bring home the tragedies of the emergency room to the family dinner table.

To help the student/client compartmentalize we suggest they purchase a small, 3.5 x 7 inch, book that will easily fit in a shirt, vest or trouser pocket or purse. Some of us just use a pocket day-timer because it has the added advantage of being used as a personal reminder book and it has a section for telephone numbers. The Quo Vadis agenda planning diary has a telephone number section that slips into the flexible cover. Buy an extra diary or just an extra telephone number refill and use the blank pages which are perfect for making a few notes. High-tech people may utilize the note making capabilities of their electronic organizer. We call the back few blank pages of this refill our SMIRB. (The front pages are used for short-term and long-term goals). SMIRB stands for: Stop My Irritating Ruminations Book. These pages are used for recording, organizing, and controlling one's intrusive worrying thoughts. We tell the client that we all tend to ruminate at times. If there were a solution to the problem they are worried about, they would have acted on it. The reason they ruminate is because, at this time, there is no acceptable solution. This recognition is often, in itself, helpful for a client who is worrying. We suggest that they give each major area of worrisome thoughts (spouse, children, finances, exams, job, future career and so on) two pages. The repetitious thoughts are to be organized and listed on the left hand page. The right hand page contains any ideas for rectifying the situation or for *reframing* the way the client thinks about it. Most of these right-hand pages will initially be blank.

Once they have their SMIB set up, the client is told to establish a time each day (they can write it in the daily agenda section) when they could sit alone and worry for ¼ to ½ an hour with a cup of tea or coffee without interruptions. The client is told that they must make an absolute decision – no exceptions - to reserve worrying for this time. If a new worrisome thought comes into their mind, then they must open their SMIB and enter it onto the appropriate list. Otherwise, when a worry comes up, the client is to reassure himself that his worry will not be forgotten because it is in his book and will be reviewed during his next 'worry-time'. In reality, most people have the same worries again and again, (finances, in-laws, weight) without many entirely new worries cropping up.

One of the nice outcomes of this SMIRB technique is that our clients get a better sleep. They make an absolute rule that no worrying is allowed in bed. If they awake worrying they are to keep their eyes closed and decide if that worry is listed in their book. If it is, they reassure themselves that they will not forget to think about it during 'worry-time' the next day. If they decide that it is not in the book, then they immediately turn on a light and carefully write it into their SMIRB. Then they think of some repetitive pleasant activity such as wind-surfing or paddling their canoe or walking through a flower garden – no people, just a pleasant scene or activity.

7. Light-Sound Stimulation & Subliminal Alpha

The field of audio-visual stimulation (AVS) has been rapidly expanding. There are many products in the market that combine photic stimulation with audio beats at particular EEG frequencies. The combined audio and visual stimulation will entrain the EEG in the same rhythm during the time of stimulation. The auditory stimulation is given through headphones and the visual is done with flashing lights that are built into goggles that resemble dark sunglasses. The manufacturer may offer goggles and programs that allow each visual field to be stimulated by a different frequency. For example, with an ADHD client, the left visual field (right brain) might be stimulated in an SMR frequency between 13 and 15 Hz for calming while the right visual field (left brain) is stimulated in a beta frequency between 16 and

20 Hz for improving attention and learning. The client sits with his eyes closed in a relaxed position while the equipment runs through a preset program. Each program has one or more preset frequencies and time lengths set for each frequency to be used. There are programs for relaxation, for alertness and for a range of states in between. It has been suggested (Siebert, 1999) that delta sessions be used to assist sleep onset, alpha sessions for relaxation and meditation, low frequency beta (SMR) for calming with ADHD students/clients and beta sessions to "perk up cognitive functioning". Research is starting to accumulate regarding beneficial outcomes with entrainment but it is still a new field and, as with regular neurofeedback, controlled studies are few. Tom Budzynski worked with AVS and Dave Sievert, a manufacturer of AVS equipment based in Edmonton, has been doing workshops at many conferences.

Because AVS is doing something to the client (providing stimulation to the brain), it is more invasive than neurofeedback. NFB, when all is said and done, is just providing information which, hopefully, assists the client to learn self-regulation. AVS tries to actively change a mental state. The results of the stimulation may differ according to the individual's baseline EEG activity so one cannot predict with certainty how a given person may react. AVS is certainly a field worth investigating and monitoring.

Some experienced practitioners, such as Paul Swingle, report shorter NFB training times when AVS is added to the NFB program. Dr. Swingle also adds other things to the training program such as the use of "subliminal alpha" – a tape or CD of pink noise (it sounds like running water) with subliminal beats imbedded into the noise that are designed to decrease slow wave (theta) activity. This subliminal alpha can be played using headphones during times when the student/client who has ADD is doing homework. Dr. Swingle suggests that you try this technique while monitoring the EEG and see if it lowers theta. Every client is different. If it lowers theta, then give the client the opportunity to try it at home and, with the cooperation of the teacher, at school. It will work for some clients and not for others. Tapes and CDs can be ordered from Dr. Paul Swingle in Vancouver, B.C., Canada.

8. SAMONAS Sound Therapy
(Spectrally Activated Music of Optimal Natural Structure)

The goal of SAMONAS sound therapy is to improve listening skills and, thereby, cognitive functioning by means of increasing first, relaxation and emotional calming, and second, acoustic perception. Relaxation of tension will increase breadth of associations, memory, recall, and efficiency of learning. Psychologically, this may be experienced as both a 'centering' and an energizing effect. Throughout history many different therapeutic approaches (yoga, relaxation training, meditation and so on) have their roots in this basic understanding. SAMONAS sound therapy appears to offer a simple, pleasant and effective way to promote relaxation.

Improvement in acoustic perception also appears to be a result of SAMONAS. At birth the human ear has the capacity to perceive distance (depth), direction and the specific character (structure) of sounds with the accuracy we marvel at in many species of animals. Much of this ability appears to be lost as we grow up in our modern environments. In addition, these components are, for the most part, lost in most recordings but are preserved by the specialized techniques developed for SAMONAS. At the highest levels of the martial arts the practitioners appear to have relearned some of these abilities. They can perceive and interpret movements and sounds which others cannot. SAMONAS sound therapy may help us to train to improve our listening skills. Improvements in this realm may in turn increase our ability to receive information detail and, combined with the relaxed reflective cognitive style which is engendered, to assimilate and more effectively and efficiently use the information we hear. This may help clients with ADD and with Asperger's syndrome however there are no controlled studies at the time of writing this book.

a. How does SAMONAS Work?
The biological faculty of hearing is innate, but the ability to listen has to be learned. Learning involves the reorganization of neural pathways. It results from emphasizing some neural pathways and de-emphasizing others. New connections among neurons in the brain are formed throughout life. Learning requires that

we exercise our brains just as we exercise our bodies to remain active and healthy. This is the basic premise underlying NFB. Similarly, SAMONAS sound therapy is built on the premise that appropriate exercise of the most fundamental organ in our bodies related to learning, the human ear (it is the first completely functional organ system and exists in its mature state at about twenty weeks of intrauterine development), can improve the total functioning of the human organism. The ear has neural connections within the brain to areas that are linked to virtually all other organs in the body. It has direct links to speech centres.

SAMONAS uses recent advances in recording technology to develop CD recordings which promote 'exercise' of the human listening/hearing pathways. It is based on the premise that improvement in the quality of sound, combined with an increase in the information the sound carries, will enable the student/client to, psychologically, not resist listening (unconsciously or automatically). The student/client, thereby, gains more information through auditory channels.

We 'learn' to tune in to meaningful sounds and tune out the surrounding *noise*. All babies babble the same but, as they grow, sounds not heard in their native tongue drop out. Similarly, native speakers of different languages show different audiograms. Italians, for example, have peak hearing in higher frequencies (4000 Hz) and French have great sensitivity around 1500 Hz which corresponds to a nasal sound. Our ear is flexible enough to adjust to the demands placed upon it. Humans hear in a range from as low as 16 Hz up to about 20,000 Hz. As we age, the higher frequencies drop out so the elderly may only be able to hear up to 10,000 Hz. We discriminate best in the 1000 to 3000 Hz range which is the key range for speech.

As we develop, there is a psychological conditioning taking place which determines what we listen to and for how long. We tune out not only noises which are uncomfortable, but also sounds which are emotionally undesirable. Sounds which are tuned out at one point in our lives for psychological reasons, may continue to be inappropriately and unnecessarily tuned out as we mature. Theoretically, SAMONAS recordings may enable us to rejuvenate this system to achieve more complete listening.

Today we are familiar with the concept of stress. With life threatening stress our ancestors had to fight or to flee. Those of our ancestors who survived developed nervous reactions which, through the sympathetic nervous system, cut down blood flow to the skin (reduced bleeding when cut) and decreased digestive activities while simultaneously increasing blood flow to the large muscle groups necessary for fight or flight. Today these body reactions to chronic stress at home, school and in the office place have no survival value and can result in a number of psychophysiological disorders. Tension producing circumstances early in our lives may lead to the inappropriate exercise of the sympathetic nervous system in this same manner. Even when these early stressors are no longer present this *fight or flight* system is activated by cues in our environment. We become tense, anxious, fatigued and even somewhat depressed without due cause. In a similar vein we may automatically block-out listening to aspects of our environment. In this area of our lives SAMONAS can also be helpful. The relaxation effects of the SAMONAS recordings are said to act directly to train us to habitually counteract these inappropriate stress related reflexes.

The SAMONAS training may also activate or reactivate unused or unexercised neural pathways which, in turn, may allow for improved reception and assimilation of information. The hope is that the student/client will continue to improve both listening and cognitive abilities because, once started, improved "listening" becomes habitual and automatic (unconscious).

b. How is "Information" Conveyed by Sound?

Particular tones seem to universally evoke certain response patterns. Low tones, for example, carry little information compared to high tones but do tend to evoke movement and even flight, which may have had survival value. Deep tones and drumming rhythms have been used to evoke group responses since primitive times. High tones, on the other hand, may be used to evoke joyous activity. High tones are also used to convey information about distance, direction and what is producing the sound.

The character of sound is contained within the harmonics or overtones. In the most basic sense, a flute, piano, violin, horn and the human voice would all sound the same if one only heard the same fundamental tone from each. However, there is no such possibility in nature. All natural sounds have complex harmonics which give the character to the source of that sound. If a sound was at a frequency of 100 Hz (cycles per second) the harmonics or overtones would be whole number multiples of the fundamental 100 Hz frequency or 200, 300, 400, 500 Hz and so on with each frequency multiple being lower in amplitude than the last. The decrease in amplitude is not simple and linear. It depends upon the source of the sound. The pattern of the amplitudes of the harmonics of a particular fundamental tone is different for each source. The pattern of the amplitudes of the harmonics is called the *formant* and is different for each instrument. It is the *formant* that makes the same note played on a flute so easily distinguished from the same tone played on a violin. Thus it is these higher amplitude harmonics of each tone which carry and convey the information, the 'colour or timbre, which tells us the unique character of the sound's source. It is the overtones that allow us to identify the tiny nuances of verbal tones which convey mood and subtle meanings.

In our modern urban world our ears are unfortunately continuously bombarded with both high and low frequency noise (e.g., cars, electrical appliances, music and so on) which for our own sanity and in order to listen to sounds which are important (e.g., speech) we must habitually tune out. We automatically train ourselves to unconsciously narrow our acoustic perception. Both in our response to stress and to sound we have to some degree become automatons and narrowed our capability for choice in our response patterns.

SAMONAS may offer clients an opportunity to relearn how to relax and to listen. It offers an opportunity for renewed choice.

c. How Does SAMONAS Promote Relaxation and Listening Skills?

SONUS: The first step was the production of recordings which differed from those made on tape and even those found on most CDs. These differed in that they reproduced the depth, direction and true natural character of the original sounds. This applied to sounds heard in nature or in the concert hall. This music did more than just sound nice for relaxing, it actually exercised listening skills in terms of giving far

more information than past recordings of the same music or sounds had been able to do using conventional recording equipment and techniques. The name *SONUS* was used to describe these recordings. *SONUS* means: System of Optimal Natural Structure.

SAMONAS: The next technological advance involved taking this system one step further to exercise our ability to listen for the information contained in the high frequency harmonics or overtones of the recorded sounds. This was accomplished through highly specialized developments in recording technology and techniques in the Klangstudio Lambdoma Studio in Germany under the direction of Ingo Steinbach. In this step they, figuratively speaking, placed an envelope around the *formant* of tones and slightly increased its amplitude. They then chose certain music to stimulate the left (cognitive processing) or the right (calming of emotions) hemispheres of the brain and increased the amplitude of these higher, information carrying frequencies to the right and left ears respectively. They then went one step further and in some recordings would exercise laterality by changing the ear to which the increased volume was directed. SAMONAS means: Spectrally Activated Music of Optimal Natural Structure. It is *SONUS* with the spectrum of harmonics for the fundamental tones activated to increase contrast and the informational content of the sounds.

In these recordings the overall volume of a piece will decrease at certain points in the music. This has the effect of attracting the attention of the listener. In the SAMONAS process there is still an increase in the information contained in the output of the recording. This is achieved by increasing the relative amplitude of the higher frequency harmonics or partial tones and increasing contrasts within the music. Steinbach's work in Germany has built upon the earlier work of the French audiologist, Tomatis. Using modern technology, Steinbach has been able to raise the high frequency formants which is particularly important because the human ear is most sensitive to sounds in the frequency range important for speech (2 to 4 KHz). Volume for frequencies higher or lower than this must be 10 to 100 times greater to enable these frequencies to be perceived.

d. Bone Conduction: It has been reported that clients may achieve faster improvement

using bone rather than air conduction. This may be due to the fact that humans are quite capable of unconsciously turning off middle ear conduction through tension of the stapedius and tympanic muscles. This tuning out is by-passed by bone conduction.

e. Evidence

There are no controlled studies using SAMONAS Sound Therapy. There is a great deal of anecdotal evidence and the theoretical rational appears reasonable. In addition, we do not know of any untoward effects. Much of the recorded music is by Mozart and there is increasing evidence that Mozart's music has rhythms which reinforce natural brain rhythms. John Hughes, a neurologist and epileptologist, has reported decreased seizure activity when patients listened to Mozart.

D. Biofeedback Assessment - Method
1. Introduction

Biofeedback of autonomic nervous system parameters and muscle tension indicators helps the client gain a relaxed, yet highly alert mental state. When combined with neurofeedback (NFB), it assists the client to improve mental flexibility and combine this with physical readiness to achieve optimal mind-body functioning. The first step in this process is to help your client make their goals for doing BFB clear. We find the easiest way to do this is to use Socratic questioning to bring out a logical and achievable set of objectives for a particular client.

It is helpful to understand the normal psychophysiological baseline pattern for the autonomic nervous system and the usual changes to this pattern when a person is subject to a stressor. A diagrammatic representation of this is given below with thanks to Marjorie Toomin. In this diagram the 'y' axis is amplitude and the 'x' axis is time. (Note: There are exceptions to the usual response to a stressor; for example, a person who has been under unremitting, chronic stress may show an atypical response - temperature rises and EDR goes flat with a new stressor.)

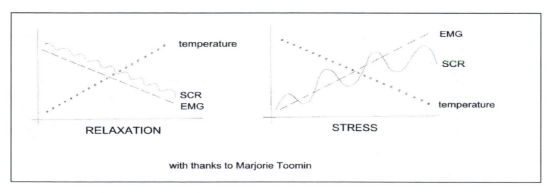

with thanks to Marjorie Toomin

2. Goal Setting With the Client

Each client should understand a little about the functions and the physiology of the ANS. The essential areas of the body served by the sympathetic and parasympathetic nervous systems have been outlined and illustrated in Section V, "Neuroanatomy".

a. Tools for Optimal Performance States (TOPS)

Before starting training with adults we discuss objectives for training. Their objectives are

clarified as work proceeds with them using a structured interview and filling in a one page questionnaire. This questionnaire correlates typical client objectives to the parameters that can be measured with combined BFB/NFB equipment. A score from 1 to 10 (high level achievement is a 10) is assigned to each area of our Biofeedback Institute's TOPS Evaluation. TOPS is our acronym of **Tools for Optimal Performance States**. Note that we use the plural, states, to reflect the reality that there is more than one optimal performance state. The state varies with task demands. This form is shown below.

TOPS Evaluation
(A structured interview.)

(<u>Describe</u> beneath or in margin <u>times when you are exactly the opposite</u> to the problem area you are working on during your training sessions. (e.g., I'm a very calm leader in catastrophic situations but I worry a lot about little things in daily life.)

A ____

A.   State of Physiological Readiness

1. **Relaxed**
   - **Objective:** To broaden associative capabilities and perspective, increase reaction time and decrease fatigue, tension and stress.
   - **Measurement:** ↑Peripheral temperature, ↓Pulse rate, ↓Respiration rate, ↓EMG, moderate EDR, ↓ 20 – 23 Hz activity.

1 ____

2. **Alert**
   - **Objective:** To efficiently respond to new information. (State of eustress)
   - **Measurement:** moderate increase in EDR (arousal & performance relate in an inverted U shaped curve), plus increases in 12 Hz & low Beta (15 - 18 Hz).

2 ____

B.   State of Mental Readiness

B ____

3. **Calm**
   - **Objective:** To allow reflection and consideration of alternative approaches.
   - **Measurement:** ↑SMR (13-15 Hz), ↓high beta (22-34 Hz); ↑peripheral skin temperature, Respiration.(diaphragmatic), ↓EMG, EDR (control), ↓Pulse, ↑RSA (synchrony) at approximately 6 BrPM.

3 ____

4. **Aware**
   - **Objective:** To broaden input range - a state of calm readiness (as in Sports: Goalie, Martial Arts, Golf, Archery…) and increase creativity.
   - **Measurement:** 11 – 13 Hz↑.

4 ____

5. **Reflective**
   - **Objective:** To increase accuracy, breadth and completeness of responses.
   - **Measurement:** Bursts of Alpha 11-13 Hz and Beta 15-18 Hz and brief bursts of theta (with memory retrieval).

5 ____

6. **Optimistic in Attitude**

6 ____

C.   State of Active Mental Work

C ____

7. **Focused**
   - **Objective:** To maintain attention to work area.
   - **Measurement:** Decreased Slow waves (ϕ & low α) - Increased fast waves (β)

7 ____

8. **Concentrating & Creative**
   Objective:
   a. To problem solve, elaborate on ideas and make decisions (↑β 16-18 Hz).
   b. To have 'fluency of ideas' and be creative (↑left hemisphere bursts of 11-13 Hz α activity; sometimes, a semi-hypnagogic state with ↑4-8Hz
   Measurement: Beta shows- controlled increase 15-20 Hz (39 - 42 Hz) + 'shifts' to high Alpha. Theta states can also be produced at will when internally and creatively oriented.

8a ____

8b ____

9. a.) Strategic Goal Oriented Approach with b.) Openness to New Innovation & a Commitment to Objectives & Time Management   9a _____

- **Objective:** To work efficiently and effectively without constricting response possibilities. Apply Active Learning Techniques (see section XII, Metacognitive Strategies) & SMIRB (Stop My Irritating Ruminations Book).   9b_____
- **Measurement:** Cognitive & Metacognitive Strategies, Goals are written down, Techniques for handling stress are utilized (especially breathing)

10.   Flexible yet Decisive

- **Objective:** Respond with openness & thoughtfulness & appropriate flexibility to   10 _____
new ideas while remaining able to make decisions & commit to a goal.
- **Measurement:** Find and weigh the positives in each new situation and decide on direction & actions.

ULTIMATE GOAL: Self-regulate to achieve 'flow'

Flow _____

⇒ **Flow** ⇐   **Flow** is as easy as ABC:

A & B - setting the stage: **C -** Performing & Producing

Put it all together, automatically, to be Efficient - Effective - Productive

---

This form is just a tool. It is used initially to structure a discussion with the client concerning their goals for combined NFB and BFB training. Some clients use it only at the beginning of their training to help them understand more clearly their goals and the kind of work they are going to do in sessions to achieve these goals. Other clients may find it helpful to use the form, and their written comments around each section, on a regular basis to guide them through the training and to decide when they have met their training goals and are ready to graduate from training.

The reverse side of this form is the "Psychophysiological Profile" (illustrated below). It lists scores for measurements in each of these areas. These scores should be put into the appropriate areas of the form with the client. This is done after completing the EEG assessment and the stress test. This is discussed again with the client in the first few sessions in order to clarify objectives for each area of feedback. It is reviewed from time to time as training proceeds.

training session. This is not a research assessment protocol. It is a practical, clinical approach to clarify what general biofeedback modalities, if any, would be important for training. We want to observe changes in respiration including rate, depth and regularity. We like to be able to see the same types of changes in heart rate: regularity, rate, and extent of variability in rate. To do this requires a screen which shows respiration and the heart rate variations that occur with inspiration and expiration as linegraphs. It is desirable, with the client, to be able to correlate these changes visually with changes in peripheral skin temperature, EDR and forehead EMG. In our center we find that the "Assessment Summary Screen" is helpful. It is illustrated below. This screen allows for a quick statistical analysis and graphic display. Using this kind of display, it takes no more than ten to fifteen minutes for the majority of our clients to see the effects of stress, contrast these with relaxation, and connect this information to their goals for training.   The process begins in the first interview with a quick stress test.

E. The Psychophysiological Stress Profile

1. Stress Assessment

A rapid stress test can be done during the EEG assessment session or at the beginning of the first

2. A Quick Stress Test

In the stress assessment we want the client to begin in as relaxed a manner as possible. They sit in a comfortable chair and close their eyes. We then explain that we are going to ask them to carry out two tasks that are meant to be emotionally uncomfortable. The first will be to think of and, if possible, mentally experience a very depressing, stressful event. After about three minutes you change the task and ask them to do mental math that will be challenging. After those two stressors they open their eyes and work on some relaxation techniques with guidance regarding how to breathe. Then we will review with them how their body's physiology responded during the test.

The steps for doing a quick assessment are as follows:

a. **Put on all the sensors** explaining as you do so what each sensor is going to measure. Tell the client that there will be a *baseline* with eyes closed and then two stressful tasks with their eyes closed: imagining (re-living) a stressful event and doing challenging mental math. This will take about 6 minutes. Then they will open their eyes and watch the screen while you teach them some relaxation techniques. When you have finished putting on the sensors and explaining what you are going to do, ask the client to relax and close their eyes.

b. **Collect data without stress** for 1 to 3 minutes to obtain a baseline for that individual. After 1- 3 minutes place a marker on the data (*marker #1*) if your instrument allows you to do this. Otherwise note the exact time. (Note: In the example given below you will note that we only used 2 markers – as long as you write down what you are doing and the times when you change tasks, you may vary the type of stress, timing, and markers.)

c. Now ask the client to **imagine a stress producing situation** (*a personally perceived potential adaptive incompetency [Thompson, 1979]*) for 3 to 5 minutes. Reassure them beforehand that they will not be telling you what it was that they were imagining. Tell them to really put themselves fully, emotionally, into this stressful image. There must not be any distracting sounds during this phase. After 3 to 5 minutes again place a marker on the data collection (*marker #2*).

d. At this point, have the client carry out a **cognitive task** which is designed to progressively increase in difficulty until it is impossible to do (In most instances you don't let the client know that this is what you are doing.) Two examples are as follows:

Use one of the following tests (or an equivalent) and after about 3 minutes again place a marker on the data collection (*marker #3*).

- **The Stroop Color Test**: This test is done with eyes open watching a special display on the computer screen. This test uses words which name a color. However, the name of the color does not match the color of the ink used to print the word. For example, the word *green* might be printed in red ink. The client must say the color the word is printed in. On one program sold by *Thought Technology*, called the *Biograph Stress Protocol*, this test is done with a very fast rate of display so that it becomes quite stressful.

- **A mental math test** for adolescents and adults: The assessor says two digits (3, 5) and the client must add them (3 + 5 = 8). The assessor then states one further digit (7). The client must now add this digit to the last digit spoken previously by the examiner (7 + 5 = 12). The series might progress as follows: 3, 5, (8); 7,(12); 2,(9); 39,(41) 63(102)…

Other, not so stressful math tests are as follows:
- Some clinicians use '**serial sevens**'. In this test you tell the client to begin at 200 (900 for teens and adults) and subtract 7. They should continue subtracting 7 until they are close to 0. They then start over again and see if they end at the same number. The advantage of this is that they do not speak during the assessment so you have less EMG artifact if you are recording the EEG. They feel stressed because you have said that they will tell you the final number they reach when the time ends or when they are close to zero.

- Another mental math test is the one Sterman recommends when doing full cap assessments, the Paced Auditory Serial Addition Task (PASAT). It can be found on the SKIL website (skiltopo.com).

e. At this juncture teach the client **methods for relaxing**. Ask the client to open their eyes and tense their shoulders hard for about 10 seconds. Then completely relax and feel their muscles relaxing from their forehead through their jaw, neck, shoulder, upper arm, forearm, to their hands. They should now feel their hands getting heavier and warmer. After about a minute, as they are doing this, again place a marker on the data collection (*marker #4*).

f. Now ask the client to continue with this relaxation and feeling of warmth while they follow your breathing. You demonstrate diaphragmatic breathing and ask if they see your shoulders move at all. They don't. Now they are to do it. They must only breathe by moving their abdomen in and out. They can pretend that they have a balloon in their tummy and are inflating and deflating the balloon. They also can pretend they have a glass balanced on each of their shoulders and they do not want their shoulders or chest to move or the glass would fall off and break. (You must judge if a particular client would find this second image stressful. If they would, omit it.)

Tell your client that you will purposely make a sound as you inhale and exhale and that you will indicate *breathing in* with your hand moving up and *breathing out* with your hand moving down. The client is to follow this paced breathing as you give soft encouragement. You breathe evenly, regularly, at 6 breaths per minute. 'Thsssssssssssss' = in, and 'phhhhhhhh' = out, then say "rest" before you begin to inhale again ('Thsssssss') and so on. Your client can watch their respiration and their cardiac variability on the linegraphs on the display screen.

Now place marker #5 on the data and do this breathing and relaxation exercise with the client for 3 to 8 minutes. With most clients you will observe the finger temperature rising, EMG, EDR and heart rate dropping and a synchrony between heart variability and their breathing. Once they are achieving an appropriate relaxed state, as indicated by the physiological variable being measured, stop the recording and save the data.

Case Example

John, age 39, was asked to think of a stressful life event after about 30 seconds of relaxing. In the example screen shown below, we did not use a marker at that point. At 3 ½ minutes (marker #1) we began the math task. At 5 ½ minutes (marker #2) we ended the math task and began the relaxation. The relaxation instructions for this took less than a minute and he began to breathe

evenly at a rate of about 5 to 6 BrPM. The EMG recording on the forehead and back of the neck in this client did not demonstrate major changes in this short time period and were left out of the above graph. Each client will demonstrate a unique combination of physiological responses to stress and relaxation. In training you will want to use those measurements that demonstrate change clearly to the client. Most often, we find that respiratory rate corresponds to the other changes in EMG, EDR, and temperature and we often use it on feedback screens. If alertness is a problem (as in clients with ADD), then EDR is also used. The client should be relaxed but also alert.

With John, when the most difficult math questions were asked, his heart rate rose as high as 96 averaging about 90. It fell to about 70 with relaxation. During the math task John's skin temperature fell from 94.5 to 91.6 degrees Fahrenheit and his EDR rose from 4.6 to 9 μMhos. Respiration became irregular, shallow and rapid rising to as high as 74 breaths per minute (BrPM). Marker #2 was placed when the math test ended and he was told that he would now learn a method for relaxing. He was then instructed on how to breathe diaphragmatically at 6 BrPM. As he did this, his peripheral skin temperature rose and his EDR fell. His pulse rate decreased. His breathing became deep and regular at 6 BrPM. There began to be symmetry between respiration (inspiration and expiration) and heart rate (increasing and decreasing). He felt subjectively calm, relaxed and alert.

3. Assessment Summary – Graphic Representation and Statistics

Now you can review the data with your client. The assessment summary graph shows a display screen from the *Procomp+/Biograph* that can be used. It graphs time against amplitude or rate for each of the parameters in a manner that allows the client to see clearly how all the parameters changed with each task or condition.

a. Summary Graph

Assessment Summary Screen for ANS Variables

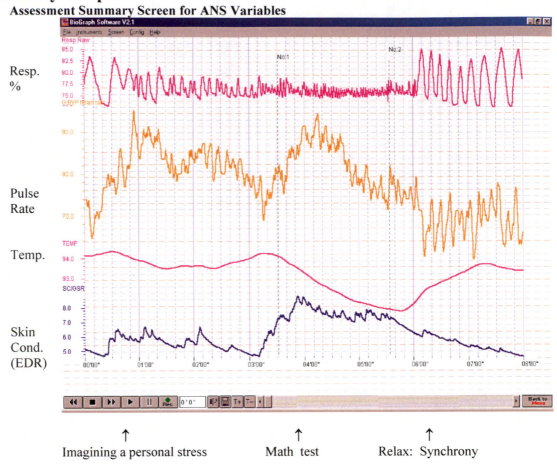

Resp. %

Pulse Rate

Temp.

Skin Cond. (EDR)

↑ Imagining a personal stress   ↑ Math test   ↑ Relax: Synchrony

Psychophysiological Feedback

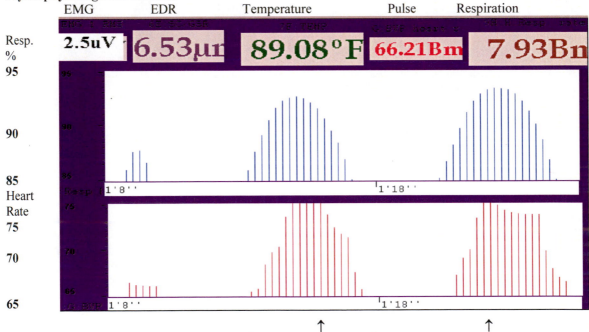

Note the synchrony (arrows) between increasing and decreasing heart rate (below) with respiratory inspiration and expiration (above).

The psychophysiological feedback is the screen that John, a 39 year old man, was looking at as he learned to relax his forehead and shoulders, warm his hands and breathe diaphragmatically and regularly at a rate of about 6 breaths per minute. His heart rate was increasing with inspiration and decreasing with expiration. In the above 20 second period he has decreased his breathing rate to 7.9 breaths per minute. He is attempting to raise his peripheral skin temperature as he relaxes. His electrodermal response (EDR) rose to 18 with stress. It should not decrease much more than the current 6.5 mhos as he relaxes or he will become less alert. His forehead EMG had risen with stress to $>9\mu V$ but is now dropping and has reached $2.5\mu V$ as he becomes calmer. With further training he did begin to hold it between $0.9 - 1.6 \mu V$ even with a mental math stress. Many clients show EMG readings on their forehead of 9 to 15 μV when they enter training and these will drop to between 1 and 2 μV with biofeedback training.

During Regular Training Sessions

In his training sessions, John had a respiration linegraph and a numerical counter (breaths per minute) on the feedback screen while he was using brain wave feedback to help him decrease nonproductive ruminating and increase a calm state of focused, problem-solving concentration.

As training progressed, John was able to think of stressful things in his life and even do a math stress test while remaining calm as evidenced both by the measured variables and by his subjective experience. John practiced the diaphragmatic breathing, muscle relaxation and hand warming when answering stressful calls at work and while listening to others in social situations.

We suggest that you carry out some type of stress assessment when you commence work with an adult client, at intervals during training, and at the end of training. The above example gives a quick psychophysiological stress profile. A more comprehensive assessment, where you give time for recovery to baseline after each stress, is described later in this chapter.

b. Recording your Data - Statistics

When you have shown your client the graphic profile (above) and they have understood how even a mild, artificial stress situation can affect so many physiological variables, then you should record the data with your client. The form displayed below is one way of doing this. You can write in your client's ratios if your equipment generates this data.

Psychophysiological Profile
Biofeedback Institute of Toronto

MEASUREMENT & Objective	PRE	POST	Associated with	COMMENTS
Neurofeedback (EEG Biofeedback) May be combined with learning metacognitive strategies.				
Theta **3 - 5 Hz** **4 - 8 Hz** ($\Downarrow$ amplitude & variability)			**Tuned out**	Variability is reduced with control of tuning out. (Example: The goal on the F1000 is ≤ 35 units on 20 overlapping 30" screens at smoothing factor of 5) Variability is a very sensitive measure but it fluctuates with time frame & averaging. Therefore, you must have a standard format for measuring this variable.
7 & 8 Hz			**Visualizing?**	Test this – ask the client to visualize

				a flower while you observe EEG.
8.5 - 9 Hz			Dissociation?	
Low Alpha 9 - 10 Hz (↓ for external focus) (↓ Left frontal in depression)			**Internal orientation,** reflection, meditation	Ratio α/β = , Relaxation
High Alpha 11 - 13 Hz (Shifts to high alpha states in the left hemisphere of right handed individuals)			**Creativity,** Broad awareness, Flow of ideas, Peak performance	Observe internal mental manipulation of ideas, concepts
SMR 13 -15 Hz (↑ if impulsive & if emotionally labile) (↑ if anxiety, Asperger's) (↑ if seizures, movement disorders - Tourettes, dystonia & Parkinson's)			**Calm self control,** **Reflection before action,** **Control movement,**	Ratio φ/SMR =
Low Beta 15 – 18 Hz (↑ in ADD & LD) (↑ left frontal in depression)			**Focused concentration,** Decision making, problem solving.	Ratio φ/β = , External input (but genius on easy task needs little time in beta - low amplitude.)
Mid Range Beta 19-23 Hz			**Anxiety, Emotionally Intense**	
High Beta 24 – 34 Hz (↓ in tense, overly intense subjects)			**Ruminations, Too Intense - "spinning your wheels"**	Like driving a car - foot pressed to floor on gas pedal but car left in first gear.
Sheer Rhythm 38 - 42 Hz (↑ focused creativity)			**Attention and Problem solving**	May be hard to measure due to EMG artifact.

BIOFEEDBACK				
May be combined with SAMONAS sound therapy & relaxation exercises.				
EDR (Electrodermal Response) (↓ if Over-arousal / ↑ if Under-arousal) Attain "Eustress" state			**Arousal level** - often low in ADD - may be labile & high if anxious, Flat with chronic stress	↑**for alertness** ↓ **if tense,** **Stabilize if labile**
Peripheral Skin Temperature (Vasodilatation / vasoconstriction - try for 94° - 96°F.)			**Low if anxious, fearful.**	⇑ **to relax -** particularly during tasks.
Pulse (also **Blood Volume** measurements)			**High if anxious**	⇓ **rate & ⇑ variation in synchrony** with inspiration and expiration
Respiration - Diaphragmatic			**Anxiety: Rate ↑,** irregular, shallow	⇓ **rate** to ≈ 6 & more **regular** with increased depth.
RSA (respiratory sinus arrhythmia) Sympathetic / parasympathetic balance			**Anxiety: irregular** breathing and heart rate which are not synchronous	**For Relaxation** ⇑ synchrony & amplitude of heart rate variation with inspiration and expiration

Note: RSA is the self regulation of breathing for maximum heart rate variability.

4. Alternative ANS and EMG Assessment Technique

a. Putting on the Sensors

Though doing a stress profile may be routine for the person providing neurofeedback and biofeedback sessions, remember that it is all new to most clients. This necessitates being careful and relaxed in your approach. Explain everything before you do it, going step by step. There are a large number of sensors when doing an ANS and EMG initial assessment. Some patients may feel a bit overwhelmed and even frightened by this. Patients attending a pain clinic may show distress if any strap feels too tight. Some patients may demonstrate psychological and/or physiological hypersensitivity even to light touch. The trainer should show each sensor to the client and briefly describe **what** it measures, **how** it does it and **why** this could be important to the client whose psychophysiology is being assessed. In addition, giving the client a simple printed sheet with an illustration showing the sensors on a person with a brief succinct description of the foregoing "what, how and why" can be very helpful. The trainer should continuously check with the client that they are comfortable with how the sensors are being put on. The trainer should obtain the client's permission for each thing they do.

The sensors are placed as described under the section on a brief ANS / EMG assessment above. An additional EMG placement may be used, however, to monitor changes in upper body tension. The ground and +ve electrodes are placed on one forearm and the –ve electrode is placed on the other forearm. Psychologist Stephen Sideroff at UCLA teaches this placement in workshops as a good way to get an overview of total upper body tension.

The purpose of this assessment is slightly different from the foregoing brief stress assessment. In the foregoing brief assessment the purpose was, first, to allow the client an opportunity to observe how the various parameters changed with stress and, second, to observe how rapidly they could bring these variables under control by following the instructor's example and instructions for relaxation for 3 to 5 minutes.

There is a third, additional objective for the more formal and lengthy assessment outlined below:

namely, to measure how long it takes the client to recover to their base line values after being given a variety of stresses. Three stressors and three recovery periods are used.

b. A Sequence of Steps for this Stress Assessment:

This assessment is done in a series of steps. After each step there is a 3 minute period of time allowed for recovery. A suggested series of steps is as follows:

1. **Base line for 3 minutes**. The client sits comfortably. They may look at the screen if they wish to.
2. **Breath rapidly for 1 minute**. This is a physiological stress. Breathing is shallow and rapid. Most clients will demonstrate a shift in baseline for a number of the parameters being measured.
3. **Base line / rest period for 3 minutes**. Clients will vary in the length of time required to recover. For some clients, some variables may not fully return to base line values.
4. **Math test.** Either use one of the math tests described previously or ask the client to subtract serial 7's from 900 (893, 886, 879, etc.) out loud after being told that they are being checked for speed and accuracy. The math tests are a real-life stress for most clients as was noted in the previous description of a stress assessment.
5. **Base line / rest period** for 3 minutes. The recovery period may be quite long for some clients. This may be particularly true for clients who demonstrate performance anxiety.
6. **Talk about a very stressful time** in their life for 3 to 5 minutes. This test is quite useful but it should, however, only be carried out with a person whom the client accepts as a therapist. If the examiner is not the client's therapist, then the client can be asked to close their eyes and try to visualize and emotionally relive a very stressful event without talking about it. Alternatively, the client can imagine an event that would be extremely stressful if it should occur in the future.
7. **Baseline / rest period** for 3 minutes. With anxious clients, the ability to

compartmentalize may be compromised and recovery after this task may be incomplete and lengthy.

8. See if the client can **learn to relax** even further than their usual baseline over a 3 –5 minute period. This final phase is the same as the previous, quick ANS assessment. The trainer models being calm and relaxed and encourages the client to breathe diaphragmatically at a rate of 6 breaths per minute. Many clients will be able to demonstrate for themselves that they are capable of changing most of the variables being monitored as they follow the trainer's instructions.

c. Examine the Data

One of the easiest variables for the client to understand is upper body tension. Most clients have experienced a feeling of tension in their neck and shoulders. *Muscle bracing*, in addition to autonomic reactivity, is a common finding. Although changes with stress may vary from one client to another, most clients will have one or two variables that show a marked shift with stress. The variable showing the largest shift, however, may not be the same one that demonstrates a slow recovery to baseline values. How well the client returns to base line is one of the most important variables for the biofeedback therapist. If you do not return to the baseline, then you will accumulate stress over the course of a day. In addition, clients will react differently to different stressors. All of these variables should be noted and discussed with the client.

John's skin temperature only varied by one to three degrees. However, it was the one variable that did not return to the original baseline during the 3 minute rest period. It, therefore, qualified as a sensitive indicator of John's ability to adjust, self regulate, and recover. The NFB trainer monitored John's skin temperature during the NFB training sessions. John found ways to associate relaxing with raising his skin temperature rapidly after stressors. John used a small portable monitor at home and work and found he could rapidly have his skin temperature recover to 94.5°F even during stressful phone calls by relaxing and using diaphragmatic breathing, both before picking up the phone and during the phone calls. He began to make better business responses to clients when he was in a calm, relaxed state. These home use temperature

monitors are readily available and are very cheap.

During the assessment the easiest variable for John to self-regulate was breathing. Obtaining good RSA was observed in the last step of the initial assessment sequence when diaphragmatic breathing at 6 BrPM was taught. Good RSA was observed to correlate with other variables returning to baseline status (except for temperature). This was the reason that John used diaphragmatic breathing to help him relax quickly during stressful events while he monitored his skin temperature. During training sessions John used both temperature and respiration feedback instruments, in addition to the NFB instruments which fed back information concerning levels of SMR and high beta. The SMR frequencies were reinforced and the high beta , in the range indicative of anxiety , was inhibited.

John was like many other clients in that he would become quite sleepy as he began to relax. This did not benefit his ability to focus, concentrate and problem solve. The trainer, therefore, had John do the feedback sessions in an upright sitting position with excellent posture. Skin conduction was monitored during each session. He had to make sure that it did not drop into a range that, for him, represented a loss of alertness. John's work performance improved and his family life became relaxed and fun as he learned self regulation techniques.

d. Theory and Objectives

Recovery to base line levels is an important indicator of good physiological and psychological health. It is important to retest this variable as BFB training proceeds. Even in normal daily living there are many periods of time between stress and no stress. Autonomic balance is best in those persons who are able to return to a calm and relaxed baseline between stressors. If you do not return to baseline, the stress becomes cumulative and you may reach the point of overload, or become "stressed-out", in layman's terms.

Some clients remain in a physiologically stressed state because they know that there will be another stress coming in a couple of hours. It is much better if your client can learn to 'compartmentalize', so that they can relax between known stressors. Persons who are able to rapidly return to a calm, relaxed physiological state are said to be 'resilient'. Thus a major goal of BFB treatment is to learn how to return to baseline, even though you know there will be another stress. This newly learned 'baseline state' should be one that is even more relaxed, with less sympathetic arousal (drive) than was observed in their original base line.

Our goal is not total relaxation, such as reclining in a chaise longue on a beach. We want the client to maintain motivation and alertness. The client should be able to enter a *eustress* state that Hans Selye discussed (Selye, 1976). Eustress is that level of stress which is optimal for a person. Remember the inverted "U" ($\cap$) eustress curve where the y-axis is performance and the x-axis is stress. Performance is poor both with low stress and high stress and is optimal in between. This can be drawn as an inverted 'u' shaped curve with performance as the 'y' axis and stress as the 'x' axis.

e. Office Environment

There should always be a relaxed time period before you begin a BFB session. If a client rushed to get to your office, their baseline measurements will reflect this physiological state. In the office you should maintain the environmental conditions to be as constant as possible as you do biofeedback. Room temperature must be comfortable. When it is cold in the winter, a time period is needed to acclimatize before a client begins their biofeedback session. If at all possible, the client should train at the same time of day. As discussed previously under NFB, circadian rhythms and our responses to stress and relaxation will change with the time of day. Some BFB therapists will train their clients to relax and then hope to have this training generalize to outside situations. In our center we have clientele who are attempting to optimize their performance in school, business or athletics. We want the office situation to vary from silent and conducive to relaxing, to being more like a normal classroom or office, busy and noisy. We, therefore, leave doors open and, as the client improves, even allow interruptions such as the telephone ringing or staff coming in to ask questions. We also ask the client to use the "attach-a-new-habit-to-an-old-habit" technique, as described previously, to assist in this generalization process.

5. Beginning Training Sessions

Start BFB sessions using muscle tension and relaxation exercises because the client can see the changes in EMG easily. Then do diaphragmatic breathing combined with pulse rate variability feedback to follow RSA. Breathing at 6 BrPM, the client can learn to rapidly turn on a calm relaxed state. Remember the phrase, "When your breathing is relaxed, you are relaxed". When doing the breathing, the client practices feeling heaviness in their shoulders and warmth in their hands.

It is important always to remember that during the early stage of training, the trainer's verbal feedback is more important than the instrument feedback. The trainer should set the instrument thresholds and the goals so that rewards are achieved readily while still having it difficult enough to make them shift in the right direction. It is important for the client to experience success in the initial stage of training.

Change, not absolute values, is the important factor in biofeedback training. For example, the same self-regulation learning is taking place if the patient moves from 24 to 9 as from 12 to 2 in the EMG values. No matter how tense the client may be, they can learn to lower muscle tension. It is very important, however, that the client sees success and that they not become discouraged at the beginning of treatment. The client must understand that training proceeds in small steps but these steps are truly significant and that, little by little, they will acquire the skill of relf-regulation.

6. Monitoring BFB Variables During a Session

It can be quite valuable to review how some of the variables you are measuring changed with different events during a regular training session. The example given below is taken from the statistics screen of an F1000 instrument. The client in this case was receiving EDR, peripheral skin temperature, and EEG feedback. In the diagram below only the EDR (green line with sharp peaks) and skin temperature (red line with handwritten words along it) recording is shown.

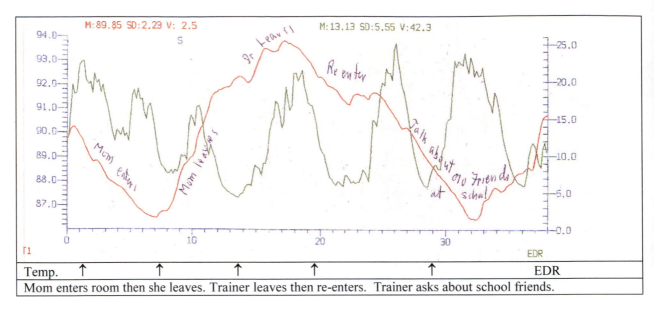

Temp.	↑	↑	↑	↑	↑	EDR

Mom enters room then she leaves. Trainer leaves then re-enters. Trainer asks about school friends.

Daniel was a bright 14 year old student/client. He was training to improve his attention span and concentration and increase his ability to remain calm and reflect before acting. Daniel had always been a loner. It wasn't that he didn't want to socialize with the other children, it was just that every time he tried he seemed to say or do the wrong thing and he would end up being teased and rejected by his peers. Daniel had learned that it was easier to stay with much younger children who would follow his interests. Daniel was quite anxious and his rather odd behaviour could be better understood if one took this into account. Daniel couldn't understand innuendo. He was very concrete in his interpretation of what others were saying and often drew the wrong meaning from expressions that were used in the school yard because he took them literally. Other children took advantage of this to encourage him to do things that he shouldn't and then laugh at him. Daniel was diagnosed with Asperger's syndrome.

In the example above, Daniel became very anxious when his mother came in to watch the session. In the above recording, skin temperature fell and EDR rose. He was greatly relieved when she left and you can see how his skin temperature rose and his EDR tended to fall as he settled back to focus just on feedback (EEG, EDR and finger temperature). The trainer then left the room for a moment to speak to his mother and his physiology indicates that he felt even calmer. When the trainer re-entered the room Daniel's EDR rose and skin temperature decreased. When the trainer then introduced the topic of how he was socializing at school his

temperature dropped precipitously and his EDR again rose. At the 32 minute mark this discussion was finished and Daniel talked about his favourite hobby. His skin temperature began to rise and his EDR fell.

In the sessions Daniel learned to associate diaphragmatic breathing with increasing his EEG sensorimotor rhythm (SMR) 13-15 Hz. He learned that when he relaxed, his skin temperature and EDR were less variable. As Daniel progressed he began to have less fluctuation in skin temperature and EDR and he was able to apply suggestions for socializing with his peers. By the time he stopped sessions he was being invited to parties given by peers. His special interest in electronics and music allowed him to help set up the music systems for these parties. In this way he turned his special interest into a socially useful attribute.

7. Biofeedback has been found to be Effective

It isn't the purpose of this text to teach biofeedback. This has been very well described in other texts such as those by Andreassi (1984), Basmajian (1989), Fuller (1984), and Schwartz (1995). Nevertheless, it is important for the reader to recognize that there are a reasonable number of studies demonstrating, for the most part, significant improvement in a wide variety of disorders using biofeedback. An excellent **review of biofeedback research** has been done by **Carolyn B. Yucha**, Associate Dean for

Research at the University of Florida with the assistance of Donald Moss and Pam Sherwill. It is likely that this will be published in 2003. We have only made a very brief overview of areas where BFB may be helpful in the outline below.

Anxiety may be decreased using EMG frontal biofeedback or EEG alpha biofeedback (Rice, 1994, Sarkar, 1999). Thermal biofeedback (Hawkins, 1980) and GSR (Fehring, 1983) biofeedback have also been shown to reduce anxiety. Astin et al. have done a review of studies using mainly thermal and EMG biofeedback for arthritis (Astin, 2002). Flor demonstrated that a reduction in pain could be maintained (Flor, 1986). Beneficial effects in asthma have been demonstrated using self-regulation of breathing for maximum heart rate variability (RSA) (Lehrer, 2000). We also recommend that the reader learn this valuable technique and combine it with neurofeedback. Richard Gevirtz gives excellent workshops on RSA at the annual meetings of the Association of Applied Psychophysiology and Biofeedback (AAPB). There are questions concerning improvement of immune function that require further study (Taylor, 1995). Chronic pain is an important area for research. Reduction in abdominal pain with thermal biofeedback has been demonstrated (Humphreys, 2000). It would be entirely logical that immune function, chronic pain and fibromyalgia could be improved by biofeedback (see Section V, J, under The *neurophysiology of the stress response*). Back pain has been helped by EMG biofeedback (Vlaeyn, 1995). Thermal biofeedback to improve blood flow has proven useful in improving the healing of non-healing foot ulcers in diabetics (Rice, 2001).

Urinary incontinence is one of the best investigated areas for traditional BFB. There are well controlled studies demonstrating its effectiveness (Dougherty 2001, Sung, 2000, Sherman, 1997, van Kampen, 2000). A review of fecal incontinence demonstrates success using biofeedback in a proportion of cases. (Heyman, 2001). Even vulvar vestibulitis has been effectively treated with BFB (Bergeron 2001).

Biofeedback may be a useful treatment modality for fibromyalgia (Hadazy, 2000). EEG driven stimulation may also be helpful (Mueller, 2001). EMG feedback for hand dystonia (writer's cramp) requires further investigation (Deepak, 1999).

Headache has been investigated for years. Thermal biofeedback for childhood migraine has been found to be particularly successful (Hermann, 2002). Frontal and trapezius EMG biofeedback has also been used for headaches (Arena, 1995). Although the degree of response to biofeedback training for hypertension does vary, BFB (EMG, thermal, blood pressure, heart rate) has been shown to be an effective treatment modality, particularly if clinic training is followed by training at home (Yucha, 2001, Henderson, 1998). Both BFB (Morin, 1998) and NFB (Hauri, 1982) have been used with some success to treat insomnia. There are indications that BFB may be useful in reducing risk for persons who have suffered a myocardial infarction (Cowan, 2001). Post traumatic stress disorder has only had limited investigation but it may prove promising. (Carlson, 1998). Raynaud's disease has been helped using thermal biofeedback (Peterson, 1983, Yokum, 1985). However, results are dependent on technique (Raynauds Treatment Study Investigators, 2000, Middaugh, 2001). Thermal biofeedback has been successfully used to treat repetitive strain injuries (Moore, 1996).

Very promising work using EMG biofeedback with spinal cord injuries requires further replication (Brucker, 1996, Petrofsky, 2001). Some hemiplegic stroke patients have also benefited from EMG biofeedback (Schleenbaker, 1993, Moreland, 1998). NFB may add a very useful dimension to the rehabilitation of some stroke patients (Rozelle, 1995, Sherin, 2003). EEG biofeedback is helpful in decreasing depression and improving memory and cognitive functioning in patients who have suffered a traumatic brain injury (Shoenberger, 2001, Thornton, 2000).

Temporomandibular pain and mandibular functioning may be helped by BFB (Gardea, 2001). Tinnitus may show some improvements with either EMG BFB (Erlandsson, 1991) or NFB to increase alpha and decrease beta (Gosepath, 2001).

SECTION VIII
Fundamentals of Intervention

A. Overview: Goal Setting, Deciding On Bandwidths, Electrode Placement and How to Begin The First Training Session.

NFB and BFB are learning procedures. Although the brain is capable of extremely fast ('one trial') learning, this is not the type of learning we are trying to achieve with NFB. Usually, one-trial learning is experienced in traumatic or highly emotional circumstances. Most learning takes time and practice. Beware of exaggerated claims of quick efficacy of some new placement or protocol. You might effect a transference 'cure' in minutes with a client yet it might not last. Certainly, anyone can experience a sudden change in their neurophysiology. Think of how you might react to news that you had won a lottery. To make matters even more confusing, a high proportion of clients with ADHD are suggestible and have been shown to have higher hypnotizability. (Wickramasekara, personal communication) This is not surprising since excess theta is the marker for ADHD.

On the other side of the coin, a consistent finding by various experienced professionals is that it is difficult to effect a significant and lasting change in children when one or other of the parents is not enthusiastically supportive or, at worst, subtly (or not so subtly) undermining the process. The undermining can be done unwittingly by an anxious, well-intentioned parent who examines in detail every school report and questions why the child, on any test, has not performed as well as they had hoped. Often these parents are quite unaware that non-verbal communication is responsible for almost 80% of human communicating and that their

child is acutely aware of their concerns even though they may have been very careful "not to say anything".

Biofeedback and neurofeedback are not stand-alone interventions. They are almost always combined with other interventions that correspond to the objectives of, and for, that client. For example: diet, sleep and exercise are very important variables that need to be discussed and managed. Two quite different examples will be used as illustrations. Each example has an overview of goal setting in terms of relating the client's EEG to their personal goals.

1. Stages in Training a Child

The first example is Jason. Jason was case #3 in our introduction to Section VI: *The Basics of Assessment and Intervention.*

Jason, age 8, was very active, impulsive and could not attend for more than a few minutes during class at school. He was very bright and tremendously creative. His doctor felt he had a problem with short term memory and when tested, it was also thought that he had a central auditory processing (CAP) problem. He loved to draw and build. His EEG demonstrated extremely high 3 to 6 Hz activity and slightly lower SMR than beta. His Theta (4 – 8Hz) / Beta (13 – 21 Hz) power ratio was exceedingly high (14). Mother was concerned that his self esteem was being affected by the negative feedback he was receiving at school.

The **objectives and steps** for working with Jason were:
1st   Enhance Self Esteem
2nd   Improve Social Interactions / Behaviours
3rd   Improve Learning and Performance

These goals correlate with a sequence of 3 groups of interventions. We encourage people to group interventions this way, as we do when giving lectures on interventions for ADHD.

Urgent (Short-Term)	On-Going	Long-Term
	+ve Family environment	Neurofeedback
		plus
Behaviour Modification	Nutrition Sleep Exercise	Biofeedback
Stimulant Medication for Hyperactivity	Tutoring School	plus
		Meta-cognitive Strategies
	Extra-curricular activities *(sports, drama, music, art and so on...)*	

Jason had a supportive family. All of the first two sets of suggestions had already been set in place well before we saw Jason. Parents had read *The A.D.D. Book* (Sears & Thompson, 1998) and had worked on the positive reinforcement suggestions contained therein and heeded the dietary recommendations. Nevertheless, Jason still displayed ADHD symptoms and they wanted to do something that could make a long term change and perhaps even decrease the amount of stimulant medication he required to function in school.

Jason was a reasonably straight-forward case. We used the EEG assessment to set the bandwidths and locations for training. We worked at both Cz and C4 locations and encouraged an increase in SMR (12-15 Hz) and a decrease in theta (3-6 Hz in Jason's case). His behaviour had begun to change in a positive direction by 30 sessions. Progress testing done after 40 sessions showed improvements on parent questionnaires, TOVA and IVA scores, and theta/beta ratios, but these measures were still indicating significant inattention. He still required medication for school though it had been stopped after school and on weekends. After 60 sessions both theta and SMR had altered appropriately on retesting. His impulsivity and inappropriate high level of

activity had decreased, his attention span had increased, his measured IQ came up by 16 points and he went to the top half of his class academically. He no longer had any discernable problem with memory and his functioning was such that there was no reason to re-do the central auditory processing (CAP) testing. His parents and their family practitioner gradually lowered his medications and he eventually came off the stimulant drug that he had been taking. He was very proud.

2. Stages in Training an Adult

Our second example is an adult with quite a different agenda.

Case # 9: Mike, age 29, wanted to return to university to do a postgraduate degree. He had completed engineering, albeit with difficulty, and was steadily employed. He was extremely anxious, particularly in performance situations. Fortunately, he usually exhibited this in a positive way with laughter. He would wake up at night worrying about his work and his social relationships. To study in his chosen field he had to succeed in the GMAT examination, one of the graduate aptitude tests taken as a prerequisite for obtaining admission to some of the better MBA programs in North American universities. This is an incredibly stress-producing exam. When he was asked to do even simple math during the psychophysiological stress profiling, he stumbled over the questions and made silly errors despite having a strong math background from his engineering years. His respiration rate rose to 40 breaths per minute (BrPM) and was shallow and irregular. His heart rate rose and was completely out of synchrony with his breathing. His skin temperature dropped, electrodermal response rose markedly and his muscles tensed as shown by the electromyogram. In the electroencephalogram measured at Cz referenced to the left ear, he showed high 'thalpha' 6-10 Hz, low SMR 13-14 Hz, and he had high beta peaks at 21 Hz and 29 Hz. His high amplitude thalpha and bursts of high amplitude, high frequency beta were also observed on a second assessment at F3.

The objectives and steps for working with Mike were:

1st   Decrease tension

2nd   Decrease his negative, non-productive ruminations

3rd   Increase his focus and concentration while remaining calm

4th   Improve strategies for learning and performing well in a test situation

Training initially emphasized relaxation. He learned to breathe at 6 breaths per minute (BrPM), raise his peripheral skin temperature and bring his forehead EMG down. As he mastered these biofeedback tasks, he began to feel more confident that he could make both physiological and behavioural changes. At this juncture he began to work on maintaining a sense of calm. He raised his high alpha (11-13 Hz) and his sensorimotor rhythm (SMR 13-15 Hz). In order to decrease anxiety and ruminating, he learned to decrease 21-32 Hz. He said that to do this he really had to clear his mind and either think only of the task at hand or think of positive experiences while relaxing.

In addition to biofeedback, he actively worked on other suggestions we had made to him. He created a section at the back of his pocket day-planner for recording and organizing his worries. This SMIRB or Stop My Irritating Ruminations Book was a technique to gain control of intrusive worrying thoughts. Each major area of worry (wife, finances, GMAT exams, university future), was given 2 pages. The repetitious thoughts were organized and listed on the left hand page. The right hand page contained any ideas for rectifying the situation or for 'reframing' the way he thought about it. He established a time each day (noted in his day-planner) when he could sit alone and worry for ¼ of an hour with a cup of tea and without interruptions. He made an absolute decision to reserve worrying for this time. If a new worrisome thought came into his mind, he would open the pocket book and enter it onto the appropriate list. Otherwise he would reassure himself that that worry would not be forgotten because it was in his book and would be reviewed during his next 'worry-time'. He said he felt reassured that to have worries was normal. But to worry all day long when he had to accomplish other things was non-productive.

However, being relaxed was necessary but not sufficient. He needed to get rid of muscle tension

and yet remain extremely alert. To do this he learned to control his EDR, keeping it high enough but not extreme. He had always tuned out in school and while doing homework unless it was a subject he was really interested in. When he tuned out, he would lose his alertness and become sleepy. To increase his ability to focus while studying relatively tedious information he decreased "thalpha", 6-10 Hz. the range that increased when he tuned out. We taught him metacognitive strategies (described in the next section) and had him do GMAT reading exercises using these strategies while he decreased "thalpha" and increased beta 17 - 18 Hz. When he was cognitively problem solving, 17 Hz would rise. He practiced becoming relaxed, with his mind free of worry, then focusing on the task. The auditory feedback reinforced his maintaining this state while he did the reading.

He sent us an e-mail immediately after getting his results on the GMAT exam. He had achieved an almost unbelievable result, 93rd % ile rank. He attributed his success to the program, beginning with pin-pointing his problems during the assessment and then helping him to overcome them during training. He said that he used the sequence of relaxed breathing, calm and focused mental state, and the use of strategies in the exam, just as he did in training and when studying.

As in our work with Jason, other techniques (relaxation techniques, SMIRB and metacognitive strategies) were important adjuncts to the neurofeedback and biofeedback done with Mike. Our clinical experience suggests that neurofeedback is probably crucial for a long term change to take place in most of the children and many of the adults that we see. **The results achieved with the addition of NFB + BFB are definitely more consistent than the results achieved in previous years with patients using psychotherapy and medications.**

3. Beginning a Training Session

The first step in every training session with a client, if your EEG instrument has this capability, is to record a raw EEG sample for approximately 1 to 3 minutes. Together with the client, you review the EEG sample and remove artifacts. This assures you that you are obtaining a clean recording without an undue number of artifacts. It allows you to review, and discuss with your client, their objectives for training and how their objectives relate to what they will be working on with respect to the EEG in today's session.

a. A Child

What is a simple EEG goal for young Jason? For an eight-year-old it must be expressed initially in simple terms. Sometimes we put up a simple diagram near the monitor. For a child with ADD, such as Jason, it looks like this. It serves as a visual reminder to him of his NFB objectives:

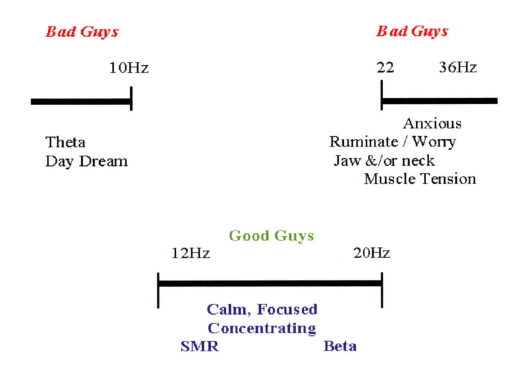

Bad Guys

10Hz

Theta
Day Dream

Bad Guys

22   36Hz

Anxious
Ruminate / Worry
Jaw &/or neck
Muscle Tension

Good Guys

12Hz   20Hz

**Calm, Focused
Concentrating**
SMR   **Beta**

To Relax
Relax shoulders
Feel hands becoming warm
Do diaphragmatic breathing at 6 BrPM

To Remain Alert
Maintain EDR at a reasonably high level
This should correspond to feeling
bright and alert

When Jason is achieving his initial NFB goals we will combine the NFB with learning metacognitive strategies. He needs to become aware of how he best learns and remembers things. Even an eight-year-old can learn to plan an approach to a task and evaluate how he is doing. (Should I subtract using my fingers or by making tally marks? Maybe I should use those flashcards with Mom every night and memorize my number facts.) Then he will practice this combination of NFB and strategic learning while doing academic exercises.

When working with children who have ADD we do not routinely use general biofeedback sensors. A practical reason is that they tend to touch and fidget with them. Relaxed breathing can be taught without a respiration strap being attached. EDR is monitored more often because arousal is a very important managing ADHD symptoms. The child earns extra tokens for keeping the hand with the EDR sensor still

b. An Adult

The goal for an older student or adult client is more often expressed in terms of optimizing functioning. This may mean a decrease in symptoms and/or an increase in positive attributes.

Three seconds of Mike's EEG from his first training session is shown below. The EEG had been paused and Mike was asked what was happening in the previous few seconds. He said that he could not recall what I had been telling him. His mind had wandered and he was thinking of something completely unrelated to the session. With this kind of review Mike started to learn about the correlation between his EEG and his mental state. We tried to find a mental state that corresponded to his goal of focusing on one task without going off topic. Using the spectral display of the first one second

of this EEG sample, he correctly pointed out that the desirable, externally focused, mental state he wanted to achieve would correspond to a decrease in amplitude and variability of his dominant slow wave activity at 9 Hz.

Looking at the EEG before the main training part of the session begins is also helpful to the trainer. The trainer might, for example, observe that even though impedance readings had been good initially, when Mike moved around in the chair, settling into a comfortable position, he had moved an electrode such that it now had a poor connection resulting in 60 hz activity being a little high. He would then readjust the electrodes before beginning the training. If a cardiac artifact was noticed, then the trainer would try moving one or more electrodes to see if it could be reduced.

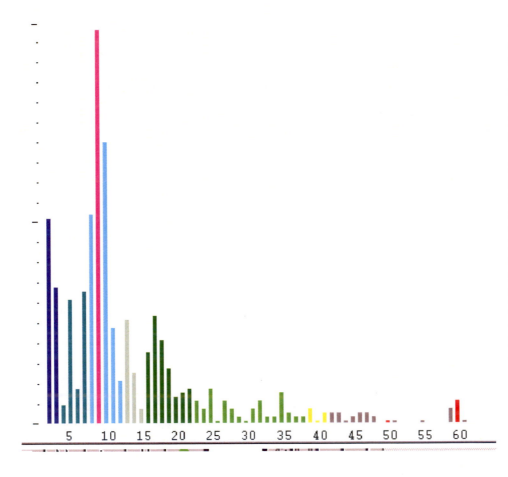

This spectral display of one second (1:38-1:39 on the above EEG) shows how Mike tunes out in low alpha.

He told us that at this moment he did not register what was told to him. He was thinking about something else (also note the high 17-18 Hz activity).

His active electrode was adjusted and the 60 Hz activity seen here dropped to almost zero.

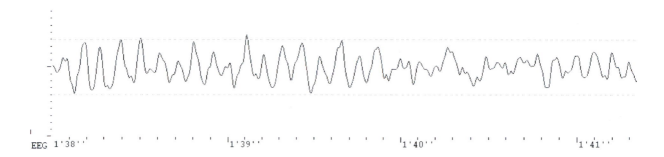

EEG 1'38'   1'39'   1'40'   1'41'

Mike tended to tune out in low alpha as is seen in the left portion of this EEG.

4. Reviewing the Client's Goals in Light of their EEG

After looking at the brief EEG profile at the beginning of each session, the trainer has the student restate their purpose for being in that session. The student states this purpose in terms of their goal for training. Then they relate this goal to what they wish to change on the EEG and in the biofeedback modalities being used for feedback, such as respiration.

For adults, such as Mike, we use a more complex diagram than the one used for children. It has a greater emphasis on optimizing performance and mood using a combination of NFB and BFB. It spells out a state which is relaxed, calm, with broad awareness yet focused concentration. We often put the following reminder sheet near the monitor.

a. Summary Sheet – Bandwidths & Mental States

**Goal: Relaxed yet alert,
calm reflective state.**

20-23 Hz ⇓	**Decrease anxiety / tension**
High Beta 24-34 Hz ⇓	**Decrease 'racing' mind / ruminating**
High Alpha 11-13 Hz ⇑	**Relax and open/broaden awareness**
SMR 12 or 13 – 15 Hz ⇑	**Calm, reflecting before acting, 'readiness state'**
Theta &/or Low Alpha (< 10 Hz) ⇓	**Remain focused**
Finger Temperature ⇑	**Relaxed**
Forehead, Jaw, Shoulders and Neck Muscle tension ⇓	**Relaxed**
Respiration @ 6 / minute	**Diaphragmatic, (Abdominal) Breathing**
Pulse ⇓	**Calm**
Respiration synchronous with pulse rate. (RSA)	**Feeling calm**
Skin conduction (EDR) fluctuating between *approx* 12-18 child; 6-12 adult	**Remain alert**

Consider an 18-year-old student who is not focusing well in school and who is impulsive. The impulsivity can extend to an impulsive approach when answering questions on exams. The goals and an approach to achieving them with such a client are outlined below:

Summary of Goals

1. **To be calm, not impulsive or irritable** and able to tolerate frustration; increase 13-15 Hz

2. **To be relaxed mentally and not ruminating**; keep 24-33 Hz at a low amplitude; as previously described, use a 'stop-my-irritating-ruminations-book' (SMIRB);

3. **To remain free from anxiety**; low amplitude of 21-24 Hz and physiologically not tense – breathing diaphragmatically at 6 BrPM (good RSA), skin temperature 94-96 degrees, skin conduction (EDR) not flat and not extreme amplitude or extreme fluctuations, forehead EMG < 4μV

4. **To remain alert**; maintain EDR at a level that reflects alertness (usually above 8, though it will be lower with older clients.

5. **To be broadly, externally focused and calm**; high 11-13 Hz (high alpha)

6. **To be able to shift to a narrow focus**; decrease dominant slow wave activity (below 10 Hz). Although reflection and memory recall and associations requires shifting in and our of theta and low alpha, these frequencies should not be dominant when a student is sitting eyes open in class or when studying.

7. **To be capable of remaining in a problem solving mental state**; increase beta in the 16-20 Hz range (often about 17 Hz).

8. Most importantly, **to be able to self regulate and to move in a flexible manner between mental states** according to task demands. (One possible feedback screen for practicing going in and out of focus at will is the sailboat screen which will be shown later in this section under H2.)

For any individual client, you must emphasize components from the foregoing which are most important for that client. The same procedures may be used for episodic conditions, such as headaches but the overall goal is stated somewhat differently. Your objective then is to decrease frequency, intensity, and duration of the undesirable events.

B. The Trainer's Task - During a NFB Session

The trainer should remain with younger clients for the entire NFB training session. The exception to this rule is at a stage during training when we are working on 'generalizing'. At this point the trainer and the student may agree to experiment and see if the client can maintain their good results without the trainer sitting beside them. The trainer might sit behind the client or stand at the door so they can still observe the computer but without the child receiving the trainer's verbal feedback and encouragement. They may also decide to have no visual or auditory feedback though still recording data while the client carries out a task. After each of these experiments, the recorded data is reviewed and compared with previous time segments when there was active coaching.

For most sessions, however, the trainer is actively involved. The trainer's task will vary with each client. It will be quite different with young children compared to adults. As a general rule, the trainer will have to be more actively involved with young children. The trainer's task is to *facilitate, enable, assist and model and always remain positive!* **Trainers are coaches and, at times, educators**. Trainers are acting as therapists only when professionally trained in psychotherapy and carrying out a psychotherapeutic intervention. This type of intervention, for example, is appropriate when using an alpha-theta protocol for patients who have addiction problems.

We want our trainers to believe in our ADD Centre motto, "You can't change the wind, but you can adjust the sails". They are not trying to change the basic personality, but rather to facilitate the student learning a new skill, the skill of self-regulation. In students with ADD the new skill allows for sustained, focused concentration on learning tasks.

The trainer's task is to encourage their learners. They are coaching but they cannot tell the person what to do to attain and maintain a particular mental state. The task is about being, rather than doing. The analogy of learning to ride a bicycle is a helpful one that most people doing neurofeedback use. You cannot tell a child how to balance when they first get on a two-wheeler. Similarly, you cannot tell a child how to concentrate. With practice and the direct "neurofeedback" of the vestibular system in the middle ear the child learns to ride his bike. With practice and the computerized neurofeedback that encourages the calm, paying attention waves and discourages the tuning out waves, the child with ADD learns what it feels like to concentrate. When the older students get discouraged or impatient for results, the trainer can remind them that brain change takes time – it is a learning process. If they consider how long it took to learn how to hit a good drive in golf, serve in tennis, skate and turn rapidly for hockey, play basketball and so on they will perhaps have more patience. It certainly took more than the equivalent of 40 sessions to master these athletic skills.

With adults or parents, the trainer can use analogies that remind them that it takes time and, with enough training, things should finally fall into place. Learning a new skill takes time and practice. Second, be patient, in the early stages it may seem that very little is changing. Some parents enjoy sayings such as: there are orchids that can take 9 years to bloom; or, ninety percent of the growth of the Chinese Bamboo tree is in the fifth year! Third, don't give up. If you stop pumping the old hand water pump when you need water, you must reprime it and start all over again.

The trainer and the parents must always remember that many of their young clients are going to become discouraged or complain that it is boring and they may even want to give up. This is the same phenomenon that every good coach is familiar with – the child is all keen to play on their first hockey team. Then they find they cannot skate and stick handle like Wayne Gretzky after one or two practices and they get discouraged and give up. The trainer, as their coach, has the task of helping their young clients stick with it, facilitating and encouraging them as

they guide them. For the children a reward system can be used. At the ADD Centre children and adolescents earn tokens over the course of a 50 minute session when they are working hard and achieving goals set for them. There is an ADD Centre Store (a large corner bookshelf) with books and toys and they can exchange tokens for prizes when they have saved enough tokens. The system is that children can earn about 10 blue tokens during their session. For children who need frequent reinforcement, white tokens can be used, and 10 white tokens equal 1 blue token. There are also red tokens (special bonus tokens worth 2 blues) that can be used for an extra good job, or for using calm focus outside of the center as evidenced by a good test result at school, for example. Tokens earned and redeemed for prizes are tracked on the student's bank account sheet. This level of extrinsic reward system is an important part of the motivational aspect of this program. As children with ADD shift towards more mature (age appropriate) brain wave patterns, they are usually more able to delay gratification and save their tokens over a number of sessions in order to earn the larger prizes.

****

Note: Throughout the remainder of this section discussion of means for lessening the effects of artifacts is followed by a description of how to decide on the appropriate placement for the active electrode(s) and how to choose the bandwidths to be enhanced or inhibited. Simple one channel and two channel feedback combined with metacognitive strategy training (operant plus classical conditioning) is then outlined. This is followed by pointers on handling more complex cases where neurofeedback is combined with biofeedback.

C. A Review of Artifacts During Feedback

1. Importance of Artifact Recognition

It is important to minimize false feedback and to be able to distinguish electrical activity of cortical origin from muscle activity and non-EEG electrical activity. Non-neuronal activity that appears in the EEG may also be caused by eye blinks or movement of an electrode. Preventing artifact from affecting feedback is an important consideration when building or evaluating a feedback screen.

As previously noted, at the beginning of every training session you always want to look at the raw EEG. If your instrument has the capability to do so, always record, artifact, and print out data concerning at least one minute of EEG. Apart from having a consistent record of changes taking place over time, this assures you that you are obtaining a quality EEG signal. You may note cardiac artifact and have to change your electrode sites. If 60 Hz is apparent but impedances are excellent, then one must investigate the wiring and the possibility of an unusual electrical source of interference. This could be things like a table lamp or an extension cord. Check the *offset* as well as the *impedance* as this will give you information about the integrity of your wires. The following examples of trouble shooting come from our clinic.

The trainer asked for some back-up, explaining, "There seems to be an EMG (45-58 Hz) reading that is too high". It was extremely high (over 25 μV). When we looked at the raw EEG, it consisted of irregular, extremely high fast waves. The spectrum showed high 60 Hz activity. If the client made even a small movement, the entire spectrum went so high as to be off the scale. The first step was to check the impedance readings. They were all over 25 Kohms. When the trainer reattached the sensors with more 10-20 conductive paste, he brought them down close to about 3 Kohms for each pairing of electrodes. Then the EEG was excellent, 45-58 Hz activity was <2 μV and 60 Hz activity was at the baseline on the spectrum. He learned 2 important lessons. First, always do impedance checks both before starting and during the session if something looks awry. (If you work with youngsters who have ADD, electrodes sometimes do shift position.) Second, always look at the raw EEG and the spectrum before beginning feedback.

The same week another trainer announced, "I don't understand it, the EEG machine worked with the last client. Now I get a flat line. If I shake a wire I see a sudden change in the EEG line so there is a connection between where I plug in the electrodes and the amplifier and the computer. All my impedances were below 5 Kohms. Why am I getting a flat line EEG?"

She had done the correct thing and begun with a screen that showed the raw EEG. She had excellent impedances. Asked what her offset readings were, however, she realized she had not done them. When she did, she found the offset between the ear electrodes was 20 but the offset between either ear and the active scalp electrode was above 120. There was a broken wire. Replacing the scalp electrode and lead resulted in a normal EEG. She has learned an important lesson. Check the offsets.

These anecdotes reveal some of the technical challenges in trying to give quality feedback. Consider the complex question of impedance. Ideally, you should check impedances and offsets every time you connect a client. Unfortunately, not all instruments are set up to allow for this and not all practitioners have invested in an impedance meter. Some manufacturers do not sell their equipment without an impedance meter. Others say the input impedance of the EEG amplifier is so high that you can still have a good EEG signal even without careful prepping and low impedance. Still others have a built-in impedance check. The most conservative approach is to verify readings with an external meter such as the Check-trode.

Next, consider the question of the integrity of your wires. An electrode and its attached wire may not appear bent or broken, but a wire inside may be loose. If you suspect a problem just replace the lead with a new one and see if that solves the problem. The length of time that an electrode lasts is very dependant on how carefully it is handled. The connection between the wire and the electrode is a particularly vulnerable spot so remove electrodes without your client trying to help.

You will always have some degree of eye movement artifact. At times the eye-blink artifact may be worse than in previous sessions. It may be that the client has worn contact lenses or allergies are bothering them. It may be that you must change from a referential to a sequential (bipolar) recording to see if the preamplifier's common mode rejection will eliminate, or at least reduce, this problem. If it does not, then you will probably just have to use an inhibit bandwidth that is not affected by eye blinks. In some clients an eye blink may only increase delta range frequencies but in others it may increase 4 Hz or 5Hz as well.

Joan, age 32, had very high amplitude eye blink artifact. It affected 2 –5 Hz but usually not 6 Hz and definitely not 7 Hz. Bipolar placement gave slightly lower amplitude readings in the 2-5 Hz. range when she blinked, but it was still significant. We could inhibit feedback every time she blinked by placing 2 threshold lines above and below the EEG linegraph and putting an inhibit-over-threshold into the system so that all feedback would cease when the large eye-blink artifact occurred. This is further described below. (This was using Procomp+/Biograph equipment and software.) However, given Joan's very frequent high amplitude blinks, this would have resulted in a very interrupted feedback session. We, therefore, decided to inhibit 7-10 Hz and reward 15-18 Hz when doing academic work. This worked well and avoided false readings due to her eye blinks while reinforcing appropriate mental states.

What can you do about artifacts produced during feedback? This is an important question because these artifacts can give your client an incorrect impression of their brain states as they are reflected in the EEG.

First, place inhibits to stop sound or visual rewards when your client is producing unacceptable artifacts. You are not actually artifacting the EEG during feedback, you are merely stopping false information from being conveyed to the client. If you save some of the data from the NFB session, remember that this data **is not** artifacted. The EEG instrument and computer were still recording the EEG, artifact and all, even though the client was not receiving feedback. Before you look at statistics you must return to a screen that shows the raw EEG and remove artifacts. We use the assessment screen

shown above, in the section on 'Assessment', to do this artifacting with the Procomp+/Biograph. We then print out or graph statistics for 25 overlapping 2 Hz bandwidths using a very precise IIR Butterworth filter for the bandwidth in question.

Because you are **not** artifacting data during feedback, you must know what major artifacts may affect NFB for each of your clients. Each client is unique. We will sometimes do the statistics both with and without the artifacted segments. In this way we can obtain an impression of the extent to which that particular client's blinking or muscle tension may affect their EEG during feedback sessions.

Jason, the client in the case example at the beginning of this section on "Intervention" (and example #3 at the beginning of Section VI, assessment of the EEG), had shown rather large excursions of the EEG with eye blinks. However, when the EEG was artifacted only 3 - 7 Hz and not 4-8 Hz activity changed with artifacting. Thus it appears that although 3 Hz activity was increased with eye blink, 4 Hz was not significantly increased. We could thus do 4-8Hz training without worrying that we were just teaching him not to blink.

2. Minimize the Effect of Eye Blink Artifact

Whenever possible, eliminate the effects **of eye blinks.** Eye blinks can falsify the amplitude of slow wave activity particularly in the 3 – 5 Hz range. As previously explained, the eye can be likened to a small battery: the retina negative, the cornea positive. When you blink, the eye rolls up and the eyelid touches the cornea, or positive end, of this little battery and a wave is observed on the EEG tracing. It usually looks like a large 'V'. In set-ups where there is a separate clinician screen (one monitor for feedback, a second monitor to show the raw EEG and statistics) the trainer can observe the raw EEG for artifact. In most children the wave is in the delta range and does not appear to have any major influence above 1 or 2 Hz. In adolescents and adults you may find that it goes up to 3 Hz or higher. Frequent blinks may have a major effect on average theta amplitude calculations. You can reduce the influence on feedback caused by eye blinks and movements reasonably efficiently by putting threshold lines on an EEG linegraph on your feedback screens as noted above.

In programs which allow you to modify the display screen you should consider placing an EEG linegraph (or a 3-62 Hz spectral display) on some of the display screens which you typically use during a session or which appear on a monitoring display screen viewed by the clinician. This is important for two reasons:

- First, you make sure through the session that you have a normal EEG (an electrode has not popped for example).

- Second, by means of threshold lines, you can stop two types of false feedback. First, you put an inhibit on movement artifact and thereby stop feedback to the client when this occurs. Second, you stop feedback when large amplitude eye-blink artifact occurs. By so doing you prevent falsely high %-over-threshold theta readings on the feedback screen. These falsely high readings can be unduly discouraging to your client who is trying to lower theta.

When recording your assessment data and during artifacting, it is important to note the frequency of blinking and the degree to which the client's eye blinks change frequencies that you hope to be inhibiting (for example in the 3 – 5 Hz range). However, despite our best efforts, we do meet clients, mostly adults, where we are not able to give any feedback in the lower range of theta.

It may be possible on your program to create an inhibit instrument, set thresholds, and then eliminate it from view during most of the session so as not to clutter the screen. This can be done with the ProComp+/Biograph at this time and, hopefully, with other instruments in the future.

3. Minimize the Effect of EMG & Electrical Artifacts

You can minimize false feedback by putting an inhibit-over-threshold on 45 – 70 Hz to prevent most **muscle activity and electrical** activity from giving a false impression of fast wave activity. Alternatively, you can put an inhibit-over-threshold on 45-58 Hz in North America to show mainly the effect of muscle activity on the EEG without concern for 60 Hz. Have your client grit their teeth to demonstrate the massive changes that muscle contraction can make on beta. Now ask your client to very gently tense their jaw, scalp and neck muscles respectively and observe the changes in SMR and beta which appear to correspond to a rise in 45 – 58 Hz activity. In Europe, Australia and China, you might use a 53-61 Hz range for muscle inhibit since their current is at 50 Hz.

In the example given below, note that the bargraph has gone above the threshold that we set for this client. The client had some tension in their jaw. This could give a false impression of high SMR or beta which might otherwise have been rewarded with sound or game feedback. We usually set the feedback options on the program to stop all feedback, both sounds and movement in a game display, when the client goes above threshold on this bargraph. We called it EMG though, strictly speaking, it is only a reflection of EMG activity. True EMG usually occurs at higher frequencies, well above 60 Hz. Our interest is in how EMG affects the amplitude of EEG activity in the SMR and beta ranges, causing it to appear (falsely) high.

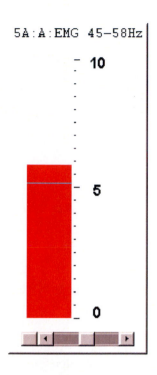

5A:A:EMG 45-58Hz

- 10

- 5

- 0

Even a small amount of jaw muscle tension can shift the beta and SMR readings upwards. We often use a 45-58 Hz inhibit in North America and a 43-48 Hz or a 53-61 Hz inhibit in Europe, Asia and Australia. We do this so that we have a better idea of the extent to which muscle activity is responsible for a rise in beta frequencies.

Note that **we do not inhibit 38-42 Hz.** This is because an increase in the EEG amplitude in this range may be associated with useful attention and cognitive activity. Activity around 40 Hz is sometimes called Sheer Rhythm after David Sheer who published in the 70's on 40 Hz being associated with some aspects of attention.

The bargraph turns 'red' when over threshold.

4. Minimize the Effect of Electrode Movement Artifact

Electrode movement will usually be different at each electrode and therefore this artifact will not be removed by the amplifier's *common mode rejection*. It is also more significant with even very small head movements if impedance readings between electrodes are high (> 5 Kohms).

The large effect of even a slight movement of the electrode can be understood if we recall Ohm's law: V (voltage) = I (current) x R (resistance) (Resistance is used for direct current. We are actually interested in resistance to the flow of alternating current which is referred to as 'z' - impedance). Because the current (I) is so small any change in impedance (z) will have a major effect on voltage (V). Even a very small movement of an electrode will massively alter 'z' and thus 'V' and it may do so in the

frequency range we are measuring, say 3 - 6 Hz since electrode movement produce a high amplitude slow wave. As previously noted above, this will mean that you may interpret the rise in theta as the client tuning out when, in fact, the increased amplitude is just due to an eye blink or a poor connection. This can be very frustrating for your client!

To minimize electrode movement try the following:

- Tuck the electrodes under a headband. It really will minimize movement artifact if you stabilize the wires. Tell children they look like a tennis star. Between sessions we keep each client's headband in their chart. (The important rule here is that nothing that touches the head of one client, touches the head of another client.)

- Keep the impedances between all the electrodes within 1 Kohm of each other.

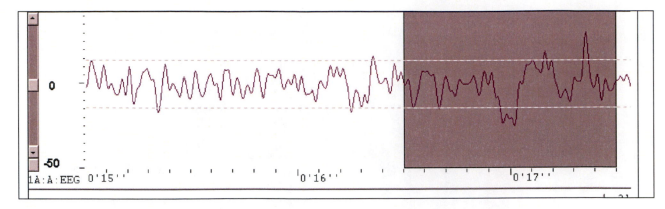

The horizontal dotted threshold lines above and below the EEG can be set so that when the EEG goes outside of these lines it will stop rewarding with feedback. In the above example, the client both blinked and moved. This example also demonstrated how, at the end of a few minutes of feedback during the session, areas with artifact can be marked on the EEG for exclusion from statistical analysis. The gray area has been marked, in this program, by drawing the mouse across the time ruler below the segment in question. The slightly lower amplitude movement artifact at 16.2 seconds was not eliminated. (Note that +ve is a downward deflection on the graph despite the scale reading on the right in the above figure. This is because we have reversed the reference and active electrodes in order to have +ve a conventional downward deflection.). Remember Bell's phenomenon: the eyeball rolls upwards when you blink. The positive cornea moves up and the consequent EEG deflection is +ve; that is, by convention this is represented by a downward direction on the electroencephalogram.)

5. Minimize the Effect of Cardiac Artifact

It is also important to watch for **cardiac waveform**s. These are regular waves at a frequency of approximately one per second. It is usually a consistent wave, the same general form each time. These complex waveforms can alter different frequency band amplitudes. This problem is rare. It is usually only seen in adults. As previously noted in the artifact section, it is more often encountered in persons who have a very short, thick neck. When it occurs, your best solution is to redo the assessment changing your electrode site until it is minimized. Moving to the top of the ear or using the mastoid placement for reference sometimes works. In some cases we have had to use a sequential (bipolar) placement to use the amplifier *common mode rejection* feature to minimize the effect. This also does not always work but it may decrease the amplitude of this artifact somewhat as shown below. (This is the same example as used previously in the section on artifating.)

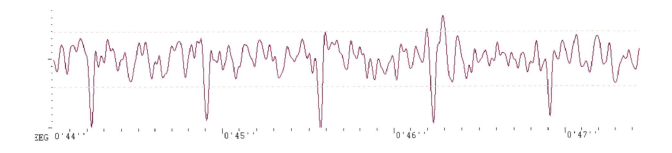

The electrodes for this client, a large man with a very short and extraordinarily wide, thick neck, were moved from the above referential placement to a sequential, Fz-Cz, placement (below). There is some decrease in the cardiac artifact amplitude.

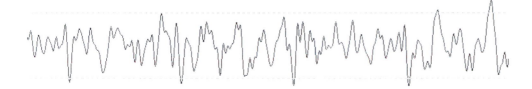

0'7''   0'8''   0'9''

The cardiac artifact is still definitely present but at a lower amplitude relative to the rest of the EEG. This is also a good example for another reason: the second EEG demonstrates, in the second EEG, how difficult it can be to see the effect of the cardiac influence on the EEG when the waves are not large. It might have been difficult to pick out the cardiac artifact if one had been rapidly moving through just the second, bipolar, sample.

In the section on assessment it was noted that the more consistent the wave, the less may be its overall effect when averaging amplitudes in different bandwidths. The heart rate effects may be a little more consistent if you train the client to relax and breathe diaphragmatically at 6 breaths per minute, (see the section on RSA (Respiratory Sinus Arrhythmia later in this book), Because the changes that cardiac artifact will make in your recording are fairly consistent over time, you can still do successful feedback. Absolute values will be affected but *relative changes* in fast and slow wave amplitudes will be reasonably correct and your client can learn self-regulation.

6. Brief Summary

Having the raw EEG on the screen is helpful during feedback as it enables you to detect interference, for example, from an electrode that has lifted slightly mid-way through a session. Without the EEG on the screen you would miss certain kinds of artifacts and the client might be receiving false, incorrect feedback.

In Summary:
- Eye blinks, rolling eyes, and other eye movements can give **a false impression of** **high theta,** as can heart beat (a consistent artifact) or any electrode movement over the skin.
- Muscle tension can give a **false impression of increased SMR or beta amplitudes**.
- Heart-beat (a consistent artifact) **can influence a number of frequencies** and every effort should be made to minimize the effects of this source of artifact. (Move the electrode or try a sequential placement.)

D. Decisions Regarding Frequency Bands and Setting Thresholds

1. Basic Principles

Your next task is to decide on which bandwidths to reward and inhibit. Then you must decide on the threshold levels for each. Bargraphs are good for setting thresholds because they are easy for a client to understand. Bargraph screens are available on many systems such as the F1000, the Autogen A620, the Procomp+/Biograph and J&J equipment. EEG spectrum displays the same information with boxes. How you determine appropriate thresholds will depends on the software you are using. The basic principle is that the client must receive enough information to learn the task. If reward rates are very high (threshold too easy), the client is not going to shift his EEG pattern because the computer is indicating he is already in the right zone. If reward rate is very low, there is not enough information about success and the client may become frustrated. You must, as always, respect individual differences. Some people need more frequent reward. This is generally the case with young children and with clients who have ADD. These two groups need a high frequency rate of reward.

The other decision with respect to thresholds is whether to set them initially with great care and leave them unchanged for the duration of training, or to employ a shaping strategy and change thresholds according to the client's performance over time. One cannot say that one approach is better. As with other decisions, it is a matter of trade-offs and depends on your goals and knowledge of you client with respect to such things as frustration tolerance. The set-and-leave-alone approach has the advantage of being able to make session to session comparisons that are meaningful using data such as microvolt amplitudes, percent-over-threshold for particular frequency bands, or number of points earned in a time period. The task for the client will be relatively hard initially and should become easier as training proceeds. With this approach the trainer will need to provide a lot of encouragement and coaching initially to augment the computer feedback, which will be harder to achieve. With the shaping procedure the amount of reward can remain at about the same level across sessions and the client's improvement will be reflected in the thresholds changing: threshold for inhibit frequencies declining and for reward frequencies increasing over time.

An analogy from training a golfer puts this in perspective. If the objective is to be able to consistently sink a 20 foot putt you could take two different approaches. The analogy to a constant threshold would be to start 20 feet from the hole and keep trying from that distance until the person can do it reliably. This will be very difficult at first and you will have to give lots of praise and encouragement for coming close to the hole since successful shots will be relatively rare. The other approach would be to start one foot from the hole and, when that is mastered, go to 18 inches away, then 2 feet away, and so on until you get out to the 20 foot mark. The latter method uses shaping, or what psychologists term *successive approximations*.

Both approaches should work whether we are dealing with golf or learning to change brainwaves. It would make a good dissertation topic to compare the two approaches with two groups of similar subjects receiving neurofeedback.

2. Setting an Inhibit Frequency Band

a. Setting Thresholds

Consider the case example of the 8-year-old boy with ADHD described at the beginning of Section VIII. On assessment Jason had demonstrated very high 3-7 Hz activity when he was not paying attention. His eye blinks affected 2-3 Hz activity but not 4 Hz. Therefore, a bandwidth of 4-7 Hz or 4-8 Hz could be inhibited in order to help him gain control of focusing and learn to focus externally when this was appropriate. The initial assessment was referential, Cz to the left ear, so this placement would be good for feedback sessions. Further assessment demonstrated that the high theta activity was over the entire frontal and central area so that placement of the electrode for feedback to inhibit slow wave activity could be helpful anywhere in the frontal or central region. The final placement decision could, therefore, be based on where it could be appropriate to reward his fast wave activity.

With the EEG Spectrum equipment you use lines above and below the EEG tracings and adjust them until the client is meeting the criteria a certain percent of the time. Thresholds can be changed without stopping feedback and the thresholds are 'remembered' in the client's disk for the next session. This is a handy feature.

Bargraph showing theta 4-8 Hz activity.

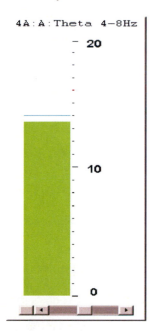

4A:A:Theta 4-8Hz

We have decided to reward our client, Jason, for keeping his theta 4-8 Hz activity below a threshold which we have set for him. We based the threshold level on his being able, initially, to keep theta below threshold between 50 and 60% of the time.

His threshold for theta had initially been at 20 µV. After 42 training sessions, Jason had progressively lowered that threshold. It was now at 14 µV.

To the left is a bargraph from a Procomp+/Biograph screen. This is one of the simplest and most useful instruments used in NFB work. We initially set most bargraph instruments so that the client can get rewarding feedback about 50% of the time. This should provide enough feedback for learning to take place without the task being too easy. We always have the colour of the *bar green when the client is meeting the objective* (focused and concentrating) and red when they are not meeting preset threshold criteria. The bargraph shows that Jason has met the criteria; he is below the threshold of 14 µV. Therefore the bar is green. If he goes over the threshold line, it will instantly turn red. Early in training we slow the movements of the bar somewhat so it is easier to follow. As training proceeds we decrease this smoothing or averaging and the movement becomes much faster than conscious thought.

If you are working with a client who has ADD, you could have both a theta inhibit bargraph and an alpha inhibit bargraph on the same screen if both were a problem. With some equipment you are able to use a different sound for below threshold (reward) for each of them. Or, you can use a *sound reward* for below threshold for one of them and use an *inhibit all feedback if above threshold* setting for the other one.

b. Using %-Over-Threshold To Follow Progress

Alternatively, and the method we most frequently employ, you can link a '%-over-threshold' counter to each bargraph. You might have three bargraphs, perhaps one for theta, one for beta and a third for the ratio of theta/beta. You and the student follow changes in all of them in this manner. One of them may also be linked to a point (reward) counter and a tone can sound for each point earned. An example of having a '%-over-threshold' linked to a bargraph is shown below. (*Display screens that do this will be shown and described more fully below.*) The A620 software has a feedback screen which shows three bargraphs (EEG reward, EEG inhibit, and EMG inhibit) with an amplitude scale, % over threshold, a timer and points.

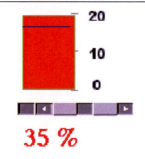

Theta, 4-8 Hz has been 35% of the time over the threshold. It is red when over threshold to signal that the client is not meeting the criteria and should try to make it green by bringing it down.

SMR, 12-15 Hz, has been over the threshold 72 % of the time. It is green when it is over the threshold as a signal that this is good. The client attempts to keep all the bargraphs green (not red).

Once you know what threshold level works well for a client, then you can use the same threshold level for any of your feedback screens. Some equipment will do this automatically for you. In others you must enter thresholds for each new screen you put up. By keeping the thresholds constant you and your client can follow progress during a session even though you change display screens. You can also compare their progress from week to week. You can develop and use a tracking client progress sheet to help with this. It is useful to track a client's progress over time. Machine generated graphs, trend reports, or even hand drawn diagrams are useful here.

When dealing with ADD, each client will have one, or perhaps two, dominant slow wave frequency bands. In young children this is usually in the theta range. In adults, tuning out may be in low alpha or in the range Lubar has called "thalpha" (6-10Hz.).

3. Setting a Reward Frequency Band
a. Choosing an Initial Site and Reward Frequency Band

Again using Jason as the example, two factors dictated the initial reward frequency for him. First, the assessment EEG showed that 13-15 Hz activity was generally lower than both 10-12 Hz and 16-18 Hz. Second, he was a very active and impulsive boy. This was confirmed by his history, clinical observations and results on continuous performance tests (TOVA and IVA). Rewarding a child for increasing SMR, 13-15 Hz across the sensori-motor strip, in most cases will result in a decrease in hyperactivity and impulsivity and an increase in reflecting before acting. Although some practitioners have suggested that a C4 placement is preferable, others have obtained good results at other locations across the central strip including C3 and at Cz. With Jason, we decided to use a C4 placement initially.

Since you are training rhythmic activity that is influenced by thalamo-cortical loops the change in the sensorimotor (12-15 Hz) activity is not localized to the area under your electrode. (Remember that the activity you record is from a scalp area of about 6 cm^2.) It should be found all across the sensori-motor strip: training at one site should also produce an increase in those frequencies at other sites. This would not be the case if you were training to increase beta, which is a desynchronized waveform largely reflective of cortico-cortical communication rather than rhythmic activity influenced by thalamic pace-makers.

(Here is another good thesis topic: measure at C3, Cz and C4 but just train at one of those sites in each of three groups to see to what extent an increase in SMR generalizes.)

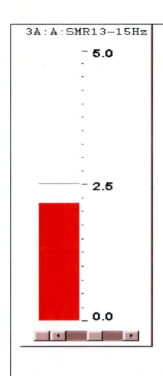

```
3A:A:SMR13-15Hz
        - 5.0
        .
        .
        .
        .
        .
        .
        - 2.5
        .
        .
        - 0.0
```

Jason is to raise SMR 13-15 Hz activity. Early on he had trouble with this and a very low threshold had to be set to give him encouragement. When it went below threshold he did not receive sound or game movement rewards.

The bargraph on the left is below threshold. Jason is not meeting the preset criterion (threshold). Therefore, the colour of the bar is red. However, the blue 62% shows that overall he has been over threshold 62% of the time in this segment of his session. To give encouragement we often place both a *% above threshold* and points on to the screen. In the square on the right hand side, below, *points* are designated as *"reward"*. Points have been *linked* to the SMR bargraph. This bargraph must be held above threshold for one second to score a point. Points are different than % above threshold because they have a time factor built in. On other screens, Jason had the points linked to theta and Jason had to hold theta below the threshold line for a full second to score a point. On still other screens, points were linked to a ratio of theta / beta. On these screens Jason had to hold the bar below threshold (green) for one second to get a point and hear a beep. In addition to the bargraph and numbers he would see an animated display – (maze, car morphing, etc.). This combination of display screens allowed for some variety during training and encouraged Jason to find and sustain a calm, focused, problem solving mental state.

% ABOVE threshold   8A:REWARD

62 %   35

b. Changing Electrode Site to Meet a new Objective

When his inappropriately high activity level and his impulsivity decreased, (evidenced by progress testing after 40 sessions that collected EEG, TOVA, IVA and questionnaire data), we moved the electrode site and changed the reward frequency. This was done to address the second objective of improving his academics. In order to achieve this he must learn to sustain activation of the area of the brain which is involved in problem solving, organizing, sequencing, and analyzing material. F3 was the site we used. Sustaining activation required that he decrease slow wave amplitude (4-8 Hz) while he increased fast wave activity (15-18 Hz). The result was sustained attention while solving problems. On the EEG we could observe an increase in 17 Hz activity while he was doing a math problem or reading.

We then paired his sustaining low 4-8 Hz amplitude and high 15-18 Hz activity with him while he carried out academic tasks including reading, math and listening to his trainer

teaching him learning strategies. If the feedback sound rewards stopped for more than a few seconds, the academic task was discontinued until the feedback indicated he was again maintaining focus.

With a two channel instrument we might decide to have one channel primarily working on increasing SMR with an active electrode at C4 and a second channel increasing 15-18 Hz (or 16-20 Hz) with its active electrode placed over the lateral aspect of the left hemisphere. This could be, for example, at F3 or at other sites if there were more specific learning disabilities. An example would be training over Wernicke's area for a child who had reading problems involving decoding. At the same time the second channel would also reward a decrease in 4-8 Hz activity. Academic exercises would be done during the feedback sessions but only while concentration was being maintained.

Below is a display example showing beta, 16-20 Hz, that has been 82% of the time above threshold.

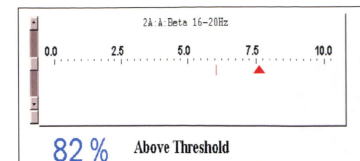

This figure shows an alternative method of displaying μV levels. Again, sound feedback, points, percent of time over threshold and games can be linked to the gauge so that Jason will be rewarded for scoring above (to the right of) the threshold line with various forms of feedback.

4. How Your Assessment Data are Used to Set Bandwidths

In the section on assessments it was recommended that you be able to look at 1 Hz bandwidths or overlapping 2 Hz bands. The reasons for this suggestion are threefold.

Wide versus Narrow Bandwidths

First, in assessments, you can miss marked differences from normal by using wide band-widths. For example, a large increase in 9 Hz activity may not show up if you are only looking at 6-10 Hz. It will definitely be missed if you look at a standard bandwidth for theta, such as 4-8 Hz. Looking at narrow bandwidths, your assessment will pick out the high amplitude at 9 Hz. You can then be quite specific and inhibit 9-10 Hz or 8-10 Hz activity. In addition, if you are using an assessment program for full cap assessments, such as SKIL, then the precise, narrow bandwidth may show important comodulation differences from a normal database. These may not show up with a wider band-width.

Second, when doing neurofeedback you may incorrectly assume you are encouraging a client to raise a specific type of brain wave when, in fact, you are encouraging quite a different waveform.

For example, a client with Parkinson's may have very high 12 Hz alpha activity and a marked dip at 14-15 Hz. Your objective is to increase SMR. In this case the assessment would indicate that rewarding 12-15 Hz would not be appropriate since that could be achieved just by increasing 12 Hz alpha activity. While this may not do any harm, it is not your objective. Given the assessment, you would narrow your training

band to 14-15 Hz in order to make it more likely that training would encourage an increase in true SMR activity. You are thus being more specific and targeting the deficiency observed in your assessment. Some instruments, such as the F1000 (unfortunately no longer on the market, but perhaps available second hand), will allow you to reward a single Hz band such as 14 Hz. (Remember in this discussion that the actual frequencies measured also depend on the filters used. Other frequencies are attenuated but not eliminated when you select 14 Hz.)

Third, in attempting to guide your client you can be misled, and even make the situation worse. For example, if you observe high 24-30 Hz activity, you might assume it reflects EMG activity when the client is actually anxious and worried. On the other hand, if your assessment looks at a wide frequency range up to 61 Hz, you may observe that there is no significant electrical interference (59-61 Hz) and no significant reflection in the EEG of muscle activity (45-58 Hz). In these circumstances, instead of telling your client to relax their jaw, forehead, neck or shoulders, (which can make them more mentally anxious and tense because they really have tried to do that), you would recognize that they had a problem with anxious ruminations as reflected by activity in those frequencies. You would not get side-tracked into working on muscle relaxation (though low EMG is always important for quality feedback).

5. Selecting Bandwidths – Discussion of Case Examples

a. Bandwidths Correspond to Mental States

In the first part of this book we gave brief descriptions of a number of different bandwidths found between 2 and 60 Hz. Each bandwidth had a specific mental state or mental activities associated with it. Rather than repeat this information we would advise you to do a quick review of that section (Section I, C.2b.). This will help you to choose the appropriate bandwidth to reinforce or inhibit, based on the triad of client's symptoms and goals, the EEG pattern, and the correlation between particular frequencies and mental states.

As a very general statement, we could say that most clients who want to optimize their performance can benefit by learning to achieve a relaxed, yet alert, calm, openly aware state with efficient problem-solving capacity and a minimum of anxiety and ruminations. We want the EEG to give us information related to these mental attributes with minimum artifact.

While it is true that low alpha (8-10 Hz) and high theta (5-7 Hz) states can be useful in meditation, memory recall, relaxation and in psychotherapy, remaining in these states for long periods of time is not normally considered useful in the board-room, classroom or in an athletic endeavour. They are internal mental states while optimal performance rests on mental flexibility that includes the ability to maintain controlled external orientation. The word 'controlled' refers to the major goal of NFB & BFB, self-regulation of mental states to optimize performance during a task. Except in *alpha - theta* psychotherapeutic work, we are usually training the student to reduce activity in the slower frequencies for reasonable periods of time. We, therefore, place an inhibit on them.

However, as with most general rules, there are well documented exceptions. Psychologist John Gruzelier, working with elite musical performing artists from the Royal Conservatoire of Music in London, England, demonstrated that increasing theta corresponded to improvements in some aspects of performing. (Gruzelier, 2002) This does not seem to contradict the work done in decreasing theta in students with ADD who underachieve academically. Such students are remaining internal-oriented in a non-productive fashion when they should be spending more of their time with an external focus, listening or reading. The high performing musical artists, on the other hand, were perhaps getting more in touch with their feelings and enhancing the creative aspects of their performance, which is an internally-oriented phenomenon. It is also

likely that these students, in contrast to those with ADHD, had no difficulty in producing beta. Also, quite likely their initial theta levels were not high and thus they demonstrated very low theta / beta ratios.

Most adult clients can identify with changing mental states while driving a car. It is quite normal and reasonable to go 'internal' in order to recall the directions to your destination. It is also a common experience to hyper-focus while trying to read a road sign as you approach an intersection. In both cases, however, one's broad attention to all the other traffic around your car is momentarily gone. That period of time, in order to drive safely, must be very brief. Longer time frames are neither safe nor reasonable while driving. These would include going internal and figuring out a problem concerning home or work, or focusing on a cell phone conversation. These longer distractions may result in the driver missing changes in traffic patterns. An accident may be the serious consequence of a longer loss of focus during the important task of driving. For a student, loss of focus means that they miss what the teacher is saying and later fail to recall material that they read.

Clients who demonstrate a relaxed state while remaining alert, externally aware and capable of quick, accurate reactions to the environment, demonstrate *'high' alpha* (11-13 Hz) activity. With athletes we may reward this bandwidth to help them more easily get in the zone for sports performance. High performing clients may also show some momentary activity in theta that is associated with memory retrieval, creativity and visualizing. Flitting in and out of theta can, therefore, be useful but remaining in this state results in being tuned out and not being consciously aware of what is happening in one's external environment. These optimal performance clients also demonstrate frequent bursts of beta, usually around 17 Hz. This is associated with analyzing information and problem solving. It can be interesting for a client to try testing out whether their mental states really do correspond to specific bandwidths. You might suggest that your client check out these "hypotheses" by creating some image in their mind, visualizing it as they do so. You pause the spectral display of the EEG when they tap the table to indicate that they really have the image. You may see a sudden rise between 7 and 8.5 Hz. Try asking them an oral math problem and pause just as you can see that they are about to answer. We have found that asking a child to multiply 7x8 results in some alpha or theta activity then a significant dip in their dominant theta frequency and a rise around 17 Hz. This is so consistent and dramatic that we often let the child demonstrate it to their parents. Perhaps we now have a way of measuring concretely the admonition to put on your thinking cap.

b. Comments on Bandwidths to Enhance

i. Rewarding 11-13 Hz

The bandwidth 11-13 Hz is associated with a mental state of *open awareness*. An open awareness implies being capable of responding to a wide range of changes in one's environment. In athletics this state is associated with fast reflexes and accurate responses. The awareness of a professional goalie in hockey or soccer, or a black belt martial artist fighting several opponents are examples. It is also associated with the mental and physical calm required in that readiness state before action. The moment prior to and during the release of an arrow is an archery example that has been studied (Landers, 1991). Open awareness appears to be an ideal mental state achieved by top performers in most any field of endeavor. It can be helpful to any of us. When clients are ruminating over problems in their lives, you may find low 11-15 Hz and high activity somewhere in the 21-32 Hz range. In these clients we have found it useful to reward decreasing the ratio 21-32 Hz/11-14 Hz or 11-15 Hz. By doing this we are discouraging ruminative activity. We are also encouraging both a calm high alpha and SMR state. Because SMR is lower in amplitude compared to alpha we will alternate this with SMR, 13-15 Hz training and/or training to decrease the ratio 21-32 Hz/13-15 Hz. The precise range used depends on assessment findings. We have clients where the dip is very specific, for example at 14-15 Hz. We also have clients where the rise in high beta is quite specific when ruminating and then a narrower high beta frequency range is used.

On the other hand, high alpha amplitudes in the 9-12 Hz range can carry over to 13 Hz and even, in rare instances, as high as 14-15 Hz and mask a low SMR. In this client you would not reinforce in the "sensorimotor" range 13-15 Hz (because from the waveform you can see that it is really alpha, albeit at a higher than usual frequency).

This kind of client may show symptoms, such as tuning out and having his mind wander from what he is reading; this clearly corresponds to the slow wave component of the EEG. The same client may also act impulsively. Since a low SMR in the assessment may have been masked by the high amplitude high alpha, then it is reasonable to set rewards assuming the true sensori-motor rhythm activity may be low. For example, a 16-year-old boy with mixed symptoms of Asperger's syndrome and severe ADHD demonstrated a very high peak at 10 Hz with typical alpha waves seen to be flowing over into the 11-15 Hz band, but not above 15 Hz. He had an average 14-15 Hz amplitude over 3 minutes that was very close to the average amplitude of 16-17 Hz beta. His symptoms included impulsivity and anxiety. We feel it is reasonable in his case to reward decreasing 9-10 Hz activity and reward increasing 14 Hz or 14-15 Hz.

The bandwidths used should be derived from your assessment. They are also changed as the client changes. For example, as a child with ADD begins to concentrate better and to mature, the dominant slow wave bandwidth may not just decrease but it may also shift to a higher frequency. For example, it may move from 5 Hz to 7 Hz and then cross into the alpha range. A shift of the dominant frequency upwards is the natural progression with age so it seems that neurofeedback training in clients with ADD is really encouraging a more mature pattern.

ii. Rewarding SMR (12-15 Hz or 13-15 Hz)

In the ADD Centre our most frequent starting point is to reward 12-15 Hz or 13-15 Hz activity with the active electrode placed at Cz or C4. The initial EEG profile typically shows very low amplitude (eyes open) at 12 Hz in most people though it may be high in some clients who have ADD or in elite athletes who have put themselves into a state of "open readiness." In clients who show high amplitude 12 Hz but a 'dip' at 13-15 or 14-15 Hz we chose the appropriate frequency outside of the alpha range when we do the settings for NFB. The rational for SMR training also includes the following considerations:

- For a broad, relaxed awareness we reinforce synchronous high alpha sine waves at a frequency around 12 Hz (11.5-13 Hz). The mental state which corresponds to this band appears to work well in athletics as discussed above. This range is used in 'peak-performance' training.

- In addition, high alpha may appear through the entire 12-15 Hz range and this waveform appears to be associated with a mental state which embodies inner 'reflection' and creative thought. (Remember, the term *alpha* refers to the morphology of the waves and not just a frequency range. Alpha waves may also appear at slower frequencies, such as 7 Hz, especially in young children. It is sometimes referred to as pediatric alpha.)

- Also in this range, perhaps more between 13 and 15 Hz, is the synchronous SMR spindle rhythm which is regulated by the thalamus. This sensorimotor rhythm appears across the top of the head along the sensorimotor strip and is associated with decreased sensory input as well as decreased motor output. (In other locations, such as frontal or occipital, 12-15 Hz activity would be low beta, not SMR.) It appears to be associated with decreased red nucleus firing, decreased muscle spindle activity and decreased muscle tension. When it is increased, the clients tend to become less hyperactive, less fidgety and less impulsive. They tend to be calm and reflect more before responding. Sleep also improves in some cases. In some clients who have emotional lability or hypomanic behaviours SMR may also be of some benefit since higher amplitudes of SMR are associated with a calming effect. SMR training is being used for pain management and in cases of fibromyalgia.

- Desynchronous beta waves associated with problem solving activity are also found at the upper end of this range, though perhaps more in the 14-17 Hz area.

These components or waveforms come from different origins (or "generators"). The brain waves observed in the EEG represent cortical electrical changes which may be influenced by both thalamo-cortical and cortico-cortical activity. The feedback loops within the brain are complex. Each of these waveforms (synchronous alpha, SMR spindles, desynchronous low beta) represents a different mental state though their frequency may be similar. All of the mental states mentioned above are desirable in the process of learning self regulation. This is particularly true when dealing with clients who present with difficulties in attention, concentration, reflection before action and calmness.

Caution #1: Some of your clients tune out in alpha. This alpha may be the predominant component of the 12 to 15 Hz band you are rewarding. If this is true, you may be rewarding your client for tuning out.

Suggestion: Look carefully at the raw EEG. When you see clear alpha waveforms, ask yourself if they go into the 12, 13 Hz range on the spectrum. Is the microvolt level of 12-15 Hz bandwidth markedly raised? If it is, consider rewarding 'SMR' at a slightly higher frequency, say 14 to 16 Hz, especially if there is a dip in this range when you generate your histogram summary of your assessment data. In addition, inhibit 7-9 or 7-10 Hz rather vigorously if this low alpha is excessively high.

Caution #2: If you inhibit 3 to 5 Hz, the predominant wave you are inhibiting may be that which is caused by eye blink. In effect you are rewarding your client for not blinking or moving their eyes. There is a large literature on eye blink rates and it is an interesting phenomenon but it is not typically what we are trying to train.

Suggestion: Look at the raw EEG carefully and note the frequencies that are increased when the client blinks. If blinking is frequent and does raise the amplitude of the 3 to 5 Hz range then you must be careful about how you interpret the EEG. In addition, it is difficult to actually 'feel' or 'sense' 3 to 5 Hz. If 7 to 9 Hz is also raised in your assessment profile, you can choose to train this down. One advantage of this appears to be that even your young children can 'sense' what it feels like to be in the 7 to 9 Hz range or out of this range. The lower frequencies may normalize (decrease) as the client learns to control the 7 to 9 Hz frequency range. You may have to down train 6 to 10 Hz if your equipment does not allow you to customize the bandwidths.

iii. Rewarding Beta 16-20 Hz (or 13-15 Hz)

The electrode placement is usually at Cz, C3, or F3 when training up 16-20 Hz as previously described. Rewarding beta is recommended in clients who demonstrate A.D.D without hyperactivity, impulsivity or labile mood. It is often the range of choice for the client who is not impulsive and who **is lethargic and has a low alertness level.** (Also consider *sleep apnoea* in the differential diagnosis if the person is lethargic to the point of excessive daytime sleepiness. Other symptoms usually include snoring. It is more common in those who are obese and have short, thick necks.) It is appropriate to encourage this range in the left hemisphere in a client who is doing academic work and in most clients with learning disabilities, particularly language based LD. It may also be desirable to reinforce this range in the left frontal region for clients with depressed mood. Of course, you always consider the client's EEG pattern plus knowledge of neuroanatomy and physiology in making decisions about which frequencies to reinforce and where to place the active electrode. In children 15-18 Hz may be more appropriate than 16-20 Hz. Remember that the dominant EEG frequencies shift higher with age.

As noted above, when you reward 13-15 Hz over the sensorimotor strip, you are usually attempting to increase SMR activity. SMR rhythm originates in the ventrobasal nucleus of the thalamus. Anywhere else over the cortex, 13-15 Hz is called low beta. When compared to SMR, desynchronous beta, 13-15 Hz, has a different waveform and a different origin. It is the result of localized neuronal activity. It may correspond to cognitive work. There are occasions when you may wish to *activate* an area of the brain in the right hemisphere but not want to encourage higher beta over 16 Hz. A *soft* encouragement of activation is used. Examples are cases of autistic spectrum disorders, including Asperger's Syndrome, where the full-cap assessment has demonstrated a localized area of slow activity at, or close to, T6. Although, at the time of writing, there were no case series in the literature, there have been a number of anecdotal reports of side effects (such as being temporarily cognitively somewhat out-of-touch with reality) in clients where 16-20 Hz activity was encouraged in this area (Jay Gunkelman, personal communications). In these children we have observed positive effects of increasing 13-15 Hz activity while concomitantly decreasing the dominant slow wave activity in the right hemisphere.

During a course he taught at the 2001 meeting of the SNR in Monterey, CA, Tom Budzynski mentioned that one should not train to increase 16-20 Hz on the left side in children who have *reactive attachment disorders* (RAS). RAS children reportedly have a worsening of symptoms with this training. (We have never seen adverse results with 16-20 Hz training on the left but we evaluated its effects on a series of clients with RAS.)

iv. Brief Review of 'Reward' Frequency Ranges

What is the most important frequency to work on? To make that decision look at the EEG profile and also keep these suggestions in mind:

- To decrease impulsivity and raise 'reflection before responding' the client should usually attempt to increase SMR 12-15 Hz (or 13-15 Hz) activity across the sensorimotor cortex.

- To increase focused concentration decrease the client's dominant slow wave. Make decisions regarding location and frequencies based on whichever location is higher than expected. Data base norms may be consulted for this purpose. Usually the dominant, eyes open, Cz frequency will be somewhere between 3-10 Hz in people who have problems with attention.

- To emphasize peak performance, broad awareness, and a calm mental and physical state, the client should be encouraged to increase 11.5-13.5 Hz activity. However, the ultimate objective is for the client to have mental flexibility, the ability to shift mental set appropriately and thus rapidly shift frequencies. The objective is not merely to increase a particular frequency range.

- To emphasize problem solving use beta 15-18, 16-19 or 16-20 Hz. You could consider attempting to increase 39-41 Hz activity but, as previously noted, this Sheer rhythm is more difficult to work with both because you must severely inhibit any muscle influence (43-58 Hz) and because the amplitude of this frequency band is usually quite low.

- Anxiety and mind *racing* with tension may be associated with increased amplitude in waves anywhere from 24 – 35 Hz. Looking at frequencies above 36 Hz. is helpful in distinguishing muscle tension from mental tension. These high beta frequencies will usually decrease if the client enters a calm state and increases SMR while concomitantly working on relaxing using biofeedback: respiration, RSA, finger temperature, EDR and muscle tension. (As previously mentioned, the clinician should be cautious about encouraging diaphragmatic breathing in a client who has a seizure disorder. If, in the learning process, such a client hyperventilates, a seizure may be precipitated.)

E. Electrode Placement for Feedback

1. Introduction

Decision making regarding placement is most easily done after doing a full cap assessment because you can then compare the relative amplitudes at each site for each frequency. You can also observe how different areas of the brain are communicating with one another by measurements of coherence or comodulation.

However, most readers will not have either the training or the equipment to do this. We will, therefore, look at some general principles and then at two common and relatively simple examples. If you are doing a 1-channel assessment, Cz is often the site chosen. It tends to have the highest amplitudes (it is furthest from the ear reference points so there is less common mode rejection) and it is also less influenced by artifact (either eye movement or jaw tension).

Shaping and Rewarding Responses at One Site may Affect Many Sites

Dr. Joel Lubar has experimented with placing electrodes at different sites for training. He found that, after training along the central cortex at Fz, Cz, Pz or at FCz-CPz, post training changes in theta/beta ratios were also noted at the other 10-20 electrode locations (Lubar in Evans & Abaranel, (1999); Lubar, (1997).

2. Case Examples
a. Electrode placement in ADD without Hyperactivity

Gains from NFB may be seen more rapidly with persons who have ADD without hyperactivity than with those who are quite hyperactive. As an aside, this parallels the finding that there is a different dose-response curve for learning as compared to sitting still for stimulant medications. It takes a higher dose to reduce hyperactivity than to improve performance in a paired-associates learning task. (see chapter 9 on medications in *The A.D.D. Book, [Sears, 1998]*)

Jane, age 17, was a 'couch potato' according to her mother. She was described as being lazy and unmotivated. When Jane was questioned, however, it turned out that she felt very discouraged. She said she knew she was bright enough but it took her so much more time studying than her girlfriends to get even close to their marks. She admitted she had just given up. She said that she would start reading a paragraph, get to the end, and realize she couldn't recall anything. Her mind had just drifted off even though her eyes may have followed the words.

We began training with the active electrode at Cz. The reference electrode was placed on the left ear with the ground on the right to emphasize the left hemisphere. After a few sessions we decided that activation in the left frontal area was important due to her discouraged and somewhat dysphoric mood. We wanted to pair activation with doing academic tasks. Placement was changed to having the 'active' +ve electrode at F3 and the -ve 'reference' electrode on the right ear. Placement of the reference electrode on the right ear gave higher amplitudes of the waves being measured. If it were placed on the left ear lobe, there would be greater common mode rejection by the amplifier and thus lower amplitudes.

Note: Occasionally you will place the active electrode either more anterior or more posterior for either a clinical reason, such as specific learning disabilities, or for an EEG reason because of findings on a full cap 19-channel assessment. You may also choose to reference to the left ear if you decide you mainly want to influence activity in the left hemisphere between your active electrode and that ear. This suggestion must be understood as purely theoretical. It has not been empirically tested. It is based on an equipment manufacturer, electrical engineer's model of the EEG. (Frank Diets, personal communications.) The theory is that you are mainly training dipoles between the active electrode and the reference electrode.

b. Electrode placement in ADD with Hyperactivity:
i. Symptoms of Brent, a 9 Year Old Boy

Assume for this example that a student has come to you with a combination of ADHD, Combined Type and dyslexia. It is important to proceed through the decision making process for each client using the decision pyramid (See the Decision Pyramid diagram in Section VI under Assessment.) This example is discussed in detail as ADHD, Combined Type. It is the most common application of NFB at the time of writing.

Brent was an extremely hyperactive and impulsive 9-year-old boy. He was in grade 3 but his reading was at beginning grade 1 level. He was a child who definitely needed either to have entirely one-on-one teaching or he had to be on a stimulant medication when at school due to his disruptive behaviour. Stimulant medication did work well for Brent as a chemical restraint. However, his mother commented that, "His eyes glaze over just as much on the stimulant as off [it]". She was not convinced it directly affected his attention span although he would spend more time working and finish more school work when, as she put it, he was 'glued' to his seat. Certainly it had not helped him learn to read. She wanted Brent to learn to control his own behaviour and concentration. She also wanted him to catch up in his reading.

The assessment first used an active electrode placement at Cz referenced to the left ear with the ground on the right ear. Brent displayed very high theta at 5-6 Hz. His theta 4-8 Hz / beta 16-20 Hz microvolt ratio was 4.

Now take Brent's case and use the decision pyramid to decide on electrode placements and bandwidths for enhance and inhibit instruments.

ii. Theoretical Approach

(1.) The decision pyramid requires that we first delineate our immediate objective from the client's history and objectives.

(2.) Second, we consider the wave pattern that corresponds to that mental state and which, therefore, must be enhanced and/or inhibited to normalize the EEG and hopefully the symptom(s).

(3.) Third, we consider the client's symptoms in the context of what is known about functional neuroanatomy / neurophysiology. This should assist in delineating the appropriate theoretical site for enhancement and / or inhibition of frequency bands. (or sites for coherence or comodulation training if 19-lead assessment data are available.)

(4.) Fourth, we see if our theoretical formulation corresponds to our findings on the EEG.

(5.) At this juncture we make a final decision on the following parameters: frequencies to be enhanced / inhibited, the site for our active electrode (or electrodes in a sequential placement), the condition(s) which should be incorporated into the feedback sessions such as reading, math, listening (or combinations of these activities in a work – rest sequence).

iii. Practical Application with Brent:

First: We must decide what is the most important symptom to deal with first. Most of us would feel we must deal with the **hyperactivity and impulsivity** before we can adequately focus on his reading. Clinically, experience has demonstrated that raising SMR along the sensorimotor strip will correspond to a decrease in hyperactivity and impulsivity in most children. The red nucleus will decrease firing when the thalamus has increased SMR output. The red nucleus is part of the extrapyramidal system with gamma motor efferents that go to the muscle spindles. Anatomical knowledge and neurophysiological theory suggests that in ADD there may be overactivity related to norepinephrine activity in the right cerebral hemisphere (Malone et al., 1994). This would support a right-sided placement. Therefore, we place the electrode, most often, at Cz or C4. Cz would be less prone to jaw muscle artifact so C4 could be used once the frequencies reflecting EMG activity are consistently low. (As an aside, it is known from experience a C3 placement can also bring good results. This is probably because SMR rhythm is generated in the thalamus and there is communication between the right and left lobes of the thalamus so that training SMR on one side of the brain can have a similar effect on the other side.)

Second: While we enhance SMR, we should increase Brent's ability to **sustain focus**. Studies have demonstrated that decreasing slow wave activity will assist with this objective (Lubar, 1995). Neuroanatomically there are studies done with subjects who have ADD demonstrating a decrease in frontal blood flow (Amen, 1997) and glucose metabolism (Zametkin, 1990). Slow wave activity is generally associated with decreased external focus and decreased problem solving activity. In addition, it is hypothesized that there is deficient dopaminergic activation of the left hemisphere in ADD which corresponds to a decrease in focused attention (Malone et al., 1994). Therefore, we will decide to reinforce a decrease in dominant slow wave activity. Studies are showing that there may be different locations for maximum theta and / or low alpha wave activity in ADD, however, high amplitude slow wave activity is usually found over a relatively wide region. Most often it is frontal or frontal and central. Since we found high theta centrally it is reasonable to lower theta in the central region (C1, Cz or C2).

We could do a second assessment and evaluate the amplitude of theta at F3 and / or Fz. If you have a two channel instrument then it is quite simple to place a second active electrode (for channel B) at F3 and use a *linked ears reference* and a *linked ground* anterior to FPz with wires to both channel A and Channel B. This allows you to assess Cz and F3 at the same time. This gives data for comparison that is collected at the same time and the procedure takes less time than moving your electrode from one site to another and taking two EEG samples.

Third: We want to ameliorate his **reading** difficulty. This will require that his brain be both focused and active, in the problem solving sense, while he is learning to read. For this we combine a theta inhibit (sustain focus), and a beta enhance (actively analyzing the reading material). Neuroanatomical understanding of dyslexia points to the optimal placement of the electrodes being over areas of the brain that correspond to reading functions which are in the left cerebral hemisphere. Reading may involve

the insula area and, perhaps, the angular gyrus at the occipital-parietal-temporal lobe junction. The latter area could be postulated to affect the **visual-spatial-language** skills involved in visual word recognition. To affect these areas the electrode placement, for most people, would be approximately in the middle of a triangle with angles at C3 –P3 -T5 or where the two diagonals would cross in a four sided box with corners at C3-P3-T5-T3. As previously mentioned, Lubar has suggested that for disphonetic dyslexia, you place the active electrode at F3 or F5 (bipolar try F3 – P3 or F7-P7 (T5) and for diseidetic dyslexia at P3 or P5 (bipolar try F3-P3 or F7-P7 (T5). In each instance the objective is to have the student increase activity in that area while carrying out the appropriate academic task.

3. Further Case Examples

Go back and review the earlier descriptions of cases such as Brad and Ben (Severe **Asperger's** Syndrome) from the standpoint of how the 'decision pyramid' was used to define both electrode sites and bandwidths for neurofeedback training. In particular, note how the 19-channel assessment finding of slowing around T6 with Brad and P4 with Ben corresponded to our neurophysiological understanding of the right brain's role in interpreting and expressing innuendo and emotions. This led to electrode placement at a posterior location in the right hemisphere. Brad and Ben both attempted to activate this area.

4. Brief Summary

At this juncture you have chosen electrode placement for a one-channel instrument. We will look at more complex cases and 2-channel training later. You have decided on the inhibit and enhance bandwidths and the thresholds for beginning training. Brent will first be rewarded for increasing 12-15 Hz activity and decreasing 5-8 Hz activity at C4. Once he is calmer, training will shift to 15-18 Hz enhance and 5-8 Hz inhibit on the left side in the middle of the equilateral triangle formed by joining C3, P3 and T5. Now you may consider the speed of feedback (termed smoothing or averaging in most instruments), the types of feedback (auditory and visual) and the screens that you may use. All this is done in order to give the client the most appropriate information to facilitate the task of changing their EEG and, thus, improving self-regulation skills. It is likely in a 9 year old that the highest theta activity will be across the central region (C3, Cz, C4). In adolescents and adults the slow wave activity is often found more frontally (closer to Fz).

F. Speed of Feedback

Some instruments such as the F1000 (Focused Technology), Procomp+/Biograph or the newer Infinity (Thought Technology) allow the operator to alter the rate of feedback; for example, how fast a bargraph moves up and down. This is variously referred to as *averaging* or a *smoothing* factor. It relates to the time period of data collection used before the feedback is updated. We find that, in the early stage of work with a client, slower changes allow the client to follow changes more easily. The jumpy movement may even irritate some clients. However, some clinicians believe that faster feedback, often beyond what one can follow consciously, may have a more dramatic effect. (Here is another empirical question for a graduate student to investigate.) Averaging is a bit like the suspension in a car. You can have it very responsive like a sports car and feel every bump or you can have it very smooth like a Lincoln Town car or a big Citroen. Jumpy will be a little more accurate (faster feedback) but some clients do not like it. You can let your client choose - do they want a smooth ride or a more responsive 'feel the bumps' sporty ride? Better still, in an instrument like the F1000, you can begin the session with a challenge to reach a certain score using a high averaging setting, then change the setting to a faster feedback with a new goal and then to even faster feedback (less averaging). This can be very challenging and we have found that it will engage even some of the most unmotivated children.

Important: 'Averaging' puts a slight delay on information. This can be confusing when you review data. Say, for example, that you are using sound feedback for a professional golfer as they putt. They wish to review the data after they make the putt to see the precise mental state they were in at specific points during a series of actions such as preparing to putt and putting. You must turn off all averaging to accurately see what was occurring at specific points in time, such as when the client made contact with the ball. (Not all equipment allows this kind of review.) If averaging were being done, then there would be

a delay and the raw EEG data would not correspond precisely to the spectrum if both were on the feedback screen.

Similarly, if you want to view a few seconds or minutes of data during an assessment and look at precise points in time, you don't want to use the spectrum because it will to average the information. You want bargraphs without averaging so that they will precisely reflect what the EEG at that instant is showing.

G. Choosing Sound Feedback

1. Use of Sound Feedback

Sound feedback is often used as a reward signal for meeting the criteria such as being below threshold for the theta inhibit. A sound reward at the instant the client achieves the preset threshold can be used in most instruments. On a bargraph, for example, the sound reward for theta is set to occur when the column moves below the threshold.

2. Type of Sound Feedback
a. Discrete Sounds

In some instruments you have further options such as setting a distinct sound. (Digitized sounds such as *chord* or *ding* can be found in 'windows media'). The sound occurs only after the client has held the criteria for a specific length of time (for example, 1, 2 or 3 seconds). In some instruments you can set it so that the reward sounds on moving above or below threshold and then, if held in that state, to sound again at specified time intervals (such as 1, 2 or 3 seconds).

b. Continuous Sound

On the other hand, you may choose to have a continuous sound, a pleasing tone or even music from the client's favourite CD, which remains on only if they continue to meet all the preset criteria. You should see what the client likes and tolerates best and also fit the feedback to the task you are asking your client to do such as reading or math. Music stopping tends to alert the client to when they *lose* rather than *achieve* the threshold criteria.

c. Timing of Sound Feedback

There are several other important considerations. First, all feedback must be <500 msec after a client's response. (The response is meeting the criteria.) Virtually any visual or auditory feedback on a NFB instrument can meet this primary criterion. In addition, you must decide what you are attempting to accomplish, (1.) feedback for discrete events meeting pre-set thresholds <u>or</u> (2.) prolonged feedback for sustaining threshold levels. Let us expand this, to answer the question of what type of feedback for what purpose.

i. Discrete Feedback

Do you want discrete feedback corresponding to each time the client attains the desired mental state? Gail Peterson, a psychologist at the University of Minnesota who teaches learning theory, outlined the criteria for adequate feedback for operant conditioning of a desired response in a guest lecture at the annual meeting of the Society for Neuronal Regulation, October 2000, in Minneapolis. These criteria may be given the acronym SURA. This stands for being **sharp** or immediate; **unique** in that it doesn't otherwise occur; **reliable** in that the equipment produces it reliably; and **ambient** meaning that it stands out distinctly from the ambient environment. No icon that we use should be identified with any previous learning. In addition, Sterman's early animal research suggests that there should be a 2 to 5 second recovery period between rewards.

Ideally we would like to meet Sterman's and Gail Peterson's criteria for successful operant conditioning. In order to do this we should first pay attention to our office setting. We want to have the least amount of clutter, not only on the screen but also around the monitor. This is done to minimize associative learning (anything associated with the stimulus may become necessary for obtaining the response). Second, we require a sharp, unique sound and a visual feedback with a delay between rewards. For the visual feedback visual displays that give a discrete, distinct movement each time the criteria are reached and allow a defined time length between movements when the criteria are

maintained would theoretically be best. What we want is discrete, clear, unique feedback.

Sterman's recommendations for feedback are based on research which concerned synaptic transmissions of impulses. More recent work has demonstrated that the postsynaptic membrane is not the only site of ionotropic receptors which receive a neurotransmitter and open an ion channel. There are presynaptic *autoreceptors* along the length of axons, for example, which bind extracellular circulating neurotransmitters. This system, involving many neurons, may be involved in *sustaining* attention. (Personal discussion with Fred Shaffer, based on material covered in his workshop about neurons given at the AAPB 2001 annual meeting.) Thus we postulate a second way to do operant conditioning may be acceptable.

ii. Sustained Feedback

You may decide to reward **maintaining the desired mental state**. To do this, set the threshold on your instrument so that it is somewhat easier to reach. You may also decide to set *averaging* to a higher figure. This will ensure that sounds or music will not cut on and off too frequently which could be quite irritating to some clients. Try to give a pleasant sound for achievement of the desired mental state. The music chosen may be either relaxing or invigorating. For example, the William Tell Overture may be quite invigorating. The slow movement from the work of Baroque and Classical composers may, on the other hand, be quite relaxing. Your choice depends on your purpose at the time.

As mentioned previously, it is arguable that this type of feedback emphasizes *losing the reward*. Thus, when the music stops suddenly, this loss of rewarding feedback may alert the client to the fact that they have lost the desired state and precipitate them working to actively re-enter the desired mental state.

iii. When to Use Music

Some equipment, as mentioned above, may allow you to use a CD for feedback. This option can allow teenagers to bring in their own CD with music they find rewarding. This provides a further opportunity for you to discuss with the teenager the effect of music on different types of study tasks. The brain can consciously work on one task at one time. We show them visual illusions, such as one where you see either two faces or a vase, and ask them if they can see both images at precisely the same instant in time. They can't. We then joke that on a canoe trip, it is possible to walk across a narrow log over a fast moving river carrying a canoe and chewing gum – just don't taste the gum. If you allow your focus to move to the gum you are likely to find yourself swimming. Music with words may be fine if the subject is one where you learn best by moving in and out of focus (like memorizing a vocabulary list). It is not so good if you are trying to solve a complex math problem or write an essay. Above all, listen to their experiences and beliefs. Try an experiment with different types of music or no music while they do a series of math problems if they would find this genuinely interesting. It is amazing how the most oppositional students will work with you in the spirit of genuine discovery about what works best for them if you approach it in a truly interested (in them) and scientific manner.

H. Sample Feedback Screens

1. Keeping Score – Points and %-Over-Threshold

Some EEG instruments allow the user to '*link*' one feedback display to another. This allows the client to keep score at the same time as they try to meet a challenge, such as keeping the ball to the right on the balance beam in the figure below.

Theta/SMR ratio is under threshold and has therefore turned green.

30 points (blue) have been attained.

These rewards are given for each 1 second the client stays below the ratio threshold.

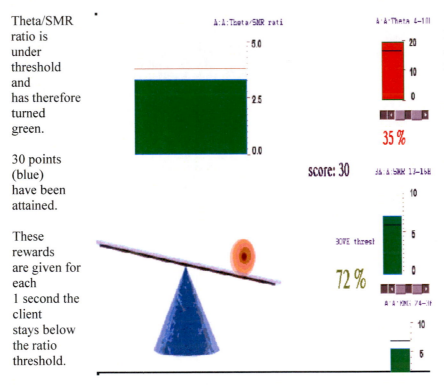

'Thalpha' 4-10 Hz It is above threshold & has therefore turned red. It has been 35% of the time over threshold.

SMR, 13-15 Hz, is above threshold & has therefore turned green. It has been 72% of the time above threshold.

An inhibit has been placed On 24-36 Hz activity. This will inhibit all feedback (sound, balance beam, %'s-above-threshold & points) if too high.

Different colours are used for meeting criteria (green) and not meeting criteria (red). Thus: Green = desired activity Red = Undesirable

The ball moves to the right when the client remains below the ratio threshold (desired result) and goes to the left when the client goes above the ratio.

Purpose of Screen

The objective is to roll the ball to the far right hand side of the balance beam and hold it there as long as possible. This screen is set so that the balance beam animation is linked to a theta / SMR ratio. It therefore requires an externally focused, calm mental state. If, instead, a theta / beta ratio were to be used, it would require a focused and actively problem solving mental state. The beta option is used (beta substituted for SMR in the above screen) during the part of a session when the student is listening to a mock academic lecture given by the trainer or when the trainer is teaching the student metacognitive strategies such as active reading, note taking, underlining or math strategies. It makes sense to train for increased beta when on task.

Screen Details

The sound feedback can be discrete, digitized sound, a chord or a ding. The sound could be set so that it requires that the mental state be held; for example, for 1 or more seconds. The points are often set so that the student is required to keep the ratio below threshold for an entire second. This makes attaining points very different than changing the percent-above-threshold. The *green* %-over-threshold is linked to the SMR (or Beta). The *red* %-over-threshold is linked to the slow wave (thalpha, 4-10Hz) in this case. The student is told that green and blue are the 'good-guy' colours –increase them. The red is a 'bad-guy' colour –decrease it. The 4-10 range is an unusually wide range that was chosen for this client because there were two slow wave peaks at 5 Hz and 9 Hz. The *dark blue* points are linked to the balance beam animation. We linked a %-over-threshold to the points and thus to the animation and the ratio but we decided we had sufficient on the screen for this client to watch so the instrument was hidden while feedback took place. %'s-over-threshold and points are recorded manually at 3-5 minute intervals on a Client Tracking Sheet. The length of time, 2 minutes, 3 minutes, etc., is determined by what seems doable for a particular client. Two minutes of sustained focus is quite a challenge for young children. We like the client to write down their own scores. We find this gets them more interested in shifting the scores in a desirable direction.

Note that the 24-36 Hz bargraph is being used on this screen as a muscle inhibit as well as an inhibit for nonproductive ruminative thinking. An EEG with threshold lines has been set and hidden in the background in order to reduce clutter on the screen. The threshold lines above and below the EEG are set to inhibit feedback if there is significant eye blink or movement artifact. This EEG linegraph can be brought on to the screen if the trainer wishes to view the EEG during the session.

A Clinical Hint: With some display screens, such as the one above try counting out seconds, in a barely audible voice, while the student maintains the desired mental state. For example, count: 1001, 1002, 1003… while the ball remains on the right side. Mark a horizontal line in seconds; say 1 to 20. Place a check mark on how far the student gets on each count. Perhaps give one token for achieving 7 seconds and two for reaching 10 seconds, 3 for 12 seconds and so on. Tokens earned are recorded in the client's bank account at the end of each session and they can use them to purchase prizes that are kept on display on a large bookshelf.

2. Empower The Client To Produce Specific Frequencies At Will

It is very empowering for a student to discover that they are able to decrease theta or thalpha on purpose or to raise SMR or beta through conscious control. The balance beam above can be used in this exercise. **If your instrument has a "work-rest" function** then you can set it so that "work" lasts for about 45 seconds and "rest" lasts for about 15 seconds. During the "work" phase the client must roll the ball to the right. During the "rest" phase the client must roll the ball to the left and keep it there. They must do this without changing any aspect of their posture and without moving their eyes or their jaw. (With special thanks to Jim Stieben, Toronto, for his work with clients refining this technique.) This technique follows an exercise model. You work on producing a particular state, then briefly rest, then try to produce the state again. Alternatively try to turn the mental state on and then deliberately turn it off. It can be likened, for the client, to doing a number of sit ups or chin ups and then resting.

The sailboat display screen (below under H2) available in the Procomp+/Biograph program is also particularly good for this purpose. This screen allows the client to build or destroy the sailboat (which fragments and goes totally black when the client loses the desired state of focus). You make it difficult to build the boat (threshold for theta somewhat challenging for that client). The client must then find and hold a focused mental state (if the boat picture is linked to theta) that "builds" the boat. This is not easy at first but attaining control can be tremendously gratifying and self-empowering.

We begin the session with the client attempting to hold theta down and thereby obtain the lowest possible %-above-threshold (in red) and the highest number of points (in blue) possible during a 3 minute period. The student will compete with himself 5 or more times. He tries to improve his scores each time. When he gains some real control over theta the trainer suggests he try a different challenge. He is told to hold the boat for a count of 5. Then he is to destroy the boat by letting his focus wander. He is to hold this lack-of-focus mental state with the boat in its blackened form for a count of 5 and then purposefully build it again and hold it built for a count of 5. He is to repeat this process several times until conscious control over theta is possible. Older students may experiment retrieving memories and see if this increases theta.

Two inhibits may be used. The first is 45-58 Hz to stop the influence of muscle tension, and the second is on 13-15 Hz and stops feedback if he client goes below threshold. These and the spectrum are sometimes hidden to make the screen less cluttered (This means the data are being recorded but the information does not appear on the screen.) Clients learn to hold all movement (EMG) at a minimum and remain calm and concentrating (to produce SMR) while they ONLY vary their focus and thereby build the sailboat and hold it built (theta below threshold) for a defined period of time. Then they let their focus go on purpose and the boat is destroyed. Then they rebuild it again. They repeat the exercise until it is entirely under their conscious control. This is an exercise for all ages. We have watched clients from age 4 to 64 enjoying it. When the client has control with theta or thalpha, they try it with SMR and then beta 16-18 Hz. Adults may try control of high beta (20-23 Hz and 24-32 Hz) activity. The sailboat is linked to an appropriate bargraph in each case. With young children, after they become proficient at this form of self regulation, we ask them if they would like to show the other staff (and then their parents) how they have control of their own brain waves.

The bottom left corner of this screen has a spectrum. One could substitute the raw EEG. This allows the trainer to see the broader picture of brain wave production and to monitor whether artifacts are interfering with the feedback.

3. Gaining Control of Slow and Fast Wave Production

During a session, it may be helpful to use a variety of screens. Each screen should have a clear purpose. In the screen shown below the client gets a real sense of making the box (which corresponds to the amplitude of the slow wave activity, *theta or "thalpha"*, smaller. They try to make it recede into the back of the screen while

simultaneously making the fast wave activity, *SMR or beta*, box large so that it seems to come out of the screen towards them. This kind of screen is simple but very effective. The percents-over-threshold can be recorded for each 5 minute time period.

Jason demonstrated that he could hold theta below threshold while maintaining SMR above threshold. In his first session both %-below-threshold figures were close to 50%. Now, in a 5 minute time frame, he was able to reach 79 % above threshold for SMR and 36% for theta. Skin Conduction (SC) was placed on his screen because he had a tendency to drop to a low level of alertness when things weren't moving quickly.

Brief Summary
Purpose:

(1.) For the client to attain, through visual and sound feedback, a distinct, dynamic sense of:

    a. the reciprocal relationship between *decreasing* slow wave and *increasing* fast wave activity;

    b. being able to find and hold the desired mental state for longer and longer periods of time.

(2.) For the client and trainer to follow progress by tracking brief time periods (two to five minutes) for changes in *percent over threshold*

of the slow and fast waves. (Changes in the %-over-threshold values change rapidly at first and then slow down over time because the calculation is an average over the period of the recording. Even after ten minutes it is difficult to shift the percent.) Points are also scored (white number at the top of the screen) for each one second that theta is held below threshold.

(3.) For the client and trainer to follow the EEG and, in particular, to note the changes in the EEG with different mental states. It is highly motivating for a client to be able to observe first hand that they are truly learning to control their brain's electrical activity.

(4.) To ensure quality feedback.

a. **Minimize muscle artifact** – 'Muscle inhibit' in this screen is 45-58 Hz. Sound feedback will stop if there is muscle activity in the head and neck region. Because EMG can be very high in amplitude, it may overwhelm filters and give a false impression that beta and/or SMR is raised. You do not want to be rewarding tense jaw muscles and think you are rewarding SMR or beta!

b. **Minimize movement artifact** from electrode movement or excessive eye movement. The movement artifact inhibit in this screen is achieved by setting the EEG threshold parallel lines at a level which allows normal EEG activity, but which will stop sound feedback should a large amplitude wave appear in the EEG. These dotted lines can be seen above and below the raw EEG signal.

(5.) **Maintain an alert mental state**. EDR is recorded. If it drops the client's alertness level may also be decreasing. They may want to adjust their posture or take some other action to maintain arousal at an appropriate level.

4. Choice of Games for Feedback Training

a. Purpose Dictates Type of Game

On the whole, children with ADD have excellent focus for games and things that are novel. Our job as neurofeedback trainers is to have them create their own internal "game" (a method for remaining alert and focused) in order to achieve *self-regulation* and be in control in boring situations. The more interesting, dynamic or 3-dimensional the feedback screen, the less useful it may be in the long run. Although using relatively boring feedback theoretically seems logical to us, it requires research studies to elucidate the variables. For example, we may use an interesting feedback display to initially catch the attention and effort of an extremely hyperactive young child or an autistic child. Certainly neurofeedback is never one-size-fits-all so you want to be able to reward learning the task of self regulation in a number of different ways. Ultimately, however, our clients must be able to sustain their concentration during boring

activities such as doing homework or listening in some classes.

b. 'Resting Waves' Review

- Think of the brain as *turning off or resting from external world involvement* when it is in theta or low alpha. These synchronous waveforms (they look like sine waves), in an oversimplified way, are thought to come mainly from thalamic generators (central area of brain) and project up to the surface of the cortex. We record their rhythmic influence on the pyramidal cells in different areas of the neocortex with sensors on the scalp.

- *Calmly resting in a very positive sense* is associated with increased SMR. These synchronous *spindle-like* waveforms, are thought to come from other thalamic generators (ventrobasal nucleus of the thalamus) and project up to the surface where cortical neurons are recruited to produce the same rhythmic activity. This cortical activity is what we record. We see higher amplitudes of this waveform when people are in a calm state, with reduced sensory input and motor output (fidgeting) and not tending to be impulsive. Remember the original research did with cats. It is the cat waiting but alert and ready to pounce when conditions are right. SMR should be considered only to be projected to, and therefore recorded over, the sensorimotor strip, immediately anterior (motor) and posterior (sensory) to the central sulcus in the left and right hemispheres. We usually record it from C3 on the left across to C4 on the right

I. Combining Operant and Classical Conditioning with NFB

(With special thanks to Dr. Joel Lubar for the clarity of his teaching about this kind of training.)

Operant and classical conditioning are more fully discussed in the first section of this book. This section briefly reviews these two learning paradigms and clarifies how these principles are applied during training sessions.

1. Objective: Transfer to Home and School

The objective is to assist the 'transfer' of training using NFB to work, home and school settings. To accomplish this objective, we want the student to unconsciously and automatically turn on a mental state of calm, focused concentration when appropriate. Training for this is carried out in two steps that involves first, operant and, second, classical conditioning.

To briefly summarize this, recall from Section I that you first use **operant conditioning.** The basic principle underlying this kind of conditioning is that when you reward behaviour you increase the likelihood of its recurrence. This is done by having the student find a mental state which results in his meeting the thresholds which have been set for the slow and fast waves in the absence of EMG induced artifact. This will cause visual and auditory feedback to be emitted. This information acts as a reward and increases the likelihood of that brain state being achieved and maintained again.

Secondly, use **classical conditioning.** The basic principle here is to pair two stimuli. In this case, pair the desired mental state with carrying out an academic task. This is done by having the student find the desired mental state using the operant conditioning paradigm above, and then introduce the academic task while retaining that state, as evidenced by continued auditory feedback. If the auditory feedback should stop, the student is instructed to return their attention to the NFB display screen. The student works at getting the appropriate feedback until they again are able to hold it steady for a reasonable period of time. This steady feedback signifies that they have the desired mental state for returning to the academic task.

For this procedure we want a non-intrusive screen such as a fractal display. Alternatively, the screen is covered and the student only receives sound feedback. The counter is usually linked to a soft *chord* or *ding* feedback that occurs at a rate of one every 1 to 3 seconds while the state is produced. You can also use a pleasant tone or music. This may sound continuously as long as the desired mental state is produced. The client, in this case, is alerted by the sudden cessation of sound.

2. The Why and When of Combining Academic Tasks with Neurofeedback

(A version of this section appeared first in the *Journal of Neurotherapy* 6(4) Clinical Corner with our permission.) Judith Lubar's comments on the efficacy of training while on task also appears in that volume.)

As we have stressed throughout this text, the practice of neurofeedback has its roots in research labs. It draws on both learning theory and empirical observations concerning outcomes. Each practitioner also brings his own background and knowledge into play. If you have a background in educational psychology, it feels natural to add the teaching of metacognitive strategies to neurofeedback training. Combining neurofeedback with the teaching of strategies and academic tasks is also supported by learning theory principles and outcome studies.

Neurofeedback is a type of learning since it involves the operant conditioning of brain wave activity. As Sterman points out in his writings (Sterman, 2000), Thorndike's Law of Effect, which states that behaviours which are rewarded have a higher likelihood of recurrence, is at the core of what we do. Operant conditioning, carefully developed by B.F. Skinner, grew out of Thorndike's trial and error learning experiments. When we reward the production of certain EEG patterns with information about success, using visual displays and auditory feedback from the computer, we increase the probability that the client will produce that pattern again. We do not know the precise mechanisms (perhaps a change in neurotransmitter release, or in receptor sites at the synapse, or structural changes involving greater dendritic arborisation over time) but we do observe EEG changes in people who learn the task (Lubar, 1997; Thompson & Thompson, 1998).

When you pair an academic task with the state of being relaxed yet focused, you are adding classical conditioning to operant conditioning. Classical conditioning, whose principles were elucidated by Ivan Pavlov through his experiments with dogs and their digestive systems, involves presenting a neutral stimulus (the conditioned stimulus) just prior to presenting a stimulus that elicits a reflexive response. Pavlov rang a bell before giving meat powder and, after a few pairings of bell and meat powder, the bell elicited salivation even if no food was given. In our work with clients who have ADD, where the goal is to improve concentration, we first use operant conditioning to train the state of being relaxed while sustaining alertness and focus. The feedback comes to reliably elicit this state so that it is like a reflex. (Remember, only reflexive, autonomic responses can be trained with classical conditioning. You use operant conditioning to train voluntary responses.) The feedback now acts like an unconditioned stimulus that produces the response of the desired physiological state (relaxed yet focused). If you now present metacognitive strategies and an academic task along with the feedback, this academic work is the conditioned stimulus that, after enough pairings, will also elicit the relaxed, yet alert and focused, state.

The academic tasks are done with an emphasis on metacognition; that is, executive thinking skills that monitor and guide how we learn and remember things. Examples include active reading strategies, techniques for organizing written work, and mnemonic devices, such as tricks for remembering multiplication facts. (For a fuller discussion see Section XII of this text and the chapter on "Strategies for School Success" in *The A.D.D. Book* by Sears & Thompson, 1998.) Metacognition is particularly important for students with ADD because they are not naturally reflective: they do not plan their approach to tasks, are not good at time management, fail to make neat and organized study notes, and they always underachieve relative to their intellectual potential. Good students, on the other hand, seem to just naturally apply metacognitive strategies (Palinscar & Brown, 1987). To have the greatest impact, you cannot just do tutoring along with neurofeedback because there is not enough time to cover much content when you see a person for two one-hour sessions a week and the main focus is on getting focused. But there is time to teach one strategy in a session and then try to apply it to an academic task. The next session you can review that strategy and either reinforce it with more practice or move on to a new one. It is a great advantage to be teaching something when you know (from the neurofeedback) that the person is paying attention. Thus you want the feedback to continue both when you are coaching the person concerning a strategy and when they are trying to apply it. If they are reading it will be the auditory feedback that is giving the information. If the feedback indicates they have tuned out, you simply stop the task and let them return to focusing on the feedback until they get back in the zone. Learning principles tell you that you do not want to pair new learning with a tuned-out state of mind.

What are the logistics of fitting in the strategies? First, obviously, you want the client to be in the right mental state before you start. Thus you pair the task with neurofeedback once the feedback is reliably eliciting the desired mental state. The timing will differ from client to client, both in terms of which session first includes strategies and in terms of when during each subsequent session they are introduced. If the client is not performing well one day, maybe due to having an infection and being on antibiotics, you might just do feedback for that session. Another day the same client might be very much in the zone and more strategies and academic work would be covered. Typically, in practice, the first twenty minutes or so are usually spent doing pure feedback – paying attention to paying attention. (This is not twenty minutes uninterrupted; indeed, it may be ten two-minute segments with a client who is struggling to maintain focus. Always respect individual differences and tailor the feedback, and the strategies, to that client and how they are performing that day.) Once the client is reliably producing the desired mental state the metacognitive strategies and their application to an academic task begins. Now they must think about thinking; that is, be aware of how they learn and remember things and apply it to an actual task.

The answer to the question of why bother with strategies/academics in the first place has to do with generalization. Generalization of a response is another concept from learning theory. It means that similar situations (or stimuli) will elicit the same response that was learned during training. In Psych. 100 you perhaps learned that when John Watson conditioned fear of a white rat in little Albert in his (in)famous experiment early in the last century, Albert also came to fear cotton wool and even Watson's white hair. With Pavlov's dogs, a bell with a different tone could still elicit salivation. When we have paired being focused with doing an academic task while receiving neurofeedback, the expectation is that the student will also get focused when they pick up a book to read at home. The student may also use metacognition, recalling the active reading strategies taught in the session. As he thinks about applying them, they should also trigger the relaxation and sustained concentration that was his physiological state when the strategies were learned. Although some of the learning that occurs with neurofeedback is clearly unconscious, we also want to encourage generalization (some of which is also unconscious) with the conscious application of strategies. Parents are impressed if they see their child calmly reading and doing schoolwork during a training session and they are even more impressed when their child starts doing this at home.

Parent notice of changes brings up the second underpinning of neurofeedback; namely, empirical observations. A further reason for pairing academic coaching with neurofeedback is that is has been observed to work. The results at our center (Thompson & Thompson, 1998) showed statistically significant gains not only in behaviour (measured by TOVA and parents' questionnaire data) but also in academic performance and IQ scores. These results parallel those of Lubar (1995; also reviewed in Lubar & Lubar, 1999), which is not surprising since the Lubars are mentors to us and many others in this field. They advocate a session structure that has five conditions: feedback alone, feedback plus reading, feedback alone, feedback plus listening, feedback alone. This approach follows the principle of getting the person focusing before you introduce the academic task.

In summary, adding metacognitive strategies and applying them to academic tasks makes sense when working with clients who want to improve their concentration, organization, and academic or work performance. The reasons for doing so are derived from learning theory principles involving operant conditioning, classical conditioning, and generalization of behaviour. The combined intervention is also supported by empirical observations of favourable outcomes using this approach. Furthermore, there is perceived value to the client because metacognitive strategies can be applied immediately in other learning situations even before the EEG changes are consolidated.

It remains an open question, however, whether adding the academic component improves outcomes and which measured outcomes are affected. It could be argued that time spent on strategies detracts from learning the EEG task. It would make a good doctoral dissertation to compare neurofeedback alone, metacognitive strategies alone, and the two in combination. Until we have such data, clinicians can justify the combined approach since it is based on established learning principles and published empirical research.

J. Two Channel Assessment and Training

1. Using 2 Channels

With two separate channels of EEG one can see what is happening at two sites simultaneously. A common use of this is with a mind mirror display, a term used by Anna Wise in her book, *Peak Performance Mind*. A mind mirror shows a frequency display for left and right hemispheres and it is place vertically (see Figure_.) It is the basic screen used in Val Brown's software for the Procomp+ equipment.

In order for the reading to be truly comparable it is ideal to use linked electrodes for reference and a common ground as shown in the diagram below. This way you know that impedance at the ground and reference sites and most artifacts will be affecting the two active sites equally. Thus differences in EEG readings at the two sites can be assumed to reflect what is happening at those sites. Of course, eye movement artifact will have more influence on frontal sites and jaw tension will affect temporal sites the most but you have at least eliminated some variance due to impedances and electrical artifacts.

Note that 2-channel training is not the same as sequential (bipolar) placement. Sequential placements have 2 electrodes at active sites plus a ground and those three sensors comprise 1 channel of EEG. With a sequential placement you know there is a difference but you cannot say with certainty which site has higher activity in a particular frequency range.

2. Two channel montage with linked ears and common ground.
Diagram of Linked Ear Reference and Common Ground Set-Up

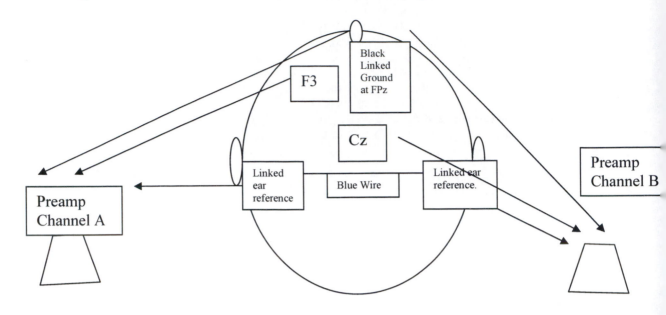

3. Examples of 2-Channel Training

Two channel training allows options which may be useful for some clients. There is not yet published research on outcomes but these suggestions make sense in terms of what we know about symptoms, neurophysiology and mental states. (See the *Decision Pyramid* Part II, Section VI A1.) A 2-channel placement may be the option of choice for a learning disabled child who is also impulsive. Channel A at F3 or C3 rewarding beta, inhibiting theta to increase left frontal activation and channel B at C4 rewarding SMR to decrease impulsivity.

A two channel training may also be considered for dysphoria combined with either anxiety or emotional lability. In these circumstances one may encourage the client to increase activity at F3 by decreasing their dominant slow wave activity and increasing beta 15-18 Hz at this site. Concomitantly they would attempt to increase SMR using channel B at C4. Three examples for the use of 2 channel feedback are described below.

Note that these *are **not** protocols*. They are suggestions for training if certain symptom pictures and EEG profiles are found in a client. This type of training should only be carried out by persons who have training and expertise in these areas. Though the suggestions are not researched, they do logically follow from what is known about brain function.

a. ADHD combined with Learning Disabilities

Learning disabilities are the most common co-morbidity found with attentional problems. If you are using a single channel for training you will address the main symptoms that are distressing to others, which usually will be hyperactivity and impulsive behaviour. This involves reducing the dominant slow wave activity and, even more important, increasing 12-15 Hz across the sensorimotor strip. Placement at Cz or on the right side at C4 makes sense in terms of calming effects corresponding to an increase in SMR activity. This is mediated by thalamo-cortical loops and can be expected to generalize to sensorimotor areas and not be limited to the training site. With 2-channel training you can simultaneously address those problems while also activating areas associated with the cognitive functions that are impaired. Most often these students have language based learning disabilities so you want to activate areas in the left hemisphere. (A good text that discusses the typical learning problems and offers teaching strategies to deal with them is *Right-Brained Children in a Left-brained World (Freed, 1997).*) Since beta activity is associated with cortico-cortico coupling and short distance loops you will choose the site according to which cognitive processes you want to activate. You do not expect beta to generalize. Activation equates to increasing 15-18 Hz (or 16-20 Hz) and reducing the dominant slow wave activity. Thus, as previously noted, for the child who has trouble decoding words, placement might be tried over Wernicke's Area in the vicinity of P3 to P5. If he has trouble reading aloud it might be near Broca's area approximately in the vicinity of F3 to F5.

Non-verbal learning disabilities may be associated with right side dysfunction. These students have problems with spatial reasoning and will thus usually have weaknesses in some aspects of mathematics, especially geometry. Some also have problems reading social cues and with emotional responsiveness, both reading emotions and expressing them with the subtle modulations you would expect. The *non-verbal LD* style has some communalities with Asperger's Syndrome. The parietal-temporal regions seem to show more slow wave activity (less activation) on brain maps done on people with AS. (This finding has been noted with a rapidly increasing number of clients by Jay Gunkelman (personal communication), plus our own findings). Thus activation of the area around P4 to T4 in the low beta range could be tried. Frequencies of 13-16 Hz may be appropriate.

Decreased activity at F3 and F4 has also been observed. However, you would not likely want to activate right frontal activity alone since that can be associated with a focus on negative thoughts and *avoidance behaviours*. However, activation of both right and left frontal activity may be tried. Increasing spectral correlation (comodulation) between the left frontal lobe and the right parietal and frontal areas may also be attempted in future as equipment is just coming on the market that will be able to do this (see www.ThoughtTechnology.com for the neuro-navigator).

To summarize the above:

- Channel 1 (A) on left side of head: usually for purposes listed above to help with learning. The site will vary depending on the type of learning disability being addressed.
- Channel 2 (B) on right side of head: usually for purposes listed above, namely to decrease the hyperactive &/or impulsive symptoms if placed over the sensorimotor strip at Cz or C4. It might also be used to increase activity in the right parietal-temporal region in Asperger's syndrome.

b. Depressed Clients

Depressed clients may show less activation of the left frontal lobe compared to the right frontal area (Robinson 1984; Davidson 1995, 1998; Rosenfeld 1996, 1997). In EEG terms it may be observed that beta is lower and theta and alpha wave amplitudes are higher on the left as compared to the right frontal areas. To remember this asymmetry, recall that one's heart (happiness) is on the left and the left pre-frontal cortex is associated with processing positive thoughts and *approach behaviour*. Robinson's original work noted that damage to the left frontal lobe was associated with *depression* while damage to the right frontal lobe was associated with *manic symptoms*. The conclusions drawn from these observations were that the left frontal area mediated positive thoughts and approach behaviour while the right frontal area mediated negative thoughts and withdrawal behaviour. Taking this a step further, a low activation of the left frontal area compared to the right may not only differentiate between depressed patients and normals (state marker), but it may also be a trait marker for vulnerability to depression (Rosenfeld 1996).

In treatment with neurofeedback, the observation is that increased activation means increased fast wave activity relative to slow wave activity. The hypothesis is that activation of the left frontal area may decrease depressed feelings. Jay Gunkelman has suggested that, along with increasing beta over the anterior portion of the left frontal lobe, one may use a second channel to encourage high alpha (11-13 Hz) in posterior regions (parietal) (Workshop, AAPB, 2001). This posterior alpha is thought to compete with the production of alpha in the frontal region. In other words, you have the alpha in a more appropriate location. The reason for paying attention to alpha in this case is that it is an inverse indicator of activation. (In adults, increased frontal alpha suggests the brain is resting, whereas less alpha suggests activation.) Alpha is used because EMG activity can produce artifact that affects the beta range but it has less effect on alpha. Beta is a much lower amplitude wave than alpha so small changes due to EMG would have a relatively larger effect on recorded amplitudes of beta compared to their effect on the much higher amplitude alpha waves.

Another way to approach the treatment of depression, developed by Peter Rosenfeld at Northwestern University is called the *alpha asymmetry protocol*. It uses two channels with the active electrodes over the left (L) and right (R) frontal regions respectively. Both channels are referenced to Cz. You can purchase Rosenfeld's protocol from him for a nominal fee. On some instruments that allow you to set parameters you could utilize the alpha asymmetry idea put forth by Rosenfeld and put in the formula (R-L) ÷ (R+L). Set up in this way means that a positive number will indicate that the client is happier because you are measuring

alpha, the inverse of activation. You want right sided alpha (R) to be higher than left sided alpha (L). You let the right side, associated with negative thoughts, rest and you keep the left side's focus on positive thoughts activated. The most important factor according to Elsa Baehr, who has done clinical work using Rosenfeld's protocol, is the percent of time during the recording session in which (R-L) ÷ (R+L) is greater than zero. This is a better discriminator of depressed vs control subjects than the (R-L) ÷ (R+L) score itself. Baehr notes that <55 percent of the time with left frontal activation suggests depression and >60 percent of the time with left higher than right suggests no depression (Baehr, 1999).

It should be noted by the reader that using a complex formula such as (R-L) ÷ (R+L) the results do not inform you as to whether changes have taken place in R or in L. A positive value only indicates a shift in a ratio but does not say if alpha on the right increased or if alpha on the left decreased. This is another question worthy of research.

2 Channel training to improve mood.

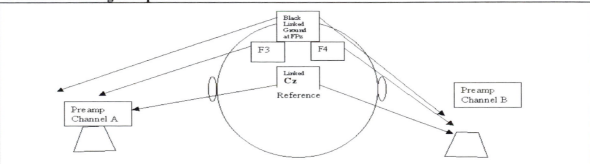

Note in the above diagram how the ground reference electrode has two wires, one for each channel. If a second electrode with two wires attached is used at Cz it could go into reference inputs on each of the two preamps for channels A and B respectfully. This would be an easy way to compare activity under the two active electrodes at F3 and F4 because the reference and ground are the same so comparisons are meaningful. Channel A would be 'L' and channel B would be 'R' in the formula (R-L) ÷ (R+L) given above. Electrodes linked in this fashion must be specially purchased from a manufacturer such as IMA in Florida.

Although a Cz reference is used by Rosenfeld, others have found that clients differ on which reference point is best and some clinicians find an ear reference can be used with equally good results. Here is another good thesis topic, to compare outcomes with different reference sites and see if it makes a difference in training outcomes. Still others have suggested that it is

more effective to just activate the left frontal area as suggested by Jay Gunkelman.

Whatever method you use, try using as your goal having a greater percent of time that left activation exceeds the level of activation on the right. Of course, you must look at your client's EEG data first. Perhaps, for example, some people who are 'true lefties' with hemispheric functions reversed will show the opposite pattern. Always respect individual differences rather than just following a protocol.

Remember that anyone with depression should first be assessed and perhaps treated by a physician. For a patient with serious depression neurofeedback would be an adjunct, not a substitute, for medical treatment. As is also true of clients with ADD, they may be on medication when neurofeedback is begun. As progress in self-regulation is made the individual may, in consultation with the prescribing physician, be able to reduce their medication use.

c. Seizure Disorders

At the seizure site there is often observed to be increased slow wave activity. Decreasing this slow wave activity at or near the seizure site would appear to be a constructive, normalizing approach. In addition, past research has demonstrated that increasing SMR activity may have a positive effect for those clients who exhibit grand mal seizures, partial complex seizures, or any type of seizures with a motor component. The analogy to setting up a 'firewall' by increasing SMR has been used by experts in this area, notably Sterman (Sterman, 2000). Thus you are both directly trying to decrease epileptiform activity and encourage competing activity so that neurons near those firing in the wrong way resist being influenced and the kindling of a full blown seizure does not occur.

To this end, the clinician might consider placing one active electrode (channel A) near the seizure site to inhibit the slow wave component. A second active electrode (channel B) would be placed along the central motor strip (possibly alternating sessions at C3 and C4, the sites where Sterman worked) and 12-15 Hz SMR activity would be encouraged.

4. Case Example of Two Channel Training

Electrode Placement in a Complex Adult Case
Each adult will be different in terms of their symptoms and it follows that there may be corresponding differences in the placement of electrodes both for assessment and for training.

The following case is sufficiently complex to allow readers to follow the kind of decision pathway they may wish to follow with their clients.

Peter, age 36, complained of a poor school history, depression with ruminating, impulsivity, and falling asleep when he tried to read text book material. With a Cz single lead assessment, the EEG demonstrated a dip in SMR at 13-14 Hz but no significant rise in slow wave activity. This did correspond to his impulsivity but not to his constant worrying or inattention.

A second, two channel, assessment was carried out using F3 and Cz placements for the active electrodes. This demonstrated very high amplitude 7-9 Hz activity, when reading or doing math, at F3 but not at Cz. The theta/beta μV ratio at F3 was 3. Clearly we now had 2 tasks. First, we to do SMR training centrally. Second, to decrease "thalpha" (7 to 9 Hz in this case, in others it might be 6 to 10) and increase beta (16-20 Hz) at F3. This would be done first while paying attention to feedback, then later while doing an academic task, such as reading. (We chose the F3 site for a comparative assessment because we knew we would not be encouraging an increase in beta in the right frontal region as it seems to be related to undesirable states in some individuals such as depression, although this supposition requires further research).

However, there was still another challenge. Peter was dysphoric and ruminated. We had seen increased 28-32 Hz activity at F3 and at Cz

We wondered if there would be a difference between activation of the two frontal lobes. Research, as noted above under depression, has found asymmetry between the left and right frontal areas with greater activation on the right. It was concluded that we tend to focus on negative thoughts in the right frontal areas and on positive thoughts on the left (Davidson, 1998). This has led to the hypothesis that, in work with NFB, we should increase beta (15-20 Hz) and/or decrease alpha (an inverse index of activation) in the left frontal area in order to increase activation of the left frontal lobe.

The investigation of the dysphoric mood and ruminating required that we again use two channels. This time we explored the question of differences between the two frontal lobes by doing a 2 channel assessment using F3 and F4.

Full-cap assessments would be excellent, however, it is more time consuming and expensive. As well, most programs for doing the full-cap, at this time of writing, are not looking at the spectrum of activity to 60 Hz. If we do not look beyond frequencies in the mid 20's you may miss some of the ruminating that is reflected in activity in the 28-34 Hz range. Finally, many readers of this volume will not yet be doing full-cap assessments on a regular basis.

We find it useful for clients who complain of ruminating and becoming internally distracted by concerns regarding matters irrelevant to the task at hand, to put the active electrode for channel A at F3 or slightly anterior to this point. The active electrode for channel B is placed at the equivalent point (F4) over the right hemisphere. Both electrodes are referenced to their ipsilateral ear lobe or mastoid or to linked ears. Although theoretically we should only require one 'ground' we have found that the results are more consistent if we use a ground for each channel. Better still is to purchase a lead for a 'common ground' as shown in the diagram above. When not using a common ground, we usually ground to the opposite ear from the reference, placing the electrode on the top of the ear. In this type of assessment the **impedance** must be almost **exactly the same** between each pair of electrodes. Otherwise, (we again remind you), any difference observed might in part be due to the different electrode connections.

Now that you have your electrodes in place, compare the 2 sites for different frequency ranges. You should graph in one or two Hz band segments. For training, use the exact bandwidth that the assessment shows to be problematic, that is, the bandwidth that has an amplitude outside the range which you would expect when compared with other bandwidths for that client and for normal subjects. (Having an idea of what normal looks like is always helpful.) For ruminating and worrying we usually find a marked increase somewhere between 23-34 Hz. We are finding that when most (but not all) of our clients think negative thoughts (ruminate) 23-34 Hz activity, measured either in microvolts or as %-time-over-threshold (which you can put on your screen with some instruments), is higher in the right frontal region. When the same client thinks positive thoughts it is either higher on the left or this activity disappears altogether. (This requires replication so please check it out with your own clients.) We also find that, when the client relaxes and becomes externally openly aware, this frequency band (23-34 Hz) drops in both hemispheres and the 11-15 Hz bandwidth amplitude rises. With intense, obsessive compulsive clients and clients who are anxious and ruminate, you may observe very high amplitudes of beta between 20 and 34 Hz along the midline Fz, Cz. (You may, less frequently, see this high amplitude beta activity at lower frequencies.) It would appear that this corresponds to a 'hot' cingulate and it does respond to neurofeedback training with a decrease in the symptoms. (Bob Gurnee has also reported this in meetings of the SNR, 2002, and FutureHealth, 2003.). We are not finding large overall differences in alpha 8-12 Hz or in 11-15 Hz or even 16-20 Hz comparing right and left hemispheres. It will take further work to define precisely which frequencies for different age ranges change. The differences between hemispheres for the high beta between 24-34 Hz, however, are remarkably large and consistent. It is not that the whole range is high but, for individual clients, the increase is somewhere in that range. It might just be 24-26 Hz or 30-31 Hz. Once again (it is worth repeating) check the individual client's pattern and customize the feedback accordingly.

Mind Mirror Type of Screen

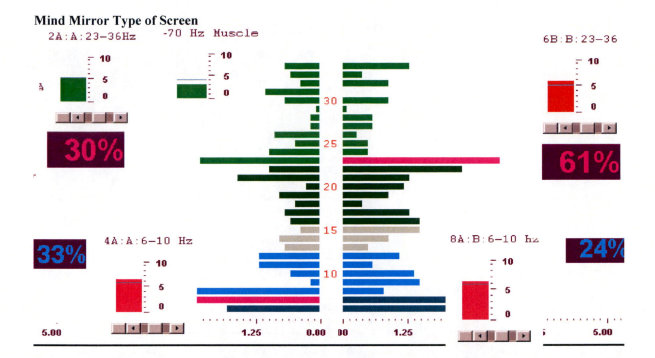

The above screen can be used to help the client see the difference between activity in the two frontal lobes. Percent of time above threshold numbers are linked to each bargraph. In this display, Peter shows higher average frontal "hibeta" (23-36 Hz) on the right and higher frontal thalpha (6-10 Hz) on the left. The %-over-threshold numbers show an average over several minutes. If this screen is used for feedback, the bargraphs are set, then placed in the background so that they do not clutter the screen. Respiration, skin temperature and/or EDR may be added as further checks on anxiety.

Peter demonstrated a combination of difficulties. Therefore, after using the above screen for a short time for feedback, another screen was made.

Given his history of tuning out when doing school-type work, we would want to decrease 6-10 Hz and increase 16-18 Hz while carrying out academic tasks. Simultaneously, considering his

rather marked impulsivity, we would use a second channel and encourage him to increase SMR at C4. We would also, due to his negative ruminations which were associated with high high-beta frequencies in the right hemisphere, want to have him decrease "hibeta" activity at this site on the right side. We did find that the high amplitude 28-32 Hz activity was easily detected at C4 as well as at F4 making it easier to choose a site for the second channel.

At the same time we used biofeedback emphasizing increasing EDR for alertness (but not too high because that, in Peter's case, corresponded to his becoming emotionally labile and excited). Peter was to try to maintain his breathing at a steady 6 BPM even when stressed. This corresponded to good RSA. Simultaneously, on some screens, we had Peter decrease his forehead EMG and increase his hand temperature. All the biofeedback modalities were based on a stress test assessment.

2-Channel Feedback to Reduce Ruminations and Impulsivity

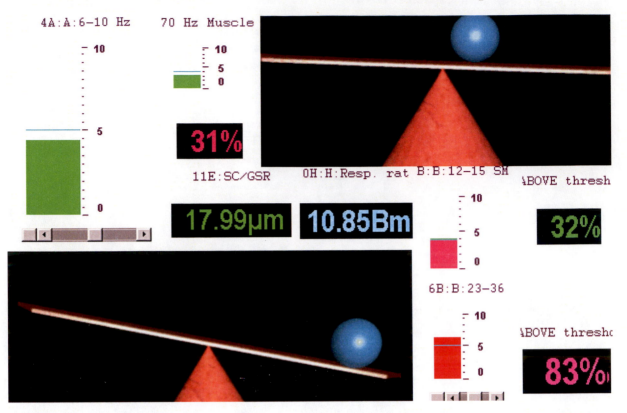

In this display, Peter tried to keep both balls to the right on the two balance beams. The bottom balance beam was linked to channel A, the left side thalpha (6-10 Hz) bargraph. He is to keep the ball to the right representing low thalpha. The red '31%' represents the time he was over the threshold for thalpha. This is good for Peter but he is trying to lower it still further. The 'muscle' bargraph at the top is actually 45-70 Hz representing both electrical and EMG effects on the EEG. It must remain very low.

The top balance beam is linked to channel B, right sided SMR. He is to keep the ball to the right representing high SMR. The green 32 % represents the percent of time he has kept SMR above threshold. Peter is encouraged to become very calm and raise this percent.

The bottom right hand corner 83% in red represents the amount of time he is over the channel B, right sided 23-36 Hz threshold. (For most clients, this is a narrower band that corresponds to a single peak found during their assessment.) He wants to drastically lower this percentage. He is to keep respiration at an even 6 BrPM. It is to be diaphragmatic without shoulder tension (EMG had been monitored on other training screens.) SC (skin conduction) or EDR (misnamed GSR on this program's display) must come down to around 10 –12. This is the range it is usually in when Peter is both calm and alert. With training Peter was able to control all these variables. Three years later, Peter telephoned to say that the training has "changed his life" and he would like to see training available in the city where he lives.

SECTION IX
Combined NFB + BFB
Intervention Fundamentals

A. Adding Biofeedback to Neurofeedback

1. Introduction

Most of a neurofeedback practitioner's time is spent working with a student/client to improve specific areas of functioning. The task is to help the student/client learn how to self–regulate. Increasing attention and concentration and decreasing tension and anxiety are often central in this process. The EEG Profile and Stress Profile assist in decision-making. For neurofeedback, the assessment dictates where electrodes should be placed and the frequency bands to inhibit or enhance. For biofeedback, the assessment will help you to decide, with your client, which instruments best reflect physiological changes that occur with stress. It will show both the modalities that demonstrate the most change as well as which ones show a slow recovery after stress. It will also help you decide on the usefulness of EDR for reflecting alertness levels.

On the basis of the assessment the practitioner discusses with the client what they may reasonably expect from NFB combined with BFB. The practitioner also discusses with the client the things that will be done in addition to NFB and BFB. For example, you will be training your clients in procedures which will help them generalize what they are learning in your office to home, school, athletic and work situations. With students you will be training them in the use of metacognitive and time management strategies for their academic work. You may be training them in quick procedures to turn on a relaxed but alert state. You never want to omit a discussion of diet, sleep and exercise since these all have a direct effect on performance. We call them the common sense variables: Eat well and take a balanced vitamin-mineral supplement. Get enough sleep. Exercise at least three times a week. It seems to be stating the obvious but remember what Covey has said in his books about successful habits: common sense is not always common practice.

2. Self-regulation: 4 Steps

There is a logical sequence of steps (a to d below) which overlap and eventually merge as the client becomes more flexible in their mental functioning and is able to shift to the appropriate mental state for the task at hand. There are further activities that help the client to generalize so that the steps they have learned in training become largely automatic. The client learns to control their own mental and physiological states. This is called self-regulation.

a. External Open Awareness

For the athlete, executive, or a tense and/or anxious student the **first step** is to learn to be externally and broadly focused, aware of everything in their environment (open awareness) yet often focused on no one thing in particular. In the martial arts this may be called "no-mindedness" or *mushin*. (It is an application of Zen in the training of these practitioners. At a high level of training, the practitioner may be instantly aware of any change in the environment surrounding him.) The professional athlete, such as a goalie in soccer or hockey, must retain both the open awareness of all players at the same time as having a singular focus on the player with the ball or the puck. This may be more accurately described as a *flicker-fusion-focus* where the mind is actually moving rapidly through the entire scene. On the other hand it may be a *soft-eyes* state (Sue Wilson's term) for really perceiving everything in a state of mental and physical *readiness*. In the latter hypothesis, it is almost as if their attention is to the *space* around them. Psychologically, when the objective is relaxation, it is important for these clients to imagine a pleasant scene or event. Physiologically the most helpful technique is to breathe diaphragmatically at a rate of 6 breaths per minute. In this state a balance occurs between sympathetic and parasympathetic systems and in natural biological oscillators (heart rate, respiration, blood pressure). There will be synchrony (coherence) between oscillators which is most easily seen by monitoring respiration and heart rate variability (RSA). At the same time the client is to relax their forehead, neck and shoulders and warm their hands. Les Fehmi has used the term "open focus" for a similar mental state. He has also produced audiotapes to help people achieve open focus.

b. Flexible Shifting of Mental State: Open Awareness to Focused Concentration

The **second step** is to use operant conditioning of brain waves so they can train themselves to consciously move from the open awareness high alpha (11-13 Hz) and SMR (13- 15 Hz) to a focused concentrating state where they lower their dominant slow wave activity and increase beta (16-18 Hz). This may require that the student shift in and out of open awareness. When they shift out of the calm, openly aware state, they move into an external narrowly focused state where they consciously produce a problem solving type of activation. In this mental state the student will decrease slow waves and increase fast waves (15 –18 Hz activity). This shift toward faster, desynchronized activity is reinforced by a visual and/or auditory signal that indicates they have met the pre-set criteria. Using this traditional operant conditioning they will train themselves to control, and perhaps to permanently change, their brain wave pattern.

c. Pair Desired Mental State with Learning

The **third step** is to link a desired activity, such as studying, to this efficient mental state using classical conditioning. Associative learning may also be occurring so the trainer must be alert to what is in the immediate environment. To pair the focused mental state with learning the feedback is altered so that the student can receive continuous auditory reinforcement for sustaining the mental state of externally oriented narrow focus while performing a task, such as scanning a textbook chapter or doing a math problem. If the feedback stops, the student immediately moves back to the operant conditioning mode, watching the display screen until the desired mental state is again achieved and sustained.

d. Generalize Techniques to Home, School and Work Environments

The **fourth step** is to train the student in procedures which will help them to generalize this ability to produce a calm, relaxed, alert, flexible, focused, concentrating mental state to home, school and work situations. Breathing techniques linked to daily habits and metacognitive strategies linked to learning new material are examples of effective methods of assisting this generalization.

3. Heart Rate Variations with Respiration – A Key Variable for Combined NFB + BFB Training

As previously noted, heart rate variability is emerging as one of the most important feedback modalities for rapidly assisting individuals to self-regulate their autonomic nervous system. Heart rate continuously changes or oscillates with healthy functioning. Controlling breathing is the simplest and most powerful means of controlling this system in a helpful manner. Breathing in (inspire) is linked with sympathetic outflow which increases heart rate. Breathing out (expire) releases the heart rhythm from the sympathetic nervous system's control and the parasympathetic system's inhibition takes over to slow the heart rate.

a. Instrument

It is helpful early in training to have a biofeedback instrument that allows your client to observe synchrony between their breathing rate and the increases and decreases in their heart rate. This is called *respiratory sinus arrhythmia* or 'RSA'. Heart rate can be detected using a photoplethysmograph taped to palmer surface of a finger tip. If your biofeedback instrument does not have this capability then you can purchase a heart rate monitor which will show a very smooth high amplitude wave form when you are producing good quality RSA. The Freeze-Framer device from Heart Math in Boulder Creek, Colorado is an example of an instrument that can be used by your client at home using their own computer. A simple $20 skin temperature apparatus can be added for monitoring finger temperature as a reflection of relaxation.

b. Begin with Biofeedback

The first step for most of our clients is to learn diaphragmatic breathing. A breathing rate of about 6 *breaths-per-minute* (BrPM) achieves a good quality RSA for most adult clients. Children breathe at a slightly faster rate. Next, they learn to raise their peripheral skin temperature, maintain a moderate skin conduction and a relaxed musculature (frontalis is a good indicator of EMG tension and a simple muscle to train) This is done as they maintain a good quality RSA. Ask them to practice this breathing, relaxation and hand warming while entering a mental state of awareness of everything in their environment. Opening and broadening their focus from an inwardly directed, narrowed, ruminative focus allows a quieting of the mind and a state of mental alertness.

Heart rate variability or change is greatest in periods of relaxation. In our early example, Jane's heart rate varied regularly from around 88 *beats-per-minute* (BPM) when she inspired to about 71 BPM when she expired when she was calm and really relaxed. On the other hand, when Jane thought of a stressful event or discussed an anxiety producing event this variation in heart rate almost immediately was reduced from the previous 17 (88 – 71) BPM to a difference of only 1 to 2 BPM. Heart rate should show approximately a ten beat difference or variation as the patient inspires and expires. This variation is lost when the client becomes overanxious. This loss in variability corresponds to an increase in overall cardiac rate with stress.

Purposefully changing one's breathing to diaphragmatic breathing at a rate of about 6 BPM is often associated with a sense of calm control. This can be very helpful in stressful situations. It can also improve efficiency of learning at school and work. Almost needless to say, it is an essential skill for a top athlete.

Now that the client is beginning to control their physiological state using BFB, introduce the NFB variables according to that client's EEG assessment.

4. Display Options for Combining BFB with NFB

You may have two, three, or four BFB variables on your screen when doing neurofeedback with adolescent and adult clients. These will vary depending on the stress assessment. The ones we most commonly use are: *breaths per minute (BrPM), temperature, forehead, trapezius or masseter EMG, and EDR. The appropriate variables for a particular client are placed on display screens with the neurofeedback instruments.* Although this is highly recommended for adolescents and adults, it may also be important for younger children who demonstrate anxiety and/or low alertness levels. The trade off is that having sensors on their hands may be distracting to some young children. They may fidget and thus distort the readings. For most of our older clients we use respiration plus one other modality. The reason we use respiration as the primary instrument is because it can change rapidly with stress and, for most clients, it corresponds to changes in other modalities. A respiration rate that is regular, deep, diaphragmatic, at a rate of about 6 BrPM corresponds to increasing peripheral skin temperature and relaxing muscles in most people. However, some clients can breathe in this manner and yet remain tense. Others can relax their muscles and breathe diaphragmatically yet have trouble raising skin temperature. Most people need to be able to change all modalities in order to genuinely self regulate and sense that they are really beginning to relax.

In order to adequately follow respiration the client can be helped with feedback using both a counter (for rate) and a linegraph. With a belt sensor around their abdomen, the linegraph allows them to see that respiration is regular, diaphragmatic and deep. Rate alone could be brought to 6 per minute and breathing still be largely thoracic and even irregular. In order to initially help your client to stop shallow thoracic breathing you may use a second respiration belt around the chest (under the armpits) or measure EMG from one forearm to the other. Both methods will demonstrate a rise in amplitude if the client expands their upper chest rather than moving the diaphragm.

Temperature changes slowly and can be adequately followed, in most people, using a simple box which recalculates every second. In some individuals, however, significant changes are very very small. Recent observations with ADHD adults showed erratic little finger temperature changes and research is underway to see if this could be used as a diagnostic test for ADHD. In these people an instrument that registers minute shifts can be quite useful. The F1000 has a temperature circle that can do this. When we are just measuring gross shifts in EMG a simple microvolt box that recalculates each second may do. However we prefer much faster updating which can be displayed on a speedometer-like line or a bargraph where the calibration can be shifted to display small changes. This kind of instrument is shown on Joan's screen below.

5. Combining Biofeedback with Neurofeedback – Case Examples

The examples below are further to ones earlier in the text that illustrated the importance of combining biofeedback (BFB) with Neurofeedback (NFB). In the section describing one- channel EEG there was the example of a university student with ADD and performance anxiety. In the section using two-channel training, an example of an older woman with ADD and agitated depression was used. Below three further examples are given. The first category involves training to optimize performance and the cases are a professional golfer and a racing car driver. The second category involves training procedures and the theoretical rational for the use of biofeedback plus neurofeedback for problems such as movement disorders (dystonia, Parkinson's, Tourette's), fibromyalgia, hypertension and headache. The third category discusses how we are training business executives to optimize their performance while improving their ability to shift mental states between work and home.

a. A Professional Golfer
i. Deciding on NFB and BFB Feedback Parameters

This example demonstrates a decision making process for using a combination of BFB + NFB to optimize performance. This combined approach was also mentioned in the example of 2-channel-training. In that case, it was important to produce a calm, relaxed yet alert mental state. The example below is one of optimizing performance in a professional golfer. What may initially appear to be a simple case of improving athletic performance, often ultimately involves a complex array of factors that are interfering with the athlete maximizing their potential. For this example we have used case #6 which is reiterated here:

Case #6: *Joan, age 28, is a golf professional. She felt her game could be improved but had no idea how to do this other than practice. She was also frustrated that some of her golf students did not seem able to improve despite many lessons over an extended period of time. The EEG showed higher than expected 5 – 9 Hz activity. When specifically asked, it turned out that Joan had been a bright student but had found it difficult to remain focused in classes. She appeared calm and certainly not at all anxious but when assessed her breathing rate was irregular, shallow and rapid. Her skin temperature was 88 degrees. Her shoulders (trapezius) became tense with the math stress test. When we discussed what occurred mentally during her approach to the ball and in the back-swing, she realized that she was ruminating and worrying about the outcome of the shot. This corresponded to increases in her 23-34 Hz activity and to an increased breathing rate and increased muscle tension in her face, shoulders and forearm. She then talked about being a very out-going person but said that this covered up the fact that she was often quite tense and anxious and a great worrier.*

Joan used the biofeedback stress assessment screen for 10 minutes in each of her first 3 sessions. She learned to produce good quality RSA with heart rate increasing with inspiration and decreasing with expiration. When she did this, her peripheral finger temperature rose and her forehead EMG dropped from 5 μV to 1.1 μV. After 10 sessions she was able to lower her thalpha (5-9 Hz in Joan's case) and sustain an external focus while maintaining diaphragmatic breathing at 6 BrPM.

Joan then began to practice putting and chip shots while she received feedback. The encoder was clipped to her belt and she set up the waiting room as a putting green. A screen was customized to meet her needs. She wanted the screen to be complex. This is not unusual, we have found that most of our optimal performance clients ask us to make a complex screen with a lot of information. They can choose for themselves what parameter to focus on at different times. She needed to:

1. Stop anxiety and worrying (decrease 20-23 and 24-32 Hz activity respectively);
2. Be very calm and externally, broadly-focused on the green, the hole and the ball (increase 11-13 and 13-15 Hz activity and maintain diaphragmatic breathing at 6 BrPM);
3. Eliminate undue and inappropriate tension in her lead forearm and her shoulder muscles. (EMG on forearm extensors and trapezius);
4. Be consistent in her shot with respect to her breathing cycle. Make the putt during the pause after exhaling and before the next inhalation.

ii. An Initial Display Screen

Golfer's Training Screen

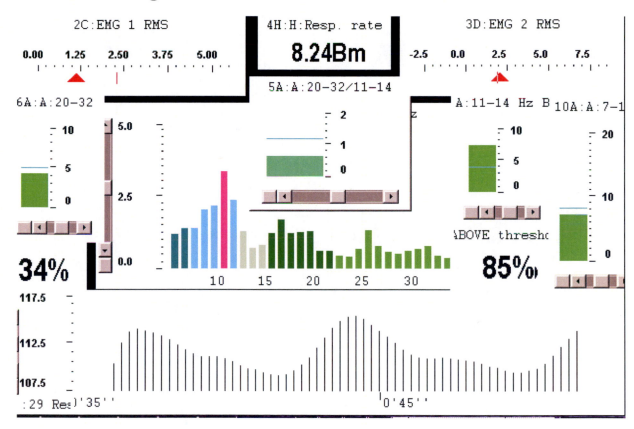

Use of the Above Screen
The above screen was used by Joan to practice changing mental states before putting. Then it was used by her coach (with sound feedback to her) while she practised putting in the waiting room. She chose the waiting room because it provided distractions similar to the audience in competition. We also felt she was a good role model for the children.

Screen Design
The display screen shown above was made to provide the feedback while she was putting. At the moment shown above, the spectral array

indicates she was in a calm (high 11-12 Hz), externally-focused (low 4-8 Hz) mental state but she was still worrying about her shot (25-32 Hz). Before putting she used the *spectrum* on the screen for feedback while she visualized herself putting and went into the desired mental state for each stage of the putt. While putting she received auditory feedback for keeping the (20-32) / (11-14) Hz ratio below threshold with a second sound to signal whenever EMG was higher than desired. (It went silent when she relaxed.) It had become clear that Joan's 20-22 Hz activity increased when she became anxious about her performance. When she thought about the people watching her or worried about her score or next shot, the amplitude of 26 – 31 Hz rose markedly and 13-15 Hz decreased. Therefore, the main sound feedback was contingent on her keeping the ratio 20-32/11-14 Hz below threshold. The secondary sound feedback was based on her keeping a chosen muscle group (usually: forearm, shoulder or forehead) below threshold. The trainer would sometimes call out the reading of variables such as EMG if they went outside of the desirable range as part of the coaching.

iii. Physiological and Brain State Changes Occur in a Sequence

Joan would mentally prepare to putt in the following sequence: She stands relaxing her face, shoulders and arms – *respiration goes to 6 BrPM, trapezius and forearm EMG to as low as 0.8µV, 20-32 Hz and 45-58 Hz(not shown) falls.* Beta at 17 Hz increases as she judges the distance, grass conditions, wind, slope and angle. At that point she bends to the correct position to putt with her eyes vertically over the ball, arms hanging totally relaxed - *EMG at 0.9 to 1.1 µV, and SMR rises.* When she is totally mentally relaxed but focused, she grips her putter a little more firmly and visualizes the putt: *7-8 Hz rises briefly.* Then she sees only the hole and the path the ball will take. She completely enters a mentally relaxed state at 11-12 Hz, shuts out all other thoughts (20-32 Hz drops and 11-15 Hz rises), and putts during the pause in her breathing after expiration. At the completion of her putt she relaxes and 9 Hz rises. Because there is mental flexibility and a sequence of EEG patterns associated with a successful putt, the record must be reviewed and analyzed over the total time period. Averages of various frequency amplitudes do not tell the story and can be misleading. For example, a raised 7-8 Hz at the wrong time could mean she was internally distracted. Produced at the correct time in the sequence it was good evidence of visualizing the shot.

iv. Joan's Changes with Training

When she increased 11–15 Hz activity and breathed effortlessly and diaphragmatically at a rate of 6 BrPM, she felt calm, relaxed and aware of all aspects of terrain, wind and distance. When she visualized the shot, activity around 8 Hz increased. When she evaluated the range and wind, 17 Hz activity increased. Joan found that, just as in her high school years, her mind sometimes wandered off what she was doing, even in competition. She, therefore, did additional training to gain control of theta activity.

Joan continued to practice diaphragmatic breathing which she knew from the stress assessment screen is associated with relaxed muscles, warm hands and a calm mental state. However, breathing was important for another reason. She had been hitting her putts at different points during the breathing cycle without realizing it. When she learned to putt always at the same time in her breathing cycle (after expiration, in a rest phase), her putts became more consistent.

Professional athletes cannot afford to be anxious, worried or ruminating, hence the emphasis on decreasing 20 – 32 Hz activity in the above screen. Note also that scores are on the screen so that she can evaluate performance. There are %-over-threshold scores for both fast and slow waves. Scores may also be used for the slow / fast wave ratio.

In the display screen shown above, the left EMG is on her leading forearm extensors and the right EMG is on her left trapezius. She found, initially, that her forearm and shoulders were quite tense as she addressed the ball. When she learned to relax and correct her posture, she discovered that she required a new putter with a shorter shaft. The length and angle of her old putter were incorrect for her height with arms relaxed. She learned to control muscle tension. Twenty training sessions resulted in a significant improvement in Joan's game.

As Joan progressed we wrote out the steps with her as follows:

v. Review of a Sequence of Mind-Body Changes for Optimal Performance in Golf.

1st Stand 3 feet away from the ball relaxing your face, shoulders and arms – *respiration should go to 6 BrPM, trapezius and forearm EMG to as low as 0.8 μV, 20-32 Hz and 45-58 Hz (not shown) should fall.*

2nd *Beta at about 17 Hz will increase* as you judge the distance, grass conditions, wind, slope and angle.

3rd Now you will step up to the ball and bend to the correct position to putt with your eyes vertically over the ball, arms hanging totally relaxed - *EMG low (around 0.9 to 1.1 μV), as SMR rises.*

4th When you are totally mentally relaxed but focused, you will grip the putter a little more firmly and **visualize** the putt: *7-8 Hz will rise briefly.*

5th At this point you are to see only the hole and the course the ball will take. You will completely enter a mentally relaxed state at 11-12 Hz and you will have shut out all other thoughts or awareness of noise and people around you (20-32 Hz will drop and 11-15 Hz will rise). At this point you will exhale (breathing has to be diaphragmatic at about about 6 BrPM) and **you will putt.**

6th At the completion of your putt you will not alter this calm mental state. For two to four seconds you will mentally follow through and calmly sense the ball going into the hole. At this point 9 Hz may rise.

At the end of this process the record is reviewed and analyzed over the time period to see if any of the stages require further practice.

The trainer could distinguish good from poor performance and predict whether the shot would go into the cup, with his back to Joan, by watching the display screen. If he saw the correct sequence of brain wave, muscle and breathing changes, he knew it would be a successful shot.

b. A Racing Car Driver
i. Deciding on NFB and BFB Feedback Parameters

Dave, a professional racing car driver, received training that was a variation on Joan's. Dave had had ADHD symptoms in school and fit the Hunter Mind style described so well by Thom Hartmann. He was excellent in competition because he entered a state of hyperfocus. His mind wandered, however, when he was alone on the track during the qualifying laps that determined pole position. His goal was to better manage his attention when there was no other car to chase and to improve his qualifying times. With Dave we had to use mental imagery since it was not feasible to physically simulate the race course. As with the golf pro, the goal was mental flexibility and control of physiological measures reflecting alertness, muscle tension, and breathing. The first emphasis in training was to be fully externally focused and problem solving even when the situation was less stimulating. He started his training by decreasing and controlling 4-9 Hz activity while keeping 17-18 Hz high. Then he practised remaining highly alert (EDR) and relaxed (diaphragmatic breathing at 6 BrPM with forehead EMG below 1.5 μV) while he imagined scanning the track and his instrument panel (11-15 Hz increased).

ii. An Initial Display Screen
Figure : Racing Car Driver's Training Screen

c. Harry, A Business Executive: Senior Vice President of a Large Corporation

Goal: Optimize Performance of a Company Executive

Problem: Many executives lack the flexibility to be in different mental states depending on where they are and what they are doing. They tend to stay in high gear. This high intensity, take-charge-rapidly state is advantageous in some work situations. In other situations, however, they would do better with a calm, receptive mental state. In this receptive state they would appear to have nothing else happening in the world other than paying attention to the person to whom they are listening. When they arrive home to greet their wife and children they need a different state again. They need to be attentive to their children's interests and participate actively in family life in a relaxed way without thinking about business.

Solution: Training emphasizes awareness of different emotional, cognitive, and physiological states. The executive is trained, using NFB + BFB + metacognitive strategies, to adapt to various work and home situations. They learn to rapidly switch mental / physiological states.

The QEEG of Harry, a senior vice president, during a math task, demonstrated very high 21 Hz at Fz and Cz and very high 11 Hz activity at T5. High 3 Hz and 9 Hz activity and a dip in 13-15 Hz activity at Cz was also noted. In a stress test, during a math task, he demonstrated shallow, irregular, fast respiration with no synchrony with heart rate, raised pulse rate, high forehead and trapezius EMG activity.

The figure below demonstrates an eyes closed comparison with the SKIL data base. It shows at 1.5 SD above the data base mean bright, high amplitude, 11 Hz, alpha activity at T5 and 21 Hz, beta activity, at Fz.

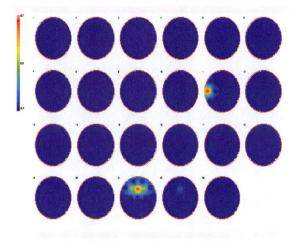

Display Screens and Training Parameters

The display screens and training parameters are determined for each individual according to their profile on EEG and psychophysiological stress assessments, their responses to life style questionnaires (designed by Vietta Wilson, Ph.D., professor, York University, Toronto) and their goals regarding their work and home situations.

Important Caution: Nothing stated below should be considered a 'protocol'. The electrode placements and bandwidths corresponding to mental states are always **hypotheses or assumptions** that <u>must be checked out with every client</u> **before** you decide on how to proceed. You check out electrode placements by looking at QEEG data as previously explained. You check out the correspondence of mental states with band widths at each of the chosen sites by asking the client to consciously sense differences in their mental state when they raise versus when they lower the amplitude of the chosen bandwidth.

Training Screens

For feedback Harry requested that there be a lot of information on any display screen that we used. He would decide on his point of focus from moment to moment and ignore the rest.

Screen #1: Initial screen

This is a typical screen used for two 3 to 5 minute periods at the beginning and end of each session. Harry was encouraged to attempt to control a number of variables simultaneously and have numerical values (% of time over threshold) to compare with previous sessions. The bandwidths used are unique to each individual and depend on their initial assessment.

Raising 13-15 Hz controls rolling the ball to the right. 70 % represents the % of time over threshold for this 13-15 Hz activity. It is coloured green to signal that the objective is to increase it.

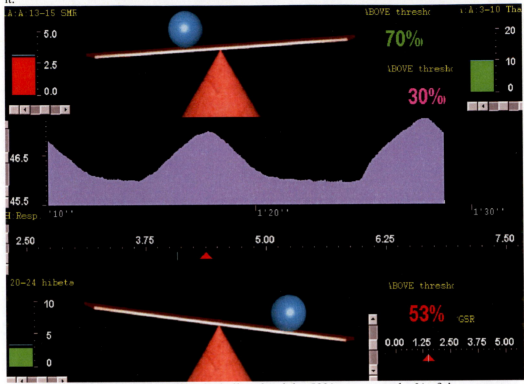

3-10 Hz has been over threshold 30% of the time.

Respiration (in blue – one breath/ 10”) is regular and at a rate of 6 BrPM.

Lowering 20-24 Hz controls rolling the ball to the right. 53% represents the % of time over threshold for this 20-24 Hz activity. It is coloured red to signal that the objective is to decrease it.

Forehead EMG is at 4 μV.

We add points later. Points are dependent on decreasing variability. The client must hold the required state for 3 seconds to receive a point. **Decreasing variability** is an **extremely powerful feedback technique** to improve self-regulation capabilities.

EDR at 1.3

Note: Lowering 20 - 24 Hz. would not be a common exercise but it matched this particular individual's profile. Most of the other executives had high 27 –32 Hz activity that corresponded to worrying and ruminating. In those cases the lower bar would encourage the client to find a relaxed mental state without worries and ruminating that corresponded to a decrease in 27–32 Hz activity. We quickly learned that his high 21 Hz activity was related to extremely emotionally and cognitively intense mental activity that was necessary for his rapid analysis of complex corporation problems. It did not relate to anxiety. This was important for him in business but this same mental state was ruining his marriage and was inappropriate for some business activities.

This screen was therefore DISCARDED for this particular executive.

This is an important lesson. You must know what the assessment shows but you do not *normalize* the EEG until you learn what a particular deviation from the database represents for that client.

Screen # 2: Control 9-10 Hz.
The objective is to be able to consciously sense activity in this range. This executive found that the activity in this range increased, and the boat disappeared, when he was internally distracted. When he focused externally and was figuring out a problem the activity decreased markedly and the boat reappeared. He became capable of doing this at will.

The sailboat jigsaw puzzle is fully formed when 9-10 Hz activity is low (as in this display).

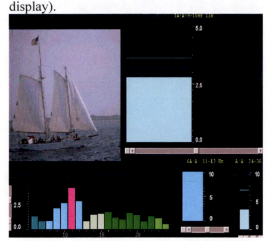

The spectrum shows where maximum activity is in the frequency range from 6 to 24 Hz. Harry was attempting to increase the 11-13 Hz bargraph, next to the spectrum, while lowering the 9-10 Hz bargraph beside, and linked to, the sailboat. He found that this would occur when he had a relaxed, calm, external, open awareness.

With training he was able to consciously turn this state off and on. If he raised the 24-36 Hz bargraph in the lower right corner, it would go red and all feedback would be inhibited. This controlled both for EMG artifact and ruminations.

Screen # 3: Goal is to control 11-15 Hz

In this step, the executive attempts to find a mental state that would raise 11-15 Hz and then to find a different mental state that would lower 11-15 Hz.

The objective was to be able to sense both states and be able to control them consciously. Harry found that he could build the sailboat puzzle (increase 11-15 Hz) by breathing at 6 breaths-per-minute, relaxing his muscles, warming his hands, and mentally going into a calm, yet alert, open awareness state.

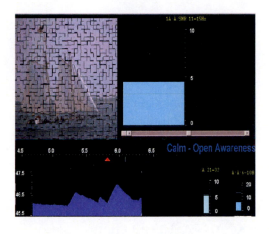

Recall that Harry had demonstrated extremely high Fz, 21 Hz and T5, 11 Hz activity.

Immediately prior to this point, Harry had been breathing in a tense, shallow, irregular manner (blue respiration linegraph) and his forehead EMG had been very high (> 7μV). At this moment his forehead EMG was decreasing. (Note that the red indicator is now below the automatic threshold which is at 6.2 μV.) 11-15 Hz activity has risen well above threshold and the sailboat (which had been totally black and gone from view) is now rebuilding. Harry became able with training to turn this state off and on. A bar-graph placed on the bottom right of the screen is for the EEG inhibits on 23-32 Hz activity.

Screen # 4: Goal is to control 21 Hz
20-22 Hz

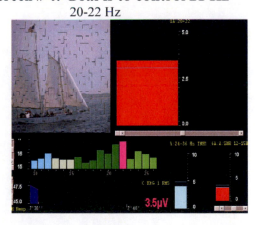

- The spectrum shows activity between 10 and 26 Hz. In the lower left corner is a respiration line graph.
- Forehead EMG activity is high at 3.5 μV. He was capable of decreasing it to 1.5 μV.
- 24-36 Hz activity (blue in the bargraph on the lower right corner) is below threshold.

- 12–15 Hz activity (red in the bargraph on the lower right corner) is too low at this juncture.
- 20-22 Hz activity is high. Harry said that emotional intensity raised this area. As previously noted, he felt this intensity was valuable when chairing meetings. On the other hand, it was not appropriate in other situations at work and it was ruining his home life. In training he learned to turn it on and off.

Screen # 5: The Mind Mirror Screen with EMG & Respiration

This screen was developed because this executive had *dissociated* in his first session when he had worked too intensely on decreasing high beta and increasing 11-15 Hz. Other factors may have contributed to this, such as not eating anything all day (it was 1:30 PM) and having a viral infection. Nevertheless, it was felt that a wise precaution would be to activate the left frontal lobe with channel A at F3 and use channel B at C4 for 13-15 SMR or at Pz to raise high alpha, 11- 13 Hz.

This screen is complex but it may be used for training with some individuals. The specific bandwidths would be modified according to the EEG assessment but the principles are the same for most individuals:

The client moves in steps. These are summarized in the *Sequence for Success* chart below. The first step is to control physiological variables, respiration and EMG. To do this the client will:

1st relax: Respiration diaphragmatic and regular at about 6 BrPM. Respiration is chosen because, for most executives, changes in respiration correspond closely to changes in other biofeedback modalities including the EMG, EDR, peripheral skin temperature and heart rate measurements, as previously explained. These other modalities may be used on other screens.

2nd Attain an alert, calm, focused state that can move between thoughtful reflection and memory retrieval with visualization (6-7 Hz) and high alpha (11-12 Hz) and calm (13-15 Hz) problem solving, focused concentration (16-18 Hz) without undue anxiety (21 Hz). (Some anxiety is a positive driving force but too much may almost paralyse the system with the complaint of *going blank* or being confused or 'disrupted'.) The client must do this without unproductive ruminating (23-35 Hz). Increased *binding rhythm* or *Sheer rhythm* (38-42 Hz) may be helpful (though muscle artifact makes it a difficult rhythm to accurately assess and reward). The bandwidths on the following screen are altered according to the goal for the executive.

The "Make a Xmas Tree" Screen
Respiration (blue line graph)
'Mind Mirror'

Channel A
Left Hemisphere

Channel B
Right Hemisphere

45-56 Hz inhibit.

Increase 16-18 Hz activity (may alternate with 14-18 Hz)

Decrease 3-5 Hz activity. – the specific frequency band depends on where the individual client is found to tune out.)

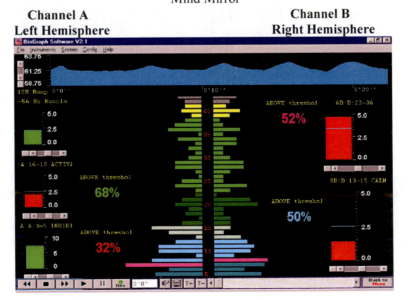

Decrease 23-36 Hz (May alternate with decreasing 19-22 Hz (intense emotional state &/or anxiety.)

Increase 13-15 Hz at C4 (But may alternate with increasing 11-14 Hz at Pz for a calm open awareness state.)

BRING   Red % ↓   Green or Blue % ↑

At this juncture Harry, our executive, had learned how different frequency bands corresponded to different mental states that he experienced. He wanted to be more active and see if he could control these states in a sequence that might correspond to his activities outside of the sessions. Like many executives he played golf so putting during the session was both fun and meaningful. More than that, putting could be directly related to the sequence we had recommended to reduce stress and tension at home after work.

The following table shows the sequence of mental steps done with Joan, the professional golfer described previously. The last column shows how this same sequence for an executive might correspond to going home after work. The reader can see how it might apply also to the sequence the executive might go through just before the start of a business meeting. It is a sequence of steps that can be practised outside of the biofeedback office to help generalize the executive's ability to enter different mental states.

d. Sequence for Success

	GOAL	*ATHLETE* **ACTION**	PHYSIOLOGY	EEG	*EXECUTIVE* **Coming HOME**
1.	Relax (IPS)	Stand 3' away from the hole. Relax forehead, face, shoulders	6 BrPM, RSA EMG ↓ Skin temp. ↑	45-58 Hz ↓	Park the car. Talk to yourself, say: "Stop", "Breathe", "Act". Relax muscles and do diaphragmatic breathing at about 6 BrPM.
2.	Solve problem	Judge the distance, grass conditions, wind, slope and angle	Retain relaxed state	17 Hz	Fill out day-planner & SMIRB
3.	a.) Empty-your-mind b.) Lose all Anxiety	Step to ball then bend, hang arms loosely, mentally have nothing-in-world but ball, green & hole	Totally relaxed – loose, calm, EMG ↓, Skin temp. ↑	13-15 SMR ↑, 24-32 Hz ↓ 20-23 Hz ↓	Think of being pleasant with the family and feeling good.
4.	Visualize or 'feel' the next step you will do	See or feel the ball going into hole. Keep eyes open	Remain relaxed, Any movement or tension is seen in EMG	7 Hz ↑	Visualize yourself, approaching family with warmth, openness & then positive interaction with kids
5.	Focus	Shut out all other thoughts or awareness of noise and people Become openly aware of the Gestalt: hole, green, ball –soft eyes.	Exhale & putt	11-13 Hz ↑ SMR ↑ Thalpha ↓ 20-32 Hz ↓ & 'binding' rhythm 39-42 Hz ↑	Go into house and focus 100 % on smiling with a relaxed posture; then listen, listen, listen and be 100% positive
6.	Follow through	Follow ball in same calm, openly aware state	Remain relaxed with 6 BrPM	9 – 11 Hz ↑ (possibly *Post Reinforcement Synchronization*)	Active play (not passive TV or video) until the kids are asleep.

In the above single channel feedback is often at Fz or Cz. Two channel feedback may be at F3 or Fz for the high beta and thalpha feedback combined with Pz for 11-13 Hz feedback.

In the feedback screen above, the client forms a 'Christmas tree' by decreasing 3-10 Hz which makes a thin trunk to the tree. Then the largest lower branches reach out at 11-13 Hz and gradually decrease in amplitude through to 18 Hz becoming narrow above 20 Hz.

Once Harry was able to consciously regulate his psychophysiological profile it was just a matter of generalizing this ability to his home and work environments. He was asked to list his daily habits. The list included: getting out of bed, showering, eating breakfast, brushing his teeth, driving to work, answering the telephone and so on. None of these activities required high emotional intensity. Therefore he would take two deep diaphragmatic breaths while relaxing his forehead and feeling his hands warm while he entered a mental state where he was aware of most things around him, relaxed, calm and still very alert. He would only enter the high intensity state for certain meetings and for studying materials when this seemed to assist his efficiency and his memory. Harry was now beginning to control his life with less stress, which had been his objective when he entered the training program. Nothing is simple, however. This takes time and other interventions such as family therapy may also be necessary.

e. Can the Client have any Untoward Experiences?

This possibility is not called a 'side effect' because the experiences do not appear to be caused solely and directly by neurofeedback. However, when you work with extremely bright, intense, fast moving executives who have 'Type A' personalities, then occasionally one of them may put himself into the initial session with such intensity that he feels 'different' later that day. The previously described executive is a good example of a tense client who only focused on bringing high beta down and SMR, 13-15 Hz up. An 'overdose' of 13-15 Hz without activation (beta) of the left hemisphere may make one feel a little 'spacey'. The result can be a single session *after-effect* where the individual has practised, not being externally alert and problem solving, but going into a state of relaxation and practicing a type of meditative total awareness. In addition, if in this effort they ignore the inhibit on 9-10 Hz and lower their alpha, they may dissociate. The temporary lowering of their peak alpha frequency from 11-12 Hz or higher, to 10-11 Hz or lower, may result in some loss of semantic retrieval. Remember, this could be for a number of reasons, one being that memory retrieval is state dependent. These affects will wear off in a few hours.

Example: As previously described, in his first session, one senior executive insisted that no one talk while he worked to become relaxed and decrease 20-28 Hz. On assessment he had a high

peak at 21 Hz. He wanted to work at lowering this and did so for 1½ hours (longer than the usual 50 minute session because he was determined to 'get-it'). He preferred trying it alone so he could really concentrate and so the trainer for the most part refrained from coaching or commenting. The client stared at the screen and really worked at decreasing the high beta and increasing 11-15 Hz. Although there was a bar for 6-10 Hz on the screen, he reported later that he did not pay attention to that. After 90 minutes he suddenly looked at his watch, realized he had to be chairing a meeting of senior staff, had the sensors removed and raced out to the meeting. It was learned later that he had not had either breakfast or lunch and it was 1:30 in the afternoon when he finished the session. His administrative assistant, a very observant woman, noted that he did not appear his usual self. He had trouble chairing the meeting in his usual efficient fashion and was a bit 'spaced out'. He described feeling intense, perhaps anxious, later in the afternoon and said he was a bit "out-of-it". In some ways it was like waking up with a mild hang-over with a slight dull headache. Reviewing his reaction at the next session, we thought it possible that he had self-hypnotized himself and perhaps he had experienced a dissociative state. (A similar response to a brief neurofeedback demonstration was described by Dan Chartier in the SNR journal.)He said later that he had gone into the session believing this was a very powerful tool and he was going to change quickly. This was despite being told it was a learning phenomenon that would take time and being given instructions to relax and 'let-it-be' and to spend the first session working on breathing and muscle relaxation.

In his second session, the trainer sat with him and discussed his experience during the session. The emphasis was placed on control, going into and out of mental states that changed the variables as described above under screens 1 to 4. There was also a discussion of hypoglycemia and the importance of breakfast and regular meals. At the end of the second session, his assistant brought him lunch. He ate this while discussing with his trainer ways to generalize relaxation techniques in appropriate situations. There was no repeat of the 'spaced out' feeling after subsequent training sessions.

A second executive had a very mild but similar experience. However, it was a week later that he had his first session and he had discussed the first executive's experiences with him. He did not have much time for his first session and, after instructions and discussion of his objectives, he only had a sample of about 5 minutes with feedback. He was in perfect shape when he left the session. It was later in the day that he reported bloodshot eyes, headache and a 'spaced out' feeling. This raises a remote possibility that perhaps both workers had a mild viral infection. We feel certain that diaphragmatic breathing and muscle relaxation, which was all we had time for, did not cause his symptoms. It is of interest that he knew of the first executive's symptoms so one wonders if there was an unconscious suggestive factor involved.

f. Side Effects – An Overview

In thousands of sessions over the past decade we have not had other clients have any changes they would call negative side-effects. Very occasionally, if you ask your adult client, they may say that after the first or second session, they felt a little different or 'spacy' for a few minutes. But this rare phenomenon seems to occur, if at all, only after the first session or very early in training and not after that. Nevertheless, the example given was a valuable learning experience. If due to the intensity with which the person applied themselves to the feedback, it is worth noting and is easily avoided.

Sometimes you will hear from some practitioners how powerful a few minutes of feedback can be. In our centre this has not been our experience, possibly because we avoid using verbal or non-verbal suggestions about what they might feel. Anyone experienced in the psychotherapies knows how powerful (and yet temporary) suggestion can be. Some people are much more suggestible than others. People with ADHD, for example, have higher hypnotizability (Wickramasekara, personal communication). Neurofeedback and biofeedback are learning experiences. Learning usually takes time and reinforcement. The amount of time and repetition will be different with different people but instant, dramatic change, or change within a few minutes, is not likely to last.

Since the foregoing example is a rare, but possible, phenomenon, it is a good idea to have a set training time and to have time to chat with your client for a few minutes at the end as you are removing sensors to ensure that they are not in a spacey state of mind. It is also important that your clients follow good nutritional habits and sleep habits.

B. Disorders Involving Muscle Spindles
1. Variables in Common to Movement Disorders and Fibromyalgia

Movement disorders and disorders such as fibromyalgia involve muscle spindles. Muscle spindle activity is influenced by SMR and by sympathetic drive. It may thus be that increasing SMR and decreasing sympathetic drive will have benefit in terms of symptom relief in a number of disorders. Results in clinical settings are preliminary but promising. Movement disorders such as dystonia, Parkinson's and Tourette's have a number of variables in common. A few of these variables are as follows:

- Dystonia, Parkinson's and Tourette's all involve involuntary muscle movements. In every case the basal ganglia (caudate, putamen and globus pallidus) are involved.
- Interactions between the basal ganglia are probably responsible for smooth, stable movements.
- Damage to the globus pallidus or the ventral thalamus may cause deficiency of movement (akinesia). Thus the globus pallidus and the ventral thalamus appear to be generally excitatory, whereas the caudate and the putamen appear to have inhibitory functions (Carlson, 1986 p. 313). Different combinations of malfunctioning in these nuclei appear to be important in movement disorders.
- In each of these movement disorders an imbalance of neurotransmitters is postulated to be at the core of the difficulty and in each case increases and/or decreases in dopamine are implicated.
- In each condition control of muscle spindle activity may be important. This control involves both gamma motor efferent input to the spindles from the red nucleus and sympathetic nervous system control.

Working with ADHD one also sees clients who demonstrate the symptoms of Tourette's disorder since the majority of those with Tourette's Syndrome also have problems with attention. In our experience, the training program described below in the example of Mary has been **just as successful for clients affected with Tourette's** as it was for this case of dystonia and Parkinson's.

Theoretically, the same combination of BFB with NFB should decrease the negative activity of trigger-points in **fibro-myalgia** (Thompson 2003). Work with fibromyalgia patients has been pioneered by Stuart Donaldson in Calgary, Alberta.

In addition, the calming result seen with increased SMR and decreased hi-beta (24-32 Hz) combined with decreasing sympathetic drive should be helpful in patients with **hypertension** and in patients who have severe **headaches** (Basmajian, 1989).

2. Parkinson's with Dystonia, a Case Example
Mary, age 47, Parkinson's and Dystonia

Mary's example also appears as Case #5 in the case examples. *Her case has been reported in the Journal of Neurotherapy (Thompson & Thompson, 2002) To recap, Mary, age 47, has both Parkinson's disease and severe dystonia. She has been treated with multiple medications, has even taken part in experimental surgery. Prior to doing NFB & BFB walking was extremely difficult and she was unable to control either dyskinesia (the sudden onset of gross motor movements) or the inability to move (freezing) when standing or even sometimes being unable to get up when lying down.*

i. Assessment and Deciding on NFB and BFB Feedback Parameters

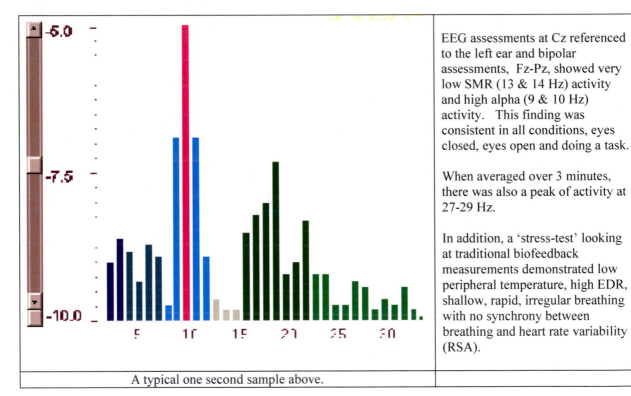

| EEG assessments at Cz referenced to the left ear and bipolar assessments, Fz-Pz, showed very low SMR (13 & 14 Hz) activity and high alpha (9 & 10 Hz) activity. This finding was consistent in all conditions, eyes closed, eyes open and doing a task.

When averaged over 3 minutes, there was also a peak of activity at 27-29 Hz.

In addition, a 'stress-test' looking at traditional biofeedback measurements demonstrated low peripheral temperature, high EDR, shallow, rapid, irregular breathing with no synchrony between breathing and heart rate variability (RSA). |

A typical one second sample above.

Medications helped Mary but not all symptoms were under control. Quality of life also suffered due to poor concentration so she had trouble completing tasks, such as reading a novel. Increases and decreases in dopamine may be part of a biochemical understanding of the problem and of a medical approach to it, but they do not answer the important question of how to control her sudden, precipitous onset of gross movements. In dystonia a noradrenergic predominance has been proposed (Guberman, A. 1994). It stands to reason that our traditional drug approach is necessary but not sufficient. In Mary's case, one obvious factor in precipitating undesirable events is stress. Increased sympathetic drive that occurs with stress is a factor. Noradrenalin is also a factor. One iatrogenic precipitator of a major dystonic episode is the injection of even a very small dose of adrenalin, as might occur in a dental procedure.

If an increase in SMR is associated with decreasing spinothalamic tract activity and a decrease in the firing rate of the red nucleus (whose activity links the gamma motor system to the muscle spindles), then it would appear sensible to see if raising this rhythm would correspond to a decrease in undesirable muscle tension, jerks and 'spasms'. Raising this rhythm has also been observed to be associated with a feeling of *calm*. Muscle spindles are involved in reflexes and in governing muscle tone. They are innervated by the motor/sensory pathways to the spinal cord, the red nucleus and basal ganglia, and by the sympathetic nervous system. We might have some constructive influence on the first half of this innervation by raising SMR. Sterman demonstrated that the red nucleus stopped firing when the thalamus started to fire in association with the production of SMR rhythm. Training Mary to relax would theoretically affect the second (sympathetic) input to the muscle spindle in a helpful manner.

ii. NFB + BFB Training
We trained Mary to breathe diaphragmatically at 6 breaths per minute. At this rate breathing became synchronous with heart rate variability. She then associated (paired) this breathing style with increasing her SMR using NFB.

Training Screen

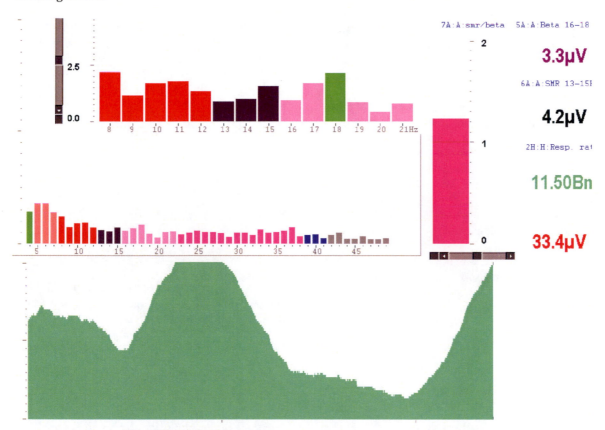

Job number one is to pay attention to respiration shown at the bottom of the screen. At the moment in time reflected here, she must relax and decrease the breathing rate from 11.5 BrPM (the number appears on the right hand side). When she has accomplished this, she will then continue to breath in this relaxed manner and focus on increasing 13-15 Hz and keeping it above 16-18 Hz. Given her initial extremely low 13-15 Hz, this was a difficult task. However, within 25 sessions she had control of this variable. The double spectrum allowed her to see the whole picture and assure herself that she was controlling the effects of EMG on higher frequencies and that she was maintaining a low level of hi-beta activity in the 20 –32 Hz range. The higher magnification spectrum from 8 to 21 Hz allowed her to focus on her primary goal of increasing SMR. Her goal was to move the green bar (representing the maximum amplitude at that instant in the 8-21 Hz range shown) to 14 Hz. Gradually she was able to do this for an increasing percentage of the time. In the figure it is at 18 Hz and she is attempting to find a mental state where it will move to 14 Hz. She was there in the frame before this, slipped out and then got back into it in the next frame. (*Note: the spectrum feedback is faster than the figures showing μV levels on the right because it does not require averaging over a one second time period.*)

iii. Mary's Changes with Training

After 40 sessions of training Mary was able to bring both 'freezing' and gross unwanted dystonic movements under her voluntary control. She did this by focusing on her breathing and putting herself into the same calm state that was associated with increased SMR during training.

Daytime alertness had been a problem for Mary and this symptom improved as excess alpha (9 & 10 Hz) came a little more under her control. Mary was formerly an avid reader but had not been able to sustain her focus in order to read a novel for four or five years. Controlling her dominant slow wave activity has resulted in her being able to concentrate well enough to finish a book and enjoy reading again.

Mary's quality of life was improved by training and she was even able to reduce the amount of L-dopa medication. Long term effects are not known (follow-up has been three years at this point). There is no pretense that one is treating the underlying disease process. But, symptom management is, in and of itself, a desirable outcome. It is a joy to see this woman doing crafts again, and, as of this writing, she is having a book published that she wrote and illustrated.

There has been a case report of a boy with Tourette's being treated using a similar approach (Daley, 2001). By raising SMR and teaching relaxed diaphragmatic, breathing the boy's tics disappeared over the course of a few months.

C. Biofeedback + 2 Channel Neurofeedback

Rationale

With adult clients one is often faced with complex objectives that require multiple feedbacks. The client's objectives may correspond to EEG differences in different areas of the two hemispheres. In these cases 2-channel training becomes important. To achieve good results quickly requires that the client be able to relax and yet remain alert. This is best achieved by combining biofeedback with neurofeedback. David is an example of such a client.

Case Example – A Business Executive

i. Deciding on NFB and BFB Feedback Parameters

David is a brilliant young executive who has developed a very dynamic company. He is doing well in business and family life. Unfortunately, he has a bipolar disorder which is unresponsive to medication and the cycles do affect his functioning. As with most persons who have periodic mood swings, depressive affect underlies both phases of the disorder. His objective in coming to the center was to gain a greater degree of self-regulation. He ruminated about things constantly. He was impulsive. He had always been easily distracted except when he was developing something himself. He wanted to be able to relax and focus on his business and home life without always thinking about immediate problems at work. He wanted to be able to remain alert even when the situation was boring.

His stress test demonstrated rapid, irregular, shallow, thoracic breathing, tense chest, neck and forehead musculature and a tendency to fall asleep if the session became the least bit boring for him. The 2 channel EEG assessment in the F4 right frontal channel and F3 left frontal channel both showed very high amplitude hi-beta activity with peaks at 22-24 Hz and 27-29 Hz. The beta activity was slightly higher in amplitude on the right side. High amplitude slow wave activity with a peak at 9 Hz was observed in the left hemisphere. When the second channel was put at Cz and then at C4 during the assessment, a dip was seen in the SMR frequency range at 13-14 Hz (compared to 11 –12 Hz and to 15-16 Hz) and 17-18 Hz was also low. High amplitude hi-beta and thalpha activity was not present at the central sites. These findings correspond to literature findings of low activation (high alpha) in the left frontal lobe in depression.

A display screen that is shown below was designed to allow David to follow his respiratory rate and forehead EMG as he attempted to relax. Relaxation increased his tendency to become bored and fall asleep. The EDR monitor on the screen forced him to find a way to remain alert. Sitting straight with good posture and on the edge of the chair, not leaning against the back, in addition to being aware of his arousal level with feedback on the screen, helped him to remain alert. His EDR rose from 1.8 in the initial two sessions to ranging between 7 and 9 after a few sessions. Learning to breathe diaphragmatically and relax his forehead EMG (from 15 to < 2μV as training proceeded) took longer. He had difficulty learning to 'empty his mind' of all the worries and insolvable problems in his life. Success in this was reflected in being able to bring down the high amplitude 22-32 Hz activity in channel A and increase SMR in channel B. As he succeeded in this self-regulation, his thalpha activity in the left frontal area decreased and he felt subjectively brighter and less dysphoric.

ii. An Initial Display Screen

Example of a display screen at the end of a 5 minute segment of training.

Channel A @ F3
Thalpha 5-10 Hz→
(Green below threshold).
The red 45% shows that it has been below threshold 45% of the cumulative time.

Channel B @ C4
SMR 13-15 Hz →

It has been over threshold 53% of the time.

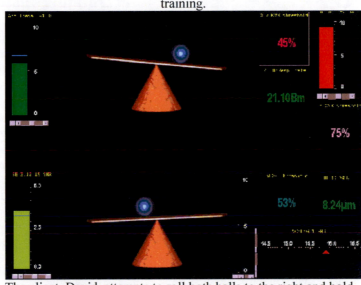

Channel A @ F3
Hi-beta 22-32 Hz is very high. It has been over threshold 75% of the cumulative time.

His breathing rate is high at 21 BrPM.

His EDR has risen to 8.24 μm and he has become more alert.

Forehead EMG is high, > 15 μV.

The client, David, attempts to roll both balls to the right and hold them there. To accomplish this he must decrease slow wave activity in the left frontal area (appropriate activation) and increase SMR at C4 (a calm mental state).

iii. David's Changes with Training

David feels that his work performance has improved and that he is better able to focus on his family life when away from the office. As with the Parkinson's client, one does **not** cure a bipolar disorder but the ability to self regulate does give more control over the symptoms and improve quality of life.

D. Tracking Client Progress

Why Track Progress?

Students are more highly motivated when they are challenged to improve and can track objective data to demonstrate the changes they are making. Within a session they can compare a few minutes of data with preceding time periods of the same length to see how they are improving. One also wants to see if there has been a demonstrable shift over a number of training sessions.

1. Within Session Tracking
a. Types of Measures – Points versus %-Over-Threshold

During each session we suggest that you record the student's scores every few minutes. With children this is usually 3 to 5 minute time frames, though with very young or very hyperactive clients it may be shorter. We use a *Tracking Client Progress* sheet and have the student fill in their own scores. We reward children for beating their last scores or their last day's scores. On some instruments, such as the Autogenics A620, a chart with statistics will appear on the screen after each time period. It is important to note that μV average, a point score and a %-over-theshold score are all different types of calculations. Thus one could conceivably improve their %-over-threshold score and yet get no points. They could improve their %-over threshold, get the same points as last time and yet not obtain as good a μV score for a particular parameter (fast or slow wave). The reason for this is that these variables measure slightly different things.

%-over-threshold depends on where you set the threshold. If it was for theta, then the student could be just below threshold for much of a 5 minute sample, and thus get a reasonable %-below–threshold score, but seldom stay below threshold for the required time (0.5 seconds or 1, 2 or 3 seconds depending on your settings) to score a point. Thus the **point score** would be very low. The average μV level could be the same in two 3 minute samples but the student might score a higher number of points in the second sample just because he held theta below the threshold for >1 second more times on his second try. Higher point scores are associated with better performance in terms of less *variability* in slow wave activity.

b. Test Ability to Hold Mental State Without Feedback

When the student has reasonably good control of their brain wave pattern, challenge them to find and hold the same mental state without feedback. You turn off the sound and the monitor and run the program for the same time period (3 or 5 minutes) recording data but not giving feedback. Compare the scores with those obtained with the feedback turned on. This is excellent practice for transferring what has been learned in sessions to home, school and work. Just as you cannot tell a person how to balance but they can learn what it feels like through feedback from the vestibular system, so you cannot tell someone how to achieve a particular mental state. They must learn what it feels like through neurofeedback.

c. Obtain Consistent and Accurate Data

To obtain consistent data within each session we suggest, first, that you record for the same time period each time and under similar conditions, feedback alone and then on task. We suggested above that this be between 3 and 5 minutes for children. Adults may want to record for longer periods. One reason we use the shorter times for children is that it becomes increasingly difficult to shift a %-over-threshold score as time progresses. Since it is calculated over the total time, it changes extremely quickly in the first few seconds and then slows down.

Pause the program whenever your client wants to move or to talk. Most programs have some simple method which allows a pause. With mature clients you can support their feeling in control by letting them use the mouse or keyboard to pause the program when they want to rest, stretch, ask a question and so on. These pauses result in the data remaining accurate for whatever time period you are using with minimal muscle and movement artifact. It also, even more importantly, emphasizes to the client that they should only do one thing at one time and they must be in control of what they decide to do: work on a task, or, conversely, fidget.

2. Comparing Different Sessions - Trend Reports

Some programs have built in mechanisms for computing a trend report. This allows the practitioner to graph trends over a number of sessions for each of the variables (theta, SMR, beta, ratios). If the equipment does not automatically generate such reports, you could still do it manually if you collect comparable data during part of each session.

a. Compare Similar Conditions

Remember to compare data that has been collected in the same way *or* to identify and compare different 'conditions' using a graph. 'Collected in the same way' means that the impedances were low between electrodes in each session, that the *active* and *reference* electrodes were on the same sites, and that the client was in the same condition (watching the display screen, reading or doing math). 'Comparing different conditions' is also possible if you have chosen to do a graph and compare each frequency or frequency band (3Hz to 60 Hz). for the two or more conditions. Trends are important so you should try to ensure that you clearly record the following information for each segment of data saved: the site, reference, time of day, activity (condition) and whether the data was artifacted. On the A620 one generally uses a standard progression of conditions, for example, watching the feedback screen, reading, watching the feedback screen and listening. On the Biograph program we use short preprinted forms to write in this information as we save each data segment. For example: Cz-L, 11A, R, ART means that the active electrode was at Cz, the reference was to the left ear lobe, the recording was done at 11 A.M., the student was reading and the data was artifacted. Comparing data that was artifacted with data that was not artifacted may be misleading. Eye blinks, for example, might raise theta and give the impression that the student was more tuned out that session compared to one which had been artifacted. SMR might appear to be higher in the unartifacted session due to muscle activity.

b. Time-of-day Effects

Include time of day because this may affect theta amplitudes in particular. Sleep latency studies show that we all produce more theta in the early afternoon. People with ADD often show more theta when asked to do a task, like reading or mental math, than when not challenged with a task. You can check for yourself how time of day and tasks affect your client.

c. Compare Artifacted Samples

If possible, do one or two artifacted segments each day, perhaps at the beginning and end of the session. This allows for a consistent trend report to be done after a number of sessions have been completed. There can be large differences in artifacted versus non-artifacted samples. Obey the simple rule: "Be consistent".

E. Summary: Areas to Target for Feedback:

1. One Channel Feedback
a. Right Brain Feedback

Feedback to encourage SMR appears to assist the client to stabilize emotions and reduce anxiety and tension, decrease impulsivity and increase calmness as well as the ability to reflect-before-responding. For this we usually place our active electrode either centrally or between Cz and C4. To increase social appropriateness in Asperger's syndrome we use an experimental approach, encouraging an increase in low beta, 13-15 Hz and a decrease in the dominant slow wave at sites identified in the full cap assessment. This has been between P4 and T6 in a number of clients. (P4 & T6 have shown less activation in the Asperger's clients we have seen, but this needs to be replicated before anything definitive can be said.)

b. Left Brain Feedback
i. Focus and Concentration

We place our electrode on or between Cz and C3 on the left side when working primarily on focus, concentration, problem solving. We encourage a decrease in slow wave activity, 3 to 10 Hz (the exact range depends on the client's profile) and an increase in beta activity in the 15-18 Hz or 16-20 Hz range.

As previously noted: A note of caution from Tom Budzynski is that training up beta frequencies on the left side in children or adolescents with reactive attachment disorders may result in angry behaviour.

ii. Dysphoria / Depression

When dysphoria or mild depression is an additional factor, we may place the electrodes more anterior around F3. The active electrode is placed over the frontal or prefrontal area on the left side to *activate* the brain. The client is encouraged to decrease the dominant slow wave and increase low beta, 15-18 Hz. In addition, if there is a peak between 21 Hz and 34 Hz they will be encouraged to "empty" their mind (of all ruminative activity) and lower this peak frequency. This has been discussed above under 'combining NFB and BFB' and also under 'two channel' training.

iii. Learning Disability - Dyslexia

Language representation is in the left hemisphere for almost all right-handed people and for approximately 75% of left-handed people (Panu & Wong, 2002). When doing NFB for dyslexia we may choose a site slightly towards the posterior third of a line drawn between C3 and P3 and somewhat inferior to it for a few sessions and then do a number of sessions between C3 and F3. In these instances we decrease slow wave and increase fast wave (beta) activity. This method is used in certain kinds of learning disabilities, particularly in training clients with reading, writing, and speech problems. The specific difficulties the client is having are considered in terms of what is presently known about the neurophysiology and neuroanatomy for these brain functions. Wernicke's area (posterior superior temporal and inferior parietal) is used for the comprehension of spoken language and for the initiation of a reply or action. Visual stimuli reach Wernicke's area through the angular gyrus. This is important for the comprehension of written language. Wernicke's

area is thus involved in *phonemic knowledge* (decoding written word and sound symbol relationships). It is connected to Broca's area by the *arcuate fasciculus*. Broca's area and Wernicke's area are, together, known as the *perisylvian language zone*. Broca's area processes meaning and sends signals to the motor cortex if one is reading aloud.

NFB training to activate these areas is still considered *experimental* at the time of writing as they are based on present knowledge and clinical experience and not on a great deal of published research.

As noted above, for some sessions we may move the electrode more posterior (closer to Wernicke's area) in some speech and language disorders and in dyslexia. For dyslexia we reference to the right ear reasoning that the insula, which has been implicated in some forms of dyslexia, is well below the surface of the scalp and we want to try to influence more than just the dipoles between C3 or P3 and the left ear.

F. Sequential (Bipolar) Training

In general it is recommended that bipolar training be carried out between different areas (frontal, central, parietal, occipital) of the brain within the same hemisphere or along the central strip. It is not usually done transversely across the hemispheres at homologous sites, such as C3 and C4. However, opinions do differ. If observations of beneficial changes are seen with a particular protocol, the next step is research to replicate the observations. This requires defining the population and the symptoms that respond. A rationale should be provided as to why such training should work. One needs to address the question of why creating a potential difference in particular frequencies between two sites would affect particular symptoms.

SECTION X
Intervention Summary
Basic Stages of Training &Tracking Progress

A. Four Basic Components of Training Sessions

1. Goals & Overview

The learning technique based on neurofeedback can be used to normalize the EEG in cases where it differs from established data bases OR it can be used to modify the EEG towards patterns which indicate mental states which are associated with improved functioning. The patterns can be adjusted according to the area of interest (work, school, relaxation, performance arts, athletic achievement). In all cases one is trying to improve mental flexibility.

The overall objective is to help the client manage symptoms and optimize their performance in areas they have defined as important at this point in their life. To do this with a student or business person we take into consideration that person's entire physiological state and carry out procedures in a logical sequence. However, the sequence or components **overlap and eventually merge** as the person becomes more flexible in their mental functioning. Shifts to the appropriate mental state for the task at hand then become largely automatic.

2. The Four Component Parts of a Typical Training Program

Note: These four components overlap. They are not to be thought of as strictly sequential 'stages'.
Component # 1. is used if appropriate to your client's assessment profile and goals. With children you typically start with Component # 2. A complete history will precede training, as will a discussion with parents of other appropriate interventions (diet, medications, sleep, extracurricular activities, educational support).

a. Component # 1: Setting-up-for-Success

As noted in the previous section, general biofeedback modalities may be combined with neurofeedback. This is particularly helpful with optimal performance clients. In the initial stage of training the student/client learns to be externally and broadly focused, aware of everything in their environment (open awareness) yet focused on no one thing in particular. It is almost as if their attention is to the *space* around them. This state closely resembles the *open focus* so well described by Les Fehmi. In its extreme form it approaches the *cosmic experience* described by E. Bucke, the Director of London Psychiatric Hospital near the turn of the last century or to the *Satori* of Zen Buddhism. This mental state is a kind of dissociation. It is psychologically important for the student to be experiencing a pleasant scene in their imagination and associate this image with a self-empowering feeling when entering this mental state. A positive inner dialogue can also be quite helpful.

Physiologically, the most useful technique is to breathe diaphragmatically at a rate of 6 breaths per minute. In this state a *balance occurs between sympathetic and parasympathetic systems* and in natural biological oscillators (e.g., heart rate, respiration, blood pressure). In this state it is postulated that there will be synchrony between oscillators. This synchrony can be seen by monitoring respiration and heart rate variability (respiratory sinus arrhythmia or RSA). Of course, one can teach diaphragmatic breathing without using biofeedback sensors but the use of feedback will usually make learning faster and more effective.

b. Component #2: Operant Conditioning

The second stage is to use *operant conditioning* of brain waves so that students/clients can train themselves to move consciously from open awareness, high alpha (11-13 Hz), and SMR (12-15 Hz) to a focused, concentrating state in which they lower their dominant slow wave activity and increase beta. This may require that they shift in and out of open awareness. When they shift out of this open or total awareness state they move in to a narrowly-focused state where they consciously produce activation. What one sees in the EEG is a decrease in slow waves and an increase in fast wave (15 –18 Hz) activity. This narrow focus is reinforced by a visual and/or auditory signal that indicates they have met the pre-set thresholds. In this traditional operant conditioning they will train themselves to control, and, perhaps, eventually to permanently change, their brain wave pattern.

Two approaches for operant conditioning of brain wave patterns have evolved. The methodology used initially, exemplified by Barry Sterman's work, involves rewarding the person, (or cat, or monkey) each time they produce a burst of the desired brain activity. The second approach involves continuous feedback, a tone or song, whenever the activity is maintained. These are described below.

i. Technique # 1: Use of Feedback to Reinforce Finding a Desired Mental State

One method of *knowing* when a desired state is being achieved is by getting almost instantaneous feedback, such as a discreet tone paired with a change in a visual display. IIR and FIR filters have a reasonably short latency time and it is assumed that the brain is receiving the feedback faster than the student can move on to their next thought. Feedback should be well within the outside limit of <500 milliseconds that is necessary for operant conditioning.

On the other hand, the sudden absence of a sound can also be effective feedback. If the client's mind wanders, the absence of tones makes them aware that they have drifted. It is felt that this kind of feedback *catches* them before they move off too far. Some practitioners believe this method may be the most efficient way to effect change.

Operant conditioning can be done either by observing a single instrument, such as a bargraph, or by simultaneously observing several instruments. (It is not really simultaneous since the brain consciously focuses on only one thing at a time; rather, it is dividing attention among various feedback components, paying attention to one and then another in a rapid sequence.) The bargraphs show amplitudes for fast and slow waves and for artifacts. Knowledge of possible artifacts permits one to distinguish changes in brain wave amplitudes that are due to *real* alterations in the subject's mental state (as opposed to changes that are merely a reflection of other processes, such as eye blinks or muscle tension). Inhibits can be set that will stop all feedback, including sound and animations, if the client moves, blinks, tenses muscles, ruminates or lets their mind wander.

ii. Technique # 2: Using Averaging and Continuous Feedback to Reinforce Remaining in a Desired Mental State over Time

Smoothing and averaging can be done by a number of EEG instruments. Slowing down the speed of feedback and using continuous sound, such as classical music, can encourage the student to find the desired mental state and hold it for longer and longer periods of time. The student is encouraged to **continuously track** how much of the time they are managing to *remain in* the desired mental state. Percentage-of-time-above (or below)-threshold combined with points that require the client to sustain feedback for 3 or more seconds are useful ways to score this kind of activity.

In this type of feedback you may decide not to have any *feedback inhibits* since it could be irritating to have the music starting and stopping frequently. With respect to the use of an inhibit, the following is true:

a. *The advantage of NOT using an inhibit is:* Clients may become quite keen to find ways to increase their scores and better their threshold levels (for example, shifting their position to increase alertness in order to decrease slow waves and increase fast waves if you are training a person with A.D.D.)

b. *The disadvantage of NOT using an inhibit is that the client may consciously or unconsciously tense muscles. This would artificially raise SMR and Beta and reward them for EMG artifact rather than their mental state:*

On the other hand, with adults who remain very still and are not clenching their jaws, muscle tension artifact is usually not a problem. With children, if you don't want to have an EMG inhibit, then *deal with the problem of muscle movement by setting the* EMG (really EEG at 45-58 Hz) instrument to a very difficult setting, link a %-over-threshold counter to it, and insist that if they remain over say 6% for more than 30 seconds you will stop feedback and start over. Children do not like stopping and starting. (They aren't getting tokens for the store in our centre when this occurs.) It is amazing how even children with extreme fidgeting will settle down and work on feedback using this technique. It is helpful if at first you go somewhat overboard in rewarding young children every few seconds for remaining so still. With some young children it may also be helpful to be animated, silly, fun and extremely positive. At the end of the time, say 3 minutes, you record (or you encourage the student to record) their scores on a tracking client progress sheet and give a token for each score that beats their last three minute period score. You can create your own sheets and graphs for tracking progress depending on which EEG instrument you use. Some instruments automatically track relevant statistics that you can print out.

c. In strict operant conditioning terms the student's/client's response is becoming linked to the feedback. However, positive response may also be linked to your actions as a trainer. If you as a trainer become psychologically (unconsciously) necessary to trigger positive responses you may have only achieved what is sometimes, in psychotherapy, called a *transference cure*. This is not permanent and is thus not the mechanism of change we are after. Therefore, you should vary your techniques for reward. At the ADD Centre we change rooms, EEG instruments, feedback screens and trainers during the course of training.

We want the gains to be within the student/client and independent of specific cues found only in the training environment. This works.

d. If you get electrical changes in the EEG pattern, results should last, according to Lubar who has reported on 10-year follow-ups with one series of children with ADD. (Lubar, 1999)

If you see positive behavioural changes in a child with ADHD but without the EEG changes, it might be due in part to the therapeutic relationship between the child and the EEG practitioner. There may be heightened self-esteem due to the positive attention and the child may behave better to please their trainer. The therapeutic alliance is important in order to make gains as rapidly as possible but the gains must be independent of that relationship by the time the child leaves training.

Here is an example of a serendipitous follow-up at our centre. This young man had been a difficult client to engage but he respected his trainer; he would work for him but not others. On the other hand, he did make electrical changes and took pride in acquiring this control.

Case Example: A strong looking, upright, impeccably dressed young man walked into our centre. I saw another student's mother audibly gasp as he introduced himself in the waiting room. He explained politely that we might not recognize him but he had been a client during the summer four years ago. Failing grades (30's and 40's) had been the reason for seeking help and he had responded well to training. He left training after only 20 sessions because he went away to a military school at the end of the summer. He said he was pleased to report that he had graduated with top marks and as a commander. He attributed his success to his training at the ADD Centre. He wanted to return this summer and finish off a further 20 sessions with us because he was entering a science program at a top university and he recognized that the training would further optimize his functioning. He arranged his sessions, shook hands and left.

The mother who had gasped in the waiting room came forward and quietly explained her astonished behaviour. He had, she said, been her eldest son's friend before he went away and he was one of the worst kids in their high school, always in trouble. She had not seen him in years and was astounded at the transformation. Obviously the military academy had been the right school environment for this young man. He, himself, felt the neurofeedback training before he began there prepared him to benefit from the experience.

c. Component #3: Classical Conditioning

The third stage is to link a desired activity, such as studying, to this efficient mental state using *classical conditioning*. To do this the feedback is altered so the student can receive continuous, auditory reinforcement for sustaining the mental state of externally-oriented, narrow focus while performing a task (such as scanning a textbook chapter, doing a math problem, organizing a business proposal or hitting a golf ball). If the feedback stops, the student immediately moves back to the operant conditioning mode (watching the display screen and/or listening to the auditory feedback) until the desired mental state is again achieved. One may use a series of discreet tones or, perhaps more effective, a continuous tone while the desired mental state is maintained.

Classical conditioning is when you pair a new stimulus (*conditioned stimulus*) with a stimulus (*unconditioned stimulus*) that already reliably elicits a response. A dog will reliably salivate when given meat (*unconditioned stimulus*). Pavlov paired a bell (*conditioned stimulus*) with the presentation of meat powder (*unconditioned stimulus*). Soon the dog reliably salivated when he heard the bell (*conditioned response*).

We use operant conditioning until we have reliably paired the desired mental state of focused concentration with auditory feedback.

Once the mental state (think of it as a physiological state, just as salivation is a physiological state) can be reliably produced in the training session using operant conditioning then the client is ready for the second stage using classical conditioning. In this second stage, we *pair* this mental state (now an unconditioned response) with doing an academic task (or a business or an athletic task) (conditioned stimulus). After a few sessions of training the new *conditioned stimulus* of doing this task will automatically and reliably elicit the appropriate mental state.

During the task, if the auditory feedback stops (reflecting that the desired mental state has been lost) the client is instructed to return to doing operant conditioning (look at the monitor) until it is regained. Then they can return to doing the task. You do not want to pair being tuned out with the task.

Summary of Learning Paradigms

Operant Conditioning:

Behavior	Reward (behavior repeats)
Mental State $\rightarrow$	*Computerized Feedback +*
	Trainer's Feedback (mental state maintained)
15-18 Hz $\rightarrow$ *tone* $\rightarrow$ *more 15-18 Hz*	

Classical Conditioning:

Unconditioned Stimulus	Unconditioned Response
Meat $\rightarrow$	*Salivation*
Feedback $\rightarrow$	*Mental State*
Conditioned Stimulus	**Conditioned Response**
Bell $\rightarrow$	*Salivation*
Academic Task $\rightarrow$	*Mental State*

d. Component #4: Generalizing

The fourth stage is to train the student in procedures which will help them to *generalize* this ability to produce calm, relaxed, alert, flexible focusing and sustained concentration to home, school and work situations.

The first step in doing this is to have the student achieve all feedback objectives without active coaching from the trainer. The second step is to have them achieve all the training objectives for neurofeedback and biofeedback both while sitting looking at a blank screen and then while doing a cognitive exercise without any visual or sound feedback. The monitor and speaker are turned off but the program is still recording data.

The final step is also an on-going step. The client is instructed early in training to practice going into the psychophysiological state, which they are learning in sessions, when they are at home and at school or work. Breathing techniques, imaging, and metacognitive strategies are examples of effective methods of triggering this mental state. They act both as behavioral cues for eliciting the desired mental state and as useful techniques for efficient functioning. Attaching this state to regular habits in daily life, such as answering the phone, reading, listening to others and driving, is an effect way to have it become a new routine component of one's daily living. Specific methods to help students, professionals and business people generalize this mental state to their academic and work tasks are giving in the chapter on metacognition. For details about metacognition see Section XII.

B. Summary of Steps in a Typical Session

1. Screens and Screen Sequences

Objectives

1. To have clients compete with themselves to remain for longer and longer periods of time in the desired mental state (focused concentration when working with clients who have ADD.) This means they get better scores (and children get more tokens if you are using that type of secondary reward system at your office).

2. To learn to 'self-regulate' and flexibly control transitions between mental states (EEG patterns, ANS & EMG variables) and achieve rapid recovery after stress.

3. To have the client end the session feeling empowered and feeling they had some fun as well.

4. To have the client generalize their learning to daily life.

Principle: The screens used and the sequence will vary with the age, stage of training and interests of the client. However, they must also meet the objectives of the training which means changing the pattern of brain-wave activity in the desired direction. They should be coupled with doing cognitive tasks appropriate to the goals of the individual client. Thus a whole session on pac-man or pong or puzzles or car racing or "picking up bags of gold" may not be what the trainer feels is giving the best feedback in the early part of the session but may be useful for enjoyable "breaks" during the training time. Perhaps favourite (game-like) screens like these are perhaps best used with young children as a reward. Less entertaining screens that clearly indicate the parameters for training should be the mainstay for conscious learning. In this manner the client will learn to consciously hold a particular mental state. In real life they must maintain their concentration even with boring tasks so this must be practiced during their session. Doing brief periods of training, 2-5 minutes, and using secondary rewards (praise, tokens) maintains motivation for the mental exercises. Even executives will say that they tune out rather quickly when reviewing documents. Doing this kind of cognitive activity while receiving feedback that is informative can be very useful. While receiving feedback, the student learns mental strategies for sustaining interest and attention.

Suggested Sequence

1. **Baseline:** Start with a brief baseline recording without feedback.

2. **Pure Feedback:** Do three to five training segments each lasting 2 to 5 minutes using a screen that shows %-over-thresholds and scores (points). The first screens used should give

simple, discrete auditory and visual feedback spaced 1 to 3 seconds apart. Adolescent and adult screens may include appropriate biofeedback measures such as EDR, respiration and EMG.

We usually do not save all the data recorded during each segment of feedback. We just record relevant scores (such as %-over-threshold and points) and compare them to previous scores. After each segment we discuss the client's own observations about their *mental state* during that segment compared to other segments where different scores were attained.

3. **Task:** After between 3 and 5 short periods (1 to 5 minutes) of pure feedback we may introduce an academic task. The academic task is only done *when the client is maintaining steady auditory feedback.* We may have to make the thresholds slightly easier in order to achieve steady feedback. This is the *classical conditioning* step in the training session. We may increase the time of an on-task segment. It might be from 5 to 10 minutes depending on the age of the client and their attention span. We ask questions about the work when we stop feedback (to avoid muscle artifact that may result from talking during feedback). We may *pause* the feedback, if we notice a change in the wave pattern, and ask the client to identify what was going on in their brain at that time. The tasks can be reading, writing, mathematics or listening to the instructor. They will have to use metacognitive strategies to remember the information for a question period which will follow the listening task. We train the students in the use of strategies for the task so that using strategies is paired with the correct mental state for cognitive work. In time the strategies will also unconsciously cue the student to turn on the desired mental state.

4. **Pure Feedback and/or** *Work–Rest* **(Self-Regulation):** Then we return to pure operant conditioning for 1 or 2 segments. At this step, if the instrument allows for it, we might have the client turn on a focused mental state for 30 seconds (or longer). This is called a *work* state. Then, the client is told to deliberately turn it off this mental *work* state and let their mind wander for 30 seconds. This second condition is called a *rest* state. At the end of several trials, compare the scores. Clients feel quite empowered when they see that the values of the different frequency

bands actually change and that they have control over this. (Be careful to make sure that there is no difference in 45-58 Hz activity between *work* and *rest* periods. A higher reading in one *state* could indicate that muscle activity was raising beta.

5. **Task:** At this juncture we may do another academic task with auditory feedback on. Once the client is showing mastery we will have them do some segments of the session with no visual or auditory feedback. The student will compare the results of these segments to similar time frames where they were receiving both feedback and secondary rewards.

6. **Positive Ending:** To finish the 50-minute session we will let the client choose their favourite screen for feedback. You want to end on a positive note and reinforce the idea that they are in control.

Other Pointers:
Some children will produce a great deal of muscle artifact. With these children you simply must have an EMG inhibit. Without such a strict EMG inhibit you would not be able to accurately reward the child for producing SMR or beta due to the very large effect that muscle activity can have on beta and SMR frequencies. These active children are often the same children who need to have you emphasize increasing SMR (12-15 or 13-15) at Cz or C4.

If you want them to also remain externally focused while they learn to increase SMR then you might put an '*inhibit-over-threshold*' on your dominant slow wave (often 3-7 or 4-8 Hz) instrument. Alternatively you might relate your primary reward to decreasing a theta / SMR ratio (if allowed by the program you are using).

2. Tracking Trends and Motivating Children
For some feedback segments it is a good idea to have the student attempt to *feel* (or 'sense') the **desired mental state and consciously change it** back and forth. This has been described previously using the example of a sailboat screen. This gives the student a real sense of self regulatory control and empowerment. At our center one of the ways to earn tokens is to demonstrate this control. Some students like it if

we use a stop watch to time how long they can maintain the picture or hold the theta in the *green zone* below the threshold line. With younger students the trainer counts out loud and we see how high he can get before he 'loses it'. We make up games with the students. For example, we might have little piles of tokens. One white token each time we reach 5 seconds; 2 tokens if we reach 8 seconds, 3 tokens for 10 seconds and 4 for 12 seconds. We will record the numbers on a special score sheet after a session segment of 3 to 5 minutes. The child may want to do it again to better their score. Making up a special game for the student is more personal and interactive and we feel this is even better than automatic machine controlled games.

Note: There has been discussion, even in the popular press, of using **interactive video games** for feedback. This can be done with attachments to some types of equipment. However, Olaf Palsson and Alan Pope have done the best-known work in this area. They pioneered this approach feeling it might improve motivation for doing the training. (Palsson, 2001) Some instruments do this as their primary mode of feedback. Other instruments have this as a secondary capability. Students with ADD/ADHD typically are past masters at video games. The can usually beat their peers in this type of activity. They go into *hyperfocus*. We see no need to train them to focus on these items. There is a place, however, for this kind of activity. We find it very useful as a reward for the young, hyperactive, non-compliant child to get them interested in working during other parts of the NFB session. It is also a useful way to attract the attention of an autistic child. It is used as a reward and as an opportunity to maintain a state of reduced theta and increased SMR, the criteria which must be met to play the games successfully. Presumably this is a different brain wave pattern than is found when playing other computer games. The main question is whether the student is able to transfer this state to an academic setting. Hopefully some follow-up studies can be done to investigate this question.

At the time of writing, however, we do not feel this is the best way to train a student to constructively handle boring classroom tasks. Until there is evidence that feedback with a video game format generalizes to classroom performance we will, for the most part, use relatively boring feedback screens, that give direct feedback about brainwave activity, as the mainstay of our feedback program.

3. Other Types of Feedback and Cueing

1. Teaching a student to be able to *self-regulate* going in and out of high **alpha synchrony** is said to result in improved cognitive performance. (Anna Wise) This kind of peak performance training can be attempted using the mind mirror type of display. Percent of time-over-threshold data for the right and left channels help the client to quantify the feedback. The mind-mirror display places the spectral array derived from FFT calculations for each hemisphere in a vertical position (see executive training, IX, 5c, Screen #5, above) so that one can see how symmetrical (or asymmetrical) the activity is on the right and left by seeing if the bars for the particular frequencies are going in and out to the same degree on both sides.

2. We encourage all students to sit up straight, rather than lean back in their chair. Good posture **increases alertness**. The increased alertness correlates with an increase in EDR and this can be recorded and shown to the student. We also teach them diaphragmatic breathing at a rate of, approximately, **6 breaths per minute**. The younger child will have a faster rate than the 6 BrPM that is best for most adults. There are individual differences at all ages with respect to what rate is best in order to achieve synchrony with heart rate variability. This combined with learning to raise their peripheral skin temperature and decrease shoulder and/or forehead muscle tension is done before starting on an academic exercise. We encourage them to use these techniques as a method of triggering ('cueing') getting into the desired, highly focused, problem solving mental state. This is the zone which they are learning to turn on and maintain for efficient learning and work production.

As noted previously, when they are in the physiological state described in 2 (above) then using a metacognitive strategy that we have taught them during training sessions will trigger the student to produce the appropriate mental state. The strategy, apart from being useful in itself, acts as an unconscious and automatic 'cue' to precipitate the appropriate relaxed, alert, focused and concentrating mental state.

SECTION XI
Alpha - Theta Therapy
Combining NFB and BFB with PSYCHOTHERAPY and RELAXATION TRAINING

Introduction

When William Penniston's study showing successful treatment of chronic alcoholics was published in the early 1990's it created considerable interest. He used a combination of temperature training, imagery and neurofeedback that encouraged slow wave activity. Due to the neurofeedback component, it came to be called alpha-theta training. Traditional alpha-theta therapy using the Penniston protocol is described in other texts (White, 1999).

The newest application of alpha-theta therapy has been to enhance the performance capabilities of music students. This is designed by John Gruzelier and his colleagues. They told the students only that they were to receive EEG biofeedback in order to induce a deep relaxation state. The feedback consisted of a pleasant tone sounding when theta activity exceeded alpha activity measured at Pz. Just twenty ½ hour sessions produced measurable improvements in the interpretative aspects of musical performance.

Alpha theta training is not really new; indeed the basic underlying techniques are very old. It is the use of computers and modern high-speed feedback instrumentation to produce the changes in the patient's attitudes and behaviour that is relatively new. The addition of biofeedback and neurofeedback has speeded the learning process tremendously. It has made learning the techniques possible for people who might never have been able to change using just teaching or psychotherapy.

At the outset, let us again emphasize that EEG biofeedback for improving attention span and for optimal performance is a completely different intervention than alpha-theta therapy. The first is a learning process that can be carried out by trainers with backgrounds in education, coaching and so on or, in some cases, by the individuals themselves. The second is a psychotherapeutic

process and, because of the state of extreme suggestibility that the client may enter, it should probably only be used by very well trained and experienced psychotherapists.

Tom Budzynski discusses the use of inducing the theta state for the purpose of having the client in a state where they are not able to resist rescripting suggestions. Hypnosis also utilizes this shift. (Hypnosis as an adjunctive technique is too broad a topic to be covered in this text. The reader is referred to experts in the field, including Eric Wilmarth in Grand Rapids, Michigan and Cory Hammond in Salt Lake City Utah.) Even a cough or a movement by the therapist may reinforce a client's recall of a real event or a fantasized one with the possibility of solidifying in their mind a false-memory. We will not have our training staff use alpha / theta training in our center unless they have extensive psychotherapy qualifications since we have an educational orientation. Nevertheless, we do feel that it should perhaps become part of the curriculum in Psychiatry and in other professions where the practitioner has supervised psychotherapy training for four or more years. The therapist must have training that equips them to deal with memories or imagery or emotions that may be relived when the patient is in the hypnogogic state associated with theta being higher than alpha with eyes closed.

In the mid 1960's a relaxation psychotherapy technique was being taught to psychiatry residents and it will be described here. Not surprisingly, the stages parallel the technique used by Penniston with alcoholics. The stages are a variation of the old *'sandwich technique'*. Think / say something positive – get to the 'meat' of the issue – think / say something positive. You use this technique continually when working with children. To demonstrate the shift from these very old techniques to modern coupling of them with what we now understand concerning brain waves we suggest you keep three stages in mind.

Preliminary Caution

Anyone who has worked extensively with autistic children will probably have come to realize how essential it is to think only that which you would like your client to 'hear'. Put simply, you will communicate your thoughts and feelings non-verbally whether you want to or not. It may even be the case that we are capable of picking up far more telepathically than scientific research has yet been able to elucidate. Whatever the mechanisms, it is important that you be aware of your own thoughts and feelings with each client and that you not work with clients when you are in a negative frame of mind. The telepathic possibilities are not a well accepted area to talk about in professional circles but this phenomenon has been reported by a number of responsible professionals, Julian Isaacs in discussing these phenomena quotes Nancy White and also references a chapter by Ullman, (1975) in Freedman, Kaplan,& Sadock, Comprehensive textbook of Psychiatry, 2nd Ed., Vol. 2, 2552-2561. Baltimore, Williams and Wilkins.

Here we suggest you keep in mind three processes that merge and run simultaneously. The suggested format is to do the NFB and BFB assessments first, then begin regular feedback and neurofeedback as required to promote relaxation and then, when the client is relaxed (as indicated by an ability to warm their hands and breath diaphragmatically at about 6 breaths per minute) begin the imagery. This is followed by neurofeedback that promotes a hypnagogic state; that is, a mental state with eyes closed in which theta activity reaches a higher amplitude than alpha in the occipital region. This is the normal state of affairs as one falls asleep but the goal in this therapeutic technique is to retain sufficient alertness that one can be conscious of the material that comes to mind and can process this material without falling asleep.

A. Start with BIOFEEDBACK / NEUROFEEDBACK Assessments / Training	B. RELAXATION (with attempted 'SATORI') TECHNIQUE	C. Addition of ALPHA / THETA THERAPY

All three processes (A, B, & C) should be carried out when doing alpha-theta therapy. They are not 'stages' in the true sense of the term because they are layered and A and B are still in process as C is added.

A. EEG & Stress Assessments and Teach Client Basic Components of Alpha – Theta Therapy

1. Stress Assessment

A stress assessment is carried out as previously described. In this assessment we record respiration, pulse rate, synchrony between pulse rate and respiration (RSA), peripheral skin temperature, skin conduction (EDR), forehead and upper body muscle tension (EMG). We suggest placing the electrodes for the first EMG measurement on the forehead and for the second EMG measurement the trapezius or masseter may be helpful. (Note, it has also been suggested that placing the positive electrode on the ventral surface of the left forearm and the negative electrode in the corresponding position on the right forearm may give an impression of overall upper body tension.)

2. EEG Assessment

Electrode Placement

With a one channel instrument the assessment may be done with the active electrode placed at Fz referenced to the left ear or to linked ears.

With a two-channel instrument use a linked ear reference and a single ground electrode attached to preamplifiers for both channel A and B. The active electrodes will be F3 and F4 initially with a second assessment comparing Fz and Cz. These sites will show whether there is a pattern suggestive of anxiety and may show high amplitude beta spindling which may be associated with obsessive compulsive symptoms. A third assessment may compare F3 and T3. (T3 is based on the theoretical hypothesis that theta activity in this area is associated with memory retrieval.)

EEG recordings may be done at the same time as the stress assessment. However, the EEG assessment is usually done separately to minimize the effects of muscle tension artifact. This is especially important in that we are primarily looking for peaks and dips in the beta range, 13- 34 Hz. This beta range we are interested in, (13 –34 Hz), is very susceptible to the effects of EMG artifact which can artificially elevate the amplitude of the waves and give a false impression of brain activity.

3. Set Objectives for NFB Training

With individuals who are anxious we may see a peak between 20 –24 Hz. If they are negatively ruminating a peak may emerge between 25- 32 Hz. In both cases there may be a concomitant dip in the amplitude somewhere between 13 and 15 Hz (SMR) when the site is along the sensorimotor strip.

We are also interested in the degree to which the client can go into high alpha, 11-13 Hz, when calm and externally focused. People with addiction problems tend to have less alpha and more beta than is found in adults without addiction concerns.

Set the EEG parameters according to assessment results.

4. Training Overview
a. Step 1: Learn Diaphragmatic Breathing combined with Relaxation.

The client is asked to close their eyes, breath deeply diaphragmatically, pretending that they have a balloon in their abdomen and imagining that they are inflating it while counting to 3 and deflating it while continuing the count to 6 then resting while they finish counting from 7 to 10. Next they are asked to tense then release the muscles in their forehead, neck, shoulder, arm, forearm and hand and to feel the difference in the two states (tension and relaxation).

Now the client is instructed to again focus on their breathing. Once this is going smoothly (RSA recording will tell you how successful they are) they are instructed to continue their diaphragmatic breathing but, in the expiration phase and the resting phase, to sense/feel heat, tingling and any other sensations in their muscles. They are to start with their forehead and then pretend that the feelings are 'energy' and they are allowing the 'energy' (tension) to move from that muscle to the next in a series moving from their face to neck to shoulder to arm to forearm to hand and then to dissipate out the end of their fingers. They may liken the energy sensations to a light which grows brighter and brighter. As the energy/ tension / light moves down, the muscle it leaves is to be completely relaxed. They are to allow the warmth to remain in their hands and fingers.

b. Step 2: Couple these exercises with BFB + NFB

Feedback is done that encourages respiration at about 6 BrPM with good synchrony between breathing and heart rate. The client is encouraged to increase peripheral skin temperature. They are to maintain EDR in a middle range without volatility. The client is to find a way to decrease EMG readings. Much of the foregoing formed a part of Tom Budzynski's twilight learning state (Budzynski, 1979).

During the feedback stage the student/client is encouraged to decrease the appropriate band width which usually lies somewhere between 21 and 34 Hz. The band 45-58 Hz must be held down to ensure that muscle artifact is not affecting the lower frequency beta bands. Concomitantly the client will increase 11- 12 or 13 Hz and 13 to 15 Hz. These are done separately because 11-12 Hz contains high amplitude alpha. 13 –15 Hz contains much lower amplitude SMR and beta.

Psychologically, in this stage, the student/client is encouraged to find a calm mental state of **'open awareness'**. This is the state athletes enter when they are well trained. For example the goalie who needs to be aware of every player around the net and yet who can instantly shift to narrow focus on the puck, the black belt martial artist who is being attacked by several opponents at the same time, the archer just prior to and during the release of the arrow and so on. Clients were encouraged to find this mental state in the

60's but only in the last decade have we understood that it corresponds to an increase in 11 &/or 12 Hz activity. Previously we could not objectively measure how successful the patient was doing but now they can have instant feedback. It is a similar state to that which Les Fehmi teaches using the term 'open focus' (Fritz & Fehmi 1982). This state allows a wider context to be sensed and defuses the narrowly focused negative ruminations of the client.

c. Step 3: Begin Using Imagery and Desensitization

In this stage the client maintains their relaxed state from Stage #1 and begins the imagery suggested below in section II. In this stage of imagery more alpha will be seen on the EEG and it may be lower in frequency (thalpha in the 6-10 Hz range) than the alpha seen initially. The client is moving to an even more internal, free association state. One may see a peak of alpha at either 7.5, 8 or at 9 Hz. This step is done with the eyes closed.

Remember that for the vast majority of our clients we are not doing psychotherapy (it is, rather, an educational intervention to learn self regulation) and we prefer **not to** have lower frequencies; indeed we discourage theta production and a big drop in EDR. We do not want the client in a state of high suggestibility. The work with alpha –theta with the most common application being with alcoholics, or those with drug addiction problems, is a different intervention than that discussed in the rest of this book. Another application of alpha-theta training would be if a highly trained psychotherapist was working with their client in long term psychotherapy and they wanted to facilitate a hypnogogic state so that there would be material to work with in therapy. In these instances all aspects of alpha + theta work would be discussed including the possibility of abreaction and an appropriate signed release obtained. With respect to the utility of increasing theta during a therapy session, there is no published data. On an anecdotal level, a Zurich trained analyst who was using the F1000 equipment mentioned anecdotally that his classic Jungian techniques when augmented with increasing theta speeded up the process of psychoanalysis so that the work could be done in 9-12 months rather than 3-5 years. Instead of waiting for the subject to have a dream that he could recall, the free associations while in the hypnagogic state of high theta (which is akin to a pre-sleep mental state)

provided the material for discussion in the therapy session. This work needs to be replicated and published.

B. Relaxation-Desensitization Technique

The client has begun to achieve a physiologically and mentally relaxed state, using the combination of biofeedback and neurofeedback described above. While the client maintains this relaxed state with eyes closed, diaphragmatic breathing at 6 BrPM, increased amplitude of 11-12 and 13-15 Hz, and decreased amplitude of frequencies between 21-32 Hz, (they are receiving soft, pleasant, auditory feedback), begin the following relaxation techniques.

The method described below is as easy as A,B,C. Other techniques can be substituted for the ones described here. The stages described below are the ones carried out and taught by the elder author for the last 25 years. However, most therapists have their own favourite techniques to aid clients with relaxation and you should use whatever you are comfortable using.

1. Deal with Major Negative Ruminations.

The client is asked to state, and the therapist writes down, a list of experiences, thoughts, or concerns about which they ruminate. Next, the client is asked to order this list from least to most personally traumatic. This is followed by the client putting each of the items on this list as a title on a separate page of their **SMIRB** (stop my irritating ruminations book) which they picture in their mind. The therapist writes these titles on separate pages. (The SMIRB has been described previously and will therefore only be summarized here.) The client is asked to state the phrases that continually reverberate through their mind when they ruminate about each area in turn and the therapist lists these phrases below their appropriate heading.

The page on the right side of this notebook is left blank for future ideas concerning actions to rectify the situation or to list different, more positive, ways of reframing it (this is similar to what is now called cognitive behaviour therapy (CBT)). Later the client will rewrite the foregoing into their own SMIRB. Then they are told that this book should always be with them. They are instructed that, for example, if they awake in the night with a negative thought they must ask themselves if the negative thought they are having is in the book. If it is, then they remind themselves that they have a worry time (perhaps a half hour with tea each afternoon) and they will not forget to worry about that thought because it is in their book. If it is not in the book then they must turn on the light and put it in. It is relatively rare, however, to have a new worry. Most people ruminate about the same things repeatedly.

Note that the SMIRB is a very small book which can fit into a small pocket or purse. The rumination section starts at the back of the book. The desirable goals and enabling objectives and actions section is in the front of the book. Writing positive goals with time lines is an old and well documented technique for achieving success. Stephen Covey's books are a resource that can be used to expand on goal setting, as is time-management training such as that offered by Charles Hobbs using Day-Timer products.

2. Imagine An 'Ideal Me'

The client is asked to make, in a very brief form, a statement describing an "Ideal Me". The therapist will carefully write this down. Then the client is to describe succinctly the sensations and feelings they would experience in that ideal state, followed by how others would react to them if they were actually like that. The therapist writes this down carefully for the client to have at the end of the session. Finally the client must describe how they would envisage their environment being (home, school, work, social) if they were in this ideal state. The therapist also notes this.

The client is told that when they are relaxing, this is the state we want them to have (be living in) for themselves. They are to take home their notes (that the therapist has made) and add, modify, or delete items. They are to repeat the imagery at specific times during the day. The times are chosen to be paired with habits that are already in place each day. This is also a technique that has been previously described – attach a new habit to an old habit and it is used

with the 'SMIRB' technique described in Section XII (and in *The ADD Book*).

The recovering alcoholic, for example, would typically describe an "ideal me" who was an abstainer. He would picture family and friends enjoying his company without any apprehension that he would drink and spoil the occasion.

3. Desensitize Yourself to Stress
a. Step 1: Imagine a Relaxing Scene

In this stage the client develops a strong positive, calm, relaxing image or scene. The client may develop their own scene. However, experience suggests that most clients want and require assistance in this phase. Therefore, the therapist may need to help them imagine themselves in the most peaceful and relaxing scene possible. You may assist this process by playing music. There are many opinions about what to play but the main thing is that the patient find it relaxing and pleasant. Piano music by a contemporary artist, such as Michael Jones' Pianoscapes or Seascapes is one option. Classical music may work for others. SAMONAS sound therapy CD's are another option (especially the ones using compositions by Mozart). Mozart music has been studied by John Hughes, an epileptologist, and he found that it corresponds best to the brain's natural rhythmicity. He has even had patients stop seizuring when Mozart's music was played (Hughes, 2002).

Similarly there are any number of dialogues on tape, though a personal approach is often better. The following is an example. Begin by telling the client, in a soft voice, that they are on a beach. The beach stretches for miles in both directions. There are no other people. The ocean is a beautiful light blue and the waves are softly lapping on to the sand. They see a lounge chair and go to lie down on it. It is like no other chair. When they are seated they cannot feel any pressure from the chair, it is like being suspended in warm, body temperature, salt water. We go on for a bit about the total comfort they are feeling (we use a very comfortable chair). Then we tell them that the only things they can see are a single white fluffy cloud and a seagull. They gull is beautiful and graceful. Without even moving its wings it circles down slowly towards the ocean only to dip its wings slightly to a different angle and rise again in great sweeping circles.

b. Step 2: Imagine Themselves Being "One with the Scene"

When they are ready they are to allow themselves to imagine that they are 'floating' out of their body and rise to become one with the sky, the soft white cloud, the gull in its gentle circular drifting. They are to feel totally relaxed, strong, aware of everything, aware without narrowing focus, a sense of complete power, a sense of total mastery and oneness.

c. Step 3: Enter a Personally Perceived Stress

At this point it is quietly suggested to the client, in their imagined scene, that they are to come back into their body on the lounge chair and, while remaining relaxed, rise and go behind the chair, off the beach and up a slight grassy hill. When they reach the top they will look down on a scene which represents for them a problem from their own life. They remain relaxed and detached and watch it unfolding. Then, if they are still able to be relaxed, they enter and correct the problem and then return to the beach and their chair. They again relax.

This is a type of progressive desensitization. The client is instructed to initially choose a scene which is only mildly traumatic and only to move progressively through more traumatic scenes as they are able to feel comfortable, calm and relaxed in so doing.

d. Step 4: Return to a Totally Physiologically and Psychologically Relaxed State

In this stage the client has returned to the beach and their chair and they again attempt to mentally become 'one with the sky' and the peaceful scene as a whole.

Remember to end the relaxation session with a gradual return to awareness of the here and now. You do not want your client leaving the session in a dissociated state.

C. Addition of ALPHA / THETA THERAPY

1. Review of Assessment and of Training Procedures

a. Stage 1: Review EEG & Stress Assessment & Autogenic Training Procedures with Client & Begin Relaxation Training

Although the original Peniston protocol used autogenic training (Green 1977) and hand warming as the first stages in training you could also use the steps described above, that is, combining BFB + NFB with traditional relaxation training. Use of finger temperature feedback alone may not be as effective as using a number of sensors for different modalities (temperature, EDR, breathing, RSA) as described above. Some practitioners do not do an EEG assessment. If you are beginning in this field, we would suggest you take the time to do careful assessments of both EEG and a psychophysiological profile.

If you are going to do alpha theta therapy and do not have a full cap EEG assessment then you may want to do at least a 2 channel assessment with electrodes placed at Fz and T3 since these may be the sites you will be using. Alternatively, if you are doing the traditional *Peniston Protocol*, you would do your assessment using an occipital site (Peniston, 1993). Then you can re-assess after training to see what effect there has been on EEG parameters.

We would suggest that you begin relaxation training using traditional biofeedback and neurofeedback as outlined above, and combine this with the modified autogenic training and imagery described above. Handwarming has received particular emphasis as being important before starting EEG biofeedback. Remember that autogenic training and other relaxation techniques can have negative side effects. Seb Streifel has stated in his AAPB workshops on Autogenic Training that about 30% of patients will experience discomfort. Begin the alpha-theta therapy after the client has mastered the relaxation techniques.

b. Stage 2: Alpha-Theta Enhancement Introduction

This has three components. First you must decide on electrode placements and whether to do one or two channel training. The theoretical considerations that may affect your decisions in this area are outlined in section A below. Then you will set your inhibit frequencies, your enhance frequencies, and thresholds.

2. Theoretical Considerations

a. Theoretical Framework – Alpha and Theta Enhancement

The essence of the alpha-theta process is the premise that alpha represents a bridge between internal and external attention. Theta is a bridge between wakefulness and sleep. Alpha and theta states are also important for and involved in memory and reflection. Training is done with eyes closed so the expected dominant frequency (particularly in the occipital region) is alpha. When the client hovers in a mental state of higher amplitudes of theta as compared with alpha (this is referred to as the alpha-theta crossover) they are capable of recovering memories with associated emotions and/or insights and/or creative thoughts. Early memories may be evoked harkening back to childhood, perhaps because, in a child, the dominant wave form is theta. This may represent a form of state dependant learning and state dependent retrieval of memories.

At the same time as this state is one of creativity and insight, it is also an unstable state in which the patient is prone to suggestion. Wisely used, this opens the door to new learning and the replacement of old and inappropriate 'scripts' laid down in early childhood. Inappropriately used by a therapist this state could lead to 'false memories'. The key principle for the therapist is be cautious, well trained in handling abreactions, and do no harm.

b. Theoretical Considerations for EEG Feedback Electrode Placements

The traditional Peniston protocol called for an O1 placement for the active electrode with a linked ear reference and a forehead ground.

However, given the theoretical considerations outlined below, there is a rationale for the use of 2-channel training with electrodes at Fz and T3. (Julian Isaacs has also suggested T3 – Fz sites but he uses a bipolar placement. With a sequential electrode placement one is less certain of what might be occurring at each site.) In this manner the alpha that is encouraged at Fz will relate to the client relaxing while the slowing at T3 may reflect a decrease in cognitive activity related to speech and language processing and correspond to memory retrieval and primary process insights.

Recently, work has been done with music students at the Royal Conservatoire in London England, with placement at Pz (Gruzelier and Egner, 2001, 2002, 2003). They found improved musicality (emotional interpretation of the music) in a group of students trained to increase slow wave activity as compared to groups who received mental strategies, Alexander techniques (posture and movement exercises), aerobic training or training to increase 15-18 Hz activity.

c. Theoretical Rationale for Using Fz and T3 Sites

Alpha projection systems are from the thalamus. Julian Isaacs has pointed out (EEG Spectrum workshop handouts 2000) that the 'specific' thalamic projections to the occipital lobe do not necessarily correspond to relaxation. On the other hand, the non-specific thalamic projections to the entire cortex do reflect relaxation. The Fz site reflects this second type of projection system. (Isaacs notes that the medial forebrain bundle projects theta from the limbic system to the frontal lobe). In addition, alpha at the T3 site may reflect the speech/language centre being inactive which may be desirable as it may mean that there is less self-talk going on. These suggestions by Isaacs appear to be well thought out and the concept of more than one alpha generator is well accepted (personal communications with Jay Gunkelman).

Since sequential (bipolar) placement can only reflect differences between the two active sites, a 2-channel feedback system might more clearly reflect the activity at each site and thereby better monitor the objectives for training at Fz and T3. However, this means that the program used must allow for computations based on channel A and channel B governing the feedback to the client. Both sites must demonstrate the desired alpha / theta state.

A practical consideration for not using O1 site is the effect on the active electrode of the client's position in the chair. For relaxation and for carrying out alpha-theta therapy one often uses a comfortable cushioned high-back chair. Putting your head back comfortably in these chairs with an O1 active electrode site may result in electrode movement or electrode pop. This will interfere with accurate recording and feedback. If you are using O1 then try using a rolled towel or a small cushion under the client's neck so that the electrode is not touching the chair's head-rest.

3. Training
a. Step 1: Use Inhibits
While doing alpha-theta therapy, the therapist should inhibit activity in the 2-5 Hz bandwidth. This is not only to inhibit movement artifact but also, and perhaps more importantly, to prevent the client from falling asleep. It is also important to maintain inhibits on fast beta wave activity. These inhibits include first, 19 - 24 Hz which may correlate with anxiety, second, 24-36 Hz which may correlate with worry and ruminations and third, 45 –58 Hz which may correlate with scalp, jaw and neck muscle tension (EMG artifact).

b. Step 2: Enhance Alpha and Theta
With all the above being carried out one will set the reward tones to encourage alpha 8 – 11 Hz initially and later 8 – 9 Hz. The reward for alpha should be a pleasant high pitch sound when alpha is over threshold. The threshold is set so that the client can achieve it about 55% to 70% of the time. This will ensure that the client does not become discouraged and will help the client increase the production of alpha for longer periods of time. In addition one will reward theta, 5- 8 Hz, with a lower tone feedback.

It would be especially helpful if, for the two enhancing signals, the pitch of the two tones blended appropriately and were proportional to the amplitude of the respective waveforms being monitored. However, these options are not yet available on most instruments.

In addition to these enhancement feedback sounds, most programs provide an auditory signal, such as a pleasant ding, when the theta band amplitude exceeds the alpha amplitude.

It is helpful if your program can graph changes in alpha, theta, and in beta. Otherwise you may choose to hand draw the changes on graph paper. In the graph, make the x axis be time and the y axis amplitude. With this arrangement high beta will be observed to decrease, alpha will increase then slightly decrease as high theta increases and a cross-over takes place.

c. Step 3: Imaging
In this stage in most alpha-theta work the client is to imagine themselves performing a task or being a part of something in the area they would most like to change. They are then asked to change this scene in a way that makes it what they wish it to be rather than what it typically is. This imagery of the situation they want to change, followed by imagery of the scene after the change has been made is done while they continue with the alpha-theta feedback.

4. Conclusion
In concluding this section we can reasonably expect that adding biofeedback and neurofeedback to standard relaxation methodologies should make the process more effective and decrease the time necessary for learning effective self-regulation considerably.

It is a good idea obey the principle of parsimony. Being parsimonious means you do the simplest, least invasive, least expensive, and least time consuming interventions which have a reasonable chance of success, first. The first thing to try for intervention is to use biofeedback and verbally instruct the student/client in relaxation techniques to use at home and also get them to implement the use of SMIRB (Stop My Irritating Ruminations Book) as has been previously described in this book. Psychotherapy and alpha + theta neurofeedback are there as a back up for those clients who require a long term therapy. There may also be a developing market for using alpha-theta training alone as a form of deep relaxation to further enhance performance in those who are already at a very high level.

SECTION XII
Metacognitive Strategies
Michael & Lynda Thompson
With special thanks to James, Aaron & Katie Thompson for their help in the development of this section.

Note: This chapter may be photocopied and used as a monograph to assist students.

An Introduction

Training to decrease slow wave electroencephalographic (EEG) activity and increase fast wave activity is necessary but not sufficient to maximize beneficial behavioural changes in clients who wish to improve their attentional processes. To work efficiently the graduates of a training program should ideally be able, at will, to put themselves into a mental state that is relaxed, alert and focused. In this state they can demonstrate concentration and engage in organized problem solving. In addition, graduates should have techniques - metacognitive strategies - which improve their ability to listen, learn, organize and remember material in a manner that allows them to efficiently and effectively accomplish tasks. These executive thinking skills can be applied with equal efficacy in academics, work and social situations.

Important Note:

This chapter is reasonably detailed and reviews some of the neurofeedback and biofeedback principles and examples given in previous sections. This has been done in order that this section can be read and used independently by learning centre / clinic staff, senior students and by parents.

1. Defining Metacognition

The term metacognition came into use in the mid 1970's at the same time as the first studies of neurofeedback for ADD were published. It was a new term for thinking skills that have always been with us. Metacognition may be understood as thinking about thinking and learning about learning. Metacognitive strategies are those executive functions of the brain that go beyond ("meta" in Greek) regular thinking (cognition) and allow one to be consciously aware of thinking processes, such as how to learn and remember things. Strategies for listening, reading, organizing and remembering are included in this training. The effective learner is able to select appropriate strategies and monitor their use. In a nutshell, metacognitive strategies boil down to a three step approach. You ask yourself; 1) What is the job here? 2) How can I best accomplish this job? and 3) How did I do? Metacognition thus involves the executive functions of the frontal lobe including planning and evaluating.

This chapter will describe an approach that combines self-regulation training with direct instruction in metacognitive strategies. Self-regulation training includes neuronal regulation (EEG biofeedback) and autonomic nervous system regulation using biofeedback of other modalities, such as respiration, temperature, and skin conduction. The examples used in this chapter mainly deal with training students who have Attention Deficit Disorder. However, the principles and strategies described apply equally well to top students, professionals and athletes who wish to further their performance. We emphasize metacognition because failing to use strategies is what separates superior students from weak ones. Awareness and teaching of strategies varies a great deal from teacher to teacher. We feel that it is an essential component of our NFB work with students. There are good articles in the literature concerning the relationship between metacognitive strategies and school performance (Chen et al 1993, Palincsar, A.S., 1987, Weins et al, 1983)

2. Combining Neurofeedback and Metacognitive Strategies

Neurofeedback training for attentional difficulties is based on observed links between brain wave patterns and particular mental states and behaviour. It trains the student in self-regulation of brain wave activity. For example, students who typically would produce an excessive amount of high amplitude slow waves are trained to decrease the amplitude of these waves while attending, reading, writing and listening. Less fluctuation in slow wave activity means attention is steadier, since bursts of theta are associated with flickering attention to external stimuli. (It is important to note, however, that theta and / or alpha waves will be briefly observed when the student is recalling information.) Simultaneously, these students increase the production of faster waves associated with activation of the brain for problem solving. When this balance is achieved, students report that they feel focused, attentive and that they organize and recall material better than they have ever done previously. It is also entirely logical to use this ideal learning state during the neurofeedback sessions and to simultaneously train these students in metacognitive strategies to further increase their learning effectiveness and efficiency. The pairing may also stimulate more rapid transfer of their training to classroom and study situations.

Teaching strategies while you are monitoring brainwave activity means you teach only when you know they are paying attention. This greatly enhances learning.

In addition to improving attentional processes and reducing impulsivity, goals for training include reducing anxiety and increasing alertness. The overall objective is to improve mental flexibility so that a person can produce a mental state appropriate to situational requirements.

3. Dealing with Anxiety

In addition to needing help with focusing and using strategies, many students demonstrate performance anxiety in classroom, athletic and social situations. It is associated with fear of failure when some performance is demanded; for example, answering a question, reading a passage, speaking in public, or skiing down a steep slope. This type of anxiety markedly inhibits performance. Often the same task could be performed easily if it were not a demand situation; for example, these children may spontaneously answer a question that is directed to the whole class but they cannot produce that same answer when singled out without warning. Going blank on a test is another example of anxiety interfering with performance. People with ADD are particularly prone to this problem and it is brain-based: SPECT scans show decreased blood flow when the child is given a stressor. (Amen, 1997). Dan Amen used a math task as the stressor and Sterman also feels that mental math is the best task for eliciting slow waves (tuning-out) in those with ADD. Decreased blood flow parallels increased theta activity. Parents often report frustration that their child knew the material when they reviewed it at home and then forgot it during the exam.

Skin temperature is one physiological measure which reflects anxiety and tension. It can be easily monitored using a tiny heat sensor placed on a finger. The finger-tip skin temperatures may initially be low, sometimes in the low 70's rather than the low to mid 90's on the Fahrenheit scale. Most clients quite quickly learn to self-regulate their temperature. They are able eventually to increase hand temperature at will and this correlates with a more relaxed state. One client, for example, began to use hand warming prior to ice-skating performances and her coach remarked on her remarkable improvement (two senior levels in a month).

Many candidates for training also demonstrate very low or labile levels of alertness. This is monitored by measuring skin conduction (EDR). Electrodermal response (EDR) is an autonomic nervous system measure which reflects arousal and alertness. Clients learn to recognize and regulate their arousal level. Instead of drifting off towards sleep when they perceive the teacher as boring, they can choose to stay alert. Both the self-regulation of the EDR and the application of metacognitve strategies help in such situations.

With modern equipment you can now monitor and give feedback on peripheral skin temperature, EDR, EMG and respiratory sinus arrhythmia while at the same time giving EEG feedback and carrying out learning exercises involving the use of metacognitive strategies.

The trainer can choose the appropriate combination of modalities for each client. Students are taught specific techniques for attaining a *eustress* physiological state wherein they remain highly alert yet relaxed. (Eustress is the term coined by Hans Selye for a level of stress that is optimal for the individual (Selye, 1976).

4. Dealing with Daydreaming

Appropriate candidates for combined NFB, BFB, and the teaching of strategies are, in particular, those who have a propensity to slip into daydreaming or drowsiness at inappropriate times. They may tune out in class, when they are doing homework, when the coach is giving instructions or even in everyday conversations. These states are associated with excessively high levels of slow brain wave activity. In most children, this slow wave activity is in the theta bandwidth (approximately 4 to 8 Hz [Hertz, shortened to Hz, means cycles per second]). In adolescents and adults it may also be associated with increases in "thalpha" (6-10Hz.) or in alpha brain wave activity (8 to 12 Hz). These EEG patterns appear to correspond to drifting off topic and brief or prolonged cessation of concentrated work on the subject matter at hand. Clients learn through the feedback of brain wave activity to self-regulate their attention, increase their concentration and maintain their focus until a task is completed. When they start to drift off, self-regulation training allows the student to recognize rapidly that they are no longer tuned into working on the subject matter, and to redirect focus back to the primary task.

5. Dealing with Learning Disabilities

Many, but by no means all, of the students with ADD also have specific learning deficiencies. They underachieve with academic performance that is low relative to their overall intelligence. All of the candidates demonstrate difficulties in working efficiently at academic tasks, although sometimes they will produce at the last minute. In the majority (exceptions often being those with high anxiety) organization and timely completion of work tasks is a major difficulty.

All of the candidates benefit from the combined training using feedback and teaching of cognitive strategies but those with specific learning disabilities need them most of all. The key in working with LD students is to develop strategies that use their strengths to help them compensate for weaknesses. Thus the child with weak spatial reasoning skills can be taught to use their stronger verbal abilities to "talk their way" through tasks where other students may just "see" the solution. One example would be learning to read maps. The visual child may just picture the compass points to orient himself. The verbal child will have an internal dialogue, "North is at the top so, if I turn the map upside down, north will be at the bottom and south is at the top." The trainer must be perceptive and figure out how the child best encodes information, or they may offer a number of ways; for example, using visual, auditory and kinaesthetic approaches to learning the letters of the alphabet.

Client Example:

C. is an 11 -year-old boy with severe learning disabilities and ADHD. His family is extremely supportive and both parents are teachers. In his history it was related that he had been called "the most profound learning disability ever seen" at a major Canadian hospital's child development clinic. Despite intensive special education his Reading and Arithmetic scores on standardized tests were only at an early grade two level when he started the program on August 8, 1994. Re-testing on November 20, 1994, after 40 sessions, demonstrated that Reading and Math were both up to a grade five level. His TOVA (Test of Variables of Attention) profile had also shifted towards a normal pattern. He sits calmly, is no longer restless and fidgety, and can listen attentively. This boy could not multiply even 2x2 and now he takes great pleasure in being able to do easily and quickly all the multiplication tables and has been learning the 13 times table on his own "just for fun". Most importantly, he no longer says, "I can't" but eagerly jumps into each new challenge and really enjoys learning.

6. Which Children Benefit most from Training?

Parents often ask if intelligence is the key factor involved in successfully dealing with ADD. It is true that, as with other kinds of learning, learning self regulation is generally easier for children who test at a high level on standard intelligence tests. However I.Q. scores do not reflect other variables that are important in achievement, such as perseverance or creativity. Intelligence tests originated with Simon Binet, who was working for the school system in Paris, France and wanted to develop a tool to help predict which children would benefit from the school system. Standardized intelligence scales like the Standford-Binet and the Wechsler scales are still used as predictors of school success. They measure skills associated with doing well in academic settings. Intelligence, in the broader sense, is made up of a number of components which include:

- Areas predicting school performance (as tested on standard IQ tests)
- Memory (short term and longer term and types of memory such as visual or auditory)
- Motivation
- Persistence (and the factors which seem to stimulate it for a particular child).
- Creativity
- Goal Setting ability
- Self confidence, "street smarts" and the ability to read social cues
- Approaches to learning and remembering
- Attention span and ability to concentrate

Goleman has termed some of these attributes "emotional intelligence" (Goleman). Each of the forgoing factors are inter-related with each of the others. Given a basic modicum of natural ability with respect to the above areas, the effective student also requires the ability to turn on:

- a relaxed (not tense) state of mind and approach to learning
- a high level of alertness
- flexibility and control of mental states (not in a meditative alpha state or a drowsy theta state when attempting to problem solve complex material)
- focus and attention with the ability to exclude irrelevant material
- concentration and a problem solving state of mind (associated with beta wave production)

- a thoughtful, reflective, considered style (not impulsive)

It is these latter factors that can be most directly affected by neurofeedback training and these, in turn, affect each of the factors listed under "intelligence" above. Outcome studies that have included pre-post testing of intelligence have reported increases in overall I.Q. scores of at least 10 points. ADD Centre retesting on the Wechsler subscales most affected by attentional factors (general information, arithmetic, digit span, coding) consistently demonstrate gains, often of 3 to 4 scale score points. (Linden, 1996; Lubar, 1995; Othmer, 1991; Thompson & Thompson, 1998). Data for 103 subjects seen at the ADD Centre is shown below. These data represent an update done late in 1998 of the case series reported in the literature.

	PRE	POST
Verbal (+ 9)	104	113
Perf. (+ 12)	105	117
Full (+ 11)	105	116

The problem with the majority of students who have ADD is that their memory, at least for subject matter covered at school, is poor. Some of these students have given up trying to remember material and use both conscious and unconscious defences to excuse their shortcomings. One of the more common defences is some variation on an "I don't care; it's all useless and irrelevant anyway, I want to quit school as soon as I'm old enough and earn money" attitude. This may be directly and confrontationally, or passive aggressively and indirectly, expressed. The passive aggressive stance is perhaps the most difficult to deal with. In this stance the student may begrudgingly agree to do the work or even smile and be quite pleasant and agree that the work will be done. Then, despite many reminders, it is not completed, completed far below their ability, or completed but just not handed in on time or at all. The terms lazy and unmotivated are often applied to these students but it really is a neurologically based problem with focusing and sustaining attention for things that are, frankly, boring for them. Over the years these students have become discouraged. Their self confidence in many academic areas is low. Many have given up.

What we do about this problem is give them hope, because once they start using strategies life becomes a little easier. Our initial job is to catch their interest in a non-threatening fashion. The initial interview, where they see their own brain waves and can even change things on the screen by focusing and concentrating, is extremely helpful in stimulating their interest. Virtually all, even the initially reluctant students, want to come back.

But Neurofeedback training takes time. Some of the students, though initially fascinated, become quickly discouraged as the novelty of training wears off and the real work of exercising the brain to make a lasting shift toward more mature patterns begins. Metacognitive strategies, apart from being an integral part of the program for maximizing the student's potential, are also a good means for catching interest and producing immediate changes in their academic endeavours. Taught without the feedback, in our past experience, the majority of students would use only a few strategies and would return rapidly to their old patterns. Taught during neurofeedback the students appear to apply many of the strategies on an on-going basis. Their initial and continuing interest in working on strategies during sessions is also completely different than when strategies were taught without neurofeedback.

B. Overview of how Metacognition fits into Training

Here is how metacognition can fit into the training program. We use 3-5 overlapping stages or steps. Some students have developed habitual counterproductive styles of coping with perceived stress. These coping styles or "bracing" techniques may include becoming very tense and anxious, displaying decreased arousal, opting out, and "distress" autonomic states. These coping patterns are usually learned very early in a child's life and are automatic and usually outside of cognitive awareness. The first two steps in training help counteract these negative coping styles. They are not necessary for all students. Most younger students go directly to step number three and do neurofeedback plus strategies with some work on diaphragmatic breathing added as needed. Adolescents and adults are more likely to receive

the total biofeedback, neurofeedback and metacognition combination.

The **first** step, learning diaphragmatic breathing with RSA feedback and raising fingertip temperature, is used with candidates who report performance anxiety. The **second** step, regulating the EDR, is emphasized in candidates who have low arousal (alertness) levels in class or work meetings and who exhibit low or labile EDR. Students report that they feel more relaxed yet alert, awake and energetic when they learn to control these parameters. These first two steps create a "eustress" state and are relatively quick to learn. They give the client a real sense of empowerment, since self-regulation of temperature and arousal is easier to learn than self-regulation of brain waves. Mastering these first two steps gives the student confidence that they will master the steps involving brain waves too. The third, fourth and fifth steps run concurrently with the first two, and are done by all clients.

In the **third** step the student is trained to hold the slow wave activity at a low microvolt level with decreased variability. Decreasing theta standard deviation and variability results in the student maintaining a steady focus on a topic for increasingly longer periods of time. Parents and students often initially ask what they should be doing in order to decrease both the amplitude and the variability of the theta wave. We use the analogy of learning to ride a bicycle to help them understand that, just as one cannot explain how to "balance", one cannot put into words how to control brain waves. In learning to ride a bicycle the brain receives direct and immediate feedback from the inner ear concerning going off balance. In training using brain waves the student is receiving direct and immediate feedback (less than 50 milliseconds delay) concerning going off focus. Given this directness and immediacy, the student trains to self-regulate and, just as in riding a bicycle, the new learned behaviour remains accessible and becomes, for the most part, automatic over time.

The **fourth** step emphasizes the student's ability to find the mental state in which they can continue to hold down the slow wave activity and increase the fast wave activity. When in this state, students report that they remain acutely aware of their surroundings but remain totally "absorbed" by a single train of thought and mental activity. We often liken this alertness and focus to the mental state of a high level expert in the martial arts. The students at the ADD Centre, when highly focused, sometimes report a concurrent sensation in their abdomen and occasionally a mild headache if they come out of this state too rapidly. The fast wave activity which is being trained may be in the SMR range (sensory motor rhythm, 13 to 15 Hz) or the Beta range (15 to 18 Hz or 16 to 20 Hz) depending both on the presenting difficulties of the child, their EEG pattern on assessment and their initial response to whichever range is initially used. The more impulsive children are usually started in the SMR range. The electrode placement is referential ("monopolar") and it is usually placed in the central Cz position with the reference and ground electrodes being placed on the ear lobes. In some children who are not impulsive and who have specific "left-brain" academic difficulties (particularly in reading or language), the electrode may be positioned on C3. Other electrode positions may be considered for special cases but are not as frequently used. Electrode placement and bandwidths enhanced or inhibited vary according to the objectives for training and the EEG assessment.

The **fifth step** is to continue doing the first four steps while reading, listening, doing math or written work in a manner that is extremely well organized and which utilizes metacognitive strategies. There is coaching done regarding strategies to increase the student's ability to assimilate, organize and recall information.

Note that the strategies are taught, modelled and practiced while the student continues to receive feedback. If they are looking at a page of math, reading or written work it is the auditory feedback that will give them information about their focus and concentration. The trainer can monitor the relevant EEG parameters and have them stop the academic work and return to pure neurofeedback whenever they tune out. Thus the metacognitive work is always paired with an alert, focused state. The initial part of a training session is always pure feedback and then strategies are begun after the client has demonstrated they are remaining focused. (For more about the timing of introducing strategies, see the section under Interventions on the structure of a session.)

The rest of this chapter is a mini-catalogue of strategies. Regard them as samples but recognize that the number of strategies is limitless. The trainer's job is often to do their own task analysis concerning a topic their client is having difficulty with, figure our which part of the task is presenting difficulties, and then come up with appropriate strategies for handling that part of the task.

C. SAMPLE METACOGNITIVE STRATEGIES:

1. Advantages of Using Metacognition

The strategies presented here are not always new to the client. Good teachers and parents may have tried to share them previously. Unfortunately the ability to enter and remain in a mental state wherein these strategies are actively and continuously used over a period of time has been a missing component. Being able to apply a strategic approach to academic tasks is almost always an entirely new experience for the students.

At the ADD Centre we typically train the students in strategies for listening, reading, math and organizing written work. We train the older students and adults in time management and any other area they desire. Most often it is reading skills. Our first adult client at the ADD Centre was a 56-year old lawyer who reported having to read things three or four times because his attention wandered and he could not recall what he had read when he got to the bottom of a page. Learning to maintain his concentration while reading increased his efficiency and shortened his working day.

2. Introducing Learning Strategies

When using metacognition you think before you jump into a task. A simple method may be used to introduce reading comprehension exercises. The student is taught to use the W-W-H-W PARADIGM. That is, "**W**hy am I doing this?" and, "**W**hat is it I wish to learn or accomplish?" "**H**ow am I going to approach this task?" strategies. These questions, explored in a simple enthusiastic manner, will engage even early primary grade students and all ages enjoy the positive reinforcement that follows the final question; "**W**hat have I learned in this session?" (At the completion of each step when working with children, tokens are awarded. Tokens can later be exchanged for prizes, including gift certificates for the local bookstore and music

store, when enough have been accumulated in the student's bank account. The bank account sheet is the first page of the student's training file and tokens are an integral part of the motivation during training.)

3. Memory

The first step towards beginning to teach strategies to students age 12 and over, begins with an exercise which is carried out to underscore the need for strategies. Memory is key for learning so the demonstration relates to their ability to remember simple material. This, in turn, has the effect of catalyzing their motivation to learn techniques which might improve their memory. The trainer then uses this opportunity to teach the student time management, study organization and a basic learning-to-remember strategy.

a. The 3 Fact Method to Improve Recall

i. Establishing the Need for Memory Strategies:

To recall facts for a test or examination, the facts must have been processed through immediate, short term, intermediate, and long term memory. Students often feel that their memory is less than it should be. Early in training students are therefore presented with a short challenge in a fun, game-like manner. They are asked if they include regular, daily review of material presented in their classes as part of a routine study time. The majority do not. They are then asked whether, if they added this to their routine, would such a habit require more or less study time. These questions usually lead to an interesting interchange.

Students are then challenged to a memory task involving telephone numbers. Most agree that they do not find it difficult to recall a telephone number. The student is then given a number to remember. It is easily recalled. Then they are given a second phone number but before they can reply they are asked to look at a picture on the wall and name 3 colours that are in it. Virtually none can then recall either the number they were just given or the number they had recalled correctly just a minute before.

They are reassured that the failure to recall the numbers when there is interfering material (the distraction of another question in this case) means they are no different than everyone else. They are then asked how this might relate to listening to a teacher talk and then being asked, even five minutes after the beginning of a lecture, what has been said. The analogy is a powerful one and usually leads to a productive discussion and motivation to improve their memory.

The telephone number demonstration has shown that they have a good immediate memory but they have also just demonstrated to themselves two other facts. First, their immediate memory will fade almost instantly unless they do something else with the information. Second, any simple quick distraction will interfere with their memory. The trainer, almost in passing, notes that when a person does even a few seconds of work on material (for example, attempting to associate it with something familiar or amusing) they usually will be able to recall it an hour later. The student is then asked to read a few lines of material, make some amusing association and recall it at the end of the training hour. They are then left with the suggestion that they may be able to learn how to recall even a large amount of material if they first learn ways of organizing it. Students are usually shocked that immediate memory fades so quickly but, upon reflection, they agree that "in-one-ear-and-out-the-other" is typical of their memory for new information. Yet they have noticed how easily they can remember amusing things that remind them of something else. This leads to a better understanding of why they must review new material at least once again the same day it is taught in order to lay it down in what we call intermediate memory. This may last longer than a minute or two, or even longer than a couple of hours or days, but it will usually fade within the week. More work must be done with the material for it to be placed in long-term memory. The trainer reassures the student that working together on memory strategies will make school life a little easier. We will ask him to do a simple - three key facts - experiment in class during the course of the next week and report back the results. Then, during our next few sessions, we will coach him in methods for reading and remembering.

ii. 3-Key-Facts Technique

This task requires that the student experiment at school by writing down three "key" facts in each class. (Of course, it may be 1 fact in one class and 10 in another.) They are told that teachers almost always give away all the questions they are going to ask in the next exam during their lectures. Teachers cannot resist emphasizing what they think are the most important things that they are teaching and will give away their feelings about important subject matter in various ways such as: saying it more than once, changing their tone of voice, gesturing, writing it on the black board and so on. Students may even notice that the teacher gets excited and their pupils dilate when it is something they find particularly interesting. Some students get really involved in playing a "beat-the-teacher" game by predicting the questions on the next test and thereby scoring a top mark in their class.

Case Example, Jane

Jane, age 19, complained that she couldn't recall anything from her classes. She had failed her last set of exams. She noted that when reading and trying to study, she couldn't even recall the material in the first paragraph by the time she reached the end of the second paragraph in a text book.

Her NFB trainer asked her to remember a telephone number. She repeated it back easily. Then a second number was given but she was interrupted before she could repeat it back by being asked to look at a painting and count the children in it. When asked to repeat the second telephone number, she couldn't. The trainer remarked that she had easily memorized the first number, so would she please repeat it. She couldn't. Putting this in the context of trying to remember things during an hour long lecture when her immediate memory was 5 to 6 seconds long convinced her she needed some mnemonic strategies.

One suggested technique was the key facts method. She would look up tomorrow's lecture topic in her text book and in the notes she had from a student who took the course last year. She would only spend a few minutes doing this before going to bed. She would scan the headings and then the subheadings and look at any picture or table that caught her interest. She would try and talk to herself about what the lecture tomorrow should cover and how it might be organized. When she got to the classroom she would sit near the front and put a small pocket notebook beside her main notepad where she took lecture notes. Every time the lecturer made a gesture or altered his tone of voice in a manner that she detected as meaning that he thought this was a 'key' fact or point, she would write it in her notes but also scribble it in short form in the small note book beside her. At the end of the lecture she would glance at this small list of facts before walking to her next class. During the class she would mentally compare the teacher's organization with the textbook and if she felt sleepy or if she was falling behind, she could ask a simple question such as, "Are you going to cover _____ today?" She knew the topic from her last evening's scanning of headings so it was relevant and not embarrassing to ask and it would serve to raise her level of arousal and get her emotionally involved in the class. In fact, she might just think about adding a question without actually doing so. This, too, would raise her alertness level and get her feeling more involved in the class.

When she got home she would put these facts neatly onto a list at the end of her notebook. When she took the same subject two days later she would add the next few 'key' facts to her list at the back of her notebook.

Somewhat to our surprise she tried this technique and reported to us that she could recall the key facts when she got home each evening and, after copying them again neatly, she could recall them a week later. At the end of the term she shared with her trainer a straight A report card. She was near the top of the class. Her succinct conclusion was that she had every exam question in every subject covered in her list of 'key' facts. How could she lose!

It is true in Jane's case that she was ADD and was also doing NFB training to help her focus so the key facts strategy was not the only intervention. Nevertheless, without a technique to help her improve her recall of relevant facts we do not think the results would have been this remarkable.

Day Planner & 3 Facts Scribbler

For some students, we suggest that they purchase a day-planning book which we call their ADD-PADD (ADD Centre Planner and Distraction Dissipater). Planners are commercially available. They can also use their school's student agenda. They use the day page for scribbling down the key facts in short form. Then they transfer the facts neatly to a summary sheet for that subject in a section in the front of the book. Alternatively, other students may choose to just write the 3 key facts from each lecture in a small pocket book and then transfer them neatly to a blank sheet in their binder for that subject. These should be facts that the student feels are likely to be asked in tests and are facts that should be committed to memory. An example in Math could be the formula for the surface area of a sphere. In History it might be several dates, names and events. In Biology it could be the definitions and critical characteristics of DNA, RNA and ribosomes. The facts from each class normally take 3 to 5 lines and the total for the day may take less than a page. The student is asked to do one more step, on the way home or while having a snack on reaching home, for 5 minutes to really concentrate and transcribe carefully each of the facts that they feel absolutely must be memorized for exams to another section of the ADD-PADD. This section is divided into school subject areas with 3 or 4 pages per subject. When the experiment is completed the full use of the "ADD-PADD" for keeping track of their school and personal dates and deadlines and maintaining sections for every major area in their life to record internal ruminations and distractions (hence the label "distraction dissipater"), is outlined and worked on with each student.

Case Example, Vince

Vince was an 18 year old, final year, high school student. He came to the centre in September, at the beginning of the school year. He had almost failed the previous year and was in the bottom 10% of his class. Testing demonstrated that he was a bright student. He found it very difficult to concentrate in class and literally fell asleep doing his homework in the evenings. Vince was at first reluctant to come for NFB training. His twin sister felt the same way. She dropped out after 4 sessions. She failed her final high school year. Vince seemed to be somewhat interested observing his own brain waves. He remained in training. The author introduced Vince to the 3 fact method, outlined above, in the second NFB training session. In January, Vince came into his first session of the new year and threw an envelope on to the author's desk. When asked what it was, he just said, "Have a look." After he started the NFB I opened the envelope and found his report card. All his subjects: algebra, calculus, physics, chemistry and English, were in the 90's. Vince stood first in his class.

I inquired as to how he accomplished this turn around in such a short period of time. He responded, "Look in my back-pack". I did so and found a rather thick day planner. I was not able to read very much of the scribbles that filled each day but it was clear they were abbreviated notes, facts and formulae. At the front of the day planner, however, were neatly demarcated sections, one section for each subject. In each section there were about 6 to 12 pages. On these pages were printed, with extreme care, lists of phrases, facts and formulae.

Vince put it quite simply, "I couldn't help but stand first. The facts listed accurately predicted nearly all the exam questions and I was ready with the answers."

Vince had made this exercise a game, a contest. He wanted to outwit the teacher. He had decided to see what percentage of the term exam questions he could guess. He guessed correctly for 100% of the questions on some of the exams. This, admittedly, is unusual, but it can happen.

Vince's story is exceptional. He was very bright and could use that strength once he had improved his ability to sustain focus during class and while doing his homework. He had made use of the other strategies outlined in the remainder of this chapter. However, he did conclude that the 3-fact-method had made a significant contribution to his scholastic success.

Vince used SMIRB

The author noted that there was another set of section markers at the back of his day planner. Vince said this was his version of SMIRB. SMIRB was another suggestion the author had made about half way through the fall after he noticed that Vince was worried about certain things that were happening in his life. He was worried for his sister but she wouldn't talk to him. He was concerned about other things that were happening in his family. He couldn't make up his mind about what to do next year. He had brought this up because he felt he was wasting a great deal of time in unproductive thinking. It was also interfering with sleep.

The suggested technique was that he make a section of his day planner into a Stop-My-Irritating-Ruminations-Book (SMIRB). This would have two pages devoted to each major worry area. He would list his concerns on the left hand page, and on the right hand page he would list possible options for future action. He would put aside one time of day for a 20 minute worry. At that time he would open this section of his book and think about things. If he began to ruminate at any other time of day or night, he was to make sure the 'worry' was listed in his book. If it were, he would forget about it and get on with his work (or sleep) knowing he could think about it later. If it wasn't listed, he would enter it in this section of his SMIRB

Vince said that this little technique had also been a positive factor in his being able to achieve high marks. It freed his mind of worries so he could focus on his studies and social life.

4. Reading
a. Four Steps for Reading
i. Overview of Four Strategic Steps for Reading

In each step outlined below the student carries out an internal dialogue in which they generate questions concerning what they wish to learn from reading a passage. Then they predict answers to their own questions. Thus reading becomes a search for the answers.

The four steps or stages for reading a textbook chapter occur:

1. Before opening the book
2. Upon first looking at the chapter.
3. While reading the chapter
4. When reviewing what was read

In this process the student is always an active participant and emotionally involved. The student should never be a passive recipient in the learning situation. The student learns that the responsibility for learning being interesting resides with them and not the teacher.

Early in training, the student is introduced to the approach outlined above for reading textbook material. The following exercise has been found to be a useful starting point. Note that strategies are integrated into a neurofeedback training session only after the feedback indicates that the student is concentrating.

ii. The "Nelson versus Napoleon" Exercise

A short example can demonstrate reading (scanning, reading for detail and chunking) and memory strategies (associations and visualization). One example that is frequently used at the ADD Centres for students at or above a grade 8 level of reading is three pages taken from a history textbook, "The British Epic". (Grade 3 –6 level students choose an animal or bird described in a National Geographic book series and carry out a similar but simplified series of steps.) The student is told that we are giving them just 2 1/2 pages of reading with large pictures on each page, that it is about a war that took place in the 1790's and that we will ask them when they finish it what they have learned. The fact that it is a war and the approximate time is given so that a good student could use learning strategies for the reading if they knew how to do this. The first question we will ask after they have read the passage is deliberately open ended and no instruction is given as to how they should go about organizing their thinking before reading or about how they should scan, read and learn, or how to review at the end of paragraphs, pages, sections and at the end of the passage. It provides a baseline for how they currently read and recall information.

This initial reading exercise has been used on hundreds of students, many of whom were in the senior years of high school, university or in postgraduate studies. Nearly all used basically the same procedure. They opened the text, went directly to the assigned page and began reading starting with the first word of the first paragraph. Only a few of them bothered to look at the titles or the author or observe the time line giving dates and events at the top of the first page of the chapter. Those with extremely high intelligence remembered a sprinkling of facts and one, a lawyer, recalled the basic strategies of the British and the French. Even though little is recalled the trainer must remain very positive. The idea is to be a coach and the strategies are presented within the framework of a game and an enjoyable challenge. The student is told that they will now try a few tricks with the trainer to see if they can increase their recall and they are going to do this in 4 stages.

iii. 4 Steps in Detail
Step 1: Before Opening The Book / Chapter
First, before reopening the book, they are to play a game with the trainer in which they think of all the things they might expect to read about in these pages given that all they knew initially was that passage is about a war in the 1790s. They are asked, "What would you like to learn? Often the trainer must model speaking aloud the thoughts that the student will later internalize. Here and throughout the following steps, you are training them to use what cognitive psychologists call *verbal mediation techniques*. In other words, they use an internal dialogue to talk their way through a task.

Generate ideas, headings, and questions and organize these into a grid: Within the framework of generating questions and organizing ideas the student is guided into forming a simple mental grid. They draw the grid on a piece of paper to provide a visual reminder. When using the grid technique the rows represent headings for grouping the information that the student wants to learn concerning each of the areas represented by the columns. In this example there may be just two columns representing the two countries: England and France. The rows would be generated by questions commonly referred to as the reporter's questions: **Why** - there should be at least one clear reason for why each country enters a war; **Who** - the Generals, Admirals, Prime Ministers, soldiers, sailors, merchants etc.; including characteristics or important facts about each; **When** - the dates for events and time frames; **Where** - the countries, oceans, cities, battles etc.; **What** - the strategies developed by each of the countries and events that occurred such as the battles, voyages and so on; **How** - the types of weapons, ships, other transportation, clothing, foods, and so on and **With What Effect**?: both on the countries at the time and on future history.

The student and the trainer attempt to predict answers for some of the questions they have generated. When their ideas are exhausted they then agree to open the book and begin scanning the author's headings.

Step 2: Immediately After Opening The Chapter

A this juncture the trainer will ask the student if he thinks that the author will cover all the topics that he has thought of and put in his grid. Then the student checks this for himself.

Scan the author's headings: Before starting to read, the student scans the table of contents of the history textbook and notes what seemed to be happening immediately before and after this time in history. They then open to the chapter, read the headings, subheadings, introduction and conclusion of the chapter, review the questions at the end of the chapter, if there are any, and glance at the pictures and their captions. This step takes only a few minutes. During it they enjoy seeing what ideas they had generated that the author had forgotten to mention and what they had missed that the author had included. They remain actively involved because they are checking out their own ideas.

Step 3: Reading and Remembering

The student has already read the required pages once in their usual fashion. However, they recalled very little information. Therefore the trainer now reads each paragraph with the student and models techniques for memorizing the important facts. (These mnemonic devices are described and illustrated in more detail in *The A.D.D. Book* by Sears and Thompson in the

chapter "Setting Up for School Success". Some will also be described later in this chapter.)

Pictures Help Recall Of Characters: The trainer may develop a picture such as the Mapping Techniques. Create a mental map (or sketch one) showing Great Britain, Europe, the Mediterranean and North Africa with the West Indies in the distance on the left and India on the right. England has a large hole in it's centre representing the Prime Minister "Pitt", Europe has dollar signs (or English Pound signs) in each of the countries surrounding France, and ships surrounding France in the English Channel, the Atlantic and the Mediterranean Sea. This represents the British strategy. The French have guns pointing at Belgium and Holland and India representing both the reason for the English becoming involved in a war and the French strategy. Students with ADD tend to be creative with good visual skills (remember Hartmann's Hunter Mind analogy) and creating mental pictures, or even sketching them, provides opportunity to use those positive attributes.

Associate Names with Known People, or Places, Things, or Amusing Pictures: Horatio Nelson is represented in a Neilson's chocolate bar wrapper standing on deck looking at a book (battle at Aboukir Bay) with a sphinx in the background (Egypt), Santa Claus on a cruise ship is by one empty sleeve (lost an arm at Santa Cruz) and an eye patch with an apple core or a small car on one eye (lost an eye at Corsica). Napoleon Bonaparte is depicted as rowing away in a small rowboat with his ships being "blown-a-part" in the background.

Students find this exercise amusing and informative.

Step 4: After Reading the Chapter

Speed-read review of the material: The trainer models a quick scanning (rereading) review of the material using the first few paragraphs. In this demonstration the trainer uses a speed reading technique that involves "chunking", grouping important words and phrases together and scanning through unimportant details to find the key words and phrases. The facts are then related to a revised 'grid' or set of mental pictures that will assist future recall of the material.

When the student is asked what they remember after using these techniques they are usually surprised at themselves in that they not only recall more detail, but they also do it in a more organized fashion. They are even more amazed, when they come into their next session and are asked to do a quick review of the passage, at the immense amount of detail they effortlessly recall in an organized fashion.

During the final review, the trainer will ask for much more detail. Taking the passage about the Napoleonic wars, for example, a question might be, "What did Nelson look like?" If they know then they are asked, "Where did he lose the use of one eye? and where did he lose his arm?" At this juncture that trainer may demonstrate, model, or develop through Socratic questions, more advanced methods for laying material down in memory using mnemonic devices that include associations and visualization. These are discussed in the following sections.

Summary of the 4 Steps for Reading a Textbook Chapter

I.   BEFORE I OPEN THE BOOK
A. Why? What is my PURPOSE?
    (set tone, get in the zone - relaxed / alert / focused / concentrating / steady)
B. MAKE ASSOCIATIONS (develop questions)
    - the tree and it's branches -

C. ORGANIZE & SYNTHESIZE
    - headings / grid & the organizing principle / the red thread -
    - scaffolding & linkages

II. Right After I Open the Book

A. SEARCH & SCAN
    - headings / subheadings / pictures / abstract / conclusions -
B. SKIM - key words / phrases – 1st line of each paragraph
C. ORGANIZE / SYNTHESIZE

III. As I Read or Listen

A. Make notes / underline / reorganize

B. Use MEMORY TRICKS
    - simultaneous visualizing -
    - sequential - the Roman room / mnemonics / rhymes / acronyms / first letter sentences / silly sequenced scenes
    - make Associations

IV. Review

A. Chunk / Key Word Review / Reorganize
B. What have I Learned ?
C. What is the PRODUCT !

Value of This Approach

Working through these initial discussions and practical experiments allows the student to discover for themselves that applying strategies really does work to make their academic lives easier.   The initial three facts and memory exercise leads to the student understanding why they should quickly review last week's material in order to further lay it down in long term memory. The reading of three relatively simple pages of history gives them basic methods for learning that do not take a lot of extra time. The seed is sown and students become willing to try learning how to learn.

The exceptions are predictable. Occasionally a student from a family where there is disruption, separation or divorce, will resist strategies just as they are resisting other learning experiences. They may be angry and resentful and not have either the motivation or the emotional energy for learning. Students with low self esteem comprise another group who may resist trying something new: if they do not try, they cannot fail. Being passive entails less risk. These students need to experience success in learning the self regulation aspects of training before they can be introduced to strategies. Working on modalities that can be quickly mastered, raising finger temperature and breathing such that the heart rate follows in synchrony with respiration (RSA) and controlling EDR is the first place to start building a sense of self sufficiency. To sell the student on strategies the trainer can comment that these methods, if faithfully carried out, make studying for final exams a faster and more enjoyable process. The student's initial success in recalling material more easily makes this statement believable. These initial steps also lead into further discussion of memory strategies. (See below under 8. Memory)

b. Basic Principles which Underlie the Four Strategic Reading / Listening Steps

As sessions proceed the students are challenged with further listening, reading, and presentation-preparation tasks. The same strategies apply when listening to a lecture as when reading a chapter. The tasks are at appropriate levels for their intellectual and academic abilities (Psychoeducational testing carried out prior to beginning training can be used to establish these levels. Failing the availability of such data, use grade placement and report card information.). These tasks allow the trainers to expand on the strategies and the principles that underlie them. The student is always encouraged to use the neurofeedback in the first half of the session to help them achieve a highly focused, relaxed,

alert state before this desirable mental state is paired with an academic task. The auditory feedback is continued while the student learns the strategies and works on the tasks and any time their focus is lost they can return to watching the screen till it is regained..

i. Generating alertness and motivation

Students must be attempting to "figure out" something which is important or interesting to them in order to maintain an optimal level of alertness, focus and concentration. This is the first of the four-strategic-steps: forming a personal challenge at the outset of each lecture or assignment. That the teacher or one's parents will invoke a consequence if one does not do the work is sufficient motivation to sit in a seat, face the front and pretend to listen or work. It is a good reason for falling asleep because if a student is forced by someone else to do something they may unconsciously sabotage the activity and sleepiness is a classic method of so doing. To be motivated to learn the student must formulate a personally meaningful reason to pay attention and concentrate. This is particularly essential for students who have ADD. This is relatively simple if some aspect of the subject matter is interesting for the student or if the subject itself is important for a secondary reason. An example of the latter is learning the cardio-pulmonary system for a student who is advancing in the Red Cross and Life Saving levels in swimming. A future airforce pilot may fail a high school math credit yet later do exceptionally well on the math required for navigation when he was a cadet. Knowing he would be dropped from flight training with out a good grade made that math a relevant challenge. Older students may motivate themselves with a challenge, such as, "By the end of this lecture I will have produced a superior and more organized outline of this topic than the presenter is about to give". This stance requires that students become exceptionally alert and form their own personal organization and grid of the material as it is being presented.

ii. Generating Questions:

When reading mysteries or thrillers there is not a problem staying engaged in the process. The nature of the stories makes one automatically generate questions, including the classic "Who dunnit?" The trick for the student is to somehow transform their textbook into the equivalent of a pageturner mystery. In the Nelson vs Napoleon example the student was encouraged to generate questions and predict answers to their own questions concerning the material to be learned. The trainer then helped the student reorganize and redesign the scaffolding organization that the student initially made in order to logically order the information. First the student "free associates", scribbling down in point form ideas that come to mind about the topic area. Generating ideas also identifies large areas where the student has only questions. This increases the effectiveness of reading and listening since they are searching for something. Students are taught to continue the process of generating questions and predicting answers throughout the scanning, reading and reviewing stages.

iii. Generating Organized Thinking:
The basic thesis is that **recall is dependent on continuously organizing and reorganizing data** that comes into one's mind. Use the analogy of the garbage bag mind.

The Garbage Bag Mind versus The Filing Cabinet Mind:
In order to emphasize the need for organization in one's life (and in one's thinking), begin with a dramatic example. The student is challenged to visualize a possible scenario in their social life such as the following: Your alarm didn't go off, you awake to find that two friends just telephoned saying their father is already in the car driving them to the ski hill charter bus. There is just barely enough time to catch the bus, and you must be ready in 5 minutes so they can pick you up en route to the bus. Otherwise you miss the planned ski day.

The student is then asked how long it will take to find their ski things if all their clothes are contained in a huge garbage bag in the middle of their room. They usually agree it would take much longer than the required 5 minutes. They are then asked for a solution. They normally suggest labelled, organized drawers or shelves with gloves in one, socks in another, and so on.

A comparison is then drawn. Equate entering a classroom or opening a textbook without a minute or two's mental preparation with the "garbage bag " (disorganized) mind. The contrast

is to a mind that is ready to take in and 'file' new information. Information is easier to recall if it is logically organized. Even the initially most unmotivated students agree they would like to make their study time more efficient, that is, spend less time for better marks. They acknowledge that they have to sit through the class anyway and they might just as well learn the material there as have the hassle of trying to retrieve it and work on it later when they would rather be doing something else.

c. Using a Grid
i. Introduction:
A grid technique can be used for organizing thinking, discussing and writing. It is a major help in creating the Filing Cabinet Mind.

In the Nelson versus Napoleon example, after generating as many ideas and questions as possible, the trainer helped the student to organize the data into headings and a grid. Gridding is only one of several organizing methods. Some students prefer to take the central idea (the topic heading), and draw highways or branches coming out from it and place the most important headings on different branches close to the central trunk. Other students will make a list and gradually add new headings. In Nelson vs Napoleon the student was encouraged to use the reporter's headings: Who, When, Where, What, Why, How and with What Effect, to get ideas flowing. More advanced students prefer to immediately make a grid with columns and rows. One of the journalist's headings may form the columns and the others the rows.

ii. Habitual 'Bracing'
In the "Nelson versus Napoleon" example the student created a simple grid. In later sessions more complex examples are used. However, regardless of age and past education, the first time most students are given such a task they become anxious and resist. The students with ADD may freeze and begin their habitual mental turn off as a part of their dysfunctional "bracing" when put under perceived academic stress. (Dan Amen's SPECT scans show decreased blood flow when students with ADD are given a math stress.) Biofeedback techniques are used to help them learn to self regulate and relax when under stress. Even if you are not doing any general

biofeedback, you can teach slow diaphragmatic breathing to counteract those old, maladaptive responses to an academic task.

iii. Examples of Organizing and Gridding Problems for Students or Business Professionals

- **Gridding Task - Design a School:**

Designing a school is a good non - threatening introduction to the grid technique. The trainer begins by asking, "What does a school have to do?" If the student "freezes" (goes blank) the trainer jokes with them and makes fun, ridiculous suggestions such as, "I guess the best thing would be to put the 1500 students in one big enclosed space with wire mesh for a roof and scatter a few teachers and black boards through the area." This is usually sufficient to provoke even the most reticent participant into suggesting that that would not be appropriate. The trainer then rapidly changes vocal tones and challenges the student, saying this is a perfectly sensible idea and would save lots of money and why shouldn't we design our school this way. The challenge becomes a game, with the trainer playing the naive straight-man. Soon the student has outlined functions that must be carried out by a school which are incompatible with all ages being grouped in a single room with no effective roof. Two key areas that must be addressed emerge: education and health or safety. Soon the structures in the design are being dictated by the needs or functions each part of the structure must achieve. Even the younger students come up with excellent needs including the need for small classes to decrease distractions and group students of equal competence together for more interesting discussions, the need for books and therefore for a library, the need for healthy exercise and learning teamwork and therefore for a gym and so on.

In this process the light soon flashes on and the student discovers for himself the equivalent of "needs / functions dictate structure". This kind of quick exercise gives an enjoyable introduction to the idea of generating ideas and organizing them into meaningful groups.

- **A 'Gridding' Task - Design An Introductory Lecture on the Cardio-pulmonary System:**

The trainer may starts with a question such as: "You must give an introductory lecture to your class tomorrow on the cardio-pulmonary system." We have had students as young as grades 6 and 7 really get interested in this challenge. Having done the first few examples they know to first ask (and we look up with them) the meaning of each of the words: cardio, pulmonary and system. They then use the same procedure of answering the questions of: "What are the needs?" This will generate a list: take in oxygen and give off carbon dioxide (or blow up like a balloon!); take in nutrients and give off waste material; the basic structures essential to these processes including tubes for transport of gas, tubes and a medium (blood) for transport through the body, a means for moving (exchange) the gas from the lung to the blood, pumps for the respiratory process and for pumping blood and so on. Students who have never taken this subject in school draw an amazingly accurate diagram of both systems without little prompting! They can move from their idea to examining a textbook illustration and will have some motivation for doing so.

- **A Gridding Task - Discuss the Great Depression**

In a history assignment another student used a GRID & the 5 W's to organize information about the great depression. This student developed a grid where the column headings went under the general heading of "WHEN", that is, a time frame: before, during & after. To help generate questions and organize information for these three time periods, the rows were labelled: WHERE (countries, urban vs rural etc.); WHAT (the economics, production, consumption etc.) and WHO (the classes of people and how they were differentially affected etc.) This student then used the questions of WHY and HOW to help expand information and discussion for every row in every column.

- **A Gridding Task - Design a Living Environment for Another World**

Gridding can be a real challenge for even post-graduate university students. It is an essential method to ensure that important areas are not being omitted before beginning an investigation. Once the grid is done, the student makes decisions concerning which areas to include and which to exclude, which to emphasize and which just to touch upon. Without a grid, the student would approach the task in a relatively disorganized manner and at worst, in a comparative vacuum with little motivation.

Case Exampe: Susan

Susan, a senior in high school, was asked to pretend that she would have to give a lecture for 30 minutes to her class the day after tomorrow. She was told to imagine that the earth's atmosphere was deteriorating and that she had unlimited funds and one year to create something to sustain life for herself and a few chosen others for the rest of time. Her topic, therefore, was "Ecology and the Biosphere". She had never heard of a Biosphere but guessed it must be some sort of container that sustained life. She was shown the cover of a book on Biosphere2 and told she could use this and the encyclopaedia. She was then asked how she would like to proceed.

*Susan had previously learned how to formulate **grids**, the importance of having an **organizing principle or "red thread"** and she had practiced the **three step procedure for giving a speech:** (Say what you are going to say - say it - say what you have said.) With guidance and encouragement, after her first exclamation that that was an impossible assignment, Susan was able to help herself go from utter confusion and a giving up attitude to using the four strategic steps and a methodical step by step approach to the problem. She looked up ecology and biosphere then began a **free association and grouping procedure.** This led to her asking herself what she and her friends would require if they were to have to begin living one year from now in a completely enclosed container with nothing being allowed out and only sunlight being allowed in. She quickly grouped together essential elements such as, air, food, water, energy, waste recycling systems, and so on. This led her to defining an underlying general principle which she would use to tie together the entire talk, "Functions dictate Structure", or "Form Follows Function" if you want to be more alliterative for ease of memory. This led to exploration of **"How"** to build the enclosure and its components. With each step she was asking herself, **"Where"** component parts should be and **"Why"** and **"When"** each part should be introduced into the system. As she thought this through - without ever opening a book - she was **generating question after question and***

*predicting a few answers and some ideas as to where she might be able to find the information. Susan decided that she would use the principle, "Functions (needs) dictate Structure", in her introductory **"Thesis"** in which she would demonstrate to the class that if one followed this principle and fulfilled all the basic needs of the humans and other creatures in this closed system that one could create a system with multiple subsystems that would constantly regenerate its own equilibrium and sustain life.*

*As she thought about it she drew small rectangles in the top left and the bottom right corners of a page to represent her **introduction and thesis** and her **summary and conclusion** (proof of thesis) respectively. In the remainder of the page she drew a rough **grid.** As she free associated she first created **rows** -which were **areas that she would need to discuss for each of her columns**- and filled in major areas mainly under What - Needs. She also had rows for Where and When but these were not developed initially. Beside each of the subheadings under What (the needs of the humans who were to live in the biosphere) she filled in ideas in her second column titled, "Supporting Ecological Systems and their interconnections". Her third column was, "How - Structures". Her fourth column was initially titled 'Why and With What Effect". She explained to the trainer that she had been **overinclusive only as a starting** point. She said that, once she had given a general overview in the beginning of her speech, she was going to tell the class that for ease of understanding and time constraints she would take one need, such as the need for fresh water and expand the biological cycle related to it. She would then list the structures that would be necessary in order to create it in a closed environment. She would use this example as a means to demonstrate how the thinking behind creating a biosphere would evolve.*

All of the above was developed over a 20 minute period and Susan correctly observed that even without opening a textbook she had enough in the way of ideas to deliver a very well organized and interesting introduction to this topic without any further study. However, she also noted that she had gone from virtually no interest and some negative feelings about this assignment to wanting to continue it on her own, just for her own interest. Susan had established her own personal motivation for completing an assignment. Sometimes a student must begin without personal motivation and plunge into the four strategic steps in order to discover for themselves a personal reason for carrying out the assignment! It is part of their job to make the task personally relevant and interesting.

- **Broader Applications of the Grid Technique**

This student created a mental image which she was continually modifying and to which she was steadily adding new information. Continuously reworking one's initial 'grid' is a procedure that is also carried out when reading. The student should review the material they are reading at the end of paragraphs, pages, chapters and so on. To review they quickly 'scan', 'chunk' and make visual images of key information. This "reviewing" technique is taught and emphasized as one of the key metacognitive strategies with all students. Why? Because it is the step good students naturally do and the one poor student always skip. Students with ADD, for example, read to get to the end and seldom want to take time for review. No wonder they feel discouraged. They were never actively involved and thus cannot remember what they read.

At times the trainer will just go through the second and third strategies as outlined above. When the student is very interested in a topic and/or has that topic as a project in school, then the trainer may begin reading a textbook chapter that the student has brought in. With older students the trainer may elect to assign a first reading of such a chapter to be done at home. At the ADD Centre, however, we very rarely assign homework. An exception might occur if the student was keen to try a new learning technique on material at home and would like us to go over it in the next session.

5. Planning a Project Time Line – a Flow Sheet

Projects and independent study assignments are being assigned starting in the junior grades (4,5 and 6) and high school students are expected to do these without much teacher guidance. Most students with ADD do not have any idea where to begin so they procrastinate. The old adage that failing to plan is planning to fail is often borne out. Coaching in how to develop a time line is like preventive medicine.

When project planning is done the trainer will develop with the student a flow sheet outlining how the student will approach the task. In this process the trainer works with the student on how to set down a time line including each step of the project. On the sheet would go the exact time(s) the student says that he will do his rough work plan, first draft of a grid (organization of headings for the paper), scanning of the text(s), reading with note taking, reformulating the draft organization for the written paper, initial draft of the paper and revisions leading to the final copy. The trainer wants to make sure the student puts down realistic times and goals for each stage of this activity in their day planner. The rule of thumb is that you spend 1/3 time researching and planning, 1/3 writing the first draft and 1/3 editing, revising and doing a final copy. Most students do not allow for that final 1/3 and those with ADD often want to call it done when they have finished the first draft. In the following sessions that follow the trainer will review what the student did and any stumbling blocks encountered.

Brief Summary

Initially we prefer to use materials that we have in the centre. Most students want us to not only be independent of the school authority network but also to 'appear-to-be' completely independent. As some students proceed with training they become more comfortable that we can be independent and yet make their school assignments easier. At this stage the student may decide to bring in their own textbooks and projects.

In the first stage of looking at material we emphasize that the student always pretend that they are the author of that text. The student is then asked to begin by imagining that their assignment is to give a lecture on that topic the next day and that they have therefore far too little time to prepare or even to begin at the first line and read the full text of the material. With this thought in mind the student works through the first step, 'before opening the book', and then compares their ideas and organization with that of the author's work that they must read for school. Then the student and trainer may go through the steps for reading, organizing and reorganizing a draft for the project.

6. The Red Thread:

The concept of the "red thread" is often elucidated while working on the foregoing gridding exercises. Older students quickly carry out the entire process on their own. Before the lecture begins or before opening a book, they generate questions, predict answers, mentally register unknown areas/definitions to look up, decide on **an overriding question** -usually a "why?" question or **an underlying principle** around which the entire area can be organized. This is the "red thread" which will tie all the factual information together into a logical sequence or Gestalt.

In the foregoing examples of designing a school, figuring out the cardiopulmonary system and creating a biosphere, function / needs dictate structure was the universal principle. In reading short stories and novels, the author's purpose in writing the story (usually a universal and timeless message for mankind) may be a thread that ties together what might otherwise be seemingly unrelated sections of the story. The students learn that when they present material this linking "thread" must be very clear to whomever is reading their work or listening to them.

7. Memory and Recall

Among countless visual techniques to assist memory and recall the following three will be discussed: The Single Picture Technique, The Roman Room and Mapping Technique, and The Cartoon Technique.

These related techniques were briefly discussed in the original example above in which the student was asked to read two and one half pages of British history concerning a naval battle between Admiral Nelson and Napoleon Boneparte. They will be expanded below.

a. The Single Picture Technique -The "Titanic" Exercise

Like the British history example, this exercise also **emphasizes the inclusion of as many essential facts in a single picture as possible.** Either a mental picture or a rough sketch can be used. **This picture** is built as the story unfolds about the sinking of the Titanic.

Jacob imagined the name of the Titanic's shipping line's President: "Ismay" as being similar to "is May" then thought of adding a "D" to make it read "dismay" because the Titanic sank. Jacob made a picture in order to remember the names of the shipping line (White Star) the ship building firm (Harland & Wolf) and the place where it was built (Belfast). He imagined a scene with a hard piece of land and a wolf sitting on this rock, in the middle of the night surrounded by white stars while a bell rang quickly in the wolf's ear. He had added a "D" not only to Ismay to make it dismay but also to Harland to make it "hard land". As he read he added to the picture and retained both the old and the new information despite that fact that new facts usually rapidly replace previously read or listened to facts.

Jacob's retention and ease of recall was due to his use of an **active process** in which all of the material was altered slightly and placed into a single mental image. He was reducing the material from **multiple units of data to a single unit of related material.** The process also entailed his own creativity, something that students with ADD have in abundance but which they seldom recruit when trying to memorize facts.

b. The Roman Room Technique

This technique requires that the student visualize a room with items placed in a logically organized fashion within it. The Roman Room technique actually goes back to Roman time and techniques used by orators of that period. The basic idea is that you picture a familiar room that you mentally go through in a particular order but familiar items have things hanging or sitting on them that trigger recall of the items to be remembered. Using this technique the student could memorize anything. Let them practice with a list of groceries. To do this the student might group the groceries into fruits, vegetables, meats and so on and place the groups of items in different sections of a familiar room. The individual items in each group might be arranged in their area of the room in the form of statues and paintings (bananas hanging on a picture frame etc.). The bigger and bolder the better for the mental images.

The **Mapping Technique** described earlier and the Roman Room technique are very similar. In the original British History example, ships blocked the French ports, ships in battle were placed near the West Indies and Egypt and dollar or English pound) signs were placed over each of the countries England attempted to use to surround and fight France as part of Britain's strategy in the war.

c. The Cartoon Technique:

This technique is a sequential extension of the above single picture, mapping and roman room techniques which creates a series of related pictures that allow a **time sequence** of changes in the data to take place. In the British history example above, the next picture in the sequence would include all the data around the battle at Trafalgar where Nelson died and the next pictures might include events leading up to the battle at Waterloo and the battle itself.

d. Verbal Techniques to Assist Memory and Recall:

Visual imaging has been emphasized up to this point because many of the students who have ADD find this particularly easy and fun to do. Some students, however, find it easier to use verbal mnemonic devices, such as rhymes or acronyms (using the initial letters of words). Another verbal technique is to **invent sentences out of the first letters of words or phrases** in order to help with later recall of information or names. Examples in music are "FACE" for the notes between the lines in treble clef score, and "Every good boy deserves fudge" for the notes on the lines of music. Some acronyms are in such common usage that they have virtually replaced the original word, like SCUBA for self contained underwater breathing device or IBM for International Business Machines. Another common example of a mnemonic trick that has been used for many years to help people learn French grammar is the phrase "Dr. (&) Mrs. Vandertamp". This acronym is used to remind the student of the French verbs that are conjugated with être rather than avoir: Devenir, Revenir, Mourir, Rendre, Sortir, Venir, Aller, Naitre, Descendre, Entrer, Retourner, Tenir, Arriver, Montre, Partir.

Sometimes the 'acronym' is a real word such as in the 'FACE' example for music given above or using the word 'HOMES' to help recall the names of the 5 great lakes in North America: Huron, Ontario, Michigan, Erie, Superior. A way to remember where Lake Superior is, is that it is above the others. (Here a visual and a word meaning are used together.)

Seeing words and images within an unfamiliar name may help later recall.

Case Example, Benny

Benny found names from different cultural groups very hard to distinguish, recall and to spell. He felt this might be due to a mild hearing problem which meant that distinguishing different and unfamiliar sounds was hard for him. In one of his classes in comparative religion, he had to learn the name of the person who developed Kung Fu. Benny could make no linkages or associations for this name to people or things in his everyday life. The monk's name was 'Bohidarama'. Benny was able to commit to memory the phrase, "Bo-hid-a-ram" and he visualized his friend "Bo" hiding an old goat.

8. Reading Comprehension

The active reading strategies outline above improve reading comprehension for a wide range of materials. There are also graded series that can be purchased to practice specific comprehension skills. These include, finding the main idea, getting the facts, drawing conclusions, inferring and using the context to understand vocabulary. The Barnell Loft Multiple Skills Series or a similar series of texts such as the Sullivan Readers which cover grades 1 to 9. Timed Readings in Literature edited by Edward Spargo takes passages from short stories and novels graded from Grade 5 to college level. These exercises are a useful beginning to encourage students to read passages carefully. The format is a short passage followed by multiple choice questions some of which require factual recall and some of which require more inferential thinking. The advantage of multiple choice format when doing neurofeedback is that the student will not produce as much movement artifact as they would when printing or writing. It also provides an opportunity to work on strategies for answering multiple choice questions which are a crucial part of test taking skills. However this multiple choice format does not require the student to synthesize and organize information. Therefore, instead of doing the questions, the neurofeedback is paused, and the student is taught how to underline the information, jot brief notes, critically analyse the facts and make inferences and summarize the information for the trainer. This will be discussed further under "Self Stimulated Recall" below.

Another excellent resource is the series by Gary Gruber called Essential Guide to Test Taking for Kids. There are editions for grades 3-4-5 and 6-7-8. Gruber is excellent at teaching strategies and he has also published books on preparing for the Scholastic Achievement Test (SAT).

Using these texts for practice is helpful but you do not just assign a passage for the student to do. The trainer is essential to provide coaching in strategies. If the child gets a main idea question wrong, perhaps because they focused on a detail mentioned in the passage, it is the trainer who will ask reflectively, "Hmm, is that what it is mostly about?"

Some children have very special difficulties. The child with Asperger's syndrome is a good example. This child, who will take things literally and have trouble understanding social innuendo, may read stories several years ahead of their grade level and answer correctly all the factual questions yet be completely unable to answer any question that required thinking abstractly and inferring something even from stories several grades behind their age and grade level. The trainer will have to help this child devise methods for answering these questions. Usually the trainer will use short simple questions that "lead" the child. Trainers should practice using **Socratic questions**. (A useful example of this type of questioning is the kind of questioning used on the old TV show, "Columbo".) It is important to use this type of teaching technique with all students. It is crucial that the trainer severely limit what they "teach or tell" the student. The trainer must not lecture but

should use a short carefully thought out series of questions to help the student learn to use similar questions of themselves ("inner dialogue") when reading..

When practicing a new strategy expect to work through four similar questions: with the first question the trainer models how to get the answers. On the second question the trainer works together with the student and they share the task. The third question is done by the student with guidance from the trainer and the fourth question is done independently.

a. Self-Stimulated-Recall / Organization of Ideas / Synthesis of Data

Three essential comprehension strategies are: self stimulated recall (as opposed to mere recognition of facts - the emphasis of the popular multiple choice format), organization of ideas and material, and synthesis of data into a logical, meaningful Gestalt. The trainers will therefore rapidly move from using the questions given at the end of passages in the type of learning material mentioned above to asking the student to recall more from their own memory. Another way to do the questions is for the trainer to read the question and the answers: a, b, c, d. The student must identify, not the answer to the question, but the letter (a to d) that preceded the correct answer. This requires exercising auditory memory.

The next step is a different type of exercise. The student is allowed to read the first sentence of the story and then carry out the four steps / strategies outlined for reading above. Even the younger children quickly catch on to generating questions that they think the story should answer. After the passage has been read the trainer asks the student to silently summarize the data in an organized fashion. Shortly all of our students give far more data in a succinct fashion than even the most difficult text questions ask. This is pointed out to the students who find this complement very gratifying. You are always looking for ways to reinforce the attitude that the student is a good learner. Self concept is an important component of successful learning. As Henry Ford reportedly said, "If man thinks he can do something, or thinks he cannot, he is right."

When it is appropriate, the final step may be to ask the student to analyse how the author has written the passage. Has the author given her thesis in the first paragraph? Has she followed this with three paragraphs each stating an argument or point and supporting that point with data? Has she summarized, discussed and given a conclusion?

b. Special Techniques for Short Stories and Novels:

The first of these techniques concerns character analysis and is labelled the **billiard game technique**. Most of the students have played pool or have heard of the game of billiards which is played on the same kind of table but it only uses three balls, red, white and an off-white 'spot' ball. The student is asked to imagine that the pool or billiard table has many sides instead of just four sides. Each of these sides represents a "flat" character or a setting. A flat character is one who never seems to change from one situation to another. It could be, for example, a man who is always angry and boasting or the opposite, always anxious. A setting might be a school or a frozen lake and so on. These are likened to the flat sides of the table. In a story there are usually only two or three "round" characters. These are likened to the three balls in the game of billiards. These characters are multifaceted. The student is told to imagine that each time one of the balls (round characters) bounces off the side of the table (a flat character or setting) or caroms off another round ball (which is rewarded with points in billiards) that something important is learned, through that interaction about a side (for example, a fault) of the round characters. (In the game of billiards the player would learn something about angle and spin.) For ease of portraying and understanding the round characters, the student is asked to only consider two important sides of each of the main characters and develop how the character's thinking and emotions govern their behaviour.

Here is an example using a short story called "A Kind of Murder" by Hugh Pentecost (Scholastic Scope Literature, 1991). The student first task is to find and recall the major facts and issues in the story.

Mary, a high school student, while reading this story made a visual picture of an emotional scene. In her scene (not an actual scene in the story) Pentecost, the author and also the principle character and narrator of the story, is waving a fist at fellow students defending Mr. Warren. Mr Warren looks weak and extremely anxious. In the actual story he is a very nervous and rather hapless new teacher at Morgan Military Academy, a boy's private school. However, in Mary's mental image, although Pentecost is waving a fist apparently in defiance and warning at the other boys in order to stand up for Mr. Warren, he is also, at the same time, anxiously turning away from Mr. Warren towards the jeering students. She has caught in her own image the two sides of Pentecost that are developed in the story. He is compassionate, thoughtful and brave but he is also anxious and concerned for his own popularity and is not immune to peer pressure. In this manner Mary developed a mental image that portrayed the double bind that Pentecost found himself in and the opposing, internally conflicting aspects of Pentecost's character.

c. The Reporter's Questions Technique for The Elementary School Student

Most of the forgoing techniques are equally effective for all ages of students. However, it goes without saying that students must be taught using a degree of complexity and language that suits their mental age and reasoning skills. Young children love to read about animals, birds and insects. The Nature's Children series is an excellent resource. Before reading about an animal the trainer may ask "Why is this animal able to survive?" Then the trainer, through Socratic questioning, helps the child to organize headings they think the author should include and questions they will be trying to answer as they read. With the younger child or with an anxious student, the trainer can model by saying, "I want to know …" and then alternate developing questions with the student. Together the trainer and the child think of 10 to 20 questions and then check their ideas against the author's table of contents.

The more advanced students may organize their thinking about an animal, bird, fish or insect using the reporter's questions: Who, When,

Where, What, Why and How. In this example, 'What' equals structure. This stimulates the child to think of the animal, bird, fish or insect from the head and working down the body to the limbs. This stimulates thoughts on various aspects of the creature: intelligence, five senses, eating/elimination, reproduction, locomotion and any special capabilities (e.g., venom, web making, etc.). They must then discuss how this creature's structure dictates their functions, such as escaping enemies and finding or capturing food. The student then considers further questions including: Who = (social & family), When = (life span) and Where = (countries & terrain).

d. An organized approach to reading complex scientific material - the Boxing Technique:

Students in computer science, chemistry, physics and other complex areas that involve formulas rather than literature may use some of the techniques described in the foregoing. Another technique called, the "blocking or boxing" technique can also be utilized to maintain concentration and remember material. In this technique the student groups together sections of scientific material into "blocks" contain **one connecting principle or unit of study**. In a calculus, physics or chemistry text each section must, or at least should, relate to the previous section. In calculus, for example, the "box" the student makes might contain only half a page of material. For the student to define it as a "box" it must contain nearly all of the data necessary to derive the equation or the principle being taught and to understand it. The student then endeavours to be clear concerning the linkages of the "box" under study to "boxes" previously studied and areas which come after it. The student may use the four strategic steps in shortened form on the material in the "box" and then take a break. Before beginning the next "box" the student should always do a quick review of the area previously studied. The student then considers how that box *links* to the next unit of study.

9. Writing Technique The Hamburger or '3-3-3' Method

One general approach can be used to accomplish many writing and speaking tasks including writing a paragraph, an essay, preparing a debate or answering an exam question. It is commonly called, 'The Hamburger Method'. This name is apt because the student organizes the material into three sections: the top bun, the meat and veggies, and the bottom bun. These sections correspond to the Introduction, the Main Body and the Conclusion of the piece. In these three sections the student follows the general principle: *Tell them what you are going to tell them, tell them, tell them what you told them*. In its simplest form, if the student is writing a paragraph the top bun is the introductory sentence, the next three sentences are the meat and condiments (you want some details to add interest not just a plain burger) and the last sentence is the bottom bun that holds it together. The top and bottom buns are the same material (topic) since you do not want to introduce something new at the end.

The three simple sections noted above become further elaborated for students in grade seven and above as they must write essays. Each section is further subdivided into three parts in the following manner:

- Introduction: Divide the Introduction into 3 sections: the introductory statement which catches an audience's attention, a thesis statement which says what you are going to discuss or prove and, third, you mention the three arguments or points that you will develop in the body of the dissertation.

- Main Body: The Body of the dissertation is also divided into three sections. These sections are for the three major arguments (points) that will be made. Each of these three arguments must be supported by at least three facts (data). The student is told that 2 arguments are insufficient and 10 arguments would be too many and quite confusing. Three to five arguments would probably be all right. If there are more points or arguments the student should sub-group them into three major headings and then each major heading could have subheadings or arguments.

- Conclusion: The third section of the dissertation is also divided into three sections. The first section is the summary, stating in brief the three arguments. In the second section the student discusses how the thesis (or hypothesis) was supported or proved. The final section is very short. In it the student makes a conclusion that wraps things up.

Case Example, Judy

Judy was given 10 minutes to develop a debate. She could either imagine that she would have to do this tomorrow morning in front of her class or that she and the trainer were the local university debating team competing against other universities. The subject was handed to her as it would be in the short topic section of a University debate, on a folded slip of paper or in an envelope. (It is more fun this way.) The subject is: "Panda Bears will become extinct".

Judy decided to introduce the topic by holding up an imaginary little panda bear which she would introduce to the audience as "Charlie". I, as her partner, was to hold up a little cap gun as if I were going to shoot Charlie. She would pull Charlie away, turn to the audience and, speaking to Charlie and the audience say, "I'm so sorry Charlie, but I don't think I can protect you for ever, you and all your friends and relatives are going to become extinct." She hoped this would startle the audience, catch their attention, and state the thesis for our side of the debate. She would then say, pointing at me, that we were going to prove today that panda bears would be killed by human actions, that they couldn't escape, and they could not reproduce quickly enough to replace the lost numbers.

In the body of the debate Judy would support the first argument (pandas would be killed) by noting that they live in a region of the world where people needed meat to live, fur to keep warm and more land on which to grow crops. Destruction of the Panda's bamboo habitat would necessarily lessen their numbers. Her second argument (panda bears couldn't escape) she would support by noting that, unlike small burrowing animals, they nest on the ground. They aren't particularly fast or fierce so they are easy prey. Her third argument (panda bears do not reproduce fast enough to fill the gap) she would support by noting that they only have one

or two babies at a time, the babies nurse with their mother for about 9 months and the offspring take at least 6 years to grow to maturity and begin to have their own babies.

In the conclusion of the debate Judy was going to summarize her three arguments in one sentence. She would then discuss the situation. First she would acknowledge the argument she was sure the other team would make concerning the success of conservation measures in various parts of the world, by saying that we, along with all those present, would hope that the world would and could convince the responsible government of the area that they should enact measures to prevent this terrible outcome. She would note, however, that the government in question had too many other pressing issues to deal with. It was highly unlikely they would act rapidly enough to avert this disaster. She would end by stating that, "Our conclusion has to be that Panda Bears will become extinct."

The trainer can make up amusing topics such as: "Cheese is the most important food in the world" and have the student put their organization of a dissertation on this subject into the hamburger design. If they use the 3-3-3 approach they should have little trouble organizing their ideas and the essay should have a good flow. They will discover that time spent planning ends up saving time because they are never twiddling their thumbs, wondering what to write next. The harder sell is getting them to spend time on editing. The rewrite typically should take as long as the first draft did. If they understand this in advance they can allocate time appropriately and not resent the editing stage. The analogy is that you do not leave your diamond in the rough. You find your piece of rock, cut your gemstone, and then polish it.

10. Studying Technique Using Packaging

Packaging is a method for Staying Up-to-date and Maximizing Recall. It is a technique for older students. We consider it an essential technique for anyone taking sciences in college or university. In this technique the student makes precise, concise, very neat notes for each section of the subject matter being taught. The student writes **definitions** for each new term. They **organize** (logical sequences of material) and **synthesize** (combine material from different sections / books / notes) to make one clear statement of the facts and conclusions for that section). Each "package" should be less than 10 hand written (or well spaced, typed) pages per section of work. A section usually corresponds to a chapter in their textbook. The student will make the "package" using information from class notes, handouts, labs, a last year's student's notes ('cook-book') and relevant chapter(s) from the text book(s). This "package" can be hand written or typed point form notes. It must be very short yet contain all the key facts in a logical order that the student can find easy to recall. The student then staples these pages together to make a "package". These become their short notes for final exam studying.

Case Example, Aaron

Aaron was busy at his desk. It was a large desk surface but he had very little on it. He had his computer, an open underlined textbook, lecture and lab notes and his 'cook-book'. To one side were neatly laid out series of packages with each title showing. I asked him why he was spending all this time every night doing this. His answer was short and simple, "I spend time to save time".

He had that, before exams, he could review the same material in ¼ the time it took his friends. It dawned on me, some time later, what he had meant. He was the elected Head of his college and participated in every possible activity. He didn't have time to cram before exams and in science the volume was far too large for that to be effective anyway. He was expanding the 'three-fact' method discussed earlier. His method was to scan each evening, the subject matter to be taught the next day. He would ask questions in class to keep up his alertness. He would scan the material covered in class when he got back to his desk that evening and then summarize everything in "packages" as the course went along. Keeping up and even keeping a little ahead actually did save time as evidenced by his participation and leadership in so many other activities.

I asked him what technique he and his top performing friends used for reading passages. Two techniques emerged. The first is the scanning technique used every day for reading a textbook. However, for these exams another technique was also used. First, they did practice

exams so that they would be familiar with the format and would not have to spend a lot of the time reading the examination instructions. Second, they would read the first paragraph of a passage twice in order to have an extremely clear picture of what that passage was about. Then they would memorize where arguments and facts could be found in the remaining paragraphs. In this way, detailed questions, demanding small factual differences, could be rapidly found in the original passage. The text would hopefully only be consulted once because the information was then distilled into a package which could be reviewed in a fraction of the time it would take to reread the textbook

Aaron's techniques are exemplary and efficient. We try through Socratic questions, to help the students at the ADD Centre formulate and experiment with similar techniques in their own studies.

11. Strategies for Mathematics
a. Introduction

In this section only a few very basic examples are used. As is true for metacognitive strategies for reading and remembering, there is no comprehensive catalogue of strategies. Rather, there are as many strategies as there are stumbling blocks. You must continually create new strategies relevant to the task. The purpose here is to illustrate some of the most common difficulties experienced by students. The mathematically gifted students usually do not have these difficulties. Students with attention span problems who are talented in math reasonig, however, will often have tuned out in class in former years when some of the very basic math concepts and principles were being taught. Now they are well beyond these levels and their teachers expect the basics of math to have been mastered previously. To help them, you must address their skill gaps which are usually a failure to learn boring things like multiplication tables, the steps for long division or fractions.

Many of the teenagers who come to the ADD centre are very bright intellectually and yet they have never learned simple, basic approaches to written math problems and to handling fractions and equations. The neurofeedback trainers teach the students a few very simple basic concepts, rules and examples. The purpose is not to teach the child math, for that is the job of the school, but rather to stop the giving-up, "Oh, I can't do that," all-or-nothing reaction of some students. When this attitude is observed our first objective is to help these children get themselves into a relaxed alert state. Then we assist the child to focus on each small section of the word problem. At this point we have the student ask him or herself: "What am I being asked in this problem? What facts have they given me?" How can I draw the facts so that I can visualize the problem? It is the approach to the question that can be the key to success. We attempt to help create a positive attitude towards this subject by increasing the student's self confidence through training. They must learn how to learn and how to think about problems in mathematics in order to genuinely understand them.

b. Grade School Math Tips:

These tips and tricks are generally only needed for those students who have a specific difficulty with math. The child who can generate excitement at the challenge of solving the problem just because it feels so good to figure it out for oneself, is the child who will progress. The following are a sampling of the kinds of tips that can be used with grade school students while working on having the student feel competent, interested and then fascinated by the challenges that math offers.

In teaching younger students math you begin with a concrete math manipulative. This does not have to be a fancy purchased set of objects. It is much better to use things in the child's natural environment like fingers, pencils or blocks. Later you use pictorial representations like tally marks or drawings. Drawings can be chocolate bars or a pie or other familiar 'fun' things that can be divided into fractions. Good mathematicians see the relationships. This is why the spatial reasoning tasks on IQ tests correlate so strongly with math skills. Only after something is illustrated with a tangible object (fingers are the easiest) and the concept is grasped, do you move to a pictorial representation, such as tally marks. After the student is comfortable with the pictorial representation you can move on to the abstract, that is, a numeric symbol. A deck of cards is very handy for both learning and practicing math

facts because it has the number in two corners but also the back-up of the illustration (five hearts or clubs, etc.). If you take the face cards and put the remaining 40 cards into two stacks and flip one over one card from each stack you have a great way to randomly practice addition and subtraction facts up to 20 or multiplication facts up to $10 \times 10 = 100$.

• Addition and Subtraction

In grade school the student must **understand** simple addition and subtraction. We see students as old as 12 years of age who have never grasped what it means to be adding $9 + 8$. $8 + 8$ is completely out of their range. To teach the concept we have them use their own fingers and the examiners and fully understand $10 +$. Fingers are a wonderful math manipulative. When this is achieved through "understanding" and not rote memory then we have them remove one thumb after doing $9 + 10$. In this manner the child gets rid of, subtracts, one digit so that the same question becomes $9 + 9$. They then do a series where they do $10 +$ and change each to $9 +$. For example, $10 + 7 = 17$ becomes $9 + 7 = 16$. Then they can do $8 +$ by changing each $10 +$ answer by subtracting 2 thumbs. In training trainers for the Centres we emphasize that they must **never assume a child has grasped a concept just because they give a rote memory correct answer!** They must see the number fact to understand it.

These students require a familiar concrete representation of number facts. Initially fingers, yours and theirs, work best. You can check that they are understanding what they are doing by first asking them to tell you if the answer is going to be "more or less" than what they had. Then they must tell you what they have done. Have them use your fingers and theirs. When they are adept at using concrete representation and explaining what they are doing, then you can move to using math manipulatives such as counters where numbers are represented by coloured plastic discs or cubes. We encourage parents to do things at home to reinforce addition facts. Games that use dice give lots of practice for addition facts up to $6 + 6$. The dots on each die give the pictorial representation of the number.

For those who have grasped the foregoing, the concepts of grouping into ones, tens and hundreds, borrowing and carrying are rapidly taught when necessary.

• Multiplication and Division

When addition and subtraction are mastered the trainer will check the child has grasped a basic concept in multiplication, namely, that we are multiplying groups times the number of things in that group. As noted above, children who have difficulty in paying attention very often miss the teaching of math concepts when they are taught in the classroom. Unfortunately we find one teenager after another who, even if they have memorized the multiplication tables, have no really clear understanding of what is meant when they multiply one number times another. The older students should, for example, be able to rapidly multiply virtually any number in their heads. Often with the teenagers we ask them to multiply such numbers as 17 times 13 or 376 times 25 and 2/3 times 3/4. To the reader it will be clear that these examples are deliberately simple if you visualize them but they are used in order to emphasize the concept of multiplying and some simple tricks for visualizing figures and fractions. (For example, to multiply 75 by 25 you multiply by 100 and divide by 4.) With the younger children we use a simple grid with houses for the columns and people for the rows. We like to use groups of objects, animals or people that the child suggests from their interests. Often the children will choose groups of horses in their stalls, teams of hockey or basketball players and so on. We can then have the columns in a grid be the team (stall for horses and so on) and the rows be the number of players (each position) on each team. The child multiplies the number of teams (groups) times the number of players (rows) on each team to find the number of players on the field if every team is lining up before a big contest like the Olympics.

Division follows the same concept using the same grid diagrams. This basic understanding of multiplication and its reciprocal, division, is necessary in order to begin fractions and algebra and it is frequently deficient even in high school students. It is therefore expanded below.

The Teams (groups) times the number of people on each team Rule:

Although you can use commercially available brightly coloured modern Math Manipulatives, the concepts are often more easily, thoroughly and lastingly assimilated using the time honoured and quite old-fashioned basic rules and hand drawn diagrams. With the younger children we start by **drawing two (then three and four and so on) little houses** which are attached to each other like row houses. **Each house is at the top of a column** and they are labelled 1, 2, 3 and so on. **We then draw a row** below the houses and put a little person or happy face into each of the resulting squares and ask how many people there are. The answer, of course, is the same as the number of houses. This is the 1x table. We note that this is the same as saying the number of houses times the number of people in each house. We **then draw a second row of people, a third, and so on**. With each addition the child notes the same general rule. They realize that multiplication is simply repeated addition.

The Reciprocal Rule

When the child clearly understands the rule we introduce the question as to whether 3 houses times four people in each house holds the same number of people as 4 houses with three in each (the reciprocal). For children with a specific difficulty in math this is a very difficult question. However, using the grid, they catch on to it quite rapidly noting that the number of people in the squares is the same. An egg carton is another way to visually display this principle. The student can **discover** that there are not only 3 groups of 4 and 4 groups of 3, but that there are 6 groups of 2 and 2 groups of 6 and one group of 12. The trainer may mention the word **factors** at this juncture. (A factor will divide evenly into another number. Two and three are factors of the number six.)

c. More Difficult Multiplication

Some simple tricks are used to help accelerate remembering tables and thus increase the child's self confidence. We start with the 7 and 9 times tables because they are usually considered difficult and the child's confidence soars when they are mastered.. First we teach the **counting trick,** 7 x 8 = 56 is learned by simply counting from 5 to 8: 5, 6, 7, 8; <u>5 6</u> = 7x8. Then we teach

3 times 7 as three sevens and we hold up 3 fingers, (the trainer uses 2 in the right hand and one on the left and the student mimics it, to make 21. Then we do the same using 6 fingers, 4 on one hand and two on the other, to make 42 for 6 'sevensies'. We call these the **finger tricks**. Seven sevens is one less than 50, i.e., 49 Alternatively, if they like football, say lucky number 7 twice (7x7) gives you the 49ers football team!. 4 sevens is taught as 3 sevens (using their finger trick) plus an extra seven making 28. The latter emphasizes the concept of one extra seven is just seven more. 5 times 7 is not a problem since they can count by 5's using seven fingers. And 2 times 7 is just 7 + 7. This just leavews 9 times 7. For the nine times table they "discover" that the tens column is always one less than the number which they are multiplying times 9 which is logical (makes sense) because they know that if they had, for example, 10 sevens it would be 70 thus 9 sevens has to be less, that is 'sixty' something. They then notice that the two figures in the answer always add up to 9 (e.g., 6+3). Then we decide that maybe we might have discovered a new rule. Have one less than the number we are multiplying by to get the first number and then the second number plus the first will always equal nine. We try it out and find that $9 \times 9 = 81$ and $8 + 1 = 9$, $9 \times 8 = 72$ and $7 + 2 = 9$ and so on. By this time most children discover for themselves that the numbers which we have conveniently placed in a column go from 9 down to 1 and from 1 up to 9 in sequence.

We then show them that they have the 9x table at their finger tips. You show the two hands on the table minus one finger trick for the nine times table. For those who don't know this little manoeuvre, try putting both your hands on the table, palms down and label the fingers one to ten starting at your far left with the little finger of the left hand. Now fold down one finger, say the fourth finger which would be the index finger of the left hand. The finger you put down (the fourth finger) stands for the number of nines. The nine fingers left on the table represents the fact you are in the nine times table. The answer to 4×9 is represented by the three fingers to the left of the one folded down finger and the 6 fingers to the right of it, that is 36. Younger children really enjoy this manoeuvre. Make sure you have your fingers held up beside theirs, not opposite them so left to right is the same.

Do not assume the student knows that 0 times anything is zero and 1 times anything is that number. Don't assume that they know that two times is just two of them added together, (doubling) or that the 10 times table just requires one to add a zero. Check each of these concepts.

The 11 times table merely requires one to place the numbers side by side, e.g., $6 \times 11 = 66$. However, ask the teenager what 11×11 is and you will often get the incorrect answer 111. You then help him use the logic you have been teaching. What are 10 elevensies? He answers, "110". Ask him if there are 11 players on each (hockey or basketball) team how many players would be on the field if 9 teams lined up (99). How many if 10 teams lined up (110 by adding a 0 to 11). Then how many are on the field if the 11th team marched out and lined up beside the 10th team? The impulsive student will still blurt out the answer as 111. You ask incredulously how he went from 110 to 111, just 1 more, when the whole team just marched on to the field. Once he slows down, stops guessing, and thinks before speaking, he calculates 121 and then you take him all the way up to 11x15 and congratulate him on really understanding what he is doing.

When we are doing times tables, most of the children are able to easily count by fives. Therefore, whenever we get to 5 times a number we teach them to reverse the question so it becomes a 5 times table question. They then use their fingers to count the number of five's as they say the series: 5, 10, 15 etc., to themselves. Very soon the children have mastered the 11, 10, 9 and 7 times tables. $8 \times 8 =$ the number of squares on a chess board. The series: six 4s is 24, six 6s is 36, and six 8s are 48, has a rhythm to it and it kind of sounds right! At this juncture they are surprised to discover that there is very little they haven't learned. In fact there are only 6 more facts to learn (3x3, 3x4, 3x6, 3x8, 4x4, and 4x8). These are quite easy and the trainer can guide the student to figure out a strategy for each. For example, for 3x you can double the number and add one more: $3 \times 3 = 6 + 3 = 9$; $3 \times 8 = 16 + 8 = 24$. for 4x you double and then double again; $4 \times 4 = 8 \times 2 = 16$; $4 \times 8 = 16 \times 2 = 32$. Most of this work can be done while they practice getting themselves into a focused and concentrating state while we put the electrodes on their head and ears. They are rewarded with lots of up-beat praise and sometimes extra points. Parents are told what they have accomplished at the end of the session and the child often will demonstrate it.

went on to learn how to add, multiply and divide fractions in the next few sessions.

Case Example, Jason

Jason, age 11, had gone to a learning centre for 2 years to learn math, especially the times tables. It was a system where the children did drill and practice but were not taught the concepts underlying math skills. They did hundreds of exercises (It takes about 800 repetitions for the average child to learn a single math fact by rote). He knew the 2 times and the 5 times tables but little else. He arrived for his first session with a very discouraged mother. In the session the author got him focusing with neurofeedback and then taught him the tricks for the 7 times, 9 times and 10 times tables. After the 1 hour session he answered questions on each of these tables accurately and rapidly for his mother. She was flabbergasted. In the second session he learned the concept of multiplication (he loved calculating using groups of ninjas). He then did the 11 times table, up to 11 x 15, for all the parents in the waiting room. Jason was very proud. He never forgot the times tables and

In this manner one continues to have children **play with numbers** in order to really be able to manipulate them and understand them. No amount of repetition of math facts will have the same beneficial effects. Also, the beautiful pictures in most school texts which are meant to teach these concepts turn out not to really be very interesting once they have been seen once by these children. We like the children to have mental pictures but we prefer that these are pictures they have developed themselves through playing with numbers. We do use repetition, however, because for a number of sessions we will go through exactly the same sequence of **"discovering"** all of the foregoing tricks and logic. In our experience students who learn their tables in this manner really become very confident about their mastery and understanding of multiplication. Older students are then willing to be challenged with otherwise seemingly impossible questions such as 13 times 17.

d. The Concept of Multiplication
– Give a student a tough problem to develop self confidence, such as 17x13.

To get the answer the trainer takes them through a logical sequence. 13 is just $(10 + 3)$, 13 x 17 is the same as writing $(13)(17)$ or $(10 + 3)(10 + 7)$. The trainer asks the student to draw the houses and people grid. (Use soldiers with rocket launchers and rockets grid for some of the more reticent boys!). For this example say there are 13 basketball teams (or columns). There are 17 players on each team. The trainer then suggests that since it is so simple to multiply 10 x 10 why not just call the first 10 players the first string. The next seven players are the substitutes. Now the child uses a red pen to outline the 10 x 10 box and write 100 in it. He then multiplies the 7 substitutes times the 10 teams and gets 70. He draws a box on the grid around players 11 to 17 for the first 10 teams in green ink and puts 70 in

this box (at the bottom of the grid). Then on the right hand side of the grid the student draws a blue box around the squares representing 3 columns (or teams 11 to 13) x 10 (rows or 1st string players for those teams) and puts 30 on the page. The only squares on the grid not enclosed in the red, green and blue boxes are in the lower right hand corner and represent 3 columns times 7 rows and the student encloses this area with a pencil and writes 21 in it. The student then **sees** simply that the answer to the problem is 100 + $(70 + 30) + 21 = 221$. It is not much of a step then to see that they could have done this in their head using the bracketed figures $(10 + 3)(10 + 7)$. The student is then encouraged to relate this method to the grid. $(10x10 + 10x7 + 3x10 + 3x7)$

	1	2	3	4	5	6	7	8	9	10	11	12	13
1													
2													
3													
4				100								30	
5													
6													
7													
8													
9													
10													
11													
12													
13				70								21	
14													
15													
16													
17													

The 13 Teams(Groups) x 17 People on each Team Grid:

e. Long Division: - Use the family rule.

For long division the hard part is remembering the steps. Unless the steps have become an automatic checklist the student is inclined to get stuck and then tune out. Memorizing a simple mnemonic can be very useful. Try using the Family Ruler, Dad, Mom, Sister, Brother and Rover (the dog), to help them with the five steps: **D**ivide then **M**ultiply, **S**ubtract, **B**ring down and **R**epeat. Tell them this family will help them remember the steps. Some children learn better using a really silly phrase they make up. One boy came up with, "**d**ead **m**onkeys **s**till **b**reath **r**egularly". (Always ask their parent if it is OK to use this example before you say it to the child)

Help the child attain a real pride in keeping their number work in neat columns so that they do not become confused. This is particularly important when working with children who have ADD. Children with ADD may be wonderfully artistic, may do script incredibly artistically and may have excellent fine motor coordination. At the same time, however, they may have a very specific hand-writing difficulty where, as they attempt to put down a great deal of material, the numbers and letters begin to change in size, shape and spacing, making their work appear messy and even illegible. Cursive writing is particularly difficult for many of them. The same difficulty may be seen when they are doing a full page or more of math. It may also be due to an impulsive carelessness. If uncorrected, this leads to negative feedback from teachers and a downward cycle with respect to motivation and effort. Using grid paper is another helpful aid for keeping math calculations neat In some European countries math note books come with grid lines rather than just horizontal lines.

• Division - the concept:

Many of the children have memorized how to carry out simple division but have never thought about what it was that they were doing. We use the **same grid that they used for multiplication to help them.** They can quickly understand that if they have a total of 12 players altogether (total for all the teams) and 4 teams then there will be 3 players on each team. As noted at he outset of the section on math, begin with something concrete, like dividing 12 pencils into groups of three, then move to a pictorial representation using the grid, and only after these two steps are consolidated do you write $12 \div 3 = 4$. The student must get to the point where they understand, and truly see, that multiplication and division are reciprocal operations. This is necessary in order to figure out what operation to use in word problems.

f. Fractions
i. Analog Time - Simple Fractions:
Many children have never learned to tell the time from an analog clock though most are familiar with digital time pieces. The trainer and the child begin by discussing how to divide a blueberry pie into 4 equal pieces. The concept of quarters and a half comes rapidly and the analogy drawn to saying quarter and half past and a quarter to the hour is easily drawn. Many of our trainers have diver's watches. Stories about SCUBA diving and how important it is to know how many minutes you have been underwater naturally follow a study of the clock face and hands. Kids enjoy the "real thing". Playing down to them with large school supply cardboard clock faces is not only boring but is actually irritating to some of these children. They can see the dial on a real diving watch very well and they love turning the bezel. The bezel gives them the chance to mark how far 15, 30 and 45 minutes are around the face of the clock. They then rapidly grasp that ¼ hr. + ¼ hr. = ½ hr. This leads, often within only one or 2 sessions, to addition of fractions and simplifying the answers (e.g., 5/4 = 4/4+1/4 = 1 1/4).

Another way to reinforce the concept of quarters is with coins: 4 quarters equal one dollar; or 2 quarters are half a dollar. Money is also a helpful way to help them understand that decimals are just another kind of fraction and you can convert between decimals, fractions and percent with all of them being equivalent. 25 cents can be written 0.25 and it equals ¼ or 25%. Explain that % means per cent, which is per 100, ('cent' is French for 100 and 'per' means divided by, as in miles per hour). You must make the new learning relevant and link it to things they already know. As a general rule, **if more than 1/3 of the facts or information is new, then no learning takes place.** Make sure **2/3 of what you say involves material or concepts they already know.**

ii. Adding Fractions
Once the student has mastered the clock face and pie analogy we can move to adding and subtracting fractions. However, it is easier for most children to visualize a rectangle (chocolate bar) than a circle (pie) when we later get to multiplication and division of fractions. We therefore move to the chocolate bar as an example at this juncture. It is not always easy for some students to perceive that if they had 2 chocolate bars (we always initially have them draw the chocolate bars under each of the fractions.) and one was divided in 2/3 and the other ¾, which one would have the bigger pieces. Always ask the student if he likes chocolate. Then, if he does, to point to the chocolate bar he would like to have a piece from. Many students choose to have a piece from the chocolate bar that is divided into 4 because they look bigger. Help these students to see that dividing it into 4 makes smaller pieces than dividing it into 3. Now they understand that if the chocolate were to be shared with friends on his soccer team, his team-mates who received the pieces from the "3/4" chocolate bar might be upset because they were smaller.

The trainer can carry the illustration further. The team and the coaches mean that there are between 15 and 17 people and we have only got 5 pieces. We need more (and therefore smaller) pieces and it is essential that everyone be happy that the chocolate is shared fairly, that is, equally. Therefore the pieces must all be the same size. It is at this juncture that we look at how we would divide a chocolate bar. The chocolate bar, or a rectangular cake of brownies, could be divided into 3 sections horizontally. What if, however, we then divided it into 4 sections vertically. Now each of us who had 1 section of the bar that was cut into three, would have our slice divided into 4. Our whole chocolate bar has how many pieces now? - (Twelve.)

We take a second chocolate bar and divide it into 4 vertical slices. Then we cut it horizontally into 3 and each of the people who formerly had one slice of the bar cut in 4 now has their piece cut into three. The total number of pieces is 12, the same as our other chocolate bar! Have the student 'discover' that now everybody will get the same size piece no matter which chocolate bar they choose from.

The **first** chocolate bar. 	The 1st chocolate bar is divided into 3 pieces. One piece is missing and therefore there are 2 pieces of chocolate left. (2/3)
The **second** chocolate bar. 	The 2nd chocolate bar is divided into 4 pieces. One piece is missing and therefore there are 3 pieces of chocolate left. (3/4)
The 1st chocolate bar is further sub-Divided. 	The 1st chocolate bar is cut vertically three more times. There are 8 shaded boxes out of a total of 12. (8/12) Thus there are 8 pieces of chocolate (8/12) in the bar where 2/3 of the bar had been left uneaten.
The 2nd chocolate bar is further sub-divided. 	The 2nd chocolate bar is cut horizontally two more times. There are 9 shaded boxes out of a total of 12. (9/12) Thus there are 9 pieces of chocolate in the bar where ¾ of the bar had been left uneaten.

Case Example, John

John, age 11, was finding math very hard. He had, in fact, given up. However, John loved chocolate and, after discussing what his favourite chocolate bars were, he was open to talking about a problem where he was pretending he was giving out a chocolate reward after his soccer game. In the above problem he was asked if the pieces were all going to be of equal size. He said, "That's obvious, we just cut them so that there are 12 pieces in each bar". I then asked how many pieces were left since he and I had each had a piece from the original 2 chocolate bars. He said, "That's easy, there are a total of 17 equal pieces of chocolate left over in the two chocolate bars". I said, "Each piece is one 'twelvsy' (1/12)". He agreed.

I then asked him to write that addition as a fraction. I asked what would go on the bottom (denominator). He said that it would be the number of pieces originally in the chocolate bar before we ate any of it = 12. I then asked what number would go on top (numerator). He said, "8". I noted that he had just said(implied that) we had 8 twelvsies = 8/12. He agreed. We did the same process for the 2nd chocolate bar and got 9/12. He added these and made 17/24. I asked him what we had nicknamed each piece. He correctly answered, "One twelvsy". I then asked how many twelvsies we were left with for the team. He said, "17 twelvsies. I asked him what that would look like as a fraction and he wrote: 17/12. His eyes lit up and he crossed out his former answer of 17/24.

We then looked at how many pieces made up one whole chocolate bar and he said, "12". I asked if he could use that answer and simplify 17/12. He correctly wrote: 1 5/12. He then showed me how he figured it out with the picture by putting pieces of chocolate from the second bar to fill up the gaps in the first and finding that 5 pieces were left over.

It was a simple matter for John to repeat this exercise a couple of times and **derive basic rules for working with fractions <u>for himself.</u>** After working with twelfths, thirds and quarters seemed easy for him.

In Summary the general principles you want to stress are the following:

- The denominator represents the total number of pieces the object is divided into.
- The numerator represents the number of pieces you have left.
- You must make sure the objects are divided into the same number of pieces before you add or subtract to find out how many pieces there are in total.
- Whatever you do to the bottom (denominator) of the fraction (e.g., multiply it by a number such as 3 or 4 in the above example), you must do to the top (numerator). The logic of this is quickly apparent to the student when they look at each of their chocolate bars or pies. They multiply the 4 pieces, in the bar or pie that is

divided into quarters, by 3 to get 12 and they multiply the 3 pieces they have shaded, by 3 and get 9.

You cannot add apples and oranges but you can group them as fruit; similarly, you cannot add thirds and quarters until you change both to twelfths.

iii. Don't Let Children with ADHD Fall Behind

These very simple examples are, of course, usually worked through in the classroom. The children we are working with, however, were not mentally there. Most of them were tuned out much of the time when the concepts were being taught. The rest of their class has long since gone on to higher levels of math. Higher math levels unfortunately assume that the basic principles are second nature to all of the children. **Once children with ADD get behind the degree to which they tune out rises exponentially!** These children could do very well in picking up some of the math facts and skills which they missed by attending a good supplementary learning centre. We often recommend that the children who do not have a significant problem with ADD do just that. Many of the children with ADD, however, have tried that or had tutoring. These children continue to fall behind in class. They have not made a **fundamental shift in the way they learn.** The problem that remains is that they have never learned how to deal with ADD in terms of increasing their attention span and concentration and, in addition, they have never learned how to learn. The neurofeedback trains them in how to pay attention, focus, concentrate, and act in a reflective and less impulsive fashion. When in this state the children learn remarkably quickly. The children can "feel" this and a brief amount of experiencing this during their neurofeedback sessions usually leads to a positive attitude towards learning in their classrooms. Then they are taught **strategies that work for their kind of cognitive style.** Skill gaps, such as learning multiplication tables or steps for long division, can be taught. The combination means that in the future they will be able to learn in the classroom.

iv. The Be Fair, Do the Same Thing to ... Rule for Fractions & Equations:

With selected students the trainer helps the student discover that the problem of multiplying 376 x 75 in your head is nothing more than a very simple example of the general rule: "If you do the same thing to the top of a fraction as to the bottom" the value stays the same. You are fair – you treat numorator and denominator the same. In this case many of the children can see that since it is easy to multiply times 100 they could multiply the 376 by 100 as long as they divided the 75 by 100. But 75 /100 is 3/4 therefore they could just divide the 37,600 by 4 and multiply by 3 to obtain 28,200. A simpler concept that can be taught first is that, to multiply by 25 you can multiply by 100 and then divide by 4 (since 25 = 100/4). Manipulations like these with the older students are used to decrease their resistance to "thinking" and "puzzling" over math problems and engender a feeling that there really can be a very pleasant sense of accomplishment when they take up these challenges.

v. Multiplication of Fractions - the "Of" Rule:

Many of our high school students have been taking fractions for a number of years. However they often do not really understand what they are doing when they are multiplying or dividing fractions. To grasp what is meant by **multiplying** fractions, the trainer asks the student to multiply 2/3 x 3/4 and then to explain in words, or by a diagram, what they have done. Most students cannot do this. The trainer then makes the problem into a little story. The trainer says, "This (shows a sheet of paper) is a tray full of brownies. One quarter of the tray must be saved for Dad, leaving three quarters available. Your mother says that you and your brother may have 2/3 of ¾ of this tray if you can figure out how much that is. The trainer then has the student fold a piece of paper into four quarters and remove ¼ (by folding it behind). The trainer asks how many quarters are left. The student answers "3". The trainer then has the student follow what mother had said by taking 2/3 of this ¾ section of pretend brownies. The student refolds the paper into thirds and folds one third behind. Now they have 2/3 of just 3 of those quarters. When they open the sheet and count all the little squares (brownies) they find that they have 6 of

12 sections or ½ of the brownies. Many students are quite intrigued by the fact that they are really taking 2/3 of 3/4. Whenever they encounter a word problem with 'of' in it they will remember that means multiplication will be the operation needed.

vi. Division of Fractions - the "How many "....sies" are there in "..." Rule:

Some of the students have actually been told that there is no way to understand division of fractions, just learn the rule, invert and multiply. They are quite confused by the fact that, with fractions, multiplication results in a smaller number and division a larger number for the answer. This is the opposite result to what you get working with whole numbers. If we have been able to peak their curiosity then we tell them that we can prove that inverting the second fraction and multiplying really does give a sensible (valid) answer. We note they will never have to do this but it is kind of interesting and fun. We ask the student to take a simple example, such as dividing 2/3 by 3/4. They are told to use the same drawing that they used for addition. They draw two chocolate bars and make all the pieces equal by changing it to 8/12 (eight 12sies in this bar) and 9/12 (nine 12sies left in this bar).

Now, off to the side, ask the student to tell you how many apples each student would get if there were 20 apples and 5 students. He will immediately answer "4". You then circle the denominator in the fraction 20/(5) and tell him that he just asked himself the question, **"How many 5sies are there in 20?".** Tell him that he is to do exactly the same procedure with the fraction division, i.e., 8/12 / 9/12. He is to ask himself, **"How many 9 12sies are there in (or can I fit into) 8 12sies?"** At this juncture he takes a highlighter and highlights the 8 squares in the 8/12 chocolate bar and the 9 squares of chocolate in the 9/12 chocolate bar. Now he draws lines to represent moving pieces of chocolate, one at a time, from the 9/12 chocolate bar, into the 8/12 chocolate bar. Only 8 pieces will fit in. He therefore concludes that the answer is that 8 out of 9 pieces, 8/9 of the chocolate, will fit into the other bar. The answer to, **"How many 9 12sies are there in (or can I fit into) 8 12sies?"** is that he can fit in 8/9ths. In school he has learned to invert one fraction and then multiply. This would become, 8/12 x 12/9 = or

8/9. He then does the same thing to the original and gets: 2/3 x 4/3 =8/9.

Now have the student see that "inverting" is merely an example of the "do-the-same-thing-to the numerator as you did to the denominator rule. You multiply the denominator (the fraction ¾) by the same fraction inverted (4/3) to get "1". Then you multiply the numerator fraction (2/3) by the same number (4/3) to get the answer (8/9).

The objective is to have the student begin playing with math in order to see it and thus understand it!

g. Word Problems:

A logical stepwise strategy takes <u>extreme focus and concentration</u> and is crucial to solving most math problems. The first rule is read carefully - then read it again putting lines into the problem to divide it into sections. Use a logical four-step approach. Not all the steps are necessary in every question. The steps are analogous to a detective investigating a crime. The detective, on coming to the scene of the crime, first wants the facts. Second, he draws the scene. Third, he wants the truth – a solution. Fourth he double-checks it to make sure he hasn't made a mistake. The method is therefore as follows:

(1.) Facts + Question. Section the question into separate statements using slashes (/).
- "What are the facts?" - List them!
- What is the question? - Circle the key word.

(2.) Draw it + Label it.
- "Can I draw the facts?" - Draw them!
- Label the drawing(s) with all the facts.
- Label the unknowns with a letter such as x or y.

(3.) The Truth? And Solve it. Put the facts into a "truth statement" which, in math, is an equation.
- Translate words into mathematical signs; e.g., "is" is an equal (=) sign, more than is a + sign, and so on. There are two types of truth statements:
    - What "truths" can I derive from the facts?

- What "truth(s)" does the question give me which relate some or all of the facts to each other

To Solve it, first recall with the student the basic rule: whatever you do to one side of an equation, you must do the same thing to the other side of the equation. (This is analogous to the rule with fractions: whatever you multiply the denominator of a fraction by, you must multiply the numerator of the fraction by the same number.) It may be helpful to draw an analogy to a simple balance scale. In order to keep a scale in balance, if you take something away from one side you must take away the same amount from the other side.

(4.) Check your answer.

Most high school problems can be thought through logically. Particularly when working with the student who has ADD, one uses **math problems to reinforce a non-impulsive, thoughtful, reflective approach.** The following problems may be solved by a formula or by a "short-cut" but many students do not know that. To these students some of these challenges may at first appear insurmountable. In their early stages of learning we emphasize the logical 4 step approach given above. **Following a defined sequence of steps helps to provide an opportunity to overcome negative "bracing".** The student knows how to get started using metacognitive strategies rather than avoiding tasks.

- **Example**
Step I. Facts and the Question
a. Section the question into separate statements using slashes (/).
  - A piece of string is cut \ into two pieces.\ The second piece is 5 cm more than twice the length of the first piece. \ If the original string is 245 cm long,\ how long is the longer piece when cut?
b. "What are the facts?"   - List them!
  - Fact #1: A piece of string is cut \ into two pieces.\
  - Fact #2: The second piece is 5 cm more than twice the length of the first piece.
  - Fact #3: The original string is 245 cm long

Step II. Draw and Label the Facts
a. "Can I draw the facts?"   - Draw them! Label them

I <----------- 245 cm. ---------------------------> I
_____

I←- x cm -→I I←---- y = 2x + 5 cm ---------→I
_____   _____

1. "What is the question being asked?"
   - How long is the longer piece when cut?
2. Label the unknowns with a letter such as x or y.
   - Let the first piece be x and the second piece be y.
3. Put the facts into "truth statements" or equations. Translate words into signs.
4. What "truths" can I derive from the facts?
   - y is 5 cm. longer than two times x (longer than is the same as a + sign)
     - Therefore: $y = 5 + 2x$

Step III. Truth Statement or Equation and Solve it
What "truth" does the question give me that relate some or all of the facts to each other.
   - $x + y$ = the whole string = 245 cm.
   - Therefore when you *substitute* for y: $x + (5 + 2x) = 245$ cm.
1. Solve it for one unknown at a time. (Do the same thing to both sides of the equation – just like on a scale for weighing gold, if you add or subtract from one side you *must do the same thing to* the other side in order to have the scale balance again.)
   - $3x + 5 (-5) = 245 (-5)$ cm. then divide both sides by 3 and get $x = 80$ cm. Thus $2x + 5 = 165$ cm.

Step IV. Check your answer.
   In this case the student would add: $x + y$ to see if they got the length of the original string (80cm + 165cm = 245cm)

It is crucial that the trainer always use the same 4 step approach and that the trainer not assume the student has the basic concepts that would allow steps to be skipped.

- **Example #2:**

Often the wording of a problem confuses the student. Some students give up rather than try to logically think through the problem. The following is an example that the reader can try.

- A line (cord) is drawn between two points, A & B, on the circumference of a circle. The radius of the circle is 3 cm. The angle formed when two lines are drawn from the centre of the circle to points A & B on the circumference, is 90 degrees. What is the area of the segment between the line AB and the shortest arc of the circle between A and B?

This is a very easy problem providing the student doesn't panic. The student must mark the 3 key facts in the question then draw a large clear diagram. Then the student must not waste time recognizing that they do not know any formula to calculate an area between an arc and a cord of this circle. Therefore they must think logically and ask themselves what area formulas they do know. They know the formula for getting the area of a circle. They also know how to calculate the area of a triangle. The student must figure out from the drawing that he/she must subtract knowns (area of the triangle from the area of 1/4 of the circle) to find the unknown (the area of the segment).

Note: The number of strategies for different aspects of math is large. There are good texts and courses that cover this material in detail. A good example is any of the SAT (Scholastic Achievement Test) preparation books by Dr. Gary Gruber. The key phrase the student must keep in mind is, "When the question looks too complicated, find a way to simplify it".

h. Brief Summary

The importance of the foregoing processes to help children with basic math concepts does **not** lie mainly in learning how to read a clock, add and subtract fractions, multiply large numbers, solve word problems and so on. These skills should be taught in school. The value of the foregoing process is to train the child to go into a high state of focused concentration and recognize that they have, within themselves, the

capability to figure out things from first principles. Our objective is to have the students change their outlook and apply strategies rather than avoiding work or giving up on something that seems hard. We don't want them to grudgingly memorize formulae for exams. We want them to feel that they can take abstract academic subject matter and make it interesting and exciting. They can use their creativity and develop their own tricks for learning and remembering things that augment the strategies taught during neurofeedback training sessions.

13. Study Hall:

The student must have a determined attitude when, (and a concrete method for), entering every period of study **and never deviate from the basic dictum that every unit of work or of time must produce a "product".** In other words, they do not just flip open a book and start, they set a goal.

We liken study hall time at home or in the library with the production of "widgets" in a factory. The student must decide before beginning on an evening of study, for example, exactly what the product should be for each unit of this study time. This may be a unit of time but preferably it would be a unit of work to be accomplished.

With a very young child the parent should ask Socratic questions to help the child develop these goals. Using an egg timer can help awareness of time and allow the child to develop their judgement about how long it will take to complete a task.

To help with setting up a profitable evening study time the parent may use a 3 step study hall procedure: First, the parent might ask, "What would you like to learn about …..". Second, they might ask, "Where can we find this information (e.g., the child's notes or school text, the encyclopaedia, the dictionary, a magazine or book etc.). Third, the parent will find and read with the child the needed material. The idea is for the parent to *facilitate.* The parent must not add to the burden. Rather the parent must be perceived as a helper, not a critic. If possible it is good if the parent can generate excitement about finding answers and generating new interesting questions as they read. Fourth, after the parent has read the material, partly with, and partly to a young child, the parent may then reward the child. The parent perhaps gives points for achievement and bonus points for new questions generated during the reading process. The points gradually accumulate towards earning something. Or the reward may be a game the child enjoys or "recreational electricity" (TV or computer time). A desired activity is a strong reward for doing a less desirable activity.

It is important that parents model for their child. The parent(s) should read, do bills or write letters, but not watch TV or play games on the computer while their child is doing homework. Then, if helpful, parent and child can take pleasant breaks together.

With older students, the parent will demonstrate very genuine interest in the student teaching them how to organize the material for study and reporting to them the essence of the units studied at the completion of each time period. It is crucial, however, that the student develop the schedule, the units to be studied, and the time frames. The parent is only a useful tool in the process. The moment the parent begins to dictate the "what, why, when, where and how" of study hall is often the moment when passive aggressive non-compliance begins. One has to sell the parents as well as students on the idea of study hall since the parent is in a position to reinforce this good habit. Tell them that if they were investing $35,000 in a good boarding school, one of the things that they would be paying for would be study hall – a period of time each week day evening (usually 7 to 9 pm for high school students) that is set aside for studying. Students who need the support of a teacher resource may study in a special hall that is supervised. Stronger students usually study in the library or in their room. Students with an A+ standing in all subjects are excused from formal study time since they have demonstrated that they know how to use effective study habits. Since this is part of the formula for success at boarding schools, why not develop a similar procedure at home? Friends soon learn to call after study time (especially if only an answering machine gets calls during study time). A call to clarify a homework problem, however, is allowed. Television shows can be taped for later viewing. A family may decide that 4 to 6 is a better time than 7 to 9. Be flexible about when and where but rigid about the expectation that there is a study hall time. No homework? The time can be spent in review, reading and test – preparation.

14. Conclusion

Many students are not very efficient learners in standard classroom settings. Students with ADD, for example, are the *'hunters'* so aptly described by Thom Hartmann in his books. They are often quite bright though they tend to underachieve in school. They are capable of hyper focus and they are often extremely creative. Simply put, they learn differently than the *'farmers'* do. Our job is to help such students to use metacognitive strategies and develop learning mechanisms or techniques that fit their cognitive style. Neurofeedback plus metacognitive strategies can help these students to learn more efficiently and effectively and it empowers the student to remember material and improve their school performance. They finally learn how to learn.

D. Metacognition – Quick Reference

<u>Cognition</u> = Thinking
- Perceiving
- Learning
- Remembering

<u>Metacognition</u> = **Thinking About Thinking**
- Guiding & Monitoring Your Cognition
- Being conscious of how you learn & remember things.
- Develop strategies to organize, plan, learn, and remember more effectively.
- Games for young children *(start techniques early - learn that learning is fun)*

Read Actively not passively using 4 Steps:

(1.) Before You Open the book or start on a chapter:
- *Predict what should be covered:* Headings and subheadings which the author should include. *Brainstorming, Gridding - Rows are questions like who, what, when, where, how, with what effect or biological, psychological and social. Columns are main areas to be discussed like: before, during and after or, in health-related matters, contributing, precipitating and sustaining factors.*
- *Generate questions* about things you would like to learn.

(2.) When You First Open the book or chapter:
- *Scan* -abstract, conclusion, headings, questions, graphs, tables, pictures
- *Skim* – a few seconds a page for first line nouns (key words) in each paragraph
- *Framework* - build the foundations, the girders, the framework of the knowedge, then fill in as you read.

(3.) While Reading
- Start with something that catches your interest, e.g., the caption under a picture or a table which summarizes the main points.
- **Highlighting & Underlining: Use 2 pens (red and blue) and a high-lighter to mark**

the essentials: – highlight very, very little and keep underlining to a minimum. Circle the major items. The red pen is only used to mark the most important items when you review the chapter. Write summaries in the margins &/or draw summary diagrams.
- <u>Only highlight</u> the thesis (purpose of the material), the key word for each of the main arguments or each new topic (new section or new paragraph).
- <u>Circle</u> The key word for each new thought within the section or argument.
- <u>Underline</u> key facts which support each area.
- *Boxing* - divide reading time and material into small units.
- *Connect* - each box to the next as you read. Connections must be logical to you.

- *Number* (sections / concepts) and *mark* (important points)

And, while reading
- Keep *Generating* questions & *Predicting* answers
- *Chunk* - Key words & Phrases into logical &/or amusing groups.
- *Pictures, Rhymes, etc.* Use tricks to assist memory and recall.
- *Review* as you read, after each page or paragraph
- *Widgets* - decide on a product-to-be-accomplished for each unit of time in your study schedule.

(4.) Review
- *Organizing, Synthesizing* - Make a **flow sheet,** an overview linking the main concepts.

- *Packaging* - Make extremely neat & well organized but brief notes - *only the exam essentials. One package per chapter. The numbering gave you your sections for each package and your marks (or high-lighting) gave you the main points to include.*

- *Lecturing* - To parents or a friend or pretend the walls are your teachers. - Teach / Teach / Teach - it's the best way to learn!

Writing An Essay, A Debate or an Exam Question. The Hamburger or '3-3-3' Method

Follow the general principle: Tell them what you are going to tell them, tell them, tell them what you told them.

- Make 3 sections – the bun, the meat and veggies, the bun (Introduction. - Body - Conclusion.)
- Have 3 Subsections for each of these sections.

- **Introduction**: Divide the Introduction into 3 sections: introductory statement which catches an audience's attention, thesis statement, then mention the three arguments you will develop in the body
- **Body**: Make 3 major arguments (points) in the "body" of the essay with 3 supporting facts (data) for each argument.
- **Conclusion**: Summarize the 3 arguments, discuss them in the light of your thesis or hypothesis and then make a wrap-up comment.

Listen Actively

- Find out from the teacher, if possible, what will be covered in each class for the next term. Buy the textbook. Obtain good cook-book notes from a high ranking student who is in the year ahead of you.

- Brief before class preparation gives you a *Filing Cabinet Mind rather than a Garbage Bag Mind. Briefly (5 - 10 minutes) the night before each class do the Predicting, Organizing, then Skimming, Scanning, and Frame-working of the text-book (see reading section above) and / or look at last year's notes from a student in the year ahead . The next day you will recall more information than your fellow students at the end of each class because your mind has been ready to assimilate the information.*
- Set up for success for in-class alertness and information recall by using the *3-fact-method. This is a method for connecting what is learned at school to reviewing the main points at home. It is a quick way to predict the questions that will be asked on the next test or exam.*

- *Scribbling each main idea/fact, or marking it specifically in the notes you are making in class will move that fact from a 6 second recall time to about a 4 hour recall. Try for three facts from each lecture.*
- *Writing each of these <u>key facts</u> neatly in a list that is kept at the back of that subject's three-ring-binder moves those key facts from a 4 hour recall to a 7 day recall.*
- *Glancing at, and/or looking up, information on those key facts a few days later moves that information to long-term memory and recall.*
- *At the end of the month or term, this list of facts may correspond quite well to the questions that the teacher will ask on the exam.*

Organize Your Time

- **Study Hall** - Your desk has files, calendar, planner and silent phone (with message machine to say you will call back at the end of the hour).
- **Planner** - Keep a calendar to help your recall of things-to-be-done: one calendar that you carry plus a large three month wall calendar for assignment due dates and test dates.
  - **Short Term** work-to-be-done must be listed for each day and seen as a *week at a glance* overview. Daily activities and homework are listed for each day.
  - **Long Term** projects should be kept on a separate page (*inserts &/or month at-a-glance pages*). This section includes projects with a plan for completing library searches, internet searches, outline, rough draft and final product with deadlines for each section of the work.

Attach a new habit *(looking at your planner)* to an old habit *(eating breakfast, eating dessert, having a snack after school, sitting in the car…)*
Keep in mind the adage that *failing to plan is planning to fail*. With neurofeedback you self-regulate your mental state and with metacognition you self-regulate your approach to learning.
Metacognition is a powerful adjunct to neurofeedback because they both empower the person to take control.

SECTION XIII
Brief Overview of Statistics and Research Design

James W. G. Thompson

Introduction

In order to gain knowledge, make advancements, and improve credibility all disciplines must have a sound scientific backing, the cornerstone of which is research. Although not a necessary requirement for all clinical practices, research is an integral component of any science and biofeedback is no different. Indeed biofeedback practitioners can be justifiably proud that their field is one that has been built on the solid foundations of scientific research.

A. Scientific Papers
1. Getting Started: Planning and Failure to Plan...

The old maxim "failure to plan is planning to fail" holds especially true in conducting scientific research. The solid foundation set out by a good plan allows the researcher to easily conduct their research, avoid pitfalls and backtracking and ensure credibility.

The key to the planning process is familiarizing yourself with the current knowledge in your field. This is the basis of the planning stage in which you gather information to help form and mould your hypothesis. As well, this familiarization with recent work will help to inform the researcher of current methods that have been successful or unsuccessful.

The planning process can be divided into four steps:

a. Write the Problem Statement

The problem statement is the backbone of the paper. It defines the area to be investigated and guides the entire research plan. The problem statement covers five main areas:

Workability – Is the research feasible given the time and resources available?
Critical Mass – Is the problem being studied of sufficient proportions to validate a study?
Interest – Is the field (and are you, yourself) interested enough in the area to warrant a research study?
Theoretical Value – Will this research fill a gap in the current literature?
Practical Value – Is there any practical value to this study?

When these questions have been satisfied, the researcher can feel confident that their research and purpose will be of value to the field. This step, although the beginning point, is not finished or complete as of this point. The problem statement needs to be continuously consulted, assessed and refined as the researcher continues to learn about their specific field of study.

b. Consult Secondary and Primary sources

This is the background research stage. The time when you truly learn how little you know about the field you are an "expert" in. It begins with the basic searches through preliminary sources. These include: reviews, encyclopaedias, abstracts and bibliographies. Once the topic and sources of information have been narrowed and keywords have been identified, secondary and primary sources can be consulted. Journals, original studies, theses and dissertations fall into this category. These sources will give you more detailed information regarding the field and will be a huge help in guiding your research. With the advent of the internet, information is so readily available that it can become overwhelming. The key is to keep the search specific. Be aware of the keywords, phrases and descriptors you use. Also, use the search engine "limits" to avoid getting hits that are not relevant to your search. Lastly, be sure to only utilize sources that are trustworthy. Some sites that have proven their worth in the scientific field include: psychinfo/psychlit, medline, eric and pubmed.

c. Read and Record the Literature

By this point you no doubt have stacks of literature very relevant to your area of interest. Now comes one of the most time consuming, yet also the most fun and interesting parts of the planning process: reading and recording the current literature. In the interest of being provident, you should keep an electronic record of all literature you found on-line, as well as hard copies of all literature you are going to read. This will avoid the tedious process of re-finding articles at a later date and will help to avoid confusion as to who said what and where.

The reading and recording is a time for an engaging challenge. It is your turn to do more than just learn. It is an opportunity to outsmart your colleagues in the field. You get to be in the driver's seat and play the role of the critic. To say "this was done well, yet I could improve on it by doing this!" There is no such thing as being too critical of a peer's work at this juncture. Whatever flaws you find and can avoid in your research will only improve your chances of success. Whatever improvements you make to something that worked previously in the field will only serve to increase the likelihood of publication of your research. It is of the utmost importance to take note of specific features of previous work. Some of the most important areas to take note of are previous hypotheses, designs, methods, subject selection and exclusion, equipment used, limitations and suggestions for future research.

You will exit this stage of the planning process with more ideas for conducting research than you even thought possible. It may even be the case that your entire problem statement has been rewritten! The ability to learn and adapt will serve you well at this stage and throughout the research process.

d. Write the Review

This final step of writing up the literature review may at first seem redundant, and unnecessary to some. It seems counter intuitive to write on a subject before performing your research, however, in the later stages you will be able to use this as the basis for the introduction of your paper. You will have therefore already written a major portion of your paper before even testing a subject. What a feeling of accomplishment!

The review should be divided into three very basic parts, the "hamburger" if you will. The introduction; which defines the area and familiarizes the reader, makes clear the problem you wish to study and attracts the reader's attention.

The body (organized around your three, or possibly four, major points); which summarizes and is critical of past research, and is detailed about explaining the need for your further investigation in this field.

The summary and conclusions; which paraphrases gaps in current literature thus lending support for the need for your research, gives the direction of your research, defines your problem statement and your hypothesis.

2. Putting the Plan into Action: Contents of a Scientific Paper

a. Overview of Putting the Plan into Action.

The research process will be described following a typical journal format divided into four sections: introduction, methods, results and discussion. The introduction will lead the reader through the necessary components of an introduction, whose purpose is to 'introduce' the reader to the subject area and the research that will follow. The methods section will outline the scientific process and will discuss areas such as subjects and the design of a study. The third section will be the results section where the data collected is analysed using statistics. Some basic statistics used in research will be discussed. The final section is the discussion section. The important aspects of a discussion, and how to write and organize this section, will be broken down and explained.

b. Introduction

The purpose of an introduction is simple. It is there to raise the reader's interest in the topic, give background information and introduce the problem. The manner in which this purpose is fulfilled is not as simple however. There are four mutually exclusive, yet equally important components to the introduction.

First, there is the problem statement. This is a brief description of the area to be studied. It is an identification and description of the variables. *Independent variables* (causes of changes and often the variables controlled by the experimenter), *dependent variables* (effects), *categorical variables* (e.g., sex and age), *controls* (e.g., time of day of testing) and *extraneous variables* (things that cannot be controlled) are all discussed in brief. At this stage the researcher should also mention assumptions, limitations and delimitations.

Assumptions are what the researchers must assume during the experiment, for instance, that the subjects will give their best effort and follow instructions. *Limitations* are shortcomings inherent with this research, such as the *generalizability* of results. *Delimitations* are limitations that are under the control of the researcher; one's that the researcher has imposed. These include such things as size of the sample and tests used.

Second is the *hypothesis*. This is the predicted outcome of the study, the expected effects. In contrast to this is the *Null Hypothesis*. The Null hypothesis is ultimately what you will be testing. This will be further explained in the results section. For now it will suffice to say that it is the inverse of your hypothesis. For example, if your hypothesis was that 20 sessions of neurofeedback would improve a students Beta/Theta ratio by 5% then the Null hypothesis

would be that 20 sessions of neurofeedback would not cause any change in the Beta/Theta ratio. In formulating a hypothesis one should keep in mind the SMART principle. **S**pecific, **M**easurable, **A**ttainable, **R**ealistic time frame, **T**angible. These guidelines will help the researcher to formulate a testable hypothesis.

Third, and directly following the hypothesis comes the *operational definition* of terms. If you are measuring *intelligence* the definition you operate with will be "what an IQ test measures" and you will specify which test. This is an observable phenomenon and a concrete description of the expected effects. It enables the evaluation of results and a discussion of the findings. It is most important to operationally define the dependent variable(s). What is stated is how the expected effects will be manifested in the subjects. As with the hypothesis these are very specific. For instance, in neurofeedback, it may be the ability to hold Beta above 5 μV for 2 minutes while performing a reading task at the grade 8 difficulty level. This is the standard against which you will measure.

Fourth, but certainly not of least importance, is the *justification* of the study. The purpose of which is to draw attention to the differences between this study and others in the same area. This component will (a) address contradictory findings currently in the literature, (b) explain how this research paper will fill gaps in existing knowledge, (c) describe existing theories and how this research will refute or support them and (d) the practical applications of the findings to the field.

After looking over the components of the introduction it should be clear how all the work that went into the planning process and writing the literature review will aid you in expediting the writing of the introduction. Each step builds on the previous in a logical progression when performing a research study. The thorough and successful completion of each step helps to ensure success in the steps that follow.

c. Methods
i. Purpose

The methods section is a very detailed and a somewhat dry section of the paper. It is a succinct description of the components of the study. It has but one purpose. That is to enable the *reproduction/replication* of the study. That is it. That *is* the sole purpose of the methods section. There are four sub-sections within the methods section. Theses are: subjects, instruments & tests, procedures and design analysis.

ii. Subjects

The section on subjects is a straight forward description of the subjects chosen and how they were chosen for the study.

First, comes the description of the number of subjects who participated in the study. It states the number of subjects used in the study and any dropouts or changes in numbers during the study. This is important to mention right at the onset since sample size contributes to a very large extent to ensuring statistical results are relevant and reliable. The number of subjects used is a major contributor to the *power* of the study. It is a relatively simple calculation and can be found in almost any basic statistics book. By definition, power is the probability that you will correctly reject a false Null hypothesis. The equation is 1 – Beta = Power. Calculations of Power, Beta and other statistical measures will be discussed in the next section. Do not be surprised if, during your study, subjects drop-out or numbers change due to other extenuating circumstances. These eventualities occur in all studies. Initial numbers and changes in numbers need to be mentioned at the conclusion of the subject's section.

Second, the researcher should describe who the subjects are. Were they chosen from a specific grade level, city or country? Are they male or female, old or young? Details of subjects sex, age ranges, race, socio-economic standing and other areas relevant to the study being performed, such as I.Q or experience in a sport, need to be described.

The selection process is one of the most important elements of a study and is described in the methods section. Proper selection techniques and assignment to groups of subjects is essential in setting up a study that will be considered valid in its findings. There are 5 concepts to be considered here.
1. *Random Sampling* from Population:
2. *Stratified Random Sampling:*
3. *Systematic Sampling*:
4. *Sectioned Sampling*: Where you randomly pick areas, then cities, suburbs, etc…

5. *Random Assignment* of Study Groups:

Different areas of study bring with them their own sampling difficulties. It is, for example, extremely difficult to define a control group in a study of ADD. This is because many children with ADD are extremely bright and creative and are functioning near the top of their class, albeit possibly below their actual potential. Therefore merely not fitting the DSM criteria is a necessary but not a sufficient criterion to be included as a control for a study that is looking at EEG differences.

It is also important that you mention how permission and co-operation were obtained. This is simply a mention of the informed consent form used and how it was administered, Internal Review Board permissions, and, in animal studies, how the animals will be protected during the study.

iii. Instruments and Apparatus (Validity and Reliability)

This section, like the subjects section, is a detailed description. Here it is a list of the type, make, model, year, etc. of all the equipment used to carry out the study. Anything used for set-up, measurement, penalties or rewards must be described in detail. In considering the design of this section, the researcher should take into account the *validity* and *reliability* of equipment and tests. Please note that the distinction between validity and reliability is very important; they are NOT synonymous. *Validity* questions whether the researcher has measured what they intended to measure. *Reliability* addresses whether your measures were accurate, that is, could they be repeated with the same result. Also under consideration should be the difficulty of obtaining the instruments, difficulty in taking the measurements, the range of scores expected and the time needed to administer the tests and experiments.

iv. Procedures

The procedures description is the meat of the methods section. Here, a step-by- step account of the process is detailed to the reader. It is like the recipe book of the experiment. There is a description of how the tests are carried out and of how the data is obtained. This section is extremely important in allowing readers to determine the credibility and validity of the study and in allowing for the replication of the study. First is the order of steps. This is important in ensuring there is a logical flow and ensuring that there are no learning effects (and if there are, they are addressed). The timeframe is also an important aspect of the procedures. Is there fatigue in the subjects (mental and/or physical)? Is there a loss of interest and therefore a decrease in test performance? Finally, the exact instructions given to the subjects must be detailed. Wording, location, time before trials, individual or in a group and many other factors can contribute to how subjects will react under test conditions. Colleagues and interested readers will scrutinize this section to the letter. If the procedures used are not clear, logical and replicable then the experiment will lose all credibility and will be deemed a failure even if results were found.

v. Design & Analysis

This portion of the methods section is particularly important in experimental (quantitative) studies. It is a description of the variables (independent, dependent and extraneous) and how each is related and controlled. For example, the fact that an EEG will vary within subjects based on time of day needs to be addressed. In this section these external factors are described and the means by which they are controlled are discussed. The cause-effect relationship is also addressed here. The researcher needs to convince the reader that changes in the dependent variable(s) are explainable only on the basis of the treatments (the independent variable). There needs to be shown a method of agreement (why does A cause B?) as well as a method of disagreement (why does B not happen without A?).

The analysis portion of this is a description of the statistical tests that will be used to determine if an effect of statistical significance occurred. It is a description of the data processing and a description of the statistics to be used and why those particular ones were chosen. For instance, why is a parametric statistical test, such as a t-test, being performed on the data. It would need to be justified by stating that interval data was being processed and that the data possessed normal distribution with an equal variance between samples on the variable being tested and that the observations were independent of one another. These criterions would justify the use

of a parametric test. Also, it would need to be noted that differences between two groups were being tested for, thus justifying the use of a t-test over another type of parametric test such as ANOVA. If this statistical jargon seems slightly over your head, please don't be alarmed. It will all be explained in the results section, which follows.

The methods section is often viewed as the 'dry section', where list after list appears. Although I cannot deny the mundane nature of the writing of this section, the content is truly exciting. This section determines everything! Without a thorough methods section an experiment will never be successful. Attention to detail is the key to conducting successful research, and nowhere is this more important than in the set-up of the study. The aforementioned adage *failure to plan is planning to fail* has never held so true as in this section. It is here that your planning shows. In summary, the methods section has four main content areas: (1) it contains information on the subjects (2) a description of the instruments, tests and apparatus used (3) an outline of the procedures and (4) briefly describes the design and analysis.

Well, with that under wraps it is time to get to the fun stuff - the results and discussion sections! Did we find an effect? Why or why not? To answer those questions, get ready to dive into the wonderful world of basic research statistics.

d. Results
i. Overview (Significance and Meaningfulness)

Let me begin with a plea to all, not to roll your eyes at the mention of the word "statistics". As researchers, statistical calculations are our friend. They will prove the worth of a well conducted study and its findings, while filtering out research that has been improperly conducted. This section, titled results, is merely an introduction to some essential terms, concepts and statistical tests that one needs to know in order to competently read research papers and prior to embarking on a research study.

Statistics tell us two very important things in research. These are: (a) the strength of an effect or relationship and (b) the significance of an effect or relationship.

It is very important to note the distinction between the two words strength and significance. A finding can be significant yet not be meaningful – the inverse does not hold true. Significance is simply a measure of reliability. It merely answers the question "did a change occur?" Meaningfulness, on the other hand, is a more difficult distinction to make. It questions whether the change that occurred is worth the input that induced the measured change. An amusing example of this is Popeye (the old cartoon character). For him, eating only one can of spinach elicited unsurpassed strength for a short period of time. For him, the change is meaningful. However, what if he had had to eat 50 cans of spinach in a row to get the same result? The experiment to deduce this would have been significant because a change did occur, however, the expense, time and effort that was incurred to elicit this change (the purchasing and eating, in this case the input) is not worth the response (the increased strength for a short duration of time) and is therefore not meaningful. This distinction is unique to all research and is determined by the experimenter and their peers.

ii. Describing the Data (See 'Statistics' below):

e. Summary, Discussion and Conclusion

The discussion section actually is comprised of a summary of the findings and some discussion and conclusions that might be drawn from the findings. It is your wrap-up and you want it to leave an impression. It is a chance to answer the question, "So what? Where is the relevance to the broader picture?" Typically you interpret the information from the results, where findings and statistical significance were reported objectively but without comment. This summary is more subjective and allows for comment on how the findings relate to the original hypothesis. There is some discussion of the limitations of the study (small sample size, certain variables not controlled for, like time of day, etc.) and the generalizability of the findings. Finally, you draw conclusions. A typical concluding sentence might run thus: Neurofeedback, when administered in such and such a manner for this many sessions, appears to be effective in improving 'x' (or decreasing 'y') in a particular population (conservatory of music students with performance anxiety, children with ADHD, athletes who have suffered concussions, or whatever group is of interest to you).

B. Statistics

1. Describing the Data
a. Measures of Central Tendency

i. Mean, Median, Mode
One of the most important basic concepts in statistics is the description of the data. Essentially there are two concepts to be discussed here: *measures of central tendency* and measures of variability.

Central tendency has three measures. These are the mean, median and mode. The *mean* is probably very familiar to all. It refers to the average of all the scores and is the sum of all scores divided by the number of scores. The *median* is the middle score. For instance, if your scores were 3,6,7,9 and 13, then the median is 7. The term *mode* refers to the score that occurs most frequently. An example here is a set of scores of 10, 15, 16, 17, 17, 21 and 22. The mode in this example would be 17. The mean is considered to be the most accurate reflection of the entire group score.

b. Measures of Variability

i. Standard Deviation, Variance, Range
Variability is defined in statistics as the degree to which each individual score differs from the central tendency score. As with central tendency, there are three measures of variability: variance, standard deviation (here referred to as SD) and Range. *Variance* and SD both measure the variability, or spread of scores around the mean. Variance is the square of the SD. SD is calculated by dividing the sum of all the squared differences between each score and the mean

score by the number of scores (n) minus one and then taking the square root of that number.

$$SD = \sqrt{\frac{\Sigma(x\text{-mean})^2}{N-1}}$$

$$\text{Variance} = SD^2$$

The *range* in a set of data is simply the distance between the lowest and the highest score. It is the "difference" (subtraction) between the high score and the low score.

The concept of variance in statistics is an extremely important one. As previously mentioned, it tells about the distribution of scores around the mean. If most of the scores are very close to the mean then you have a fairly homogeneous group with respect to the variable being measured and you will calculate a low variance within the group or between the groups. If you have a very diversified group on the variable being tested then you will end up calculating a high inter or intra-group variance due to the diverse nature of the scores.

2. Types of Data & Tests
a. Nominal, Ordinal, Interval

In research there are three types of data: Nominal, Ordinal and Interval. (As an aside, remember that *data* is plural. The singular is *datum*. In Latin, 3rd declension nouns range from 'um' to 'a' endings for the plural as in medium to media.) *Nominal data* are data which are categorical, for example, males and females. The data fit into categories set by the researcher. Ordinal data refers to data that are ranked. If for instance, the best score of ten participants was 13.5/15 and the lowest score was 5.25/15, then the highest of the ten scores may be ranked as 1 and the lowest may be ranked as 10. In this type of data scoring the order is significant, yet the quantitative distance between scores is not meaningful. The third type of data is Interval data. This is the type of data we most often see in scientific or quantitative research. With this type of data the relative distance between data points is meaningful. An example could be in the long jump where a score that is .25 meters greater than another score shows a quantitative difference in ability.

b. Categories of Tests

The explanations of data types should elicit in you the question, "When in statistics does it matter what type of data we have?" The answer lies in the tests we use. There are two general categories of statistical tests: Non-parametric and Parametric. Non-parametric tests are tests that are used on data that are either nominal or ordinal in nature. Parametric tests, on the other hand, are used when data is of an interval nature and three assumptions regarding the data are met. These assumptions are:

(1) the population data are *normally distributed* (this can be inferred from your sample of the population). This means that the curve plotted by the recorded data is a normal (or '*Bell*') curve.

A normal curve meets specific criteria:
    1) the mean, median and mode are all at the same point (have the same value)

    2) 68% of all the scores fall within 1 standard deviation, 95% of scores fall within 2 SD's and 99% are within 3 SD's.

(2) the samples being compared have *equal variance*. (Normal curves can be drawn with different heights and widths.) The curves of the samples being compared must be equal in height and width.

(3) observations made during the research are *independent* (one variable cannot affect another). The influence of one variable cannot have an effect on another variable being measured. For example, if a first pill is taken and results are recorded, then a second pill is taken, the first pill can in no way have an affect on the outcome of the second pill. If the first pill did affect the results of taking the second pill, the outcome of the second pill would be said to be dependent on the first and this would negate the third assumption of independent observations.

c. Hypotheses
i. Null Hypothesis

All research is based on statements called hypotheses. A *hypothesis* is a statement whose validity the research is being conducted to test. In all research there are least two hypotheses, the (primary) hypothesis (H_1) and the null hypothesis (H_0). The hypothesis is the statement of what the researcher believes will be the treatment effect. The *Null hypothesis* is the inverse of the hypothesis. It states that there will be no effect found. For example, if the research hypothesis is that taking a pill 3 times a day for one year will permanently turn blond hair to red, then the null hypothesis would simply be that taking the specified pill 3 x/day for one year will not turn blond hair permanently red. The null hypothesis is important in that it is the statement against which research results are tested. Based on the research findings the null hypothesis will either be accepted or rejected. If the null hypothesis is proven to be true (the treatment has no effect) then we say that we accept the null hypothesis. If a treatment effect is found it is expressed as a rejection of the null hypothesis.

ii. Probability and Alpha

Statistical tests use tests on samples to infer things about a population which that sample is assumed to represent. As with any inference, there is a chance of making an improper assumption. Statistics uses the term **alpha** to define what the researcher thinks is an acceptable hprobability of making the error of finding a non-existent effect. In other words, alpha is the chance of your research finding an effect in the sample even though in the population there would not be an effect.

Let's go back to our discussion of hypotheses to tie this together. By accepting or rejecting the null hypothesis, we are making a statement about the effects of the treatment. At this stage two types of error can be made. If H_0 is actually true but is rejected then we have committed a *type 1 error (false positive, alpha)*. If, on the other hand, H_0 is not true but is accepted anyway, a *type 2 error (false negative, Beta)* has been committed. A simple chart will help to clarify.

	H_0 true	H_0 false
Accept H_0	correct decision	Type 2 error (false negative, Beta)
Reject H_0	Type 1 error (false positive, alpha)	correct decision

In the literature it is the alpha value that is always stated as the accepted error level.

Ordinarily, alpha is set at either 1% (.01) or 5% (.05), however, there are times when a researcher will set alpha at 10% (.1). These alpha levels or probability statements are called the *P-value*. For an alpha level of 5%, the P-value would be written as p<.05. P<.05 means that the probability of finding an effect in the sample, given that there is no effect in the population, is smaller than 5%. In other words, there is a one in twenty chance that the effect you found is not real.

iii. Power

The Beta value discussed in the chart above is used in determining the power of the study. Power is defined as the probability that you will correctly reject H0 (probability that you will find an existing effect). Power is calculated as 1-Beta. This is logical since, by definition, Beta is the chance of making a type 2 error (conclude that there is no effect when there actually is one). If then, you have a low chance of making a type 2 error (Beta is low), then the Power of your study will be high. Generally, an acceptable level of power for a study is 0.8. The power of a study can be increased by manipulating one or all of three major factors. These are:

1) increasing sample size
2) decreasing overall variance (make the within group variance of both groups smaller)
3) increase alpha (by increasing alpha from .05 to .1 you are testing at a lower confidence limit and increase your chance of making a type 1 error from 1 in 20 to 1 in 10. The effect of this is a decrease in the chance of making a type 2 error).

iv. Effect size

Now I'm sure you're wondering where this all leads. Here it is. The Effect size is the number that a prudent researcher needs to calculate to ensure that they are "set for success". The Effect size is the standardized value of the practical importance, or meaningfulness, of a study.

The *effect size* is calculated by measuring the difference between groups based on means and standard deviation. The calculation for effect size is:

$$ES = \frac{(M1 - M2)}{SD}$$

M1 – the mean of group 1
M2 – the mean of group 2
SD – the standard deviation of the control group.
(It should be the case that the SDs of the two groups are the same since, it is an assumption of parametric statistics that the within group variances of the test groups are the same.)

A calculated effect size of 0.2 is considered small, 0.5 is considered moderate and an ES of 0.8 is considered large.

v. Merit of a Study

The interaction between effect size (ES), sample size (N) and power is best represented by a chart.

Schematic Representation of the Sample Size, Effect Size, and Power Relationship

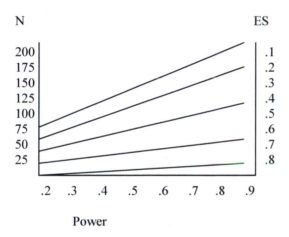

Power

As you can see, having a small effect size will necessitate a larger sample size to maintain a high power for the study.
In conclusion, the merit of a study is determined by four factors:
1) Alpha level being tested at
2) The effect size
3) Power
4) Sample Size (N)

C. A Short List of Related Concepts and Terms

This section will comprise a list of additional terms that the reader may encounter when reading the literature in this field. Only a brief definition or description is given for each of these terms. For further information it is recommended that the reader refer to any standard undergraduate textbook on statistics.

Alpha level: The probability of making a Type I error, that is, a false positive, or rejection of the null hypothesis when there really is no difference or effect.

Beta level: Beta level is the probability of making a type II error, that is, a false negative. (Your study, for example, concluded that neurofeedback did not have an effect on your sample when it actually does have an effect in the larger population.)

Correlation. This is the degree to which two variables vary together. It is usually calculated as a correlation coefficient designated as 'r'.

Sensitivity. This term refers to the ability of a test to identify true cases.

Specificity. This refers to the ability of a test or procedure to correctly distinguish one diagnosis from another.

Test Power: The power of a test is the probability that a type II error will not be committed. This is calculated as '1-beta'. It addresses the question of whether a test has the ability (power) to detect a difference that exists.

Pre & Post testing: In this text the authors have recommended that all practitioners do pre and post testing appropriate to the client's goals and the type of BFB work that they are doing. In NFB work, for these measures to be accurate, the practitioner should keep in mind the following variables, although some of the suggestions made here may be impractical in a busy clinical practice. Some objective testing is, for the most part, better than no testing. Tests commonly used with clients who have ADHD include: continuous performance tests (Conner's, IVA, TOVA), EEG measures (theta/beta ratios), intelligence tests, and academic achievement measures.

- Testing should be at the same time of day. In NFB work this will help control for the influence of circadian rhythms on theta.
- Most clients will be more consistent if testing is done early in the morning.

- Be sure to control for variables that could conceivably affect the results including: caffeine, meals, smoking, medications and sleep. If stress factors differ then you must note that when recording results.

Terms Related to Test Characteristics:

Criterion - Referenced Test. This is a test that allows its users to make score interpretations in relation to a functional performance level, as distinguished from those interpretations that are made in relation to the performance of others. A grade equivalent score is criterion referenced.

Norm - Referenced Test. This is a test that allows its users to make score interpretations based on the comparison of a test taker's performance to the performance of other people in a specified group. Intelligence tests, for example, are age-normed; each score is compared to the norms for that person's exact age.

Reliability
- **Reliability.** The term 'reliability' refers to the degree to which test scores are consistent, dependable, or repeatable, that is, the degree to which they are free of errors of measurement.

- **Reliability Coefficient.** This is a coefficient of correlation between two administrations of a test. The conditions of administration may involve variation in test forms, raters, or scorers, or passage of time.

  These and other changes in conditions give rise to qualifying adjectives being used to describe the particular coefficient including:
  - *parallel form* reliability
  - *inter-rater* reliability
  - *test - retest* reliability

Validity
- **Validity.** The term 'validity' refers to the degree to which a certain inference from a test is appropriate or meaningful. Does the test measure what it purports to measure.

- **Validity Coefficient.** This is a coefficient of correlation that shows the strength of the relation between predictor and criterion. If you were checking the validity of a new intelligence measure, you might compare the scores with those obtained o the Wechsler scale.

- **Concurrent Criterion.** This refers to having evidence of criterion - related validity in which predictor and criterion information are obtained at approximately the same time.

- **Content - Related Evidence Of Validity.** This refers to having evidence which shows the extent to which the content domain of a test is appropriate relative to its intended purpose. This would require, for example, that one have a representative sample of content and a clear exclusion of content outside that domain.

- **Criterion - Related Evidence Of Validity.** This refers to having evidence that shows the extent to which scores on a test are related to a criterion measure.

Differential Prediction. This term refers to the degree to which a test that is used to predict people's relative attainments yields different predictions for the same criteria among groups with different demographic characteristics, prior experience or treatment.

Error Of Measurement. This term refers to the difference between an observed score and the corresponding true score.

Psychometric. This refers to tests that pertain to the measurement of psychological characteristics such as abilities, aptitudes, achievement, personality traits, skill, and knowledge.

Standard Error Of Measurement. This is the standard deviation of errors of measurement that is associated with the test scores for a specified group of test takers. (For example, this may be thought of as an indication of just how variant scores would be if the test were given to the same subjects an infinite number of times.)

True Score. In classical test theory, this refers to the average of the scores earned by an individual on an unlimited number of perfectly parallel forms of the same test.

Measures Of Dispersion.

Range. The lowest to the highest score. (Highest - Lowest + 1)

Standard Deviation (SD). This is a unit of measurement. With normal distributions, scores can be expressed in terms of standard deviation units from the mean. (It is useful to note that:
over 68 % of scores fall between $\pm 1 \sigma$ from the mean
over 95 %............................. $\pm 2 \sigma$ from the mean
over 99 % ....$\pm 3 \sigma$ from the mean

Variance. This is a measure of variability. It is the average squared deviation from the mean (the square of the standard deviation). (*Note the difference in this formal statistical term from the term 'variability' which may be used in NFB work, for example, to rate changes in scores for theta over time. Variability is the standard deviation / mean x100. This measurement is useful to help compare (approximately) measurements of a variable that varies with age like theta because it relates the amplitude to the mean. (A child has much higher amplitudes of theta and much wider deviations from the mean when compared to an adult.) Note that in most instruments you must define a standard time and a standard averaging or smoothing factor before you can compare variability in one subject over several sessions. In NFB work with ADHD the client attempts to decrease both the amount of theta and its variability. (For example, using the F1000 by Focus Technology, we use 30 seconds and a smoothing factor of 5 and have both adults and children attempt to get more than 15 out of 20 consecutive 30 second segments having a variability of less than '35'. This can be an extraordinarily sensitive measure of a client's ability to self regulate focus and attention. At the beginning of training most clients meet this criterion on only one or two segments out of twenty. By the end of training most clients score twenty out of twenty.*) (The reader should note that 'variability' is not a standard statistical term.)

Normative Scores
Scores Of Relative Standing.

T - Score. This is a derived score on a scale having a mean score of 50 units and a standard deviation of 10 units.

Standard Score. A score that describes the location of a person's score within a set of scores in terms of its distance from the mean in standard deviation units.

Z - Score. A type of standard score scale in which the mean equals zero and the standard deviation equals one unit for the group used in defining the scale.

Percentile Rank. This refers to the percentage of scores in a specified distribution that fall at or below the point at which a given score lies. If a child scores at the 98th percentile rank, his score exceeds or equals 98% of the population. He is in the top 2%.

Stanine. This term refers to a form of standard score that is based on a distribution of the raw scores into 9 equal parts. *[A score of '5' puts the subject in the centre of the distribution]*.

SECTION XIV
Multiple Choice Questions

Note 1: These questions have been written as a teaching tool. To this end the questions often have a longer stem than would be found in a typical exam. Many questions may also often be rather self evident to a knowledgeable reader. These are included as a review of the basics.

Note 2: Selected references are included in the answer section that follows the questions. All questions are based on text found in the book but selected questions, where we felt the reader might want to do further reading, are referenced further. The questions are ordered, for the most part, according to sections of the Biofeedback Certification Institute of America (BCIA) blueprint. BCIA required hours as of 2003 are noted for most sections for the convenience of those intending to become certified. Not all of the sections have written questions. Some sections are more appropriate for demonstration and oral examination. For more details on certification consult the BCIA website (www.bcia.org).

1. Introduction To EEG Biofeedback
Required Hours: 4

1. Electrical activity in the mammalian brain was first measured, using a string galvanometer, by this scientist, with the findings being published in 1875 :
    a. Richard Caton
    b. Marie Curie
    c. James Maxwell
    d. Hans Berger

2. In the 1920's a German psychiatrist recorded a pattern of uniform electrical waves from the human scalp that he labeled first order waves. This came to be known as *alpha rhythm,* with reference to the first letter of the Greek alphabet. He also observed periods when these waves were absent and the pattern of waves was smaller and desynchronous. This pattern became known as *beta.* His name was:
    a. Richard Caton
    b. Han Aufreiter
    c. Heinrich Hertz
    d. Hans Berger

3. In the 1950's, an American psychologist, using careful scientific methods, demonstrated that a person could correctly identify when they were producing alpha waves but subjects were not able to say precisely how they were making that discrimination. His name was:
    a. Barry Sterman
    b. Joe Kamiya
    c. John Basmajian
    d. Tom Budzynski

4. An American psychologist working with cats in the late 1960's at the University of California Los Angeles, demonstrated that they could be trained, using a method called "operant conditioning", to increase a specific spindle-like brain wave pattern which ran at a frequency between 12 to 19 cycles per second. He gave the spindle like activity between 12 and 15 Hz. the name *sensorimotor rhythm (SMR).* Closely following on this discovery was his observation that cats who had increased their SMR activity were resistant to seizures. His name was:
    a. Barry Sterman
    b. Joe Kamiya
    c. Joel Lubar
    d. Tom Budzynski

5. It has been established that measuring the theta / beta ratio was helpful in differentiating between normal and ADHD clients. The first researcher to propose and investigate this was: His name was:
    a. Barry Sterman
    b. Keith Conners
    c. Joel Lubar
    d. Vince Monastra

2. Learning Theory Relevant to EEG Biofeedback:

6. Operant conditioning or instrumental learning is based on _____ which can be simply stated thus: *When you reward behaviour you increase the likelihood of its recurrence.* This law was first stated by Edward Thorndike in 1911. He mainly studied cats in puzzle boxes. This law is also called trail and error learning. Which "law" fits the bank above?
    a. Thorndike's Law
    b. Watson's Law
    c. The Law of Effect
    d. The Law of Consequences

7. Classical conditioning is a term that refers to a type of learning. It was originally described by_____ as a conditioned, or learned, reflex. Who was this investigator:
    a. Thorndike
    b. Watson
    c. Skinner
    d. Pavlov

8. In what kind of learning does the conditioned stimulus *automatically elicit* a conditioned response after it has been paired a sufficient number of times with an unconditioned stimulus (that elicits an autonomic response)
    a. operant conditioning
    b. classical conditioning
    c. associative learning
    d. conditioned response learning

9. In classical conditioning, motivation is:
    a. very important
    b. somewhat important
    c. usually downplayed
    d. for the most part, irrelevant

10. What term usually refers to conditioning by successive approximations? (Rewarding a behaviour or a sequence of neurophysiological occurrences, _____ the contributing components of that sequence in a way that results in an increased frequency of that sequence occurring.)
    a. generalizing
    b. shaping
    c. conditioning
    d. associating

11. What kind of learning occurs when things get unintentionally paired with reinforcers. (For example, a coloured light that indicates an artifact, such as eye-blink or muscle activity, on a neurofeedback screen.)
    a. classical learned response
    b. incidental or associative learning
    c. operant conditioning
    d. unintentional learning

12. In its simplest form, what term means that what the client learns in the office doing neurofeedback will also occur at other times, places and with other people and tasks. (The ability to do this is severely impaired in some disorders such as autism.)
    a. conditioned learning
    b. operant learning
    c. shaping
    d. generalization

13. If a student who is doing neurofeedback learns to use metacognitive strategies during the feedback session when he is in a mental state that is producing positive rewards for low slow wave activity and higher beta activity (15-18 Hz), then using those strategies while doing homework will be:
    a. less likely to elicit focus and concentration
    b. more likely to elicit focus and concentration
    c. irrelevant in terms of eliciting focus and concentration
    d. produce interference with respect to memorizing new material.

14. The rationale for pairing diaphragmatic breathing at a rate of about 6 breaths per minute with the production of SMR rhythm in patients who have dystonia and Parkinson's disease has been reported to be based on the fact there is a double innervation of the muscle spindles by:
   a. the parasympathetic nervous system and gamma motor efferents
   b. the parasympathetic nervous system and corticobulbar efferents
   c. the sympathetic nervous system and gamma motor efferents
   d. the sympathetic system and pyramidal efferents

15. Coaches may have the athlete use self-cueing of some kind, like a word or an image that has been paired with the production of the desired state, to produce:
   a. a classical response
   b. shaping
   c. generalization
   d. high beta rhythm

16. What may occur when the conditioned stimulus is no longer paired with the unconditioned stimulus over a number of trials. (In operant conditioning it may occur when a behaviour is no longer reinforced.)
   a. shaping
   b. extinction
   c. a classically conditioned response
   d. an operantly conditioned response

3. Research

17. Central tendency has three measures. These are the mean, median and mode.
The term mode refers to
   a. the sum of all scores divided by the number of scores.
   b. the score that occurs most frequently.
   c. the most accurate reflection of the entire group score.
   d. the middle score.

18. Variability is defined in statistics as the degree to which each individual score differs from the central tendency score. As with central tendency, there are three measures of variability: variance, standard deviation (here referred to as SD) and range. Variance and SD both measure the variability, or spread of scores around the mean.
Variance is:
   a. the sum of all the squared differences between each score and the mean score divided by the number of scores (n) minus one and then taking the square root of that number.
   b. the square of the SD.
   c. the sum of all the squared differences between each score and the mean score
   d. the average of the standard deviations divided by the mean times 100

19. There are two general categories of statistical tests: Non-parametric and Parametric. Non-parametric tests are tests that are used on data that are either nominal or ordinal in nature. Parametric tests are used when data is of an interval nature. One or more assumptions regarding the data are made. Which of the following is/are included as an assumption:

   a. the population data is normally distributed
   b. the samples being compared have equal variance.
   c. observations made during the research are independent (one variable cannot affect another).
   d. all of the above

20. A normal curve meets which specific criteria:
   a. the mean, median and mode are at different points (have different values)
   b. 88% of all the scores fall within 1 standard deviation
   c. 95% of scores fall within 2 SD's
   d. all of the above

21. The Null hypothesis
   a. is a statement of what the researcher believes will be the treatment effect.
   b. states that there will be no effect found.
   c. is a statistically invalid proposition
   d. states that no hypothesis is possible

22. Statistics uses the term *alpha* to define what the researcher thinks is:

    a. an unacceptable probability of finding an existent effect

    b. an acceptable probability of finding a non-existent effect.

    c. the probability of an event occurring

    d. the probability of an event not occurring

23. If H_0 is actually true but is rejected then we have:

    a. a *type 2 error (false negative, Beta)*

    b. a *type 1 error (false positive, alpha)*.

    c. an inconclusive result

    d. a misuse of statistics

4. Basic Neurophysiology and Neuroanatomy

Required Hours: 4

a. Neuroanatomy

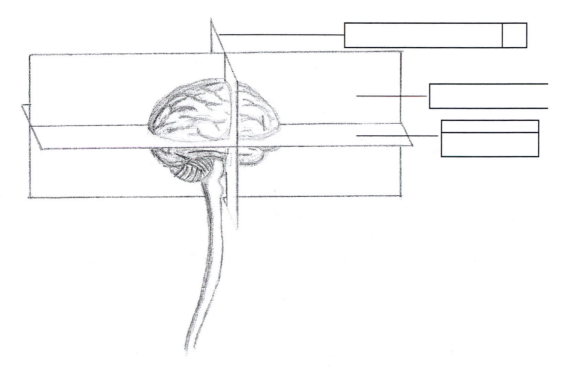

24. Place the following names on the correct lines in the above diagram:

    a. Sagittal Plane

    b. Horizontal Plane

        c. Transverse Plane

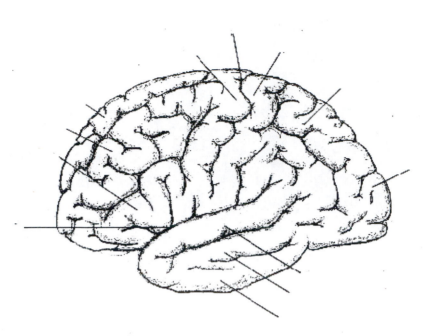

Note that there are more lines on the drawing than labels listed below.
When you are labelling be sure that it is clear to which line you have attached your label.

25. Put the following labels (or the correct number) next to the appropriate line on the above drawing:
    1. Parietal lobe
    2. Postcentral gyrus
    3. Inferior temporal gyrus
    4. Superior frontal gyrus
    5. Lateral sucus
    6. Central sulcus
    7. Inferior frontal gyrs
    8. Superior temporal gyrus
    9. Occipital lobe
Then outline, shade and label approximately where you think the following areas would lie:
Wernicke's
Broca's
Exner's
Auditory cortex

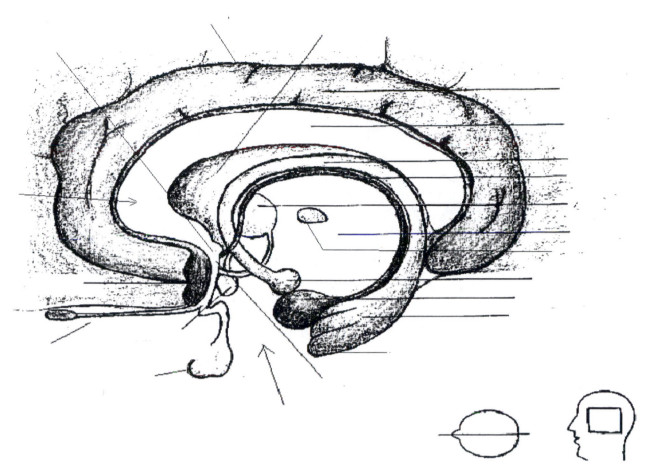

Sketch of a Midsagittal Section of the Human Brain

This is counted as 2 questions with 2 bonus marks available. One correct answer for 5 correct labels and a second correct answer for a further 5 correct labels. A bonus mark for a further 5 and a second bonus mark for 18 or more correct labels. Note that there are more lines on the drawing than labels listed below.

When you are labelling be sure that it is clear to which line you have attached your label.

26. Put the following labels (or the correct number) next to the appropriate line on the above drawing:

1. olfactory tract
2. anterior thalamic nucleus
3. thalamus
4. septum
5. amygdala
6. massa intermedia
7. hypothalamus (on this sketch it is small, roundish and immediately posterior to the lamina terminalis and the septal area)
8. lamina terminalis
9. entorhinal cortex

10. pituitary
11. anterior commissure
12. fornix
13. corpus callosum
14. stria terminalis
15. cingulate gyrus
16. sulcus cinguli
17. mammilary body
18. an arrow pointing to the approximate site of the anterior perforated area

27. In the spinal cord and peripheral nervous system, the white matter is on the outside and grey matter on the inside – the reverse of the cerebral hemispheres where the grey matter is on the outside. This statement is:

a. true
b. false

28. When there is a head injury the grey and white matter will move at different speeds due to their different densities and the resultant sheer forces lead to diffuse axonal injury (DAI). This type of injury can be detected in the EEG.

a. true
b. false

29. The area responsible for interpretation of the meaning of language and the assemblage of letters in phonemes is called:
   a. Wernicke's
   b. Broca's
   c. Exner's
   d. Penfield's speech area

30. The area responsible for assemblage of information into intelligible speech is called
   a. Wernicke's
   b. Broca's
   c. Exner's
   d. Penfield's speech area

31. Wernicke's area is in the
   a. Right parietal-temporal cortex
   b. Left parietal-temporal cortex
   c, Basal ganglia
   d. Left frontal region

32. Broca's area is in the:
   a. Right parietal-temporal cortex
   b. Left parietal-temporal cortex
   c. Basal ganglia
   d. Left frontal region

33. Executive attention is believed to be, in part, organized by the:
   a. Right parietal-temporal cortex
   b. Anterior cingulate gyrus
   c. Thalamus
   d. Red nucleus

34. The *anterior perforated area* (APA) is an area which is perforated by small blood vessels which supply corpus striatum. This area forms the inferior medial part of the innominate substance of the lenticular nucleus. It borders posteriorly with the _____. The _____ is continuous anteriorly with the innominate and with the putamen. It is also connected to the *uncus*. In part the grey matter of the uncus is continuous with gray matter of the _____.
Anterior to the anterior perforated area, the lentiform nucleus joins the caudate.
The one correct nucleus to fill all of the blank spaces is the:
   a. substantia nigra
   b. locus coeruleus
   c. claustrum
   d. amygdala

35. Fibers connect the anterior perforated area, the septum, and the amygdala to the _____. The _____ lies below (inferior to) the thalamus and is continuous with the septal area and with the anterior perforated substance.
The one correct term to fill all of the blank spaces is the:
   a. substantia nigra
   b. locus coeruleus
   c. hypothalamus
   d. caudate

36. The _____ is critical in the regulation of blood pressure, pulse rate, body temperature and perspiration. It is involved in all the body homeostatic mechanisms. It is important in hunger, thirst, water balance, sexual behaviour and lactation. It is important for our biological clock and thus our circadian rhythms. It is, with the amygdala, an integral player in our fight or flight responses.
The one correct term to fill the blank space is the:
   a. substantia nigra
   b. locus coeruleus
   c. hypothalamus
   d. caudate

37. The cortex (gray matter) of the _____ has only three layers as compared to the neocortex which has 6 layers. At its anterior end this archicortex connects with the amygdala and the anterior perforated area. Posteriorly it is continuous with what is termed *entorhinal cortex* in the wall of the _____ sulcus and this gives rise to the fibers of the fornix that eventually connect with the hypothalamus. The *fornix* or 'arch' also connects the _____ with the anterior thalamic nuclei and the mammillary body. In addition, the _____ has connections with the frontal, parietal and temporal lobes.
The best term to fill all of the blank spaces is the:
   a. substantia nigra
   b. claustrum
   c. hippocampus
   d. putamen

38. The _____ has connections to the areas concerned with emotions, the autonomic nervous system, the endocrine system and consciousness. It plays a key role in the laying down of memories. It is the _____ that allows the animal to compare the present situation with past memories of similar situations. This is an important function for survival.
The best term to fill all of the blank spaces is the:
  a. substantia nigra
  b. claustrum
  c. hippocampus
  d. putamen

39. The subcallosal gyrus + the parolfactory area + the cingulate gyrus + the parahippocampal gyrus + the hippocampal formation together form the _____.
The best term to fill the blank space is the:
  a. substantia nigra
  b. claustrum
  c. limbic lobe
  d. putamen

40. The hippocampal cortex connects with the entorhinal cortex anterior to it and to the bulb of cortex there called the uncus which is continuous with the amygdala and the anterior perforated area. This entorhinal cortex is the origin of the _____. The _____ contains *commissural fibers* that cross to the other cerebral hemisphere allowing (hippocampal commissure) for connections between the right and left hippocampal formations.
The best term to fill the blank space is the:
  a. corpus callosum
  b. superior longitudinal fasciculus
  c. uncal fasciculus
  d. fornix

41. The cortex has *extrapyramidal motor* areas (premotor). The pathways from these areas have many intervening synapses in different areas of the motor system. These areas include the nuclei within the _____ (including the lenticular nucleus (putamen & globus pallidus)) which send fiber bundles to the *subthalamic* nucleus. The first bundle pierces the posterior limb of the internal capsule (lenticular fasciculus) and the second courses around the anterior border of the internal capsule (ansa (loop) lenticularis).
The best term to fill the blank space is the:
  a. cingulate gyrus
  b. hippocampus
  c. fornix
  d. corpus striatum

42. The neocortex has *extrapyramidal motor* areas (premotor). The pathways from these areas have many intervening synapses in different areas of the motor system. They course through some of the nuclei of the basal ganglia and descend to connect, in the midbrain, with the _____, the *substantia nigra,* and the *reticular formation* and from there descend to influence (extrapyramidal) the striated muscles.
The best term to fill the blank space is the:
  a. red nucleus
  b. hippocampus
  c. fornix
  d. corpus striatum

43. The voluntary motor pathways descend through the internal capsule to the *crus cerebri* on the lateral aspect of the diencephalon to become the *basis pedunculi* of the midbrain running in this basal or ventral position through the pons segment to become the _____ on the lateral surface of the medulla, from whence they enter the spinal cord and *cross over* to the opposite side to become the *lateral corticospinal tract.*
The best term to fill the blank space is the:
  a. inferior longitudinal fasciculus
  b. hippocampal formation
  c. fornix
  d. pyramid

44. The _____ are involved in executive functions: the voluntary control of attention, the inhibition of inappropriate and/or unwanted behaviour, the planning of actions and executive decision making. They have a role in the maintenance of arousal and the temporal sequencing of complex entities such as the expression of compound sentences.
The best term to fill the blank space is the:
  a. inferior posterior portion of the temporal lobes
  b. prefrontal areas of the cortex
  c. anterior portion of the parietal lobes
  d. the pyramid

45. The _____ is involved in speech, articulation and writing. It has a major role in auditory and verbal representation. Object naming and word recall requires activation in this area. It is also involved in the representation of visual images evoked by auditory input.
The best term to fill the blank space is the:
    a. left cerebral hemisphere
    b. right cerebral hemisphere
    c. fornix
    d. medial portion of the right temporal lobe

46. The _____ is important in sensing the Gestalt (image of something) and in parallel processing. It attends to spatial relationships. It is to a large extent responsible for the representation of geometric forms. It is also responsible for orientation in space and holistic perceptions.
The best term to fill the blank space is the:
    a. left cerebral hemisphere
    b. right cerebral hemisphere
    c. the angular gyrus
    d. medial portion of the left temporal lobe

47. _____ dominance is usually thought of as being characterized by distractibility, stimulus seeking behaviour, seeking novelty and change, being emotionally involved and expressive and extroverted. There may tend to be external locus of control. There may be more of a tendency for hysterical, impulsive and even manic behaviours. Processing tends to be fast and simultaneous in keeping with the Gestalt or holistic tendencies.
The best term to fill the blank space is the:
    a. left cerebral hemisphere
    b. right cerebral hemisphere
    c. left temporal lobe
    d. right temporal lobe

48. For the most part, the _____ controls the emotional aspects of language, such as the information conveyed by intonation.
 The best term to fill the blank space is the:
    a. left cerebral hemisphere
    b. right cerebral hemisphere
    c. left angular gyrus
    d. medial portion of the right occipital lobe

49. The area responsible for auditory processing and, on the medial aspect, for short term and working memory is?
    a. prefrontal areas of the frontal lobes
    b. hippocampal formation
    c. fornix
    d. temporal lobes

50. _____ dominance is usually thought of as being characterized by a lack of emotion, introversion, goal directed thinking and action with an internal locus of control. Processing may tend to be slow and serial in keeping with the tendency to be careful and sequential. The aptitudes tested on IQ tests are largely _____. The dominant neurotransmitter is dopamine.
The best term to fill the blank spaces is the:
    a. left cerebral hemisphere
    b. right cerebral hemisphere
    c. left temporal lobe
    d. right temporal lobe

51. Damage to the **right frontal lobe** can result in euphoria and emotional indifference. The affected person seems to ignore, and even be completely oblivious to, paralysis of their left side. The term used to describe this problem is:
    a. anosognosia
    b. associative visual agnosia
    c. prosopagnosia
    d. apperceptive agnosia

52. _____ means 'without action'. It is the inability to execute a learned movement. Constructional _____ refers to an inability to construct or even to draw an object. It is due to lesions in the right parietal cortex.
The best term to fill the blank space is the:
    a. agnosia
    b. apraxia
    c. alexia
    d. abulia

53. Understanding speech involves the inferior parietal lobe and the auditory association area of the superior temporal gyrus. If there is damage to this area speech will still be fluent with good grammar, but the person will **speak nonsense.** This area, which is important for understanding speech, is called:
    a. Jenson's area
    b. Wernicke's area
    c. Broca's area
    d. Exner's area

54. Damage to _____ interferes with the individual's ability to instruct the motor cortex and results in defects in the articulation of speech. Damage to this area and its **association areas** may result in the person being able to understand what has been said to him and being conscious of what he wants to say, but he **cannot say it**. This person may substitute staccato nouns and verbs so that the flow is lost and it sounds like a telegram. Ungrammatical speech and writing errors may be observed.

The best term to fill the blank space is the:

    a. Jenson's area
    b. Wernicke's area
    c. Broca's area
    d. Exner's area

55. The _____ is a region of one of the lobes of the brain. This region sits at the *occipital-parietal-temporal* junction behind (posterior to) the lateral fissure. It involves *visual-spatial-language* skills and therefore **visual word recognition.** This region in the left hemisphere, called the _____, is required for reading. Damage to this area can result in **alexia** (inability to read) and in **agraphia** (inability to write).

The best term to fill the blank space is the:

    a. medial aspect of the orbital cortex
    b. inferior lateral temporal gyrus
    c. angular gyrus
    d. cingulate gyrus

56. When a client has dyslexia the neurofeedback (NFB) training usually involves increasing the activation of certain areas of the cerebral hemispheres. This is done by increasing fast wave activity (low beta often between 13 and 19 Hz) and decreasing the dominant slow wave activity (theta or thalpha).

Two types of dyslexia, disphonetic (trouble sounding out) and diseidetic (trouble with visual processing of the letters) are approached differently in NFB. It is commonly suggested that, for diseidetic dyslexia you might first place your active electrode(s) at which of the following sites?

    a. Fp2 or F4 (sequential try F4-P4 or F8-P8 (T6)
    b. F3 or F5 (sequential try F3 – P3 or F7-P7 (T5)
    c. P3 or P5 (sequential try F3-P3 or F7-P7 (T5)
    d. O2 or T6 (sequential try P4-O2 or F4-O2

57. When a client has dyslexia the neurofeedback (NFB) training usually involves increasing the activation of certain areas of the cerebral hemispheres. This is done by increasing fast wave activity (low beta often between 13 and 19 Hz) and decreasing the dominant slow wave activity (theta or thalpha).

Two types of dyslexia, disphonetic (trouble sounding out) and diseidetic (trouble with visual processing of the letters) are approached differently in NFB. It is most commonly suggested that for disphonetic dyslexia, you place the active electrode(s) at which of the following sites?:

    a. Fp2 or F4 (sequential try F4-P4 or F8-P8 (T6)
    b. F3 or F5 (sequential try F3 – P3 or F7-P7 (T5)
    c. P3 or P5 (sequential try F3-P3 or F7-P7 (T5)
    d. O2 or T6 (sequential try P4-O2 or F4-O2

58. With Injury to the Visual Association Cortex the person can still see but will be unable to recognize objects unless they are able to touch them.

Injury to another portion of the Association Cortex can result in difficulties perceiving the shapes of objects that cannot be seen. Drawing or even following a map may become difficult. What is this part of the Association Cortex called?

    a. limbic
    b. temporal
    c. somatosensory
    d. supramarginal

59. In normal people the _____ gyrus specializes in the recognition of human faces. This _____ gyrus lies on the medial aspect of the temporal lobe between the parahippocampal gyrus above, and the inferior temporal gyrus below.

The name of this gyrus (and the best term to fill the blank spaces) is the:

    a. superior frontal gyrus
    b. inferior orbital gyrus
    c. fusiform gyrus
    d. supramarginal gyrus

60. The fusiform gyrus lies on the medial aspect of the temporal lobe between the parahippocampal gyrus above and the inferior temporal gyrus below. The fusiform gyrus has been show to be important for:

    a. hand writing
    b. speech
    c. recognition of faces
    d. integration of auditory inputs

61. The _____ comprises a bundle of long association fibers that lie within the cingulate and parahippocampal gyri. It is at the core of the limbic lobe. It is involved therefore, in the conscious perception of emotions. (A surgical procedure to remove tissue in this area (cingulotomy) could tame a wild animal. In humans cutting certain fibers in this area (cingulectomy) has been used to treat depression, anxiety and obsessive behaviour.)
The best term to fill the blank space is the:

    a. inferior longitudingal fasciculus
    b. superior longitudinal fasciculus
    c. uncal fasciculus
    d. cingulum

62. Connections between the ventral tegmental area of the mid brain through the medial forebrain bundle to the nucleus accumbens and the cortex are most often thought of as being involved in the experience of _____.
(The nucleus accumbens is a region of the basal forebrain adjacent to the septum and anterior to the preoptic area.)
The best term to fill the blank space is the:

    a. pain
    b. pleasure (reward)
    c. displeasure (aversion)
    d. rage

63. Neurofeedback studies have demonstrated that increasing alpha activity in the _____ compared to the other hemisphere, the so-called alpha asymmetry protocol, has a positive effect on depression. In this approach the alpha is used as an inverse indicator of activation.
The best term to fill the blank space is the:

    a. left frontal cortex
    b. right frontal cortex
    c left parietal cortex
    d. right parietal cortex

64. The arterial supply from the vertebral basilar system is linked with the internal carotid system in a 'circle' at the base of the midbrain and diencephalon.

    a. true
    b. false

65. The _____ nervous system is involved in processes that activate and expend energy (catabolic). The cell bodies of the _____ system are located in the thoracic and lumbar regions of the spinal cord. The axons exit through the ventral roots of the spinal cord. The majority if these preganglionic fibers synapse in ganglia in the _____ chain or trunk or in ganglia of the prevertibral plexus.
The best term to fill the blank spaces is:

    a. parasympathetic
    b. extrapyramidal motor
    c. corticospinal
    d. sympathetic

66. For the most part the _____ nervous system is involved in processes that inhibit and those that produce or conserve energy (anabolic). The nerves of the _____ system leave the CNS in cranial nerves 3, 7, 9, & 10 and in sacral nerves 2, 3, & 4. The cell bodies or ganglia of the _____ system are located in close to the organ which they supply.
The best term to fill the blank spaces is:

    a. parasympathetic
    b. extrapyramidal motor
    c. corticospinal
    d. sympathetic

67. The synapses within the _____ ganglia are acetylcholinergic. However, the terminal 'buttons' on the target organs are noradrenergic. An exception to this, which you might predict, is the innervation of the sweat glands which is acetylcholinergic.
The best term to fill the blank spaces is:

    a. parasympathetic
    b. extrapyramidal motor
    c. corticospinal
    d. sympathetic

68. The terminal buttons of both the pre and postganglionic fibers of the _____ system are acetylcholinergic.
The best term to fill the blank spaces is:

    a. parasympathetic
    b. basal ganglia
    c. locus coeruleus
    d. sympathetic

69. Episodic memory, or memory of a recent happening is easier to recall if associated with emotions. These conscious memories are stored like 'films', and are thought to be encoded and held for about 2 to 3 years in the _____. (The _____ is part of the limbic system. It is situated in the medial temporal lobe. Profound stress has been shown to have a detrimental effect on the_____. _____ memory includes working memory.

The best term to fill the blank spaces is:
    a. putamen
    b. hippocampus
    c. amygdaloid
    d. tegmentum

70. Alzheimer's Dementia is due primarily to deterioration of the_____. Recent memory is gone and these patients often can't find their way around and get lost.

The best term to fill the blank spaces is:
    a. putamen
    b. hippocampus
    c. amygdaloid
    d. tegmentum

71. The term_____ is applied to a condition found in alcoholics where there is an inability to form new memories (*anterograde amnesia*). The person can still recall old, long term memories. It is associated with deterioration of the mammillary bodies and the dorsomedial nuclei of the thalamus.

The best term to fill the blank spaces is:
    a. senile dementia
    b. Korsakoff's
    c. Alzheimer's
    d. amyotropic lateral sclerosis (ALS)

72. Some authors have hypothesized the following theoretical frame work for the production of excess theta in ADHD. Decreased blood flow to, and metabolic activity in the cells in the frontal / prefrontal areas (including the motor **cortex**) may *lead to r*educed excitation by the cortex (layer VI) of the inhibitory cells in the **putamen.** Two parallel pathways are then postulated. The first involves a direct effect of the putamen on the substantia nigra while the second is more indirect involving an external globus pallidus – subthalamus –(internal globus pallidus)-substantia nigra pathway. Either way,

the substantia nigra would be released to increase its inhibition of which thalamic nucleus or nuclei?
    a. ventral lateral (VL)
    b. ventral anterior (VA)
    c. centromedian (CM)
    d. all of the above

73. One hypothesis concerning a source of theta comes from animal (rat) studies and shows involvement of limbic areas. In these studies theta is said to be paced by _____pathways that project from the septal nuclei to the hippocampus. If true in humans this finding would correspond to the observed involvement of theta in memory retrieval. Recall of words corresponds to synchronization of theta. This is thought to represent hippocampal theta. Which type of neurotransmitter is, for the most part, found in this pathway?
    a. noradrenergic
    b. acetylcholinergic
    c. dopaminergic
    d. serotonergic

b. Neurophysiology:

74. For the most part, the process of myelinization in the cortex is generated by:
    a. Schwann cells
    b. Stellate cells
    c. Oligodendroglia cells
    d. Basket cells

75. Norepinephrine arises principally from neurons located in the locus coeruleus. It has connections through the medial-forebrain-bundle to the hypothalamus. Its primary excitatory function in the central nervous system (CNS) is related to arousal and attention. It is released during stress and may be a part of the fight or flight response. It is also thought to have a role in learning and the formation of memories. Too little norepinephrine may be associated with depression and too much with:
    a. mania.
    b. anxiety
    c. fear
    d. all of the above

76. Serotonin (5-hydroxy-trypamine [5-HT]) is produced in the brain stem and released by the Raphe nuclei. It is primarily an inhibitory neurotransmitter. It is involved in the regulation of pain, mood, appetite, sex drive and in falling asleep. It may also be involved in memory. It is a precursor for melatonin which, in turn, is important in biological rhythms. Low levels of serotonin are thought to be related to a number of psychiatric disorders including: obsessive compulsive disorder (OCD), aggression and:

    a. mania
    b. depression
    c. schizophrenia
    d. ADHD

77. The 'amino acids' group of neurotransmitters includes two inhibitory transmitters: gamma amino butyric acid (GABA) and glycine. It also includes glutamate and aspartate, which are an excitatory transmitters. The anxiolytic medications (benzodiazepines), alcohol, and barbiturates may exert their effects by potentiating the responses of GABA receptors. GABA will open both potassium and chloride channels and thus:

    a. hypopolarize the neuron
    b. hyperpolarize the neuron
    c. neutralize the neuron
    d. none of the above

78. Glutamate is important in learning and memory and in an important process called '*long term potentiation' (LTP)*. Long term potentiation is the process whereby which of the following is postulated to be occurring

    a. the post synaptic cell changes (is enhanced) in response to a constant stimulus such that it can depolarize more in response to a neurotransmitter
    b. depolarization of the post synaptic membrane due to glutamate
    c. an influx of Ca^{2+} results in the activation of other 'messenger' pathways and the release, by the post-synaptic cell of a '*paracrine*'
    d. all of the above

79. 'Neuropeptides' are short chains of amino acids. They are responsible for mediating sensory and emotional responses. The 'endorphins' are neuropeptides. They function at the same receptors that receive heroin and morphine and are thought of as naturally occurring analgesics and euphorics. They are found in the limbic system and the midbrain. The ventral tegmental area of the midbrain and the nucleus accumbens in the frontal lobe have this type of receptors called 'opiate' receptors.
Another neuropeptide '*Substance P*' mediates the perception of pain. Measurements of substance P in the cerebral spinal fluid (CSF) are assisting clinicians in the diagnostic work-up of persons suffering from pain associated with:

    a. phantom limb
    b. stroke
    c. fibromyalgia.
    d. Charcot Marie Tooth

80. Amphetamines and cocaine are catecholamine agonists. Their effect in the nucleus accumbens may be important in understanding the excitatory effects of these drugs and their ability to result in a chemical 'high'. (Alcohol, nicotine and caffeine can also increase one of the following neurotransmitters in this nucleus.) Which of the following statements is most true concerning the effect of amphetamines and cocaine:

    a. they increase the reuptake of dopamine and noradrenaline
    b. they block the reuptake of dopamine and noradrenaline
    c. they increase the effects of GABA (gamma amino butyric acid)
    d. they block the effect of serotonin at the post synaptic membrane

81. When cats are trained to increase their 12-15 Hz activity (SMR), which of the following is **NOT** true:

    a. There is an increase in the SMR in the baseline EEG.
    b. There is a reliable increase in sleep spindle density and decreased awakenings during non-REM sleep.
    c. Activity in the polysynaptic digastric muscle is reduced. (This is the jaw opening muscle and it lacks muscle spindle afferents.)
    d. Neck muscle activity is suppressed in strict association with emergence of the sensorimotor rhythm (SMR).

82. The suppression of neck muscle activity in cats, without posture change and occurring abruptly just prior to the appearance of SMR bursts (12 to 15 Hz.), suggests there is:

a. a specific reduction in muscle tone

b. a change in length of the innervated muscle

c. a change in gamma motor neuron activity

d. a & c

83. It has been demonstrated in cats that, during SMR activity;

a. cell discharge rates in the red nucleus are suppressed.

b. ventrobasal thalamic nucleus firing bursts increase

c. the thalamus produces synchronized, recurrent activity bursts which are observed in the EEG as 12-14 Hz spindles.

d. All of the above

84. It has been demonstrated in cats that during SMR activity;

a. ventrobasal (VB) thalamic relay cells change their behavior to recurrent, oscillatory bursting.

b. bursting discharge of the ventrobasal thalamic cells results in hyperpolarization of the relay cells

c. there is attenuation (decrease) of the conduction of somatosensory information to the cortex.

d. all of the above

85. During SMR activity there is:

a. decreased motor excitability

b. decreased motor reflex excitability

c. decreased muscle tone

d. all of the above

86. Motionlessness in the context of attention produces altered motor output to thalamus and brainstem resulting in:

a. decreased red nucleus activity

b. decreased stretch reflex activity

c. decreased muscle tone

d. all of the above

87. Operant conditioning to increase SMR (12-14 Hz activity) can:

a. produce sustained changes with respect to increased sleep spindle density.

b. destabilize sleep states

c. inhibit ruminative thinking

d. all of the above

88. Epileptic syndromes have in common the favouring of recurrent abnormal and excessive synchronous discharge in neuronal populations. Therefore effective intervention, such as operant conditioning of SMR (12 to 14 Hz.), might be expected to:

a. reduce neuronal excitability in relevant tissues

b. blunt the impact of transient neuronal discharge

c. stabilize state characteristics

d. all of the above

89. When an action potential depolarizes the membrane of an axon's presynaptic terminal it triggers the influx of a cation which initiates a series of steps culminating in the release of neurotransmitter into the synaptic space. This cation is:

a. K+

b. Na+

c. Ca+

d. Mg+

90. If you think that you may be observing the wicket shape of a mu rhythm at C3 or C4, but you are not sure, then you can test to see if it can be suppressed by voluntary movement such as closing the fist on the opposite side of the body from the observed rhythm or by asking the client to open their eyes and watching to see if the rhythm disappears. Mu doesn't disappear when the client opens their eyes.

Testing to see if the rhythm is mu or alpha is important because:

    a. mu rhythm indicates a seizure disorder

    b. mu rhythm indicates a space occupying lesion

    c. If the rhythm doesn't disappear and is of high amplitude it could be alpha and correspond to difficulties with attention span

    d. mu rhythm is usually observed at Pz and is not observed at C3 and C4.

91. A wicket shape rhythm at frequency of about 7-11 Hz at C3 and/or C4, which is suppressed by voluntary movement such as closing the fist on the opposite side of the body from the observed rhythm and which is not suppressed by asking the client to open their eyes and watching to see if the rhythm disappears, is called?

    a. lambda

    b. K-complex

    c. alpha

    d. mu

c. Neurophysiology – Nerve Transmission - Origin Of The EEG

92. The speed of transmission in a nerve fiber is increased by:

    a. increased axon diameter

    b. *salutatory* conduction

    c. myelinization

    d. all of the above

93. For the most part, the process of myelinization in the peripheral nervous system is associated with:

    a. Schwann cells

    b. Stellate cells

    c. Oligodendroglia cells

    d. Basket cells.

94. In the spinal cord, brain stem and mid brain as opposed to the cerebral hemispheres the white matter is:

    a. medial to the gray matter

    b. lateral to the grey matter

    c. mixed fairly evenly with the gray matter

    d. none of the above

95. Comparing EEG and magnetic resonance imaging (MRI) techniques, which of the following is true?

    a. the EEG has better temporal resolution than MRI.

    b. MRI has less spatial resolution

    c. traditional EEG procedures and MRI have about the same spatial resolution

    d. none of the above

                            c.

96. If thalamo-cortical connections are cut, the brain is most likely to produce:

    a. delta

    b. theta

    c. alpha

    d. beta

97. Changes in cortical loops (patterns of firing - connecting - among neurons) can change the firing rate of thalamic pacemakers and hence change their intrinsic firing pattern. It is also noted (Lubar) that changes in this intrinsic firing pattern may correspond to changes in mental state. This process may be facilitated by:

    a. learning

    b. emotion

    c. neurofeedback

    d. all of the above

98. The pyramidal cells and their surrounding support cells (stellate and basket cells) are arranged in groups. Each vertical column contains hundreds of pyramidal cells. The columns are parallel to each other and at right angles to the surface of the cortex. Many adjacent groups may receive the same afferent axonal input and thus fire in unison allowing for a sufficiently large potential to be measurable at the surface of the scalp. These 'groups' may be called:

    a. pyramidal formations

    b. cortical loops

    c. macrocolumns

    d. oligodendroglial resonant groups

99. A standard electrode on the scalp measures the activity of what area of cortex underneath it:
   a. 0.5 cm^2
   b. 2 cm^2
   c. 6 cm^2
   d. 12 cm^2

100. The cortex works in terms of three major resonant loops. They are:
1. Local: This loop of electrical activity is between macrocolumns. It appears to be responsible for high frequency, (> 30Hz), gamma activity.
2. Regional: This loop of electrical activity is between macrocolumns which are several centimeters apart. It appears that this activity is in the range of intermediate frequencies: alpha and beta.
3. Global: This loop of electrical activity is between widely separated areas, for example, frontal-parietal and frontal-occipital regions. Areas can be 7 cm apart. The activity produced is in the slower frequency range of delta and theta activity.
All three of these resonant loops:
   a. can not operate independently of thalamic pacemakers
   b. can operate spontaneously or be driven by thalamic pacemakers.
   c. only operate as independent entities without thalamic pacing.
   d. can only operate with the influence of thalamic and other diencephalic and midbrain pace-making activity

101. The wicket shape of a mu rhythm is usually observed at
   a. F3 and/or F4
   b. C3 and/or C4
   c. P3 and/ or P4
   d. O1 and/or O2

102. If you observe the wicket shape of a mu rhythm at C3 or C4, you can check if it is truly a mu rhythm by observing if it can be:
   a. increased in amplitude when the client closes their fist on the opposite side of the body to the observed rhythm
   b. decreased in amplitude when the client closes their fist on the same side of the body to the observed rhythm
   c. increased in amplitude when the client closes their fist on the same side of the body to the observed rhythm
   d. decreased in amplitude when the client closes their fist on the opposite side of the body to the observed rhythm

103. In broad general terms the approximate percent of communication activity in the human brain is:
   a. 50% between cortical areas and 30% thalamo-cortical
   b. >90% between cortical areas and 5% thalamo-cortical
   c. 20% between cortical areas and 60% thalamo-cortical
   d. 45% between cortical areas and 45% thalamo-cortical

104. On the recorded EEG, similarly appearing waves occurring at the same moment in time at non-adjacent sites probably originate from the same generator. If there is a time delay then this probably indicates:

   a. a synapse and therefore a different cellular origin.
   b. cellular damage
   c. a space occupying lesion
   d. an arterio-venous malformation

105. It has been noted (Lubar), "Neocortical states associated with strong corticocortical coupling are called hypercoupled and are associated with global or regional resonant modes." Hypercoupling means that there are large resonant loops. Biochemically it appears that the dominant neurotransmitter in this type of coupling is:
   a. dopamine
   b. acetylcholine
   c. serotonin
   d. noradrenalin

106. Corticocortical hypercoupling is said to be appropriate for states such as:
   a. focused attention
   b. reading & math
   c. hypnosis & sleep
   d. none of the above

107. Corticocortical <u>hypocoupling</u> is associated with small regional and local resonant loops and thus higher frequencies. Biochemically it appears that the neurotransmitters principally involved in this type of coupling are:
    a. acetylcholine, norepinephrine, and dopamine.
    b. acetylcholine, and gamma amino butyric acid (GABA)
    c. serotonin, GABA, and dopamine
    d. noradrenalin, glycine and serotonin

108. Corticocortical hypocoupling is said to be appropriate for:
    a. complex mental activity and increased attention.
    b. rapid eye movement (REM) sleep
    c. hypnosis and meditation
    d. Stage III sleep

d. Waveforms and the EEG Spectrum - Correspondence of Band Widths To Mental States

109. The transformation from the *time related domain* of the raw EEG to the *frequency domain* for statistics is carried out by a mathematical calculation that is based on the fact that any signal can be described as a combination of sine and cosine waves of various phases, frequencies and amplitudes. The breaking apart of a complex wave into its component sine waves may be called a:
    a. Nyquist principle
    b. Fast Fourier Transform (FFT)
    c. common average referencing
    d. Helmholtz solution

110. Observing the spectrum of an EEG recording (Fast Fourier Transform (FFT)) without the raw EEG may be deceptive because:
    a. the FFT shows too many artifacts
    b. a few very high amplitude waves may give the same value as extensive lower amplitude bursts of the same frequency
    c. low amplitudes on the FFT may correspond to a combination of muscle and eye blink artifacts
    d. all of the above

111. Morphology of a waveform refers to:
    a. the amplitude of a wave
    b. the power of a wave
    c. the shape of a wave
    d. the ratio of positive to negative power of the wave

112. A *complex* wave form is:
    a. usually monophasic but not triphasic
    b. a sequence of 2 or more waves which is repeated and recurs with a reasonably consistent shape
    c. a sequence of 6 or more waves which is repeated and recurs with a reasonably consistent shape
    d. a sequence of 2 or more waves which is repeated and recurs with an inconsistent shape and amplitude

113. A "transient" wave is one that stands out as:
    a. similar to the background activity of most of the EEG
    b. pathological
    c. different against the background EEG.
    d. evidence of a seizure disorder

114. Waves of similar morphology and frequency that are not in phase may be said to have a time delay. This delay may be expressed as a *phase angle*. If the peaks point in opposite directions it would be called a *phase reversal* and the peaks would have a phase angle of:
    a. 45°
    b. 90°
    c. 180°
    d. 360°

115. If the same kind of waves occurred simultaneously on both sides of the head (different channels) and in a constant time relationship they would be said to be:
    a. out of phase and asynchronous
    b. in phase and bisynchronous
    c. asymmetrical
    d. lateralized

116. Normal alpha rhythm frequency should exceed 8 Hz. Its amplitude may be higher on the right but the right to left difference should not exceed:
    a. 1.5 times
    b. 2 times
    c. 2.5 times
    d. 3 times

117. If alpha never exceeds 8 Hz in an adult this is probably abnormal and a difference of 1Hz in frequency of the dominant alpha rhythm between the two hemispheres indicates an abnormality
    a. in the basal ganglia
    b. in the hemisphere with the higher frequency
    c. in the hemisphere with the lower frequency
    d. in the ipsilateral locus coeruleus

118. Normal alpha rhythm is found predominantly in which region:
    a. anterior (frontal)
    b. central
    c. lateral (temporal)
    d. posterior (occipital)

119. Beta activity is found >13 Hz in adults. It is almost always a sign of normal cortical functioning. Asymmetry in beta between hemispheres should be no more than a certain percentage of the amplitude of the side with the higher amplitude. If the difference is greater than this then the side with the lower amplitude may be abnormal. What percent difference is the maximum allowable before it may be considered abnormal:
    a. 10%
    b. 22%
    c. 35%
    d. 50%

120. Amplification is rated in terms of *sensitivity* and *gain*. Thus amplifiers have known *sensitivities* which are recorded as a number of $\mu v/mm$. The need to use a higher sensitivity indicates:
    a. low amplitude recording
    b. high amplitude recording
    c. higher frequency waves will be exaggerated
    d. the low-pass filter will function abnormally

121. 'Gain' refers to a ratio of the voltage of a signal at the output of the amplifier to the voltage of the signal at the *input* of that amplifier. Thus a gain of $10V / 10\mu v = 1$ million. You will see *gain* mentioned in the specifications for your amplifier. It will probably be recorded in *decibels*. A gain of 1 million (or 10^6) is
    a. 20 decibels
    b. 60 decibels
    c. 120 decibels
    d. 200 decibels

122. Wave forms characteristic of an absence (petit mal) seizure are:
    a. bursts of high amplitude spikes followed by spike and wave complexes
    b. focal bursts of 2 per second spike and wave 'pairs'
    c. generalized 3 per second spike and wave 'pairs'
    d. uniform 6 per second spike and wave 'pairs'

123. Sharp waves do not have as sharp a point as 'spikes'. They have a duration of:
    a. 30-70 ms
    b. 70-200 ms
    c. 100 –300 ms
    d. 200-400 ms

124. *Complexes* containing spikes and sharp waves which are repeated may represent *interictal* (between seizures) epileptiform activity.
    a. true
    b. false

125. The term 'paroxysmal hypnogogic hypersynchrony' refers to synchronous, slightly notched, sine waves that are higher in amplitude than surrounding waves and run at about 3-5 Hz. The burst may last for a couple of seconds. This type of wave:
    a. indicates a seizure disorder
    b. is a warning of a space occupying lesion
    c. may be observed in normal children when they are sleepy
    d. is a particularly prominent finding in Asperger's syndrome

126. Sleep spindles look like SMR spindles and are in the same frequency range: 12-15 Hz. Like SMR they are maximal over the central regions. Apparently they arise from a different generator. They are frequently observed:
    a. only in sleep (stage II)
    b. during sleep and during physical exercise
    c. only in rapid eye movement (REM) sleep
    d. in autistic children both when awake and asleep

127. K complexes are sharp, negative, high amplitude waves followed by a longer duration positive wave. They are seen:
    a. in rapid eye movement (REM) sleep
    b. in stage II sleep
    c. in ADHD children when awake
    d. as interictal activity in seizure disorders

128. The tentorium is a large in-folding of dura matter (connective tissue) separating:
    a. the two cerebral hemispheres
    b. the cerebellum below from the cerebrum above
    c. the corpus callosum from the diencephalon
    d. the precentral gyrus from the postcentral gyrus

129. Deep lesions (e.g., in the internal capsule) generally demonstrate:
    a. focal delta
    b. hemispheric or bilateral delta.
    c. focal beta spindling
    d. diffuse beta spindling

130. In an alert resting adult delta waves may appear intermittently in bursts and be higher in amplitude than surrounding wave forms. This phenomenon may be due to:
    a. diffuse white matter damage
    b. diffuse gray matter damage
    c. dopamine overactivity
    d. noradrenergic overactivity

131. In relative terms, the communication going on in our brain between cortical areas compared to to thalamo-cortical connections is, in very general terms, approximately:
    a. cortical-cortical 5 % - thalamo-cortical 90 %
    b. cortical-cortical 50% - thalamo-cortical 40 %
    c. cortical-cortical 25 % - thalamo-cortical 70 %
    d. cortical-cortical 90 % - thalamo-cortical 5 %

132. Which of the following is a mathematical process which looks at surface EEG information and infers what activity is occurring in areas a little deeper in the cortex.
    a. PET (Positron Emission Tomography)
    b. MRI (Magnetic Resonance Imaging)
    c. LORETA (low resolution electro-magnetic tomographic assessment)
    d. SPECT (Single Photon Emission Computerized Tomography)

133. An event related potential (ERP) is a measure of:
a. brain electrical activity which occurs as a response to a specific stimulus.
b. spontaneous and on-going activity of the brain..

c. a brain response unrelated to any specific stimulus
d. a brain response that is time-independent

134. With Attention Deficit Disorder the slowing of the EEG parallels decreased _____ recorded by Positron Emission Tomography (PET scans) and decreased blood flow on Single Photon Emission Computerized Tomography (SPECT) scans in the frontal region. The best phrase to fill the above blank is:
    a. PCO_2 levels
    b. glucose metabolism
    c. adensoine triphosphate (ATP) levels
    d. creatinine metabolism

5. EEG and Electrophysiology
Required Hours: 8

135. A microvolt is:
    a. One tenth of a volt
    b. One hundredth of a volt
    c. One thousandth of a volt
    d. One millionth of a volt

a. Wave forms - Morphology
136. In which age group is theta the dominant wave form?
    a. 3 - 7 years
    b. 8 - 16 years
    c. 17 - 23 years
    d. 24 - 30 years

137. Match the appropriate frequency band in column 1 (letter "a" to "j") with the best description of expected corresponding mental state in column 2 by putting the appropriate letter from column 1 beside the answer in column 2. Example:

| a. butter is placed on: | Hamburgers(b) |
| b. relish is placed on: | bread (a) |

Column 1	Column 2
a. delta activity, 0.5 –3 Hz	- found in sleep and also in conjunction with learning disabilities and brain injury.
b. Theta waves 4-7 Hz	- seen in drowsy, states which are also states in which some quite creative thoughts may occur.
c. Low alpha, 8-10 Hz	
d. High alpha, 11-12 Hz	
e. Sensorimotor rhythm frequencies, 13 – 15Hz over the sensorimotor cotex.	- may correspond to jaw, scalp, neck or facial muscle activity
f. Low Beta waves, 13-15 and 16-20 Hz,	- found in dissociative states, some kinds of meditation, and tuning out from external stimuli (daydreaming).
g. higher beta frequencies (20-23 Hz)	- often called 'Sheer' rhythm or a 'binding' rhythm. Corresponds to cognitive activity
h. 24- 33 Hz	-can be found associated with creative reflection as well as relaxed calm states of optimal performance.
i. 38-42 Hz	
j. 52-58 Hz	
Note: There is overlap in the frequency bands (theta is often defined as 4-8 Hz, for example but experts often use 4-7 or 3-7 Hz) and there are also shifts with age, moving to the right along the spectrum. In young children, for example, alpha wave forms may be found at a frequency of 7 Hz.	- implies being motorically calm with reflection before action.
	-associated with singular focus, external orientation and problem solving
	- may be elvated with anxiety
	- may be associated with rumination

138. Increased activity around 40 Hz (39-41 Hz) has been found experimentally to be associated with:

a. dissociation
b. catching one's balance
c. intense emotion
d. advancing age

139. The beta frequency range, 38 – 42 Hz, is sometimes referred to as 'Sheer' rhythm after David Sheer who did some work in the 1970's concerning enhancing 40 Hz activity. One of the effects of raising this particular rhythm has been observed to correspond to:

a. decreased learning capacity
b. improving attention where the subject is bringing together different (binding) aspects of an object into a single percept
c. increased appetite
d. low muscle artifact activity

140. 'Beta spindling' refers to bursts of beta waves in a rising and falling spindle-like pattern. Although it can be less than 20 Hz, most spindles involve fast beta, above 20 Hz. They can be associated with epileptic auras. It may be due to a disease process and cortical irritability. It can be seen in ADHD and in obsessive compulsive disorders. When neurofeedback (NFB) is used for this pattern the logical NFB intervention would be to:

a. counterbalance the increased hi-beta amplitude on one side of the head by training up the same frequency of beta at the corresponding site on the opposite side
b. train down that range of beta in the area involved
c. nullify the effects of this disproportionate beta activity by training up theta rhythm on the same site
d. counterbalance the effects of this disproportionate beta activity by training up alpha rhythm on the same side.

141. **Mu** waves may fool you. They look like alpha waves and are usually found in the 7-11 Hz frequency range. They are usually observed at C3 and C4. When the subject opens their eyes:
    a. both alpha and Mu are blocked
    b. alpha is reduced but Mu will remain in the central region
    c. frontal alpha is increased and Mu disappears from the central region
    d. occipital alpha remains steady and Mu will increase in the central region

142. **Spikes:** These waves have a duration of :
    a. 10 –20 ms
    b. 20-70 ms
    c. 70-100 ms
    d. 90-120 ms

143. *Focal epileptiform* activity often consists of localized spikes and sharp waves. This activity may be surrounded by irregular slower waves or followed by an aftergoing slow wave. Focal spike and sharp waves may appear before and after a generalized discharge. These spikes and sharp waves are:
    a. always generalized and seen throughout all channels
    b. are generally just observed in a single channel
    c. are often seen just in a few neighbouring electrodes
    d. are most often seen at Cz and Fz

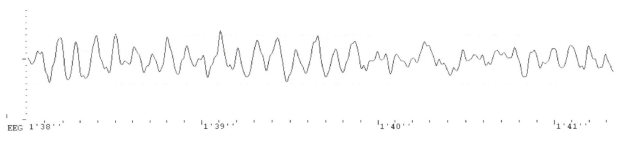

144. The dominant wave form in the first one second above is:
    a. delta
    b. theta
    c. alpha
    d. beta

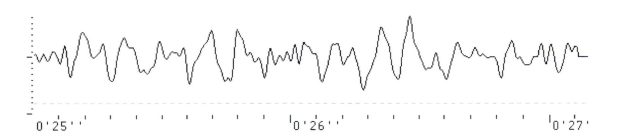

145. The dominant wave form in the first one second above is:
    a. delta
    b. theta
    c. alpha
    d. beta

Eyes open looking at a dot.

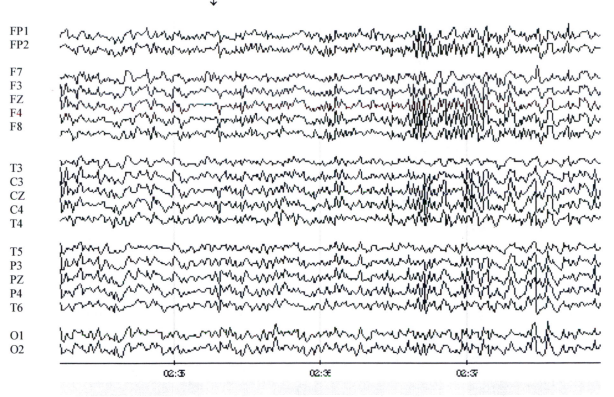

146. In the figure above, the group of waves in the prefrontal and frontal leads, under the arrow, that are higher in amplitude than the foregoing EEG, are called:

    a. alpha
    b. spike and wave
    c. sharp waves
    d. Sheer rhythm

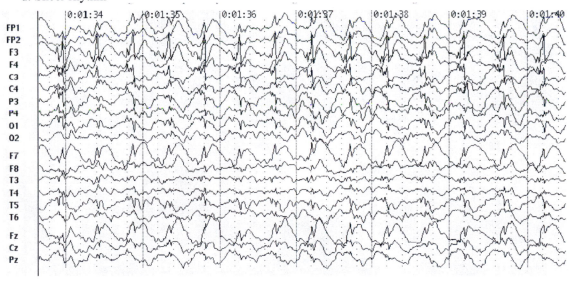

147. The group of waves seen best at F3, are called:

    a. alpha
    b. spike and wave
    c. sharp waves
    d. beta

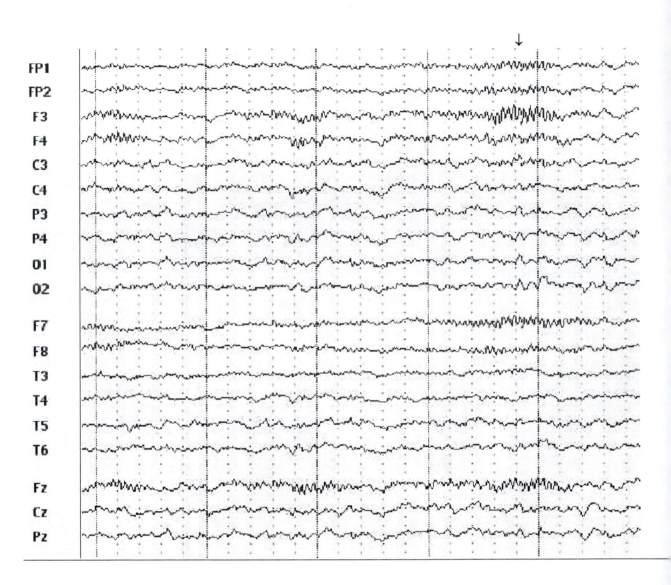

148. The wave group seen best at F3, under the arrow, is termed:
    a. spike and wave
    b. epileptiform spike paroxysm
    c. alpha transient
    d. beta spindling

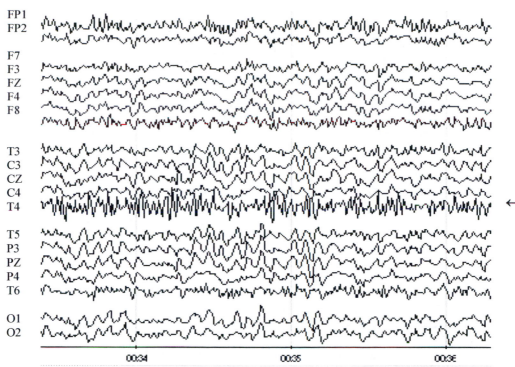

149. The waves observed at T4 are most likely:

a. epileptiform spikes

b. absence seizure waves

c. muscle artifact

d. paroxysmal burst of fast beta

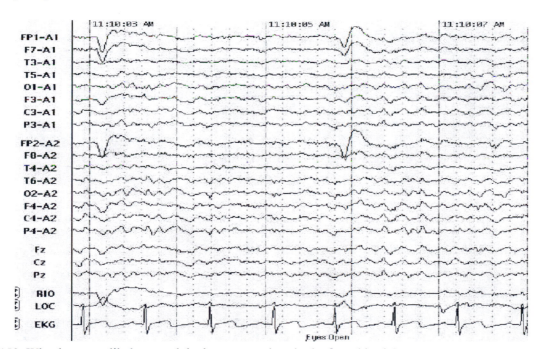

150. What has most likely caused the large excursions in the frontal leads?

    a. muscle tension

    b. raising the eye brows

    c. eye blink

    d. myoclonic seizure bursts

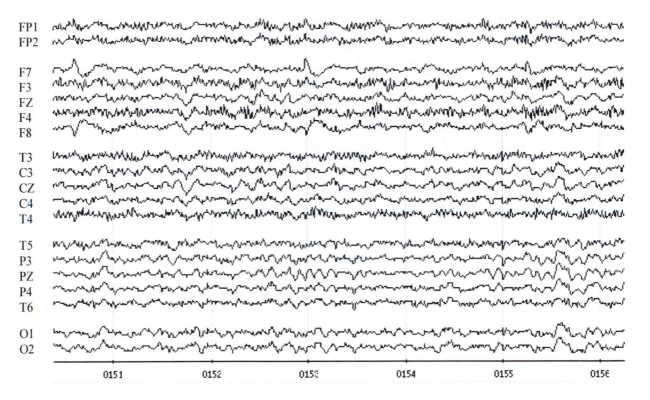

| | 0151 | 0152 | 0153 | 0154 | 0155 | 0156 |

151. In F7 and F8 large deviations of the wave pattern are seen just prior to 0151 and again at 0153. These are most likely due to:

    a. eye blink

    b. isolated absence seizure (petit mal) bursts

    c. lateral eye movement when reading

    d. digastric muscle movement

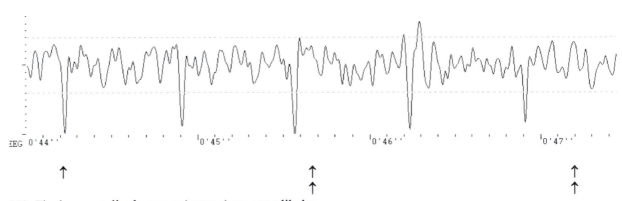

152. The large amplitude waves (arrows) are most likely:

    a. absence seizure activity

    b. eye movement

    c. cardiac artifact

    d. muscle activity when speaking

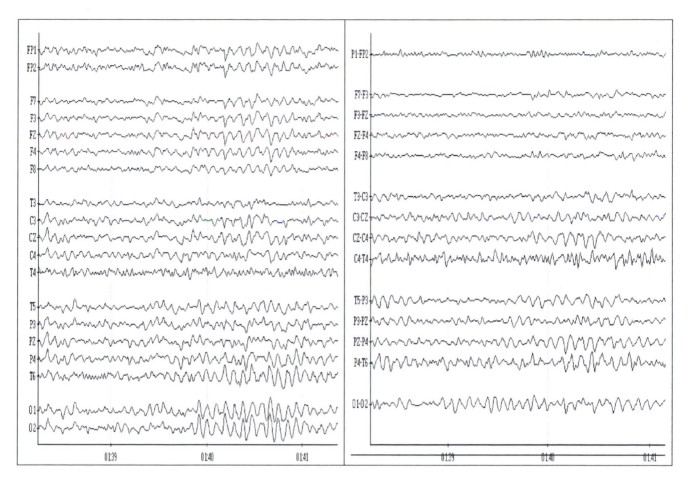

153. The referential and sequential montages above show the same patient's EEG at the same moment in time. The origin of the activity observed in the FP1 and FP2 leads (below the arrow) most likely should be interpreted as being evidence of:

    a. prefrontal theta
    b. prefrontal alpha
    c. temporal alpha
    d. paroxysmal alpha bursting

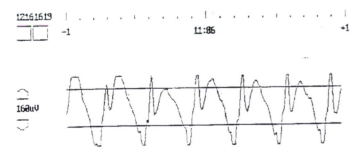

Amplitude > 160 µV, Two seconds of recording in a single channel referential recording, Cz to the left ear with right ear ground.

154. The wave form observed above is most likely the result of:

    a. grand mal seizure
    b. partial complex seizure
    c. absence seizure
    d. evenness suggesting an electrical artifact

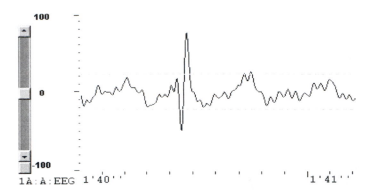

1A:A:EEG 1'40''   '1'41''

The electrode was placed 1 cm above a point, 1/3 of the way along a line drawn from external ear canal to the lateral canthus of the eye in a patient with a known partial complex seizure disorder. (This is an appropriate placement for picking up interictal activity). There were no similar waves in the next 10 seconds of the recording. The reference was to linked ears.

155. The very large amplitude wave is most likely:
    a. spike indicating a possible seizure disorder
    b. sharp wave transient
    c. lateral rectus muscle spike
    d. wave representing myoclonic seizure activity

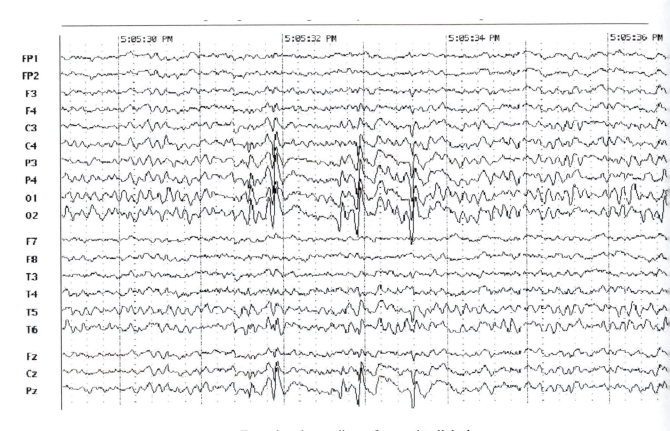

Eyes closed recording referenced to linked ears.

156. The bursts of higher amplitude waves are most likely:
    a. absence seizure complexes
    b. normal alpha wave bursts
    c. lateral rectus muscle spikes
    d. epileptiform paroxysmal discharge

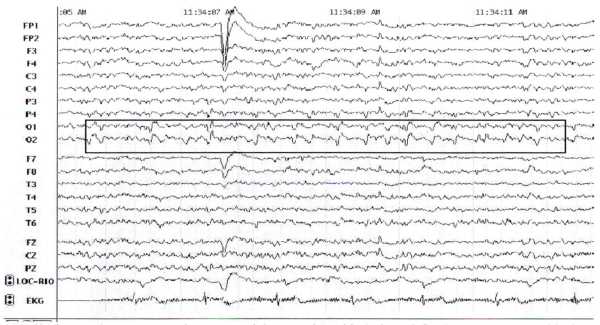

157. The box encloses an area where repeated downward (positive) sharp deflections are seen repetitively in the occipital leads. Which of the following is the best term that could describe these:

    a. mu waves

    b. lambda

    c. absence seizure complexes

    d. eye movement artifact

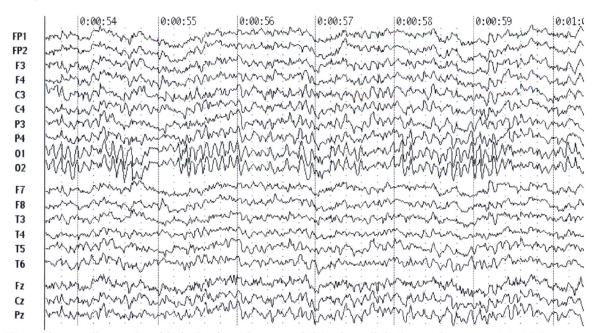

158. In this recording made with the Lexicor Neurosearch 24 using a linked ear reference and the high pass filter on, the large rolling excursions observed particularly in the prefrontal leads are most likely due to:

    a. raising the eyebrows

    b. sweat artifact

    c. repetitive eye blinking

    d. eye movement with reading

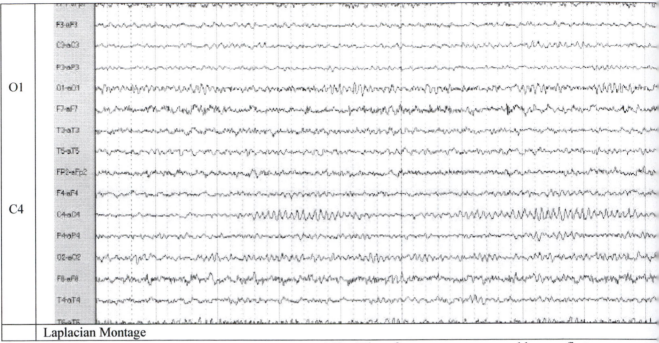

O1	F3-aF3
	C3-aC3
	P3-aP3
	O1-aO1
	F7-aF7
	T3-aT3
	T5-aT5
C4	FP2-aFp2
	F4-aF4
	C4-aC4
	P4-aP4
	O2-aO2
	F8-aF8
	T4-aT4
	T6-aT6

Laplacian Montage

159. In the EEG (Laplacian montage) above, note the wicket shape activity at C4. This type of activity is termed:

    a. lambda

    b. mu

    c. sharp wave transient

    d. paroxysm

160 a. Deep lesions (e.g., in the internal capsule) are likely to produce:

    a. focal delta

    b. hemispheric or bilateral delta.

    c. focal beta spindling

    d. diffuse beta spindling

160 b. Superficial lesions in the cerebral cortex are likely to produce:

    a. focal delta

    b. hemispheric or bilateral delta.

    c. focal beta spindling

    d. diffuse beta spindling

161. In the awake subject what would sudden, brief, increases in frontal 1 to 2 Hz activity usually represent?

    a. muscle tension in the jaw or neck muscles

    b. increased problem solving cognitive activity

    c. eye blink

    d. a meditative state

162. What frequency range would you first expect to see increasing with muscle tension in the jaw, neck, or forehead?

    a. 4 - 8 Hz

    b. 8 - 12 Hz

    c. 13 - 17 Hz

    d. 18 - 25 Hz

163. When a sequential placement is used with electrodes at site A and site B on the scalp; a decrease in 4-8 Hz (theta) activity, measured in microvolts, could result from:

    a. A decrease in 4-8 Hz voltage of the same magnitude at both sites, A and B.

    b. A disproportionate increase in 9-12 Hz (alpha) activity.

    c. Site A is more in phase with site B.

    d. Movement artifact affecting both sites equally

164. Which sites, using the 10-20 electrode placement system, would show the highest levels of sensorimotor rhythm (SMR) activity during eyes open conditions:

    a. F3 & F4

    b. C3 & C4

    c. P3 & P4

    d. O1 & O2   c.

165. Which sites, using the 10-20 electrode placement system, would show the highest levels of alpha rhythm activity (8-12 Hz) during eyes closed conditions:
    a. F3 & F4
    b. C3 & C4
    c. P3 & P4
    d. O1 & O2

166. When you reinforce 12-15 Hz activity at C4 what types of brain wave activity are you encouraging?
    a. sensorimotor rhythm (SMR), high alpha and gamma
    b. high alpha and ipsilon spindles
    c. sensorimotor rhythm (SMR), high alpha and low beta
    d. sensorimotor rhythm (SMR), 'J' complexes and desynchronous beta

167. 15 minutes sound and light stimulation in an alpha frequency may result in the following frontal EEG changes 30 minutes after the stimulation has ceased:
    a. Increased Theta 4 - 8 Hz
    b. Increased Alpha 8-12 Hz
    c. Decreased Alpha 8-12 Hz
    d. Increased Beta 13-21 Hz

168. 15 minutes sound and light stimulation in twice the dominant frequency (usually beta 20-21 Hz), has been shown to result in the following frontal EEG changes 30 minutes after the stimulation has ceased:
    a. Increased Theta 4 - 8 Hz
    b. Increased Alpha 8-12 Hz
    c. Decreased Alpha 8-12 Hz
    d. Increased Beta 13-21 Hz.

b. Electrophysiology:

169. In the resting state, neurons have what is called a *resting potential*. The resting potential represents the potential difference between the inside and the outside of the cell. When at rest this potential inside the cell is about how many millivolts (mV):
    a. – 20 mV
    b. + 20 mV
    c. –70 mV.
    d. + 70 mV

170. *The EEG is defined as the difference in voltage between two different recording locations plotted over time.* The pyramidal cell postsynaptic potentials from large groups of cortical pyramidal cells form an *extracellular dipole layer*. The EEG is generated by the synchronous activity of postsynaptic:
    a. inhibitory potentials
    b. excitatory potentials
    c. inhibitory and excitatory potentials
    d. action potentials generated by the pyramidal cells

171. Action potentials which travel down the axons or dendrites of these cortical cells have a very short time duration (1ms). Postsynaptic potentials have a long time duration (15-200 ms). These potential changes summate and the EEG records the potential (+ve or –ve) directed towards the electrode on the surface of the scalp. The charge will differ depending on whether an excitatory post synaptic potential (EPSP) or inhibitory post synaptic potential (IPSP) has been generated in the area of the cortex beneath the electrode. To obtain a reliable scalp EEG recording how many cm^2 of cortex with predominantly synchronous activity is necessary?
    a. $0.5\ cm^2$
    b. $2\ cm^2$
    c. $6\ cm^2$
    d. $10\ cm^2$

172. *The influx of sodium into the neuron at the postsynaptic membrane site makes for what is known as an active sink at the level of the synaptic input from another cell's axon.*
If the simultaneous discharges of axon terminals results in excitatory post synaptic potentials (EPSPs) at the distal end of a sufficient number of adjacent pyramidal cell dendrites, what charge would be detected by a scalp electrode placed over that area of the cortex and referenced to a second neutral site?
    a. negative
    b. positive

173. The pyramidal cells and their surrounding support cells and stellate and basket cells are arranged in groups called macrocolumns. In a macrocolumn neurons are arranged in a group of cells several mm in diameter and 4-6 layers deep. Each vertical column contains hundreds of pyramidal cells. The columns are parallel to each other and at right angles to the surface of the cortex. Each pyramidal cell may have thousands of synapses. The EEG electrode is detecting electrical activity from:

    a. single pyramidal cells

    b. the extracellular charge surrounding one macrocolumn

    c. the action potentials produced by the pyramidal cells of many adjacent macrocolumns that receive the same afferent axonal input and thus fire in unison.

    d. the extracellular charge surrounding the tips of the dendrites (near the scalp) of many adjacent macrocolumns.

174. Anatomically it has been found that, of the fibers entering the gray matter of a hemisphere in the cerebral cortex, the percentage that arise from the thalamus is:

    a. less than 5 %

    b. about 10 %

    c. about 15 %

    d. greater than 25 %

175. Which of the following statements about coherence is NOT correct:

    a. Coherence is a measure of shared activity at two different locations

    b. Coherence between two sites can be evidence of a functional connection between cortical areas.

    c. As coherence increases within an interhemispheric region, it will also increase between the intrahemispheric regions.

    d. Decreased frontal coherences may be related to increased cortical differentiation

176. Hypocoupling favors small regional and local cortical loops which lead to faster frequencies, including beta and gamma (especially 40 Hz.) activity, which are said to be important for detailed information acquisition, complex mental activity and increased attention. Such hypocoupling may be related to an increase in which neurotransmitter(s):

    a. Acetylcholine, Norepinephrine and Serotonin,

    b. Norepinephrine, Dopamine and Serotonin

    c. Acetylcholine, Dopamine, and Norepinephrine

    d. Acetylcholine, Dopamine, and Serotonin

177. Hypercoupling of large resonant loops which leads to slower frequencies, sleep spindles, theta and delta activity, and decreased attention, is related to an increase in which neurotransmitter?

    a. Serotonin,

    b. Dopamine,

    c. Acetylcholine

    d. GABA (gamma amino butyric acid)

178. Very low coherence between two sites (lower than a recognized statistical data base) implies that these areas are:

    a. functionally highly connected

    b. functionally disconnected

    c. not differentiating related functions properly

    d. connected by non-myelinated fibers

179. Very high coherence (greater than a recognized statistical data base) between two sites that are expected to be related in function suggests:

    a. the individual has high intelligence

    b. the two areas are functionally disconnected

    c. the two areas are not differentiating related functions properly

    d. the individual is highly focused on a task

180. Known resonances of brain electrical activity include:

    a. Local, between macro columns of cells producing EEG frequencies above 30 Hz (gamma)

    b. Regional, between macro columns that are several centimeters apart producing EEG frequencies in the alpha and beta range.

    c. Global, between widely separated areas (e.g., frontal and occipital) producing frequencies in the delta and theta range.

    d. All of the above

181. An event related potential (ERP) is a measure of brain electrical activity which occurs as a response to a specific stimulus. It is usually defined as being *time-locked* to a specific stimulus.

(There are exceptions to this. For example an ERP can be found at the exact time when a stimulus was expected but when there was no actual external stimulus present.)
    a. True
    b. False

182. Most often event related potentials (ERP)s are measured at FZ, CZ, and PZ and amplitude and scalp distribution are among the variables measured. Amplitudes are usually:
    a. highest frontally and lowest in the parietal region
    b. highest in the parietal region and lowest frontally
    c. the same frontally and parietally
    d. highest in the central region

183. Research has shown that event related potentials (ERP)s can distinguish between different clinical conditions so they are used in diagnosis. The most common application is the use of ERPs by:
    a. dentists to identify dead nerve tissue
    b. dermatologists to identify malignancy
    c. audiologists to test hearing
    d. ophthalmologists to detect retinal lesions

184. Most event related potential (ERP)s are only made visible by averaging many, many samples (at least twenty and sometimes several hundred samples). Specific ERPs, in a given individual, come a set time interval after the stimulus and are always:
    a. spike and wave morphology
    b. the same wave form.
    c. a different wave form
    e. 3 per second waves

185. It is acceptable to think of four types of event related potentials (ERP): sensory, motor, long-latency potential and steady-potential-shifts (as discussed by Vaughn). The sensory ERPs are those evoked by sight, sound, smell and touch. Auditory ERPs occur with a negative peak at about 80 – 90 msec, and a positive peak at about 170 msec, after the stimulus. It is called the N1-P2 complex. This is most easily observed:
    a. in the frontal cortex, Fz
    b. in the auditory cortex in the temporal lobe
    c. in the parietal cortex at Pz
    d. in the occipital cortex

186. Motor event related potentials (ERP)s precede and accompany motor movement and are proportional in amplitude to the strength and speed of muscle contraction. They are seen in the:
    a. limbic cortex
    b. precentral area
    c. prefrontal area
    d. temporal lobe

187. Long-latency potentials reflect subjective responses to expected or unexpected stimuli. They run between 250 and 750 msec after the stimulus. The most often mentioned event related potential (ERP) is a positive response called the P300. It comes approximately 300 msec after a (an) _____, although it can be later, depending on variables such as age and processing speed. A (an) _____ refers to a stimulus which is different than the other stimuli in a series. It indicates that the brain has noticed something.
The best term to fill the blanks is:
    a. red alert
    b. odd-ball stimulus
    c. unexpected sentence ending
    d. semantic deviation

188. One important negative long-latency potential is the N400. It occurs as a response to:
    a. unexpected endings in sentences or other semantic deviations.
    b. auditory stimulation
    c. visual stimulation
    d. an "odd-ball" stimulus

189. An example of a *steady-potential shift* is one that occurs after a person is told that they must wait after a signal (warning) and then respond to an event. It is a kind of *anticipation* response. It is seen as a negative shift which occurs between the warning signal and the event. This type of steady-potential shift is called:
a. an early warning stimulus (EWS)
b. an abulic response (AR)
c. a contingent negative variation (CNV)
d. an odd-ball contingent

190. An event related potential (ERP) can help to distinguish response differences in ADHD children and normals. In a 'go' condition the subject performs an action in response to a cue. A green light is an example of a cue that says you can cross the street. A 'go' stimulus produces alpha desynchronization. In a 'nogo' condition the subject withholds acting in response to a cue that indicates he is not to act. A red light at a street corner is an example of a cue that says you must not cross the street. In this case the subject must suppress a prepared action. There is motor inhibition. Following a 'nogo' stimulus there is:

    a. an initial desynchronization followed by synchronization in the frontal and occipital areas

    b. an initial synchronization followed by desynchronization in the frontal and occipital areas

    c. an initial desynchronization followed by synchronization in the central and parietal areas

    d. an initial synchronization followed by desynchronization in the central and parietal areas.

191. GO and NO-GO event related potential (ERP) responses are impaired in ADHD. The ERP amplitudes are higher in normal subjects. It has been demonstrated that 20 sessions of beta training, in subjects diagnosed with ADHD, can result in:

    a. no increase in the ERP response
    b. a dramatic increase in the ERP response
    c. a dramatic decrease in the ERP response
    d. no change in ERP

192. The observation that increased cognitive or sensory workload results in a decrease in rhythmic slow wave activity and an increase in _____ beta activity is termed:

    a. post-reinforcement-synchronization (PRS)
    b. event related potential (ERP) response
    c. event-related-desynchronization (ERD)
    d. positron emission tomography (PET)

193. When the task is completed there is _____ of the EEG. M. Barry Sterman describes these phenomena in his work with pilots. He notes that this _____ phase is self-rewarding. The best term to fill in the blanks are:

    a. post-reinforcement-synchronization (PRS)
    b. event related potential (ERP) response
    c. event-related-desynchronization (ERD)
    d. slow cortical potential (SCP)

194. _____ are very slow waves that indicate a shift between positive and negative. These shifts underlie the electrical activity we are usually measuring. There is great interest in this meticulous work. Birbaumer has been able to teach subjects with severe amyotrophic lateral sclerosis (ALS or Lou Gehrig's disease), who could not speak or move or otherwise communicate, to consciously make a response.

    a. slow cortical potentials (SCP)
    b. event-related-desynchronization (ERD)s
    c. post-reinforcement-synchronizations (PRS)s
    d. event related potentials (ERP)s

6. Patterns associated with different clinical presentations

195. In a right handed client with A.D.D., in which cortical area would you reasonably expect to see EEG slowing (increased theta &/or alpha activity) when carrying out a boring cognitive task:

    a. occipital cortex
    b. left parietal cortex
    c. right central cortex
    d. frontal cortex

196. Which frequency range does one usually train down (decrease) in children with Attention Deficit Disorder without hyperactivity (ADHD: Inattentive Type)?

    a. 4 - 8 Hz
    b. 8 - 12 Hz
    c. 13 - 17 Hz
    d. 18 - 25 Hz

197. Which of the following frequency ranges would you wish to reward (increase) in children with Attention Deficit Disorder <u>without</u> hyperactivity (ADHD: Inattentive Type)?

    a. 4 - 8 Hz
    b. 8 - 12 Hz
    c. 12 - 15 Hz
    d. 15 - 18 Hz

198. Which frequency range would you usually choose to reward (increase) in Attention Deficit Disorder <u>with</u> hyperactivity and impulsivity (ADHD: Combined Type)?

    a. 4 - 8 Hz
    b. 8 - 12 Hz
    c. 13 - 15 Hz
    d. 15 - 18 Hz

199. What may the sudden appearance of an <u>extremely</u> high amplitude spike and wave form (at approximately 3 Hz), represent?

    a. muscle tension in the jaw or neck muscles
    b. increased problem solving cognitive activity
    c. eye blink
    d. absence seizure (petit mal epilepsy)

Figure 1: Sample of Eyes Closed Resting EEG - Linked Ear Montage

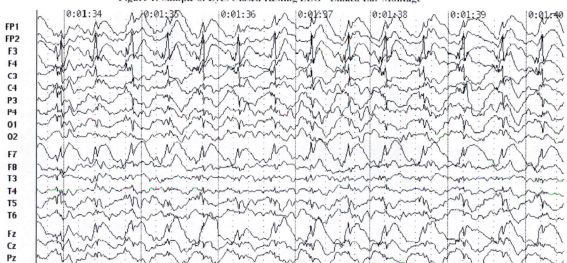

200. The EEG pattern above is most likely consistent with:

a. Generalized Absence Seizure activity
b. Partial complex seizure activity particularly in the left frontal region
c. Generalized grand mal seizure activity
d. Electrical artifact

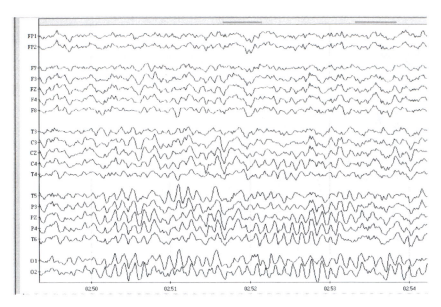

201. In the above client's EEG the most consistent pattern observed was low frequency alpha at P4 and T6. (T6 is oriented for spatial and emotional contextual comprehension, and non-verbal memory.) The subject had symptoms of one of the following disorders. Which is the most likely?
a. Depression
b. Wernicke's Aphasia
c. Asperger's syndrome
d. Anxiety with Panic Attacks

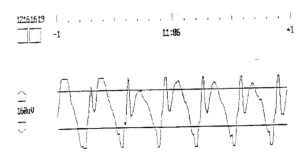

202. The EEG pattern above is most likely consistent with:
a. Absence Seizure activity
b. Partial complex seizure activity particularly in the left frontal region
c. Generalized grand mal seizure activity
d. Electrical artifact

7. Instrumentation
BCIA Required Hours: 6

203. Impedance is measured using what type of current and band width:
    a. Direct current in theta range
    b. Direct current in alpha range
    c. alternating current in beta range
    d. alternating current in alpha range

204. The formula: Voltage (V or E) = Current (I) x Impedance (z) Impedance is a more complex construct than resistance because its calculation requires measurements of not only the resistance of the conductor but other factors. These factors are:
    a. capacitance, inductance and the frequency of the alternating current
    b. capacitance, and the frequency of the alternating current but not inductance
    c. inductance and the frequency of the alternating current but not capacitance
    d. capacitance and inductance but not the frequency of the alternating current

205. Current flows due to the potential difference between source (-ve site) and destination (+ve site).
   a. true
   b. false

206. Opposition to electron flow is high in substances such as rubber where most of the atoms contain outer electron layers that are full. This increases the resistance of the electron in the outer layer to being dislodged. These substances make good insulators and very poor conductors:
a. true
b. false

207. Current measures the rate of transfer of electric charge from one point to another.
   a. true
   b. false

208. The electrons in the outermost layer of the atom are responsible for electricity. This electron layer may be incompletely filled. When this is the case, the electrons in that layer are less tightly held in place and collisions may dislodge them. Imagine that a loose electron acts like a billiard ball. It collides with another electron, is captured by the atom it collided with but that atom's electron is sent off on a different course to strike the next atom and so on in a chain reaction. It is this sequence that is responsible for what we know as:
a. an electric current.
b. potential difference
c. capacitance
d. inductance

209. To measure the amplitude of a wave we usually measure from the top of the positive part of the wave to the top of the negative part of the wave and we term this a:
   a. root mean square measurement
   b. peak to peak amplitude measurement
   c. logarithmic measurement
   d. power measurement

210. *Calibration* of a full cap EEG instrument is done by applying a standard voltage to all input channels. This ensures that the voltage read is accurate and that all inputs are amplifying and filtering the signal in the same way.
   a. true
   b. false

211. The differential amplifier detects and amplifies differences between 2 inputs. It amplifies changes in the signals to each input to the same degree. The amplifier only amplifies this difference between the two inputs and not what is in common. Hence it is correctly called a differential amplifier. In this way the amplifier is said to 'reject' signals that are in common to both inputs. This is called 'common mode' rejection. It, for the most part, cancels out common inputs by:
   a. conducting any common amplitude to the ground
   b. taking all waves that are in phase and putting them through a high input resistance.
   c. reversing the polarity of the second input so that the two currents are effectively subtracted
   d. amplifying the first input by 100,000 but not amplifying the second input.

212. The *common mode rejection ratio* is the ratio of the common mode input voltage divided by the output voltage. This ratio should be >10,000 and often it is higher than 100,000 in newer instruments. In the neurofeedback practitionner's work, failure of this system to eliminate external common mode artifact is most likely due to:
a. similar impedances between the two `electrodes and/or a poor 'ground' connection
b. a difference in impedance between the two `electrodes and/or a poor 'ground' connection
c. a faulty amplifier input ground
d. a failure of the ground wire to connect with the wall socket electrical ground connection

213. A high pass filter is not an all-or-none type of filter. It will gradually attenuate the amplitude of waves that come in at a frequency:
   a. above its cut off point
   b. below its cut off
   c. over 60 Hz
   d. over 50 Hz

214. A low pass filter is not an all-or-none type of filter. It will attenuate the amplitude of waves that come in at a frequency:
   a. above its cut off point
   b. below its cut off
   c. over 60 Hz
   d. over 50 Hz

215. The term band pass filter usually refers to a filter that allows:
   a. a defined frequency range (e.g., 4 to 8 Hz) to pass wile frequencies above and below the range are attenuated.
   b. a filter that keeps out high frequency artifact
   c. a filter that keeps out low frequency artifact
   d. all of the above

216. A band pass filter:
   a. must be > 2 Hz
   b. must be < 8 Hz
   c. lets pass a range of frequencies
   d. all of the above

217. The maximum frequency that can be accurately reconstructed in a filter is determined by the *Nyquist* principle. This frequency is what proportion of the sampling rate?
   a. one tenth
   b. one quarter
   c. one half
   d. three quarters

218. A sampling rate which is too slow will make the analog signal incorrectly appear to be running at a slower frequency than it actually is. This effect is called
   a. the Nyquist effect
   b. shaping
   c. aliasing
   d. retarding

219. The number of 'bits', or 'bit number', refers to the number of amplitude levels that can be resolved. An 8 bit analogue to digital conversion (ADC) will have 2^8 or 256 amplitude levels. This would be $\pm$ 128 discrete voltage levels in the voltage range allowed by that ADC. Too few *bits* means that:
   a. small increases in voltage will be overemphasized

   b. small increases in voltage will be underemphasized
   c. large increases in voltage will be overemphasized
   d. none of the above

220. The FIR filter computes a moving average of digital samples. The number of points which are averaged is termed the:
   a. range of the filter
   b. order of the filter.
   c. amplitude of the filter
   d. bits of the filter

221. When you use an FIR filter to sample a certain frequency range, say 4-8 Hz, the frequencies outside that range are attenuated but not entirely eliminated. In particular, the frequencies in each end of the range will get through to a certain extent due to the shoulders (degree of slope) on either end of the range.
   a. true
   b.false

Montages refer to different types of 'spatial' filtering. Sequential filtering is best to view highly localized activity and filter out coherent waveforms of similar amplitude and phase (Fisch p73).

222. Column 1: Match the description given below, in this column, to the correct term in column 2.	Column 2 Place the correct letter a, b, ... beside the term to which the description best corresponds.
a. Reference of an 'active' electrode to an average of all the other electrodes	1. Laplacian montage. (*Laplacian montage*, Hjorth, 1980)
b. Reference of an 'active' electrode to the average of the electrodes immediately surrounding it.	2. *sequential (bipolar) montages*
c. Reference of an 'active' electrode to an ear or linked ears.	3. *average reference montage*) 4. *common electrode reference montage*
d. Adjacent pairs of electrodes are referenced to each other. This may be transverse or longitudinal **Note:** Each *montage* is just a mathematical reworking of the data which can easily be done by the computer	
	Ref topographical EEG interpretation, Amer. J. EEG Technol. 20: 121-132)

223. The *bipolar* and *Laplacian* montages are good for different procedures than the *common reference montage*. The common reference montage is often considered better for:
a. detecting localized activity
b. locating the origin of seizures activity
c. analyzing asymmetry and detecting artifacts
d. finding a small space occupying lesion

8. Psychopharmacology Considerations

Required Hours: 2 224. QEEG measures of theta (4-8 Hz) and beta (13-21Hz) taken at 19 sites in children with Attention Deficit Hyperactivity Disorder when on and off stimulant medication (Ritalin) demonstrate that, on medication, there is:
a. increased alpha activity in the occipital area
b. decreased theta activity in the frontal regions
c. little change in theta/beta power ratio at any site
d. a decrease in theta/beta ratio in the frontal area

225. Sedatives and tranquilizers produce an increase in which EEG frequency range:
a. delta
b. theta
c. alpha
d. beta

226. Selective serotonin reuptake inhibitors (**SSRI's**) are most likely to:
a. increase beta activity and may decrease alpha.
b. decrease beta activity and increase alpha
c. increase theta and delta activity
d. none of the above

227. Excessive alcohol consumption can:
a. increase beta (usually above 20 Hz) and decrease "thalpha" and alpha.
b. decrease high frequency beta
c. decrease high frequency beta but increase theta and alpha
d. none of the above

228. The use of Lithium for the management of bipolar disorder can result in:
a. raising the frequency band for alpha
b. generalized asynchronous slowing, increased theta, and some slowing of alpha.
c. increase beta (usually above 20 Hz) and decrease "thalpha" and alpha.
d. decreased SMR 13-15 Hz with an increase in 12 Hz alpha

229. Tricyclic antidepressants may produce:

a. decreased SMR 13-15 Hz with an increase in 12 Hz alpha

b. generalized asynchronous slow waves and spike and wave discharges. Although they decrease alpha and also perhaps low beta, they may increase high beta.

c. a rise in the frequency band for alpha

d. decreased high frequency beta but increase theta and alpha

230. Marijuana will typically:

a. increase beta

b. increase 38 - 42 Hz activity

c. increase alpha

d. decrease alpha

Effects of Drugs on Learning Tasks

231. State dependent learning refers to which of the following?

a. information (or skill) acquired in one physiological state is best recalled when again in that state

b. the finding that when in a drugged state people cannot learn

c. the observation that a repeated operant will produce a consistent response

d. the repeated finding since the 1970's that children learn better on Ritalin

9. Treatment Planning

Required Hours: 6

232. It has been hypothesized that in ADD there is reduced dopamine in the fronto-mesolimbic system in the left hemisphere. The type of cognitive processing which is affected and deficient is that which requires slow, serial effort. It is this kind of processing that may be improved with stimulant medication. Training using neurofeedback in the left frontal area for clients with ADHD may be done to:

a. increase SMR

b. increase high beta (26-34 Hz)

c. decrease high alpha (11-13 Hz)

d. decrease the dominant slow wave

233. Dopaminergic overactivity is thought to be associated with blunting of affect, excessive intellectual ideation and introversion. Pathologically it may underlie disorders including: paranoid states, anxiety, hallucinations; psychosis, including the +ve symptoms of schizophrenia such as paranoia; Tourette's syndrome; overly excited states including euphoria and mania and also in

a. attention deficit disorder

b. obsessive compulsive disorder (OCD)

c. Parkinson's disorder

d. none of the above

234. Too little dopamine has been reported to be associated with: Parkinson's disease with its tremor and inability to start movement; the negative symptoms of schizophrenia including lethargy, misery, catatonia & social withdrawal, addictions, and with which of the following:

a. obsessive compulsive disorder

b. paranoid states

c. adult ADHD

d. anxiety

235. In obsessive compulsive disorder (OCD) the pathophysiology is hypothesized to involve an overactive *loop* of neural activity between the **orbital prefrontal cortex,** which is involved in *feeling that something is wrong,* to the **caudate nucleus,** which gives the *urge to act on personal memories or on instincts such as cleaning or grooming,* to the **cingulate,** which is important in registering conscious emotion and *which can keep focus or attention fixed on the feeling of unease.* The caudate nucleus is involved in automatic thinking; for example when you check that you closed the fridge, turned off the stove, locked the door. Overactivity of this circuit means constantly checking and rechecking. Brain scans show that when a person with OCD is asked to imagine something related to their compulsion (such as dirt if it is someone who must compulsively clean) their caudate and prefrontal cortex light up. In NFB we tend to:

a. decrease high amplitude beta activity frontally

b. increase 24- 29 Hz activity frontally

c. decrease delta frontally

d. increase Sheer rhythm 38-42 Hz activity frontally

236. In Tourette's syndrome the **putamen** is overactive. The putamen is related to the *urge to do fragments of preprogrammed motor skills.* The putamen is linked to the **premotor cortex** which governs the production of the actual movements. Instead of the relatively complete procedures seen with compulsions, the motor and vocal tics appear in Tourette's Syndrome as fragments of known actions. In neurofeedback and biofeedback work we will attempt to reduce and/or modulate the firing of the fusiform fibers in the muscle spindles by:

- a. increasing sympathetic drive and decreasing SMR
- b. decreasing sympathetic drive and increasing SMR
- c. decreasing RSA and increasing high beta (22-32 Hz)
- d. increasing EDR and decreasing theta

237. Which of the following areas is involved in the general maintenance of attention and arousal which is said to be "wide" to extra-personal space. This area regulates information processing which requires peripheral vision, spatial location, rapid shifts in attention. These aspects of attention appear to involve the noradrenergic system.

- a. the left cerebral hemisphere
- b. the right cerebral hemisphere
- c. the diencephalon
- d. the basal ganglia

238. In ADHD there might be excessive locus coeruleus norepinephrine production and excess noradrenergic stimulation to which area. (This has been suggested because clonidine affects α_2 (inhibitory) receptors (locus coeruleus) and helps to decrease the symptoms of ADHD).

- a. left cerebral hemisphere
- b. right cerebral hemisphere
- c. the diencephalon
- d. the hypothalamus

239. People with ADD seem to have automatic processing which is fast and simultaneous. This style of attention is biased towards novelty and change. It has been posited that the positive effect that dexadrine has on some people with ADHD is due to its effects on alpha2 inhibitory receptors in the locus coeruleus. It has also been noted that overactivation of the noradrenergic system in the which of the following areas is associated with extroversion, histrionic behaviour, impulsivity and manic behaviours.

- a. left cerebral hemisphere
- b. right cerebral hemisphere
- c. the diencephalon
- d. the hypothalamus

240. Stimulants, in animal studies, have been found to do which of the following:

- a. decrease right hemisphere processing speed
- b. facilitate release of dopamine (but not norepinephrine) from the striatum (which includes the caudate)
- c. increase left hemisphere processing speed
- d. all of the above

241. A model of cortico-thalamic feedback that may be relevant to understanding and treating ADHD clients with neurofeedback, suggests that decreased blood flow to, and metabolic activity in, the cells in the frontal / prefrontal areas (including the motor **cortex**) may *lead to* reduced excitation by the motor cortex (layer VI) of the inhibitory cells in the **putamen** which, in turn, may affect the activity of the substantia nigra (either directly or indirectly via the external globus pallidus and the subthalamus). Either way, the substantia nigra would increase its inhibition of areas of the thalamus resulting in the thalamic relay cells producing bursts of activity and then, by projection to the anterior association cortex (layer IV), a wave form and rhythm of activity that we pick up in the EEG. What is this rhythm?

- a. delta
- b. theta
- c. high alpha
- d. beta

242. A model of cortico-thalamic feedback that may be relevant to understanding and treating ADHD clients with neurofeedback, suggests that decreased blood flow to, and metabolic activity in, the cells in the frontal / prefrontal areas (including the motor **cortex**) may lead to reduced excitation by the motor cortex (layer VI) of the inhibitory cells in the **putamen** which, in turn, may reduce its inhibition of the inhibitory cells in the **substantia nigra** which would result in the substantia nigra being released to increase its inhibition of the **thalamus.** The net result of this model is thought to be increased inhibition of the ventral lateral (VL), ventral anterior (VA) and the centromedian (CM) nuclei of the thalamus. These cells would depolarize then repolarize in a slow rhythmic manner. This would begin an oscillatory process that would be conveyed to the cortex. The end result of this cycle in the EEG would be:

    a. delta

    b. theta

    c. beta

    d. Sheer rhythm

243. A commonly "inhibited" frequency range in ADHD students may sometimes represent constructive brain activity and not just tuning out. This wave frequency may be paced by cholinergic pathways that project from the septal nuclei to the hippocampus. This would correspond to the observed involvement of this wave form in memory retrieval. Recall of words can correspond to synchronization of this frequency wave. This is thought to represent hippocampal production of this wave. Which of the following frequencies is this discussion referring to?

    a. higher frequency delta

    b. theta

    c. high alpha (12-14 Hz)

    d. low beta (15-18 Hz)

244. This area of the cortex and prefrontal cortex is said to be involved in inhibiting inappropriate action. Also in tests of intellectual and/or attentional functions this area appears to have decreased functional activity. The most likely area referred to in the above statements is:

    a. right temporal cortex

    b. medial posterior cortex

    c. left orbito-frontal cortex

    d. Exner's area in the left frontal cortex

245. In which area of the brain have SPECT scans of subjects with ADHD demonstrated a decrease in blood flow during a continuous performance task. (Found in about 65% of the ADD subjects compared to 5% of the controls in one study)

    a. Broca's cortex

    b. prefrontal cortex

    c. supramarginal gyrus

    d. hippocampal cortex

246. The amygdala strongly connects to an area of the cortex where emotions are experienced and meaning is bestowed on perceptions. Which area is this:

    a. prefrontal cortex

    b. ventromedial frontal lobe cortex

    c. ventrolateral frontal lobe cortex

    d. right parietal cortex

247. This area of the cortex focuses attention and facilitates tuning in to one's own thoughts. Increased blood flow on the right side of this area may correspond to attention being focused on internal events. This area distinguishes between internal and external events and is under-active in schizophrenia where the subject is unable to distinguish their own thoughts from outside voices. These statements most likely apply to:

    a. the left parietal lobe

    b. the substantia nigra

    c. the anterior cingulate

    d. the red nucleus

248. The area that is thought to be principally involved when you **hold** a thought in mind, **select** thoughts and perceptions to attend to, **inhibit** other thoughts and perceptions, **bind** the perceptions into a unified whole, endow them with **meaning**, **conceptualize**, **plan** and **choose** is:

    a. the left parietal lobe

    b. the substantia nigra

    c. the anterior cingulate

    d. dorso-lateral prefrontal cortex

249. People who have ADD may have a genetic alteration in the dopamine D4 receptors. These differences may lead to reduced dopaminergic activity (LaHoste et al, 1996). Deficiency in dopamine related functions in the frontal-striatal system is the basis of some theories as to the emergence of ADHD symptoms. (Charcot et al, 1996, Malone et al, 1994, Sterman, 2000).

Stimulant medication such as Ritalin (methylphenidate) is thought to:
- a. increase dopamine production
- b. block the re-uptake of dopamine.
- c. increase receptors for dopamine
- d. decrease the need for dopamine

10. Understand Procedures / Initial Assessment

250. Place in the following two figures the abbreviations (e.g., O1, P4.) for the 10-20 sites indicated by ovals and circles.

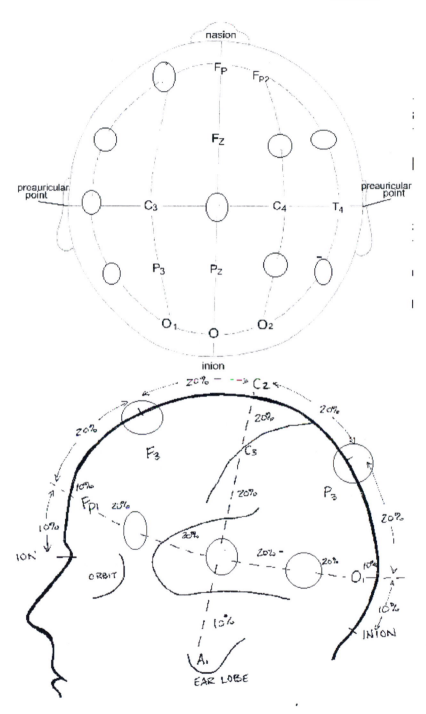

11. Artifacting the EEG:

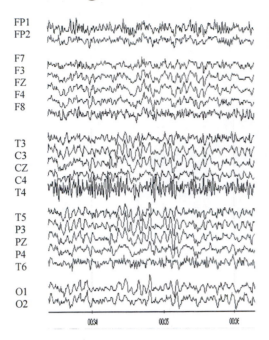

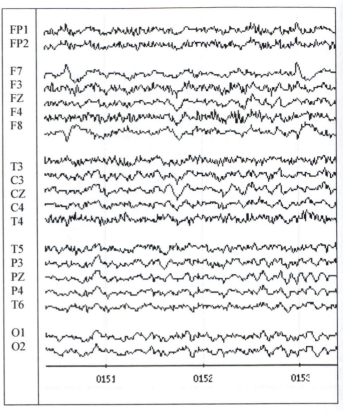

251. The above tracing at T4 is an example of:
   a. eye flutter
   b. spiking epileptiform activity
   c. muscle artifact
   d. severe beta spindling

253. In the above figure, the relatively high amplitude sharp excursion upwards followed by a downward flowing wave at F7 just prior to 0151 and again at 0153 represents:
   a. eye blink artifact
   b. cardiac artifact
   c. single epileptiform spike and wave
   d. lateral eye movement

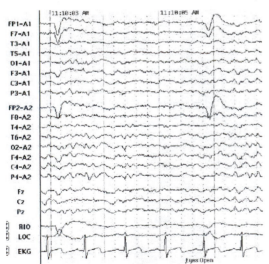

252. In the above figure, the two large downward excursions followed by a wave in the tracings at FP1-A1 and FP2-A2 represent:
   a. eye flutter
   b. spike and wave epileptiform activity
   c. muscle artifact
   d. eye blink artifact

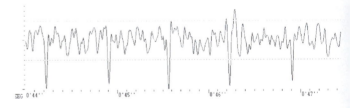

254. In the above figure, the 5 large downward excursions most likely represent:
   a. eye blink artifact
   b. cardiac artifact
   c. single epileptiform spike and wave
   d. lateral eye movement

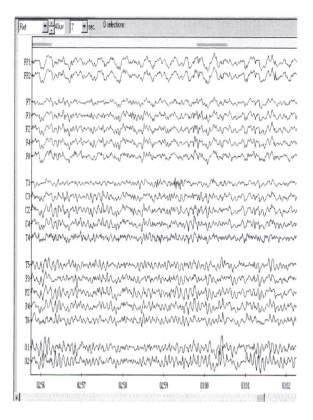

255. In the figure opposite, from the EEG (eyes open, referenced to linked ears) from an 11 year old boy, the waveform seen at FP1 and FP2 most likely may represent:

    a. repeated eye blink artifact

    b. delta activity associated with a learning disability

    c. eye flutter

    d. frontalis muscle artifact

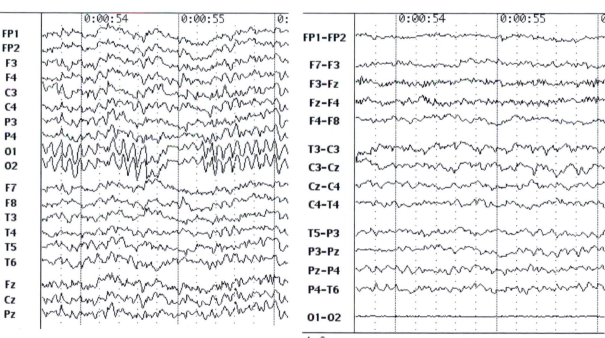

256. In the above recording (above 2 figures), displayed with two different montages, the activity seen in the left hand montage at O1 and O2 most likely represents:

    a. high amplitude alpha at sleep onset

    b. "salt bridge" artifact

    c. normal occipital alpha which is the same in both channels

    d. occipitalis muscle artifact

427

4. QEEG (Single channel QEEG and multi-channel Brain Mapping)

a) Interpretation: databases, montages, comparison to databases using parameters such as frequency, amplitude, coherence, phase and asymmetry

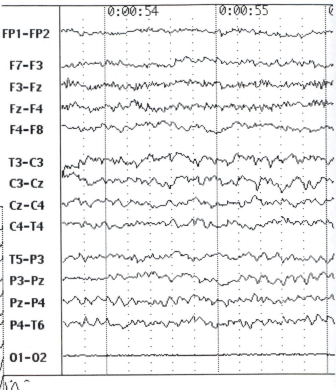

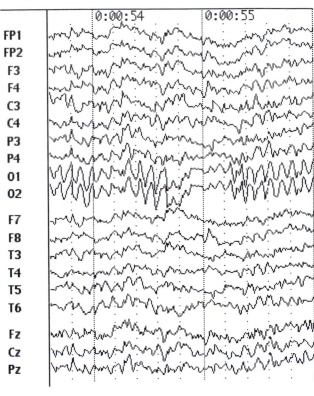

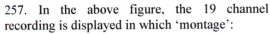

257. In the above figure, the 19 channel recording is displayed in which 'montage':
    a. Longitudinal sequential
    b. Transverse sequential
    c. Linked ear referential
    d. Laplacian or Hjorth

258. In the above figure, the 19 channel recording is displayed in which 'montage':
    a. Longitudinal sequential
    b. Transverse sequential
    c. Linked ear referential
    d. Laplacian or Hjorth

259. Electrodes record electrical activity produced by the neurons (nerve cells) in the brain. The best statement of what an EEG instrument measures is:
    a. the voltage under each electrode
    b. the current under each electrode
    c. the potential difference between pairs of electrodes
    d. the potential difference between the electrode and ground

260. The term 'LORETA' refers to:
    a. electro-magnetic resolution of neuronal orientation
    b. a mathematical process which looks at surface EEG information and infers what activity is occurring in areas a little deeper in the cortex
    c. glucose metabolic activity detected by positron emission from a radioactive form of oxygen
    d. blood flow perfusion detected by a scan procedure

12. Treatment Protocols

261. Biological markers for Attention Deficit Hyperactivity Disorder include:
   a. increased glucose metabolism in frontal and certain subcortical regions as recorded in PET scans.
   b. increased slow wave activity (4-8 Hz)in frontal and central cortical regions
   c. increased blood flow as recorded in SPECT scans
   d. all of the above

262. Positive features found in most people with Attention Deficit Disorder do NOT generally include:
   a. spontaneity
   b. ability to hyperfocus
   c. constant reflection
   d. creativity

263. In the United States in the mid 1990's, the proportion of the school age population taking stimulant drugs, such as Ritalin (methylphenidate), for Attention Deficit/Hyperactivity Disorder approximates:
   a. less than 1%
   b. 3%
   c. 7%
   d. 10 %

264. Research supports the finding of long term benefits after cessation of treatment, measured by behavioral questionnaires (sampling behavior, attitude, homework completion, grade averages and relationships), in children with Attention Deficit Hyperactivity Disorder for:
   a. stimulant drug therapy
   b. behavior modification
   c. EEG biofeedback
   d. nutritional supplements

265. Students who have Attention Deficit Disorder when expected to sustain attention during a cognitive task (such as listening to the teacher or doing homework) often experience:
   a. A decrease in EDR (electrodermal response)
   b. An increase in peripheral skin temperature
   c. Deep diaphragmatic breathing
   d. An increase in 28 - 35 Hz EEG activity at Cz

266. Successful EEG biofeedback training for students who have Attention Deficit Hyperactivity Disorder is **NOT** associated with significant increases in:
   a. reading comprehension
   b. intelligence test scores
   c. attention span (measured by continuous performance tests)
   d. theta activity (3-7 Hz)

267. After 40 sessions of EEG biofeedback, students who have Attention Deficit Disorder were found to demonstrate the following pattern on Wechsler Intelligence Scale testing:
   a. an increase in overall IQ but no significant improvement on sub-tests for arithmetic, coding, digit span, information.
   b. sub-test scores for arithmetic, coding, digit span, and information increase significantly but remain lower than other sub-test scores.
   c. sub-test scores for arithmetic, coding, digit span, information increase significantly and are no longer lower than other sub-test scores.
   d. sub-test scores for arithmetic, coding, digit span, information get worse, though other scales do make a significant improvement.

268. EEG biofeedback for Attention Deficit Disorder usually requires:
   a. More sessions for students with co-morbidity of specific Learning Disabilities
   b. Fewer sessions for students who have associated hyperactivity
   c. The addition of intense individual psychotherapy
   d. Fewer sessions for students who have Asperger's Syndrome.

269. Successful EEG biofeedback training for depression has utilized:
   a. at Cz, decreasing theta 4-8 Hz activity and increasing SMR (12-15 Hz) activity
   b. at F3, decreasing dominant alpha relative to F4 alpha in the same frequency band
   c. at T6, increasing low frequency beta, 13 – 16 Hz activity and decreasing dominant slow wave activity
   d. at P5, deceasing dominant theta activity and increasing beta 15-18 Hz activity.

270. Successful EEG biofeedback training for Asperger's syndrome that may help to improve interpretation of social cues and abstract thinking may utilize:
   a. at Cz, decreasing theta 4-8 Hz activity and beta 20-24 Hz activity
   b. at F3, decreasing dominant alpha relative to F4 alpha in the same frequency band
   c. at T6, increasing low frequency beta, (13–16 Hz activity) and decreasing dominant slow wave activity
   d. at P5, deceasing dominant theta activity and increasing beta 15-18 Hz activity.

271. Successful EEG biofeedback training in conjunction with appropriate teaching strategies for dyslexia has utilized:
   a. at Cz, decreasing theta 4-8 Hz activity and increasing SMR (12-15 Hz) activity
   b. at F3, decreasing dominant alpha relative to F4 alpha in the same frequency band
   c. at T6, increasing low frequency beta, 13 – 16 Hz activity and decreasing dominant slow wave activity
   d. at P5, deceasing dominant theta activity and increasing beta 15-18 Hz activity.

272. Successful EEG biofeedback training for athletic performance, as reported in professional meetings, has utilized:
   a. at Cz, decreasing theta 4-8 Hz activity and increasing SMR (12-15 Hz) activity
   b. decreasing high EMG activity, diaphragmatic breathing and increasing peripheral skin temperature, while increasing 11-13 Hz and 13-15 Hz activity at PCz and decreasing 21- 32 Hz activity in central and frontal regions
   c. at T6, increasing low frequency beta, 13 – 16 Hz activity and decreasing dominant slow wave activity
   d. at P5, deceasing dominant theta activity and increasing beta 15-18 Hz activity.

273. Successful EEG biofeedback training for dystonia combined with Parkinson's disease has been reported utilizing:
   a. at C4, decreasing 24-32 Hz beta spindling activity
   b. at F3, decreasing dominant alpha relative to F4 alpha in the same frequency band
   c. promoting diaphragmatic breathing at 6 BrPM and RSA while concomitantly increasing 13-15 Hz in central regions (C3, Cz, C4)

   d. at P5, deceasing dominant theta activity and increasing beta 15-18 Hz activity.

274. Successful EEG biofeedback training for seizure disorders has utilized:
   a. at Cz, decreasing theta 4-8 Hz activity and increasing SMR (12-15 Hz) activity
   b. decreasing the dominant slow wave activity near the seizure site while concomitantly increasing SMR (13-15 Hz) activity in the central regions (C3, Cz, C4)
   c. at T6, increasing low frequency beta, 13 – 16 Hz activity and decreasing dominant slow wave activity while doing diaphragmatic breathing at 6 BrPM
   d. increasing beta 16-22 Hz activity near the seizure site while concomitantly increasing SMR (13-15 Hz) activity in the central regions (C3, Cz, C4)

275. Successful EEG biofeedback training to improve musical performance (musicality and emotional interpretation) has been reported using:
   a. at Cz, decreasing theta 4-8 Hz activity and increasing SMR (12-15 Hz) activity
   b. increasing high frequency theta activity at Pz to the point where theta amplitude just exceeds alpha activity at the same site
   c. at T6, increasing low frequency beta, 13 – 16 Hz activity and decreasing dominant slow wave activity while doing diaphragmatic breathing at 6 BrPM
   d. increasing beta 16-22 Hz activity at Fz while concomitantly increasing SMR (13-15 Hz) activity in the central regions (C3, Cz, C4)

276. Successful EEG biofeedback training to decrease anxiety and tension has been reported using:
   a. at Cz, decreasing theta 4-8 Hz activity and increasing SMR (12-15 Hz) activity
   b. at T6, increasing low frequency beta, 13 – 16 Hz activity and decreasing dominant slow wave activity
   c. increasing high alpha (11-13 Hz) and SMR (13 – 15 Hz) while decreasing high beta (20-23Hz and 24-32 Hz) plus hand warming and diaphragmatic breathing at 6 BrPM.
   d. increasing beta 16-22 Hz activity at Fz while concomitantly increasing SMR (13-15 Hz) activity in the central regions (C3, Cz, C4)

13. Other Treatment Techniques

Required Hours: 4

a. Psychotherapy

277. Mechanisms of defence are mental processes that are defensively motivated in an attempt to obtain relief from emotional tension, anxiety and to resolve conflict. They are:
   a. conscious but automatic
   b. unconscious and automatic
   c. conscious efforts to relieve emotional pain
   d. require thought and motivation to enact but become automatic

278. A detached and intellectual awareness and understanding of feeling, emotions and behaviour of another person is termed:
   a. sympathy
   b. empathy
   c. transference
   d. psychic awareness

279. The _____ is a combination of defence mechanisms including, projection, repression, identification and rationalization. It is that unconscious process (defence mechanism) whereby one has an extreme negative reaction to another person who has characteristics that are really disowned aspects of ones own self (physical, behavioural, and/or personality characteristics). These are aspects of self that are unacceptable to ones own self image and which one does not consciously recognize. These aspects of self are seen (projected on to) in the other person and adamantly reacted to without any recognition of the inappropriateness of that reaction.
This process is important for trainers and therapists to recognize when they have a very strong reaction to someone they are working with. It is called:
   a. displacement
   b. transference
   c. countertransference
   d. the King David Reaction

280. _____ is a defence mechanism outside of conscious awareness in which emotional feelings are 'transferred' from their appropriate (now 'internal object') to an external one. (phobia is an example). Substitution + _____ may result in minor similarities between a person in one's present life and a significant other in earlier life, to cause reactions towards the person in the here-and-now "as if" they were the person from the past. The defence mechanism that fits in the above blank spaces is called:
   a. rationalization
   b. suppression
   c. repression
   d. displacement

281. The unconscious transfer to another person of feelings that were originally felt towards another (important) person earlier in life is called:
   a. counter transference
   b. projection
   c. reaction formation
   d. transference

282. The transfer (partially or wholly unconscious) of emotional responses of a therapist to a patient, that may in part be due to the patient's transference and/or based on the therapists early relationship with an important other, is called:
   a. transference
   b. projection
   c. countertransference
   d. King David Reaction

283. A special kind of collaborative relationship between therapist and client to promote meaningful progress in psychotherapy is called:
   a. counter transference
   b. therapeutic alliance
   c. reaction formation
   d. transference

284. A mental mechanism operating outside of and beyond conscious awareness by which the emotional significance and affect is separated and detached from an idea, situation or object is called:
   a. counter transference
   b. dissociation
   c. reaction formation
   d. transference

285. _____ is unconscious and defensively intended to help maintain the lack of awareness of one's rejected and disowned ideas, wishes, impulses and motives. The best term to fill in the blank is:
    a. counter transference
    b. repression
    c. reaction formation
    d. transference

286. _____ directs outwardly and attributes to others one's disclaimed and objectionable character traits, thoughts, feelings, attitudes, motives, and desires. It distorts one's understanding of the outside world and enables people to remain blind to important dynamic factors in their own personality.
    a. counter transference
    b. suppression
    c. reaction formation
    d. projection

287. A mechanism beyond conscious awareness in which the ego justifies or attempts to make otherwise unacceptable impulses, needs, feelings, behaviour and motives into ones which are consciously tolerable and acceptable is called:
    a. counter transference
    b. therapeutic alliance
    c. reaction formation
    d. rationalization

288. Unconscious mental mechanism by which needs, complexes, attitudes and motives are developed in large areas of the personality which are the reverse of consciously disowned ones. Personally an socially acceptable goals are developed which are the antithesis of the hidden, previously disowned ones. This is called:
    a. counter transference
    b. therapeutic alliance
    c. reaction formation
    d. transference

289. _____ is the conscious effort to subjugate (remove from conscious recognition) unacceptable thoughts or desires. One directs attention away from undesirable thoughts, objects, or feelings and is aware of so doing.
    a. counter transference
    b. repression
    c. reaction formation
    d. suppression

b. Cognitive Interventions

290. A metacognitive strategy is:
    a. an unconscious strategy learned by repetition of an exercise
    b. an executive thinking function that consciously monitors learning and planning
    c. a mathematical exercise usually learned in calculus
    d. a philosophical term applied to advanced theological learning

291. Research has demonstrated that metacognitive strategies are:
    a. used by good students and not by poor students
    b. not a differentiating factor between good and poor students
    c. often accompanied by increased 32-35 Hz activity.
    d. improved in high stress situations

c. Regular Biofeedback:

292. The human normal reaction to stress involves a release of norepinephrine from the locus coeruleus which causes the hypothalamus to increase its output of:
    a. ACTH
    b. Acetylcholine
    c. Cortisol
    d. Serotonin

293. Increase in peripheral skin temperature is correlated with:
    a. peripheral vasoconstriction
    b. a decrease in sympathetic nervous system arousal
    c. increased heart rate
    d. anxiety

294. Increase in electrodermal response (EDR) is correlated with:
    a. parasympathetic nervous system arousal
    b. an increase in skin resistance measured in ohms
    c. an increase in skin conduction measured in 'mho'
    d. decreased sweat gland secretion

295. Which of the following physiological changes might you expect to observe in a client who feels very tense and anxious:
   a. EMG decrease in the trapezius muscle groups
   b. Diaphragmatic breathing pattern
   c. Synchrony between changes in heart rate and the inspiration and expiration phases of breathing.
   d. Decreased peripheral skin temperature

d. Relaxation Techniques

296. There are 6 standard exercises in a classic form of relaxation training. They are limb heaviness, limb warmth, cardiac, respiration (diaphragmatic breathing), solar plexus warmth and forehead cooling. The term used for this is:
a. progressive relaxation
b. guided imagery
c. autogenic training
d. 6 step meditation

****

B. Answers for the Multiple Choice Questions

All questions are covered in the text with the exception of the questions on *Mechanisms of Defence*. Additional references are mentioned for a few of the questions.

1. a
2. d.
3. b.
4. a.
5. c.
6. c.
7. d.
8. b.
9. d.
10. b. (Sterman, 2000)
11. b.
12. d.
13. b.
14. c. (Thompson & Thompson JNT, Nov. 2002)
15. c.
16. b.
17. b.
18. b.
19. d.
20. c.
21. b.
22. b.
23. b.
24. See diagram in text, p.71
25. See diagram in text, p.71
26. See diagram in text, p.85
27. a.
28. a.
29. a
30. b.
31. b.
32. d.
33. b. (Amen, 1997)
34. d. (Smith)
35. c.

36. c.
37. c.
38. c.
39. c.
40. d.
41. d.
42. a.
43. d.
44. b.
45. a.
46. b.
47. b. (Malone et al)
48. b.   (Carlson from Tucker, 1977)
49. d.
50. a.
51. a. (Carlson p674 after Babinski 1914)
52. b.
53. b.
54. c.
55. c.
56. c. (Reference: Joel Lubar workshop handout of applications supported by peer reviewed journal papers.)
57. b. (Reference: Joel Lubar workshop handout of applications supported by peer reviewed journal papers.)
58. c.
59. c.
60. c.
61. d.
62. b. (Olds, Milner, 1954)
63. b. (Rosenfeld, 1997)
64. a. (Smith)
65. d.
66. a.
67. d.
68. a.
69. b.
70. b.
71. b.
72. d. (Sterman 2000, DeLong 1990)
73. b.   (Klimesch et al., 1999). (Thatcher, personal communication)
74. c.
75. d.
76. b.
77. b.
78. d.   (Silverthorn, Dee Unglaub (1998)
79. c.
80. b.
81. c. Sterman, 2000
82. d. (Sterman, 2000)
83. d. (Sterman, 2000)
84. d. (Sterman, 2000)
85. d. (Sterman, 2000)
86. d. (Sterman, 2000)
87. a. (Sterman, 2000)
88. d. (Sterman, 2000)
89. c. (Campbell, 1996, pp 971)
90. c.
91. d.
92. d. (Campbell, 1996)
93. a.
94. b.

95. a.

96. a. (Stermam)

97. d. Joel Lubar, 1997 after Nunez)

98. c.

99. c. (Dyro, 1989)

100. b. (Lubar)

101. b.

102. d.

103. b.

104. a. (Fisch, p. 16, 1999)

105. c. (Lubar)

106. c.

107. a.

108. a. (Lubar)

109. b. (Fisch, p.125)

110. b.

111. c.

112. b. (Fisch, p.145)

113. c.

114. c.

115. b. (Fisch, p. 152)

116. a. (Gibbs, F.A. and Knott, J.R., 1949)

117. c. (Fisch, p185, 187)

118. d.

119. c. (Fisch, p. 181)

120. a. (Fisch, p. 45, p. 149)

121. c.

122. c.

123. b.

124. a.

125. c.

126. a.

127. b.

128. b.

129. b. (Fisch, p. 349)

130. b.

131. d.

132. c.

133. a.

134. b.

135. d. (Schwartz, 1987, p. 76)

136. a. (Niedermeyer & Da Silva)

137. See table in text

138. b.

139. b.

140. b.

141. b.

142. b.

143. c.   (Fisch p271)

144. c.

145. b.

146. c.

147. b.

148. d.

149. c.

150. c.

151. c.

152. c.

153. c.

154. c.

155. c.

156. d.

157. b.

158. b.

159. b.

160a. b. (Fisch, p.353)

160b. a. (Fisch p. 352)

161. c.

162. d.

163. c.

164. b. (SMR by definition is only over the central area)

165. d.

166. c.

167. d. (Lubar)

168. d. (Lubar)

169. c.

170. c. (Fisch, 1999)

171. c. (Dyro, 1989.)

172. a.

173. d.

174. a.   (Thatcher, 1986, 64: 123-143)

175. c.   (Thatcher, 1986, 64: 123-143)

176. c. (Lubar, 1997)

177. a. (Lubar, 1997)

178. b.

179. c.

180. d. (Lubar, 1997)

181. a. (Sutton, Teuting, Zubin & John. 1967).

182. b.

183. c.

184. b.

185. b. (Vaughn & Arezzo, 1988).

186. b.

187. b.

188. a. (Kutas & Hillyard 1980).

189. c. (Walter, Cooper, Aldridge, McCallum &Winter 1964)

190. a.

191. b. (Grin-Yatsenko, Kropotov, 2001)

192. c.

193. a.

194. a.

195. d.   (Mann, 1992)

196. a.   (Lubar, 1995; Thompson & Thompson, 1998)

197. d   (Lubar, 1995; Thompson & Thompson, 1998)

198. c.   (Lubar, 1995, Thompson & Thompson)

199. d.

200. b.

201. c.

202. a.
203. d.
204. a.
205. a.
206. a.
207. a.
208. a.
209. b.
210. a.
211. c.
212. b.
213. b.
214. a.
215. a.
216. c.
217. c.
218. c.
219. a.
220. b.
221. a.
222.   1=b
        2=d
        3=a
        4=c
223. c. (Lubar)
224. c.
225. d. (Fisch p. 414)
226. a.
227. a.
228. b.
229. b.
230. c.
231. a
232. d.
233. b.
234. c.
235. a.
236. b.
237. b. (Malone, 1994)
238. b.
239. b. (Tucker)
240. d. (Malone)
241. b. (Sterman 2000, DeLong 1990)
242. b. (Sterman 2000, DeLong 1990)
243. b.   (Klimesch et al., 1999)
244. c. (Sterman, Child Study, 2000)
245. b.   (Amen et al, 1997).
246. b.
247. c.
248. d.
249. b.
250. See diagram in text
251. c.
252. d.
253. d.
254. b.

255. c.
256. b.
257. c.
258. b
259. c.   (Lubar, Thompson)
260. b.
261. b. (Zametkin, A.J. 1990, Mann, 1992, Amen)
262. c. (Thompson & Thompson, 1998)
263. b. (Thompson & Thompson, 1998 after Safer 1996)
264. c. (Lubar in Schwartz)
265. a. (Thompson & Thompson, 1998)
266. d. (Thompson & Thompson, 1998, Lubar, 1995)
267. b. (Thompson & Thompson, 1998)
268. a.
269. b.
270. c. (Thompson, 2003; Jarascewicz, 2002)
271. d.
272. b.
273. c. (Thompson, 2002)
274. b. (Sterman, 2000)
275. b. (Grazelier)
276. c.
277. b. (Introduction to Psychiatry. George Washington University Medical School, Washington D.C.)
278. b.
279. d. (Laughlin, 1967)
280. d.
281. d.
282. c.
283. b.
284. b.
285. b.
286. d.
287. d.
288. c.
289. d.
290. b.
291. a. (Thompson & Thompson, 1998 after Cheng 1993)
292. a. (Smith-Pellettier)
293. b. (Schwartz, 1987, p 98)
294. c. (Schwartz, 1987, p 98)
295. d. (Schwartz, 1987, p 98)
296. c.

References

Note: A helpful listing of articles is the Comprehensive Neurofeedback Bibliography organized and kept current by D. Corydon Hammond. It is arranged according to disorders (epilepsy, ADHD, anxiety disorders, depression, etc.) and is accessible under the heading Neurofeedback Archive on the web site of the International Society for Neuronal Regulation, www.isnr.org.

Alhambra, M. A., Fowler, T. P., & Alhambra, A. A. (1995). EEG biofeedback: A new treatment option for ADD/ADHD. *Journal of Neurotherapy, 1*(2), 39-43.

Amen, D. G., Carmichael, B. D., & Thisted, R. A. (1997). High resolution SPECT imaging in ADHD. *Annals of Clinical Psychiatry, 9*(2), 81-86.

Amen, Daniel G. (1998). *Change bYour Brain: Change Your Life.* New York: Times Books division of Random House, Inc.

Amen, Daniel G. (2001). *Healing ADD.* New York: G. P. Putnam's Sons.

Anderson, P., & Anderson, S. A. (1968). *Physiological basis of the alpha rhythm.* New York: Appleton.

Andreassi, John L. (1995). *Psychophysiology, Human Behavior & Physiological Response - Third Edition.* New Jersey: Lawrence Earlbaum Associates.

Andreassi, John L. (1995). O*p. cit.,* after Sakai, L., Baker, L., & Dawson, M. (1992). Electrodermal lability: Individual differences affecting perceptual speed and vigilance performance in 9 to 16 year old children. *Psychophysiology, 29,* 207- 217.

Andreassi, John L. (1995). *Op. cit.,* after Ekman, P., Levenson & Friesen, W. V. (1983). Autonomic nervous system activity distinguishes among emotions. *Science, 22,* 1208-1210.

Andreassi John L. (1995). *Op. cit.* p. 327, after Blanchard, E. B., Theobald, D. E., Williamson, D. A., Silver, B. V., & Brown, D. A. (1978). A controlled evaluation of temperature biofeedback in the treatment of migraine headaches. *Archives of General Psychiatry, 41,* 121-127.

Andreassi, John L. (1995). *Op.cit.,* p. 326, after Cohen , J. & Sedlacek, K. (1983). Attention and autonomic self regulation. *Psychosomatic Medicine, 45,* 243-257.

Andreassi, John L. (1995). O*p. cit.,* p.156 after Fridlund, A. J., Cottam, G. L., Fowler, S. C. (1984). In search of a general tension factor: Tensional patterning during auditory stimulation. *Psychophysiology, 19,* 136-145.

Andreassi, John L. (1995). *Op. cit.,* p. 318, after Denkowski, K. M., Denkowski, G. C., Omizo, M. M. (1984). Predictors of success in the EMG biofeedback training of hyperactive male children. *Biofeedback and Self Regulation, 9,* 253-264.

Andreassi, John L. (1995). *Op. cit.,* p.176 after Yuille, J. C., & Hare, R. D. (1980). A psychophysiological investigation of short term memory. *Psychophysiology, 17,* 423-430.

Arena, J., Bruno, G., Hannah, S. L., & Meader, K. J. (1995). Comparison of frontal electromyographic biofeedback training, trapezius electromyographic biofeedback training, and progressive muscular relaxation therapy in the treatment of tension headache. *Headache, 35*(7), 411- 419.

Arena, J., Bruno, G., Brucks, A. (1997). The use of EMG biofeedback for the treatment of chronic tension headache. *The Biofeedback Foundation of Europe,* <www.bfe.org>.

Arnsten, Amy F. (2001). Dopaminergic and noradrenergic influences on cognitive functions mediated by prefrontal cortex. In Mary V. Solanto, Amy F. T. Arnsten & F. Xavier Castellanos (Eds.) *Stimulant Drugs and ADHD Basic and Clinical Neuroscience.* New York: Oxford University Press, p. 186.

Astin, J. A., Beckner, W., Soeken, K., Hochberg, M. C., & Berman, B. (2002). Psychological interventions for rheumatoid arthritis: A meta-analysis of randomized controlled trials. *Arthritis and Rheumatism.* 47(3), 291-302.

Attwood, Tony (1997). *Asperger's Syndrome: A Guide for Parents and Professionals.* London: Jessica Kingsley Publications.

Ayers, M. E. (1995). Long-term follow-up of EEG neurofeedback with absence seizures. *Biofeedback and Self-Regulation, 20(3), 309-310.*

Baehr, E., Rosenfeld, J. P., Baehr, R., & Earnst, C., (1999). Clinical use of an alpha asymmetry neurofeedback protocol in the treatment of mood disorders. In J. R. Evans & A. Abarbanel (Eds.) *Introduction to Quantitative EEG and Neurofeedback.* San Diego: Academic Press.

Banks, Sonja L., Jacobs, David W., Gevirtz, Richard, Hubbard, David, R., (1998). Effects of autogenic relaxation training on electro-myographic activity in active myofascial trigger points. *Journal of Musculoskeletal Pain, 6* (4), 23-32.

Barnell Loft, Ltd., *Multiple Skills Series – Second Edition.* (1990) New York: SRA Division of MacMillan/McGraw-Hill School Publishing Company.

Basmajian, John V. (1989). *Biofeedback: Principles and Practice for Clinicians - Third Edition.* Baltimore: Williams and Wilkins.

Basmajian, John V. (1989). Anatomical and physiological basis for biofeedback of autonomic regulation. In John V. Basmajian, *Op cit.*, pp 33-48.

Basmajian, John V. (1989). O*p cit.*, p. 179, after Stoyva, J. M. (1986). Wolfgang Luthe: In memoriam. *Biofeedback and Self Regulation, 11,* 91-93.

Basmajian, John V. (1989). *Op.cit.,* p. 207, after Mitchell, K. R. & Mitchell, D. M. (1971). Migraine: An explanatory treatment application of programmed behavior therapy techniques. *Psychosomatic Research, 15,* 137-157.

Basmajian, John V. (1989). *Op. cit.,* p. 77 after Morgan, W. P. (1896). A case of congenital word blindness. *British Medical Journal, 2,* 1612.

Bergeron, S., Binik, Y. M., Khalife, S., Pagidas, K., Glazer, H. L., Meana, M., et al. (2001). A randomized comparison of group cognitive-behavioral therapy, surface electromyographic biofeedback and vestibulectomy in the treatment of dyspareunia resulting from vulvar vestibulitis. *Pain, 91(3), 297-306.*

Boddaert, N. & Chabane, N. (2002). Temporal lobe dysfunction in childhood autism. *Journal of Radiology, 83,* 1829-1833.

Budzynski, T. H. (1979). Biofeedback and the twilight states of consciousness. In D. Goleman & R. J. Davidson (Eds.) *Consciousness in Brain States of Awareness and Mysticism.* New York: Harper & Row.

Bauer, G. & Bauer, R. (1999). EEG drug effects and central nervous system poisoning. In E. Niedermeyer & F. Lopes Da Silva (Eds.) *Electroencephalography: Basic Principles, Clinical Applications and Related Fields.* Baltimore: Williams & Wilkins, pp. 671-691.

Blum, K. & Cummings, D. (1996). Reward deficiency syndrome. *American Scientist, 84.*

Boyd, W. D. & Campbell, S. E. (1998). EEG biofeedback in the schools: The use of EEG biofeedback to treat ADHD in a school setting. *Journal of Neurotherapy, 2(4), 65-71.*

Brucker, B. S. & Bulaeva, N. V. (1996). Biofeedback effect on electromyography responses in patients with spinal cord injury. *Archives of Physical Medical Rehabilitation.* 77(2), 133-137.

Byers, Alvah P. (1998). *The Byers Neurotherapy Reference Library – Revised Second Edition.* Wheat Ridge, Colorado; Association for Applied Psychophysiology and Biofeedback.

Campbell, Neil A., Reece, Jane B., Michell, Laurence G. (1996). *Biology - Fifth Edition.* New York: Addison Wesley Longman, Inc., pp 960-974.

Cantor, David S. (1999). An Overview of Quantitative EEG and Its Applications to Neurofeedback. In J. R. Evans & A. Abarbanel, *Introduction to Quantitative EEG and Neurofeedback.* New York: Academic Press.

Carlson, J. G., Chemtob, C. M., Rusnak, K., Hedlund, N. L., & Muraoka, M. Y. (1998). Eye movement desensitization and reprocessing (EMDR) treatment for combat-related posttraumatic stress disorder. *Journal of Traumatic Stress, 11*(1), 3-24.

Carlson, Neil, R. (1986). *Physiology of Behavior - Third Edition.* Toronto: Allyn and Bacon Inc.

Carmody, D. P., Radvanski, D. C., Wadhwani, S., Sabo, M. J., & Vergara, L. (2001). EEG biofeedback training and ADHD in an elementary school setting. *Journal of Neurotherapy, 4*(3), 5-27.

Carter, Rita (1998). *Mapping the Mind.* London: Weidenfeld & Nicolson.

Castellanos, F. Xavier (2001). Neuroimaging Studies in ADHD children on Stimulant Drugs. In Mary V. Solanto, Amy F. T. Arnsten & F. Xavier Castellanos (Eds.) *Stimulant Drugs and ADHD Basic and Clinical Neuroscience.* New York: Oxford University Press, p.243-258.

Chabot, R. J. & Serfontein, G. (1996). Quantitative electroencephalographic profiles of children with attention deficit disorder. *Biological Psychiatry, 40*, 951-963.

Chabot, R. J., Orgill, A. A., Crawford, G., Harris, M.J., & Serfontein, G. (1999). Behavioural and electrophysiological predictors of treatment response to stimulants in children with attention disorders. *Journal of Child Neurology, 14*(6), 343-351.

Chabot, R. J., di Michele, F., Prichep, L., & John, E. R. (2001). The clinical role of computerized EEG in the evaluation and treatment of learning and attention disorders in children and adolescents. *Journal of Neuropsychiatry & Clinical Neurosciences. 13*(2), 171-86.

Cheng, Pui-wan (1993). Metacognition and Giftedness: The state of the relationship. *Gifted Child Quarterly, 37* (3).

Clarke et al., 2001. *Psychophysiology, 38,* 212-221.

Cohen, Bernard (1989). Basic biofeedback electronics for the clinician. In John V. Basmajian, *Biofeedback Principles and Practice for Clinicians - Third edition.* Baltimore: Williams and Wilkins.

Congedo, Marco, Ozen, Cem, Sherlin, Leslie (2002). Notes on EEG resampling by natural cubic spline interpolation. *Journal of Neurotherapy, 6*(4), 73-80.

Contreras, D., Destexhe, A., Sejnowski, T. J., & Steriade, M. (1997). Spatiotemporal patterns of spindle oscillations in cortex and thalamus. *Neuroscience, 17*(3), 1179-1196.

Courchesne, E., Karnes, C. M., Davis, H. R., Ziccardi, R., Carper, R. A., Tigue, A. D., Chisum, H. J., Moses, P., Pierce, K., Lord, D., Lincoln, A. J., Pizzo, S., Schreiban, L., Haas, R. H., Akshoomoff, N. A., & Courchesne, R. Y. (2001). Unusual brain growth patterns in early life in patients with autistic disorder: An MRI study. *Neurology. 57*(2), 245-54.

Cowen, M. J., Pike, K. C., & Budzynski, H. K. (2001). Psychosocial nursing therapy following sudden cardiac arrest: Impact on two year survival. *Nursing Research, 50*(2), 68-76.

Davidson, R. J. (1995). Cerebral asymmetry, emotion and affective style. In R. J. Davidson & K. Hugdahl (Eds.) *Brain Asymmetry.* Cambridge, MA: MIT Press, 369-388.

Davidson, R. J. (1998). Anterior electro-physiological asymmetries, emotion, and depression: Conceptual and methodological conundrums. *Psychophysiology, 35,* 607-614.

Davidson, R.J., Abercrombie, H., Nitschke, J.B., & Putnam, K. (1999). *Current Opinion in Neurobiology, 9,* 228-234.

Deepak, K. K., & Behari, M. (1999). Specific muscle EMG biofeedback for hand dystonia. *Applied Psychophysiology and Biofeedback, 24*(4), 267-280.

DeLong, M.R. (1990). Primate models of movement disorders of basal ganglia origin. *TINS, 13*(7), 281-285.

Dougherty, M. C., Dwyer, J. W., Pendergast, J. F., Boyington, A. R., Tomlinson, B. U., Coward, et al. (2002). A randomized trial of behavioural management for continence with older rural women. *Research in Nursing and Health, 25*(1), 3-13.

Duffy, F. H., Iyer, V.G., & Surwillo, W.W. (1989). *Clinical Electroencephalography and Topographic Brain Mapping: Technology and Practice.* New York: Springer-Verlag.

Duffy, F. H., Hughes, J. R., Miranda, F., Bernad, P., & Cook, P. (1994). Status of quantitative EEG (QEEG) in clinical practice. *Clinical Electroencephalography, 25,* vi-xxii.

Dyro, Frances M. (1989). *The EEG Handbook.* Boston: Little, Brown and Co., p. 18.

Erlandsson, S. I., Rubinstein, B., & Carlsson, S. G. (1991). Tinnitus: Evaluation of biofeedback and stomatognathic treatment. *British Journal of Audiology, 25*(3), 151-161.

Elliott, R., Sahakian, B. J., Matthews, K., Bannerjea, A., Rimmer, J., & Robbins, T. W., (1997). Effects of Methylphenidate on Spatial Working Memory and Planning in Healthy Young Adults. *Psychopharmacology, 131,* 196-206.

Fehring, R.J. (1983). Effects of biofeedback-aided relaxation on the physiological stress symptoms of college students. *Nursing Research, 32*(6), 362-366.

Filipek, P. A., Semrud-Clikeman, M., Steingard, R. J., Rendshaw, P. F., Kennedy, D. N., Biederman, M. D. (1997). Volumetric MRI analysis comparing attention-deficit hyperactivity disorder and normal controls. *Neurobiology, 47,* 618-628.

Frank, Y. & Pavlakis, S. G. (2001). Brain imagining in neurobehavioural disorders (Review). *Paediatric Neurology, 25*(4), 278-87.

Fried, R. (1987). *The Hyperventilation Syndrome: Research and Clinical Treatment.* Baltimore: Johns Hopkins University Press.

Fisch, Bruce J. (1999). *Fisch and Spehlmann's EEG Primer: Basic Principles of Digital and Analog EEG - Third revised and enlarged edition.* New York: Elsevier.

Flor, H., Hagg, G., & Turk, D. C. (1986). Long-term efficacy of EMG biofeedback for chronic rheumatic back pain. *Pain, 27*(2), 195-202.

Freed, J. & Parsons, L. (1997). *Right Brained Children in a Left-Brained World.* New York: Simon & Schuster.

Freedman, J. (1993).*Failing Grades.* Society for Advancing Educational Research: Full Court Press Inc.

Friedman, M. & Rosenman, R. H. (1974). *Type A Behavior and Your Heart.* New York: Knopf.

Fritz, & Fehmi, L. G. (1982). *The Open Focus Handbook.* Princeton, NJ: Biofeedback Computer.

Fuchs, T., Birbaumer, N., Lutzenberger, W., Gruzelier, J. & Kaiser, J., (2003). Neurofeedback treatment for attention-deficit/hyperactivity disorder in children: a comparison with methylphenidate. *Journal of Applied Psychophysiology and Biofeedback, 28*(1), 1-12.

Fuller, George D. (1984). *Biofeedback: Methods and Procedures in Clinical Practice.* San Francisco: Biofeedback Press.

Gardea, M. A., Gatchel, R. J., & Mishra, K. D. (2001). Long-term efficacy of biobehavioral treatment of temporomandibular disorders. *Journal of Behavioral Medicine, 24*(4), 341-359.

Gibbs, F. A. & Knott, J. R. (1949). Growth of the electrical activity of the cortex. *Electro-encephalography and Clinical Neurophysiology,* 223-229.

Goleman, Daniel, (1995) *Emotional Intelligence.* New York: Bantam Books.

Gosepath, K., Nafe, B., Ziegler, E., & Mann, W. J. (2001). Neurofeedback in therapy of tinnitus. *Hals-Nasen-Ohrenärzie, 49*(1), 29-35.

Green, F. & Green, A. (1977). *Beyond Biofeedback.* New York: Knoll Publishing.

Grin'-Yatsenko, V. A., Kropotov, J. D., Ponomarev, V. A., Chutko, L. S. & Yakovenko, E. A. (2001). Effect of biofeedback training of sensorimotor and beta-sub-1 EEG rhythms on attention parameters. *Human Physiology, 27*(3), 259-266.

Gruzelier, J. (2002). Neurofeedback training to enhance musical performance. *Proceedings of the AAPB Annual Meeting*, Las Vegas, NV, March 2002.

Gruzelier, J. & Egner, T. (2003). Theta/Alpha neurofeedback training to enhance musical performance. *Proceedings of the combined annual meetings of the European chapter of iSNR and the Biofeedback Foundation of Europe,* Udine, Italy, February 2003.

Gruzelier, J. H. & Egner, T. (2003). Ecological validity of neurofeedback modulation of slow wave EEG enhances musical performance. *Neuroreport, 14*(1).

Guberman, Alan (1994). Hyperkinetic movement disorders. In Alan Guberman, *An Introduction to Clinical Neurology*. New York: Little, Brown & Co.

Gunkelman, Jay, Personal communications. www.Q-metrx.com

Grassi, C., Filippi, G. M., & Passatore, M. (1986). Postsynaptic alpha 1- and alpha 2- adrenoreceptors mediating the action of the sympathetic system on muscle spindles in the rabbit. *Pharmacological Research Communications, 18*(2), 161-170.

Gruber, Gary (1986). *Dr. Gary Gruber's Essential Guide to Test Taking For Kids*. New York: William Morrow and Company.

Hadhazy, V.A., Ezzo, J., Creamer, P., & Bergman, B. M. (2000). Mind-body therapies for the treatment of fibromyalgia. A systematic review. *Journal of Rheumatology, 13*(3), 487-492.

Hammond, D. Corydon & Gunkelman, Jay, (2001). *The Art of Artifacting*. Merino, CO: Society for Neuronal Regulation.

Hauri, P. J., Percy, L., Hellekson, C., Hartmann, E., & Russ, D. (1982). The treatment of psychophysiologic insomnia with biofeedback: A replication study. *Biofeedback and Self Regulation, 7*(2), 223-235.

Hawkins, R. C. II, Doel, S. R., Lindseth, P., Jeffers, V., & Skaggs, S. (1980). Anxiety reduction in hospitalized schizophrenics through thermal biofeedback and relaxation training. *Perceptual & Motor Skills. 51*(2), 475-482.

Hebb, D. O. (1949). *The Organization of Behavior.* New York: Wiley-Interscience.

Heller, W., Etienne, M. A., & Miller, G. A. (1997). Patterns of regional brain activity differentiate different types of anxiety. *Journal of Abnormal Psychology, 104,* 327-333.

Henderson, R. J., Hart, M. G., Lai, S. K., & Hunyor, S. N. (1998). The effect of home training with direct blood pressure biofeedback of hypertensives: A placebo controlled study. *Journal of Hypertension, 16*(6), 771-778.

Hermann, C., & Blanchard, E. B. (2002). Biofeedback in the treatment of headache and other childhood pain. *Applied Psychophysiology and Biofeedback, 27*(2), 143-162.

Heymen, D., Jones, K. R., Ringel, Y., Scarlett, Y., & Whitehead, W. E. (2001). Biofeedback treatment of fecal incontinence: A critical review. *Diseases of the Colon and Rectum, 44*(5), 728-736.

Hjorth, B. (1980). Source derivation simplifies topographical EEG interpretation. *American Journal of EEG Technology, 20,* 121-132.

Horwitz, B., Rumsey, J. M., Grady, C. L., Rapoport, S. I. (1988). The cerebral metabolic landscape in autism: Intercorrelations of regional glucose utilization. *Archives of Neurology, 45*(7), 49-55.

Hughes, John R. & John, E. Roy (1999). Conventional and quantitative electroencephalography in psychiatry. *Journal of Neuropsychiatry and Clinical Neuroscience, 11* (2).

Hughes, John R. (2002). The Mozart Effect. *Proceedings of the 10th Annual Conference of the Society for Neuronal Regulation.* Scottsdale, AZ, September 2002.

Humphreys, P. A., & Gevirtz, R. (2000). Treatment of recurrent abdominal pain: Components analysis of four treatment protocols. *Journal of Pediatric Gastroenterological Nutrition, 31*(1), 47-51.

Hynd, G. W., Hern, K. L., Novey, E. S., & Eliopulos, D. (1993). Attention deficit hyperactivity disorder and asymmetry of the caudate nucleus. *Journal of Child Neurology, 8,* 339-347.

Introduction to Psychiatry. Washington, D.C.: George Washington University Medical School.

Jacobson, E. (1970). *Modern treatment of tense patients.* Springfield, IL: Charles C. Thomas.

Jantzen, T., Graap, K., Stephanson, S., Marshall, W., & Fitzsimmons, G. (1995). Differences in baseline EEG measures for ADD and normally achieving pre-adolescent males. *Biofeedback and Self Regulation, 20*(1), 65 - 82.

Jarusiewicz, Betty (2002). Efficacy of neurofeedback for children in the autistic spectrum: A pilot study. *Journal of Neurotherapy, 6*(4), 39-49.

Jasper, H. (1958). Report of the committee on methods of clinical examination in electroencephalography. *EEG and Clinical Neurophysiology, 10, 374.*

John, E. R., Prichep, L. S., & Easton, P. (1987). Normative data banks and neurometrics: Basic concepts, methods and results of norm constructions. In A. S. Gevins & A. Remond (Eds.), *Handbook of Electroencephalography and Clinical Neurophysiology. Vol. 1.*

John, E. R., Prichep, L. S., Fridman, J., & Easton, P. (1988). Neurometrics: Computer-assisted differential diagnosis of brain dysfunctions. *Science, 239*, 162-169.

John, E. R. (1989). The role of quantitative EEG topographic mapping or 'neurometrics' in the diagnosis of psychiatric and neurological disorders: The pros. *Electroencephalography and Clinical Neurophysiology, 73*, 2-4.

Kaiser, D. A. & Othmer, S. (2000). Effect of neurofeedback on variables of attention in a large multi-center trial. *Journal of Neurotherapy, 4*(1), 5-15.

Kamiya, J. (1979). Autoregulation of the EEG alpha rhythm: A program for the study of consciousness. In E. Peper, S. Ancoli, & M. Quinn. (Eds.) *Mind Body Integration: Essential Readings in Biofeedback.* New York: Plenum Press, pp 289-298.

Klimesch, W., Pfurtscheller, G., & Schimke, H. (1992). Pre- and post-stimulus processes in category judgement tasks as measured by event-related desynchronization (ERD). *Journal of Psychophysiology, 6*, 185-203.

Klimesch, W. (1999). EEG alpha and theta oscillations reflect cognitive and memory performance: A review and analysis. *Brain Research Reviews, 29*, 169-195.

Koelega, H. S. (1993). Stimulant drugs and vigilance performance: A review. *Psychopharmacology, 111*, 1-16.

Kropotov, J. D. & Etlinger, (1999). *International Journal of Psychology, 31*, 197-217.

Kropotov. Juri D. (1997). *Russian Journal of Physiology, 83*, 45-51.

LaHoste, G. L., Swanson, J. M., Wigal, S. B., Glabe, C., Wigal, T., King, N., & Kennedy, J. L. (1996). Dopamine D 4 receptor gene polymorphism is associated with attention-deficit hyperactivity disorder. *Molecular Psychiatry, 1*, 121-124.

Landers, D. M., Petruzzello, S. J., Salazar, W., Crews, D. J., Kubitz, K. A., Gannon, T. L., Han, M. (1991). The influence of electrocortical biofeedback on performance in pre-elite archers. *Medicine and Science in Sports and Exercise, 23*(1), 123-128.

Laughlin, Henry P. (1967). *The Neuroses.* Washington: Butterworth Press, p.76.

La Vaque, T. J., Hammond, D. C., Trudeau, D., Monastra, V., Perry, J., Lehrer, P., Matheson, D., & Sherman, R. (2002). Template for developing guidelines for the evaluation of the clinical efficacy of psychophysiological interventions. *Applied Psychophysiology and Biofeedback, 27*(4), 273-281. Reprinted in *Journal of Neurotherapy, 6*(4), 11-23.

Lehrer, P.M., Carr, R., Sargunaraj, D., & Woolfolk, R.L. (1994). Stress management techniques: Are they all equivalent, or do they have specific effects? *Biofeedback and Self-Regulation, 19*(4), 353-401.

Lehrer, P., Smetankin, A., & Potapova, T. (2000). Respiratory sinus arrhythmia biofeedback therapy for asthma: A report of 20 unmedicated pediatric cases using the Smetankin method. *Applied Psychophysiology and Biofeedback, 25*(3), 193-200.

Linden, M., Habib, T., & Radojevic, V. (1996). A controlled study of the effects of EEG biofeedback on cognition and behavior of children with attention deficit disorder and learning disabilities. *Biofeedback and Self Regulation, 21*(1), 106-111.

Love, A. J. & Thompson, M. G. G. (1988). Language disorders and attention deficit disorders in a child psychiatric outpatient population. *American Journal of Orthopsychiatry, 58*(1), 52-64.

Lubar, J. F. (1997). Neocortical dynamics: Implications for understanding the role of neurofeedback and related techniques for the enhancement of attention. *Applied Psychophysiology and Biofeedback, 22*(2), 111-126.

Lubar, J F. (1995). Neurofeedback for the management of attention-deficit/hyperactivity disorders. In Mark S. Schwartz and Associates, *Biofeedback: A Practitioner's Guide - Second Edition.* New York:Guilford Press, pp 493-522.

Lubar, J. F., Swartwood, M. O., Swartwood, J. N., & O'Donnell, P. H. (1995). Evaluation of the effectiveness of EEG neurofeedback training for ADHD in a clinical setting as measured by changes in TOVA scores, behavioural ratings, and WISC-R performance. *Biofeedback and Self Regulation. 21*(1), 83-99.

Lubar, J. F. & Lubar, J. (1999). Neurofeedback assessment and treatment for ADD/ hyperactivity disorder. In James R. Evans & A. Abarbanel *Introduction to Quantitative EEG and Neurofeedback.* San Diego: Academic Press.

Lubar, Joel, White, J. N., Swartwood, M. O., & Swartwood, J. N. (1999). Methylphenidate effects on global and complex measures of EEG. *Pediatric Neurology, 21*, p.633-637.

Malone, M. A., Kershner, J. R., & Swanson J. M. (1994). Hemispheric processing and methylphenidate effects in attention-deficit/ hyperactivity disorder. *Journal of Child Neurology, 9*(2), 181-189.

Mann, C. A., Lubar, J. F., Zimmerman, A. W., Miller, C. A., & Muenchen, R.A. (1992). Quantitative analysis of EEG in boys with attention-deficit/hyperactivity disorder: Controlled study with clinical implications. *Pediatric Neurology, 8*(1), 30-36.

Marosi, E. et al., (1992). Maturation of the coherence of EEG activity in normal and learning-disabled children. *Electro-encephalography and Clinical Neurophysiology, 83*, 350-357.

Matsuura, M., Yamamoto, K., Fukuzawa, H., Okubo, Y., Uesugi, H., Moriiwa, M., Kojuma, T., & Shimazomo, Y. (1985). Age development and sex differences of various EEG elements in healthy children and adults – Quantification by a computerized waveform recognition method. *Electroencephalography and Clinical Neurophysiology, 60*, 394-406.

Mehta, M. A., Owen, A. M., Sahakian, B. J., Mavaddat, N., Pickard, J. D., & Robbins, T. W. (2000). Methylphenidate enhances working memory by modulating discrete frontal and parietal lobe regions in the human brain. *Journal of Neuroscience, 20*, 1-6

Mehta, M.A., Sahakian, B. J., & Robbins, T. W. (2001). Comparative psychopharmacology of methylphenidate and related drugs in human volunteers, patients with ADHD and experimental animals. In Mary V. Solanto, Amy F. Arnsten, & F. Xavier Castellanos (Eds.) *Stimulant Drugs and ADHD Basic and Clinical Neuroscience.* New York: Oxford University Press, p.303-331.

Metcalfe, J. & Shimamura, A. P. (Eds.) (1996). *Metacognition.* Cambridge, MA: MIT Press.

Middaugh, S. J., Haythornwaite, J. A., Thompson, B., Hill, R., Brown, K. M., Freedman, R.R., et al. (2001). The Raynaud's treatment study: Biofeedback protocols and acquisition of temperature biofeedback skills. *Applied Psychophysiology and Biofeedback, 26*(4), 251-278.

Minshew, N. J., Luna, B., & Sweeney, J. A. (1999). Oculomotor evidence for neocortical systems but not cerebellar dysfunction in autism. *Neurology, 52*, 917-922.

Mitchell, K. R. & Mitchell, D. M., (1971). Migraine: An explanatory treatment application of programmed behavior therapy techniques. *Psychosomatic Research*, *15*, 137-157.

Monastra, V. J., Lubar, J. F., Linden, M., VanDeusen, P., Green, G., Wing, W. et al. (1999). Assessing attention deficit hyperactivity disorder via quantitative electroencephalography: An initial validation study, *Neuropsychology, 13* (3), 424-433.

Monastra, V. J., Monastra, D., & George, S. (2002). The effects of stimulant therapy, EEG biofeedback and parenting on primary symptoms of ADHD. *Applied Psychophysiology and Biofeedback, 27*(4), 272-250.

Moore, L. E., & Wiesner, S. L. (1996). Hypnotically-induced vasodilation in the treatment of repetitive strain injuries. *American Journal of Clinical Hypnosis, 39*(2), 97-104.

Morin, C. M., Hauri, P. J., Espie, C. A., Spielman, A. J., Buysse, D. J., & Bootzin, R. R. (1998). Nonpharmacological treatment of chronic insomnia. An American Academy of Sleep Medicine review. *Neuroscience and Behavior Psychology, 28*(3), 330-335.

Moreland, J. D., Thomson, M. A., Fuoco, A. R. (1998). Electromyographic biofeedback to improve lower extremity function after a stroke: A meta-analysis. *Archives of Physical Medical Rehabilitation, 79*(2), 134-140.

Morrow, L., Urtunski, P. B., Kim, Y., Boller, F. (1981). Arousal responses to emotional stimuli and laterality of lesion. *Neuropsychologia, 19*, 65-72.

Moss, Donald & Gunkelman, Jay (2003). Task Force on Methodology and Empirically Supported Treatments: Introduction. *APB, 7*(4). Reprinted, *Journal of Neurotherapy, 6*(4), 7-10.

Muel, S., Knott, J. R., Benton, A. L. (1965). EEG abnormality and psychological test performance in reading disability. *Cortex, 1,* 434.

Mueller, H. H., Donaldson, C. C., Nelson, D. V., & Layman, M. (2001). Treatment of fibromyalgia incorporating EEG-driven stimulation: A clinical outcomes study. *Journal of Clinical Psychology, 57*(7), 933-952.

Munoz, D. P., Hampton, K. A., Moore, K. D., Armstrong, I. T. (1998). Control of saccadic eye movements and visual fixation in children and adults with ADHD. *Proceedings of the Society for Neurosciences,* Annual meeting, Los Angeles, CA.

Nature's Children (1985) Publisher: J. R. DeVarennes, USA: Grolier Limited.

Norris, Louise S. & Currier, Michael (1999). Performance enhancement training through neurofeedback. In James R. Evans and Andrew Abarbanel, *Introduction to Quantitative EEG and Neurofeedback.* San Diego: Academic Press.

Olds, M. E. & Milner, P. (1954). Positive reinforcement produced by electrical stimulation of septal area and other regions of the rat brain. *Journal of Comparative and Physiological Psychology, 47*, 419-427.

Othmer, S. F. & Othmer, S. (1991). EEG biofeedback training for ADD, specific learning disabilities and associated conduct problems. Encino, CA: EEG Spectrum, Inc.

Pacak, K et al. (1995). *Endocrinology, 136*(11) 4814-4819.

Palincsar, A. S., Brown, D. A. (1987) Enhancing instructional time through attention to metacognition. *Journal of Learning Disabilities, 20*(2).

Panu, Neety & Wong, Sunny (Eds.) (2002). *MCCQE Review Notes & Lecture Series.* Toronto: University of Toronto Press.

Papez, (1937). *Archives of Neurology & Psychiatry,* 725.

Pascual-Marqui, Roberto (2000). *Proceedings of the annual meeting of the Society for Neuronal Regulation,* Minneapolis, MN, October 2000.

Patrick, G. J. (1996). Improved neuronal regulation in ADHD: An application of fifteen sessions of photic-driven EEG neurotherapy. *Journal of Neurotherapy, 1* (4), 27-36.

Paulesu in Brain (1996) (brain imaging and dyslexia)

Pavlakis, Frank Y. (2001). Brain imaging in neurobehavioral disorders. (Review) *Paediatric Neurology, 25*(4), 278-287.

Peniston, E. G. & Kulkosky, P. J. (1989). Alpha-theta brainwave training and beta-endorphin levels in alcoholics. *Alcoholism: Clinical and Experimental Research, 13*(2), 271-279.

Peniston, E. G. & Kulkosky. P. J. (1990). Alcoholic personality and alpha-theta brainwave training. *Medical Psychotherapy, 3*, 37-55.

Peniston, E., Marrinan, D., Deming, W., & Kulkosky, P. (1993). EEG alpha-theta brainwave synchronization in Vietnam theatre veterans with combat-related post-traumatic stress disorder and alcohol abuse. *Advances in Medical Psychotherapy, 6*, 37-50.

Pentacost, Hugh (1991). A kind of murder. In Katherine Robinson (Ed.) *Scholastic Scope Literature*, New York: Scholastics Ltd., 730 Broadway, New York, N.Y., 10003.

Pepper, Eric & Tibbetts, V. (1997). Electro-myography: Effortless diaphragmatic breathing. *The Biofeedback Foundation of Europe*, www.bfe.org.

Peterson, Gail (2000). Operant Conditioning. *Proceedings of the Society for Neuronal Regulation annual meeting*, October 2000, Minneapolis.

Peterson, L. L. & Vorhies, C. (1983). Reynaud's syndrome: Treatment with sublingual administration of nitroglycerin, swinging arm manoeuvre, and biofeedback training. *Archives of Dermatology, 119*(5), 396-399.

Petrofsky, J. S. (2001). The use of electromyogram biofeedback to reduce Trendelenburg gait. *European Journal of Applied Psychophysiology, 85*(5), 491- 495.

Pierce, K., Muller, R.-A., Ambrose, G., Allen, G., Courchesne, E. (2001). Face processing occurs outside the fusiform 'face area' in autism: evidence from functional MRI. *Brain. 124*, 2059-2073.

Prichep, E. S., Mas, F., Hollander, E., Liebowitz, M., John, E. R., Almas, M., DeCaria, C. M., Levine, R. H. (1993). Quantitative electroencephalographic subtyping of obsessive-compulsive disorder. *Psychiatry Research: Neuroimaging*, **50**, 25-32.

Ramos, F. (1998). Frequency band interaction in ADD/ADHD neurotherapy. *Journal of Neurotherapy, 3*(4), 27-36.

Reynaud's Treatment Study Investigators (2000). Comparison of sustained-release nifedipineand and temperature biofeedback for treatment of primary Reynaud's phenomenon. Results from a randomized clinical trial with 1-year follow-up. *Archives of Internal Medicine, 160*(8), 1101-1108.

Rice, K.M., Blanchard, E.B., & Purcell, M. (1993). Biofeedback treatments of generalized anxiety disorders: Preliminary results. *Biofeedback and Self-Regulation, 18*(2), 93-105.

Rice, B., Kalder, A. J., Schindler, J. V., & Dixon, R. M. (2001). Effect of biofeedback-assisted relaxation therapy on foot ulcer healing. *Journal of the American Podiatric Medical Association, 91*(3), 131-141.

Robbins, Jim (2000). *A Symphony in the Brain.* New York: Atlantic Monthly Press.

Robinson, R. G., Kubos, K., Starr, L. B., Rao, K., & Price, T. R. (1984). Mood disorders in stroke patients: Importance of location of lesion. *Brain, 107*, 81-93.

Rosenfeld, J. P., Baehr, E., Baehr, R., Gotlib, I., & Ranganath, C. (1996). Preliminary evidence that daily changes in frontal alpha asymmetry correlate with changes in affect in therapy sessions. *International Journal of Psychophysiology, 23*, 241-258.

Rosenfeld, J. P. (1997). EEG Biofeedback of frontal alpha asymmetry in affective disorders. *Biofeedback, 25*(1), 8-25.

Rosenfeld, J. P. (2000). Theoretical implications of EEG reference choice and related methodological issues. *Journal of Neurotherapy, 4* (2), 77-87.

Rosenfeld, J. P. (2000). An EEG biofeedback protocol for affective disorders. *Clinical electroencephalography, 31*(1), 7-12.

Ross, E. D. (1981). The aprosodias: Functional-anatomic organization of the affective components of language in the right hemisphere. *Archives of Neurology, 38*, 561-569.

Rossiter, T. R. & La Vaque, T. J. (1995). A comparison of EEG biofeedback and psychostimulants in treating attention deficit hyperactivity disorders. *Journal of Neurotherapy, 1*(1), 48-59.

Rossiter, T. R. (1998). Patient-directed neurofeedback for AD/HD. *Journal of Neurotherapy, 2*(4), 54-63.

Rourke, Byron P., Tsatsanis, Katherine D. (2000). Nonverbal learning disabilities and asperger's syndrome. In Ami Klin, Fred R. Volkmar, & Sara S. Sparrow (Eds.) *Asperger Syndrome*. New York: Guilford Press.

Rozelle, G. R., & Budzynski, T. H. (1995). Neurotherapy for stroke rehabilitation: A single case study. *Biofeedback and Self-Regulation, 20*(3), 211-228.

Sarkar, P., Rathee, S. P., & Neera, N. (1999). Comparative efficacy of pharmacotherapy and biofeedback among cases of generalized anxiety disorder. *Journal of Projective Psychology & Mental Health. 6*(1), 69-77.

Saxby, E., & Peniston, E. G. (1995). Alpha-theta brainwave neurofeedback training: An effective treatment for male and female alcoholics with depressive symptoms. *Journal of Clinical Psychology, 51*(5), 685-693.

Schleenbaker, R. E. & Mainous, A. G. (1993). Electromyographic biofeedback for neuromuscular re-education in the hemiplegic stroke patient: A meta-analysis. *Archives of Physical Medical Rehabilitation, 74*(12). 1301-1304.

Schultz, Robert T., Romanski, Lizabeth M., & Tsatsanis, Katherine D. (2000). Neurofunctional models of autistic disorder and Asperger syndrome, clues from neuroimaging. In Ami Klin, Fred R. Volkmar, & Sara S. Sparrow (Eds.) *Asperger Syndrome*. New York: Guilford Press.

Schwartz, M. S. & Associates (1995). *Biofeedback: A Practitioner's Guide - Second Edition*. New York: Guilford Press.

Sears, William & Thompson, Lynda (1998). *The A.D.D. Book: New Understandings, New Approaches to Parenting Your Child*. New York: Little, Brown and Co.

Sella, Gabriel E. (1997). Electromyography: Towards an integrated approach of sEMG utilization: Quantitative protocols of assessment and biofeedback. *The Biofeedback Foundation of Europe*, <www.bfe.org/protocol/prol3eng.htm>

Selye, H. (1976). *The Stress of Life - Revised Edition*. New York: McGraw-Hill.

Shaffer, Fred (2002). The Neuron. Workshop presentation at the AAPB annual meeting. Los Vegas, NV.

Shain, R.J. (1977). *Neurology of Childhood Learning Disorders - Second Edition*. Baltimore: Williams & Wilkins.

Sheer, D. E. (1977). Biofeedback training of 40 Hz EEG and behavior. In N. Burch & H.I. Altshuler (Eds.) *Behavior & brain electrical activity*. New York: Plenum.

Sherin, Leslie (2003). Recovery after stroke, a single case study. *Procedings of the AAPB annual meeting*, Jacksonville, Florida.

Sherman, R. A., Davis, G. D., & Wong, M.F., (1997). Behavioural treatment of exercise-induced urinary incontinence among female soldiers. *Military Medicine, 162*(10), 690-704.

Shouse, M. N. & Lubar, J. F. (1979). Sensorimotor rhythm (SMR) operant conditioning and methylphenidate in the treatment of hyperkinesis. *Biofeedback & Self-Regulation, 4*, 299-311.

Sichel, A. G., Fehmi, L. G., & Goldstein, D. M. (1995). Positive outcome with neurofeedback treatment in a case of mild autism. *Journal of Neurotherapy, 1*(1), 60-64.

Sieb, R. A. (1990) *Medical Hypotheses, 33*, p.145-153

Sievert, David (1999). *David User's Guide*. Edmonton, Alberta: Computronic Devices Limited.

Silverthorn, Dee Unglaub (1998). *Human Physiology, An Integrated Approach*. New Jersey: Prentice Hall.

Smith, C. G. (1962). *Basic Neuroanatomy*. Toronto, Canada: University of Toronto Press.

Smith-Pellettier, Carolyn (2002). The Hypothalamic-Pituitary Adrenal Axis. Paper presented at the Canadian Medical Association annual meeting.

Snowdon, David (2001). *Aging with Grace: What the Nun Study Teaches Us About Leading Longer, Healthier, and More Meaningful Lives.* New York: Bantam Books.

Solanto, M. V., Arnsten, A. F. T., & Castellanos, X. F. (Eds.) (2001). *Stimulant Drugs and ADHD Basic and Clinical Neuroscience.* New York: Oxford University Press.

Steriade, M., Gloor, P., Llinas, R. R., Lopes da Sylva, F. H., & Mesulam, M. M. (1990). Basic mechanisms of cerebral rhythmic activities. *Electroencephalography and Clinical Neurophysiology, 76,* 481-508.

Sterman, M. B. (1996). Physiological origins and functional correlates of EEG rhythmic activities: Implications for self-regulation. *Biofeedback and Self-Regulation, 21,* 3-33.

Sterman, M. B. (1999). *Atlas of Topometric Clinical Displays: Functional Interpretations and Neurofeedback Strategies.* New Jersey: Sterman-Kaiser Imaging Laboratory.

Sterman, M. B. (2000). Basic concepts and clinical findings in the treatment of seizure disorders with EEG operant conditioning. *Clinical Electroencephalography, 31*(1), 45-55.

Sterman, M. Barry (2000) EEG markers for attention deficit disorder: pharmacological and neurofeedback applications. *Child Study Journal, 30*(1), 1-22.

Stoyva, J. M. (1986). Wolfgang Luthe: In Memoriam. *Biofeedback and Self Regulation, 11,* 91-93.

Sullivan, M. W. (1970) *Comprehension Readers.* Box 577, Palo Alto, California, 94302: Behavioural Research Laboratories.

Sung, M. S., Hong, J. Y., Choi, Y. H., Baik, S. H., Yoon, H. (2000). FES-biofeedback versus intensive pelivic floor muscle exercise for the prevention and treatment of genuine stress incontinence. *Journal of Korean Medical Science, 15*(3), 303-308.

Swanson, J. M., McBurnett, K., Wigal, T., Pfiffner, L. J., Williams, L., Christian, D. L., Tamm, L., Willcutt, E., Crowley, K., Clevenger, W., Khouam, N., Woo, C., Crinella, F.M., Fisher, T. M. (1993). The effect of stimulant medication on children with attention deficit disorder: A "Review of Reviews". *Exceptional Children, 60*(2), 154 - 162.

Schwartz, Mark (1987). *Biofeedback: A Practitioner's Guide.* New York: Guilford Press.

Tansey, M. A. (1993). Ten year stability of EEG biofeedback results for a hyperactive boy who failed fourth grade perpetually impaired class. *Biofeedback & Self Regulation, 18,* 33-44.

Taylor, D. N. (1995). Effects of behavioural stress-management program on anxiety, mood, self-esteem, and T-cell count in HIV positive men. *Psychological Reports. 76*(2), 451-457.

Thatcher, R. W. et al., (1986). Cortico-cortical associations and EEG coherence: a two compartmental model. *Electroencephalography and Clinical Neurophysiology, 64,* 123-143.

Thatcher, R. W., Walker, R. A., Gerson, I., Geisler, F. H. (1989). EEG discriminant analysis of mild head trauma. *Electroencephalography and Clinical Neurophysiology, 73,* 94-106.

Thatcher, R. W., Biver, C., McAlaster, R., & Salazar, A. (1998). Biophysical linkage between MRI and EEG coherence in closed head injury. *Neuroimage, 8,* 307-326.

Thatcher, R. W. (1999). EEG data base-guided neurotherapy. In James R. Evans and Andrew Abarbanel, *Introduction to Quantitative EEG and Neurofeedback.* New York: Academic Press.

Thompson, Lynda M. (1979). *The Effect of Methylphenidate on Self-concept and Locus of Control in Hyperactive Children.* A Thesis submitted in conformity with the requirements for the Degree of Doctor of Philosophy in the University of Toronto.

Thompson, L. & Thompson M. (1998). Neurofeedback combined with training in metacognitive strategies: Effectiveness in students with ADD. *Applied Psychophysiology and Biofeedback, 23*(4), 243-263.

Thompson, M.G.G. (Ed.) (1979). (Editorial Board - Dr. S. Woods, Los Angeles; Dr. D. Langsley, Cincinnati; Dr. M. Hollander, Tennessee; Dr. F. Lowy, Toronto; Dr. H. Prosen, Manitoba; Dr. K. Rawnsley, Great Britain; Dr. R. Ball, Australia) *A Resident's Guide to Psychiatric Education.* New York: Plenum Publishing.

Thompson, M.G.G. & Havelkova, M. (1983). Childhood Psychosis. In Paul Steinhauer & Quentin Rae-Grant (Eds.) *Psychological Problems of the Child in the Family.* New York: Basic Books, Inc.

Thompson, M.G.G. & Patterson, P.G.R. (1986). The Thompson-Patterson scale of psychosocial development: I - Theoretical Basis. *Canadian Journal of Psychiatry, 31*(5).

Thompson, M.G.G. (1990). Developmental Assessment of the Preschool Child.In J. A. Stockman (Ed.) *Difficult Diagnoses in Paediatrics.* Toronto: W. D. Saunders.

Thompson, M. & Thompson, L. (2002). Biofeedback for movement disorders (dystonia with Parkinson's disease): Theory and preliminary results. *Journal of Neurotherapy, 6*(4), 51-70.

Timed Readings in Literature. (1989) Edward Spargo (Editor). Providence, Rhode Island: Jamestown Publishers.

Traub, R. D., Miles, R., Wong, R. K. S. (1989). Model of the origin of rhythmic population oscillations in the hippocampal slice. *Science, 243*, 1319-1325.

Tucker, D. M., Watson, R. T., Heilman, K. M. (1977). Affective discrimination and evocation in patients with right parietal disease. *Neurology, 27*, 947-950.

Tucker, D. M. & Williamson, P. A., (1984) Asymmetric neural control systems in human self regulation. *Psychological Review, 91*, 185-215.

Ullman, M. (1975). In A. M. Freedman, I. Kaplan, & B. J. Sadock, *Comprehensive Textbook of Psychiatry –Second Edition, Vol. 2*, 2552-2561. Baltimore: Williams and Wilkins.

Vanathy, S., Sharma, P. S. V. N., & Kumar, K. B. (1998). The efficacy of alpha and theta neurofeedback training in treatment of generalized anxiety disorder. *Indian Journal of Clinical Psychology, 25*(2), 136-143.

Van Kampen, M., De Weerdt, W., Van Poppel, H., De Ridder, D., Feys, H., & Baert, L. (2000). Effect of pelvic-floor re-education on duration and degree of incontinence after radical prostatectomy: A randomized controlled trial. *Lancet, 355*(9198), 98-102.

Vlaeyen, J. W., Haazen, I. W., Schuerman, J. A., Kole-Snijders, A. M., & van Eek, H. (1995). Behavioural rehabilitation of chronic low back pain: Comparison of an operant treatment, an operant-cognitive treatment and an operant-respondent treatment. *Clinical Psychology, 34*(1), 95-118.

Wadhwani, S., Radvanski, D. C., & Carmody, D. P. (1998). Neurofeedback training in a case of attention deficit hyperactivity disorder. *Journal of Neurotherapy, 3*(1), 42-49.

Weidmann, G., Pauli, P., Dengler, W., Lutzenburger, W., Birbaumer, N. & Buckkremer, G. (1999). Frontal brain asymmetry as a biological substrate of emotions in patients with panic disorders. *Archives of General Psychiatry, 56*, 78-84.

Weins, W. J. (1983). Metacognition and the adolescent passive learner. *Journal of Learning Disabilities, 16*(3).

Westmoreland, B. F., Espinoa, R. E., & Klass, D. W. (1973). Significant prosopo-glosso-pharyngeal movements affecting the electroencephalogram. *American Journal of EEG Technology, 13*, 59-70.

Westmoreland, B. F. & Klaus, B. W. (1998). Defective alpha reactivity with mental concentration. *Journal of Clinical Neurophysioogy, 15*, 424-428.

White, N. E. (1999). Theories of the effectiveness of alpha-theta training for multiple disorders. In James R. Evans & Andrew Abaranel *Introduction to Quantitative EEG and Neurofeedback.* San Diego: Academic Press.

Wing, L. (2001). *The Autistic Spectrum.* Berkeley, CA: Ulysses Press

Wyrwicka, W. and Sterman, M. B., (1968). Instrumental conditioning of sensorimotor cortex EEG spindles in the waking cat. *Physiology and Behavior, 3,* 703-707.

Yocum, D. E., Hodes, R., Sundstrom, W. R., & Cleeland, C. S. (1985). Use of biofeedback training in treatment of Reynaud's disease and phenomenon. *Journal of Rheumatology, 12*(1), 90-93.

Yucha, C. B., Clark, L., Smith, M., Uris, P., Lafleur, B. & Duval, S. (2001). The effect of biofeedback in hypertension. *Applied Nursing Research, 14*(1), 29-35.

Zametkin, A. J., Nordahl, T. E., Gross, M., King, A. C., Semple, W. E., Rumsey, J. H., Hamburger, S., & Cohen, R. M. (1990). Cerebral glucose metabolism in adults with hyperactivity of childhood onset. *New England Journal of Medicine, 323*(20), 1361-1366.

INDEX

The reader should also consult the Table of Contents, which is constructed in a very detailed manner. This was done in the hope that it would assist newcomers to this field to find and consult different sections quickly and thus increase their speed of learning.